H. Sathya

PUBLIC TRANSPORTATION: PLANNING, OPERATIONS, AND MANAGEMENT

PUBLIC TRANSPORTATION: PLANNING, OPERATIONS, AND MANAGEMENT

Editors

GEORGE E. GRAY
Chief, Division of Mass Transportation
California Department of Transportation

LESTER A. HOEL

Professor and Chairman
Department of Civil Engineering
University of Virginia

PRENTICE-HALL, INC., *Englewood Cliffs, New Jersey 07632*

Library of Congress Cataloging in Publication Data
Main entry under title:

Public transportation.

    Includes bibliographies and index.
      1. Urban transportation—Addresses, essays, lectures.
2. Local transit—Management—Addresses, essays, lectures.
3. Transportation planning—Addresses, essays, lectures.
I. Gray, George E., date   II. Hoel, Lester A.
HE305.P8   388.4   78–11618
ISBN 0–13–739169–2

Editorial/production supervision and interior design
    by Art Lizza and Virginia Huebner
Cover design by Frederick Charles Ltd.
Manufacturing buyer: Gordon Osbourne

Printed in the United States of America

10 9 8 7 6 5 4 3 2 1

PRENTICE-HALL INTERNATIONAL, INC., *London*
PRENTICE-HALL OF AUSTRALIA PTY. LIMITED, *Sydney*
PRENTICE-HALL OF CANADA, LTD., *Toronto*
PRENTICE-HALL OF INDIA PRIVATE LIMITED, *New Delhi*
PRENTICE-HALL OF JAPAN, INC., *Tokyo*
PRENTICE-HALL OF SOUTHEAST ASIA PTE. LTD., *Singapore*
WHITEHALL BOOKS LIMITED, *Wellington, New Zealand*

Dedicated to the many who helped put this together,
but especially to Benita H. Gray—who did the most.

CONTENTS

PART II: SYSTEMS AND TECHNOLOGIES

PART III: COMPARING TRANSIT MODES

PART IV: PLANNING PUBLIC TRANSPORTATION SYSTEMS

PART V: MANAGING AND OPERATING PUBLIC TRANSIT SYSTEMS

PREFACE

As we enter the last quarter of the twentieth century there is little doubt that the current degree of mobility of the industrialized world, especially in these United States, is higher than that enjoyed by human beings in any other age. The automobile, the airplane, and other forms of transportation provide comparatively economical and rapid access to all parts of the developed world. In most areas the automobile supplies an overwhelming percentage of trips that involve a mechanical means of travel. In this country the average person travels about 10 times as many miles in a lifetime as did his/her grandfather, and an estimated 25 times as many miles as did the average person in 1900. However, there are overwhelming indications that unless there are substantial changes in the facilities to provide this mobility, we may soon reach our mobility zenith—if we haven't already.

Continued use of the automobile in the United States and much of the developed world as the dominant mode to provide travel is causing severe impact problems, especially in our urban areas—problems which are so serious that it appears that changes are mandatory. Among the pressures leading to this conclusion are:

1. Increased congestion, which lowers auto utility so much that in some of the world's major cities individually owned and operated autos really are not a practical means of travel.
2. Increasing air and sound pollution.
3. The growing cost of petroleum products, coupled with the knowledge that such resources are finite.

4. Concerns that the social and economic costs of extending or expanding the necessary attendant facilities, such as highways and downtown parking, are too high and are disruptive to some of society's other goals.
5. The realization that overdependence on the auto is depriving many people of an adequate level of mobility.

Many of our elderly, young, disabled, and others without full access to an automobile are being forced to live an even more isolated life than did their grandparents, since public transportation in many areas has deteriorated. For these and other reasons, it is evident that we must give increased emphasis to improving alternatives to the auto for transportation in both our urbanized areas, where these impacts are most severe, and our rural areas, where often there is no alternative to existing auto-oriented travel.

We cannot take a laissez-faire approach to transportation and just keep on doing as we have in the past—providing more highways with only enough public transit investment to relieve critical congestion and provide for the transit captive. It is painfully obvious that fossil fuels *are* limited, that air pollution *is* affecting our lives, that congestion *is* causing wasted time and resource use, and that added facilities are often becoming prohibitively expensive. Transportation costs are climbing for all modes, which adds emphasis to the need for reassessment of our present practices. On the other hand, we cannot hide from the problems and do as Everyman desired—stop the world. The auto performs a very vital and needed function and we must learn to mitigate its harmful effects—make it cleaner, more efficient, smaller, and quieter. But even with these changes to the auto we have to do more, such as improve transportation services and options, encourage more trips by transit, discourage unnecessary auto use, and reduce the need to travel (when practical), to harbor our dwindling financial and physical resources.

Implementing new transportation services is not easy in our increasingly complex society. The reasons for this are themselves complex and are more related to social, environmental, political, and financial factors than to the technical/physical problems. Many of these inhibiting factors are rooted in a failure of the general population to understand public transportation—its potential and its limitations. Before decisions can be made on how best to provide for public transit, it is preferable to understand these and other aspects of such systems. This is the prime reason for this book. In addition, the work is designed to serve as an introduction for those who propose to be involved directly or indirectly in this rapidly developing field, which is so in need of innovation and creativity.

WHAT'S THE MAJOR THEME?

Before commitments can be made to implement new systems, be they relatively low-cost bus or high-cost, heavy-volume, sophisticated systems, many basic questions need to be addressed—at least to some degree. In fact, many argue that the decision on the type of technology to use in a given situation is secondary to certain basic questions. Unfortunately, in many communities the discussion of type of system for their area has become the major issue, with little understanding, or at least agreement, as to the community goals expected to be enhanced through development of any improved public transportation.

The major theme of this work is that public transporation can be provided through a variety of technologies and institutional arrangements. Many of the chapters will not address this topic directly, but this thought should build within readers as they progress through the presented material. Technology is not a major problem in providing high-level transit; goal determination and institutional arrangements are much more difficult to address and are the basic inhibiters in providing new systems. The subjects covered in this book are not especially mysterious. To the contrary, they are pretty well known through a great deal of writing by many very competent individuals, who, while they do not always agree on all aspects of transit, have considered a full spectrum of systems methods and policy considerations. This work brings much of the established information together in one place—where it is, hopefully, easier to find. Most chapters are followed by selected bibliographies, which can be used for further reference.

WHAT ARE MAJOR QUESTIONS INVOLVED IN TRANSPORTATION DECISIONS?

Naturally, there are many factors that should be considered in the process of determining local goals for public transportation, and these are not constant but will vary according to the particular area. The question of desired urban form as an area develops is one of the basic determinants for a transportation system. Land-use patterns are closely tied to available access, and without coordination between these two factors, neither land-use controls nor provisions for mobility are apt to be successful. Throughout most of this country, land-use controls have been so weak that such coordination has usually failed. The result has often been haphazard growth, which is difficult and expensive to serve with public transit. To mitigate this in the future, which would seem to be a desirable goal, much stronger land-use controls may be necessary. However, our existing life-style is based, to a large degree, on suburban sprawl, which is the result of poor land-use controls—and to change this is a difficult and generally unpopular endeavor which may be politically impossible under the present conditions.

This, then, leads to a key issue facing decision makers involved in public transportation—should transportation reinforce existing life-styles, or should it encourage or force changes in life-styles? This issue has not received much study until recently, even though it is probably the key transportation question facing us. Land-use regulation, communication advances, and a host of other developments can cause changes in future travel demands, but local, state, and national goals based on the answers to the basic question are needed. Until such goals exist and are accepted for implementation, improved transit services, auto disincentives, carpooling, improved auto emissions, and similar programs will continue to have conflicting effects. Evidence based on recent travel investigations indicates that increases or decreases in transportation use by mode of travel will be minimal unless other factors, such as implementation of a new system (e.g.,Washington,D.C.'s Metro) or severely limited fuel availability, make such changes highly attractive or mandatory. Of course, even if possible to accomplish, a program of shaping land use through providing transportation would conflict with other goals of society which may be paramount in a particular area. However, a severe crisis, as we eventually will face with the lack of adequate economical energy, may rapidly change the order of magnitude of our various goals.

Other major questions readers should keep in mind as they progress through this book are:

1. Should we focus on short- or long-range solutions to transporation problems? Or can we do both?
2. How should we pay for transit service? Who should pay—the user, the local taxpayer, or the national taxpayer? In what proportion?
3. Who should make decisions relative to providing service? The federal, state, regional, or local government? At present the responsibilities of the various government levels are clouded and the drive for available funding from categorical programs often forces an answer that may not be optimum.
4. How much mobility is necessary? We have a tremendous capacity in this country now—with about three seats available for our use at any particular moment —but our use of this capacity is very inefficient. This leads to a similar question.
5. How do we coordinate services to make them more effective and efficient? The transportation systems management (TSM) element of the required transportation improvement plans (TIPs) for urban areas presents an excellent basis for such coordination, however, the institutional difficulties are awesome.

HOW IS THE BOOK ORGANIZED?

Hopefully, the chapter titles are self-explanatory. Assuming that, we will not delve into their subject matter to any depth here. However, some general comments on organization by sections would seem to be in order and may help readers to determine which sections might be of special interest to them. Each section is introduced with a general summary which gives details about the contents of that section.

Part I (Historical Development) covers the history of public transporation development in the United States. The chapters are in chronological order historically and tie the actual events to causes and effects.

Part II (Systems and Technologies) is intended to expose readers to the attributes of the various modes used presently to provide public transportation service and how the modes interrelate. The introductory chapter gives the necessary conceptual framework and definitions needed to comprehend various system attributes.

Part III (Comparing Transit Modes) concentrates on the factors to consider in alternative analyses studies of transportation systems.

Part IV (Planning Public Transportation Systems) covers the vital planning area, including the historical development of planning; significant current issues regarding the planning process; the newest planning tool, the TSM; planning for small systems as found in rural areas; and how system planning for public transportation differs from transportation planning per se.

Part V (Managing and Operating Public Transit Systems) delves into the important field of managing an area of growing concern. The increased development of the industry through expansion and new systems is putting a severe strain on the trained management market. This aspect of public transit is not presented in great depth, however, as many of the current problems are site-specific and difficult to address in a logical manner.

Part VI (Policy Considerations) goes into the specifics of various factors that influence public transit services. The thoughts presented by the various authors are not always in agreement, but they should give readers a good perspective of the factors to consider when establishing goals.

Part VII (The Future) looks at the future from several viewpoints, and is well described by the chapter titles.

One final note. Terminology for this book is based on the Transportation Research Board publication, *Glossary of Urban Public Transportation Terms*. That publication is suggested as a supplemental resource for those seriously interested in the subject.

GEORGE E. GRAY

LIST OF TABLES

PART I

Historical Development

INTRODUCTION TO PART I

The purpose of this section is to develop the historical context of public transportation from the emergence of cities to the present day. The role that transportation has had in the growth and development of cities, beginning with waterborne transportation, is well known, and even today many cities are located near rivers, lakes, and oceans. Later, the railroad became a prime factor in city development and in the twentieth century, highways and air transportation significantly influenced the development and pattern of cities.

The ability of cities to expand in size depended heavily upon the available means of public transportation. Originally, travel on foot, or by crude land-based means, severely limited the ability of cities to develop. With the industrial revolution came the wherewithal to invent and perfect public transportation systems that would move large numbers of people at speeds heretofore unknown. Beginning with the horse-drawn omnibus on city streets and the later improved version with steel wheels on steel rails, public transportation moved into its heyday with the electrically powered streetcar first introduced in the late 1800s. Electric propulsion, steel wheels, and rails soon eliminated the horse-drawn streetcar and the cable car from serious use in public transportation.

The decades from the late nineteenth to early twentieth century witnessed the expansion of cities and the construction of public transportation facilities, including interurban streetcars, rapid transit, commuter railroads, and ferryboats. The construction of underground railways, first in London and later in Boston, New York, Chicago, and Philadelphia, permitted these cities to expand in size and population.

The advent of the automobile saw the gradual decline in public transportation, both streetcars and rapid transit. During the 1920–1950 period, motorbuses were replacing streetcars and subway construction had come to a virtual halt. The causes of the decline in public transportation fortunes are also attributed to overcapitalization, unwillingness by operators to adopt innovations, and to restrictive franchise rules. Other external forces were governmental regulation, limitations on public utility ownership of transit lines, the federally insured home mortgage program, and the federal highway program.

The construction of the San Francisco Bay Area Rapid Transit (BART) system in 1962 marked the first new construction of a rail rapid transit system in 50 years. Federally funded programs in public transportation began in earnest with passage of the Urban Mass Transportation Act of 1964, and today the federal share of transit obligations in cities is 47% of the total, although transit riding accounts for less than 3% of urban passenger trips. The reasons for the resurgence in public transit support include traffic congestion, economic vitality, mobility for the carless, energy conservation, and environmental protection. Transit has become the mode for all seasons, supported by conservatives and liberals alike, in the belief that these attributes will be distributed equitably with little inconvenience or change in lifestyle to the traveling public.

LESTER A. HOEL, Professor and Chairman,
Department of Civil Engineering,
University of Virginia

Chapter 1

THE DEVELOPMENT OF PUBLIC TRANSPORTATION AND THE CITY*

GEORGE M. SMERK, *Professor of Transportation, Graduate School of Business, Indiana University*

The city is the hallmark of a civilization. History is full of exploits of battle, discovery, endurance, and victory over the hostility of nature that took place away from cities and urban places. Yet the true progress of mankind is measured by the felicity of the good life; the excitement of great adventures of the mind; the glow of creativity as expressed in music, poetry, and the graphic arts; the formulation of law to protect men from one another and from overly rapacious government; the fellowship of society; and the greater productivity possible from the sharing of talents and skills—such progress is apparently possible only in an urban place.

IN THE BEGINNING: THE CITY

Cities as permanent places of habitation are a product of the first great turning point reached by mankind: the agricultural revolution. Early mankind hunted and gathered locally available foodstuffs and other materials necessary for human survival. Even a rich area was soon depleted of animals fit for food or of berries or other wild edibles, which meant that the human residents were forced to move on in order to survive. When man learned how to plant crops and domesticate certain animals, he could exchange the role of wanderer for that of urban dweller.

The agricultural revolution by itself was not sufficient to cause the development of major urban centers. The growth, development, and shaping of cities in their modern

---

*A previously published article on this subject is: GEORGE M. SMERK, "200 Years in Transit," *MASS TRANSIT*, 3, no. 7 (July–August 1976), 4–9.

form is closely related to the availability of transportation. To begin with, in order to grow to any great size, an urban place requires an external transportation system because urban dwellers tend to be specialists in tasks other than raising food and gathering supplies. Since the beginning of larger-scale urbanization, urban residents necessarily have traded the fruits of their specialization for the surpluses of foodstuffs and supplies brought in from other areas. How large a population of specialists a city may support is, therefore, directly related to the size of the hinterland that an urban place may tap for its food and supplies.

In ancient times, before mechanical means of transportation or engineered transportation improvements were possible, land travel was difficult and slow. Wheeled vehicles were scarce because they were expensive and difficult to make; roads were rough and difficult to use if they existed at all. With capital always scarce, primitive societies simply could not afford to take the time and effort—nor were the skills available—to provide good land transportation. On the other hand, rivers, lakes, streams, and the oceans provided natural means of transportation that enabled large quantities of goods to be moved, in early times on simple rafts and later by means of more sophisticated vessels. Urban places located on waterways thus had the potential to grow because their available hinterland was larger than that of an urban location away from water. For example, a budding community located in a river basin, especially if it was downstream, was in an excellent position to grow; the closer to the mouth of a river, the larger the hinterland that might be tapped. In an age without mechanical transportation, heavy materials could be moved easily downstream only with the current. Cities located at the mouth of a river at the sea had the potential of supporting a large population; they not only had access to the surplus of the entire river basin upstream, but could also trade with the other seashore cities.

Because of the importance of water transportion to help supply cities, even today most of the major cities of the world are located on waterways or on large lakes. However, nonwaterside locations also became attractive for modern urban locations, since railroads, highways, pipelines, and airplanes can move the supplies and foodstuffs necessary to support a large population. Water transportation is no longer a prerequisite for the growth of a large city, although the momentum of an early start has allowed water-oriented cities to continue growing, and most major U.S. cities are located on water.

THE GENESIS OF URBAN MASS TRANSPORTATION: THE AGE OF THE OMNIBUS

As long as an urban area was small in scope, residents could make their way about on foot and goods could be carried or moved with relative ease by simple and even crude means of transport. With increased city size, however, getting about on foot became a different proposition, greatly limiting the size of internal markets for goods and services, and making difficult the process of gathering a labor force from throughout the whole of the community. If a city grows large enough, limitations on the means of internal circulation of people, as well as goods, can have a decided dampening effect on urban growth and development. On the other hand, given good external and internal transportation, growth is affected not only by transportation, but by other economic, social, cultural, and geographic factors. Furthermore, over time, the means of internal transportation can have an impact on shaping the growth of an urban area.

The idea of providing a land-based public conveyance for passengers within an urban area can be dated back at least 300 years. In 1662 the eminent French mathematician Pascal began to operate a horse-drawn omnibus line in Paris. In the early period of its operation, the omnibus operated free of charge. Pascal's brainchild became popular and it was quite the rage for people of quality, as well as others of less elegant status, to utilize the new means of urban transportation. When a fare was finally charged, after a time of free operation, the public rebelled and patronage fell off so sharply that Pascal was forced to quit the omnibus business.

With the industrial revolution came both the rapid growth of cities and the separation of home and work place. The worker no longer possessed the tools of a trade that he plied at home; he worked at a machine in a factory, both of which belonged to someone else. The need to travel regularly between home and factory made the now familiar peak-hour trip a common feature of urban life. As the leader in industrialization, by the early 1800s London was awash with a tidal wave of humanity at the beginning and end of each working day as tens of thousands of working people, from the highest position to the lowest, crowded the streets, walking back and forth to work.

Mass transportation finally came to the British capital in 1829, when an enterprising coach builder named George Shillibeer introduced the first modern omnibus. The vehicle was designed for the regular pickup and drop-off of passengers and was operated by Shillibeer along a regular route from Paddington Green to the Bank. Although Shillibeer's company did not stay in business very long, the idea of the omnibus caught on; soon these vehicles crowded the streets of the great cities of the world, beginning with London and gaining popularity in Paris, New York, and elsewhere during the 1830s.

The omnibus was a high-wheeled wagonlike vehicle, with the entrance at the rear. Seats inside, for perhaps as many as 18 to 20 passengers, were arranged longitudinally along the walls so that the passengers sat facing one another. The rear entrance, with a step down to the ground level, made it possible to enter and exit with relative ease compared to a stagecoach.

Omnibuses had few amenities for the passengers apart from what was usually a fancy and brightly painted exterior. There was, of course, no heat in cold weather and passengers had to be content with straw piled on the floor in which to snuggle their feet. Omnibus drivers were known for their large vocabulary of profanity as they questioned the heritage and other habits of fellow omnibus drivers in mad dashes to the curb to pick up potential passengers. Accidents were common as the number of omnibuses grew along with the rise of other street traffic. Crowding soon grew so bad in London that to provide greater mass transportation capacity, the double-decked

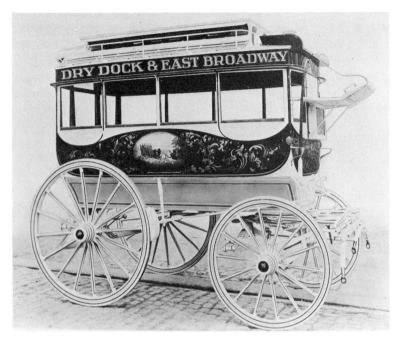

Figure 1-1 *Early omnibus. Used in New York City. (courtesy of American Public Transit Association)*

omnibus became a common feature, as a forerunner of the present-day, double-decked bus of London.

In several cities—particularly in Europe—the omnibus allowed people of modest income to live beyond walking distance from work. This opened up the possibilities of better climate and better housing for a great mass of population on the outskirts of the city. At the same time, omnibuses were usually more expensive to ride than the streetcar that appeared on the scene a bit later. Omnibuses were not heavily used in the United States except in a few of the largest cities, but they were especially popular and long-lived in New York City. New York saw its first omnibus in 1831, when Abraham Brower began to operate a line between the Battery and Bond Street along Broadway.

Where it was utilized, the omnibus strengthened the central business district (CBD) of cities, helping to make the central area a focal point for internal travel. However, because of their limited speed of about 5 km/h (3 mi/h), they could not penetrate long distances into relatively undeveloped urban areas within a reasonable travel time, nor help to open up new portions of a city. The horse-drawn omnibus, in almost its original form, continued in use in many cities throughout the world until the early 1900s; in those places where they were used so long, it was usually because of local restrictions against laying rail in certain streets. As a result, omnibuses were often directly replaced by motorbuses, as was the case on Fifth Avenue in New York.

The omnibus had the virtues of relatively low capital cost and inherent flexibility. Balanced against the advantages were the discomfort of operations on poor road surfaces, low speed, and very limited passenger capacity. As useful as it was, the omnibus was a mode of mass transportation with decided limitations. It is small wonder, then, that its use was never as extensive—at least in the United States—as was its successor in time, the horsecar.

THE MASS TRANSIT REVOLUTION: THE AGE OF THE STREET RAILWAY, 1830–1920

The streetcar as a mode of mass transportation was introduced, almost as an afterthought, in New York City in November 1832. A line of track had been laid along Fourth Avenue to bring the cars of the New York and Harlem Railroad into the heart of the city. City restrictions prohibited the use of steam locomotives in the streets of lower Manhattan, so the passenger cars were pulled by horses from Harlem into the downtown area. The enterprising promoters of the Harlem Railroad saw the potential for hauling local passengers in regular urban transit service, in addition to pulling the steam railroad coaches downtown. Lightweight cars were built and the Fourth Avenue line became the world's first streetcar service.

Figure 1-2 *Horsecar. Used in Philadelphia in 1880.* (*courtesy of American Public Transit Association*)

The horse-drawn streetcar had a number of advantages over the omnibus. Metal wheels operating on metal rails possessed a low coefficient of friction and the cars were thus much easier to pull by a given amount of horsepower. Horsecars could therefore be somewhat larger than omnibuses, with a larger payload of passengers, and yet still require only one or two horses. Because they were easier to pull, a horsecar could maintain a speed of about 6.4 km/h (4 mi/h), which was about 1 mi/h faster than the average of the omnibus.

By the late 1840s, after a slow start outside New York City, the horse-drawn streetcar appeared in a number of other American cities. By the time of the Civil War and immediately thereafter, almost all American cities and towns of any size, or those with even a modest delusion of metropolitan grandeur, had horse- or mule-powered street railway companies. As with the omnibuses, there were many competitors in a business—urban mass transit—usually thought of as a natural monopoly. Typically, there was no single city transit company operating all the omnibuses or streetcars; service on each street was usually offered by a separate firm having a franchise granting monopoly power to operate over given streets. The possibility of a multiplicity of transit operations in a town was often a fact. Philadelphia, at one time, had 39 streetcar companies all operating at virtually the same time. The public was not generally well served in the broad civic sense by competition among several local horsecar companies. Each firm served only a limited area; longer trips required changing vehicles and paying separate fares each time a different company was used. Long trips were discouraged if more than one company was involved.

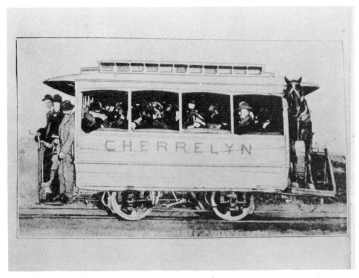

Figure 1-3 *Fifty-fifty. On this archaic line, in the outskirts of Denver, a horse pulled the car up hill and then rode down on the rear platform. He was on the job so long that his shoes wore grooves in the flooring.* (*courtesy of American Public Transit Association*)

Mergers between the street railway companies began to take place slowly but surely during horsecar days; as the transit industry moved toward mechanical means of transportation, the increased need for capital was one of the spurs to merger, since larger, more stable companies fared better in the capital market.

Horsecars required a larger capital investment than did the omnibus because track had to be laid in the streets. The horsecars themselves were of light construction and, depending on size, ranged in cost from about $600 to $1000. The horses, as with the omnibus, were, over time, the most expensive part of the investment. The usual cost was about $200 each and the horses were usually kept for 5 years. Horses in street railway service could be worked for only about 5 hours a day; thus, to keep a single car in service for a 15-hour day would take from three to six horses, depending on whether one or two horses were used per car. Additional trace horses helped the regular teams climb grades.

Because tracks were constructed in public streets, franchises were usually necessary so that the public thoroughfare could be used for private enterprise. Often, cities required that an annual franchise tax be paid. In addition, there were often duties required by the street railway company as part of the franchise agreements. For example, it was common to demand that the street railway pave the area around its tracks, and the railway was responsible for clearing snow from the paved track area in winter. If that were the only cleared portion of the street, as was commonly the case, wagons and buggies soon cluttered up the streetcar right-of-way. In some cases, the street railway company was required to pave the entire street from curb to curb, which could be a substantial financial burden and, in later years, aided and abetted the buses and automobiles that competed with the street railways. Another requirement was spraying the unpaved part of the street with water in the summer to help keep down the dust. In the electric railway days, streetcar companies often had to maintain public bridges upon which their cars operated. Another typical franchise precept was that the fare imposed on the public be no more than 5 cents. The nickel fare proved to be lucrative in most places during the last 30 years of the nineteenth century, when prices were relatively stable.

The horsecar operated at an average speed of 6.4 km/h (4 mi/h). If one uses a rule of thumb of no more than a half-hour for commuting time, one can travel 2 miles within that half-hour; therefore, it was possible for the nineteenth-century commuter of the horsecar age to find a pleasant area to live several miles from his downtown work location and enjoy the benefits of better or cheaper housing without having to bear the burden of inordinately long walks or travel time. The horsecar helped to stimulate the outward growth of the city, but the growth tended to be relatively compact. There were few long fingers of growth out into undeveloped areas. The street railways added to the importance of the established downtown area by helping to make it the most accessible place in the city and, thus, the prime location for most economic, social, and cultural activities.

Despite its many advantages over the omnibus, there was no denying that street railway managers were not happy with the horse-drawn streetcar. Many attempts were made to find some sort of mechanical power to replace the horse. The first real answer to the problem of motive power came with the successful operation of cable cars in San Francisco in 1873. Invented by Andrew Hallidie in 1869, the ingenious part of the cable car was the grip that allowed a cable, running continuously in a slot between the tracks and beneath the street, to be grasped and released so that cars could start and stop. For propulsion, the cars could rely on the power of giant engines harnessed to the moving cable. The cable car, therefore, had great potential for mass movement.

The cable railway first commended itself to attention as a means of mounting San Francisco's formidable hills; the areas on Nob Hill, Russian Hill, and to the north and west of Market Street were immediately opened for urban development. But the cable car was not merely a street railway vehicle for a city with steep hills. The passenger-carrying capacity of a cable railway system was substantial because of the power available. Cities without the problems of hill-climbing soon adopted the new type of urban transportation. Indeed, Chicago, a city not known for hills, had the largest cable car operation in the United States. Grip cars pulling up to three trailers, and traveling at close headways, provided the capacity to move thousands of people into a central location. The importance of downtown Chicago as the great and vibrant business district and major place of employment was actually made possible by the cable car, long before the elevated railway loop (the Loop) was built in the central business district.

What made the cable car attractive, particularly in large cities with many people to

Figure 1-4 *Cable car. San Francisco cable car in 1952, and still going strong. (courtesy of American Public Transit Association)*

move, was that it had a much lower operating cost than the horse-powered railway. However, if the cable railway provided relief from operating cost, the formidable capital investment required—probably a minimum of $100,000 per route-mile and perhaps much more—meant that the cable car was practical only where there were large masses of people to move.

Because of its relatively high speed potential, the cable car helped draw city development out along its routes. Of course, the need for a dense traffic level meant that most cable lines were located in well-built-up sections of a city, usually as a replacement for busy horsecar lines. The development attributable to cable traction would have been even greater had the cable car not so soon been superseded by another and better form of mass transportation.

For many years, people fascinated with electricity had been attempting to devise some method of electrically propelling a vehicle along rails. Early experiments used battery-powered cars and were not particularly successful. It was not until dynamo-generated current was perfected in the late 1860s and 1870s and the transmission of power over a relatively great distance through wires became possible that electrically propelled transportation was at all practical.

A number of pioneers experimented with electric locomotives or electric railway cars with more or less success during the early 1880s. In 1883 Charles Van Depoele operated an experimental electric line in Chicago, and on heels of that success operated a service at the Toronto Exposition in 1885. The spring-loaded pole pressing on the bottom of the wire, with the return circuit made through the running rails, was perfected by Van Depoele. The early electric cars were crude and undependable. Most were nothing more than converted horsecars, with the motor placed on the platform next to the driver, now dubbed a motorman. The rheostatic control was rough and chain drive was used to power the wheels of the car. Vibration was a major problem and the weight of the motor caused the platform of the car to buckle.

In 1888, however, the state of the art was greatly improved when Frank J. Sprague electrified a portion of the horsecar lines in Richmond, Virginia, and brought together all the elements that were necessary for the successful operation of electrically powered streetcars. Sprague used overhead wire with a bottom-contact, spring-loaded trolley pole to collect the current; the return circuit was through the rails. Sprague also devised an improved control system so that the cars were easier to operate. He also developed a means of suspending the electric motors so that there would be a minimum of wear and tear on the motors and gears from vibration, and the operation of the cars would be relatively smooth and trouble free.

The electric streetcar precipitated a revolution in urban public transportation. Within two years of the completion of Sprague's electrification project in Richmond, the electric railway was rapidly taking over the horsecar and cable operations, and better than 1900 km (1200 mi) of electric street railways were in operation in the United States. From a cost viewpoint, the electric railway car was far superior to both the cable car and the horse-powered street railway. It simply cost a great deal less to install track and the overhead wire and power distribution system for an electric railway than it did to put in the costly and complex cable system. If the capital cost was

Figure 1-5 *CBD in transportation transition. Los Angeles at the turn of the century. Horse, electric, and gasoline vehicles vie for the right-of-way. (courtesy of Southern California Rapid Transit District)*

lower than that of the cable railway, operating cost was lower than that of the horse railway.

The electric railway car was capable of an average speed of at least 16 km/h (10 mi/h) and had the potential for even more. This permitted street railways to be extended far out from central business districts and still bring in people to work or to shop in half an hour. Within a few years, the electric streetcar played an important role in shaping the city it served as the population oriented itself to the location of the expanding street railway system. It should also be added that, since many of the streetcar companies were also in the real estate business, the city shaping was deliberate in many cases. The electric traction promoters would buy large tracts of land in promising outlying territory and then extend the streetcar line to the land that they owned. The transit company stood to profit by people buying its land, building or buying houses, as well as becoming regular streetcar customers.

The coming of the electric streetcar also had an impact on the structure of the transit industry. The multiplicity of street railway operations that were common during the horsecar days—that is, many separate firms operating in a single city— were ruled out as a practical matter when it became both possible and necessary to electrify. Generally, there were wholesale mergers as dispersed companies pulled together to form what was often called the Union Traction Company of whatever city was involved. The larger company was better able to attract capital for the purposes of electrification than were separate, small, independent horse-railway companies. However, many small companies not only were overcapitalized, but much of the capital was in the form of debt. When mergers were consummated the surviving company had embraced the capital structure of the absorbed firms and was usually burdened by capitalization that greatly exceeded the value of the assets.

The shaky financial situation in the transit industry was widespread, although it did not include the entire industry. However, as long as prices and costs were stable—as they were for most of the last 30 years of the nineteenth century—and patronage continued to grow, the transit industry could function as a safe, stable, and seemingly profitable institution. At the same time, the overcapitalized transit firms were, in reality, on the edge of financial disaster if prices in general should rise or if patronage plummeted.

By the time of World War I, the electric streetcar had had a major impact on the growth and structure of cities. The huge influx of immigrants from abroad and from rural areas of the nation into American cities had helped swell urban growth, and the development of the urban area was often channeled along the streetcar lines. Like the arms of a starfish, the streetcar lines projected out as far as 8 km (5 mi), and even more in some cities, from the central business district. The electric streetcar provided the basic transportation for American cities before the coming of the auto age. Service was good, fares were relatively cheap, and the streetcar was a part of everyday life for citizens of all classes, occupations, ages, and economic levels. It is fair to say that the streetcar had the most decisive effect upon the shaping of American cities of any factor up to the coming of the automobile age and the almost universal use of the private car for urban transportation.

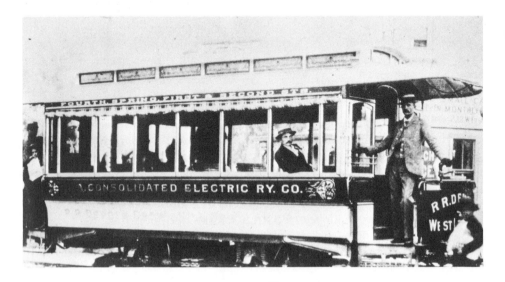

Figure 1-6 *Early streetcar, Sacramento, Calif. (courtesy of Southern California Rapid Transit District)*

Figure 1-7 *Downtown congestion. Dearborn and Randolph Streets, Chicago, 1910 —congestion! (courtesy of Federal Highway Administration)*

Figure 1-8 *Downtown congestion. Same location fifty-six years later. (courtesy of Federal Highway Administration)*

Through the first two decades of the twentieth century, large U.S. cities were streetcar cities. Their internal mobility was almost totally dependent upon the streetcar. The central focal point was, of course, the bustling downtown. Strip shopping streets developed along the streetcar's radial arteries. Local shopping centers formed where several streetcar lines intersected. Housing, to be convenient and marketable, had to be within no more than two or three blocks of the streetcar line. Large factories or major employment centers of any kind had to locate where there was either the existence or potential of streetcar service. The public-transit-oriented city was relatively compact and population was relatively concentrated. Lesser densities were possible out along the suburban and interurban electric lines or the commuter railroads, but even there homes tended to cluster.

THE MASS TRANSPORTATION AGE: FERRIES, COMMUTER RAILROADS, INTERURBANS, AND RAPID TRANSIT

In discussing transportation by rail and by omnibus in the early days of the development of modern cities, one must not forget the ferryboat and its role in urbanization. A number of American cities were faced with water barriers; urbanization across those barriers would have been impossible without the ferry. Early engineering knowledge and available structural materials were so limited that it was not possible in the early days to construct bridges across the Hudson and the East Rivers in New York, the Delaware River in Philadelphia, or Boston Bay and San Francisco Bay. The ferry provided a means of crossing water barriers quickly and at relatively low cost. Thus, the ferry made possible in certain locations the expansion of urbanization from an original core city to many other adjacent areas. Like the street railway, it permitted persons of ordinary means the opportunity to find good housing and, perhaps, a more favorable environment than were available in the major city center. The ferry, along with the other modes of public transportation, allowed cities to develop horizontally at a time when engineering skill and the quality of materials precluded vertical development of high-rise housing.

Commuter railroads must be included in any discussion of urban mass transportation and city growth. Generally, commuter rail service had its inception when enterprising nineteenth-century railroad management noted that it was possible to pick up additional passengers on trains already being operated if those trains entered the city in the morning hours coinciding with the beginning of work and departed in late afternoon at the end of the workday. Obviously, if a railroad was already operating a long-distance passenger train into the city, the extra cost of stopping at the outskirts was virtually nil; the revenue collected from the passengers was almost sheer gravy. In the nineteenth century railroads encouraged this kind of traffic. Some involved themselves in land development schemes, much like the early street railway companies, in order to encourage suburban development. In any event, to be attractive to the would-be suburban passenger, the railroads typically cut, or commuted, a part of the fare. Thus developed the name "commuter" for the regular, shuttling passenger on the railways and, indeed, for all who traveled back and forth regularly.

Eventually, in some places, the commuter or suburban railroad operations became very large in scope as cities expanded. The development of Long Island beyond Queens and Brooklyn is a case in point; its growth was due to the substantial commuter operations of the Long Island Rail Road. Like the ferry, the commuter railroad permitted persons of ordinary means the opportunity to find good housing and, perhaps, a more favorable environment than were available in the major city center. In Boston, Philadelphia, Chicago, and along the peninsula in San Francisco, commuter rail service fostered a great outward spread of population. It should be noted, however, that the pattern of development was different from that fostered by the streetcar. Because of the economics and operating nature of the steam locomotives originally used as the motive power in commuter rail operations, growth was not along a solid corridor adjacent to the railroad, but, rather, resembled beads spaced out on a string. It was uneconomical to start and stop steam locomotives much more often than about every 3 or 5 km (2 or 3 mi); the stops therefore tended to be spread out. Around the railway stations, housing would develop. In many cases, these communities strung out along the railway remained enclaves of suburbanization in otherwise rural areas and did not grow together until well after the coming of the automobile age.

In the Midwest, in particular, there was another variation of the growth pattern wrought by the commuter railroad. In the late 1890s interurban electric railway lines were developed linking smaller cities, often 80 km (50 mi) or more distant, with a larger regional city. The interurban cars, while closely related in technology to the local streetcar, were larger and more comfortable and capable of relatively high speeds. The economics and technology of the interurban were such that stops could be efficiently spaced at intervals as short as a quarter of a mile (0.4 km) apart where necessary. A beads-on-a-string type of development, similar to the commuter railroads, took place in the outskirts of many cities served by interurbans, but because the separate clusters of housing were closer together, the process of growing together into a long suburban arm of development was more likely to take place.

In some places the growth of a city and its population was so great that it became evident more than a century ago that some means of fast transportation utilizing other than the street surface was necessary. Street traffic had reached such formidable proportions in London by the 1850s that mobility was seriously threatened and it was obvious that some new form of fast transportation had to be developed on a grade-separated right-of-way. The British response was the 1863 opening of the Metropolitan Railway's steam-powered underground line in London from Farringdon Street in the city to Bishop's Road, Paddington. Shortly thereafter, in 1868, and for the same reason of surface congestion and the need for faster movement, the first elevated railway was opened in New York City. As with the earlier London subway, the New York elevated trains were propelled by steam locomotives.

With the coming of electrification after 1888, and Frank Sprague's invention of multiple-unit train control in the 1890s, rapid transit became even more popular for handling large crowds with swiftness denied the surface modes. With electrification, unlucky pedestrians need not worry about hot ashes falling on them from an elevated railway and Londoners traveling on their underground railway system did not have to worry about suffocating or bearing on their clothes and faces the environmental pollution of steam locomotives. By the first decade of the twentieth century, a network of electric elevated railways covered parts of Brooklyn and Manhattan. Chicago enjoyed the services of several steam-powered elevated railways in the 1890s; with the coming of electrification, the systems were greatly extended and linked together in the famous downtown Loop. The first American subway was a streetcar subway in Boston, opened in 1898, and soon followed by a subway built for trains. New York's first subway was opened in 1904 and construction of additional subways proceeded rapidly for the next 35 years. Philadelphia's first subway opened in 1907 and Chicago began using its first underground railway not long before World War II. Cleveland started construction of a rapid transit system in the 1920s; delayed by the Great Depression and World War II, it was finally opened in the 1950s. The San Francisco Bay area built its rapid transit system in the 1960s and 1970s as an antidote to the automobile.

Rapid transit was feasible only where the population was very large and dense and where street crowding was so overwhelming that there was no choice but to move to some high-capacity, rapid means of public transportation. Generally, rail rapid transit systems were built only in the developed parts of a city and, therefore, their impact on spreading growth was relatively modest. However, some of the earliest of New York's elevated railways were built out from the most highly developed parts of the city and strongly influenced growth in the Bronx, Brooklyn, and Queens. Locations around the rapid transit stations were often choice spots for high-density development of apartment buildings, factories, or mercantile establishments. In the London area, however, beginning in the teens and especially the twenties of the century, the underground rapid transit railway system was extended far into the suburbs on the north side of the Thames. Today people may travel as far as 56 km (35 mi) by "underground"—mostly running on the surface, of course—to find their way eventually into downtown London. The new Bay Area Rapid Transit District system in the San Francisco area resembles the London system in its ability to shape and stimulate growth well out into the suburbs, as well as serving as a backbone of public transportation in the more densely populated parts of Oakland, Berkeley, and San Francisco.

MASS TRANSPORTATION IN THE HIGHWAY AGE: THE MOTORBUS AND TROLLEYBUS, 1920 TO THE PRESENT

With the construction of subways in many parts of the world in the 1920s, the first great age of public transportation came to an end. Insofar as urban growth and development was concerned, the major transportation force of the next 50 years—especially in the United States—was the private automobile. The rapidly rising costs of the World War I period forced the overcapitalized transit systems to the wall. Even though patronage broke all records, the franchise-regulated fare of a nickel limited revenues while debt capital still demanded payment of bond interest. There was not enough revenue in many places to pay operating cost and capital obligations. By 1918 half of the street railway mileage in the United States was in bankruptcy. Even with financial reorganization, the transit firms of the nation were in poor condition to meet the challenge of the automobile age that dominated the years after 1920. This does not, of course, mean that development of new forms of transit was at an end.

In the 1930s, members of the transit industry allied to produce a new type of streetcar. The PCC (Electric Railway Presidents' Conference Committee) car was the superb result, the end product of the first systems engineering effort in U.S. history. As good as it was, the PCC car could not turn the tide in the United States against the move away from fixed-facility surface transportation with its burden of track and overhead wire maintenance cost.

The motorbus and the trolleybus are the major transit innovations of the mid-twentieth-century move away from the street railway. The motorbus is an obvious offshoot of the development of the automobile and the truck. The first regular use of buses by an existing transit firm took place in New York in 1905 when the Fifth Avenue Coach Company replaced some of its omnibuses with imported motorbuses. In 1912 Cleveland Railways began to use buses as feeders to its streetcar lines. These vehicles were often crude and uncomfortable and suffered from the same uncertainties as the early automobile.

What was needed for the real development of the motorbus was a conveyance that was easy to get into and use. The Fageol brothers provided such a vehicle in the early 1920s with the construction of front-engine buses that were designed from the ground up to be motor carriers of passengers. These buses had relatively low entrance steps,

Figure 1-9 *Early bus—the later streetcar killer.* (*courtesy of Southern California Rapid Transit District*)

doors that could be operated by the driver, and—except for the engine location—were very much like smaller versions of the buses of today.

Over the years, bus design and reliability improved greatly and by the late 1930s all the elements of the modern motorbus, with the exception of air conditioning and air suspension systems, were brought together in a single vehicle. By 1939, the motorbus that was to become typical was powered by a large, powerful diesel engine mounted at the rear and driving the vehicle through an automatic transmission. Buses by that time were produced up to a length of 12 m (40 ft) with a capacity of more than 50 seated passengers. Some gasoline-powered—and, later, propane-powered buses—continued to be produced into the 1950s, but the diesel soon became the standard.

The great advantage of the motorbus is, of course, its flexibility, since it can go anywhere there is a decently paved street. Happily, the motorbus does not require any sort of overhead power distribution or the installation and maintenance of rails in the street as did the streetcar, and is thus a truly independent vehicle. Better yet, the cost of the street surface that the motorbus uses is shared with all the other vehicles that operate on that street. The advantage of not having to pay the entire cost of the streets they use is marred for the transit bus by having to share that surface with all other motor vehicles; the bus wallowing in automobile traffic is a typical modern sight. As a result, service is often slow and undependable.

Small buses began to make inroads on streetcar operations in the 1920s. The street railway companies, sometimes burdened with motorbus competition, but often going into the motorbus business themselves when they recognized its advantages for service on lightly traveled lines, soon adopted the bus as a regular part of their operations. Starting in the 1920s, shuttle streetcar lines and light-traffic suburban lines began to be converted into bus operations. With the advent of the large diesel-powered buses in the late thirties, even major streetcar lines with heavy patronage soon fell to the conquering modern relative of the omnibus.

Another twentieth-century innovation is the trolleybus, a combination of both the electric streetcar and the bus. Equipped with twin trolley poles to gather electricity from overhead wires, the trolleybus enjoys the quiet power of electric traction. At the same time, since it travels on rubber tires like a bus, there is no need for the expensive business of laying track in the street. Moreover, the trolleybus, since it is free to move at some distance from under the center line of its wires, can easily get around obstacles in the street that would block conventional rail-bound streetcars. Many conversions from streetcar to bus operations in the United States enjoyed an interim period of a switchover to the trolleybus. The reason behind this intermediate move was the advantage to the transit property of being able to continue to utilize its major investment in power stations and power distribution equipment for several more years after the abandonment of the street railway. When the necessity for repairs or modernization of the power distribution system became substantial enough, the trolleybuses were typically replaced with motorbuses.

It is very difficult to find evidence that either the motorbus or electric trolleybus had any part in shaping the growth of modern American cities; this is so because recent urban growth came at the same time as the whirlwind upsurge in use of the private automobile. It is the automobile that has been the prime factor in shaping and developing recent urban growth, so whatever impact the bus or trolleybus may have had is virtually invisible.

There is much being written about the possible virtues and growth-shaping possibilities of new and exotic forms of urban mass transportation. Regardless of what may actually happen, it is unlikely that in the foreseeable future any of the new means of public transportation now under development will have any greater impact on urban growth than did the streetcar in the United States.

The decline of public mass transportation will be covered in the next chapter. But, to end this chapter on a cheerful note, one should remark that all over the world increased attention is being directed to upgrading and improving mass transportation. It is likely that over the next half-century mass transit will once again become a potent force for shaping cities as well as serving them.

SELECTED BIBLIOGRAPHY

CORLISS, CARLTON, JR., *Main Line of Mid-America*. New York: Creative Age Press, 1950.

DAY, JOHN R., *The Story of London's Underground*. London: London Transport, 1963.

GILMORE, HARLAN W., *Transportation and the Growth of Cities*. Glencoe, Ill.: The Free Press, 1953.

GRAS, NORMAN S. B., *Introduction to Economic History*. New York: Harper & Brothers, Publishers, 1922.

HILTON, GEORGE W., *The Cable Car in America*. Berkeley, Calif.: Howell-North Books, 1971.

———, AND JOHN F. DUE, *The Electric Interurban Railways in America*. Stanford, Calif.: Stanford University Press, 1960.

MIDDLETON, WILLIAM D., *The Interurban Era*. Milwaukee, Wis.: Kalmbach Publishing Co., 1961.

———, *The Time of the Trolley*. Milwaukee, Wis.: Kalmbach Publishing Co., 1967.

MILLER, JOHN ANDERSON, *Fares, Please!* New York: Dover Publications, Inc., 1960. (Published originally in 1940.)

MUMFORD, LEWIS, *The Culture of Cities*. New York: Harcourt, Brace and Company, 1938.

PFEIFFER, JOHN, "Man's First Revolution," *Horizon*, 5 (September 1962), 6.

ROWSOME, FRANK, JR., *Trolley Car Treasury*. New York: Bonanza Books, 1956.

SEBREE, MAC, AND PAUL WARD, *Transit's Stepchild: The Trolley Coach*. Cerritos, Calif.: Interurbans, 1973.

Chapter 2

THE DECLINE OF TRANSIT*

ARTHUR SALTZMAN,† *Director, Transportation Institute, North Carolina A & T State University (on leave at University of California, Irvine, 1976–1978)*

It is difficult for younger persons living in the auto-oriented society of the 1970s to conceive of the important role that transit once played in urban America. To the urban dweller of the first quarter of the twentieth century, transit was as pervasive a travel mode and sociological phenomena as the automobile is today.

America's urbanization in the early part of the twentieth century was shaped to a great degree by the electric street railway. The patterns of land use and population dispersion that took place followed the spokelike patterns of new street railway lines, which allowed workers not only to commute in and out of the city but also to enjoy the open spaces for their families. Transit, in some cities, captured the imagination of the most prestigious citizens, who recognized that commercial and residential development would follow the transit tracks. Elevated railways and subways in the larger cities were among the largest public works of their time. They commanded the attention of financiers, who saw transit as a public utility that would yield a reasonable return on their investment. Widows and others who needed stable investments were advised to invest in the "transit trusts" because they were such a reliable source of income.

The street railway system not only provided access to downtown areas for urban residents during their 6-day workweek, but also allowed the urban family to visit the

*This chapter partially draws on work by the author done in collaboration with Richard Solomon. ARTHUR SALTZMAN AND RICHARD J. SOLOMON, "Historical Overview of the Decline of the Transit Industry," in *Public Transportation and Passenger Characteristics*, Highway Research Record 417 (Washington, D.C.: Highway Research Board, 1972), pp. 1–11.

†The author gratefully acknowledges the resources made available to him by the School of Social Sciences and the Institute of Transportation Studies of the University of California, Irvine, while he was revising this chapter in the spring of 1977. Early drafts of the chapter profited from reviews by William Millar, Edson Tennyson, John Swindler, James Perry, James Ortner, and Karen Lundegaard.

amusement parks at the end of the transit line on Sundays. Cemeteries were also often found at the end of the street railway lines, and many family outings would include a visit to the grave of a deceased relative, followed by a picnic, and a visit to the amusement park. A true transit habit was ingrained in most urban dwellers of all ages. There were few safety or security problems, and, by the time they were ready to go to school, most urban children had already been taught how to use their local transit system. Many youngsters, who developed the transit habit going to and from school, maintained it for going to work after their school years were over.

But even as the majority of travelers were making virtually all their trips by transit, wealthier urban residents were testing the new mode that eventually would be the aspiration of all Americans and become the symbol of mobility and a suburbanized life-style. At first the automobile was considered a rich man's toy, but the reduction in auto purchase prices caused by mass production and the increasing affluence of the public soon made auto ownership possible for an increasing portion of the population.

Transit simultaneously lost its glamour and pervasiveness as it lost its patronage. Instead of serving all types of trips, transit became the preferred mode only for the journey to work, and then gradually it even lost predominance in this area, being largely replaced by the private automobile for every type of trip. Transit rapidly became the conveyance only of those who had no other choice.

Competition from the automobile is often cited as the reason for the decline of transit. Although auto competition is certainly a major factor, there were also institutional, regulatory, and financial factors that affected the transit industry's performance. The transit industry has been chastised for its lack of innovative management and preoccupation with operational problems to the exclusion of marketing efforts.[1] Much of this criticism is justified, but as subsequent sections of this chapter will show, external forces over which the industry had little control were far more important in determining the destiny of transit than local ineptness.

The industry at times has tried to respond to changing travel demands, but sources of new ways of doing things have come primarily from outside the industry. Attempts at innovation from within the industry have been infrequent and, generally, have not been widely adopted. For instance, between 1916 and 1921 many street railway operators tried to raise their service level by using a smaller, lighter streetcar called the Birney Safety Car, which was equipped to operate with one man instead of the traditional two. The savings in labor were used to increase the frequency of service. Several experiments showed ridership increases ranging from 34 to 59% after the headway was decreased from 15 to 8 minutes.[2] After 1921, however, it became obvious that the Birney cars were not large enough to cope with either heavy rush-hour traffic or snow and ice; thus, they lost their popularity as rapidly as they had gained it.

Motorbuses were a major innovation to the transit industry. The street railway industry was slow to take advantage of this new technology because it was not a rail

---

[1]LEWIS M. SCHNEIDER, *Marketing Urban Mass Transit: A Comparative Study of Management Strategies* (Boston: Harvard University Graduate School of Business Administration, Division of Research, 1965).

[2]WILLIAM D. MIDDLETON, *The Time of the Trolley* (Milwaukee, Wis.: Kalmbach Publishing Co., 1967), p. 125.

system. However, by 1930, many operators had accepted the motorbus, at least for service into new territory.

Experimentation with motorbuses was widespread, ranging from every possible vehicle configuration, including double-decked and articulated buses. Even luxury routes at first-class fares were tried. Unfortunately, few new ideas took hold. In the late 1930s most transit companies exhibited little incentive to do very much more in the way of innovation than to continue to convert their street railway routes to almost identical bus routes.

The transit picture was, and still generally is, one of a large number of operators each having a monopoly in their own area. Like most utilities, the structure of the transit industry ruled out direct competition and operators were not prone to adopt successful innovations that were developed in other cities. The major exception to this was the Electric Railway Presidents' Conference Committee (PCC) car, which was developed by the industry in the mid-1930s. Unfortunately, this standardized trolley was introduced just as motorbuses were replacing most street railway systems.

There was little innovation between the end of the war and the early 1960s. The industry began a downward cycle of decreasing ridership, which led to reduced revenue. This caused reductions in service in order to reduce cost. Lower service levels inevitably led to more passengers finding another mode and, thus, the cycle would begin again. The declining ridership experienced by public transportation that started in 1945 continued into the mid-1970s. It is difficult to say that widespread adoption of innovations during this period could have reversed the trend, but perhaps at least it could have mitigated it somewhat.

The remainder of this chapter reviews the various forces that have influenced the transit industry. Ridership trends and the change of emphasis from streetcars to motorbuses is discussed. The financial and ownership problems of the transit industry are reviewed. The final section concerns the effect of government activities on the decline of transit.

TRANSIT RIDERSHIP TRENDS

Accurate historical data on ridership are difficult to find. Although the industry was criticized for the lack of adequate and accurate data as early as 1917, ridership figures, until quite recently, are not reliable.

In Fig. 2-2 the data covering the period before 1921 were obtained from the Electrical Industry Censuses of 1902, 1907, 1912, and 1917 Except for those years, most data are speculative. The U.S. Census did not distinguish between interurban and urban electric railway passengers until 1937, and did not account for non-street-railway-company-operated buses until 1932. Other estimates of motorbus patronage before 1932, fortunately, are low enough not to skew the data noticeably; however, intercity patronage and the lack of standardized accounting for transfer passengers (the definition apparently changed every 5 years) can make as much as a 10 to 20%

Figure 2-1 *Early double-deck bus (restored) next to "new look" bus of the 1950s. (courtesy of Southern California Rapid Transit District)*

difference in urban revenue passengers. Other data used to prepare Fig. 2-2 come from Barger,[3] who corrected for interurban passengers, and various corporate entries in Moody's *Public Utility* and *Transportation Manuals*.[4] Passenger data are usually reported as *revenue passengers*, which refers to initial boarding passengers only, and *total passengers*, which includes all transfer, charter, and nonrevenue rides. Thus, the peak ridership in 1945 was reported by the American Public Transit Association (APTA) as 23,254 million total passengers (18,982 million revenue passengers.)[5]

Given these problems with the data, they are still useful in depicting ridership trends of the transit industry. To review these trends, it is useful to distinguish among four time segments. These are the initial rapid growth from 1900 to 1919; a period of stabilization from 1920 to 1939; the war-induced growth of 1940 to 1945; and finally, the recent lengthy decline covering the period 1946 to 1970.

INITIAL RAPID GROWTH (1900–1919)

During the period 1900 to 1919, per capita ridership rose faster than the urban population. The introduction of electricity to the horse railways has been offered as

---

[3]HAROLD BARGER, *The Transportation Industries, 1889–1946: A Study of Output, Employment, and Productivity* (New York: National Bureau of Economic Research, 1951).

[4]FRANK J. ST. CLAIR, ed., *Moody's Public Utility Manual* (New York: Moody's Investors Service, Inc., 1969), and FRANK J. ST. CLAIR, ed., *Moody's Transportation Manual* (New York: Moody's Investors Service, Inc., 1969).

[5]AMERICAN PUBLIC TRANSIT ASSOCIATION, *Transit Fact Book*, 1975–76 ed. (Washington, D.C.: American Public Transit Association, 1976), pp. 30–32.

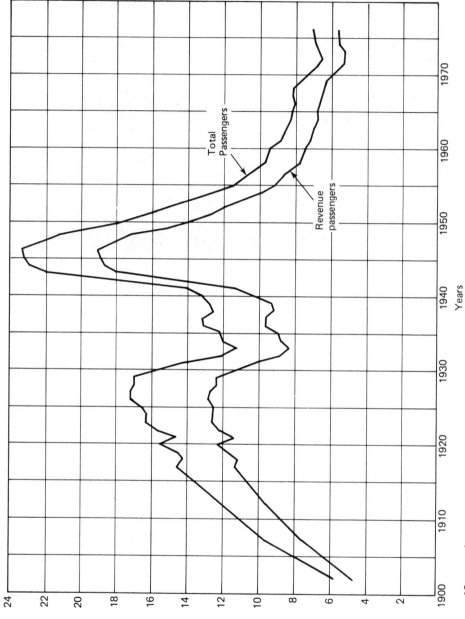

Passengers (in billions)

Years

*See text for source

Figure 2-2 *Trends in transit patronage in the United States, 1902–1976.*

the primary explanation for this.[6] The higher average speeds and capacity of line-haul electric railways permitted cities to greatly expand their urbanized areas. This dispersion necessitated more transit travel than the compact nineteenth-century city required.

STABILIZATION (1920–1939)

At the end of World War I, ridership growth stopped. Except for minor fluctuations, patronage stabilized at between 12 and 13 billion passengers per year from 1920 to 1930. Because of the increasing urban population, this unchanging passenger count actually represents a decreasing share of the urban transportation market.

Between 1929 and 1933 the lower income and loss of employment related to the Great Depression caused about a 20% decline in revenue passenger. Much of this loss was regained by the industry as the country started to climb out of its financial depression in the late 1930s.

WAR-INDUCED GROWTH (1940–1945)

A war-induced spurt of ridership started in 1939 because of gas rationing, wartime industrial production, and automobile tire and parts shortages. By 1945 ridership had climbed to almost twice its prewar level.

LENGTHY DECLINE (1946–1970)

An enormous latent demand for automobiles with their inherent flexibility had been suppressed by the war. When automobile manufacturing facilities resumed production in 1946, the affluent public started demanding more autos than were available. The establishment of the auto as the dominant urban transportation mode was spurred on by changing land-use patterns and higher incomes; and the transit industry was virtually decimated. The 5-day workweek and the reduced number of employed were also factors. Except in the large, congested urban areas, transit became the mode only for those who had no other choice. "Transit dependents" and peak-hour commuters are the only substantial markets that transit has retained.

VARIATIONS BY CITY TYPE

While the decline in transit ridership has been pervasive, it has not been uniform. Until recently, virtually every urban area lost transit ridership, but in the smaller cities, both the increase during World War II and the subsequent loss of patronage has been more severe than in the larger ones.

The increased percentage of transit patronage during the war was greatest in the smaller cities. Ridership in cities of 50,000 to 100,000 almost doubled between 1940 and 1950, while in cities of less than 50,000 population, the increase was a phenomenal

---

[6]*Proceedings of the Federal Electric Railways Commission*, 3 vols. (Washington, D.C.: U.S. Government Printing Office, 1920), pp. 2163–78.

150%.[7] In smaller cities, less transit service had been offered, and the per capita transit ridership had been comparatively low before the war. Consequently, gasoline rationing and other shortages during the war spurred transit ridership to a greater degree in the smaller urban areas.

The decline in ridership from 1945 to the 1970s has been, predictably, most severe in the smaller cities. Not only have riders opted for the auto, but the decreased ridership has caused the demise of many small transit systems altogether. The attractive travel times of rail rapid transit and the high parking costs in congested larger cities are the major factors that have kept up their transit ridership. Patronage in the dispersed smaller cities, where congestion and parking fees are not as onerous to the auto driver, has dropped more precipitously.

PEAK-HOUR DOMINANCE

Since a high percentage of its ridership is associated with work trips, transit suffers from a demand profile that is severely peaked. It is difficult to utilize vehicles and drivers efficiently where the transit traveling public takes up to five times as many rides per hour during morning and evening peak hours than during the off-peak hours. Unfortunately, this peaking phenomenon has been exacerbated during the period of transit decline. Proportionately, more off-peak riders have stopped using transit than peak-hour patrons. Transit operators have attempted to recoup some of this loss of off-peak riders by offering reduced fare to non-peak-hour riders, but usually to no avail. The journey-to-work trip which causes the peak in transit demand has maintained its patronage, while nonwork trips, which tend to be more evenly distributed throughout the day, have decreased markedly. So, while ridership and revenue have dropped, there has not been a corresponding opportunity for reductions in cost. This worsening peaking problem is further complicated by labor work rules, which give little opportunity for the operator to reduce his work force during the middle of the day.

FROM STREETCARS TO BUSES

Accompanying the decline in patronage has been a shift in modes. Table 2-1 shows that streetcars, now known as "light rail," were used for 94% of urban passenger trips in 1907. Rail rapid transit accounted for virtually all the other riders in that year. It was not until the 1920s that bus ridership became a discernible portion of the total.

The first application of the internal combustion engine to public transport occurred soon after the introduction of the gasoline-powered automobile in both Europe and America near the turn of the century. By 1905, motorbuses, not too dissimilar from contemporary streetcar physical designs albeit somewhat smaller, were running on

[7]Wilfred Owen, *The Metropolitan Transportation Problem*, rev. ed. (Washington, D.C.: The Brookings Institution, 1966), pp. 70–73.

TABLE 2-1
Trends in Methods of Transit in the
United States, Selected Years, 1907–1970 (billions of total passengers[a])

Year	Streetcar Passengers	Streetcar % of Total	Rapid Transit Passengers	Rapid Transit % of Total	Trolley Coach Passengers	Trolley Coach % of Total	Bus Passengers	Bus % of Total	Total Passengers
1907	8.9	94	0.7	7	–		–		9.5
1912	11.2	93	1.0	8	–		–		12.1
1920	13.7	88	1.8	12	–		–		15.5
1925	12.9	77	2.3	14	–		1.5	9	16.7
1930	10.5	67	2.6	17	–		2.5	16	15.6
1935	7.3	60	2.2	18	0.1	1	2.6	21	12.2
1940	5.9	45	2.4	18	0.5	4	4.2	32	13.1
1945	9.4	40	2.7	16	1.2	5	9.9	42	23.3
1950	3.9	23	2.3	13	1.7	10	9.4	55	17.2
1955	1.2	10	1.9	16	1.2	10	7.2	63	11.5
1960	0.5	5	1.8	19	0.7	11	6.4	68	9.4
1965	0.3	4	1.9	23	0.3	4	5.8	70	8.3
1970	0.2	3	1.9	26	0.2	3	5.0	68	7.3
1975	0.1	1	1.7	24	0.1	1	5.1	72	7.0

[a]Total passengers include transfer, nonrevenue, and charter passengers as well as revenue passengers.

Sources: American Public Transit Association, *Transit Fact Book*, 1975-76 ed. (Washington, D.C.: American Public Transit Association, 1976). Data for 1907-1940 are from Wilfred Owen, *The Metropolitan Transportation Problem*, rev. ed. (Washington, D.C.: The Brookings Institution, 1966), Appendix Table 16. Because of rounding, figures may not add to totals.

regular routes in London and New York. A 34-passenger double-decked bus had been imported to the United States in 1905 for a trial, and in 1907, the Fifth Avenue Coach Company in Manhattan had 14 more in service.[8]

It is true that early buses were noisy and uncomfortable, and quite a bit more expensive than later versions (to both the operator and the passenger, who often paid a double fare on a bus), but their use in New York, London, and many other European cities indicated that satisfactory equipment for innovation was available. In fact, by 1914, the London horse-drawn omnibuses had been entirely supplanted by more than 3000 motorbuses designed, built, and operated by the London General Omnibus Company.

In contrast, horse-drawn streetcars remained in service on some cross-town routes in Manhattan until 1923 because the operator could not afford to electrify, nor was the service especially amenable to the motorbus. The horsecars were later replaced with battery-powered streetcars. In Europe the motorbus was very competitive with the streetcar, a condition that was not entirely unnoticed in the United States. In a paper read at the Sixth National Conference on City Planning in May 1914, John A. McCollum stated that:

----

[8]FRANK H. MOSSMAN, ed., *Principles of Urban Transportation* (Cleveland, Ohio: Press of Western Reserve University, 1951).

Figure 2-3 *New York's Fifth Avenue double-deck buses—1930s. (courtesy of American Public Transit Association)*

The operating efficiency of the motorbus in London . . . probably exceeds the efficiency of many street railway systems. In Paris there are more than 1,000 vehicles of a type unlike those in London, operating under different conditions, but performing nevertheless an efficient passenger service. New motorbus routes are being established daily in European cities. Some are being added to street railway systems and are designed to supplement the railway services by extension into districts where the traffic does not warrant the permanent investments of the large sums necessary for the operation of a railway.[9]

Probably, the main reason that motorbuses did not take immediate hold was that the so-called "transit trusts" had vast sums invested in their streetcar lines and were not willing to make their investment obsolete or to take a chance on new technology. These operators, with some exceptions, seemed to take the attitude that they were in the electric railway industry as opposed to being in the business of providing urban transportation.[10]

A member of the motorbus industry attended an American Electric Railway Association Convention in 1922 as the representative of a bus manufacturer in Chicago. He reported that there was enough ill feeling toward the motorbus industry

---

[9]JOHN A. McCOLLUM, "Utility of the Motor Bus and Municipal Problems Pertaining to Its Operation" (unpublished paper read before the Sixth National Conference on City Planning, Toronto, May 1914), p. 5. This paper was transmitted to the Board of Estimate and Apportionment, and the Mayor of the City of New York by the Bureau of Franchises where its author was Assistant Engineer.

[10]MARTIN G. GLAESER, *Public Utilities in American Capitalism* (New York: The Macmillan Company, 1957). © The Macmillan Company, 1957.

at the convention that he was "testing the hardness of some red apples being comforted in their possibilities as weapons of defense, if necessary in covering our retreat from the convention."[11] However, a few years later in 1925, the same representative was to praise the progress made by the street railway industry in changing its attitude toward the motorbus.[12]

Although consistent and accurate statistics are not readily available on independent lines, the use of motorbuses by electric railway companies accelerated from 370 buses on 1130 rte.-km (700 rte.-mi) in 1922 to 8277 buses on 23,000 rte.-km (14,300 rte.-mi) in 1927.[13] In 1925, as indicated in Table 2-1, buses carried 1.5 billion total passengers, which was only about 9% of the total of 16.7 billion urban passengers for the entire industry. The urban transit industry hit its peak ridership in 1927, with about 17.2 billion total passengers (12 to 13 billion *revenue* passengers); buses accounted for 2.3 billion; streetcars and rail rapid transit carried the remainder.

Streetcar companies were eventually forced to make the change to the motorbus. By the 1930s, streetcar equipment was badly in need of replacement, but investment money had been difficult to attract because the industry's growth had been stemmed after World War I and, even more so, during the Great Depression. Buses were generally cheaper to purchase than streetcars; so with the restricted capital available, the wisdom of changing over to the motorbus became clearer. However, *most of the impetus for change came from outside the established industry*. This was caused primarily by the lack of financial and management resources within the transit companies, exacerbated, perhaps, by the vacuum created during the forced divestures of operating properties from the power trusts, which will be discussed in a subsequent section of this chapter.

In some colorful reporting in 1936 by *Fortune* magazine, the virtues of the bus are contrasted with the streetcar.

> Over the past fifteen years or so, the city bus has clawed, butted, and fought its way through traffic-glutted streets, through spongier and more perilous politic-glutted operating franchises, until it is, today, a phenomenon of mass transportation. You see city buses everywhere—mastodonic metal hulks gliding in and out of traffic with a soft hissing of air brakes, a rich sound of balloon tires on asphalt, a resonant hum of engines concealed within their structures. And the main reason this almost brand new vehicle became a phenomenon is because the faithful electric trolley had sunk into such a state of obsolescence as to be scarcely tolerable. During the fifteen years the bus was growing, the trolley, as an invention, virtually stood still. It just grew older and the street it was still suffered to haunt grew noisier with its clanking decrepitude. Half the trolleys now in use are twenty years old or older: the average age is around sixteen.[14]

The streetcar industry did band together, beginning in 1929, to build an ideal trolley. As previously indicated, this industry group, called the Electric Railway

---

[11]T. R. DAHL, "The Field of the Motor Bus in the Trolley Industry," pamphlet from *American Electric Railway Association Magazine*, March 1925.

[12]Ibid., pp. 3–5.

[13]JOHN SHERMAN PORTER, ed., *Moody's Manual of Investments American and Foreign: Public Utility Securities* (New York: Moody's Investors Service, 1937).

[14]"Yellow Truck and Coach," *Fortune Magazine*, 14, no. 1 (July 1936), 63–65.

Presidents' Conference Committee (PCC), did an extremely good job in producing the PCC car. By the late 1930s, PCC cars were in wide use, and they proved to be capable performers. Drivers, operators, and the public all liked the PCCs, but their introduction did not greatly avert the steady abandonment of streetcar lines.

The replacement of trolleys by buses ("bustitution" as it is acrimoniously described by trolley fans) has almost been complete in the United States, although there are still operations in a few cities, notably Boston, Newark, Pittsburgh, Philadephia, San Francisco, and New Orleans.

Rail rapid transit has been the most stable of the transit modes. Its ridership peak during World War II and its subsequent decline have been moderate compared with total transit passenger counts. This stability can be ascribed to the same forces which caused ridership in larger urban areas to fluctuate less than those in smaller cities. Rail rapid transit primarily serves the journey-to-work trip in the largest, densest, and oldest cities, where congestion and high parking fees act as a deterrent to automobile usage. Table 2-1 clearly shows that rapid transit ridership has always fluctuated less than that of the industry totals.

FINANCIAL PROBLEMS AND FORCED PUBLIC OWNERSHIP

Early street railway operators went to great lengths to secure exclusive franchise rights. Their resulting monopoly positions encouraged them to be inflexible. Given the absence of competition, transit operators counted on their rapidly increasing total ridership to pay for the conversion from horsecars to electric street railways. This conversion often resulted in an excessive valuation of equipment, land, and franchises. Further overcapitalization occurred when local street railways merged to provide a unified system in each urban area. Behling, for example, noted that "mountainous capitalization created in the more severe days of strong monopoly, have resulted in inflexibility and have made the traction companies loath to adjust fares to changed conditions of demand."[15]

Heavily watered stock and other abuses led much of the public, and their political leaders, to mistrust the "transit trusts." Much of the lack of public empathy with the industry's problems could be traced to the commonly held image of the companies—that they were socially and financially irresponsible. This was often true and was constantly reiterated by local politicians and newspapers.[16]

Another problem faced by the transit industry was that it was not possible to raise fares rapidly enough to keep pace with rising costs. The concept of a fixed fare was often written into the franchise at the request of the street railway companies as a

---

[15]BURTON N. BEHLING, *Competition and Monopoly in Public Utility Industries*, Illinois Studies in the Social Sciences, vol. 23, nos. 1–2 (Urbana, Ill.: University of Illinois Press, 1938).
[16]EDWARD S. MASON, *The Street Railway in Massachusetts: The Rise and Decline of an Industry*, Harvard Economic Studies, vol. 37 (Cambridge, Mass.: Harvard University Press, 1932) and DALLAS M. YOUNG, *Twentieth-Century Experience in Urban Transit: A Study of the Cleveland System and Its Development* (Cleveland, Ohio: Press of Western Reserve University, 1960).

hedge against future political pressures to reduce fares.[17] The public accepted this concept and later believed that the early 5-cent fare was their right. Ex-President Taft once testified that "if you inquired of a great many (of the public) you would find some such idea . . . that (the 5¢ fare) was guaranteed to them in the Constitution; that anything above 5¢ would indicate a return to investors that was outrageous. So strong is the question of fares that few politicians today would enthusiastically endorse a fare raise."[18]

It is not surprising that average fares were still only 6.9 cents in 1945. However, post-World War II inflation finally caused transit fares to start rising rapidly. By 1965, the average fare was almost 20 cents and the industry was still barely able to cover operating expenses from the fareboxes. In 1968, the first year the industry reported a net operating loss, average fares had risen to almost 23 cents. In 1975 average fares were 33 cents but the revenue generated by passengers only covered 43% of operating expenses.[19]

Early street railway operators wanted profits and thought a fixed fare could guarantee them. However, by World War I the industry was "caught between the upper millstone of the customary and franchise-fixed fare of five cents and the nether millstone of rapidly rising wartime costs."[20] While ridership and revenue remained relatively consistent, operating costs were increased by severe inflation during the war. By 1919 one-third of the operating companies were bankrupt. So serious was the plight of the industry that in 1919 President Wilson appointed the Federal Electric Railways Commission to publicize and investigate the problem.[21]

A massive restructuring of the transit industry occurred during the 1920s. What emerged were large utility holding companies which controlled the transit operating organization in addition to holding majority stock of other utilities, such as electric power and gas. The street railways were able to use the credit of the holding companies for capital requirements and, as a result, continue to offer a reasonably high level of transit service. As will be indicated later, federal antitrust regulations interceded and stopped this cross-subsidization in the late 1930s.

Public ownership of transit was thus unusual during the first half of the twentieth century. While there were still private operators willing to provide service, there was little incentive for municipal governments to own or operate transit. However, by midcentury, private companies, faced with increasing deficits, petitioned local officials to either provide an annual subsidy or purchase the operation.

It was the larger cities which first became publicly owned. By the 1970s virtually all of the larger city operations had passed from private to public ownership. The properties that remained under private control were found in the smaller cities and carried a relatively small proportion of the industry's total patrons. For example, in 1973,

---

[17]MASON, *The Street Railway*, p. 119, and YOUNG, *Twentieth-Century Experience*, pp. 12–20.

[18]*Proceedings Electric Railways Commission*, p. 4.

[19]These data are derived from AMERICAN PUBLIC TRANSIT ASSOCIATION, *Transit Fact Book*, pp. 28–42.

[20]GLAESER, *Public Utilities in American Capitalism*, p. 86.

[21]MOSSMAN, *Principles of Urban Transportation*, p. 6. The three-volume *Proceedings of the Federal Electric Railways Commission* are an excellent source of information on the problems which descended upon the transit industry during World War I.

although only 18% of the 1023 transit companies in the United States were publicly owned, this segment carried 91% of the annual revenue passengers. Even in most of the remaining private systems, public funds were used to provide the difference between farebox receipts and operating costs. Whether publicly or privately owned, transit properties had become dependent on government financial support.

GOVERNMENT ACTIVITIES

A number of public policies which were not directed toward public transit have directly influenced the industry's performance. It was not until recently that federal policy intentionally was directed to the industry. Virtually every study that discusses the federal role in urban mass transportation indicates that 1961 was the first year that there was any significant planned federal influence. For example, George Smerk, in 1974, suggested that there had been "a little more than a decade of federal participation in urban mass transporation."[22] He and others suggest that this period began when Congress passed the Housing Act of 1961, which contained three provisions affecting mass transportation. These provisions were a demonstration program, requirements for including mass transportation as an integral part of comprehensive urban planning, and a loan program for mass transportation agencies. First administered by the Department of Housing and Urban Development (HUD), these and subsequent urban transportation programs were transferred in 1968 to the Department of Transportation's Urban Mass Transportation Administration (UMTA).

Although 1961 was the first time there was direct congressional activity in mass transit, there have been other federal activities which either involved other institutions than Congress or were not primarily directed at mass transit but had an impact on that industry, nonetheless. An example of the former category is the antitrust prosecution of General Motors, National City Lines, and others which was initiated by the Justice Department in 1947. The latter category is exemplified by the Public Utility Company Holding Act of 1935 and federal policies toward housing and highways. The effects of each of these will be explored. Clearly, the antitrust prosecutions and the Public Utility Holding Act have had less influence on the industry than the investment-oriented policies which encouraged highway building and home ownership. However, no analytical framework has yet been developed that would allow an assessment of these effects. Indeed, such precise analysis may be academic only, as well as impossible to perform.

PUBLIC UTILITY HOLDING COMPANY ACT OF 1935

Utility holding companies had played a key role in the provision of capital for electrification of the street railways. By acquiring utilities, holding companies would control power, gas, water, and transit in many cities. Often a large holding company

---

[22]GEORGE M. SMERK, *Urban Mass Transportation: A Dozen Years of Federal Policy* (Bloomington, Ind.: Indiana University Press, 1974), p. 2.

had control over utilities in several dispersed urban areas. A Federal Trade Commission (FTC) study of the power, gas, and oil industry estimated that power holding companies directly controlled transit operations serving 878.9 million revenue passengers in 1931, about 10% of the nationwide total.[23] The study also identified 171 transit companies, representing one-fourth of the total, which were indirectly controlled by interlocking directorates among some dozen power trusts.

Congressional hearing and an FTC investigation did not adequately consider the potential effect the Public Utility Holding Company Act of 1935 would have on the transit industry and the act was passed. The act's key provision stated that "after Jan. 1, 1938 . . . each registered holding company . . . (must) limit (its) operations to a single integrated public utility system."[24] The Security and Exchange Commission (SEC) could modify this provision where economies of scale were demonstrated, but few holding companies requested an exemption from the act.

Because the transit operations of the power companies were showing consistent losses, the power trusts seemed pleased to find an excuse to dispose of the transit companies without incurring the wrath of local communities. They were able to eliminate the need for cross-subsidizing transit and, therefore, improve the profit of their basic operation.

Removal of the support of the power trusts was a severe blow to transit. Within a few years after the act took effect in 1938, there were only a few transit companies left in the hands of power trusts. In New Orleans, for example, the power company has been subsidizing the transit operation as part of New Orleans Public Service's utility franchise agreement with the locality. The high per capita ridership which this property has recorded for many years—second only to New York—is one indication of the effect of the 1935 act on public transit.[25] Only recently has this service been divorced from the utility's control. One can only speculate on what would have happened if Congress and the SEC had better anticipated the effect of this legislation.

ANTITRUST PROSECUTION OF GENERAL MOTORS, NATIONAL CITY LINES, ET AL.

Moving into the vacuum created by the divestment of the power trusts, General Motors Corporation (GMC) and several other motorbus, parts, and gasoline suppliers entered the transit business. They acquired stock in operating companies in exchange for capital and management services. This was similar to the techniques power com-

---

[23]FEDERAL TRADE COMMISSION, *Utility Corporations*, issued in parts from 1928 to 1937 and published as Senate Document no. 92, 70th Congress, 1st Session, 95 vols. *Index*, vol. 84-D, index to Parts 21 to 84-C (Washington, D.C.: U.S. Government Printing Office, 1937).

[24]CHARLES W. THOMPSON AND W. R. SMITH, *Public Utility Economics* (New York: McGraw-Hill Book Company, 1941), p. 494.

[25]It has been demonstrated by Fred A. Tarpley that the total household expenditure for gas, electricity, and transit in New Orleans ranks lowest of the 42 largest cities in the United States. (Although regional factors must be taken into account, there is a case for imaginative cross-subsidization of utilities.) Furthermore, New Orleans ranks, in Tarpley's view, as one of the highest in transit service, defined by indices for route density and headway. See FRED A. TARPLEY, "The Economics of Combined Utility and Transit Operations" (unpublished Ph.D. dissertation, Tulane University, 1967), particularly pp. 292–360.

panies had used to electrify, and eventually control, the street railway companies. For example, Yellow Bus and Coach, the bus-building subsidiary of GMC, had been the leader in sales since buses came on the scene in the 1920s. Its primary customers were the fleets controlled by its own subsidiary, the Hertz Omnibus Company.

Hertz, originally in the taxi business, extended its control of transit operations to many different cities and converted all of them from streetcars to buses. Hertz also was linked to the National City Lines (NCL), which, by 1946, had acquired some 46 transit systems. The acquisitions were financed almost entirely by stock shares sold to GMC and Firestone Tire and Rubber and, through the NCL subsidiary, Pacific (later American) City Lines, to Phillips Petroleum, Standard Oil of California, and Mack Manufacturing Corporation.

In 1947, the Justice Department sought an injunction against NCL and its suppliers, accusing them of being in violation of antitrust laws. The case was ultimately settled 19 years later when GMC signed a consent decree which severely curtailed its involvement in transit operations.

At a time when large injections of capital were needed to replace the worn-out fleet of transit vehicles that had limped through the peak ridership of World War II, an application of federal statutes had once again deprived transit of a source of funds. It appears, in retrospect, that the Justice Department did not consider the plight of the transit industry. One could conjecture what would have happened if a strong federal Department of Transportation had been available to argue the case of the transit industry or to supply alternative solutions to the court mandate. Again, although there is no analysis available, it is doubtful that the current ridership or profit picture would be significantly different if NCL, GMC, and the others involved in the case had been allowed to continue their involvement in transit. The basic forces of affluence and suburbanization which caused the decline of transit probably would have dominated any potential capital improvements they may have made; and most of the firms involved could obtain better returns on their funds by riding the auto surge.

Parenthetically, it is interesting to note the attention paid to the role of GMC as the villain in a plot to decimate transit. During the spring of 1974, much publicity was generated by the hearings on this issue which were held by the Senate Subcommittee on Antitrust and Monopoly. A report by Bradford Snell, a Senate staff member, suggested that GMC, Ford, and Chrysler had purposefully suppressed the bus and rail transit industry.[26] He reported that the social consequences of the monopoly position of GMC have been very costly. "The motorization of Los Angeles and dieselization of the New Haven Railroad are two of the most appalling episodes in the history of American transportation. These and other shocking incidents, however, were the inevitable outgrowth of concentrated economic power."[27]

---

[26]"American Ground Transport," pp. A-1 to A-103, and "The Truth About 'American Ground Transport'—A Reply by General Motors," pp. A-107 to A-144, in *The Industrial Reorganization Act Hearing Before the Subcommittee on Antitrust and Monopoly*, United States Senate, Part 4A—Appendix to Part 4, 93rd Congress, 2nd Session (Washington, D.C.: U.S. Government Printing Office, 1974). The study, "American Ground Transport," by Bradford C. Snell was financed by the Stern Foundation.

[27]Ibid., p. A-3.

Snell was dramatic and premature in his observation that "we are witnessing today the collapse of a society based on the automobile," and his depicting of General Motors as "a sovereign economic state."[28]

General Motors' response to this attack pointed out that the demise of the street-cars started long before GMC was involved in the operation of transit companies.[29] It is probable that GMC did not, in any underhanded way, cause the demise of street railways but, rather, was ready to supply transit operators with motorbuses which were both cheaper to buy and operate than streetcars and which also allowed the transit operators more flexibility in their routing of vehicles. On the other hand, there is little indication that they attempted to preserve the rail systems.

FEDERAL POLICIES TOWARD HOUSING AND HIGHWAYS

Transportation analysts usually point to auto competition as the primary cause of transit decline. They suggest that the affluent American demanded and received more and better roads, which were then clogged by an increasing number of vehicles. Thus, an induced demand for roads was perpetuated by patterns of increased auto ownership, the demand itself being primed by the addition of new roads.

It is doubtful that anyone in the Veterans Administration or the Federal Housing Administration thought that they were going to create increased suburbanization and urban sprawl by their federally insured home mortgage program. Yet it is clear that these programs were a major force in the establishment and growth of low-density areas around dense urban centers. Mortgage guarantees and government purchases of mortgages were some of the instruments used between 1945 and 1960 to induce housing construction and, more specifically, allow as many Americans as possible to own homes.[30]

As a way of maximizing the security of these loans, the lenders looked for safe investments. As Alan Altshuler has pointed out, conventional wisdom holds that security is found in single-family homes, relatively far from lower-class racial-minority areas, and in areas of social and racial homogeneity.[31] In short, lenders preferred to invest in homes that were in the suburbs, which are difficult areas to serve with conventional transit. As a result, a policy aimed at providing better housing had the effect of placing more persons in areas that were relatively expensive and inefficient to serve by public transit.

The rapid growth of highways further enhanced the auto in comparison to transit. This growth was clearly spurred on by federal policies, starting with Work Progress Administration (WPA) and Public Works Administration (PWA) efforts during the 1930s, which were begun primarily as relief from the Great Depression. But it was not until the late 1950s that federal highway funding became a major factor.

---

[28]Ibid., p. A-7.

[29]Ibid., pp. A-107 to A-127.

[30]Personal correspondence from Alan Altshuler dated September 9, 1975. Also see Chapter 3, "The Decision-Making Environment of Urban Transportation," by ALAN A. ALTSHULER.

[31]Ibid.

Administered by the Bureau of Public Roads, the National System of Interstate and Defense Highways was to become the largest public works project in the history of the world.[32] Again there was no malice toward transit in the proposals of the highway lobby. Indeed, the interstate program, and more highway building in general, had overwhelming support among virtually every sector of American society. Nonetheless, these massive road-building efforts further enhanced the auto, so that most current transit riders are those without ready access to the auto and who, consequently, are "captive" to the system. Few citizens, except in the very dense urban areas, lack ready access to an automobile. Even among groups who are generally considered transportation disadvantaged—elderly, handicapped, and poor persons—the auto mode dominates.

CONCLUSION

This chapter has reviewed the many factors that led to the decline of transit as a pervasive mode of travel. During this century, as affluence led to increased auto ownership, a demand was also generated for more and better roads. A more mobile life-style, which included single-family homes, suburban shopping centers, and industrial parks, resulted in dispersed trip-making patterns which were best served by the automobile operating on high-speed roads, and which were likewise difficult for transit to serve. Government policies in housing and highway development also contributed to this dispersion.

Unfortunately, the transit industry was not able to respond to changing public transportation needs. This was partly due to the industry's conservative approach to innovation, which was more acceptable when the industry was in a monopoly situation. Before the mass production of automobiles, transit did not have to compete for its share of the urban transportation market and urban dwellers had a well-developed "transit habit." Once mass-produced automobiles became available, the transit industry started to lose its share of the travel market and did little to attract new passengers or to keep its old ones.

With restrictions on automobile travel caused by World War II, transit ridership started to grow again. The transit industry almost doubled its patronage during the war years, but this induced ridership was an aberration.

Exacerbating the problems of the transit industry were the 1935 Public Utilities Holding Company Act and antitrust prosecution against major bus suppliers. These actions initiated by the government tended to restrict the flow of investment capital into the transit industry at a time when the increased patronage of the war years had left transit equipment in a severely deteriorated state.

As soon as wartime shortages ended, a new wave of suburbanization and automobile buying began. Reduced employment had its effect on ridership and the change from a 6-day to a 5-day workweek cut into weekend trip making.

---

[32]Ibid.

Public ownership and government subsidies were the remedies for transit. The results were limited. Transit ridership appeared to level off in the early 1970s, and then, aided by gasoline shortages, patronage increased slightly in 1974 and 1975. But along with this success in stopping the decline in patronage was a dramatic increase in operating expenses. It remains to be seen whether the industry can continue to attract more passengers while abating escalating costs. Public funds are not limitless and the industry cannot expect to continue to increase its share of public resources while providing only a small portion of total urban trips.

SELECTED BIBLIOGRAPHY

"American Ground Transport," pp. A-1 to A-103, and "The Truth About 'American Ground Transport'— A Reply by General Motors," pp. A-107 to A-144, in *The Industrial Reorganization Act Hearing Before the Subcommittee on Antitrust and Monopoly*, United States Senate, Part 4A—Appendix to Part 4, 93rd Congress, 2nd Session. Washington, D.C.: U.S. Government Printing Office, 1974.

BEHLING, BURTON N., *Competition and Monopoly in Public Utility Industries*, Illinois Studies in the Social Sciences, vol. 23, nos. 1–2. Urbana, Ill.: University of Illinois Press, 1938.

FEDERAL TRADE COMMISSION, *Utility Corporations*, issued in parts from 1928 to 1937 and published as Senate Document no. 92, 70th Congress, 1st Session, 95 vols. *Index*, vol. 84-D, index to Parts 21 to 84-C. Washington, D.C.: U.S. Government Printing Office, 1937.

GLAESER, MARTIN G., *Public Utilities in American Capitalism*. New York: The Macmillan Company, 1957.

MASON, EDWARD S., *The Street Railway in Massachusetts: The Rise and Decline of an Industry*, Harvard Economic Studies, vol. 37. Cambridge, Mass.: Harvard University Press, 1932.

MIDDLETON, WILLIAM D., *The Time of the Trolley*. Milwaukee, Wis.: Kalmbach Publishing Co., 1967.

MOSSMAN, FRANK H., ed., *Principles of Urban Transportation*. Cleveland, Ohio: Press of Western Reserve University, 1951.

OWEN, WILFRED, *The Metropolitan Transportation Problem* (rev. ed.). Washington, D.C.: The Brookings Institution, 1966.

Proceedings of the Federal Electric Railways Commission, 3 vols. Washington, D.C.: U.S. Government Printing Office, 1920.

ST. CLAIR, FRANK J., ed., *Moody's Public Utility Manual*. New York: Moody's Investors Service, Inc., 1969.

———, *Moody's Transportation Manual*. New York: Moody's Investors Service, Inc., 1969.

SALTZMAN, ARTHUR, AND RICHARD J. SOLOMON, "Historical Overview of the Decline of the Transit Industry," in *Public Transportation and Passenger Characteristics*, Highway Research Record 417, pp. 1–11. Washington, D.C.: Highway Research Board, 1972.

SCHNEIDER, LEWIS M., *Marketing Urban Mass Transit: A Comparative Study of Management Strategies*. Boston: Harvard University Graduate School of Business Administration, Division of Research, 1965.

SMERK, GEORGE M., *Urban Mass Transportation: A Dozen Years of Federal Policy*. Bloomington, Ind.: Indiana University Press, 1974.

TARPLEY, FRED A., "The Economics of Combined Utility and Transit Operations" (unpublished Ph.D. dissertation, Tulane University, 1967).

THOMPSON, CHARLES W., AND W. R. SMITH, *Public Utility Economics*. New York: McGraw-Hill Book Company, 1941.

"Yellow Truck and Coach," *Fortune Magazine*, 14, no. 1 (July 1936), 61–66, 106–15.

YOUNG, DALLAS M., *Twentieth-Century Experience in Urban Transit: A Study of the Cleveland System and Its Development*. Cleveland, Ohio: Press of Western Reserve University, 1960.

Chapter 3

THE DECISION-MAKING ENVIRONMENT
OF URBAN TRANSPORTATION*

ALAN A. ALTSHULER, *Chairman, Department of Political Science, and Professor, Department of Urban Studies and Planning, Massachusetts Institute of Technology*

The most striking feature of the decision-making environment of American urban transportation is the predominance of private market choice within it. Nearly 90% of urban transportation spending is in the private sector[1] (see Table 3-1). It should come as no surprise that 10% has great difficulty shaping and steering 90%—even when it tries. Bearing in mind that the American political system is highly responsive to interest group and popular desires, it should come as no surprise, either, that the 10% has rarely *sought* deliberately to steer the 90%, but has far more typically sought to accommodate it.

It is appropriate, therefore, in considering the types of decisions that have shaped the American pattern of urban transportation, to distinguish the following:

- Individual decisions in the marketplace.
- Public investment and subsidy decisions.

*The preparation of this chapter has been supported by U.S. Department of Transportation Contract No. DOT-S-50240: New Perspectives in Urban Transportation Project, Center for Transportation Studies, Massachusetts Institute of Technology. A slightly different version of this chapter appeared previously as ALAN A. ALTSHULER, "Changing Patterns of Policy: The Decision Making Environment of Urban Transportation," *Public Policy*, 25, no. 2 (Spring 1977), 171–203. Copyright © 1977 by the President and Fellows of Harvard College. Reprinted by permission of John Wiley & Sons, Inc.

[1]Another 7% consists of highway user tax payments, which are built into the market prices of privately produced goods and services, but which are received by governments rather than by the private producers. The main actors in the highway policy arena have traditionally viewed these taxes as part of a quasi-market system, in which highway users were implicitly purchasing the public provision of highway services rather than simply contributing to the general pot of revenues available for political allocation. This perception, although dubious in principle and increasingly controversial in practice, has been of central political importance during most legislative efforts to enact and allocate user taxes, and has likewise deeply influenced highway planning and administrative practices.

	Dollars (billions)
Automobile	
Vehicles: 1) Capital (includes purchase of vehicles, interest on debt, purchase of tires and accessories; excludes excise taxes)	37.5
2) Operation (includes fuel, maintenance, insurance, rentals, parking, and tolls; excludes excise taxes and registration fees)	55.6
Public highway expenditures attributable to auto use	7.5
Subtotal—auto	100.6
Local transit	
Operating revenues: Bus	1.5
Rail rapid transit	0.5
Commuter rail	0.3
Public operating subsidies: Bus and rail rapid transit	1.4
Commuter rail	0.3
Current capital expenditures (public)	2.0
Subtotal—transit	6.0
Subtotal: auto and local transit combined (94.4% auto, 5.6% transit)	106.6
Other	
Truck (including personal use):	
Vehicle purchase and operation (includes purchase of vehicles, interest on debt, fuel, repairs, driver wages, etc.; excludes excise taxes and registration fees)	44.1
Public highway expenditures attributable to truck use	2.8
Subtotal—truck	46.9
Taxi revenues	1.6
School bus	0.5
Other bus	0.6
Total	156.2

Sources and explanatory notes: see Appendix A at the end of this Chapter.

- Public decisions aiming to structure the framework of market regulatory constraints and price incentives within which private consumer decisions are made.

INDIVIDUAL DECISIONS IN THE MARKETPLACE

Acting as individual consumers, Americans have shifted in overwhelming numbers from transit to automobile travel in the period since World War II. As of 1975, estimated auto passenger mileage in urban areas stood at 559% of the 1945 level, transit passenger mileage at 29%. (The 1945 figures were, of course, reflective of special wartime conditions. Thus, 1950 is frequently used as the base year for comparison. Urban auto passenger mileage in 1975 stood at 333% of the 1950 level, transit passenger mileage at 42%.) Transit, which had accounted for 35% of total passenger mileage in 1945 (a war-inflated figure) and 18% in 1950, accounted in 1975 for only 2.8% (see Table 3-2).

TABLE 3-2
Trends in Urban Transit and Automobile Travel

Year	Transit Passenger-km (mi) (billions)	Auto Passenger-km (mi) (billions)	% Transit
1945	209 (130)	386 (240)	35
1950	145 (90)	649 (403)	18
1955	97 (60)	829 (515)	10
1960	77 (48)	1009 (627)	7
1965	69 (43)	1265 (786)	5
1970	66 (41)	1753 (1089)	4
1975	61 (38)	2158 (1341)	3

Sources: See Appendix B at the end of this chapter.

In the course of achieving this overwhelming dominance, the automobile appears to have become (contrary to popular belief) the less-expensive mode for most purposes as well as the more rapid, convenient, and flexible. As near as I have been able to estimate, expenditures for urban automobile and transit travel in 1975 (public and private, capital and operating) totaled $106.6 billion. The transit share of this combined total was 5.6% (Table 3-1). As noted previously, the transit share of urban passenger mileage was 2.8% (Table 3-2).

This finding must be qualified, however, with reference to the specific travel functions performed by transit. Most transit travel occurs during peak hours along the most heavily traveled corridors of large urban areas. Although precise figures are unavailable, it is clear that automobile travel is at its most expensive in such circumstances. Thus, it by no means follows that because automobile travel is less expensive on average nationally, it is also less expensive in the corridors where most transit service is currently provided. In any event, these figures do suggest that careful analysis is in order before concluding that major expansions of transit service, and diversions of current automobile travelers to the transit mode, would reduce the real dollar cost (public and private combined) of the urban transportation system.

Although acting separately, consumers have made their modal choice decisions over the decades within a common framework of culture and public policy. Culturally, American urban residents have always sought, within the limits set by their incomes and the speed of available modes of commutation, to combine key elements of the rural life-style with their urban means of earning a livelihood. In particular, they have sought low-density living in single-family homes on generous, privately owned plots of land. The poor, who in many cultures squat on the fringes of urban development, have tended in America to occupy the older, high-density areas close to the core.

The American propensity for urban dispersal was well established before 1945, as was also the popularity of the automobile. Between 1910 and 1930, when the nation's road system and its consumer credit mechanisms were both extremely primitive, automobile registrations grew from under 0.5 million to 23 million—from one for every 200 Americans to nearly one for every 5 Americans. As of 1975, the *number* of auto registrations had risen to nearly 5 times the 1930 level, but the *ratio* had risen by less than 2.5 times since 1930, from 1 : 5.3 to 1 : 2.0 (Table 3-3).

TABLE 3-3
U.S. Auto Registrations and Population

	Auto Registrations[a] (millions)	Population[b] (millions)	Ratio
1910	0.46	92.0	1:200
1930	23.0	122.8	1:5.3
1950	40.4	150.7	1:3.7
1970	88.8	203.2	1:2.3
1975	106.1	213.0	1:2.0

[a]Includes private and commercial vehicles but not publicly owned or military vehicles.
[b]Does not include U.S. nationals overseas.

Sources: The auto registration figures are from Federal Highway Administration, *Highway Statistics (various years)* (Washington, D.C.: U.S. Government Printing Office, various years), Table VM-1. The population figures are from U.S. Bureau of the Census, *Statistical Abstract of the United States: 1976,* 97th ed. (Washington, D.C.: U.S. Government Printing Office, 1976), p. 5.

There is much to be said, then, for the view that the postwar shift in travel patterns was a simple product of consumer preferences, delayed in the period 1930–1945 by the Great Depression and then by wartime shortages and rationing, but waiting to burst forth as soon as these restraints were removed.

PUBLIC DECISIONS AS A REFLECTION OF CONSUMER PREFERENCES

Public policy played a significant reinforcing role, however, in the quarter-century following World War II. These were years of rapid urbanization and population growth. Consequently, the pattern of *new* development during these years was able to establish itself as the predominant form of American urbanization. From 1950 to 1970 (precise 1945 data are unavailable), urbanized area population increased by 71%, from 69.2 to 118.4 million. During the same period, urbanized land area increased by 176%, from 32,978 km² (12,733 mi²) to 90,859 km² (35,081 mi²).

In considering the explosion of motor vehicle use and of urban sprawl in the decades that followed World War II, it is useful to ask whether anyone in government

—whether any public policies or institutions—deliberately sought to create the patterns of urban sprawl, transit decline, and automobile dominance. As near as one can tell, these were *not* deliberate public objectives. Government did not act in this period pursuant to a conscious urban development policy. Rather, it responded in a wide variety of policy arenas to organized pressures, to conventional wisdom, and to widespread public aspirations. In practice, of course, the result was consistently to accommodate and reinforce the majority taste for low-density living and for auto-mobility.

Yet, during the period in which postwar patterns were most decisively shaped—from 1945 to 1960—urban highway construction was extremely limited. The interstate program was enacted by Congress in 1956, but it did not provide many new facilities that motorists could drive on until the 1960s. The most important urban development policies between 1945 and 1960 were those that affected housing. The federal government, acting as regulator of the banking industry, as buyer and seller of mortgages, and as direct insurer of mortgages, became the most important single factor in the credit structure of the housing industry. Its explicit objectives were to relieve the postwar housing shortage, to satisfy the widespread desire for home ownership, and to maintain a high level of activity in the home building industry. Within the framework of these objectives, however, the primary motive of federal housing officials was to minimize risk. Delay, red tape, poor planning, even charges of racial and economic discrimination, were unlikely to get officials in trouble during this period. But to be perceived as responsible for high default rates was a very serious matter indeed.

The conventional wisdom of the period—among bankers, economists, and all others concerned with urban real estate markets—was that property values were generally most secure in areas characterized by the following: resident-owned single-family homes, inhabitants who had stable incomes adequate to support these homes and who were racially and ethnically homogeneous, locations distant from concentrations of lower-class and racial-minority population, and adequate parking space for family automobiles. If these were indeed the safest areas in which to lend and invest (and they probably were), the reason was that most Americans with money wanted to buy these amenities. A more aggressive set of public policies might have tapped certain minority markets. The government might, for example, have introduced and encouraged condominium development in the older parts of our urban areas. But it did not. It did what government and industry do most characteristically in the United States—which is to aim at the heart of the mass market and to neglect minority markets.

As for regional land-use policy, it did not exist in the forties and fifties (and it is extremely weak even today). Land-use planning and regulation were viewed exclusively as local government functions and rarely functioned effectively until *after* development was far advanced—when property owners had acquired a sense of collective economic interest and when both government and citizenry had acquired some sophistication in dealing with the complexities of urban life. In urban as well as rural areas, moreover, the proper objective of government in regulating land use was viewed as the protection of property values, not the achievement of collective community visions. It was one thing to prevent commercial or industrial users from invading a stable residential neighborhood. It was quite another to prevent a farmer from making a large profit by selling his land to a developer.

In this situation. although individual localities might hold the line against development pressures, such resistance had almost no significance within the broad emerging pattern of urban sprawl. What impact such resistance did have was generally to *accelerate* sprawl. Developers were likely to find land beyond the urban fringe less subject to regulation and red tape, as well as much cheaper, than vacant parcels within the zone of existing development. When they opted for "leapfrog" development, they could generally count on public agencies to pick up the pieces after them by providing schools, utilities, and improved highway access for the citizens to whom they made their sales.

PUBLIC INVESTMENT DECISIONS I:
THE GREAT ERA OF HIGHWAY BUILDING

In this context, the great era of highway building got under way in the late 1950s. Both this policy, and the neglect of mass transit by American governments until very recent years, were squarely in the American public tradition of following the private market. The highway program, in particular, was consistently defended by its supporters on the ground that it served a visible public demand, as demonstrated in the marketplace, on the highways, and in the voting booths.

Needless to say, there were great political forces at work. We do not get a program as massive as the interstate highway program simply because it seems likely to be popular. A great campaign to mobilize, direct, and translate into law the latent public support for highway construction was successfully undertaken by the industries and labor unions with the most to gain. It is important to keep in mind, however, that there *was* widespread public support, and that the market forces to be served by highway construction were already sweeping the field in the marketplace. Thus, the political actors who lobbied successfully for increased highway construction were able to operate within a highly congenial framework of popular taste, market behavior, and apparent political predisposition.

The best evidence of support at the ballot box is that constitutional amendments setting up highway trust funds were adopted in more than half the states by referendum in the late 1940s and early 1950s. In my own state, Massachusetts, the "Good Roads Amendment" was approved by a popular vote of 6 : 1 in 1948. In 1974, the Massachusetts electorate voted by a substantial margin to authorize expenditures from the highway trust fund for mass transit purposes, but it would be unwise to read the popular sentiments of 1974 into the interpretation of events a quarter-century earlier.

By the early 1950s the automobile industry was intensely concerned that motor vehicle sales, which had been on a steeply rising curve since 1945, would have to stagnate or decline unless the highway system was expanded to keep pace with the growth of motor vehicle usage. Along with such major allies as the oil, steel, rubber, and trucking industries, together with their labor unions, the auto industry began to orchestrate a public clamor for vigorous public action to deal with the congestion problem. If one reads the media of the time, one must immediately be struck by the apparently uncontroversial nature of the campaign. The material generated by the auto industry and its allies was printed in every popular journal of general circulation, month after month. Dissent was virtually nonexistent. The same pattern prevails in the record of congressional hearings on the interstate highway program. There were disputes about financing, but none about the desirability of the program itself.[2]

The Eisenhower administration came into office in 1953 with particularly close ties to the automobile and oil industries. Its central domestic policy was to roll back the size of the federal government. In line with this policy, it announced a policy of "no new starts" in the domestic public works field during 1954 and 1955. During this same period, nevertheless, it prepared and submitted to Congress the enabling legislation for the largest domestic public works program in the history of the world, the Interstate System.

As of 1955, the year prior to enactment of the interstate program, combined federal and state expenditures for urban highway construction totaled $718 million, only 22% of overall federal and state highway expenditures. By 1962 federal and state expenditures for urban highway construction had nearly tripled, to $2.07 billion, and the urban share of the combined federal–state total had increased to 35%. Most of the increase involved expressway construction on new rights-of-way, and substantial highway investment was being focused for the first time on the inner, densely developed portions of large urban areas.[3]

Highway interests were generally viewed in the 1950s and 1960s as constituting one of the two or three most powerful lobbies in American politics. The most significant assets of this lobby (or, more precisely, network of allied lobbies) were as follows:

First, it had numbers. The litany is familiar, but still impressive. Roughly one-sixth of all American businesses, employing one-seventh of all American workers, were (and are) involved in the production, marketing, service, and commercial use of automobiles, trucks, and highways.

Second, it had geographic distribution. These businesses and workers were spread fairly evenly across every congressional district. By contrast, 61% of all transit (including commuter rail) patronage as of 1975 was in ten metropolitan areas. New York and Chicago alone accounted for 42%—including 88% of all rapid transit and 85% of all commuter rail patronage.

Third, it had leadership. Not only were its small businesses and groups of employees spread throughout every congressional district; it also included the largest com-

[2]GARY T. SCHWARTZ, "Urban Freeways and the Interstate System," *Southern California Law Review*, 49, no. 3 (March 1976), 406–513, a superb political analysis of the origins of the interstate program and particularly of its urban elements.

[3]ALAN A. ALTSHULER AND ROBERT W. CURRY, "The Changing Environment of Urban Development Policy—Shared Power or Shared Impotence?" *Urban Law Annual*, 10 (1975), 6–7. The article as a whole appears on pp. 3–41.

panies in the nation. Of the top fifteen in *Fortune*'s annual ranking of the largest industrial companies, two-thirds were (and are) automobile, oil, and steel companies. Additionally, Dupont, the leader of the chemical industry and one of the top fifteen itself, in the 1950s owned a controlling interest in General Motors (since relinquished pursuant to an antitrust decree).

Fourth, it was excellently equipped to forge strong ties between the national companies and the smaller companies spread throughout the nation. A substantial proportion of the small businesses in the highway-related sectors of the economy were franchisers of the major national firms—particularly automobile dealerships, service stations, and many roadside businesses. Others were suppliers. The 1967 Census of Manufactures reported that the automobile manufacturers directly purchased $13 billion worth of goods annually from a total of 50,000 other companies.[4] Still other institutions had major investments at stake. The banks, insurance companies, mutual funds, and pension funds all had major investments in highway-related sectors. Indeed, it was an article of faith among businesspeople that any slowdown in automobile production tended quickly to generate recession and unemployment throughout the economy.

Fifth, the highway lobby included organized labor. The construction trades, of course, have historically been among the most powerful of unions and the most active in state and local politics. National behemoths such as the Teamsters, the Auto Workers, and the Steel Workers unions perceived a major stake in the highway program as well. In labor, as in business, moreover, the universal sentiment was that prosperity for the highway-related sectors was a *sine qua non* of prosperity for all other sectors.

Sixth, the highway lobby had money. The oil and automobile industries were among the largest financial factors in national politics. The highway contractors everywhere were among the largest contributors to state and local campaigns. Nor should it be forgotten that the enormous advertising expenditures of the national companies and of auto dealers in every locale were bound to be of help in securing favorable media coverage.

Finally, the highway lobby had a receptive popular audience. There is no denying that Americans enjoy their cars and the experience of free-flow driving. If one is a transit executive or (as I have been) a transportation official associated in the public mind with stopping highways, it has to be sobering to have a son. Somehow, there is nothing little boys want more than model cars, and nothing big boys want more than real cars and driver's licenses.

Needless to say, Americans also have an enormous investment in their cars. It is commonly said that the second largest investment made by the average American household is in cars, after housing. In fact, if one includes depreciation, automobiles clearly rank first. Over the past 40 years, at least, most American households have seen

---

[4]U.S. Bureau of the Census, *Census of Manufactures, 1967* (Washington, D.C.: U.S. Government Printing Office, 1971).

their homes appreciate in value. Their cars, by contrast, depreciate rapidly and must be replaced.

PUBLIC INVESTMENT DECISIONS II:
THE GROWTH OF MASS TRANSIT CAPITAL ASSISTANCE

As one reviews all these factors that have made the highway interest so powerful, it is difficult to imagine how the policy shift of the mid-1970s away from expressway construction in urban areas and toward dramatically increased support for mass transit could have occurred. In practice as well, the shift is one that caught virtually all observers by surprise. Even as the decade of the 1960s drew to a close, such a sharp policy reorientation appeared all but inconceivable.

Throughout the 1950s, even as the interstate highway program was getting under way, the conventional wisdom was that all transit costs, capital as well as operating, should be financed from the farebox. This wisdom held in the vast majority of American urban areas, not merely in the White House and the halls of Congress. There were a few exceptions, most notably among a few northeastern cities that had historically been highly dependent upon rail transit, but they were indeed exceptions. Even in Chicago and Cleveland, the two areas outside the Northeast with rapid transit, the doctrine of finance from the farebox held sway.

At the national level, it was considered sufficient justification for federal neglect of urban mass transit to note that few transit trips crossed state lines. Federal disinterest in the decline of transit was reinforced by the general conviction that transit was a dying industry, rooted in obsolescent technologies and urban land-use patterns. A popular analogy was that subsidization of mass transit would be akin to public spending for the revival of horse-and-buggy travel.

By contrast, the primary justification for federal participation in the costs of highway construction was that an integrated national system was required. Historically, even farm-to-market secondary roads had been viewed as of interstate significance because they carried agricultural products to railheads and other distribution points for national and international distribution. By the 1950s even the most hidebound conservative could accept the case of a national line-haul expressway network developed pursuant to the traditional federal responsibility for promoting interstate commerce. It was widely accepted as well, although without much critical analysis, that an improved highway system would be of great value for national defense purposes. Thus, the new freeway system authorized in 1956 was justified in terms of federal responsibility for national security as well as for interstate commerce, and it was officially labeled the National System of Interstate and Defense Highways.

Moving forward a decade, to the mid-1960s, the period in which the Urban Mass Transportation Act of 1964 was enacted, the predominant view was that transit had a continuing, although minor, role to play in the nation's urban transportation system. The transit function was highly important in a few metropolitan areas, of course, but it served a shrinking minority of trips, even in these areas.

The proper role of government, it was generally believed at the time, should be to provide capital for needed transit expansion and modernization, while continuing to impose the "discipline" of self-support upon transit operations by requiring them to cover all *but* capital costs with farebox revenues. Even in those areas where existing transit already required operating subsidies, the prevailing ideology was that new transit investments should be confined to those which would not increase the operating deficit burden.

Thus, when the voters of the San Francisco Bay area were presented with the BART proposal in 1962, they were assured that no operating subsidies would be required. Similarly, when the Massachusetts Legislature in 1964 created the Massachusetts Bay Transportation Authority (reorganizing a predecessor agency and expanding its jurisdiction from 14 to 79 localities), it also authorized a major program of rapid transit extensions into the Boston suburbs. Although the existing system being taken over by the new Authority already required a subsidy of about $21 million annually, the 1964 legislation specified that extensions should be supported by studies demonstrating that they would not add to operating subsidy requirements.

Needless to say, this attitude guided the development of the Urban Mass Transportation Act as well. Enacted in 1964, the Mass Transportation Act provided only for capital assistance (along with planning, research, and development activities related to transit capital investment).

As a footnote, I cannot refrain from noting that, even in the 1970s, numerous rapid transit proposals have been placed before the voters of urban regions with assurances that construction would be paid for with federal capital grants and that no operating subsidies would be required thereafter. Such forecasts were, for example, characteristic of the successful Denver and Atlanta referendum campaigns. A new wrinkle in some of the recent rapid transit campaigns, in areas that have already become accustomed to substantial bus operating deficits, has been to promise that required transit operating subsidies *with* rapid transit will be lower than without it. Such, for example, is the current official forecast in Miami.

In a closely related field, parenthetically, Congress set up Amtrak in 1971 with a mandate to become self-supporting, and sought to deal with the Northeast rail crisis in 1973 by means (mainly reorganization and start-up capital assistance) that it claimed would avert the need for continuing operating assistance.

Although implausible to most dispassionate observers, each of these forecasts has obviously played a significant part in mustering the support required to get its program approved.

A FURTHER STEP: FEDERAL TRANSIT OPERATING SUBSIDIES

The promises of operating self-support for new and reorganized systems often do not seem terribly different in the seventies, then, from those of the sixties. But predominant ideologies with respect to transit and the public acceptance of the need for transit operating as well as capital subsidies has become general. Large-scale federal operating assistance for mass transit was authorized in 1974, although highway assistance is still confined to capital investment purposes. Transit aid has been one of the most rapidly growing of all federal programs since 1970. And indeed, even the promises made on behalf of new systems in recent years generally seem intended more to establish a tone, to communicate a hope and a recognition of taxpayer concerns, than to convey firm guarantees.

How can one account for the crumbling of public resistance to transit operating subsidies, and for the meteoric growth of public transit budgets in the 1970s? Moreover, how can one account for the decisive shift away from expressway construction that has occurred in most of the nation's large urban areas?

It is striking that the federal transit program was first proposed by big-city, liberal Democrats in the late 1950s, that the first president to champion the cause was President Kennedy, and that the Mass Transportation Act of 1964 was viewed as a major liberal triumph when enacted under the auspices of President Johnson. It was a new spending program, a program for the big cities, and a program generally viewed as conferring its greatest benefits on relatively disadvantaged groups.

Yet the greatest flowering of the transit program has occurred since 1969 under two Republican presidents, both generally viewed as quite conservative. In fiscal year 1970, federal transit aid obligations totaled $108 million. The estimate for fiscal 1978 is $3.2 billion, a growth of more than 30 times in 8 years (and roughly 19 times in constant dollars).

By contrast, the highway program, which grew rapidly in the late fifties and early sixties, has actually declined slightly in real-dollar terms since then. Federal highway aid obligations in fiscal 1964, the year the transit program was first enacted, were $4.3 billion. The estimate for fiscal 1978 is $7.9 billion, an increase of 84%. During this period, however, prices have roughly doubled.

The Federal Highway Administration estimates that 38% of federal highway spending is in urban areas. Assuming that this ratio is valid, combined federal highway and transit obligations in urban areas will total $6.2 billion in fiscal 1978. The transit share will be 52%, although transit accounts for under 3% of urban passenger travel and for 0% of urban freight movement.

These figures tell only part of the story, however, because the nature of highway expenditures in large urban areas has changed substantially in recent years. Perforce as resistance to new expressway construction has spread across the country, the focus of highway spending has shifted to improvements of existing streets and highways. The antihighway revolt, it bears emphasis, has by no means been limited to older, high-density urban areas in the 1970s. Expressways have been killed and future construction planning has been drastically curtailed in many of the newer, auto-oriented metropolitan areas as well, regions as diverse as Denver, Miami, Tucson, Atlanta, and Portland (Oregon). Long-committed expressway projects are still moving forward in many regions, particularly in suburban corridors that have not yet experienced intense development, but it seems apparent that the era of major urban highway expansion is drawing toward a close.

WHY THE RECENT CHANGES IN URBAN TRANSPORTATION POLICY?

No definitive explanation of these recent shifts in urban transportation policy emphasis seems possible at the present time. As we seek a rough understanding of how they came about, however, I believe that it will prove most fruitful to focus on the following factors.

First, there have been major changes in national domestic preoccupations from the fifties, when the great period of highway expansion began, to the seventies. The urban "problem" was defined in the 1950s in terms of traffic congestion, the decline of downtown, the supposed cultural sterility of suburbia, and so on. The leading work on urban transportation of the decade was Wilfred Owen's *The Metropolitan Transportation Problem*. Owen, reflecting the spirit of the decade, defined the urban transportation problem unambiguously as one of highway traffic congestion. The first two sentences of this seminal work accurately convey its predominant perspective:

> American cities have become increasingly difficult to live in and to work in largely because they are difficult to move around in. Inability to overcome congestion and to remove obstacles to mobility threaten to make the big city an economic liability rather than an asset.[5]

More general works that reflected the dominant tone of urban criticism in this decade included William Whyte, Jr.'s, *The Organization Man* (New York: Simon and Schuster, 1956), John Keats' *The Crack in the Picture Window* (Boston: Houghton Mifflin Company, 1956), and Robert C. Wood's *Suburbia: Its People and Their Politics* (Boston: Houghton Mifflin Company, 1959).

Political leaders and the media, needless to say, likewise had little disposition to focus in this period upon the nation's more profound domestic problems, such as race, poverty, crime, and environmental degradation.

In the 1960s, attention shifted dramatically to issues of race, poverty, and urban violence. In the 1970s, the issues of environment and energy have claimed increasing attention. The Nixon–Ford years witnessed a turning away from many of the anti-poverty and antidiscrimination priorities of the sixties—and nowhere was this de-emphasis more striking than in the priorities of the national adminstration. Yet the same administration played a key leadership role in bringing about the shifts in urban transportation policy with which we are here concerned.

The explanation, I think, lies in the fact that transit proved to be a policy for all perspectives on the urban problem. Although its direct constituency was relatively small, its ideological appeal proved to be extremely broad. Whether one was for the economic vitality of our cities; for protecting the environment and stopping highways; for energy conservation; for assisting the poor, the elderly, and the handicapped; or simply for getting the other guy off the road so as to be able to drive faster, transit was

---

[5]WILFRED OWEN, *The Metropolitan Transportation Problem*, rev. ed. (Washington, D.C.: The Brookings Institution, 1966), p. 1.

a policy that could be embraced. This is not to say that transit was an effective way of serving all these objectives, simply that it was widely believed to be so.

Thus, the Nixon administration, while striving to disengage itself from the big-city, big-spending, pro-black, welfare-state image of the Johnson administration in domestic affairs, felt comfortable promoting a rapid increase in the scale of federal mass transit spending. Transit turned out to be an ideal centerpiece for the urban policy of a conservative administration. Although clearly of high priority to urban spokesmen, it did not stir class and racial antagonisms. Quite the contrary, it attracted support from every portion of the urban ideological spectrum.

The main weakness of the transit program in Congress was its narrow geographic base. As noted previously, ten metropolitan areas account for nearly three-fifths of the nation's entire transit patronage. The Urban Mass Transportation Administration (UMTA) has done a marvelous job of sprinkling buses upon nearly every urban area in the country, but this alone cannot account, in my judgment, for the remarkable flowering of the mass transit program. After all, the vast preponderance of transit aid has still gone to a very few regions, and every member of Congress is aware of this fact. From the beginning of the federal transit program in 1964 through September 30, 1977, five urban regions received 61 % of all capital grant dollars committed, and ten regions received 80%.

Perhaps the single factor most responsible for the rapid growth of the transit program has been the growing strength of antihighway sentiment—among liberals and "good-government" types generally, rather than simply among active environmentalists and neighborhood residents directly threatened by highway projects. Highway advocates, traditionally contemptuous of transit, have found advocacy of increased transit spending to be an effective means of protecting their own vital interests. In 1973 the Senate and House Public Works Committees succeeded in adding transit to their long-standing jurisdiction over highway legislation, and in making a combined highway-transit bill the vehicle for simultaneous achievement of the following objectives: (1) reestablishment of near-unanimous congressional support for the highway program; (2) achievement of similar security, with the promise of increased spending potential, for the transit program; and (3) enhancement of state and local flexibility, by providing a new option to trade urban highway (including interstate) aid allocations for transit capital grants. The key point to bear in mind here is that the first of these three objectives was the only one favored as of early 1973 by most members of the two public works committees. The representative and senator who played the key roles in forging the new strategy were from Texas and West Virginia, respectively. Along with nearly all of their committee colleagues, they were perennial champions of the highway program who had minimal interest in transit per se. Their central concern was that urban expressway controversies had become a significant threat to the consensual and veto-proof dominance of the highway coalition in Congress. By extending the program concept to include transit and to permit local flexibility in choosing between highway and transit projects, they not only reestablished legislative harmony in the highway policy arena, but they also enhanced their own reputations as congressional "statesmen." (One of the two, Congressman Jim Wright, became House

Majority Leader in January 1977.) This is by no means to minimize the victory achieved by urban antihighway and transit interests in the 1973 legislation and jurisdictional shift within Congress. But it is to emphasize that they were minority actors who achieved influence by maximizing their nuisance potential. Their triumph occurred when a few farsighted leaders of the highway coalition, which remained politically dominant, discerned that a mutually beneficial solution was possible and persuaded the rest of the coalition to accept it.

Before leaving this brief discussion of the sources of transit support, we should note that transit has never ranked as a very high priority for groups representing the poor, racial minorities, the elderly, and other disadvantaged groups. Doubtless part of the reason is that transit subsidies do not go predominantly to the very poor. The income distribution of transit patrons in those urban areas where most transit ridership occurs is not very different from that of highway users. (The situation is different in those urban areas where very few employees commute by transit, and where transit patronage is therefore confined overwhelmingly to the very poor, the elderly, and children.) Moreover, the largest subsidies tend to be absorbed by those who take the longest transit trips—who are usually the most affluent riders. Finally, most federal transit aid has gone to finance the construction of new rapid transit systems and extensions, intended to serve the most affluent end of the potential transit market spectrum.[6] It is also true that spokespersons for blacks, the poor, the elderly, and the handicapped have generally had more urgent priorities than transit. Welfare, health programs, nutritional support programs, antidiscrimination efforts, and so on, have commanded most of their attention. Nonetheless, they *have* supported transit aid, and it is a rather unusual program that unites downtown company presidents, construction workers, environmentalists, and spokespersons for the various disadvantaged groups of urban society.

In short, shifting national priorities and the ideological breadth of the transit coalition provide a significant part of the explanation for recent shifts in urban transportation policy. Several other factors, however, deserve close attention as well.

A third key factor has been the gradual maturation of a learning process about the impact of programs that entail large-scale eminent domain. One of the most striking characteristics of the American pattern of government has always been its great respect for private property. Eminent domain on more than a spot basis is a post-New Deal phenomenon. Urban redevelopment, beginning in 1949, and the interstate highway program, beginning in 1956, were the first two national programs ever to involve massive eminent domain. In aiding construction of the turnpike, canal, and railroad systems of the nineteenth century, American governments had for the most part

---

[6]The most carefully studied new system has been the San Francisco Bay area's BART. Findings to date from the full range of BART studies are brilliantly analyzed in MELVIN M. WEBBER, "The BART Experience—What Have We Learned?" *The Public Interest*, no. 45 (Fall 1976), pp. 79–108. Webber reports that in 1975 the average BART rider paid only one-sixth of the cost of each trip, and received a subsidy of $3.76. Forty-eight percent of BART riders reported incomes greater than $15,000, vs. 17% who reported incomes under $7000. In the BART district as a whole, only 25% of the population enjoyed household income over $15,000, whereas 34% had incomes under $7000. [These figures are from an extended version of the article— MELVIN M. WEBBER. *The BART Experience—What Have We Learned?*, Monograph no. 26 (Berkeley, Calif.: University of California, Institute of Urban and Regional Development and Institute of Transportation Studies, October 1976).]

granted rights to land that was already in the public domain. For reservoirs, toll roads, and other public facilities, large takings had more recently been made in rural areas. But major takings in highly developed urban areas had been extremely rare until the enactment of the redevelopment and interstate programs.

Ben Kelley, who spent two years as Director of Public Information for the Federal Highway Administration, has reported on highway program takings during one 18-month period in 1965–1966. Fifty thousand properties were taken across the country for federally aided highway construction during this period.[7] Not surprisingly, both the urban renewal program and the highway program began to encounter vigorous resistance as the news of their eminent domain activities spread. The urban renewal program was able to adapt more quickly than the highway program. Initially a clearance and redevelopment program, it gradually became a rehabilitation program, and then produced offshoots in the antipoverty and model cities programs. Originally a program designed to remake neighborhoods for new populations, it became a series of programs intended to improve neighborhoods and life opportunities for existing residents.

The highway program, with its interstate centerpiece, was far more resistant to change. As long as most federal aid was for interstate construction, the program inevitably had an enormous appetite for property. And its requirements were inflexible. Land had to be taken in straight or gently curving corridors that connected with one another throughout each region. Highway planners could seek to minimize political resistance by searching out corridors with substantial amounts of public open space and/or corridors in which the residents (particularly, racial minorities and the very poor) were relatively powerless. This strategy conserved highway dollars as well as political resources. But there was no way that highway planners could avoid stepping on an extraordinary number of toes.

The federal highway program was able to ride roughshod over the growing opposition to its eminent domain appetite for substantially longer than the urban renewal program, because its base of support throughout the nation was far more powerful. The 90% federal matching ratio was irresistible to most state and local officials; in controversial cases, affirmative local approval could generally be dispensed with (although local veto was permitted by the laws of some states); and an essential part of the program "ideology" was the alleged need for system uniformity and connectivity throughout the nation. Thus, project controversies normally sufficient to paralyze the governmental process typically had little impact on the highway program. And the national scope of the program, with 87% of Interstate System mileage outside of urban areas entirely, tended to dwarf the significance of controversies in a few big cities.

In the 1970s, however, even the highway program has had to adapt. The federal funding emphasis, particularly in urban areas, has gradually shifted away from freeway and expressway construction toward improvements within existing rights-of-way. The Federal-Aid Highway Act of 1973 provided additional flexibility by authorizing the use of urban highway-aid allocations, including those for interstate

---

[7]BEN KELLEY, *The Pavers and the Paved* (New York: Donald W. Brown, Inc., 1971), p. 145.

construction, for mass transit purposes. The Federal-Aid Highway Act of 1976 liberalized these provisions even further; it provides for inflationary adjustments during the period required to bring substitute projects to the point of construction, and it permits the use of interstate allocations for alternative highway as well as mass transit projects.

A fourth factor meriting attention has been the growing militancy and mobilization of aggrieved groups in American society. One can spot the immediate origins of this trend in the civil rights activities of the late 1950s and early 1960s. It quickly spread to numerous other groups, so that by the mid-1960s even civil disobedience by organized public employees, including law enforcement officials, had become commonplace. In consequence of this development, and also of various statutory provisions requiring citizen participation that have been enacted over the past decade, it is now essential for transportation planners to win the support of ordinary citizens at the neighborhood level before projects can be viewed as serious candidates for implementation. In the fifties and early sixties, by contrast, it was generally enough to consult with key local elected and public works officials, and with the professional representatives of large enterprises that might be affected by transportation investment decisions (e.g., businesses, hospitals, universities).

Citizen participation has been a humanizing and democratic influence. It merits note, nonetheless, that it has also been an extremely conservative influence. I use the term "conservative" here in its classic sense: resistant to change. Established institutions participate in politics almost as much to serve their expansion needs as to avert threats. In the field of urban transportation, for example, business and labor interests typically press for increased construction activity. The primary mobilizing incentives for individual citizens who participate in transportation planning, on the other hand, tend to be fear and indignation. The objective of improved service is rarely sufficient to motivate sustained or energetic participation. Citizens expend the time and energy required for effective participation mainly in order to protect their homes and immediate community environs. The result has been to challenge development agencies (1) to figure out ways of implementing their mandates *without* destroying neighborhoods or public open spaces, and (2) where this is not feasible, as with respect to urban expressway construction, to rethink the very nature of their missions.

THE EMERGING FISCAL CRISIS OF TRANSIT

A wide variety of political factors, then, appear to be militating in favor of expanded mass transit spending and against urban expressway investment Paradoxically, however, transit is in some respects as endangered today as it was a decade ago. A more sophisticated opposition to transit spending increases is developing, one that may prove more difficult to deal with. There is a growing perception that the fiscal appetite of public transit is voracious and nearly impossible for elected officials to control. Further, there is a growing awareness that the shifts in public spending emphasis in favor of transit have not significantly altered urban travel behavior and are unlikely to do so in the future.

Federally aided transit investment has focused predominantly on improving service for downtown employees, particularly for those who live in suburbs. But even in the nation's largest urban regions, those with more than 1 million people, only 9% of employed residents worked in central business districts (CBDs) in 1970. Only 4% both worked in CBDs and lived in suburbs. To some degree these figures understate the transit potential, because the Census Bureau tends to define CBDs narrowly. On the other hand, there is no conceivable way that transit will capture the entire downtown-oriented market. Thus, these figures may properly be taken as rough indications of the extent to which urban dispersal has already imposed very stark limits on the patronage potential of fixed-route transit service.

An independent analysis conducted for the Office of Technology Assessment of the U.S. Congress has recently concluded that a doubling of the transit vehicle mileage operated each day throughout the nation would bring about only a 20 to 40% increase in ridership. According to the same study, total elimination of transit fares would be likely to generate a 50 to 70% increase in ridership.[8] The study did not estimate the ridership increase that a strategy combining both initiatives might generate, but a figure in the range of 60 to 100% would seem most plausible. I have calculated that the additional public cost of such a combination strategy in 1975, over and above the current level of transit subsidization, would have been about $6 billion. The proportion of total urban passenger mileage attracted from the automobile to mass transit would have been in the range of 1.5 to 2.5%.

Quite aside from the potential cost of such ambitious new transit enhancement initiatives, the fiscal burdens associated with transit subsidization and modernization have been growing at a rapid rate. The transit industry as a whole first fell into operating deficit in 1963. Thereafter, the deficit rose rapidly to $288 million in 1970 and $1.7 billion in 1975. The rate of increase from 1970 to 1975 was 44% per year. During this same period consumer prices rose by 7% per year and overall public spending by 11% per year.

Transit advocates note, of course, that the high rate of deficit increase has in large part been a statistical aberration, and one that will gradually dissolve over time. When the deficit is small relative to total expenditures and revenues are static, a very modest expenditure increase can generate an extremely large percentage increase in the deficit. Thus, in looking ahead, the key point to note is that transit operating expenditures grew by 13% per year from 1970 to 1975, while operating revenues rose at an annual rate of only 3%. Should these trends continue to 1985, revenues in that year would cover only 22% of operating expenditures (vs. 86% in 1970 and 54% in 1975), and the national transit operating deficit would be $9.95 billion. The average rate of deficit increase in this scenario would be 22% between 1975 and 1980, and 17% between 1980 and 1985. While well below the recent rate of increase, these projections are still far in

---

[8]SKIDMORE, OWINGS AND MERRILL AND SYSTEMS DESIGN CONCEPTS, INC., *Energy, the Economy, and Mass Transit: Summary Report*, prepared for the Senate Committee on Appropriations, Transportation Subcommittee (Washington, D.C.: U.S. Congress, Office of Technology Assessment, June 1975), pp. 31, 39.

excess of the recent rate of inflation, and their realization would entail rapidly growing *absolute* dollar commitments (even as the *percentage* rates of increase gradually declined).

To date, however, increasing government involvement in the public transportation industry has tended to be a force for spending acceleration. The politicization of transit has strengthened the hand of organized labor, has intensified pressure for the maintenance of lightly patronized routes and for the development of new routes, and in many areas has promoted stable fares to the status of a sacred cow. The disciplines imposed by the farebox have been replaced by those related to the maintenance of broad political support, with highly inflationary consequences. Illustratively:

1. In order to obtain federal transit aid, local transit authorities must convince the Department of Labor that no employees will have their circumstances adversely affected.[9] Generally, the Department will grant certification only if all potentially affected unions concur. The result has been to minimize laborsaving as an objective of transit modernization programs, and to help embed obsolete and expensive work practices ever more deeply into the fabric of the industry.
2. The Davis–Bacon Act requires that highest prevailing union wage rates be paid to workers on all federally aided construction projects.
3. If competitors are threatened by publicly aided service improvements, they are generally entitled to be compensated or bought out. UMTA has established, moreover, that even bankrupt enterprises with no hope of earning a profit will be paid for their assumed value as "going businesses" in addition to the market value of their physical assets.
4. Federal and state operating subsidies have in many instances greatly reduced the pressure on local officials to engage in hard collective bargaining, particularly since transit labor unions are increasingly powerful forces in the local political process.
5. In order to utilize federal operating assistance, transit operators must permit riders over 65 to ride at half-fare during off-peak hours.
6. Extremely stringent federal requirements for accessibility by the physically handicapped mean that very large sums must be added to public investment programs in fixed-route systems—although virtually all students of transit agree that the intended beneficiaries would be far better and less expensively served by subsidized taxi or dial-a-ride services (which, it should be noted, are also increasingly encouraged and assisted by the federal government).
7. In many local circumstances, the need to establish a regionwide constituency in order to obtain political approval for major transit investments has generated massive logrolling and gold-plating—both to ensure that all parts of the urban region get their "fair shares" of the benefits and that each group of potential objectors is bought off with expensive design or service solutions.

---

[9]The provision in question is Section 13(c) of the Urban Mass Transportation Act of 1964 as amended. ALAN ALTSHULER, "The Federal Government and Paratransit," in *Paratransit*, Special Report 164 (Washington, D.C.: Transportation Research Board, 1976), pp. 97–102. The article as a whole appears on pp. 89–104.

And so it goes. Until recently, the tensions between budgetary imperatives and the forces making for transit cost inflation were obscured by several factors. First, the absolute level of transit subsidization was quite low until the past several years, so that large percentage increases had only a modest impact on the sums available for other programs. Second, the political triumph of Keynesian economic principles and the high elasticity of federal progressive income taxes have made it possible in recent years for federal elected officials to vote major increases in benefits while actually appearing to lower taxes. With progressive tax rates, receipts normally rise more rapidly than private incomes and prices. The acceptance of Keynesianism has permitted a decade or so of ebullient growth in federal deficits, to the point where the deficit in fiscal year 1976 was $65.6 billion. Third, at the state and local level, where operating budgets are still generally required to be in balance, outstanding debt (mainly for capital outlay) in 1975 was 5 times greater than in 1955.

We seem, however, to have just about exhausted these special opportunities for rapid expenditure growth. It seems likely that further increases in the federal deficit will be generally viewed as inflationary, and that both investors and taxpayers will resist further dramatic increases in the level of state and local debt. (President Carter, it bears note, has pledged to bring the federal budget into balance by fiscal 1981.) The absolute level of transit budgetary requirements has now reached a point, moreover, where large percentage increases will inevitably be cause for deep concern in most jurisdictions. It remains to be seen whether these tensions between the newly invigorated forces of fiscal austerity and those fueling transit cost inflation will prove susceptible of resolution in the years ahead on terms compatible with a continuing transit revival. The alternative would appear to be a new spiral of transit decline, consisting of widespread service cutbacks and fare increases designed to hold down the public budgetary requirements of transit.

GOVERNMENT DECISIONS ABOUT THE STRUCTURE
OF THE TRANSPORTATION MARKET

As noted previously, private-sector behavior has played the predominant role in shaping the American pattern of urban transportation. The framework of market and cultural incentives since World War II has made it highly rational for most Americans, in their market behavior, to pursue low-density automobile-reliant life-styles. Public institutions have had no explicit policy with respect to these tendencies, but numerous policies aimed at other objectives have tended strongly to reinforce them.

Nevertheless, in the mid-1970s—as the environment, energy, and mass transit entered the mainstream of American political dialogue, and as it became increasingly clear that "carrots" alone will not lure Americans into transit or other forms of ride-sharing—a public discussion finally got under way about whether government should act decisively to change the framework of urban transportation incentives. Through 1977, all proposals have floundered on the shoals of public, as translated into legislative, resistance. The two most serious efforts have involved air pollution control and energy conservation.

The Clean Air Act Amendments of 1970 established specific standards and time-tables for air quality improvement. Both transportation and stationary source (e.g., factory and power plant) emissions were to be controlled. The regulation of business has proven controversial; there have been many technical disappointments; and numerous postponements have been allowed. But the policy thrust, and public support, appear to have remained fairly strong. Supplemental regulations aimed directly at the individual consumer, however, have generated a much more negative reaction. The prospect of regulation designed to reduce vehicle-miles of travel has stirred deep resistance among the electorate, ridicule in the media, and fearful second thoughts by elected officials.

Two means have been identified to bring about significant reductions in automobile travel—pricing and the creation of shortages (most notably, of parking space and/or gasoline) by direct regulation. During 1973, the Environmental Protection Agency (EPA) promulgated plans for 20 metropolitan areas that required reductions in vehicle-miles of travel in order to comply with the Clean Air Act targets.[10] A number of these relied heavily on the imposition of increased tolls and parking charges. Late in 1973, a congressional conference committee agreed on legislative language to prohibit EPA from imposing any regulations involving pricing—on the ground that only Congress could impose taxes. Although the bill in question died in the rush to congressional adjournment, EPA judged that similar language would be adopted in 1974 unless it rescinded its pricing order. In January 1974, it did so.

EPA officials then shifted to a greater emphasis upon direct regulation of parking-space availability. In Greater Boston, for example, EPA proposed a 25% rollback in the amount of parking provided by employers for their employees, elimination of on-street parking (except by residents) until 10 each morning in much of the inner portion of the region, and maintenance of a 40% vacancy rate in central-area off-street parking facilities until 10 a.m. These proposals were to become effective, as per the statutory deadline, on May 31, 1975.

Late in 1974, however, Congress attached a provision to the EPA appropriation bill for fiscal 1975 prohibiting EPA from making any expenditures to implement parking restrictions. This provision was continued in EPA's appropriations for fiscal 1976 and 1977. Thus, the second of the two significant means available for EPA to change the incentive structure within which consumers make their urban travel decisions had been eliminated. The transportation control plan sections of the Clean Air Act, while officially remaining on the books, had effectively been nullified.

Since the Arab oil embargo (winter of 1973–1974), the debate about whether and how to shape consumer incentives has increasingly focused on energy. Here the issue is not "simply" public health or amenity. It is the strength of the national economy, the balance of payments, and national security itself. The United States is today more dependent on imported oil than just prior to the embargo. Forty-seven percent of U.S. oil consumption was imported in 1977, as against 36% in 1973. (The oil share of total U.S. energy consumption was unchanged at 47%). The nation's oil import bill in 1977

---

[10]The total number of transportation control plans promulgated was 38, but only 20 of these entailed reductions in vehicle-miles of travel.

was $45 billion, up from $3 billion in 1970. Imports from the Organization of Petroleum Exporting Countries (OPEC) have doubled since 1973, from under one-sixth to roughly one-third of U.S. oil consumption. A panel of the National Academy of Sciences reported in 1975 that (1) significant increases in domestic oil and gas production are most unlikely, and (2) American reserves are probably no more than half of previous estimates. The economic consequences of these trends have, to date, been relatively muted, for the following reasons: (1) the U.S. has been successful in building exports of real wealth (i.e., goods and services) to balance the vastly increased cost of oil imports; (2) the oil nations have invested heavily in liquid American securities, such as Treasury notes and bank certificates of deposit; and (3) virtually all the other non-Communist industrial nations, which produce little or no oil, have been hit even harder than the United States by the recent world oil price increases. But the largest category of increased exports to the OPEC nations has been armaments, which are viewed by many observers as a potential destabilizing influence on Middle Eastern politics. And Arab investments in U.S. securities could be redeployed quickly if the Arab nations were determined at some future point to bring diplomatic pressure to bear on the United States.

In the face of these developments, there has been a great deal of talk in the United States about energy conservation, and legislation has been enacted that may begin to yield energy savings in the late 1970s. The only constraint on personal travel behavior that has been adopted is the 88 km/h (55 mi/h) speed limit—originally enacted early in 1974 as the mildest energy conservation proposal available during the oil embargo, and made permanent after it had gained recognition as the main factor responsible for the 17% decline in highway fatalities that accompanied its first year of operation. The Federal Energy Administration (FEA) estimates that the reduced speed limit is currently saving about 150,000 barrels (23,848 m³) of oil per day, 0.9% of overall daily consumption.

Following two years of inaction in the immediate aftermath of the embargo, Congress took four significant actions bearing upon oil consumption in 1975:

1. It mandated fuel economy standards for new automobiles beginning with the 1978 model year. The 1978 standard, however, is slightly below that already achieved on the 1977 models. The standards will apparently have little or no independent effect until after 1980, when the sales-weighted fuel economy average (as measured by EPA) will be required to rise above 8.5 km/l (20 mi/gal). The target for 1985 is 11.7 km/l (27.5 mi/gal). Given the history of the Clean Air Act, however, many people remain highly skeptical that the current schedule will remain unchanged if it proves to entail substantial cost or consumer inconvenience.

2. It extended oil price controls, first imposed in 1973, through early 1979. Although the new control scheme was billed in some quarters as a form of "phased decontrol," in fact it was nothing of the kind. The new control formula permits substantially higher prices than the old; but whereas the old formula applied only to oil production from any field up to the 1972 level, the new formula applies to the sales-weighted average of all domestic oil marketed. The

combined result of these changes, over the 40-month life of the control authorization, is expected to be average oil prices that are lower than they would have been under the previous system of control. (Although the authorization expires in April 1979, it is of course impossible to say whether Congress will in fact permit controls to expire at that time.)

3. It successfully brought pressure to bear on President Ford to remove the $2 surcharge on oil imports that he had imposed.

4. It eliminated the oil depletion allowance, long an incentive to oil exploration but also a prime target of tax reformers on equity grounds. The rationale for repeal at this time was that increased oil prices since 1973 offer ample incentive for oil exploration.

Considering these actions on balance, it seems clear that their immediate impact is negative with reference to the proclaimed objectives of energy conservation and reduced reliance on oil imports. The automobile fuel economy standards have a major long-term potential for positive impact, as does the possibility that oil price controls will be lifted in 1979. As the standards begin to bite (sometime after 1980), however, and as the price control expiration date approaches, we may anticipate that pressure on Congress to defer the former and extend the latter will be intense.

Why has there been such apparent resistance by the American political system, at least over the short run, to strong energy conservation measures—and particularly to measures that would involve widespread behavioral adjustment by transportation consumers? The core of the problem, I believe, is readily apparent. Given that the life patterns of most American households are built around the automobile, any program designed to reduce its use will inconvenience a large share of the electorate. Any program, moreover, will visit its impact differently on different regions of the country and different types of households, in ways that many people are bound to consider inequitable. Tax schemes, for example, even though in theory they can be designed to avoid it, tend in practice to affect most painfully those rural and low-income households that are well enough off to have cars. Additionally, they compound inflation over the short run. Rationing schemes tend to become bureaucratic nightmares as they seek to accommodate special needs.

Public opinion polls suggest that the public doubts that there even *is* a serious energy problem, except as a plot by the oil companies to increase their profits. In this situation, it is no surprise that elected officials have concentrated on eliminating special tax benefits for the oil companies and demanding lower fuel prices, while so far refusing to bite any significant conservation bullets.

CONCLUSION

We are faced, then, with a fascinating paradox. The urban public, speaking collectively, has brought about a remarkable shift in transporation investment priorities over the past decade. Speaking individually in the market place, on the other hand, Americans continue to congest the highways and resist the lures of transit.

And finally, the same public, speaking collectively again, is perceived by its elected officials as thoroughly hostile to any scheming by government to reduce automobile use by restructuring market options and incentives.

Is there a constant theme running through these apparent contradictions? I believe there is. Typical urban Americans do not want government to interfere with their lives. They are receptive to having government provide improved service (e.g., transit), but they will oppose having government disrupt their neighborhoods, harm their environment, or make it more difficult for them to drive.

The status quo seems to be the objective. Citizens oppose new highways because they disrupt existing neighborhoods, social patterns, and natural ecologies. They oppose programs to reduce auto travel because such programs would disrupt established life-styles and travel habits. They can and do adjust to inconvenience when they must. But they are likely to take out their annoyance on elected officials whom they feel failed to avert the need—or even worse, deliberately created it.

In short, American governments can spend great sums to provide "carrots," even when they appear to be relatively ineffective. But they find it extremely difficult to apply even very gentle and cost-effective "sticks" when these would visit discomfort on large numbers of voters. This disposition toward serving rather than controlling constituents is perhaps the most significant charm of the American political system, but it also accounts in predominant part for its ineffectiveness in shaping the urban transportation pattern.

APPENDIX A

Table 3-1 is based on the following sources and calculations:

1. Automobile and truck capital and operating costs (other than automobile insurance), school bus and "other bus" costs, and taxi revenues are as reported in: Transportation Association of America, *Transportation Facts and Trends*, 13th ed. (Washington, D.C.: Transportation Association of America, August 1977), pp. 4, 5.

2. Auto insurance costs have been estimated for 1975 by averaging the Federal Highway Administration estimates for 1974 and 1976 from L. L. Liston and R. W. Sherrer, *Costs of Operating an Automobile* (Washington, D.C.: Federal Highway Administration, April 1974) and L. L. Liston and C. A. Aiken, *Costs of Owning and Operating an Automobile, 1976* (Washington, D.C.: Federal Highway Administration, n.d.).

3. Public highway expenditures attributable to auto and truck use have been calculated from Kiran Bhatt, and others, *An Analysis of Road Expenditures and Payments by Vehicle Class (1956–1975)* (Washington, D.C.: The Urban Institute, 1977), p. 62 and Appendices I and VIII. The estimated amounts include the following subtotals: capital ($3.3 billion attributable to autos, $1.2 billion to trucks), maintenance ($1.0 billion auto, $1.0 billion truck), administrative costs of highway agencies and traffic police ($0.7 billion auto, $0.1 billion truck), and

police and judicial system costs attributable to auto-related crimes and tort actions ($2.5 billion auto, $0.5 billion truck).

4. Rail rapid and bus transit revenues and operating subsidies are as reported in American Public Transit Association, *Transit Fact Book*, 1976–77 ed. (Washington, D.C.: American Public Transit Association, 1977), Table 4, p. 22.

5. Commuter rail revenues are as reported in *Transportation Facts and Trends*, p. 5. Commuter rail operating subsidies are as reported in John Pucher, "Losses in the American Transit Industry . . . , 1973–1976," New Perspectives on Urban Transportation Project, Center for Transportation Studies, MIT, May 1977, Table 2-1.

6. Transit capital expenditures are as reported in U.S. Department of Transportation, *National Transportation Trends & Choices (to the Year 2000)* (Washington, D.C.: U.S. Government Printing Office, 1977), Table XI.4, p. 316.

APPENDIX B

The passenger mileage estimates presented in Table 3-2 were derived as follows:

Transit passenger mileage was calculated separately for bus, rail rapid, and commuter rail. Trip length estimates of 3.93 miles for bus and 6.57 miles for rail rapid transit were obtained from U.S. Department of Transportation, *1974 National Transportation Report: Urban Data Supplement* (Washington, D.C.: U.S. Government Printing Office, 1976), Tables D-23 and D-30. These estimated trip lengths were then multiplied by estimates of total unlinked trips for each year by mode from American Public Transit Association, *Transit Fact Book*, 1976–77 ed. (Washington, D.C.: American Public Transit Association, 1977), Table 7, p. 26. Commuter rail passenger-miles for 1975 are from Association of American Railroads, *Operating and Traffic Statistics, Class I Line-Haul Railroads in the United States* (O.S. Series No. 217, 1975). Commuter rail passenger-miles for other years have been estimated from Association of American Railroads, *Yearbook of Railroad Facts*, 1977 ed. (Washington, D.C.: Association of American Railroads, 1977), p. 32.

Auto passenger mileage was derived for each year by multiplying FHWA's estimate of auto vehicle mileage in urban areas by 2.2, the latter figure representing average occupancy per urban vehicle-mile as reported in the Nationwide Personal Transportation Study (NPTS): Federal Highway Administration, *Highway Statistics (various years)* (Washington, D.C.: U.S. Government Printing Office, various years), Table VM-1 and Harry E. Strate, *Nationwide Personal Transportation Survey (Study), Report no. 1: Automobile Occupancy* (Washington, D.C.: Federal Highway Administration, April 1972), Table 1, p. 7.

Regrettably, the estimates contain several probable sources of error which we have been unable to quantify. On balance, it appears that correction of these errors would modestly reduce the transit modal shares indicated in Table 3-2. Specifically:

1. NPTS is the only nationwide source for estimates of urban auto occupancy and is available for only one point in time (1969–1970). Thus we have assumed a constant occupancy throughout the period covered, though fragmentary data

indicate that average auto occupancies have been declining over time. Correction for this factor would tend to raise the auto travel estimates for the years prior to 1970.

2. The *National Transportation Report*, which examined transit trip lengths as of 1971, is the only source for nationwide estimates. Thus, again, we have assumed constant trip lengths throughout the period covered, though it seems clear that average transit trip lengths have been increasing over time. Correction for this factor would tend to depress the transit travel estimates for earlier years.

3. Commuter rail passenger mileage estimates prior to 1971 involve considerable uncertainties due to the passenger classifications ("commutation and multiple ride," "coach," and "parlor and sleeping car") used by the Interstate Commerce Commission. The Association of American Railroads has for many years summed the commutation and multiple-ride patronage (i.e., passengers using discounted "commutation" tickets) reported by the individual railroads and has presented this total as commutation patronage. However, when Amtrak assumed almost all intercity service in 1971 it became clear that a considerable number of commuter rail patrons were riding on single-trip tickets. In 1975 commutation tickets accounted for an additional 1.25 billion. We have assumed that this pattern prevailed in earlier years as well.

4. The auto estimates do not include personal travel by light truck and van because precise estimates of such usage are unavailable. Indisputably, however, such travel has increased rapidly during the 1960s and 1970s. Illustratively, the proportion of trucks and vans used "primarily for personal transportation" (urban and rural combined) rose from 25% in 1963 to 41% in 1972, suggesting that it may be in the 50% range as of 1978. Meanwhile, the truck/van proportion of total motor vehicle registrations rose from 16% in 1965 to 21% in 1975. The average truck used primarily for personal transportation was driven 9800 miles in 1972 (compared with 10,200 miles for the average auto). Thus, it appears that correction for this factor would add 8 to 10% to the auto passenger mileage figures presented for 1970 and 1975. The upward adjustment in earlier years would be considerably smaller, but it is impossible to say (even approximately) how much smaller with any confidence.

SELECTED BIBLIOGRAPHY

ALTSHULER, ALAN A., JAMES P. WOMACK, AND JOHN R. PUCHER, *Politics, Innovation, and Urban Transportation Policy*. Cambridge, Mass.: The M.I.T. Press, 1979.

——, and ROBERT W. CURRY, "The Changing Environment of Urban Development Policy—Shared Power or Shared Impotence?" *Urban Law Annual*, 10 (1975), 3–41.

KEMP, MICHAEL A., AND MELVYN D. CHESLOW, "Transportation," in *The Urban Predicament*, pp. 281–356, eds. William Gorham and Nathan Glazer. Washington, D.C.: The Urban Institute, 1976.

OWEN, WILFRED, *Transportation for Cities: The Role of Federal Policy*. Washington, D.C.: The Brookings Institution, 1976.

SCHWARTZ, GARY T., "Urban Freeways and the Interstate System," *Southern California Law Review*, 49, no. 3 (March 1976), 406–513.

WEBBER, MELVIN M., "The BART Experience—What Have We Learned?" *The Public Interest*, no. 45 (Fall 1976), pp. 79–108.

PART II

Systems
and Technologies

INTRODUCTION TO PART II

The purpose of this section is to describe the present modes of public transportation in terms of definitions and characteristics, and the application of each to urban travel needs. Public transportation modes are characterized by extent of right-of-way separation; the technology of its guidance, support, propulsion, and control; and the type of service offered.

Street or surface transit uses modes such as buses, paratransit, trolleybuses, and streetcars in the same traffic lanes as autos. Semirapid transit excludes mixed traffic except at grade crossings, and rapid transit modes operating on an exclusive right-of-way may be furnished by buses, guided rubber-tired vehicles, or rail. Public transit modes may also be considered in terms of capacity. Low-capacity modes are paratransit (e.g., taxis, dial-a-ride, and jitneys); medium-capacity modes are regular bus, trolleybus, and streetcar; and high-capacity modes are semirapid transit bus, light rail transit, rubber-tired rapid transit, rail rapid transit, and regional rail. Each mode has a role to play in furnishing transit services, and the task of the engineer and planner is to integrate each into a coherent system of public transportation.

Steel rail and flanged wheel railways have been the most prevalent fixed guideway mode in use, despite attempts to supplant them with vehicles supported on monorail, rubber tires, or air cushions. The simplicity of the rail, ease in switching, reliability, low cost, and continual perfection of the roadbed and track are features that have maintained its competitive position. Construction of rail transit has been extensive both in the United States and in other countries, and its versatility is demonstrated in applications of modern light rail, rail rapid transit, and commuter railroads.

Conventional bus transit is the most prevalent mode and carries over 70% of all transit travel. The inherent advantage of bus transit is the ability to be routed along any street or highway, and for this reason buses serve many land-use densities and urban configurations. Bus capacities range from small vehicles used for paratransit to large articulated coaches used in heavily traveled corridors. As the "workhorse" of public transit, the bus lacks glamour, but its attributes of reliability, availability, flexibility, and economy indicate that it will remain as the most popular mode of public transportation for years to come.

Conventional bus and rail transit are being augmented by a variety of transit services collectively known as paratransit. Two of its features are that vehicles use existing streets and highways, and that all services are available to the public. Examples include taxis, vanpools, dial-a-ride, jitneys, and carpools. Paratransit services that have been particularly helpful in transporting elderly and handicapped are taxis and other demand-responsive services. Commuter travel has become more efficient, with ridesharing programs such as vanpools and carpools. Every paratransit mode requires a mechanism to match the service to the user's need, in both space and time, and the communications network that links the system with the rider is an essential element of this mode. Institutional problems involving regulatory matters, insurance, and labor are issues to be resolved if paratransit is to achieve its potential.

The pedestrian is generally not listed as a public transportation mode, although walking is a major element of any transit trip. Pedestrian flow characteristics, such as speed and density, govern the design of transit facilities. Maximum walking distances define the catchment area for bus stops, and planned pedestrian systems can be designed to augment transit services. A well-planned city will include facilities for pedestrian movement, such as malls, auto-free zones, skyways, and moving walkways.

The urban transportation system is comprised of an intricate and complex arrangement of various public transportation modes, and there are many elements and factors that should be considered in assuring that each mode operates harmoniously to produce a high level of transit service.

LESTER A. HOEL, Professor and Chairman,
Department of Civil Engineering,
University of Virginia

Chapter 4

URBAN PASSENGER TRANSPORT MODES

VUKAN R. VUCHIC, *Professor of Transportation Engineering,*
University of Pennsylvania

This chapter presents a systematic classification of concepts and definitions of terms in urban public transport, focusing mainly on transit. Features of the basic mode characteristics, such as guided vs. nonguided technologies, small vs. large vehicles, are applied to a comparison of different transit modes.

TRANSIT CLASSIFICATIONS AND DEFINITIONS

Classification of modes and concepts can be done on several different bases. Some of the classifications are interdependent. For example, mode, often identified with system technology only, actually also incorporates characteristics of rights-of-way and operations. All major classifications are given here, from the basic classification of all urban travel to the definitions of physical system components.

CLASSIFICATION BY TYPE OF USAGE

There are three basic categories of transportation by type of operation and usage: private, for-hire, and public or common carrier. The main characteristics, typical modes, and optimal operating domains of these categories are shown in Table 4-1.

Private transport consists of privately owned vehicles operated by owners for their own use, usually on publicly provided and operated streets. Private auto is the most common mode, but motorcycle, bicycle, and, of course, walking also belong in this category.

TABLE 4-1
Classification of Urban Passenger Transport by Type of Usage

Characteristic \ Usage Type	Private	For-hire	Public or Common Carrier
Common designation	Private transport	Paratransit	Transit
Service availability	Owner	Public	Public
Service supplier	User	Carrier	Carrier
Route determination	User (flexible)	User (carrier)	Carrier (fixed)
Time-schedule determination	User (flexible)	User (carrier)	Carrier (fixed)
Cost-price	User absorbs	Fixed rate	Fixed fare

	Individual			Group
Carrier type / Modes	**Private (Individual)**	**Private (Group)**	**For-hire (Individual)**	**For-hire (Group)**	**Public or Common Carrier (Group)**
	Automobile	Carpools	Taxi	Dial-a-ride	Street transit (bus, trolleybus, streetcar)
	Motorcycle	Vanpools	Rented car	(Jitney)	Semirapid transit (semirapid bus, light rail transit)
	Bicycle			Charter bus	Rapid transit (rail, rubber-tired, regional rail)
	Walking				Special and proposed modes

Optimum (but not exclusive) domain of operation:

Characteristic	Private (Individual)	Private (Group)	For-hire	Public or Common Carrier
Area density	Low-medium	Origin: low / Destination: high	Low	High-medium
Routing	Dispersed	Radial	Dispersed	Concentrated (radial)
Time	Off-peak	Peak only	All times	Peak
Trip purposes	Recreation, shopping, business	Work only	Business	Work, school, business

69

For-hire urban passenger transport is commonly designated as *paratransit*. It is transportation service provided by an operator and available to all parties who meet the conditions of a contract for carriage [i.e., pay prescribed prices (rates)], but which is adjustable in various degrees to individual user's desires. Most paratransit modes do not have fixed routes and schedules. Taxi, dial-a-bus, and jitney are examples.

Common-carrier urban passenger transport is known as *transit, mass transit*, or *mass transportation*. These are transport systems with fixed routes and schedules, available for use by all persons who pay the established fare. Most common representatives are bus, light rail, and rapid transit, but there exist a number of other modes.

Paratransit modes with routes and schedules that change with the desires of individual users are referred to as *demand-responsive*; when the difference is pointed out, transit is described as *fixed-route, fixed-schedule* service.

Urban public transportation, strictly defined, includes both transit and paratransit categories, since both are available for public use. However, since public transport is frequently identified with transit only, inclusion of paratransit is often specifically emphasized.

A secondary classification of travel categorizes transport as individual or group. *Individual transport* refers to systems in which each vehicle serves a separate party (person or organized group); *group transport* carries unrelated persons in the same vehicles. As Table 4-1 shows, the former is predominantly private transport, the latter is transit, while paratransit encompasses modes from both categories.

TRANSIT MODES

A transit mode is defined by three characteristics:

- Right-of-way (R/W) category.
- Technology.
- Type of service.

Modes vary with each one of these characteristics. Contrary to the common belief that technologies mostly determine modal characteristics, the R/W category has the strongest influence on both performance and costs of modes. For example, streetcar service is more similar to surface bus than to rail rapid transit service.

Rights-of-way. Transit R/W is the strip of land on which the transit vehicles operate. There are three basic R/W categories, distinguished by the degree of their separation from other traffic.

1. *Category C* represents surface streets with *mixed traffic*. Transit may have preferential treatment, such as reserved lanes separated by lines, or special signals, or travel mixed with other traffic.
2. *Category B* includes R/W types which are *longitudinally physically separated* (by curbs, barriers, grade separation, etc.) from other traffic, but with grade crossings for vehicles and pedestrians, including regular street intersections.

3. *Category A* is a *fully controlled* R/W without grade crossings or any legal access by other vehicles or persons. It is also referred to as "grade-separated" or "exclusive" R/W. In exceptional cases the R/W may have widely spaced grade crossings with signal override and gate protection of the tracks, and yet be considered as category A, since such crossings have little effect on line performance.

Technologies. Technology of transit modes refers to the mechanical features of their vehicles and ways. The four most important features are defined here.

1. *Support* is the vertical contact between vehicle and riding surface which transfers the vehicle weight. The most common types are rubber tire on concrete, asphalt, or other surface, and steel wheel on steel rail. Other types of support are vehicle body on water (boats and hydrofoils), air cushion (hovercraft), and magnetic levitation (not yet operational).

   Technologies with support under the vehicle body are *supported*; those with support above the vehicle body are *suspended*. The latter type is very rare.
2. *Guidance* refers to the means of lateral vehicle guidance. Highway vehicles are *steered* (by the driver) and their lateral stability is provided by wheel/support adhesion. Rail vehicles are *guided* by flanges and the conical form of the wheel surfaces. A distinct feature of rail technology is that its wheel/rail assembly combines both support and guidance. Externally guided rubber-tired vehicles in all forms must have additional wheels and surfaces for guidance.
3. *Propulsion* refers to the type of propulsion unit and method of transferring acceleration/deceleration forces. Its major components are:
   a. *Type of propulsion unit*—the most common ones are diesel internal combustion engine (ICE), used on buses and some regional rail; and electric motors, used on trolleybuses and most rail modes. Gasoline ICE dominates small highway vehicles, while the gas turbine, steam engine, linear induction motor (LIM), and others are still under development.
   b. *Methods of transferring tractive force* include friction/adhesion (dominant), magnetic, cable, and propeller, among others.
4. *Control* is the means of regulating travel of one or all vehicles in a system. The most important control is for longitudinal spacing of the vehicles, which may be manual/visual, manual/signal, fully automatic, or various combinations of these.

Conventionally, transit technologies were defined only by the techniques of support and guidance. Such definitions are not precise enough to distinguish bus from trolleybus, or light rail from rapid transit. With support, guidance, propulsion, and control, all technologies can be defined to any desired degree of precision.

Service types. There are many different types of transit services. They can be classified into groups by three characteristics:

First, by the *types of routes and trips served*:

- *Short-haul transit* is defined as low-speed services within small areas with high travel density, such as central business districts (CBDs), campuses, airports, and exhibition grounds.
- *City transit*, the most common type, includes transit routes serving the entire city. They may operate on any R/W category (A, B, or C).
- *Regional transit* consists of long, high-speed routes with few stops, serving long trips within the metropolitan region. Regional rail and some express bus routes exemplify this category.

Second, classification by *stopping schedule*:

- *Local service* is with all vehicles stopping at all stops (or as required by passengers).
- *Accelerated service* is when successive vehicles skip different sets of stations on a predetermined schedule (e.g., skip-stop and zonal service).
- *Express service* is with all vehicles on a route stopping only at widely spaced stops. These routes often parallel local service but serve fewer stops/stations, making express/local service.

The third classification is by *time of operation*:

- *All-day service* is transit operated during most daily hours. This is the basic transit service, and it includes a great majority of transit lines.
- *Peak-hour service* or *commuter transit* refers to routes operated during peak hours only. They are usually radial from suburbs, focusing on the CBD, designed for work trips only (e.g., Shirley Busway in the Washington, D.C., area). *Commuter transit is a supplement to, but not a substitute for, all-day, regular transit.*
- *Irregular service* is transit operated only during special events, such as sport events, exhibitions, or public celebrations.

Generic classes of transit modes. There is no rigorous definition of what differences in R/W, technology, or service make a separate mode, but it is common to consider systems as different modes if they differ substantially in one or more of the three characteristics. Thus, bus and trolleybus operating the same type of service on the same R/W are different modes because of their substantial technological and performance differences; but standard and articulated buses operating under the same conditions would not be considered different modes. An express bus line is a different mode than a shopper shuttle, even if the vehicles are identical, because of the drastically different services; but skip-stop rapid transit service during peak hours is not considered a different mode than the same line operating locally at other times because the two services are quite similar.

The best known classification of transit modes is into three generic classes, based mostly, but not entirely, on R/W type. They are defined here.

1. *Street transit* (also known as *surface transit*) designates modes operated on streets with mixed traffic (R/W category C); its reliability is often low because of various interferences, and its speed is lower than the speed of traffic flow, owing to the time lost at passenger stops: buses, trolleybuses, and streetcars are in this class.

2. *Semirapid transit* consists of modes utilizing mostly R/W category B, but C or A may also be used for some sections. This class includes a wide range of modes from those with B and C categories, such as buses and light rail transit (LRT) operating on separated R/W and streets on the low side, to largely grade-separated LRT (B and A) on the high side. Performance of these modes depends greatly on the degree and locations of R/W separation; it is particularly important that transit is separated from other vehicular traffic in central, congested urban areas. Another factor is technology; rail modes can operate in short trains and have higher safety through automatic signalization than buses. Higher types of semirapid transit (with little or no C category R/W) can match or exceed speed and reliability of auto travel.

3. *Rapid transit* modes operate exclusively on category A R/W and have high speed, capacity, reliability, and safety. All existing rapid transit systems utilize guided technologies (rail or rubber tire), which permit operation of trains (high capacity) and automatic signal control (high safety). Strictly, "bus rapid transit" does not exist since a bus line operating entirely on R/W category A would have much lower capacity, higher operating costs (single vehicles), and lower safety (steering instead of guidance, no automatic signals) than rail modes.

Most transit modes belong to one of the three generic classes. The exceptions are such modes as ferryboats, aerial tramways, and inclines. The latter two do have exclusive R/W, but they have no other features of rapid transit. These modes are therefore classified as *special transit*.

A matrix of mode classification by R/W category and major technological features (mainly support and guidance) is given in Table 4-2. Other technological and some service variations are given in individual matrix boxes. In addition to all street transit modes, category C contains also water- and airborne modes. Semirapid transit modes are in category B, while all rapid transit modes belong, by definition, in category A. This category includes, however, also all guided non-rail modes, since they cannot tolerate grade crossings. Inclines and aerials are also included. Thus, the generic classes correspond closely, but not exactly, to the R/W categories.

An overview of the preceding mode definitions, classifications, and characteristics is presented in Fig. 4-1.

TRANSIT SYSTEM COMPONENTS

Physical components of the transit systems are generally classified into the following items:

Vehicles or *cars*, referred to collectively as *fleet* for buses and *rolling stock* for rail

TABLE 4-2
Classification of Urban Public Transport Modes[a]

R/W Category	Technology	Highway— Driver-Steered	Rubber-Tired— Guided, Partially Guided	Rail	Special
C		*Paratransit* *Shuttle bus* *Regular bus* *Express bus* *(on streets)*	*Trolleybus*	*Streetcar* Cable car	*Ferryboat* Hydrofoil Helicopter
B		Semirapid bus	Dual mode*	*Light rail transit*	
A		Bus on busway only*	*Rubber-tired RT* Rubber-tired monorails Automated guided transit GRT PRT*	*Light rapid transit* Schwebebahn *Rail rapid transit* *Regional rail*	*Incline* Aerial tramway Continuous short- haul systems

[a]Modes extensively used are in italic type. Modes that are not operational are designated by asterisks.

Determinant Factors	Categories/Types	Basic Characteristics		Individual Modes*	Generic Classes
Separation from other traffic	C B A	Right-of-way Categories		(Paratransit modes) Shuttle bus Regular bus Express bus/street Trolleybus Streetcar Cable car	Street transit
				Semirapid buses Light rail transit	Semirapid transit
Support Guidance Propulsion - Motor/Engine - Traction Control	Highway—driver steered Rubber—tired—guided, semiguided Rail Special	Technology		Light rapid transit Schwebebahn Rubber-tired monorails Rubber-tired RT Rail RT Regional rail	Rapid transit
Line length Type of operation Trips served	Short-haul Regular Regional Local Accelerated Express	Type of Service		Automated guided transit Ferryboat Helicopter Inclines Belt systems	Special transit

TRANSIT MODES

*The list is not exhaustive.

Figure 4-1 *An overview of transit mode definition, classification, and characteristics*

75

vehicles. A *transit unit* (TU) is a set of vehicles traveling together; it may be a *single vehicle* unit or a *train* with several vehicles.

Ways, travel ways, or *rights-of-way* may be common streets and highways, reserved lanes (designated only), exclusive lanes (physically separated), transit streets, busways (grade-separated roadways for buses only), tracks in roadways, on partially or fully controlled R/W at grade, above grade (embankments and aerials), or below grade (cuts and tunnels).

Locations and facilities at which vehicles stop to pick up and drop off passengers can be of several types. *Stops* are locations along streets with simple facilities (signs, shelters, etc.); *stations* are usually buildings below, on, or above ground with facilities for passengers and system operation. *Terminals* are end stations of major transit lines. *Transfer stations* serve more than one line and provide for passenger interchange among them. *Multimodal transfer stations* are served by several modes. *Interface* is another term for a transfer station.

Bus garages or *depots* and *rail yards* are buildings or areas for vehicle storage. *Shops* are facilities for vehicle maintenance and repair.

Control systems include vehicle detection, communication and signal equipment, as well as any central control facility. *Power supply systems* on electrically powered modes consist of substations, distribution wiring, catenary or third-rail structures, and related equipment.

Except for the vehicles, all these items constitute *fixed facilities* of transit systems, or their *infrastructure*.

Transit route or *transit line* is a designated set of streets or separated rights-of-way that transit vehicles regularly serve. The term "route" is commonly used for buses, "line" for rail modes and for sections on which several routes overlap, but the two terms are sometimes used interchangeably. The collection of all routes/lines in a city is its *transit network*.

TRANSIT SYSTEM OPERATIONS, SERVICE, AND CHARACTERISTICS

Transit operations include such activities as scheduling, crew rostering, running and supervision of vehicles, fare collection, and system maintenance. They produce transportation which is offered to potential users.

Transit service is the transit system as seen by its actual and potential users.

Transit system characteristics are classified in four categories.

1. *System performance* refers to the entire set of *performance elements*, the most important ones being:
   a. *Service frequency* (f), number of transit unit departures per hour.
   b. *Operating speed* (V_0), speed of travel on the line which passengers experience.
   c. *Reliability*, expressed as a percentage of vehicle arrivals with less than a fixed time deviation from schedule (e.g., 4 minutes).
   d. *Safety*, measured by the number of fatalities, injuries, and property damage per 100 million passenger-km (passenger-mi), or a similar unit.

e. *Line capacity* (*C*), the maximum number of persons transit vehicles can carry past a point along the line.

f. *Productive capacity* (*P_c*), the product of operating speed and line capacity. As a composite indicator incorporating one basic element affecting passengers (speed) and one affecting operator (capacity), productive capacity is a very convenient performance indicator for mode comparisons.

g. *Productivity*, the quantity of output per unit of resource [e.g., vehicle-km (-mi), space-km (-mi), or person-km (-mi) per unit of labor, operating cost, fuel, R/W width, etc.].

h. *Utilization*, also the ratio of output to input, but of the same unit, for example, person-km/space-km (person-mi/space-mi) offered.

2. *Level of service* (*L/S*) is the overall measure of all service characteristics that affect users. L/S is a basic element in attracting potential users to the system. Major factors comprising L/S can be divided into two groups:

a. *Performance elements which affect users*, such as operating speed, reliability, and safety.

b. *Service quality* (*SQ*), consisting of qualitative elements of service, such as convenience and simplicity of using the system, riding comfort, aesthetics, cleanliness, and behavior of passengers.

3. *Impacts* are the effects transit service has on its surroundings and the entire area it serves. They may be positive or negative. *Short-run impacts* include reduced street congestion, changes in air pollution, noise, and aesthetics along a new line. *Long-run impacts* consist of changes in land values, economic activities, physical form, and social environment of the city.

4. *Costs* are usually divided into two major categories: *investment costs* (or capital costs) are those required to construct or later make permanent changes in the physical plant of the transit system. *Operating costs* are costs incurred by regular operation of the system.

Evaluation and comparative analysis of transit systems must include all four categories: performance, L/S, impacts, and costs of each system. The preferred mode is usually not the one with the highest performance or lowest costs, but the one with the most advantageous "package" or combination of the four.

THE FAMILY OF TRANSIT MODES: DEFINITIONS AND COMPARISONS

Transit modes can be ordered into a "family," ranging from taxis to regional rail systems. Brief definitions and characteristics of the commonly used modes are presented here. Several pairs of modes "adjacent" to each other in the family of modes are compared. More detailed methodology for their comparison is presented in Chapter 13.

Taxis are automobiles operated by a driver and hired by users for individual trips. The service they offer is tailored entirely to the user's desire. The use of a taxi may involve longer waiting than with a private car, but there is no parking problem. The user avoids the financial responsibility of owning a car, but the out-of-pocket cost of taxi travel is the highest of all modes. Since most of the cost covers the driver's time, the high price is inherent in this mode.

Dial-a-ride or *dial-a-bus* consists of minibuses or vans directed from a central dispatching office. Passengers call the office and give their origin, destination, and desired time of travel. The office plans the bus routings so that as many passengers as possible are served on a single trip.

Dial-a-bus usually operates within geographically delineated low-density areas. It serves trips that have one common end ("one-to-many") or both ends dispersed ("many-to-many"). Thus, this mode provides a service between those of taxi and regular bus.

Compared with *taxi, dial-a-ride* offers:
+ Lower-cost service.
+ More comfortable ride (larger vehicles).
− Slower, less direct travel.
− Less personalized service.
− Service within a limited area only.

Experience has shown that in most cases dial-a-rides have low average vehicle occupancies, which result in high cost per passenger. Where moderate fares are required to attract a substantial number of riders, dial-a-ride may require a considerably higher public assistance per rider than typical transit services.

Jitneys are privately owned large passenger cars or vans (8- to 15-seat vehicles) which operate on a fixed route (in some cases with minor deviations), without fixed schedules. They pick up and drop off passengers along their route by request. Because of their small capacity, jitneys operate in large numbers; because they stop frequently, they often contribute to traffic congestion. Jitneys typically offer less safety and comfort than regular transit and are used primarily in countries with inadequate transit service.

MEDIUM-CAPACITY MODES: STREET TRANSIT

Regular bus (*RB*) service consists of buses operating along fixed routes on fixed schedules. Buses comprise by far the most widely used transit mode. With vehicles varying in capacity from minibuses (20 to 35 spaces) to articulated buses (up to 130 spaces) and the ability to operate on nearly all streets, arterials, and freeways, buses provide services covering a wide range of L/S, performance, costs, and impacts.

At the lower end of their application range, regular buses serve low-volume suburban routes, overlapping somewhat with dial-a-ride. In marginal cases it is possible to operate regular buses as dial-a-bus service during hours of low demand. The more the travel demand is concentrated along corridors, the more advantageous the regular bus becomes.

Compared with *dial-a-ride*, the *regular bus* offers:
+ Higher reliability (fixed schedule, predictable waiting times).
+ Lower cost per passenger (lower fares and/or lower public assistance).
− Less personalized service (not door-to-door).
− Less frequent (not by request) service.

The most typical bus services are street transit routes, which may represent the entire transit network (small and most medium-size cities) or supplementary and feeder services to rail networks. At the upper end of their application range, regular buses overlap with the LRT domain: they can serve lines with 3000 to 5000 persons/h, exceptionally with even higher volumes. However, their largest overlap is with the domains of trolleybuses and streetcars.

Express bus service is provided by fast, comfortable buses on long routes with widely spaced stops. It is characterized by higher speed, more comfortable travel, but between fewer points and sometimes at a higher price than regular buses. Its reliability of service is dependent on traffic conditions along the route.

Trolleybuses (*TB*) are the same vehicles as buses except that they are propelled by an electric motor and obtain power from two overhead wires along their route. The trolleybus can basically be used for the same services as regular bus. It involves a higher investment cost and more complex operations, which some operators do not like. The advantages the trolleybus offers include higher riding quality (smooth vehicle motion) and excellent environmental features (extremely low noise, no exhaust). However, since these factors are not reflected in the operator's revenues, financial problems of transit agencies have often led to substitution of buses for trolleybuses.

Streetcars (*SCR*) or *tramways* are electrically powered rail transit vehicles operating mostly on streets. Their tracks and distinct vehicles give transit service a strong identification. Spacious vehicles and comfortable ride are also popular with the passengers. However, operation on the streets with congested traffic causes considerable friction with other vehicles, impeding both the streetcars and the auto traffic. A number of street design and regulatory traffic engineering techniques exist which can alleviate these problems and even provide a better flow for streetcars than buses. But without such measures, buses do offer superior speed and reliability in street operation. For this and several other reasons streetcars, which used to be the basic transit mode, have been either replaced by buses or gradually upgraded into higher-performance rail modes in most cities.

> *Streetcars* compared with *buses* have:
> + More comfortable ride.
> + Quieter, pollution-free operation.
> + Better vehicle performance.
> + Higher labor productivity (larger vehicles).
> + Higher line capacity.
> − Higher investment cost.
> − Less reliable street operation unless transit enjoys priority treatment.
> − Less flexible operation (detours, use for charters, etc.).
> − Higher maintenance of way and power supply system.
> − Greater impedance of other traffic.

HIGH-PERFORMANCE MODES: SEMIRAPID TRANSIT AND RAPID TRANSIT

Transit modes in the upper range of the "mode family" are better characterized by high overall performance than specifically by high capacity. They all offer high speed and reliability, but their capacity and productivity vary greatly between the two extremes, semirapid buses and rail rapid transit.

Semirapid transit includes only the following two modes:

1. *Semirapid buses* (*SRB*) are regular or high-performance buses operating on routes that include substantial sections of R/W categories B or A. Performance of such systems depends greatly on the following factors:
   a. Proportion and locations of separated R/W sections: their provision in congested areas is more important than in outlying, low-density areas.
   b. R/W types: bus lanes, reserved streets, or busways.
   c. Types of operation: routings, transfers, stop spacings, speed, frequency, safety, and reliability of service.

The concept of *buses on busway*, exemplified by the Shirley Express Bus Service in the Washington, D.C., area has been suggested for several cities. It consists of a busway in a freeway median which is utilized by a great number of bus routes converging during the commuting hours from suburban areas. Buses travel on the busway with few or without any stops to the CBD, where they use streets for distribution. All routes are purely radial, terminating in the CBD, and have few coordinated transfers with other routes. In the afternoon peak the same operation occurs in reverse. Busways have few or no stations and they can be traveled in one or both directions. Most often they are used only during peaks; sometimes a few routes operate throughout the day. Thus, *buses on busway typically represent commuter rather than regular transit.* They are an efficient mode for peak-hour service, but offer a lower type of service, if any, in the off-peak hours. The main reason for this deficiency is that since they follow freeway alignments, busways are not optimally located with respect to transit demand. Moreover, they provide high-speed travel in outlying, low-density areas, but the service drastically deteriorates in slow distribution and frequent delays in the CBD.

These deficiencies of buses on busways are not necessarily inherent in the SRB mode. If properly designed, SRB could utilize different types of reserved or exclusive R/W, including busways, that follow alignments of major passenger travel. Its routes could be simpler (similar to rail lines), have stop spacings of 300 to 800 m (1000 to 2500 ft), transfer with other routes, and operate with reasonable frequencies throughout the day.

Because of the separated R/W, SRB requires a considerably higher investment than regular buses for its infrastructure, but it offers a higher L/S and system performance.

2. *Light rail transit (LRT)* is a mode utilizing predominantly reserved, but not necessarily grade-separated R/W. Its electrically propelled rail vehicles operate singly or in trains. LRT provides a wide range of L/S and performance characteristics.

LRT takes advantage of a unique feature of rail technology; although guided, it can have grade crossings and even run on streets. This gives LRT the ability to utilize all types of R/W on the same route, and yet have the advantages of guided technology: high capacity, high labor productivity (train operation), comfortable ride, and so on. Street running is least desirable because of the disadvantages described before for streetcar operation; fully controlled R/W is the most desirable, but the most capital-intensive one. A typical LRT network, therefore, would have tunnels under the most congested central area, while its degree of separation decreases toward outlying areas where congestion is not a problem. LRT can also operate in pedestrian malls. The lower noise, absence of exhaust fumes, and a better safety record make LRT more compatible with pedestrian environments than buses. Because of the limited speed, however, mall running can be used only on short sections.

LRT is a higher investment/higher performance mode than streetcars. Its relationship with regular buses is similar to that with streetcars: their comparison would show that LRT is superior in nearly all L/S and performance items, but that it requires a much higher investment and, therefore, has a more limited network and longer access distances. Hence, the most important comparison is between LRT and SRB, since both utilize similar R/W categories but have different technologies.

> *Light rail transit* compared with *semirapid buses* on the corresponding alignments is characterized by:
> + Easier securing of B or A R/W (less pressure to mix with other traffic).
> + Stronger image and identity of lines (rail technology).
> + More spacious, comfortable vehicles.
> + Higher passenger attraction (result of the preceding two).
> + Lower noise, no exhausts.
> + Better vehicle performance due to electric traction.
> + Higher system performance (capacity, productivity, reliability, etc.).
> + Ability to operate in tunnels.
> + Ability to upgrade into rapid transit.

> — Lower service frequency for a given demand due to larger vehicles.
> — Somewhat higher investment for the same alignment.
> — For new applications, a need to introduce new facilities for a different technology.
> — Lower ability to branch out, requiring more transfers.
> — A longer implementation period.

This comparison shows that as the extent of B and A R/W on a transit line increases, LRT becomes more advantageous than the SRB. Since most of the investment is required for R/W construction, a small additional investment for LRT brings its very significant advantages over SRB in L/S, performance, operating costs, and impacts.

Another factor to consider in comparing modes is the type of network. Buses have the greatest ability to operate on interconnected and overlapping routes; rail rapid transit is the least capable of that. Its networks usually consist of independent lines with few (usually two) branches. They rely on easy transfers among frequent services or simultaneous passenger exchange across platforms. The trade-off between fewer transfers in interconnected networks and higher frequency, greater simplicity, schedule adherence, and use of optimal equipment on each section on independent lines varies among locations. In some cases direct routing of buses prevails; in others, regimes on branches, and trunk lines are so different that use of different modes (bus feeder with rail on trunk) or different vehicles (minibus feeders, regular or articulated buses on trunk) offers a much more reliable and economical service. LRT is between these two modes and it often is a good compromise of these features.

Rapid transit includes the following four modes:

1. *Light rail rapid transit (LRRT)* or *light rapid transit* represents small-scale rapid transit; it consists of light rail vehicles (LRV) operating on R/W category A only. There are presently very few of these systems in operation (the Norristown line in Philadelphia and line 8 in Göteborg, Sweden, are the best known ones). But the significance of this mode is likely to increase greatly when full automation is introduced.

2. *Rubber-tired rapid transit (RTR)* consists of moderately large vehicles (gross floor areas between 36 and 53 m²—380 and 570 ft²) supported and guided by rubber tires, running on wooden, steel, or concrete surfaces in trains of 5 to 9 cars. The cars also have steel wheels for switching and for support in the case of a tire failure.

3. *Rail rapid transit (RRT)* typically consists of large four-axle rail vehicles (area up to 70 m²—750 ft²) which operate in trains of up to 10 cars on fully controlled (A) R/W which allows high speed, reliability, capacity, rapid boarding, and fail-safe operation (in the case of driver's error or disability, the train is stopped automatically). Some RRT systems are further characterized by a high degree of automated operation.

Although the main representatives of semirapid transit, LRT, and of rapid transit, RRT, are extremely similar technologies and can have compatible operations, the full R/W control gives RRT several significant distinctions, as the following brief comparison of the two modes shows.

> *Rail rapid transit* compared with *light rail transit* has:
> + Higher L/S (speed, reliability, comfort, etc.).
> + Higher system performance (capacity due to long trains, productivity, efficiency).
> + Higher safety (signalized, fail-safe).
> + Stronger image (separate R/W *and* rail technology).
> + Higher passenger attraction and land-use impact (result of the above).
> − Higher investment.
> − Lower ability to fit into urban environment.
> − Less conducive to stage construction.
> − Longer implementation.

Rail rapid transit represents the ultimate mode for line-haul transport (i.e., for serving a number of points along a route). Trains of spacious vehicles with several doors on each side board passengers from high-level platforms without fare collection delays at rates of up to 40 persons/second, many times higher than any other mode; with train capacities, where required, often exceeding 1000 spaces and up to 40 trains/h passing a point, the capacity of RRT greatly exceeds those of other modes; full R/W control allows the most reliable and safe travel at the maximum speeds that station spacings and passenger comfort permit. In all these features there is no physical way that a major further improvement in performance can be achieved for line-haul service. This highest performance is achieved, however, at an investment cost higher than for any other mode; provision of its major item, a fully controlled R/W through urban areas, requires a considerably higher cost than any other R/W type.

4. *Regional rail* (*RGR*), usually operated by railroads, has high standards of alignment geometry. It utilizes the largest vehicles of all rail transit systems (up to 80 m²—860 ft²) which operate in trains, on longer routes, with fewer stations, at higher speeds than typical for RRT. Thus, RGR functionally represents a "large-scale RRT" which serves most efficiently regional and longer urban trips.

The two basic physical features of rapid transit modes, guidance and fully controlled R/W, are also shared by the proposed modes designated as *automated guided transit* (*AGT*).[1] Table 4-3 gives classification of both classes of modes by vehicle size and guidance technology.

---

[1]"Automated *guideway* transit" is conceptually incorrect: *systems* are automated, not guideways.

TABLE 4-3
Classification of Guided Modes with R/W Category
A by Vehicle Size and Guidance Technology[a]

Guidance Technology \\ Vehicle Size	Small	Medium	Large
Rubber-tired	Rubber-tired PRT* (Aramis, CVS, Kabinentaxi, Monocab)	GRT or people mover systems (Skybus, Airtrans, VAL, Transurban*)	Monorails (Alweg, Safege*) *Rubber-tired RT* (Paris, Montreal, Mexico City)
Rail	Rail PRT* (Palomino, Minitram)	Light rapid transit	*Rail rapid transit Regional rail*
	Automated guided transit	Rapid transit	

[a]Modes extensively used are in italic type. Modes that are not operational are designated by asterisks.

AGT modes consist of two groups: *personal rapid transit (PRT)*, with small vehicles serving individual parties only, and *group rapid transit (GRT)*, also known as *people mover systems (PMS)*,[2] with somewhat larger vehicles (15 to 50 spaces) designed mostly for short-haul medium-capacity lines. Similar to "bus rapid transit," the term "rapid transit" in PRT and GRT is given to enhance their image, but it is technically not justified because these modes do not have the high performance that characterizes rapid transit. Because of their limited applications, presently for short-haul lines only, AGT is classified as *special transit*, together with other proposed and specialized modes.

Fully automated operation (transit units without crews) is technically feasible for all guided modes on R/W category A. However, for AGT modes such operation is a *sine qua non* for their economic feasibility, since the small size of their transit units would make labor costs prohibitively high; for RT modes full automation is desirable but not crucial, because of their inherently high labor productivity.

Referring to Table 4-3, it can be seen that the large-vehicle modes (third column) are by far the most common ones. Applications of medium-vehicle modes are likely to increase as automation improves and smaller rail vehicles are designed. Small-vehicle modes are entirely experimental, and there are no realistic prospects that they will become technically and economically feasible in the foreseeable future.

[2]The term "people mover system" was used liberally for all short-haul modes except conventional bus and rail. Since the start of the "Downtown People Mover (DPM)" program, this term is identified with GRT modes only.

84

A systematic overview of the categories and types of characteristics for all major modes defined here is presented in Table 4-4. Characteristics of the factors determining modes (see Classification by Type of Usage and Fig. 4-1) are ordered in the sequence of increasing performance; modes are also ordered ascending from the lowest performance up; the correlation between the two shows in the table as the diagonal set of "×" marks. The frames designate the lowest and the highest performance sets in the family of modes. It is emphasized, however, that performance refers to absolute values of system capacity, productivity, and efficiency and does not imply evaluation of modes; the lowest and highest performance modes are by no means "the worst" and "the best" in the family; they are only best suited to the minimum and maximum demand conditions, respectively.

Several other comparisons of modes and their generic classes are given in the following three tables and three figures. The ranges given encompass all existing systems, with the exception of some extreme values found in very special cases. Since individual systems seldom have several extreme values (e.g., maximum transit unit capacity *and* maximum frequency), the maximum values of derived performance measures (capacity and productive capacity) are less than the products of the maximum values of their components. Thus, the boundaries of modal characteristics depicted in the diagrams are neither absolute nor precise limits; they represent the ranges of values derived from existing systems.

Table 4-5 gives ranges of the basic technical, operational, and system characteristics of the most important modes, classified into the three generic classes: street transit, semirapid, and rapid transit. Private auto is included for comparison. Several modes that are similar in the given characteristics to the selected ones are not included (e.g., taxi is similar to auto, trolleybus to bus, RTR to RRT).

Table 4-6 summarizes the values from Table 4-5 by generic classes and presents several numerical examples of systems typical for each class. This table is the basis for Figs. 4-2, 4-3, and 4-4, which graphically show such basic characteristics as capacity, speed, cost, and productive capacity. Both representative systems and ranges of values for each class are plotted. Other important aspects, including L/S and impacts, cannot be shown graphically. They are discussed in Chapter 13.

Figure 4-2 shows the relationship between transit unit capacity, maximum line frequency, and line capacity (as area) for different modes. The diagram shows that, starting from the auto (taxi) toward higher performance modes, maximum frequencies decrease while transit unit capacities increase. The most common values form a hyperbolic set of points (dashed lines) with rapidly increasing line capacities.

Since a comparison of capacities is incomplete without consideration of speed, Fig. 4-3 shows mode capacities, speeds, and productive capacities (as areas). The diagram clearly shows the large differences in all these performance elements among the classes; street transit has far lower capacity and operating speed than semirapid and rapid transit. The last has by far the highest performance and the broadest range of performance values.

TABLE 4-4
Review of Basic Features of Urban Public Transit Modes

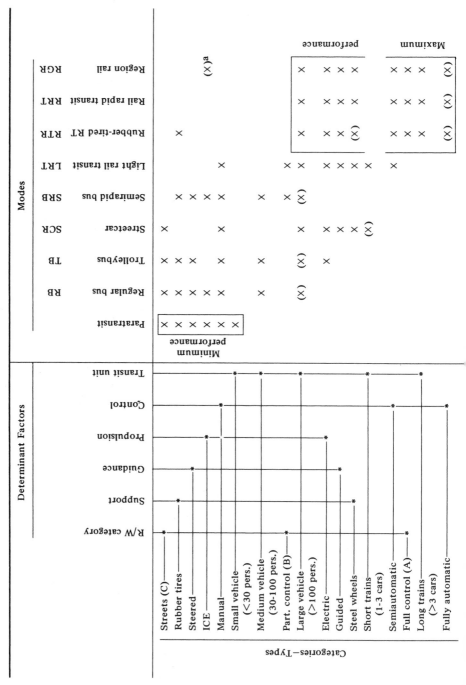

TABLE 4-5
Technical, Operational, and System Characteristics of Urban Transport Modes[a]

Generic Class		Private		Street Transit		Semirapid Transit		Rapid Transit	
Characteristic	Mode Unit	Auto on Street	Auto on Freeway	RB	SCR	SRB	LRT	RRT	RGR
1. Vehicle capacity, C_v	sp/veh	4-6 total, 1.2-2.0 usable	4-6 total, 1.2-2.0 usable	40-120	100-180	40-120	110-250	140-280	140-210
2. Vehicles/transit unit	veh/TU	1	1	1	1-3	1	1-4	1-10	1-10
3. Transit unit capacity	sp/TU	4-6 total, 1.2-2.0 usable	4-6 total, 1.2-2.0 usable	40-120	100-300	40-120	110-600[b]	140-2000	140-1800
4. Maximum technical speed, V	km/h	40-80	80-90	40-80	60-70	70-90	60-100	80-100	80-130
5. Maximum frequency, f_{max}[c]	TU/h	600-800	1500-2000	60-120	60-120	60-90	40-90	20-40	10-30
6. Line capacity, C	sp/h	720-1050[b,d]	1800-2600[d]	2400-8000	4000-15,000	4000-8000	6000-20,000	10,000-40,000	8000-35,000
7. Normal operating speed, V_o	km/h	20-50	60-90	15-25	12-20	20-40	20-45	25-60	40-70
8. Operating speed at capacity, V_oC	km/h	10-30	20-60	6-15	5-13	15-30	15-40	24-55	38-65
9. Productive capacity, P_c	(sp-km/h²) × 10⁻³	10-25[b]	50-120	20-90	30-150	75-200	120-600	400-1800	500-2000
10. Lane width (one-way)	m	3.00-3.65	3.65-3.75	3.00-3.65	3.00-3.50	3.65-3.75	3.40-3.75	3.70-4.30	4.00-4.75
11. Vehicle control[e]	—	Man./vis.	Man./vis.	Man./vis.	Man./vis.	Man./vis.	Man./vis.-sig.	Man.-aut./sig.	Man.-aut./sig.
12. Reliability	—	Low-med.	Med.-high	Low-med.	Low-med.	High	High	Very high	Very high
13. Safety	—	Low	Low-med.	Med.	Med.	High	High	Very high	Very high
14. Station spacing	m	—	—	200-500	250-500	350-800	350-800	500-2000	1200-4500
15. Investment cost per pair of lanes	($/km) × 10⁻⁶	0.2-2.0	2.0-15.0	0.1-0.4	1.0-2.0	3.0-9.0	3.5-12.0	8.0-25.0	10.0-25.0

[a]Metric conversion: 1 km = 0.62 mi. Abbreviations: sp, spaces; veh, vehicles; TU, transit unit.

[b]Values for C and P_c are not necessarily products of the extreme values of their components because these seldom coincide.

[c]For auto, lane capacity; for transit, line (station) capacity.

[d]For private auto capacity is product of average occupancy (1.2-1.3) and f_{max} since all spaces cannot be utilized.

[e]Abbreviations are for: manual, visual, signal, and automatic.

TABLE 4-6
Performance Values for Generic Classes of Modes
(Based on Table 4-5) and for Several Typical Systems[a]

Generic class

Characteristic	Unit[b]	Private auto on Street	Freeway	Street transit	Semirapid transit	Rapid transit
1. Transit unit capacity	sp/TU	1.2-2.0[c]		40-300	40-600	140-2000
2. Maximum frequency, f_{max}	TU/h	600-800	1500-2000	60-120	40-90	10-40
3. Line capacity, C	sp/h	720-1050	1800-2600	2400-15,000	4000-20,000	10,000-40,000
4. Operating speed, V_o	(km/h)	20-50	60-90	5-20	15-45	24-70
5. Productive capacity, P_c	(sp-km/h²) ×10⁻³	10-25	50-120	20-150	75-600	400-2000
6. Investment cost per pair of lanes	($/km) ×10⁻⁶	0.2-2.0	0.2-15.0	0.1-2.0	3.0-12.0	8.0-25.0

Typical systems[d]

Characteristic	Unit[b]	System "s"	System "f"	RB-1	RB-2	SCR	SRB	LRT-1	LRT-2	RRT-1	RRT-2	RGR
1. Transit unit capacity	sp/TU	1.3	1.3	65	75	140	100[e]	180	430	800	1100	1000
2. Maximum frequency, f_{max}	TU/h	700	1800	120	90	90	100	90	40	30	35	28
3. Line capacity, C	sp/h	910	2340	7800	6750	12,600	10,000	16,200	17,200	24,000	38,500	28,000
4. Normal operating speed, V_o	km/h	35	80	20	18	16	26	30	33	38	36	50
5. Operating speed at capacity, V_oC	km/h	20	40	10	12	11	18	23	25	38	34	48
6. Productive capacity, P_c	(sp-km/h²) ×10⁻³	18.2	93.6	78	81	138.6	180	372.6	430	912	1309	1394
7. Investment cost per pair of lanes	($/km) × 10⁻⁶	0.6	8.0	0.2	0.3	1.6	7.0	8.0	9.0	12.0	20.0	18.0

[a] The systems shown are assumed to be heavily loaded, but somewhat below capacity of respective mode.
[b] Metric conversion: 1 km = 0.62 mi.
[c] Maximum number of spaces that can be utilized.
[d] Designations used in Figs. 4-2, 4-3, and 4-4.
[e] Articulated buses.

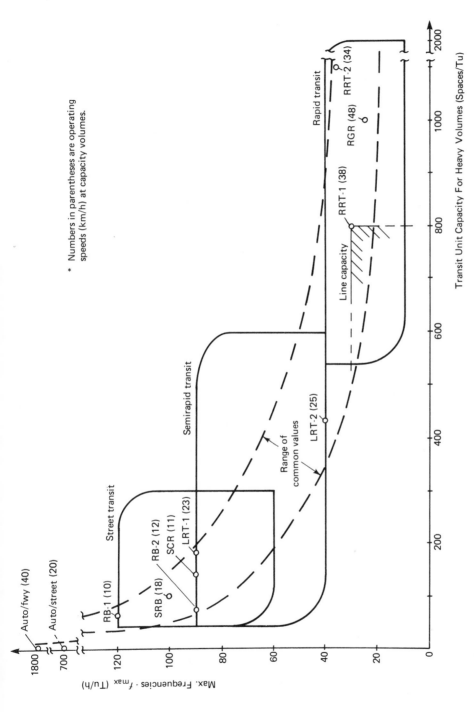

Figure 4-2 *Vehicle capacities, maximum frequencies, and line capacities of different modes*

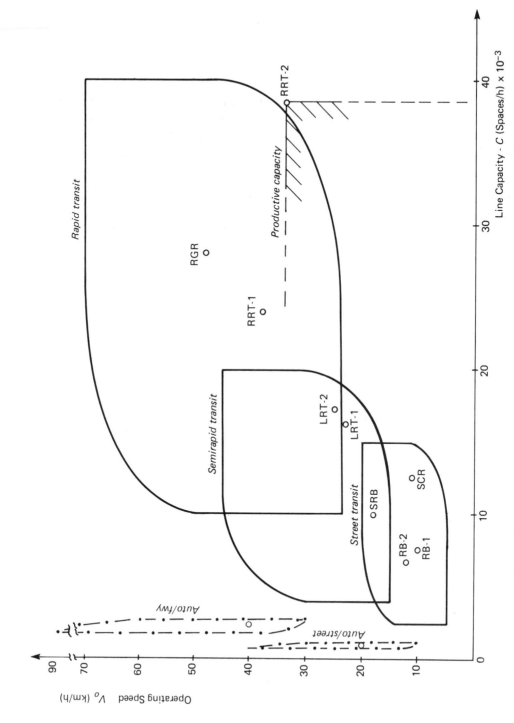

Figure 4-3 Line capacities, operating speeds, and productive capacities of different modes

The most important factor for mode evaluation, relationship of performance and investment costs, is presented in Fig. 4-4. Productive capacity is plotted as the best representative of performance: it is the product of speed, affecting primarily passengers, and capacity, important for the operator.

Similar to Fig. 4-3, the differences among classes are major. There is a jump in investment cost between street and semirapid transit, then a continuous investment range through rapid transit, with a rapid increase in productive capacity. Maximum productive capacity increases from street to semirapid transit by a factor of 4, to rapid transit by about 13. The low performance of the auto/highway mode is conspicuous.

The diagram shows that although RRT can be designed for 40,000 persons/h, 50 km/h, and cost 25×10^6/km, it can also have much lower values of all these items. Its particularly broad range stretches from high-performance systems such as San Francisco's BART (by its design specifications it would have 2.16×10^6 space-km/h², i.e., above the upper boundary) to low-performance systems such as some lines in Chicago which overlap with high-performance LRTs (e.g., Boston's Green line).

Another important modal characteristic is passenger attraction, which is a function of L/S. Since L/S is generally strongly correlated with system performance, passenger attraction of transit modes increases significantly from street to rapid transit, as the conceptual dashed lines in Fig. 4-4 indicate. Street transit, always inferior in L/S to that of auto, mostly serves captive riders. Rapid transit, usually superior to auto in the same corridor, attracts most of the trips and generates additional travel.

It is clear from Fig. 4-4 that comparisons of modes based on costs only can be highly deceptive; they compare ordinates of modes, disregarding their abscissa values. For modes with similar performance the error caused by disregarding abscissa values may not be great, but for modes as diverse as street and rapid transit, the error is always very large.

Mode comparison must include many different factors, but the major ones are illustrated in Fig. 4-4 by hypothetical systems I, II, and III. System III can be easily eliminated as inferior to system II; it has a higher cost, much lower productivity, and attracts fewer passengers. A comparison between I and II must evaluate the trade-off between the higher productivity (ΔP_c) and passenger attraction (ΔP) of system II against the lower cost (ΔK) of system I.

Observing modal characteristics in the three diagrams (Figs. 4-2, 4-3, and 4-4), it is interesting to note that the relative positions of the plotted 11 systems vary considerably; LRT-1 and LRT-2 are remote in the first, but close in the second and third diagrams. However, they all fall in the ranges of their generic classes. The overlaps between classes also vary among the diagrams, but in all three they clearly show the same sequence from low to high performance. Most modes fall in the central zone of the class areas (e.g., dash lines in Fig. 4-2), forming a nearly continuous *family of transit modes*. The extreme corners have been rounded off on the diagrams since they represent either extremes impractical to operate (e.g., smallest transit unit and lowest maximum frequency) or a nonoptimal combination (e.g., highest investment and lowest performance).

Another way of illustrating differences in modal capacities is by a sketch of facilities required for transporting 15,000 persons/h by different modes, shown in Fig. 4-5.

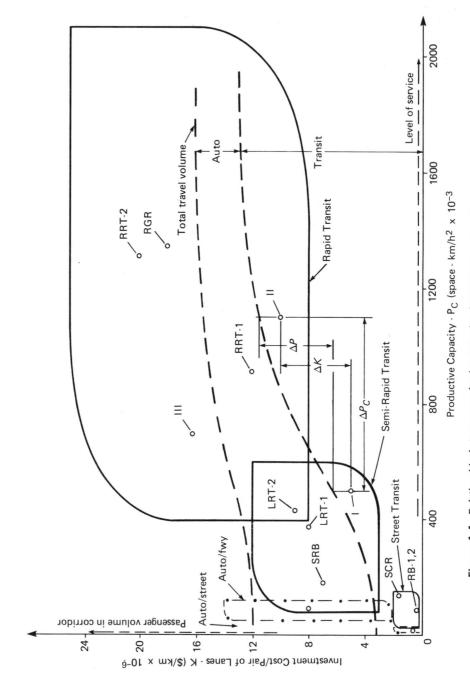

Figure 4-4 *Relationship between productive capacity, investment cost, and passenger attraction of different generic classes of transit modes*

Mode	Schematic of R/W	Line Capacity Reserve	Terminal Area Requirements
Private autos on street (Persons/vehicle: 1.3 Maximum freq.: 700)	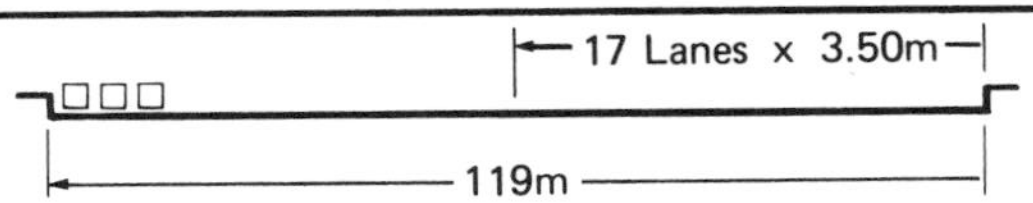 17 Lanes × 3.50m	None	Parking: 23 m²/person For 15,000 people 34.5 ha (85 acres)
Private autos on freeway (1.3 : 1800)	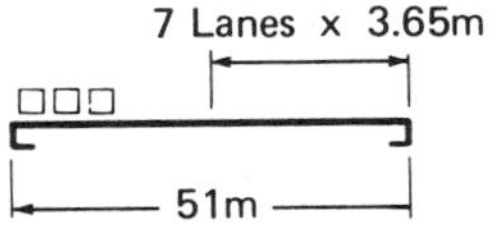 7 Lanes × 3.65m — 51m	None	Same as above, plus interchanges
Regular buses (75 : 100)	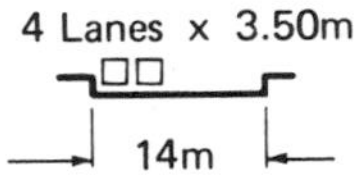 4 Lanes × 3.50m — 14m	None (station and way capacities reached)	Each station 20 × 80m on the surface
Semirapid buses (artic.) (100 : 90)	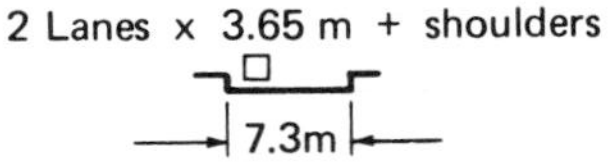 2 Lanes × 3.65 m + shoulders — 7.3m	None (station capacity reached, way capacity not)	Each station from 25 × 100
Light rail transit (400 : 50)	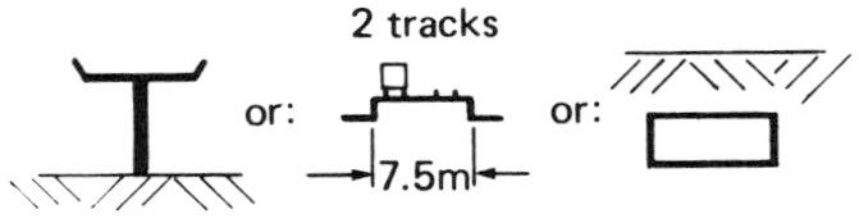 2 tracks — 7.5m or:	33%	Each station from 12 × 50m on the surface to 20 × 90 grade separated
Rail rapid transit (1000 : 25 RGR, 1000 : 40 RRT)	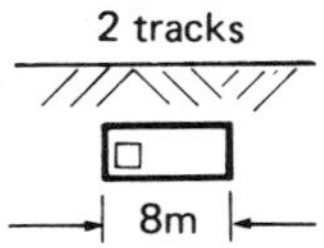 2 tracks — 8m	67 - 167%	Each station from 20 × 100 to 25 × 210m grade separated. No surface occupancy

Figure 4-5 *Areas required for transporting 15,000 persons per hour by different modes*

This volume is found in many cities since even facilities carrying only 5000 to 7000 persons/h obtain *rates of flow* of 15,000 to 20,000 persons/h for a 15 to 20 minute period, determining the design volume. Line capacity reserves are also given since they influence L/S (comfort). Terminal areas are quoted as a significant component of space efficiency of modes. The table clearly shows the superiority of high-capacity modes in serving high-density areas, particularly when their much lower terminal area requirements are also taken into account.

In conclusion, this review of the family of modes shows that all major transit modes have optimal domains of application; "adjacent" modes overlap their domains to some extent (dial-a-ride and RB, or LRT and RRT), but modes as remote from each other as taxi and bus, or bus and RRT, should never be competitive, but complementary. For example, there is no way in which it can be more efficient and economical to transport 40 persons from point A to point B at one time in 20 taxis than in one bus, or 750 people in 15 buses than in one train, unless the lower-capacity mode is operated by underpaid drivers, has low comfort and safety standards, and is indirectly subsidized; while the higher-capacity mode is excessively luxurious, inefficiently operated, and driven by overpaid drivers. Similarly, it can never be more efficient to transport a single passenger from one suburb to another by a bus than by a taxi. As a matter of fact, when such remote modes are competitive, it is a clear sign that the conditions (policies, financing, planning, regulation, design, etc.) are greatly distorted against the mode which should be optimal in that application. That is the case in many cities where auto travel into the CBD during peak hours is not only competitive, but superior to bus service or even to RRT.

This analysis also shows that there can never be a single "optimal" mode for all urban transportation. Conditions and requirements for urban travel vary so much that in most cities, except very small ones, the optimal (sometimes referred to as "balanced") transportation system should consist of several complementary modes coordinated in a single multimodal system.

COMMUTER TRANSIT

In addition to the regular public transport services operated by the modes previously defined, some cities have separate commuter services that use standard transit technologies as well as other modes. In small cities commuter transit represents a significant share of public transport; many bus routes operate during the peaks only. As city size increases, the relative role of these services decreases. In large cities commuter transit should be only a minor supplement to regular transit if the latter adequately serves as the main carrier of public transport throughout the city at all times of the day. The great attention given to commuter transit in U.S. cities is a consequence of the extremely unsatisfactory condition of regular transit.

The modes used for commuter transit are as follows.

Carpooling is travel of different parties (2 to 6 persons) together in a private car on a regular basis. Since carpooling is private transport, it cannot be organized, scheduled, or regulated by an agency, but its use can be encouraged by such measures as assistance in establishing contacts among potential users, reduced or eliminated toll and parking charges, provision of special lanes, and so on.

Carpools are socially more desirable than individual travel by car because they take less space and cause fewer negative side effects. However, their use is limited to commuting because they require that travel of the participants in each pool coincides in origin, destination, time of departure, and time of return. Moreover, carpooling is usually a greater deprivation of privacy than transit travel; it involves precise travel coordination, cost sharing, and joint ride in private cars of persons who may have nothing else in common but travel habit.

Vanpools are privately or publicly provided vans (8 to 18 seats) transporting groups of persons to and from work on a regular basis. Owing to their lower unit transportation cost and space occupancy, vanpools are even more socially desirable than carpools. However, they require a more formal organization for vehicle purchase, maintenance, driving, and so on.

Subscription bus is bus service provided for persons who subscribe for a time period (month, week) to travel every working day at the same time on the same route (commuting).

Express commuter bus, express bus service operated during peak hours only, is the most common mode of commuter transit. Usually, express commuter bus routes operate locally in suburbs and then use arterials and freeways for fast travel into the CBD.

Commuter rail is regional rail operating during peak hours only.

Commuter buses that utilize busways, and commuter rail, have fixed facilities used for transit during peak hours only. This represents a poor utilization of facilities which can often be greatly improved by introduction of properly marketed and efficiently operated regular transit services.

Figure 4-6 shows corridor service by regular transit and by commuter transit and lists their characteristics. The figure shows that regular transit offers service between any two stops on feeder routes or stations on the trunk line, while commuter transit serves only the trips between the suburban collection area and CBD. Moreover, each one of the m collector routes offers service to only one of the n CBD distributors. Transfers to the other distributors can be organized if all routes use the same freeway exit, but this is seldom the case. Direct connection between all feeders and all distributors would require $m \cdot n$ routes (33 in the example), resulting in very low frequencies on each one of them. A schematic of the network in Fig. 4-7 shows that commuter transit serves an even smaller fraction of all urban trips than corridor trips. The more decentralized the city is, the more important is the role of regular transit relative to commuter transit. Equally important is the fact that regular transit operates at all hours, commuter transit only during the peaks.

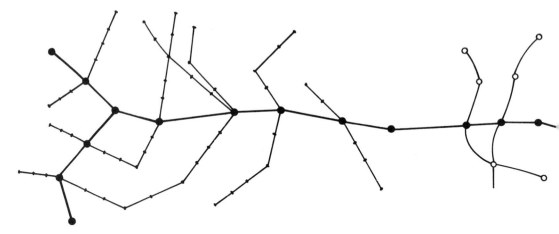

(a) Regular transit: high-frequency, trunk-line service,
transfers to feeders; all-day service

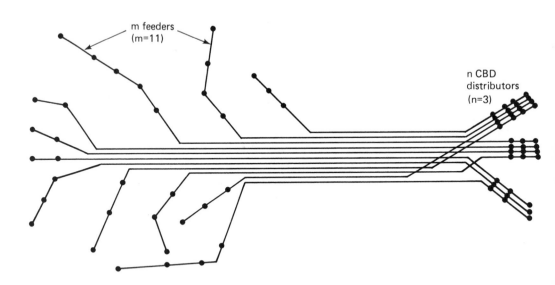

m feeders
(m=11)

n CBD
distributors
(n=3)

(b) Commuter transit: feeders travel directly to CBD:
no transfers; low frequency, no service along trunk
section; peak-hour service only

Figure 4-6 *Corridor service by regular transit and by commuter transit*

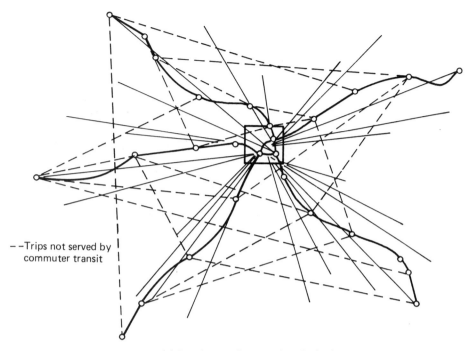

- -Trips not served by
commuter transit

(a) Regular transit network and trips it can serve

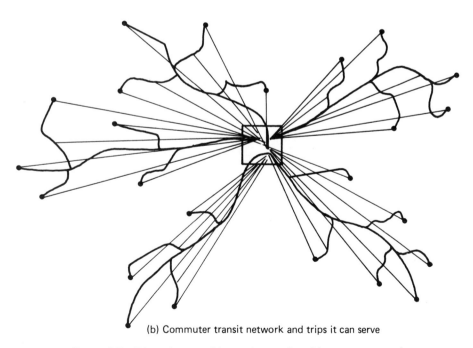

(b) Commuter transit network and trips it can serve

Figure 4-7 *Urban trips served by regular transit and by commuter transit*

SELECTED BIBLIOGRAPHY

BUNDESMINISTER FÜR VERKEHR, *Forschung Stadtverkehr*. Bonn, West Germany: Kirschbaum Verlag, 1976.

INSTITUTE OF TRAFFIC ENGINEERS, *Transportation and Traffic Engineering Handbook*, ed. John E. Baerwald. Englewood Cliffs, N.J.: Prentice-Hall, Inc., 1976.

INSTITUTE OF TRANSPORTATION AND TRAFFIC ENGINEERING, *New and Novel Transportation Systems: Planning Principles, Operating Characteristics, and Costs*, Special Report. Berkeley, Calif.: University of California, Institute of Transportation and Traffic Engineering, 1970.

LEIBBRAND, KURT, *Transportation and Town Planning*. Cambridge, Mass.: The M.I.T. Press, 1970.

PUSHKAREV, BORIS S., AND JEFFREY M. ZUPAN, *Public Transportation and Land Use Policy*. Bloomington, Ind: Indiana University Press, 1977.

RICHARDS, BRIAN, *Moving in Cities*. Boulder, Colo.: Westview Press, Inc., 1976.

VUCHIC, VUKAN R., "Place of Light Rail in the Family of Transit Modes," in *Light Rail Transit*, Special Report 161, pp. 62–76. Washington, D.C.: Transportation Research Board, 1975.

———, AND R. M. STANGER, "Lindenwold Rail Line and Shirley Busway: A Comparison," in *Evaluation of Bus Transit Strategies*, Highway Research Record 459, pp. 13–28. Washington, D.C.: Highway Research Board, 1973.

Chapter 5

RAIL TRANSIT

J. W. VIGRASS, *Superintendent of Equipment, Port Authority Transit Corporation of Pennsylvania and New Jersey*

This chapter will provide an overview of rail modes as they are applied to urban transportation. Included is rail rapid transit, fully grade separated, with various degrees of automation. Second is the light rail transit mode, which has received renewed interest in the United States, sparked by the construction of a new vehicle for use in Boston and San Francisco. Third and last is railroad commuter service, best exemplified in the Chicago, Philadelphia, and New York areas of the United States and in Toronto in Canada.

The general physical and operational characteristics of these three mode will be briefly explained and a few examples of each cited and described. The intent is that planners, engineers, and other interested individuals will obtain an overall picture of what each submode can do in the urban and suburban environment.

The rail guideway is the only form of guideway in general use throughout the world. Every generation or so, various forms of monorail are rediscovered and promoted, and each time, their inherent drawbacks are learned anew by those who have neglected to study the history of technology as applied to urban transportation. It has been said that monorail is the mode of the future; it always has been; and probably always will be!

The Wuppertal Schwebebahn or Suspended Railway in Germany has often been cited by monorail enthusiasts. It has been in successful operation since the very early twentieth century. From time to time it has been provided with new rolling stock. But it has not been extended. Increased transit provided in the area has been by surface light rail or by suburban railroad. If the suspended monorail had all the merit many of its proponents claim, it would seem that its originators in Germany would have expanded it.

A few automated, rubber-tired guideway systems have been developed since the mid-1950s, but with a few exceptions, they have not proven very successful in revenue operation. Several shuttle systems are in use at major activity centers such as airports. Because of technical limitations, no extensive systems were in reliable service by the mid-1970s. The chapter on new technology looks deeper into the features of rubber-tired systems. Here we will only discuss the rubber-tired vehicles developed by the R.A.T.P. in Paris and used there, as well as in Montreal, Mexico City, and in a few other cities. These systems rely on conventional railway track (in addition to the vertical third and fourth rails for guidance) for switching and ground return. There have been serious problems with fires, some caused by the rubber dust common to the systems and others to tire blowouts, which have resulted in shorting the third rail by the steel belting in the tires.

The Montreal system is being expanded and is quite successful, as is the Mexico City system, even with these handicaps, but the rubber-tired lines in Paris are not being expanded. Instead Paris Metro has ordered 1000 new steel-wheel cars to replace older cars on steel wheel/steel rail lines.

Let us look at the components of urban railways. Be they conventional rail rapid transit, light rail transit, or a commuter system, they have certain common features. First, there is the track and second, the flanged wheel. The steel rail and flanged steel wheel were devised in the early nineteenth century for intercity railroad use. They were well developed by the latter part of that century, and during its last three decades, steam-powered urban railways were built in a number of cities. The elevated railways in New York and Chicago were built during this period. They used 22.5-metric ton (25-ton) steam locomotives that could pull six light coaches at about 40 km/h (25 mi/h). This merited the term "rapid transit" when compared to the horse-drawn traffic below.

During the same period, indeed beginning in the 1830s and 1840s, horse-drawn street railway systems were built in many cities. By the late nineteenth century, thousands of horse-drawn cars were in use. Practical application of electricity as motive power to replace the costly horses developed quickly after pioneer installations proved workable. By 1900, many street and elevated railways had been converted to electric power, and by 1910, this conversion was essentially complete. New routes followed rapidly until a peak was reached in the early 1920s. The street railway blossomed forth into the suburbs—and far beyond—in the form of the interurban electric railway. The latter is best exemplified by the once-great Pacific Electric Railway of the Los Angeles region, then the world's largest interurban railway under one management. During this period, the flanged steel wheel on steel rails was refined to a highly reliable system with many special devices to meet specific needs.

From 1930 to the mid-1950s, a rapid decline in urban surface street railways took place, owing to the greatly increased use of private automobiles in urban areas, with motorbuses often taking over the ridership of the replaced street railways. However, rapid transit held up relatively well. Streetcar lines having private rights-of-way also held up well because they had a competitive advantage over private automobiles or street-bound buses. The resurgence of interest in transit has focused attention on the modes and submodes that did hold up well during the decline of transit, namely the grade-separated or semiseparated rail modes.

THE GUIDEWAY

The railway track is formed of T-rails which weigh, for modern applications, 42 to 65 kg/m (85 to 132 lb/yd). Track gauge is generally 1.435 m (4 ft 8.5 in), a dimension inherited from England, which in turn inherited it from the Romans. However, light rail and rapid transit have various gauges from one meter (3.3 ft) in Europe to 1.632 m (5 ft 4.25 in), Baltimore's former streetcar guage; San Francisco Bay Area Rapid Transit (BART) uses 1.676 m (5 ft 6 in), while Los Angeles Railways streetcar lines used 1.067 m (3 ft 6 in) for economy of construction. Anything reasonable will work, but, generally, standard guage 1.435 m (4 ft 8.5 in) has been used because of the easy availability of railroad hardware.

Railroads and most existing urban railways have used wood ties, with rails spiked to the ties. Construction in the 1970s began to favor concrete ties with various kinds of spring clips to hold the rail. Concrete promised to last longer, and because of their weight, such ties hold the rails down more firmly. Concrete slabs under track are being tested in Europe, and a short segment on a Pittsburgh light rail route has been in successful use since the 1930s.

The U.S. Department of Transportation has built a test facility near Pueblo, Colorado, for railroad and rail transit. Several types of track were installed, arranged as several test loops and a stub-end impact track. Included is a small loop of 7.7 km (4.8 mi) circumference with curves of up to 5° and grades up to 2%. It is labeled the FAST track, for Facility for Accelerated Service Testing. A "typical" freight train operates 16 hours per day to produce 1,000,000 ton-miles per day on this track to life-test both track and rolling stock. Another objective is to learn more about train/track dynamics. Roughly 1 year at FAST is equal to 10 years of real-world testing.

The Pueblo facility also includes a 14.6-km (9.1-mi) oval to test urban and suburban rapid transit and light rail vehicles. It is electrified with a conventional 600-volt third rail, and part of it was also temporarily equipped with catenary at the same voltage to test light rail vehicles.

The outcome of the railroad and light rail transit testing at Pueblo should be improved life and reliability for a mode that already has typically long service life and high reliability for its components.

Use of the flanged steel wheel on the rail has provided a positive guidance system for over 150 years. Switches and crossings are fully designed and proved reliable. Railroad track may be ordered from catalogs and is suitable for most rapid transit and many light rail applications. Older street and interurban railway geometric designs may still be quite suitable for proposed new light rail installations. Some innovation in trackwork has appeared in Europe, and could be duplicated in the United States should it be desired to emulate the smoothness of European trackage.

The metallurgy of the rail and wheel has been thoroughly studied, particularly for railroad use, and both items are fully engineered and available. Their service life is known, so that costs and operational ability can be forecast with confidence. Railway track can be, and has been, installed on (1) private right-of-way on the surface, as ordinary railroad track; (2) on elevated or aerial structure; (3) in subways; (4) in median strips on boulevards or freeways; and (5) in paved streets as streetcar track or light rail track. This type of guideway is both versatile and fully proved.

SOURCE OF ENERGY

Urban railways have almost always been electrically operated, usually employing 600 volts direct current (dc) or some variation of it, such as 700 or 750 volts dc. In a very few cases, self-propelled equipment using internal combustion engines has been used (e.g., the diesel-electric streetcars of Sapporo, Japan). Such arrangements are possible but are seldom used in actual practice. The use of a moderately low voltage direct current has distinct advantages. Only one current collector is needed on the vehicle. The rails act as the ground return. The simplicity of this single collector should not be ignored. Some of the more novel modes which have been promoted use three-phase alternating current, typically 480 volts. These need at least three collectors, and in one case five (two more for ground and signaling), all of which adds to complexity and, in turn, unreliability. A considerable amount of equipment is already developed and available for the usual 600 volts dc system.

Suburban railroad service most commonly uses diesel-electric locomotives to haul trains, but in New York City, Philadelphia, and Chicago electric power is used. Some rail diesel cars are self-propelled.

Suburban railroad service can be defined as having routes approximately 24 to 80 km (15 to 50 mi) in length, with frequent stops, typically 1.6 to 4.8 km (1 to 3 mi) apart. It is distinctly different from intercity high-speed railroad passenger service such as the Metroliners in the Northeast corridor of the United States or the New Tokaido line in Japan. The latter routes are several hundred kilometers long with stops 80 to 160 km (50 to 100 mi) apart.

Railway track, as a guideway, and existing forms of propulsion provide a combination that has not been equaled by other modes. The railway track with the flanged wheel, having a proved and reliable switching and crossing system, is available to any planner or engineer. If the railway type of guideway had been developed recently as a result of government-funded research and development, it would have been heralded as a great breakthrough! It exists. Use it!

CONVENTIONAL RAIL RAPID TRANSIT

In the United States, that form of urban rail transit that presently carries the most people per year is rail rapid transit. This mode is characterized by full grade separation, electric propulsion, multiple-unit trains, and speeds of 72 to 121 km/h (45 to

75 mi/h) maximum, and 32 to 80 km/h (20 to 50 mi/h) overall schedule. The very exten-sive New York City Transit Authority (NYCTA) subway system has nearly 7000 cars, and represents, by itself, the majority of rail rapid transit in this country. Its use of four track routes with local and express trains is unique, as is its common use of 10-car trains. Crowding in NYCTA trains is legendary, and official standards call for 255 passengers per 18-m (60-ft) car, at 0.2 m² (2.3 ft²) of floor area per passenger—this may be the most important dimension a person has in New York. Thus, a 10-car train will handle 2550 persons, and on some routes, such trains operate every 2 minutes in the peak, carrying passengers at the rate of 76,500 per hour past a given point. This rate is seldom achieved for more than 15 to 30 minutes, however.

Such volumes are not found elsewhere in this country, so the student of urban transportation need not be overly concerned with the unique New York problems. Other cities, such as Boston, Philadelphia, and Chicago, have rail transit systems dating from the same period as New York's, about 1905–1940, and have some very recent extensions. Routes in these cities typically handle from 50,000 to 300,000 passengers per day, with perhaps 15 to 20% of the day's travel during each rush hour.

In older intraurban systems, stations are typically 0.4 to 0.8 km (0.25 to 0.5 mi) apart. Chicago's average spacing is 1100 m (3700 ft). In more modern systems, center-city stations are similarly spaced, but in the suburbs, spacings of 1.6 to 3.2 km (1 to 2 mi) are more common. In past years, planning was based on walk-on patrons or transfer riders from surface streetcar lines. Emphasis in the suburbs now is on highway access by park-and-ride, kiss-and-ride, or feeder bus service. Boston had a highly developed streetcar feeder system with streetcars operating down into subway stations or up onto elevated stations. Several such stations have been converted for trolleybus and motorbus access to provide what is often considered the most convenient trans-ferring of any U.S. system.

Fare collection on these older systems is mostly by cashiers in booths, assisted by coin-operated turnstiles. In Chicago, during the off-peak on lightly used routes, conductors hand-collect fares on two-car trains in a manner not seen elsewhere for many decades. Conductors collect fares on board trains at certain unattended stations in Philadelphia during "owl" (midnight to 5 a.m.) hours.

Operating costs of traditional, labor-intensive rail rapid transit systems tend to be high because of two-man (motorman and conductor) train crews and the attended stations necessary for fare collection. However, with very high volumes (found in only a few places), cost per passenger is sometimes quite low.

MODERN RAIL RAPID TRANSIT

Modern rail rapid transit is an evolutionary development of traditional rapid transit. It is fully grade separated and uses railway track and direct-current electrifica-tion at moderate voltages, 650 to 1000 (up from the older 600 volts dc). It stresses high-performance trains with running speeds of 121 to 129 km/h (75 to 80 mi/h), averaging 56 to 80 km/h (35 to 50 mi/h), and employs some forms of automation. These systems, exemplified by the Bay Area Rapid Transit (BART) in the San Francisco area of California and the Port Authority Transit Corporation (PATCO) connecting Philadelphia to southern New Jersey, were designed specifically to compete with the private automobile. They feature fast, frequent service and convenient highway access, with large park-and-ride lots at outlying stations.

Trains are one-man-operated to reduce operating expenses, this being made feasible by various forms of automatic train operation (ATO). Automatic fare collection in the stations keeps all money under lock and key and minimizes station staff.

BART's designers chose a broader-than-standard track gauge at 1.676 m (5 ft 6 in) to achieve better lateral stability in high winds. They selected 1000 volts dc for electrical engineering reasons: the higher voltage delivers more power with less loss, and requires fewer substations. It is a nonstandard voltage, however, and requires custom-built equipment on board the trains. BART also chose a newly developed form of signaling and train control, the reliability of which is still not completely demonstrated. To attain the very high frequency (short headways) of a train every 90 seconds, BART's designers opted for a central computer so that trains from a three-branch system could funnel into the Transbay Tube from Oakland to San Francisco with a minimum of delay. It should be noted that subsequent changes to BART's signaling system preclude attainment of 90 second headways.

While BART has had highly publicized problems in its train control equipment and in the cars themselves, it nonetheless has proved to be automobile-competitive and has captured many new riders for transit in its region. Its trains do average about 80 km/h (50 mi/h); they have operated at 124 to 129 km/h (77 to 80 mi/h) running speed, passing vehicular traffic on nearby freeway lanes; and its filled parking lots and crowded trains attest to its popularity. Its technical and institutional problems must—and will—be solved in due course.

In contrast to the vast BART undertaking of providing a regional system as essentially one overall effort, the Delaware River Port Authority (DRPA) developed a single line to connect the suburban borough of Lindenwold, New Jersey, with center-city Philadelphia, a distance of 22.9 km (14.2 mi). The DRPA had little choice; that was all it could afford using its own resources in 1962. A three-branch system had been proposed, and is still the objective, but so far only the central line has been built. The designers chose evolutionary development of the conventional, partly because the new line was to use the existing 6-km (3.75-mi) Philadelphia–Camden Hi-Speed Line over the Benjamin Franklin Bridge, a route opened in 1936 using a heavyweight, deluxe subway-type car. Standard gauge track with a conventional third rail was already in place. There was little reason to change it, since it could easily provide the performance desired: a 121 km/h (75 mi/h) running speed, 1.3 m/s² (3.0 mi/h/s) acceleration, with an average speed of about 64 km/h (40 mi/h), the latter influenced by sharp curvature and steep grades on the older part of the line.

The new construction, from Camden to Lindenwold, used the right-of-way of the Pennsylvania–Reading Seashore Lines, a jointly owned ($\frac{2}{3}:\frac{1}{3}$) subsidiary of the Pennsylvania Railroad and the Reading Company. This line had been very much underutilized and was finally abandoned and the land sold to the Delaware River Port Authority. Much of the original railroad track was at grade, but DRPA converted it to

Figure 5-1 *BART—MacArthur Station, Oakland, California (courtesy of Bay Area Rapid Transit District)*

Figure 5-2 *BART—Rohr rapid transit cars. (courtesy of Rohr Industries, Inc.)*

a fully grade-separated facility. The inner part is on embankment or concrete aerial structure, a short segment through Haddonfield is in a walled cut, and the outer 9.7 km

(6 mi) is at grade, passing over a few streets, with one road passing over the line. A shop and yard at the outer terminus complete the physical plant.

Stations feature fully automatic fare collection, with no employees permanently assigned to any given station. Roving supervisors check each station frequently, and part-time employees manually sell tickets during the morning rush hour at a few very busy stations, but generally stations are unattended. They are under closed-circuit TV surveillance from Center Tower, PATCO's control center in Camden, New Jersey. The TV monitors who observe the screens can communicate with passengers by using a public address system or through a "call-for-aid" telephone in each station. Unattended stations allow PATCO to have the highest ratio of passengers to employees of any transit facility in the United States, about 170 passengers per day per employee. During most of its first years (1969–1975) of operation, PATCO earned its operating expenses from the farebox.

PATCO's cars have four series-wound dc motors and use a cam controller with resistors. A General Electric ATO (automatic train operation) system working in conjunction with a 100-Hz (hertz) Westinghouse Air Brake Company (WABCO) cab-signal system controls the trains. The 100-Hz system has been in use since 1925, having been pioneered by the Pennsylvania Railroad. While PATCO's version had improvements, the principles were already well proved. The cars were built by The Budd Company and are almost completely stainless steel. They have proved to be extremely strong and have stood up remarkably well.

Since it opened, PATCO has operated 24 hours per day, 7 days per week, continuously. Trains run every $7\frac{1}{2}$ minutes in midday, every 2 to 6 minutes in the rush hour, every 10 minutes in late evening, and hourly all night. On Sundays, a 15-minute headway is provided, using one-car trains. One of PATCO's purposes is to provide an around-the-clock service that people can count on. There is no "last train" to catch. A patron can always get back to his or her automobile parked in PATCO's lot. Meanwhile PATCO's own police will look in on the car from time to time, to minimize theft or vandalism.

PATCO takes pride in the fact that it has operated 98.15% of its trains "on time" (within 4 minutes of timetable) on a yearly basis. It runs 70 of its present 75 cars in each rush hour, 5 days a week. Only five cars are not needed for scheduled service, and of these three or four are in scheduled maintenance; thus, only one or two cars are available as spares most days. PATCO cars are designed for quick changeout of defective components; that is the key to running 70 of the available 75 cars twice a day. And that is why DRPA and its subsidiary, PATCO, plan on continuing with evolutionary improvements of the conventional. It has worked well in practice. Expansion to three routes is planned, to be funded by state and federal governmental agencies; preliminary feasibility and engineering have been completed, but funding has not yet been resolved.

Modern rapid transit systems are under construction in Washington, D.C., Baltimore, and Atlanta. These will share major concepts with BART and/or PATCO: high performance with automation to varying degrees. Washington Metro began operation of a short (8-km) segment of its projected 158-km (98-mi) system in 1976. Ridership on this initial portion exceeded preliminary estimates. It has been relatively free of significant technical failures such as those affecting BART. Metro's consultants selected standard gauge, conventional third rail, and a 750 volts dc power supply, along with a conventional resistance controller used in conjunction with automatic train operation. Installation of an automatic fare collection system has been implemented but on the initial segment fares were collected in bus-type fareboxes under the eyes of a station attendant. Metro plans feature bus-to-train transfers, park-and-ride lots, and fast, frequent service. Metro has been plagued by very high construction costs, with consideration having been given to truncating the planned system, but construction continues and other segments were opened in 1977 and 1978.

Modern rapid transit is expensive to build, but the three modern operating properties have proved that the American motorist can be attracted to transit, if the service is fast, frequent, and reliable. (For example, over 90% of PATCO's daily riders start their trip by getting into a private automobile and driving, or being driven, to a station, then getting out of the automobile and into a train for the remaining journey to town.)

Figure 5-3 *Washington, D.C., Metro—Rhode Island Avenue Station. Note convenient feeder-bus access. (photo by Phil Portlock, courtesy of Washington Metropolitan Area Transit Authority)*

Major corridors carrying large volumes of passengers between a relatively small number of points are the best places for modern rail rapid transit. Good highway access is essential, as is good downtown distribution from relatively closely spaced stations to provide convenient pedestrian egress. Environmental impacts can be slight,

Figure 5-4 *Washington, D.C., Metro—Metro Center Station. (photo by Paul Myatt, courtesy of Washington Metropolitan Area Transit Authority)*

and in many cases favorable. The ride can be pleasant as well as fast. People like it and will use it. It can be a very positive asset to a metropolitan region.

LIGHT RAIL TRANSIT

Light rail transit is an evolutionary development of the street railway toward modern rapid transit. It uses a railway track, usually with overhead electric power distribution, and employs cars much like streetcars, but possessing higher performance. Its track is usually segregated from traffic, but not necessarily grade-separated throughout. Often median strips of boulevards or freeways are used. If vehicular traffic is light, track can be in the street. In congested city centers, subway or aerial structure often provides full grade separation. In many European cities, the track area is reserved solely for light rail vehicles, or the entire street is reserved for light rail and pedestrians.

San Francisco Municipal Railway (Muni) has implemented a true light rail system with subway under Market Street in center city, using car-floor-height platforms, and at-grade track in the outlying residential areas. However, in these outlying areas, although the track is at grade, some is on private right-of-way, some is on a median strip, while some is in a paved street but separated from vehicular lanes by roughened paving. Vehicles can drive on this rough paving in emergency, but normally the area is

Figure 5-5 *Boeing-Vertol light rail vehicles. A two-car train at Longwood Station on Boston's Riverside line on a test run in 1976. These cars entered revenue service during January 1977. (courtesy of Boeing-Vertol)*

reserved for the light rail vehicles. In still other places, the light rail vehicles run as ordinary streetcars. The cars are trainable and have convertible steps to allow loading from floor-height platforms or street level. There are five lines in the system which merge into a single line that runs under Market Street. Up to four-car trains are possible, and the highest planned volume is 9000 passengers per hour. Speeds of up to 88 km/h (55 mi/h) are attainable in the subway, but only 40 to 64 km/h (25 to 40 mi/h) are planned on the surface portion. The motorman (train operator) needs a positive signal indicated by the "green light" (using the 100-Hz cab-signal system, the rails carrying the signal) to be able to achieve the higher speed in the subway. In the absence of that signal, the vehicle cannot go over a set speed, say 64 or 56 km/h (40 or 35 mi/h). Muni's full use of the light rail concept merits careful study and observation. Several other U.S. urban areas are contemplating such systems.

The light rail vehicle often operates as its own feeder. Access is very convenient, so that even though the lack of grade separation enforces lower speeds than for modern rail rapid transit, overall door-to-door speeds may be quite attractive. In 1960, Frankfurt, Germany, studied three alternative systems for providing improved transportation. The three alternatives were: supported monorail (Alweg), light rail transit, and conventional rapid transit, mostly in subway. Table 5-1 gives information on the salient features of the three systems.

It is interesting to note that in this study it was determined that the total peak passenger travel time is less for the light rail transit alternative. This is a result of the self-feeding feature.

TABLE 5-1
Comparison of Monorailway, Light Rail Transit, and Conventional
Rapid Transit Systems Designed for Frankfurt[a]

Item	Monorailway	Light Rail Transit	Conventional Rapid Transit
Route length of railway (mi)			
In tunnels	2.83[b]	13.15	23.76
On elevated way	36.30[c]	4.42	15.42
On separate roadbed	—	46.48	—
Total	39.18	64.03	39.18
Length of bus routes (mi)	99.30	71.91	90.73
Year of completion	1968	1974	1981
Number of rail stations	82	192	91
Average distance between stations (ft)	2,387	1,686	2,099
Total number of stations and stops	307	349	316
Average speed for rail system (mi/h)	17.76	16.02	17.53
Number of peak-hour passengers	95,600	95,600	95,600
Percentage of peak-hour passengers			
Not transferring	21.0	36.7	24.6
Making 1 transfer	44.3	47.8	45.3
Making 2 transfers	29.3	14.1	24.3
Making 3 transfers	5.4	1.4	5.6
Total peak transfer movements	113,500	76,519	106,812
Total peak passenger travel time (h)	52,200	49,300	50,300
Adjusted annual cost of system for first 10 years (no interest)	$22,900,000	$16,100,000	$22,700,000
Annual cost as percentage of present street railway costs	95	47	93

[a] Metric conversion: 1 mi = 1.6 km; 1 ft = 0.305 m.
[b] With alternative plan: 4.29 mi (6.9 km).
[c] With alternative plan: 34.67 mi (55.8 km).

Source: Gordon J. Thompson, "Light Rail Transit Social Costs and Benefits," in *Light Rail Transit,* Special Report 161 (Washington, D.C.: Transportation Research Board, 1975), p. 149. From translation by Charles J. Lietwiler of K. Leibbrand, "Stadtbahn Frankfurt-am-Main—Planerische Gesamtubersicht," City of Frankfurt-am-Main, Germany, 1960.

Light rail, having evolved from the streetcar, can accommodate very sharp curvature, steep grades, and a variety of station configurations, from the simplest to the most grandiose. Grades of up to 9% and horizontal curvature of 13 m (42 ft) can be taken by the articulated new Boeing-Vertol light rail vehicle built for Muni and Boston. Older streetcar equipment such as PCC streetcars can take an 11-m (36-ft) radius, at low speed, of course. Such curves and grades are found in paved street trackage.

Nearly all existing light rail lines in the United States and Canada are operated with these PCC streetcars. The initials PCC stand for the Presidents' Conference Committee of street railway company presidents that was formed in the early 1930s to supervise the creation of a radically new street railway vehicle to stem the decline in ridership then afflicting the transit industry. A sum of about $700,000 (eventually to reach about $1,000,000) was raised from member street railway companies and from suppliers, nearly all of whom were in difficult financial straits. C. F. Hirschfeld of the Detroit Edison Co. was chosen to head the project team.

Hirschfeld's team attacked the problem using one of the first applications of systems analysis. First, the physics of motion were studied, including what changes in the rate of acceleration and deceleration a standing passenger could tolerate. Next, sources of noise were studied. Then the duties of the motorman were analyzed. Other factors were studied intensively. A truly integrated design resulted. The car body, trucks, and propulsion were designed as a "system," not merely a collection of different manufacturers' parts as had been the industry practice.

It was recognized that one car size could not meet the needs of every operator; therefore, a limited number of variations was made available. While the standard car was single-ended, a few were built for double-end operation, and while most PCC cars were single-unit streetcars, some were built for multiple-unit (MU) operation, with couplers. Many of these MU cars remain in operation.

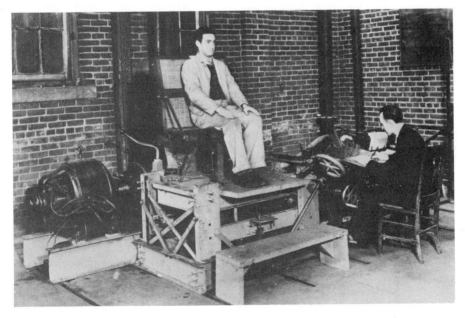

Figure 5-6 *PCC testing. Engineers are shown making tests to obtain data to improve riding comfort for the PCC car. (courtesy of American Public Transit Association)*

The two major electrical suppliers, General Electric and Westinghouse Electric, designed control and propulsion equipment to meet Hirschfeld's specification. While design of the controllers was different, they were compatible in performance and could run in multiple-unit trains together. Over 6000 such cars were built for use in the United States and Canada between 1936 and the mid-1950s. Several builders in Europe were licensed to build them, and construction has continued in Belgium and Czechoslovakia.

Light rail trackage, electrification, and structures are generally much lighter and less costly than for rail rapid transit. Nowadays the cars themselves are not notably lighter or cheaper; the big savings are in the civil engineering features. Because it requires less investment, light rail is often justified in corridors having much lighter traffic than is required to justify investment in full-scale rapid transit. Further, light rail can be upgraded one segment at a time to provide performance nearly equal to grade-separated rapid transit. The investment need not be made all at once.

Light rail is versatile and flexible, and can be designed to meet a very wide demand. While Muni is building a major semimetro system, the other end of the spectrum should also be examined. Dillard's Department Store in Fort Worth, Texas, has its own light rail line, the "M & O Subway," named after Marvin and Obediah Leonard, the store's founders and previous owners. Over 10 years ago, Obie Leonard bought five ex-Washington, D.C., PCC streetcars, laid about 2.4 km (1.5 mi) of track, reworked the cars to make them appear new, added air conditioning, built a huge parking lot along the flood plain of a river, dug a very short subway to the basement of the store, and happily hauled thousands of people into the store every day.

The track is about on a par with a railroad industrial siding. Speeds are low, 24 to 40 km/h (15 to 25 mi/h). The power supply is said to be ex-U.S. Navy submarine generators, war surplus. The trolley poles are short mine-type, so they will fit in his subway. The whole system is a triumph of ingenuity, but the subway is especially so. The street was opened (various buildings of the Dillard's complex front on both sides) and war-surplus Quonset huts were installed end to end. Then the street was backfilled —an instant subway with arched roof. It leaks a bit, but it works.

No Urban Mass Transportation Administration funds were involved, nor were local government funds. No large-scale professional consulting engineer reports were made. The work was largely done in-house by company maintenance forces who converted the old District-of-Columbia trolleys from single-end streetcars to double-end, air-conditioned, high-platform light rail vehicles. It is a marvel of practical ingenuity, and it works. The parking-lot-shuttle type of operation could be quite useful in a variety of situations in smaller communities where a planner might not normally consider rail transit of any kind.

Another rail variation is the Skokie Swift line of the Chicago Transit Authority (CTA), an 8-km (5-mi), 6-minute shuttle line using one-car one-man trains. It feeds the northern terminal of the Chicago mainline subway/elevated line from the suburban village of Skokie. It has but two stations, a park-and-ride station in Skokie and the Howard Street terminus of the "El." It is popular, economical to operate, and a worthwhile addition to Chicago's rapid transit system. While it uses high-platform rapid-transit-type cars, CTA considers it light rail because of the one-car trains and at-grade construction of much of the line—an abandoned interurban electric railway taken over by CTA for this purpose.

Figure 5-7 *Skokie Swift. Chicago's articulated "Paul Revere" in Bicentennial livery is used as a one-man operated unit on the suburban line. Skokie trains are equipped with both third rail and catenary current collection. (courtesy of Chicago Transit Authority)*

LIGHT RAPID TRANSIT

A composite of light rail and rapid transit is exemplified by the Greater Cleveland Regional Transportation Authority (GCRTA) 30-km (19-mi) route from Winderemere in East Cleveland to Cleveland Hopkins Airport on the far-southwest side of that industrial city. The GCRTA rapid is fully grade-separated, uses overhead electrification and high platforms, and runs one-car trains in the base hours, one-man-operated with fare collection on board. During rush hours, three- and four-car trains are operated with station collection of fares. Speeds are moderate, 88 km/h (55 mi/h), and headways relatively frequent, 6 to 10 minutes. The GCRTA rapid hauls about 40,000 persons per day, and until the 1970s, made its operating expenses from the farebox.

About 4.2 km (2.6 mi) of its track is shared with the Shaker Heights line which operates PCC cars utilizing low-platform loading. The Shaker Heights line is also owned and operated by the GCRTA, but it was originally constructed in 1919 as a transportation link between downtown Cleveland and a new land development.

Cleveland was a pioneer in large-scale park-and-ride lots, along with extensive and well-coordinated feeder bus lines. It has shown that rapid transit can be successfully provided in areas of moderate population density and high auto ownership. Most of the areas served by GCRTA rapid and the Shaker Heights light rail are single homes, with a modest sprinkling of apartments.

Commuter railroad service exists on a major scale in New York, Philadelphia, Boston, Chicago, and San Francisco. A number of other cities have a few trains per day on one or a few routes, using ordinary mainline railroad coaches pulled by locomotives.

In the New York and Philadelphia metropolitan areas, most commuter trains consist of electrically powered multiple-unit cars. Many of these were built recently and have performance approaching that of modern rail rapid transit. Commuter rail cars are typically 26 m (85 ft) long, 3 m (10 ft) wide, and 4 m (14 ft) high, and seat from 90 (in 2-2 seating) to 130 (in 3-2 seating). Some use 600 to 650 volts dc third rail; others use catenary overhead at 11,000 volts ac, 25 Hz; and one, the New Haven, uses both. New York area stations have floor-level platforms since the systems use high-platform cars. Philadelphia favors ground-level loading at most stations.

Figure 5-8 *General Electric Silverliner IV. These suburban commuter cars are used on SEPTA lines in the Philadelphia area. They also have provision for a high platform, center door. (courtesy of General Electric)*

For the newer equipment, acceleration is in the range of 0.67 to 0.98 m/s² (1.5 to 2.2 m/h/s). Top speed is generally 137 km/h (85 mi/h), but certain cars were designed to reach 160 km/h (100 mi/h). However, only the "Jersey Arrow" cars running between Trenton, N.J., and New York City (Penn Station) regularly approach that speed. For longer suburban journeys of about 80 km (50 mi), such high speeds can reduce trip times substantially, but only if the number of stops is strictly limited.

In the Boston area, an extensive and moderately intensive service is operated by

ConRail (Consolidated Rail Corporation) and the Boston & Maine Railroad for the Massachusetts Bay Transportation Authority (MBTA). Both Budd multiple-unit rail diesel cars (RDCs) and locomotive-drawn coaches are used, the latter in peak hours. All use ground-level platforms. Acceleration of such equipment is slower than electric, but top speed is comparable.

In Chicago, most suburban railroad service is with bilevel coaches seating 140 to 160, pulled or pushed by medium horsepower diesel-electric locomotives. These load from ground-level platforms. A driving cab is located in the rearmost car of the train to remotely control the locomotive in the "push" mode. This minimizes switching and fosters fast turnaround. These bilevel cars are 26 m (85 ft) long, 3 m (10 ft) wide, and some 5 m (16 ft) high, a height that cannot be accommodated in the below-ground terminals in eastern cities.

Two Chicago railroad companies are electrified. The Illinois Central Gulf (ICG) uses a 1500 volts dc catenary system, running south from the Chicago Loop, along Lake Michigan's shoreline. A fleet of bilevel high-platform cars was acquired in the early 1970s, partly with public funds. These are augmented in rush hours by single-deck high-platform cars built about 1925. ICG's top speed is about 105 km/h (65 mi/h). Sufficient bilevel cars were ordered in the mid-1970s to replace all remaining old ICG cars.

The Chicago South Shore & South Bend Railroad (a subsidiary of the C&O/B&O System) has a single route from South Bend through Michigan City and Gary to downtown Chicago, using ICG rails within Chicago. The South Shore line is largely in Indiana, and received no financial aid from Indiana sources until 1978. Plans to replace its 121-km/h (75-mi/h) 1925 electric cars have been stifled by lack of funds. The lack of public funds has restricted the development of this service in jeopardy, although recent proposals for public funding may resolve the South Shore's situation.

In the West only one area, San Francisco, has extensive commuter railroad service. It is provided by the Southern Pacific Transportation Company's commute service to San Jose via the Peninsula. A frequent rush-hour service is provided, with an almost-regular interval service all day of about a train every hour. Diesel-electric locomotives are used in the conventional (pull) manner. Coaches include a number of bilevel cars built in the mid-1950s and having center doors plus a fleet of well-maintained, but very old (1920s), single-level coaches.

Toronto, Canada, has one of the most efficient and effective rail commuter systems. It is operated by the Canadian National Railways (CN) for the Province of Ontario, hence is known as GO Transit (for Government of Ontario). Like many North American cities, Toronto had grown in area greatly following World War II. While it always possessed a very effective urban transit system, it depended largely on buses for outer suburban service, with a few scheduled local passenger trains operated at an out-of-pocket loss by the two railways, the CN and CP (Canadian Pacific Rail). By the early 1960s it was evident that an outer suburban service on private right-of-way was highly desirable. The high cost of urban freeways caused further pressure to seek an alternative to more freeways. In 1965, GO Transit was authorized, and service was inaugurated in May 1967.

Figure 5-9 *GO Transit train. Leaving Toronto Union Station, it's headed by an auxiliary power unit cab, an ex-F97 locomotive (freight/passenger). (courtesy of Toronto Area Transit Operating Authority)*

Figure 5-10 *GO Transit train. Passing Sunnyside Park area, Toronto, pulled by a diesel-electric locomotive. (These are leased to Canadian National Railways on weekends for freight duty.) (courtesy of Toronto Area Transit Operating Authority)*

GO Transit provides regular interval service between Pickering 33.6 km (20.9 mi) to the east and Oakville 34.4 km (21.4 mi) to the west via Toronto's Union Station, a total route of 68.1 km (42.3 mi). A few trains are extended beyond Oakville to Hamilton, 63.25 km (39.3 mi) from Toronto. A basic hourly service is provided, with trains every 20 minutes during the rush hours. Most trains have a locomotive at one end with either a driving cab or a former locomotive used as an auxiliary power car with controls at the other end. A small fleet of self-propelled rail diesel cars provides efficient short trains (two or three cars) for evening and weekend service.

Ridership has risen steadily, with additional rolling stock being added periodically to accommodate it. Trains of up to 10 cars are operated, length being limited by station platforms. To accommodate even greater ridership, a number of double-decked cars were ordered for delivery in 1977–1978. These are true two-floor cars and are not "gallery cars" such as those used in Chicago and San Francisco. Expansion of GO's system to the northwest came in the 1970s, beginning with three round trips per day. Routes to the north and northeast are planned, as is more frequent service throughout the system.

GO Transit is a composite of railroad and transit practices. Fare collection is at the stations, allowing a minimum-size train crew. Fares are distance-related. Doors are power-operated by one conductor, as on rapid transit.

Also included in GO Transit are express buses furnishing direct connections from Oakville to Hamilton on the west and Oshawa on the east. These are not merely "feeder buses," but are a continuation of a specific train schedule and stop at stations having park-and-ride lots and enclosed waiting rooms. It is, perhaps, the most effective bus–train service anywhere. These buses are operated by Gray Coach Lines (subsidiary of Toronto Transit Commission) under contract to GO Transit. The combination provides excellent regional coverage at reasonable cost.

Typically, railroad commuter services have very heavy peak-hour service with little, or even no, off-peak service. Regular interval service of a train every 30 or 60 minutes in the off-peak periods is generally considered good, with rush-hour trains every 10 to 30 minutes. It is not uncommon for a certain area to have only three inbound trains in the morning and three outbound at night. A number of medium-size cities had or have one train each way daily on certain routes. This all means that most, indeed all, railroad commuter services are heavy losers economically if evaluated of and by themselves. However, they often handle "the peak of the peak," and so reduce the need for investment in plant and equipment to handle a peak load by some other mode, be it highway or transit.

If freight train conflicts can be reduced or eliminated, commuter service can begin to approach rail rapid transit. As long as trains are operated by railroad employees represented by railroad unions, traditional labor practices ensure high operating expenses, and a high probability of significant deficits. Nonetheless, at times it is still an attractive alternative financially, and is nearly always popular with passengers. Because underutilized railroad track exists in many places, it is often possible to run a few peak-hour trains by providing only added locomotives, cars, and labor. The expensive fixed plant, a right-of-way through an urban area, is already there. Therefore, to a public transit agency, contracting for railroad commuter services may at times be an attractive alternative to massive investment in other modes.

CONCLUSION

The rail mode is versatile. It has provided a 2.4-km (1.5-mi) parking lot-to-department store shuttle, the 114-km (71-mi) Bay Area Rapid Transit system, urban systems covering major metropolitan areas, light rail systems serving busy center-city commercial districts and exclusive suburban residential areas, and far-flung suburban railroad commuter operations.

Off-the-shelf applications have been proven and can be implemented with minimal research and development. If evolutionary development of what has been successful is adopted by the planner and engineer, there is a very high probability of successful operation. Construction and operating costs are known and can be projected.

Rail transit has also been proven, and it can do many jobs in the urban and suburban environment. It can use electric power effectively, reducing pollution and improving the general quality of life. It can win motorists to transit. The opportunities to use rail transit effectively should be kept constantly in mind by the transit planner and engineer.

SELECTED BIBLIOGRAPHY

Many citations are no longer available from their original source. These citations are often available from the National Technical Information Service, U.S. Department of Commerce, 5285 Port Royal Road, Springfield, Va. 22161. We have verified the order numbers for many of these citations, and they are found at the end of the citation. Prices are available through NTIS at the address above.

DIAMANT, E. S., AND OTHERS, *Light Rail Transit: (A) State of the Art Review*, prepared for UMTA. Chicago: De Leuw, Cather & Company, Spring 1976. Now available as PB 256 821.

DOVER, A. T., *Electric Traction* (4th ed.). London: Sir Isaac Pitman & Sons Ltd., 1963.

GOVERNMENT OF ONTARIO TRANSIT, *(The) GO Transit (Story)*. n.p.: Toronto Area Transit Operating Authority, November 1974.

MADIGAN, RONALD J., *Urban Rail Supporting Technology Program Fiscal Year 1975*, *Year End Summary*, prepared for UMTA by Transportation Systems Center. Washington, D.C.: U.S. Department of Transportation, December 1975. Now available as PB 250 447.

MILLER, JOHN ANDERSON, *Fares, Please!* New York: Dover Publications, Inc., 1960. (Published originally in 1940.)

TRANSPORTATION SYSTEMS CENTER, *Urban Rail Supporting Technology: A Five Year Progress Summary, 1971–1976*, prepared for UMTA. Washington, D.C.: U.S. Department of Transportation, June 1976. Now available as PB 259 090.

PERIODICALS

The following periodicals are suggested for those interested in the rail mode. They offer both historical information and current activities.

Electric Traction, The Urban Transit Magazine for Australia. Australian Electric Traction Association, G.P.O. Box 1017, Sydney, NSW, 2001 Australia. (monthly)

Headlights. The Electric Railroaders Association, Inc., 4 West 40th Street, New York, N.Y. 10008. (monthly, actually irregular)

MASS TRANSIT. MASS TRANSIT, 538 National Press Building, Washington, D.C. 20045. (monthly)

MODERN RAILROADS. MODERN RAILROADS, 270 St. Paul Street, Denver, Colo. 80206. (monthly)

Modern Tramway and Light Rail Transit. Ian Allen Ltd., Terminal House, Shepperton TW17 8AS, England. (monthly)

Railway Age. Railway Age, Subscription Department, P.O. Box 530, Bristol, Conn. 06010. (semimonthly)

Railway Gazette International. Railway Gazette International, Subscriptions, Oakfield House, Perrymount Road, Haywards Heath, Sussex RH16 3BR, England. (monthly)

Chapter 6

BUS TRANSIT

ROBERT W. KOSKI, *Director of Planning and Marketing,*
Sacramento Regional Transit District

This chapter will focus on planning, operational, and scheduling considerations of urban fixed-route bus transit systems.

While rail modes, demand-reponsive, and paratransit operations are receiving increasing emphasis,, conventional fixed-route bus systems are still the most prevalent form of urban transit in the United States. As an indication of the importance of fixed-route bus systems, the 1975–1976 *Transit Fact Book*[1] shows the following equipment totals for member transit systems:

Passenger Vehicles Owned and Leased (First Week of September 1975)

Heavy rail cars	9,608
Light rail cars	1,061
Trolley coaches	703
Cable cars	39
Inclined plane cars	4
Personal rapid transit (PRT) cars	45
Motor buses	50,811
Total passenger vehicles owned and leased	62,271

The advantages of bus systems over rail systems include:

- Relative ease of adjustment to meet changing travel patterns.
- Comparatively low capital costs.
- Relatively short time required to inaugurate or expand systems.

---

[1]AMERICAN PUBLIC TRANSIT ASSOCIATION, *Transit Fact Book*, 1975–76 ed. (Washington, D.C.: American Public Transit Association, 1976).

- A proven, relatively trouble-free technology.
- Ease of bypassing barriers (accidents, fires, etc.) in the normal route.

Among their disadvantages (compared to rail), which become increasingly important in larger urban areas, are:

- Lower capacity in high-volume travel corridors.
- Limited ability to reduce labor cost in high-volume corridors.
- Susceptibility to delays from other vehicles, except where exclusive bus lanes are provided.
- Less "visibility" to the route network (compared to rail), frequently resulting in less public awareness and understanding of available service and coverage.

Even in the largest cities with dense and heavily used rail networks, buses are needed to supplement the rail routes and to feed into rail terminals. For example, New York City operates 6700 rail cars and 4540 buses, and the Chicago Transit Authority operates 1100 rail cars and 2440 buses.

It appears that even with a resurgence of interest in rail systems in higher-density areas, and a growing interest in dial-a-ride and paratransit operations, fixed-route bus networks will continue to provide an essential "middle-ground" role in the spectrum of available transit technologies.

EQUIPMENT AND FACILITIES

TYPES OF BUSES

Transit buses may be grouped into three broad classifications: standard, minibuses, and high capacity. The two manufacturers of standard-size buses in the United States (General Motors and Flxible) produce standard 35-ft (11-m)- and 40-ft (12-m)-long vehicles. Depending on seating arrangements, a 35-ft (11-m)-long bus typically seats 41 to 45 passengers; whereas a 40-ft (12-m)-long vehicle seats 49 to 53 passengers. The buses may be either 96 in (2.4 m) or 102 in (2.6 m) wide. The wider buses provide for either wider, more comfortable seats or wider aisles. Recently, great attention has been devoted to upgrading standard bus design by providing lower floors, wider doors, wheelchair lifts or ramps, and other features designed to make them more accessible to the elderly and handicapped.

Minibuses are being produced by a large number of American and foreign manufacturers. The configurations vary widely, and there appears to be a high degree of experimentation under way. This proliferation of models, mostly produced in small quantities, has been sparked to a great extent by the recent increase in interest and concern over service to the elderly and handicapped, dial-a-ride services, and service to rural and low-density areas. Perhaps in time there will be a move toward more standardization of smaller buses, as is now the case with standard-size buses.

Figure 6-1 *Various buses at San Francisco's East Bay Terminal. Standard "new look" buses behind an earlier AC Transit bus of a model no longer in service. (courtesy of California Department of Transportation)*

A common misconception among members of the lay public is that somehow minibuses would be cheaper to operate than standard-size buses in fixed-route service. These people fail to realize that the largest single item of expense is the driver's wage, which is usually the same no matter what size of bus is being driven. There is very little difference in fuel costs. While the initial cost of a minibus may be less, this is offset by a typically shorter life span. Thus, the operating costs of standard-size and minibuses are nearly the same. If only one trip per day requires standard-size seating capacities, it would be cheaper to operate one larger bus all day with many empty seats during most of the day than to have to operate a second minibus with driver for the peak trip. Nevertheless, minibuses play important roles where volumes are always low, and where maneuverability is paramount, as in dial-a-ride operations.

Recently, the United States has witnessed increased interest in high-capacity buses, long used in Europe and elsewhere. The high-capacity bus, despite its much higher initial cost, is frequently attractive economically on high-density routes because of savings in labor costs. The two basic types are the double-decked bus (several are being operated experimentally in Los Angeles and in New York City) and the articulated (bending) bus. Several hundred of the latter have recently been ordered by U.S. transit operators.

FIXED FACILITIES

The key facilities every bus system requires are an administrative office and one or more storage, servicing, and maintenance bases. The administrative offices may or may not be in conjunction with a maintenance facility. Routine servicing includes

Figure 6-2 *Argosy Minibus ready for dial-a-ride service. (courtesy of Argosy)*

fueling, removal of farebox receipts, interior cleaning, and exterior washing. Other maintenance functions include engine overhauls, repair of malfunctioning equipment, body painting, and repair of damaged seats and other interior furnishings. The dispatching function at each storage and servicing base (often called a "division" by transit operators) involves assigning buses and drivers to the various schedules on each route assigned to that base.

A typical division in a medium-size transit system may support 200 to 300 buses. Above that number of buses, the savings from centralization of functions and avoidance of duplication should be measured against the potential operating savings of an additional division through reduction of "deadhead" bus mileage between the storage area and the start of in-service trips. There is, of course, no magic formula; each geographical and scheduling situation is unique. In any event, all service facilities should be carefully placed in relationship to the transit route network so as to minimize deadheading. A middle ground between centralization and decentralization would be to provide routine servicing at all divisions, but to concentrate the other maintenance functions requiring specialized equipment, manpower, and parts inventories at only certain division locations.

Park-and-ride lots are becoming an increasingly important aspect of bus transit systems in a number of cities. They provide convenient access to transit via auto or bicycle for those persons who do not live within convenient walking distance of a bus line. By concentrating boardings at a single point, a more frequent level of service can be supported. Most park-and-ride lots are used primarily by commuters headed for

Figure 6-3   *AM General/MAN articulated Bus.* (*courtesy of California Department of Transportation*)

central business districts or other major employment centers. By far the most successful lots are the ones that are large enough to support frequent bus departures during the peak hours. Usually, the best locations are near freeways where fast rush-hour express service can be provided to employment centers.

In many cases, buses may perform normal residential neighborhood pickup, making their last stop at a park-and-ride lot, and then operate in the express mode. In this style of operation, several pickup routes could converge at one park-and-ride lot and support very frequent and attractive service at that location. It is desirable to locate park-and-ride lots on an all-day bus route (not necessarily express) in order that commuters will not be isolated from their autos during noncommuting hours.

Other facilities in an all-bus system might include passenger waiting shelters or stations, and even bus-stop signs should not be overlooked. Increased emphasis has been placed on the attractiveness, usefulness, and clarity of design of bus-stop signs.

TYPES OF BUS NETWORKS

Perhaps the most important factor in the quality and adequacy of service provided by a fixed-route bus system is the design of the network of routes. This section describes the major types of bus networks; in actual practice, most urban bus systems will employ some attributes of several of the network types. Following the description of network types is a listing of factors that apply generally to all route networks.

Figure 6-4 *San Bernardino Busway—El Monte Station. Present eastern terminal of busway, showing station and parking. (courtesy of California Department of Transportation)*

RADIAL PATTERNS

In many older cities, laid out in the streetcar era when most major activities were concentrated in the downtown area, streetcar lines typically fanned out in a radial pattern from the central business district into the suburbs. We find all too often that when the streetcars were phased out, the buses tended to follow the same routes. Of course, minor adjustments have been made. As new suburbs are added, the routes are extended out a little farther, and "cross-town" lines may be established. Nevertheless, many local bus transit systems still follow a basically radial pattern.

This pattern serves the work trips to downtown if there is still a reasonable concentration of employment there, but, as is frequently the case, if shopping has abandoned downtown to the suburban shopping centers, this type of transit network may have forfeited convenient access to those new shopping centers. In such cases, instead of being able to go shopping downtown from every neighborhood, you can easily get to one of the new shopping centers by transit only if you happen to live in the same transit corridor.

Not only has shopping decentralized in the typical city, but other major activities have as well, including employment, medical facilities, college campuses, and entertainment. These basic changes in land use in the typical American city have made it difficult for a radially oriented bus network to provide adequate service for more than a small percentage of desired trips. Clearly, new approaches are needed.

Figure 6-5 *San Bernardino Busway—El Monte Station. Shows bus loading facilities, SCRTD bus with water bumpers. (courtesy of Roger Marshutz Photography)*

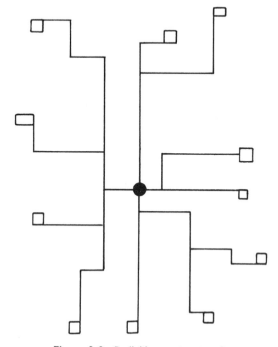

Figure 6-6 *Radial bus route network*

Grid-type bus route networks feature relatively straight, parallel routes spaced at regular intervals and crossed by a second group of routes with similar characteristics. They generally require a minimum of geographic or topographic barriers and an even-spaced network of arterial streets suitable for bus operations.

An example of a grid-type network can be found in Chicago, where surface bus operations of the Chicago Transit Authority follow primarily a grid pattern but inter-connect with rail rapid transit and commuter railroad networks which follow a radial pattern. Other examples of a grid bus network are those operated by the Southern California Rapid Transit District in Los Angeles and by the Toronto Transit Commission.

A major advantage of a grid-type system for an area that has scattered its activity centers widely is that riders can get from almost anyplace to almost anyplace else with one transfer, without having to funnel back through a central point such as the central

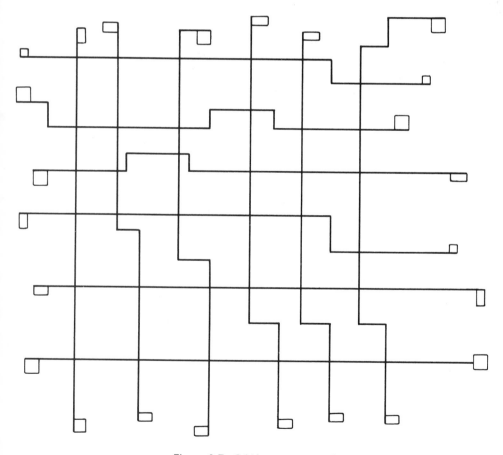

Figure 6-7 *Grid bus route network*

business district. Another advantage to the rider is relative simplicity of understanding the system. A key disadvantage of the grid system is that in order to get from anyplace to almost anyplace else, one transfer is usually necessary. For example, let us assume a high volume of trips between two points diagonal to the grid. In a pure grid system, all passengers would be required to make the one transfer; whereas in another kind of network, the high volume of trips between two points might be recognized by more direct routing.

For a grid system to work well, it should have frequent service on all the lines: hopefully, every 15 or 20 minutes, or even less. A grid system will not work well with half-hour headways because it is mathematically impossible to schedule more than a few key locations for convenient transfer connections. The remaining locations will involve long waits for transfers. (The theoretical average wait is 15 minutes.) A successful grid system depends on random connections and frequent headways. If population density or ridership is low and will not support frequent headways, it is doubtful that a grid system will be very successful.

RADIAL CRISS-CROSS

One way to obtain certain characteristics of a grid system and still maintain the benefits of a radial system is to criss-cross the lines and provide additional focal points for lines to converge, such as at shopping centers or colleges. In the diagram example, Fig. 6-8, all four lines operate directly from the central business district (CBD) to an

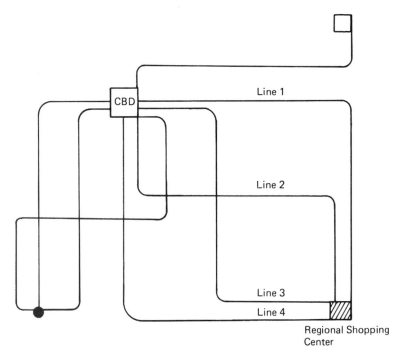

Figure 6-8 *Radial criss-cross bus route network*

outlying regional shopping center. By criss-crossing, the lines also provide grid-type transfer opportunities to intermediate locations. Under a pure grid system, there would be no direct service from the CBD to the shopping center.

TRUNK LINE WITH "FEEDERS"

The "trunk line with feeder" system is based on a strong major transit artery, either bus or rail, serving a major travel corridor. Because of the topography, geographical barriers, street patterns, or other reasons, under this system it is preferable to provide "feeder" service to the major trunk line rather than to run bus lines all the way to the ultimate major destination. A major disadvantage is the necessity for most passengers to change vehicles. An advantage is that a system of feeders can support a higher level of service on the trunk line than if it were supported only by passengers walking to stops.

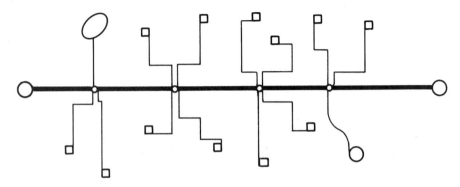

Figure 6-9 *Trunk line with feeders*

Examples of trunk lines with feeders include the bus–rail connections of the Cleveland Transit Authority, connections between Alameda–Contra Costa Transit buses and Bay Area Rapid Transit (BART) in the San Francisco Bay area, low-density neighborhood shuttle-bus connections to main bus lines in many cities, and even the Postal bus system in Switzerland, which feeds into, but is prohibited by law from paralleling, the Swiss National Railways.

TIMED-TRANSFER NETWORKS

Timed-transfer networks require an unusually high degree of coordination between route planning and scheduling. Most transportation networks have certain locations where vehicles are scheduled to "meet," or at least intersect in timed sequence, to allow interchange of passengers. In a timed-transfer network, entire systems or major segments of systems are laid out to facilitate such transfers. At a limited number of locations, from several up to many bus lines may converge at "passenger interchange points," frequently located at regional shopping centers or other such major activity centers. All lines serving a given interchange point operate at the same frequency, and are all scheduled to arrive at about the same time and leave at the same time, after up to a 5-minute period allowed for passengers to change buses. The advantages to the passenger include not having to go downtown for transfers, as in a radial system, or having to rely on random transfers at perhaps inhospitable street corners, as in the grid system. Within the timed-transfer network, most transfers can be made within a short period of time and under favorable conditions.

A timed-transfer network, however, can be extremely complicated to design and requires very careful scheduling. Among the problems that must be resolved are:

1. Possible differences in running times between several routes operating between the same pair of interchange points.
2. Scheduling conflicts between the demands of the interchange points and those of intermediate points, such as class-break times at schools and colleges.
3. Differences in running times by time of day due to traffic congestion.
4. Differences in passenger volumes by time of day on some routes serving the passenger interchanges, making evenspaced headways unsuitable.
5. Unsuitable relationships between running times and frequency of service, causing wasted vehicle and operator hours.
6. One or more lines serving a passenger interchange point being subject to fluctuating and unpredictable traffic delays, resulting in either missed connections or, if it is the policy for buses to wait for connections, one delayed bus causing an entire group of buses to be delayed.

LAYOVER OR RECOVERY TIME

There are several reasons why "layover" time is scheduled at one or both ends of each line:

1. To give the driver a rest.
2. To maintain schedule reliability. Traffic conditions vary from day to day; maybe there's an accident, unusual congestion, or a freight train blocks the street for several minutes. For any other number of reasons, the running time from one end of the line to the other may be different from one day to the next. It is necessary to have a time cushion to allow the bus to leave on time on the next trip.
3. To maintain reasonable headways. It is better practice to run a bus every 30 minutes than every 27 minutes, even if it means the driver has 3 additional minutes of layover time each trip.

BRANCHES AND LOOPS

As the service area of any transit system expands, it becomes increasingly difficult to provide adequate route coverage to the most remote areas. One approach to serving the outermost fringes of a radial network is to "branch" the lines. For example, a route may have a 15-minute frequency on the trunk portion, a 30-minute frequency on each of two branches, and hourly frequency on each of four subbranches.

One way to cover more territory without reducing frequency is to put in a loop.

Loops have some advantages and some disadvantages. The basic trade-off to passengers is the increased frequency of service made possible by the loop as compared to the increased riding time. A rider living near the beginning of a loop would be faced with a longer trip in the morning on the way to work, and one living near the end of a loop would have a longer ride in the evening coming home. If layover or recovery time is included in the schedule for the loop, the situation becomes even more undesirable in terms of passenger service. Therefore, if possible, all or most recovery time should be scheduled at the end of the line opposite from the loop, and lines with loops at both ends should be avoided. As a general rule, very infrequent headways argue for loops as a substitute for branches. The more frequent the headway, the more desirable branching becomes as a substitute for loops.

THROUGH ROUTING

Some bus systems bring all buses from all neighborhoods to downtown, loop them around, and send them back. This results in a lot of turning movements downtown, but each line can be operated as an individual entity. Through or combined routing can reduce mileage, turning movements, congestion, and transferring.

In order to through-route it is necessary to balance the characteristics of the combined lines so that the frequency and hours of service needed on each are the same. Obviously, it is not feasible to through-route a line on a 10-minute headway with one on a 15-minute headway. It is possible (although not ideal) to through-route a line on a 30-minute headway with another on a 15-minute headway, and have alternate buses turn back.

Another consideration in through-routing is the relationship between headways and the lengths of the lines and running times. For example, consider a hypothetical single line that would take 62 minutes to run a round trip without recovery time, with passenger loadings justifying about a half-hour headway. Allowing for layover, it is not desirable to run two buses at 35- or 37-minute headways, for reasons that will be outlined later. Running three buses at a 30-minute headway would result in excessive layover. One solution to the problem would be to through-route with another line that takes somewhat less than 1 hour for a round trip so that four buses could maintain an even 30-minute headway on the through-route combination.

DETAILED FACTORS IN ROUTE PLANNING

The following section is intended to serve as a checklist and very brief description of route-planning details which should be applied to any of the types of networks previously described.

GOALS AND STANDARDS

The goals, standards, and service criteria adopted by the transit agency should be the starting point for route planning. For example, what policy has been adopted with regard to the degree of effort that should be directed toward serving the needs of the transit dependent population versus the degree of effort devoted to serving the needs of commuters, who are apt to be choice riders? An emphasis on the former will be more directed toward meeting the social needs of the community; whereas an emphasis on the latter would undoubtedly mean greater concern for goals such as energy conservation and reduction of congestion and air pollution.

DEMOGRAPHIC DATA

Maps of key demographic factors by census tract or other convenient subarea should be prepared for the transit service area as a basic reference in laying out the route network. Examples would include the percentage of population without cars, percentage of population over age 65, average income, and residence location of college students. These data give useful insight into the "home" end of home-based trips.

MAJOR ACTIVITY CENTERS

All major activity centers in the community should be mapped, including major shopping centers, major employers, schools and colleges, and hospitals and clinics. A convenient way to accomplish this is to indicate a *precise* location for each activity center, with the size of the symbol being proportional to the number of person-trips generated per day. This precise mapping is far more useful in transit-route planning than the generalized level of activity by zones, which is the typical mapping technique used by regional planning agencies for transportation and land-use planning purposes. This more precise mapping is necessary because the bus routes must travel within a short distance of the entrance to these activity centers if they are to be used.

LAND-USE PLANNING

Close liaison must be maintained with local and regional planning agencies to ascertain land-use planning policies as they may relate to the layout of future transit routes. Increasingly, planning agencies will be called on to pursue such policies as the clustering of activities which facilitate transit use.

RESIDENTIAL DENSITY

Careful attention must be paid to average residential density. The higher the density, the more closely spaced and/or more frequent the level of transit service that may be supported. It is useful to arrange with local planning commissions to obtain copies of proposed subdivision plats in order to have an early-warning system of areas where route extensions may be needed in the near future.

WALKING DISTANCE AND ROUTE SPACING

A commonly used rule of thumb is that transit patrons should not be required to walk more than 0.4 km (0.25 mi) to reach the nearest bus stop. This would result in parallel routes being spaced about 0.8 km (0.5 mi) apart. In low-density suburbs, this goal may have to be compromised if there is an insufficient density of housing to support this close a network of lines.

STREET CONTINUITY, WIDTH, AND LOAD-CARRYING CAPACITY

This factor is closely related to the previous one, and if existing streets which meet minimum standards are not available, routing compromises will have to be made. Of course, it is desirable for the transit operating agency to have a role in the decision-making process regarding street layout and design as new subdivisions are being planned.

PEDESTRIAN ACCESS

Pedestrian access is becoming an increasingly important factor, particularly in newer subdivisions designed with curvilinear streets to discourage through traffic. Increasingly, transit route planners are faced with situations where routes might be within the standard 0.4 km (0.25 mi) of each residence "as the crow flies." The shortest path from some houses to the nearest bus stop, however, might actually be much longer through the maze of streets that must be followed. Transit representatives should maintain contact with local planning agencies to call attention to the need for convenient and direct pedestrian access to streets carrying transit lines. This may be provided by pathways.

SAFETY CONSIDERATIONS

Safety factors include the avoidance of potentially hazardous turns and the availability of traffic signals and stop-sign protection. For example, left-turn entries into busy arterials should be made only at intersections with traffic signals.

FINANCING CONSTRAINTS

Included in this category is not only the obvious constraint of the total budget, but also the limits of which alternative routings would produce the greatest revenue per mile. In some cases, regional operators may have formula restrictions regarding allocation of levels of service among various jurisdictions served.

MARKETING STRATEGY

Included in this factor are considerations as to which market or neighborhood or line would be easiest to sell. Depending upon the circumstances in a particular community, it might be an important factor to concentrate initially on lines most likely to quickly succeed in terms of increased patronage in order to be able to point to success as a springboard for future success.

ESTABLISHED RIDERSHIP PATTERNS

While existing routings that may date back to streetcar days are not sacrosanct, care should be taken in tinkering with long-established lines so that entrenched transit

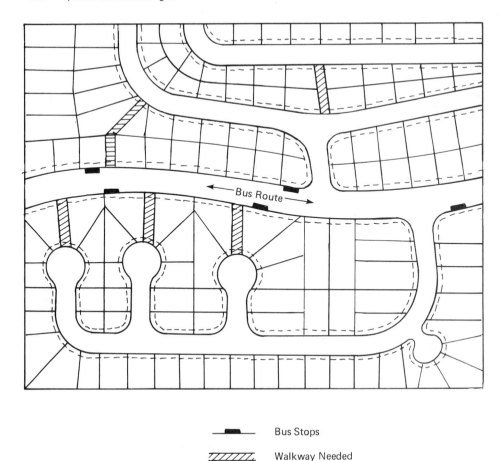

▬▬	Bus Stops
⧄⧄⧄	Walkway Needed
- - - - -	Sidewalks Needed

Figure 6-10 *Subdivision plan showing pedestrian access*

ridership patterns are not unduly disrupted. Without caution, one could, in the hope of gaining 100 passengers, lose 500 already riding the existing service.

TRAVEL PATTERNS AND COMPUTER MODELING

While overall travel patterns within the community, most of which are probably by auto, are undoubtedly important, methods of analyzing these patterns for purposes of designing street and highway networks, frequently using computer modeling as a tool, are only partially helpful for transit route planning. Travel patterns are typically aggregated by analysis zones too large to help in the detailed microplanning necessary in laying out transit routes. These broad travel patterns must, of course, be analyzed and understood in determining general corridors and major travel flows, but they are only one factor. As for computer modeling of transit networks, one must first lay out a network or series of networks to be tested by the model in order to lay out a service network with some chance of success. In this process, the other factors listed take on prime importance.

PROVISION OF CONVENIENT TRANSFER CONNECTIONS

The various lines of a transit-route network cannot be analyzed independently. Each must be thought of in terms of how it relates to others in the network. Provision of convenient locations for transfers is an especially important factor.

SCHEDULING CONSIDERATIONS

Factors such as headways, running times, number of vehicles, loops, and short turns should be taken into consideration. If the route planner has an option of extending either of two routes into a new subdivision, scheduling considerations might be the deciding factor regarding which of the routes should be extended.

SIMPLICITY AND CLARITY

The objective of simplicity and clarity to the user should not be overlooked in an effort to consider all the other factors. An intricate, sophisticated network that works on paper will be a failure if it attracts no riders because it is too complex for the public to understand.

POLITICAL CONSIDERATIONS

The degree of public support for alternative proposals and the level of requests and petitions for alternative transit improvements must always be considered.

Transit needs usually do not match up closely with city and county boundary lines. It is not unusual for a single transit line to pass through several political jurisdictions. Depending on financing arrangements and decision-making authority and procedures, reaching agreement among all the concerned parties may be time consuming and difficult.

SCHEDULING

POLICY HEADWAYS

The frequency of service on a given route is usually based either on a formally adopted or unstated policy regarding the minimum level of service to be provided ("policy headway"), or on the frequency of service necessary to handle the passenger loads, or on some combination of the two. Policy headway is more apt to be used during nonpeak hours, passenger loads during peak hours. Typical policy headways may be every 60, 30, or 20 minutes. There may be considerable unused midday capacity on lines operating policy headways, and one could argue that costs could be cut by reducing service. In a typical system, decision makers may have determined, however, that every 30 minutes may be the minimum acceptable level of service for most lines. During peak hours and on more heavily traveled lines, the frequency of service is more apt to be a function of passenger volume. Since additional drivers and buses are usually required to handle peak-hour loadings anyway, the out-of-pocket costs of providing a higher level of partially used midday service can be more easily justified.

It is very desirable to have any headway less frequent than every 10 minutes evenly divisible into 60 (i.e., 60, 30, 20, 15, 12, 10). Similar headways are necessary for facilitating transfer connections, with or without a full-scale timed-transfer network. Departure times of any headway divisible into 60 repeat themselves each hour, and riders can more easily remember them. It is much easier for a telephone information clerk to tell a caller that a bus "leaves at 10 and 40 minutes past each hour" (30-minute headway) than to have to say the bus "leaves at 9:10, 9:37, 10:04, 10:31, and 10:58" (27-minute headway). Also, it is important to coordinate schedules with class starting and ending times at local colleges, etc., which are usually on a 1-hour cycle.

At headways more frequent than every 10 minutes, the preceding factors become relatively unimportant, since riders no longer need to rely on timetables and are apt to appear at the bus stop at random times.

PEAK-TO-BASE RATIO

The peak-to-base ratio of a transit system is the ratio between the number of vehicles operated during the rush hour compared to the number scheduled during the midday or "base" period. Some systems with a high proportion of transit-dependent riders, who may use the system primarily for shopping, doctors' appointments, and similar purposes, are able to handle passenger volumes without adding any additional buses during the "rush hour." The peak-to-base ratio in such a case would be one (1).

The more successful a system is in capturing home-to-work trips, the more extra buses must be added to handle the higher rush-hour volumes. These additional buses are less productive since they operate fewer hours per day. Even more important, it becomes increasingly difficult, even with split shifts, to arrange a full day of productive work for all drivers. Many transit systems help fill part of the midday gap in demand for buses and drivers by scheduling service to schools (usually just after the morning commuter rush and just before the evening commuter rush), special midday shopper shuttles, and charter and sightseeing services.

STAGGERED WORK HOURS

One partial solution to the problem of equipment and driver utilization during peak travel hours is the encouragement of staggered work hours. To the degree that staggered work hours reduce traffic congestion and thereby increase speeds and schedule reliability, they, of course, benefit transit. For the staggered hours to have significant impact on equipment utilization, however, the spread between the first and last starting and ending work shifts must be great enough for "tripper"[2] buses to travel to the end of a line and return for second trips. As cities sprawl and bus lines get longer, this becomes increasingly difficult. More "second trips" can be produced by "deadheading" some buses back nonstop in the low-volume direction, or by "short-turning" alternate buses before the end of the line on high-frequency lines.

Surprisingly, staggered work hours even work to the detriment of transit in some circumstances. First, if the "spread" between work hours is great enough to allow a large number of "second trips" by tripper buses, then it becomes increasingly difficult to meet restrictions contained in most bus-driver labor contracts, which limit the "spread" between the start of the first piece of work and the end of the last piece of work of split shifts.

Second, in some isolated low-density suburbs, there may be only one or two bus loads of commuters destined for a given employment center. With standardized work hours, direct express service might be provided. With staggered work hours, either the bus schedules will not match work times, or extra half-empty buses would have to be operated to meet the additional shift change times.

FARE COLLECTION

FLAT FARES

Flat, or uniform, fares for the entire system have the advantages of simplicity, understandability, marketability, and ease of collection. The major disadvantages of flat fares are in questions of equitability and forfeiture of potential revenues, particularly on longer trips. Fares differ by class of passenger: one of the requirements for transit systems to be eligible for federal subsidies is that they charge not more than half the regular fare to elderly and handicapped persons during nonpeak hours. Most systems also provide reduced rates for youth or school riders. Some systems charge higher fares during peak hours in recognition of the higher costs incurred in providing peak-hour service and as an incentive to those having the option to ride during nonpeak hours, thus tending to level demand.

In recent years, 25 cents has been a common level of flat fare. It has the advantage to customers' convenience of being a "single-coin" fare which can also be paid by multiple coins; this factor is of increased importance since most transit systems, for security reasons, have adopted an "exact-fare" policy with drivers no longer carrying change. As inflation causes the 25-cent fare to be a thing of the past, tokens worth odd amounts, such as 35 cents, take on added importance for customer convenience, and additional transit system energies should be devoted to providing convenient sales outlets for them.

---

[2]Buses used during rush hours only.

Newer rail systems, such as BART and the Washington, D.C., Metro, have established elaborate fare-collection hardware to make it possible to charge by the length of the ride, which most people will agree is equitable. Lacking, thus far, the necessary automated equipment, the closest that bus operators can come to charging according to the length of ride is through use of a zone system, which is a tremendous headache to administer.

Usually, a zone system consists of one large central zone surrounded by several concentric outer zones. A basic fare (for example, 25 cents) is charged upon boarding, and additional zone charges (for example, 5 or 10 cents) are collected for each zone line crossed.

There are two basic methods of collecting the extra zone charges. The first relies on driver memory and works best in radial-type networks. It assumes that "inbound," most passengers have a destination in the central zone. Most passengers on boarding inbound pay the full fare, including zones charges to the central zone. Any passenger intending to get off before crossing one or more zone lines would so inform the driver, who would collect the lesser fare, and then be expected to see that the passenger gets off within the proper zone.

Outbound, the basic fare is collected upon boarding in the central zone, and once the first zone line is crossed, zone surcharges are collected as passengers leave the bus. Passengers boarding in outer zones are issued receipts noting their boarding point so that they are not charged for zone lines not crossed. Obviously, this system is cumbersome to drivers and passengers alike, and very confusing.

Outbound in outer zones it is not possible to use the rear door for exit, as all leaving passengers must file past the farebox to deposit their zone surcharges. This slows down operating speeds. Having to pay twice on the same trip (with multiple coins) is also very inconvenient to passengers.

The other method of collecting zone charges is for passengers to pay the full fare upon boarding, with the driver issuing a receipt for any zone fares paid. The bus is stopped at each zone crossing, and the driver then passes through the bus to collect zone receipts. This method is more workable in grid-type bus networks, and eliminates the need for the driver to remember which inbound passengers promised to get off before crossing zone lines. The rear door may also be used for exit at all times. But the delays at zone crossings can be extensive.

Zone systems can be inequitable, too. Short trips crossing zone lines cost more than longer trips that may be entirely within one zone. Obviously, some technological breakthroughs are needed in bus fare-collection systems.

FARE-FREE ZONES

Several cities, including Seattle and Portland, Oregon, have set up fare-free zones in their downtown business districts. They were installed to facilitate circulation within the CBD and to reduce traffic congestion, and have generally been considered succesful. Operationally, they are made possible by paying on entering the bus inbound and paying on exiting outbound. Loading and unloading is speeded up in the CBD, since both front and rear doors may be used to either enter or leave the bus. Any time saved is lost on the outbound trip, however, since after leaving the CBD, only the front door may be used.

TRANSFERS

Most bus systems issue transfers to passengers so that they may continue their journeys when a single bus line does not serve both trip origin and destination. Usually, transfers are free, although some systems charge small sums such as 5 cents for them. Usually, transfers have both a time limit and complex rules regarding acceptance designed to reduce opportunities for riders to make a round trip on a single fare. Complex transfer acceptance rules tend to foster confrontations between drivers and passengers regarding their interpretation. Such rules are an inheritance of the days when transit was a profit-making, private enterprise, and "cheating" with transfers was considered a drain on revenues.

With increased emphasis on transit as a public service, assuming increased public benefits with increased usage, cheating with transfers has become less of an issue, and there is a trend toward liberalizing transfer rules. Perhaps the ultimate in this trend was reached when the Sacramento Regional Transit District abolished transfers entirely in 1973, substituting all-day passes sold by the driver at twice the regular fare, with no time or travel restrictions whatever.

FARE PREPAYMENT

In recent years, transit operators have been giving increasing emphasis to fare prepayment plans, generally involving passes good for unlimited riding during a given period, usually a month. Daily, weekly, and annual passes are also used. Seattle Metro Transit offers a youth pass good for the summer school vacation season. From a marketing standpoint, these passes encourage additional riding, they eliminate the inconvenience of having to carry a pocketful of coins, and they emphasize the low monthly cost of transit riding compared to driving an automobile.

Such prepayment schemes also offer possibilities of payroll deduction by employers who desire to encourage transit use and thereby reduce parking needs.

To the transit operator, they offer benefits such as reduced coin-handling expenses and slightly improved cash flow by providing "payment in advance." Balanced against these advantages must be the costs of the pass-distribution system.

As transit systems strive to compete with the private automobile in whatever manner possible, the convenience of fare prepayment systems compared to having to deposit multiple coins in the farebox and having to worry about restrictive transfer rules takes on considerable importance.

CONCLUSION

Conventional fixed-route bus systems are the most prevalent form of urban transit in the United States, in terms of number of vehicles, number of passengers carried, and route-miles. With recent intensified interest and research in new operational methods, such as dial-a-ride, and in improved rail technologies, we should not lose sight of the important basic role played by conventional bus routes. Nor should we neglect opportunities for improving service and efficiency on such systems. They may lack glamour in some person's minds, compared to other aspects of transit, but they nevertheless deserve further development and improvement as a vital aspect of public transportation.

Figure 6-11 *AM General Transbus. (courtesy of AM General)*

SELECTED BIBLIOGRAPHY

Many citations are no longer available from their original source. These citations are often available from the National Technical Information Service, U.S. Department of Commerce, 5285 Port Royal Road, Springfield, Va. 22161. We have verified the order numbers for many of these citations, and they are found at the end of the citation. Prices are available through NTIS at the address above.

AMERICAN PUBLIC TRANSIT ASSOCIATION, *Transit Operating Report for Calendar/Fiscal Year 1975*. Washington, D.C.: American Public Transit Association, 1977.

INSTITUTE OF TRAFFIC ENGINEERS, *Change-of-Mode Parking—A State of the Art*, an informational report. Arlington, Va.: Institute of Traffic Engineers, January 1973.

——, *Transportation and Traffic Engineering Handbook*, ed. John E. Baerwald. Englewood Cliffs, N.J.: Prentice-Hall, Inc., 1976.

KEYANI, BARBARA IBARRA, AND EVELYN S. PUTNAM, *Transportation System Management: State of the Art*, February 1977, prepared for UMTA by INTERPLAN Corporation. Washington, D.C.: U.S. Government Printing Office, n.d.—report date September 1976. Now available as PB 266 953.

LEA TRANSIT COMPENDIUM, *Bus Transit*, vol. I, no. 7, 1974. Huntsville, Ala.: N. D. Lea Transportation Research Corporation, 1974.

————, *Bus Transit*, vol. II, no. 7, 1975. Huntsville, Ala.: N. D. Lea Transportation Research Corporation, 1975.

————, *Passenger Admission Processing Equipment*, vol. III, Special Issue, 1976–77. Huntsville, Ala.: N. D. Lea Transportation Research Corporation, 1976.

————, *Roadway Transit Equipment*, vol. I, no. 9, 1974. Huntsville, Ala.: N. D. Lea Transportation Research Corporation, 1974.

————, *Roadway Transit Equipment*, vol. II, no. 9, 1975. Huntsville, Ala.: N. D. Lea Transportation Research Corporation, 1975.

LEVINSON, HERBERT S., AND OTHERS, *Bus Use of Highways: State of the Art*, NCHRP Report 143. Washington, D.C.: Highway Research Board, 1973.

MURIN, WILLIAM J., *Mass Transit Policy Planning: An Incremental Approach*. Lexington, Mass.: D. C. Heath and Company, Heath Lexington Books, 1971.

ORAM, RICHARD L., *Transportation System Management: (A) Bibliography of Technical Reports*, prepared for UMTA and FHWA by UMTA. Washington, D.C.: Urban Mass Transportation Administration, May 1976. Now available as PB 257 273.

PRATT, RICHARD H., NEIL J. PEDERSEN, AND JOSEPH J. MATHER, *Traveler Response to Transportation System Changes: A Handbook for Transportation Planners*, prepared for FHWA and UMTA. Kensington, Md.: R. H. Pratt Associates, Inc., February 1977. Now available as PB 265 830/OWT.

THOMPSON, GREGORY LEE, "Planning Considerations for Alternative Transit Route Structures," *Journal of the American Institute of Planners*, 43, no. 2 (April 1977), 158–68.

THURLOW, VIRGIL S., JOHN A. BACHMAN, AND C. DENVER LOVETT, *Bus Maintenance Facilities: A Transit Management Handbook*, prepared for UMTA by The Mitre Corporation. Washington, D.C.: U.S. Government Printing Office, November 1975. Now available as PB 250 475.

TRANSPORTATION RESEARCH BOARD, *Bus Transportation Strategies*, Transportation Research Record 606. Washington, D.C.: Transportation Research Board, 1977.

URBAN MASS TRANSPORTATION ADMINISTRATION, Office of Transit Management, *Transit Marketing Management Handbook: Marketing Organization*, prepared for UMTA by LESKO Associates and Smith and Locks Associates, Inc. Washington, D.C.: Urban Mass Transportation Administration, November 1975.

————, *Transit Marketing Management Handbook: Marketing Plan*, prepared for UMTA by Grey Advertising, Inc., and Chase, Rosen & Wallace, Inc. Washington, D.C.: Urban Mass Transportation Administration, April 1976.

————, *Transit Marketing Management Handbook: User Information Aids*, prepared for UMTA by Ilium Associates, Inc. Washington, D.C.: Urban Mass Transportation Administration, November 1975.

WARD, JERRY D., AND NORMAN G. PAULHUS, JR., *Suburbanization and Its Implications for Urban Transportation Systems*. n.p.: Urban Transportation Information Service, 1976.

Also see the bibliography of Chapter 33.

PERIODICALS

The following periodicals are suggested for those interested in the bus mode. They offer both historical information and current activities.

Bus Ride. Friendship Publications, Inc., P.O. Box 1472, Spokane, Wash. 99210. (bimonthly)

MASS TRANSIT. MASS TRANSIT, 538 National Press Building, Washington, D.C. 20045. (monthly)

Transit Journal. American Public Transit Association, 1100 17th Street, N.W., Washington, D.C. 20036. (quarterly)

Chapter 7

PARATRANSIT

Daniel Roos,* *Professor, Civil Engineering, Massachusetts Institute of Technology*

During the 1960s, public transportation was generally equated with the "transit industry," which operated fixed-route bus and rail systems. Paratransit options rarely received attention even though some services, such as taxis, were playing a significant role in the provision of public transportation service. Since 1970, a significant broadening in recognition of public transportation options has occurred with a shift in emphasis from a "transit industry" orientation to a "transportation service" orientation. Options besides fixed-route bus and rail service and service providers besides transit operators are now being considered.

This broadening has been motivated in part by changes in urban structure and travel which have occurred during the past several decades. People and activities have shifted from high-density central cities to lower-density suburban areas. The largely radial, central business district (CBD) oriented travel which characterized the pre-World War II decades has been superseded by new, more dispersed travel patterns, often "cross-haul" or "back-haul" in nature, along much-lower-density travel corridors. The change in travel patterns has been both complemented and, in part, directly caused by an increasing reliance on the private automobile.

The private automobile, while fulfilling the expectations and desires of most of the travel-consuming public better than any other alternative, also has attributes that often conflict with currently accepted social values. The private automobile demands a high allocation of scarce resources in the midst of an "economy of scarcity": it is land- and energy-intensive and often results in negative environmental impacts.

*The author gratefully acknowledges the contributions of David Alschuler in the preparation of portions of this chapter.

Furthermore, the increasing acceptance of a basic right to mobility for every member of society highlights the mobility needs for those groups without easy access to an automobile (i.e., the elderly, the physically and mentally handicapped, the young, and the poor).

These concerns have refocused national attention on transportation alternatives to the automobile. Conventional fixed-route transit plays an important role in providing line-haul transit along high-density corridors; however, it is often rather inefficient for the collection and distribution portions of a trip. Furthermore, fixed-route transit often cannot efficiently serve dispersed noncorridor travel in lower-density areas. Different transit services are required to satisfy these two needs. In addition, services that are more accessible than fixed-route service to special market segments with limited physical mobility are needed.

In many ways, fixed-route transit and automobile travel are at polar extremes. Fixed-route facilities operate in finitely defined time and space, with little privacy and few amenities, using paid professional labor, and (generally) public ownership of the capital facilities. The automobile operates in variable time and space, with complete privacy and significant amenities, with labor contributed as an "in-kind" payment for service, and (generally) using privately owned capital equipment. Recently, attention has been focused on transit service options which fall midway between the polar extremes represented by fixed-route, fixed-schedule transit service and the completely flexible automobile. The service options have been categorized as "paratransit." The options and service concepts represented in the spectrum of paratransit, while containing certain untested concepts or elements, are primarily composed of operating concepts which are known and, to varying extents, existing elements of the transportation service sector: carpooling, vanpooling, subscription bus, "premium" taxi, shared-ride taxi (or dial-a-ride), jitney (or route-deviation) service.

It is not the intent of this chapter to describe specific paratransit service options. Peak-hour ridesharing options, including carpooling and vanpooling, are discussed in Chapter 9, while demand-responsive options, including dial-a-ride, taxi, and route- and point-deviation services, are discussed in Chapter 8. This chapter is concerned with general issues and relationships between paratransit concepts.

PARATRANSIT DEVELOPMENT

Paratransit alternatives (particularly exclusive-ride taxicab service) have been generally available and functioning for years. However, despite the fact that they have played a significant role in overall urban travel, they have, until recently, received surprisingly little systematic research, study, and analysis or comparison to other forms of passenger transportation. The current interest in paratransit is largely due to the emergence of a new set of values relating to mobility and a new set of economic and environmental realities. Specifically, paratransit is viewed as a potential way of (1) providing an attractive, high-quality alternative to the automobile which can induce a net savings in vehicle-miles of travel, thereby reducing time-related congestion costs, direct costs, energy consumption, and travel-related vehicle emissions; and (2) ensuring mobility and access to opportunity for those individuals who are unable (by virtue of age, physical disability, or economic inability) to use a private automobile or conventional transit.

These goals basically reflect two different orientations toward paratransit. The former view is service-oriented. It focuses on issues of efficiency and is framed by an orientation toward inputs (resources consumed) and outputs (service provided); level of service, economic efficiency, and vehicle-miles of travel are the basic measures. The latter goal is essentially derived from social welfare norms, and is oriented toward specific market segments. Its measures are framed in terms of equity (accessibility and utilization) rather than efficiency (input/output measures).

Paratransit does not have well-organized vocal constituencies. Rather the paratransit sector is fragmented, uncoordinated, and unorganized. Paratransit services often are provided by small-scale "Mom and Pop" operators with limited capital resources and limited management expertise. Preoccupied with their own operations and short-term problems, these operators rarely concern themselves with influencing opinion or policy on a regional, statewide, or federal level. The taxicab and limousine industries have nationally-based trade organizations, but these organizations have only recently begun interacting with the federal government. Paratransit services such as carpooling and vanpooling, which are not industries in the conventional sense, are seldom organized beyond a local or regional basis. The paratransit sector, lacking an organized constituency, has not undertaken lobbying efforts, so that legislators and policy makers are largely unaware of the needs and potential of paratransit.

The awareness and interest in paratransit has increased recently as a result of new government policies and new active roles of the taxi and transit industries. Government involvement in paratransit has come primarily from the Urban Mass Transportation Administration, Federal Highway Administration, and Federal Energy Administration. Numerous Urban Mass Transportation Administration policy statements have emphasized that paratransit services must be considered in an alternatives analysis and that capital and operating assistance funds may be applied to paratransit services. The Urban Mass Transportation Administration's interest in paratransit is consistent with its emphasis on low-capital-intensive alternatives, incremental planning and implementation, the involvement of private operators, and improved transportation management. Paratransit is an important component of the new transportation systems management element (TSME) of the transportation improvement program (TIP) which must be submitted to the federal government by all urban areas.

The energy crisis and gas shortages of 1973 were the primary reasons for the increased involvement of the Federal Highway Administration and the entry of the Federal Energy Administration into paratransit. The Emergency Highway Energy Conservation Act of 1974 provided funding for carpool demonstrations. 1976 legislation has broadened the program to include and encourage vanpooling.

Some of the most active interest in new paratransit services has come from the taxicab industry. Although taxicabs have played a vital role in providing public transportation, that role has only recently been acknowledged and appreciated. The taxicab industry has concentrated on exclusive-ride taxi service and has not actively sought government funding. Four events occurred which changed their attitude. First was the squeeze on profits in the taxicab industry caused by inflation and the escalation in gasoline prices. Taxi companies were unable to obtain corresponding rate increases. Second, dial-a-ride services were initiated and subsidized by public transit organizations. Although these dial-a-ride operations represented only a minuscule portion of service provided by public transit companies, the taxi industry was concerned that a threat existed. They felt that publicly subsidized companies should not provide taxilike service, or that the taxi industry should also be subsidized. Third, operating assistance was introduced in the National Mass Transportation Assistance Act of 1974. While the benefits of capital assistance to the taxi industry were debatable, the benefits of operating assistance were clear-cut. Fourth, several aggressive, innovative taxi operators rose to positions of leadership within the industry and argued convincingly that the industry should explore new shared-ride paratransit service opportunities.

The transit industry initially was indifferent or opposed to paratransit services. Their reasons included greater interest in expanding conventional bus and rail systems, concern about the reliability of small vehicles used for paratransit service, and fear that these new services would divert people from existing conventional transit. Recently, through American Public Transit Association (APTA) leadership, the industry has shown considerably more interest in paratransit. The American Public Transit Association Task Force report on paratransit concludes, "Our cities with their varied forms require a mixture of conventional transit and paratransit providing a family of services, services that can be designed or shaped to fit market needs of a particular portion of the community."[1]

In the fall of 1975, the Urban Mass Transportation Administration sponsored a paratransit conference which brought together 100 experts with different backgrounds to examine paratransit. The principal finding of the conference was, "The ideal urban transportation system is a cooperative mix of paratransit and conventional transit with highly coordinated services and with the possiblity of varied ownership of different modal components. Such a system would allow greater overall operating efficiency and increase transit patronage by allowing each mode to do what it does best."[2]

CHARACTERISTICS OF PARATRANSIT ALTERNATIVES

It is important to be able to compare and differentiate between various paratransit services. Although many different classification schemes are possible,[3] the most appropriate for our purpose is to differentiate by time and space characteristics. The family of paratransit services represents different spatial and temporal service responses

---

[1]AMERICAN PUBLIC TRANSIT ASSOCIATION TASK FORCE ON PARATRANSIT, "Paratransit in the Family of Transit Services," *Transit Journal*, 2, no. 2 (May 1976), 5.

[2]SANDRA ROSENBLOOM, ed., *Paratransit*, Special Report 164 (Washington, D.C.: Transportation Research Board, 1976), p. 13.

[3]See Chapter 4 for other types of classification.

to travel desires. Some trips taken by an individual are periodic—occurring between the same origin and destination pairs on a predictable, recurring basis; other trips occur infrequently or between scattered and nonrepeating origin–destination pairs. For example, conventional transit operates in what may be called fixed time ("the schedule") and fixed space ("the route"). On the opposite extreme, the taxi operates in completely "flexible" time and space. These attributes of time and space can be utilized to define the complete spectrum of paratransit and transit alternatives (see Fig. 7-1).

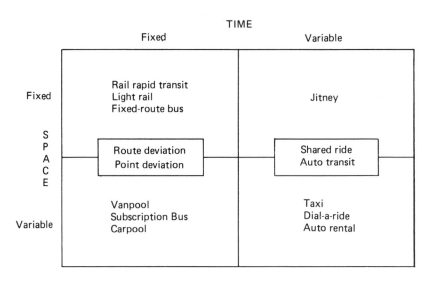

Figure 7-1 *Temporal-spatial characteristics of urban transportation alternatives*

Conventional transit, at one extreme, operates on fixed schedules. The private automobile, on the other extreme, operates in completely flexible time and space, providing point-to-point service on request. Jitney services, operating on high frequency along defined corridors, operate in semivariable time and fixed space; while vanpools and subscription buses operate on a generally prearranged schedule, with flexible routing for both the feeder and line-haul segments of the trip. Route- or point-deviation services similarly offer (limited) spatial flexibility within the basic constraints of a fixed-time schedule. Dial-a-ride, shared-ride taxi, and exclusive-ride taxi offer spatial flexibility comparable to the automobile for many trips, but may fall short of the time responsiveness of the private auto due to either length of in-vehicle travel times or wait times necessary for "immediate" service.

The dimension of time responsiveness can be further defined by the flexibility offered in utilizing service. For example, subscription bus service, vanpools, and certain dial-a-ride service operate on an "advance-booking" requirement. Taxis, shared-ride cabs, and other dial-a-ride services may offer "immediate service on request," although the actual immediacy of response is a function of the system-operating parameters (i.e., demand/supply equilibrium). Similarly, space responsiveness can be further defined through the concepts of "dynamic routing" and "prescheduled" routing, generally corresponding to "on-request" and "advance-booking" time characteristics, respectively. The time/space attributes result in trade-offs of certain user-perceived level-of-service attributes. Scheduled subscription buses or vanpools may offer limited time flexibility, but the limited flexibility allows for greater vehicle productivity (generally translated into lower user cost and less in-vehicle travel time than dynamically routed vehicles offering service on request).

The disaggregation of the different components of a total trip (feeder, line-haul, distribution) can be the basis of different paratransit service concepts. Paratransit alternatives can serve as a single part of the overall trip—generally the feeder or distributor components—or they may encompass all three components and provide the entire trip.

The spatial characteristics of service may be organized to define a number of distinct types of spatially oriented operating concepts. Spatial responsiveness may be limited, such as "many-to-one" or "many-to-few" feeder services, or it may be unlimited as in "many-to-many" services. Subscription bus, vanpools, and feeder-oriented dial-a-ride services fall into the former category, while shared-ride taxi and some more comprehensive dial-a-ride systems fall into the latter category.

PROVISION OF SERVICE

The manner in which service is provided represents another dimension to differentiate between paratransit alternatives. For example, shared-ride taxi service and many-to-many dial-a-ride service provided by a transit company are conceptually similar with respect to the service provided, but considerably different with respect to operational and institutional implications. Also, carpooling, vanpooling, and subscription bus service are similar with respect to service, but differ with respect to who provides the service and the type of vehicle used.

A wide range of management options exist for the operation of paratransit services. These include:

1. *Public transit service*. The same operator who provides conventional transit can also provide paratransit services. Many dial-a-ride services are currently operated in this manner.
2. *Other public operation*. A human services organization could provide paratransit service. This option is commonly used in providing specialized services for the elderly and handicapped.
3. *Private company*. Private companies are predominant in the taxi industry and also play a major role in providing specialized services.
4. *Corporate*. Large corporations are coordinating and operating vanpooling programs. Corporations also play a major role in many carpooling programs.

5. *Individual.* The individual entrepreneur has principally operated in the taxi industry, special service markets, and carpooling.

INSTITUTIONAL CONSIDERATIONS

Although there are many formidable technical issues relating to paratransit service, the institutional considerations are currently more significant. Technical considerations impact the service potential and cost efficiency; whereas institutional considerations determine whether the service can be provided at all, and in what manner it can be provided.

Some of the primary institutional considerations are regulation, labor provision, and competition and coordination of services.

REGULATION

Regulation of common carriers (i.e., taxis) is generally undertaken in order to protect the public welfare by ensuring:

- Adequate distribution (availability) of service.
- Reasonable pricing of service (rate structure).
- Safe provision of service (vehicle safety, driver qualification, and insurance).

Paratransit services suffer from both overregulation and underregulation. Overregulation generally takes the form of restrictive statutes which may impede efficient provision of service or prevent innovative or integrated service. Underregulation generally takes the form of lack of precise legal definition resulting from statutes with anachronistic attributes which are not flexible enough to deal appropriately with innovative concepts. Local taxi industry regulations influencing the supply and pricing of taxicab service frequently embody the former problem. Regulations—or lack of regulations—affecting vanpools exemplify the latter problem.

In the mid-1920s, local regulatory authorities came under the increasing influence of the private owners of street railways. As a result, jitneys were largely regulated out of existence "to prevent unfair competition." Most taxis operating today are prohibited from providing ridesharing service, for largely similar reasons.

More recently, with the growth of publicly owned mass transportation systems, regulatory control over fixed-route common-carrier operations has, in many cases, been shifted over to public transportation authorities, often with regional (rather than municipal) geographic bases. These authorities generally have control over service aspects (routes, hours, service types, fares) while safety powers (such as driver licensing and vehicle safety requirements) remain vested in the state.

As a result of the recent growth of the transportation authorities, publicly offered services in many areas fall under the regulatory aegis of two independent agencies: conventional transit operations are regulated by the authority, while many private operators (particularly taxis and private carriers) may fall under the jurisdiction of the local police department or public utilities commission. Even worse, some private fixed-route operators may be controlled by both an authority and the public utilities commission—the former may control routes, while the latter may control fares, licensing, and equipment standards.

The exclusion of many paratransit alternatives from enabling legislation leaves certain paratransit services in a regulatory vacuum. For example, if a private taxi operator begins offering shared-ride service, does he need a "certificate of public convenience" from the local transportation authority? If the same service were to be offered by a private bus company under a different name ("dial-a-ride"), such a certificate would undoubtedly be required. When does a taxi stop being a "taxi" and become a "bus"? Who should regulate the provision of publicly offered shared-ride services: local public utilities commissions or regional transportation authorities? The two groups generally bring markedly different philosophies to the regulatory environment, which will significantly affect the cost, quality, nature, and quantity of service provided.

Vanpooling efforts have incurred similar problems. Does vanpooling, in which the driver charges his passengers for the cost of providing service, constitute a "for-hire" service, and as such become subject to common-carrier standards of care, insurance, liability, licensing, route approval, and fare regulation? Existing statutes do not conceptually relate to vanpooling and are simply not definitive as to intent. As a result, many states have modified their regulations to include vanpooling.

There are other regulatory inconsistencies. Insurance requirements and costs differ radically between states. Taxation rulings of the Internal Revenue Service influence the provision, and profitability, of service.

Public policies with respect to paratransit, regardless of the governmental level, should share a common framework of goals:

- Provide a range of different service alternatives.
- Ensure the availability of services at an equitable price.
- Coordinate services in order to promote efficient utilization of resources.
- Protect passenger welfare in areas such as liability insurance, protection from crime, safety, etc.
- Protect vehicle operators in terms of working conditions, job security, and safety.
- Provide an equitable distribution of governmental assistance funds, including protection of the property and rights of private enterprise.
- Ensure equitable taxation and regulation of all service operations.

This common framework of goals, as translated into legislation, regulations, and policy, can be used to affect the provision, nature, and availability of service in three basic ways. First, it can act to constrain undesirable characteristics through either prohibition or disincentive. Second, it encourages desirable characteristics through incentives and regulatory flexibility. Third, it defines the relationships between different regulatory authorities and the different service alternatives, and in doing so, becomes a principal determinant of the interrelationships between alternatives.

The first strategy, constraint, is exemplified by state and local safety, insurance, and service regulations pertaining primarily to operators. The regulations set minimum standards designed to protect the public welfare, private enterprise, and the rights of workers.

The second strategy, incentive, includes fare and regulatory structures that provide incentives for ridesharing to both passengers and operators. Regulations and policies that encourage integration of services also fall into this category, as do planning process regulations which are tied to financial incentives.

The last strategy, definition, is exemplified by state-enabling legislation which delegates regulatory authority between legal jurisdictions for different services and circumscribes those services through the promulgation of certain legal definitions.

A positive regulatory framework has three important charactertistics:

- Consistency and relevance of regulations.
- Appropriate nonconflicting, nonoverlapping roles for regulatory agencies.
- Simple and quick procedures to appeal and change both the regulations and powers of the regulatory agencies.

Few regulatory agencies and structures conform to these characteristics. Regulatory organizations are not likely to participate in their own reform with respect to regulation. Regulatory bureaucracies often become so powerful and so entrenched that it is difficult to modify them even if their shortcomings are widely perceived.

LABOR

Since all paratransit services are labor-intensive, the manner in which the service is provided and, in particular, the role of the driver, has significant impacts on the cost of service. For some services, such as carpooling, vanpooling, and car rental, the driver is one of the passengers who is providing an "in-kind" service. Provision of service through utilization of voluntary labor has three important constraints:

- The necessity to promote, arrange, route, and control a shared-ride system.
- The requirement that service be highly reliable.
- The fact that volunteers often need strong incentives to provide labor and reliability.

The first and second issues generally limit the services offered utilizing self-driver labor pools to prearranged regular (or cyclical) trips. Carpools, buspools, and vanpools using regular workers as drivers exemplify this option. Transportation-related work hours are 100% utilized in productive service, which is in contrast to professional drivers who—whether full- or part-time—generally must incur nonproductive time and mileage costs ("deadheading") in order to move the vehicle from its storage site to the point where it can begin productive service. Clearly, the ability to minimize deadheading will improve service productivity and economic efficiency. Employee-driven vanpools, in which the vehicle is stored at either trip terminus while not in use (and the driver has productive uses for his time, albeit nontransportation related uses), represent the ultimate minimization of deadheading. If no additional uses for the vehicle are available during the midday and evening hours, this may represent a substitution of capital for labor (most likely a very cost-effective substitution). If other uses can be found for the vehicle, the cost effectiveness of the alternative becomes even more favorable, owing to minimized deadheading and the efficient use of capital.

The use of paid professional labor clearly implies incurring deadheading costs. Minimization of deadheading costs is an effective way of increasing both driver and vehicle utilization. Paratransit, or a mix of paratransit and conventional transit, probably offers better opportunities for this than conventional transit.

Those services utilizing a paid professional driver have considerable variations with respect to salary scale, method of compensation, and work rules. Transit companies usually have union drivers with high wage rates, generous fringe benefits, and strict work rules which prohibit the use of part-time employees. Taxi companies may lease vehicles to drivers, utilize nonunion drivers on a commission basis, are usually not bound by strict work rules, and often make liberal use of part-time drivers.

As a result of these differences, paratransit services operated by transit companies generally cost considerably more than similar services operated by taxi companies; but taxi companies often suffer from poorly skilled drivers and very high turnover rates.

The labor situation is extremely complex, often generating strong emotional reactions. Organized labor is viewed with suspicion and frequently blamed for preventing new paratransit services because of unrealistically high wages or unrealistic work rules. Considerable wage increases might make certain viable paratransit services infeasible. However, many of these "viable" services are currently operated in a substandard manner because of the low wages and the type of drivers being attracted at those wages.

Labor difficulties often arise from presupposing labor opposition and by approaching labor unions with suspicion and mistrust. There has been a tendency to exaggerate labor problems and thus establish potential conflict situations between labor and management. Several experiences, such as the Rochester and Cleveland dial-a-ride projects and the Knoxville vanpooling project, demonstrate that if a labor union is involved from the beginning and treated with respect, reasonable arrangements can be developed. In these cases, successful innovative labor arrangements were made by transit companies for paratransit services.

Labor problems do exist. The impact of Section 13(c) of the Urban Mass Transportation Act of 1964[4] assistance program on taxi operators has not yet been determined. Escalation of wages is of concern to the entire transit industry, not just paratransit. Work-rule arrangements for transit are often restrictive and pose major problems when applied to paratransit operations. Unions should realize that there are basic differences between providing transit and paratransit services. In the same way that there are different work rules for transit drivers and mechanics, there should be different work rules for transit and paratransit drivers.

---

[4]URBAN MASS TRANSPORTATION ADMINISTRATION, *Urban Mass Transportation Act of 1964 and Related Laws*, as amended through February 5, 1976 (Washington, D.C.: U.S. Government Printing Office, 1976).

Different organizations view paratransit from their own perspectives. For example, the transit industry is interested in paratransit primarily as a complement rather than as competition to conventional transit. The industry has expressed concern about paratransit whenever a potential threat of ridership loss exists. Memories of jitneys operating cream-skimming routes in the early 1900s cause great concern among transit operators whenever paratransit is discussed.

Does a new paratransit service divert existing transit riders or does it divert people from automobiles and/or create new trip making? Taxi operators and other private providers share the same concerns. We have very little evidence of what really happens, and that evidence is conflicting. In certain cases when new public transportation service was initiated, taxi patronage decreased, in other cases it remained constant, and in other cases it increased. It is essential that we better understand the ridership diversion impact of new paratransit service concepts on existing services.

Few transit operators currently view diversion of peak ridership in a positive sense, even if it can be shown to be economically desirable. They view their primary measure of success to be ridership, and the greatest period of ridership is the peak. As deficits and public concern increase, cost effectiveness will, no doubt, become more important, and the attitude toward diversion of peak ridership might change. That is already occurring in certain areas, such as Sacramento, California, and Knoxville, Tennessee. The transit operators are discouraging additional peak transit riders, encouraging the peak-hour use of carpooling and vanpooling, and placing major emphasis on encouraging off-peak transit ridership.

Certain cases exist where the transit industry supports the use of overlapping paratransit service. The most obvious example is service for the elderly and handicapped. This marketplace has such unique service requirements that the benefits of paratransit are obvious. With time, conventional transit operators will change their view regarding provision of overlapping paratransit service to other specialized markets.

Potential conflicts do exist between conventional and paratransit alternatives. However, these can be grossly exaggerated and should not inhibit intelligent implementation of integrated systems. Existing conventional transit is serving an extremely limited market—the CBD-oriented work trip which generally comprises only 10 to 20% of travel in a metropolitan area. Why concern ourselves with conflicts over that limited marketplace when the other 80 to 90% is unserved? For example, when new vanpool programs are initiated, they could be concentrated in outlying areas where no transit options exist, rather than competing with existing transit service.

The challenge is to develop combinations of services that are compatible with respect to service quality and complementary with respect to system utilization. System and service components should be integrated in a balanced manner that satisfies customer demands, provides for customer choice of different service levels at different costs, and utilizes the various system components in a highly efficient manner. The concept of an integrated system does not imply a single operating agency. Many different services should be offered by different transportation providers, both public and private, in a manner that achieves system coordination and integration, while maintaining the independence of the various operators.

An example of how integrated services with different operators could function is the Allegheny Airlines Commuter System. Over 10 small commuter operators have entered into contract with Allegheny Airlines to augment line-haul service provided by Allegheny. The customer using one of the commuter lines perceives that he is flying with Allegheny—he uses the Allegheny computer reservation system, flights are listed on the Official Airline Guide, Allegheny personnel transfer luggage to connecting flights, and so on. These services are normally not available to a commuter airline service. Allegheny does not chose to operate the commuter lines. It does, however, provide the coordination role.

Coordination of urban public transit services is, of course, far more complex than the Allegheny example. Each of the urban transportation services (e.g., transit, taxi, limousine, and specialized services) has acted in the past as a separate culture with its own procedures and traditions. Thus, there is wide variation in how these industries are structured and function. The private sector operates in a competitive environment with profit maximization as a primary goal. Public-sector operations are typically based on a single service provider, with the primary concern being social benefits.

It is important to differentiate between interest in providing paratransit services and the ability to provide service. An existing provider may be totally committed to a new paratransit concept but lack the organizational flexibility and management expertise to adjust to new service and operational requirements. This is true of both public and private providers. A more serious situation occurs when a provider is asked to implement plans they do not fully comprehend and to which they are not totally committed. Some providers view paratransit as a vogue that will pass and as a diversion from their major interest and true mission. In such instances, failure of new paratransit services becomes a self-fulfilling prophecy.

The brokerage concept has been proposed as a mechanism for service coordination. The idea of having a neutral organization matching together those who need service with those who provide service has much merit. We should realize, however, that we are not dealing with a free market situation in urban transportation. Rather, urban transportation is a public service. While opening up more service options and providers is desirable, basing the choice of options and providers solely on economic criteria can be dangerous. Is it fair to deprive existing public transit companies of more favorable operations, when another (lower-cost) operator can provide a more cost-effective service if, at the same time, we require the public transportation company to be the provider of last resort for important but very unprofitable service?

Another basic issue is whether we should utilize an evolutionary or revolutionary change process. An evolutionary process would utilize an existing organization to coordinate service, whereas the revolutionary approach would introduce a new organization. Primary responsibility for coordination of transportation frequently resides in a regional transportation authority. The charters of these regional transportation authorities are extremely broad, covering far more than conventional transit.

However, necessity to cover ever-increasing deficits has forced many regional transportation authorities to concentrate on existing transit operations. Often a regional transportation authority becomes defensive and adopts a protectionist attitude toward its transit operations. It ceases being an organization concerned with broad transportation responsibilities and becomes a transit operating company.

Regional transportation authorities should broaden their roles, seek involvement with other transportation providers, and assume overall responsibility for coordination of transportation services. Many regional transportation authorities have already begun new activities, such as carpool and vanpool programs and subsidization of private carriers for paratransit service. The federal government should encourage and reward such authorities which take positive steps to become more broadly based. This can be accomplished by providing incentives, such as considering carpool and vanpool passengers formed as a result of transportation authority coordination as increased ridership which could be rewarded by increased federal funding.

If a regional transportation authority is unwilling or unable to assume a more neutral position, then we must look either to other existing organizations, such as metropolitan planning organizations or councils of government, or create some new organizational structures within metropolitan areas that can coordinate planning, regulation, funding allocation, and operation.

Is there any one best solution for coordination? Probably not. In the same way that different service concepts are appropriate in different urban areas, so too organizational relationships between providers will vary between urban areas. It is premature at this time to specify what is best. Rather, a variety of different approaches should be tried, so that the benefits of different alternatives can be determined.

We cannot realistically expect an optimal integration of transit and paratransit services to occur quickly. The following three stages of development are most probable:

1. *Separate systems.* Paratransit services will be provided in areas where there is little or no conventional transit service.
2. *Combined systems.* Paratransit services will augment existing conventional transit in a complementary manner (e.g., feeder systems to line-haul transit). However, few changes will be made to conventional systems to reflect the available paratransit options.
3. *Integrated systems.* A basic restructuring will occur where conventional services are modified and combined with paratransit services in a coordinated manner.

The process of innovation is a slow one. In 1978, we are somewhere between levels 1 and 2. One would anticipate at least a decade to be able to achieve level 3.

SUMMARY

Paratransit has been described as a bridge between the conventional auto and conventional transit. Certain concepts, such as taxi service and carpooling, have developed from the automobile end of the spectrum; whereas other concepts, such as subscription bus service and dial-a-ride, have developed from the opposite extreme. As the continuum of service concepts develop, and there is movement from each end of the spectrum toward the center, certain conflicts are inevitable. Two major cultures, privately operated taxi companies and publicly operated transit companies, who have previously operated independently and differently, must now learn to understand each other's environment and work together. However, to view the problem as simply as taxi versus transit or public versus private is naive. As in all situations involving the assimilation of different cultures, patience, time, and understanding are required. Paratransit is a melting pot of different approaches, where gradual assimilation will occur while fundamental differences remain. Paratransit provides the opportunity to increase available options with respect to both the service and the providers of service. Service can be successfully integrated—at one level, by interfacing paratransit services with each other, and at a higher level, by interfacing paratransit with conventional fixed-route transit in a complementary manner.

SELECTED BIBLIOGRAPHY

Many citations are no longer available from their original source. These citations are often available from the National Technical Information Service, U.S. Department of Commerce, 5285 Port Royal Road, Springfield, Va. 22161. We have verified the order numbers for many of these citations, and they are found at the end of the citation. Prices are available through NTIS at the address above.

KIRBY, RONALD F., AND OTHERS, *Para-Transit: Neglected Options for Urban Mobility*. Washington, D.C.: The Urban Institute, 1975. Also available as PB 234 320.

LEA TRANSIT COMPENDIUM, *Para-Transit*, vol. I, no. 8, 1974. Huntsville, Ala.: N. D. Lea Transportation Research Corporation, 1974.

————, *Para-Transit*, vol. II, no. 8, 1975. Huntsville, Ala.: N. D. Lea Transportation Research Corporation, 1975.

ROSENBLOOM, SANDRA, ed., *Paratransit*, Special Report 164. Washington, D.C.: Transportation Research Board, 1976.

SALTZMAN, ARTHUR, "Para-Transit: Taking the Mass Out of Mass Transit," *Technology Review*, 75, no. 8 (July–August 1973), 46–53.

Also see the bibliographies of Chapters 24 and 33.

Chapter 8

DEMAND-RESPONSIVE TRANSPORTATION

DANIEL ROOS, *Professor, Civil Engineering, Massachusetts Institute of Technology*

Fixed-route transit services have been the primary form of public transportation in most urban areas. These services generally are designed to transport large numbers of passengers along corridors of high demand at a relatively low cost per passenger. Passengers using a single fixed-route service can rarely get direct door-to-door service. Some other mode, usually walking, must often be used to get to and from the fixed-route service, and transfers between fixed-route lines may be required. Therefore, although the level of service for the line-haul fixed-route portion of a trip is typically excellent, the level of service for the total trip is often poor in comparison with automobile travel. Furthermore, many demands in an urban area cannot be satisfied by fixed-route service where no service is provided to link particular travel desires. Thus, fixed-route service plays an important role in urban transportation, but certain service voids exist.

An alternative approach is to respond to customer demands as they occur and provide a more direct service between customer origins and destinations. Conventional taxi service is an example of this approach. Many similar, but less direct, types of service are possible where either the spatial and/or temporal service characteristics are variable rather than fixed. These services, classified as demand-responsive transportation, are discussed in this chapter. In contrast to fixed-route services, demand-responsive services generally carry fewer people at a higher cost per trip, providing a superior level of service and more extensive geographic coverage.

SERVICE CLASSIFICATION

Demand-responsive services can be classified in two broad categories, flexible and hybrid services. With flexible service, both time and space characteristics are variable, thus allowing maximum system responsiveness to customer demand. Hybrid systems combine fixed- and flexible-route characteristics; they, therefore, tend to be less responsive than purely flexible systems. Numerous specific examples of each of these service types exist. Some of the principal ones are described as follows.

FLEXIBLE SERVICES

1. *Exclusive ride.* A single trip is served directly from origin to destination. This type of service is the predominant mode of operation for most taxicab operations.
2. *Group ride.* Several trips with the same origin and destination are grouped together.
3. *Shared-ride.* Trips with different origins and destinations are combined together. The trips are grouped so that only minor detours are made to pick up or drop off passengers. Service can be provided on an areawide *many-to-many* basis (many origins to many destinations) or a more limited *many-to-one* basis many origins to one destination or vice versa). Shared-ride services have often been referred to as "dial-a-bus," "dial-a-ride," or "shared-ride taxi."

HYBRID SERVICES

1. *Route-deviation service.* Vehicles operate on a fixed route, but will detour from the route to pick up or drop off passengers. After the customer is serviced, the vehicle will return to the fixed route. Many jitney services operate in this manner.
2. *Limited-stop service.* Vehicles operate with a limited number of origin and/or destination points. Examples include limousine service, where passengers are typically distributed from one origin point to a limited number of destinations (or vice versa), and peak-hour subscription bus service, where customers are picked up at their homes each morning and brought to the same employment center. (The reverse trip is made in the afternoon.)
3. *Point-deviation service.* A number of checkpoints are established, corresponding to principal activity centers. Vehicles stop at these checkpoints at specified times to pick up or discharge passengers. In between the checkpoints, the vehicles can pick up or drop off passengers on request at any point as long as there is sufficient time to arrive at the next checkpoint on schedule.

Selection of which type of service should be provided is a complex issue depending on many factors, including market needs, economic implications, and institutional factors. Generally, the more flexible service is, the better the level of service provided and the higher the cost per trip. Quite frequently, different services are provided at different times of the day. In the peak hours, where travel volume is high and travel habits are more repetitive, a less responsive service is provided (such as fixed-route or subscription service). In the off-peak periods, when travel tends to be more random in time and spatially dispersed, a more responsive service is provided.

MARKETS AND APPLICATIONS

Demand-responsive transportation services can be utilized to satisfy the following needs:

1. *New service.* In low- and medium-density areas, where little or no transit service exists, demand-responsive transportation can provide intra-area service and/or collection-distribution service to conventional fixed-route service. Because of low densities and widely dispersed travel desires, it is often difficult and expensive to serve these lower-density areas with conventional fixed-route, scheduled service. However, if a demand-responsive service is successful and demand increases, consideration should be given to substituting conventional fixed-route services along the corridors of highest demand.
2. *Additional higher-quality service.* Demand-responsive transportation supplements conventional fixed-route service by providing higher-quality service to specific market groups. The justification for these services is based on the premise that conventional "mass" transit satisfies "mass" rather than individual needs, serving all needs in an adequate manner instead of particular needs in an optimal manner. Before the major growth in availability of the automobile, conventional transit was sufficient, since it was the primary or sole travel alternative. The combined effects of automobile availability, increased affluence, and more dispersed, lower-density urban development suggest the need for additional personalized forms of urban transportation that provide higher levels of service.
3. *Substitute service.* During off-peak periods, when demand is light (particularly late evenings and weekends), demand-responsive services can be substituted for conventional fixed-route transit.
4. *Special markets.* Certain market segments, such as the elderly and handicapped, prefer or require direct door-to-door service because of mobility limitations. The combination of social concern and government regulations have focused attention on the needs of these limited-mobility groups.

An unresolved question in 1978 remains whether the needs of the elderly and handicapped are best served by retrofitting conventional fixed-route vehicles to make them accessible or to providing specialized door-to-door demand-responsive service. Whereas most transportation professionals favor the demand-responsive approach on the basis of better service and lower cost, numerous special interest groups and recent government policies insist on full accessibility of existing fixed-route systems.

HISTORICAL DEVELOPMENT

The first examples of demand-responsive transportation coincide with the introduction of the automobile in the early 1900s. Exclusive-ride taxi services were initiated, and they have continued to play a major role throughout the years. Jitney service was prevalent in the United States during the early 1900s, until it was declared illegal in most urban areas. The transit industry argued that jitneys were "cream-skimming" operations paralleling the most profitable transit routes. Although there are few jitneys that currently operate in the United States, jitneys continue to provide important public transportation services in many foreign countries.

Until the 1960s, exclusive-ride taxi service was the only significant form of demand-responsive service in the United States. Thus, there were essentially two public transportation alternatives available: exclusive-ride taxi service (provided by taxi companies) and conventional fixed-route and scheduled bus and rail service (provided by transit companies).

In the mid-1960s, when the transit industry was experiencing acute problems of decreasing ridership and increasing deficits, a series of new system studies were undertaken by the federal government to determine if new types of urban transportation systems could be developed to reverse these trends.[1] Out of these studies emerged the concept of dial-a-bus, a service designed to bridge the gap between conventional fixed-route, scheduled service and exclusive-ride taxi service. As originally conceived, dial-a-bus would provide many-to-many service and utilize computer and communications technology to schedule and dispatch customer requests for service; early studies heavily emphasized the use of technology.

FIRST-GENERATION SYSTEMS

Several major dial-a-bus research and development efforts were initiated in the late 1960s by such organizations as the Massachusetts Institute of Technology, General Motors Corporation, Ford Motor Company, and the Institute of Public Administration. These efforts identified that dial-a-bus was not a specific system but rather a family of different service concepts. Thus, the focus of research efforts evolved from the single many-to-many dial-a-bus concept to a broader demand-responsive perspective. This broadening was reflected in the initial demand-responsive system implemen-

---

[1]Leon Monroe Cole, ed., *Tomorrow's Transportation: New Systems for the Urban Future* (Washington, D.C.: U.S. Department of Housing and Urban Development, 1968).

tations which began in 1969. During the next several years, approximately 100 new demand-responsive systems were implemented in North America, having the following common characteristics:

1. *Small-scale systems*. The systems involved the operation of 10 or fewer vehicles in small urban areas, generally with populations of 20,000 or fewer people.
2. *Manual dispatching*. Dispatching of vehicles was performed using manual techniques in a manner similar to conventional exclusive-ride taxi service. No new technological advances were introduced.
3. *Flexible operations*. Most operations involved the use of nonunionized personnel who were employed with few work rules and lower wage rates than prevailed for unionized drivers working within conventional transit companies.
4. *Different services*. Many different service concepts were implemented, including, but not restricted to, many-to-many service. In several cases, hybrid services were introduced; and in almost all cases, different services were provided during the peak and off-peak periods.
5. *No transit service*. The areas into which demand-responsive service were introduced had little or no existing transit service. In several cases, the demand-responsive service replaced conventional fixed-route service which had low patronage and/or high cost.
6. *Low fares*. Fares charged were typically 25 to 50 cents a trip. These fares were consistent with fare levels for conventional fixed-route transit service. In a relatively few cases, premium fares were charged to reflect the higher level of service being provided and the higher cost of service delivery.
7. *Increased ridership*. Where a demand-responsive system replaced a fixed-route system, the ridership increased. Relative ridership increases were high, but the absolute numbers were small since the systems replaced carried very modest numbers of riders.
8. *Varied productivity*. Productivity varied from approximately 5 to 20 passengers per vehicle-hour. The highest productivities (10 to 20) were achieved with hybrid systems, while the lower productivities (5 to 10) were achieved with flexible systems.
9. *Varied economics*. Considerable variation in the cost per trip was observed with the range typically $0.50 to $1.50. The lower costs were associated with the systems utilizing nonunion drivers. In all cases, the systems were not designed to break even, and most managed to meet their economic objectives.

The number of small-scale, manually dispatched demand-responsive systems has continued to increase. These systems play an important role in rural areas, towns, and small cities. For example, the state of Michigan has undertaken an ambitious program to implement demand-responsive urban transportation systems in cities under 50,000 population. Since the Michigan DART (Dial-A-Ride Transportation) program was initiated in 1974, 40 new demand-responsive systems had been implemented in the state by 1977, with more planned.[2]

EXAMPLE SYSTEMS

Two brief examples of first-generation systems follow. The first is a flexible many-to-many service in Batavia, New York, a small city of 18,000 approximately midway between Rochester and Buffalo, New York (58 km, or 36 mi, from each). In 1971, a small-scale four-vehicle demand-responsive service replaced a three-vehicle fixed-route service. A comparison of the two after 1 year's operation indicates[3]:

- Ridership increased 40% on the demand-responsive system over the previous fixed-route ridership, even though the fare charged on the new service was more than twice the fixed-route fare.
- The demand-responsive service covered over 75% of its costs out of the farebox in its first year of operation.
- The average cost per trip was approximately 70 cents.

While fares in Batavia have increased only slightly, costs have increased considerably, primarily as a result of inflation. In 1976, the cost per trip was approximately $1.50, with 50% of the operating costs covered by farebox revenue.

The demand-responsive system implemented in Merrill, Wisconsin (population 9000), in 1976 is a hybrid system with fixed- and flexible-route components. A vehicle stops at specified times at 11 checkpoints located near major activity centers. Customers can get on or off the bus at these checkpoints in the same way they would use a conventional fixed-route service. In addition, the bus will, on request, provide doorstep pickup or dropoff service between checkpoints. The fare structure is determined by the service provided in the following manner:

- Checkpoint to checkpoint: 25 cents.
- Checkpoint to doorstep (or vice versa): 40 cents.
- Doorstep to doorstep: 50 cents.

During the first year of operation in 1976 the system had the following characteristics[4]:

- Ridership was 160% higher than the previously existing fixed-route service ridership during its last year of operation.

---

[2]MICHIGAN DEPARTMENT OF STATE HIGHWAYS AND TRANSPORTATION, *Michigan DART Program Status Report* (Lansing, Mich.: Michigan Department of State Highways and Transportation, February 1976).
[3]Discussion with officials of Rochester–Genesee Regional Transportation Authority.
[4]MULTISYSTEMS, INC., *Merrill Project Final Report*, Wisconsin Urban Mass Transit Demonstration Program, prepared for the State of Wisconsin (Cambridge, Mass.: Multisystems, Inc., 1977).

- The average cost per passenger was $1.20. Farebox revenues covered 22% of the operating cost.
- Approximately 55% of all passengers used the checkpoint-to-checkpoint service, 30% used the checkpoint-to-doorstep (or vice versa) service, and 15% used the doorstep-to-doorstep option.

SECOND-GENERATION SYSTEMS

By 1973, "second-generation" demand-responsive transportation systems began to develop. These new systems differed from first-generation systems in several significant ways:

1. *Scale.* First-generation systems utilized 10 or fewer vehicles; the second-generation systems have 10 or more vehicles.
2. *Setting.* First-generation systems were implemented in small cities; second-generation systems were implemented in larger metropolitan areas.
3. *Integration with conventional transit.* First-generation systems were implemented in areas with little or no transit service; second-generation systems were implemented in areas where conventional transit service was available.
4. *Control.* First-generation systems utilized manual dispatching; second-generation systems utilized some degree of automation.

Second-generation systems incorporated an integrated-system concept, utilizing both fixed-route and demand-responsive components. The typical approach utilized is to reconfigure the existing fixed-route system to reflect shifts in customer travel demands that have occurred in the urban area. Demand-responsive services are utilized for intra-area service in lower-density areas and feeder service to line-haul fixed-route services. The fixed-route services dominate in the higher-density urban areas.

Second-generation systems have been implemented in Regina, Saskatchewan; Ann Arbor, Michigan; Santa Clara and Orange Counties, California; and Rochester, New York. The Santa Clara system, an overly ambitious and poorly planned project, was not able to satisfy demand with a reasonable service level and was discontinued approximately 8 months after implementation. The other systems are still in operation. New demand-responsive systems are currently planned in the Chicago, Cleveland, and Minneapolis–St. Paul metropolitan areas.

The initial second-generation system implementations utilized existing transit operators to provide both the fixed-route and demand-responsive services. The rationale was to maximize the potential for coordination and system integration. However, experience in operating under this arrangement has revealed the following problems:

1. *Cost.* Union wage rates and fringe benefits are extremely high. The cost per trip of a unionized operation is typically 50 to 100 % greater than for a nonunionized operation.
2. *Work rules.* Most transit companies have rather rigid work rules oriented toward a fixed-route operation. These work rules often constrain the operation of a demand-responsive system.
3. *Orientation.* The management, operation, and approach of most large transit systems are geared toward fixed-route operations. Management often finds it difficult to adjust to different needs associated with demand-responsive service.

A major change that is now developing is to provide coordinated service with fixed and demand-responsive components where the fixed-route components are provided by the public transit operator and the demand-responsive components are provided by a private paratransit operator. In many cases, a taxicab operator is an obvious choice for the demand-responsive service. The taxicab operator has labor costs often 50 % less than those of a transit operator, more flexible work rules, and an incentive pay scale for drivers to encourage improved productivity. To stay competitive, transit labor is now proposing different labor arrangements for demand-responsive services, featuring lower wage rates, use of part-time personnel, and more flexible work rules. A precedent-setting labor arrangement of this variety has been developed by the Greater Cleveland Regional Transportation Authority with its labor union.

Westport, Connecticut, provides a good example of how a privately operated demand-responsive service can be combined with a publicly operated fixed-route service. In April 1977 the Westport Connecticut Transit District inaugurated a "Maxytaxi" shared-ride taxi service to complement the existing bus service. The transit district contracts with a local taxi operator paying on a cost-plus-fixed-fee basis with an additional incentive fee based on passengers carried, productivity, and safety performance.

Preliminary results for the first half-year of operation are:

1. Ridership on the shared-ride service increased from 400 passengers the first week to over 2500 passengers per week in mid-December.
2. The service is recovering 60 % of its costs, with the recovery percentage increasing with increasing ridership. The goal of a near break-even operation appears feasible if ridership increases continue at the same weekly rate.
3. Ridership on the regular Minnybus service has increased in comparison with the previous year. The increase appears to be related to the new Maxytaxi service.
4. Only 10 % of the users of the shared-ride taxi service previously used the exclusive-ride taxi service; a new market has been developed rather than an existing market being diverted.
5. There has been a 30 % ridership decrease in exclusive-ride taxi service for the company supplying the shared-ride service. However, both gross revenues and

profitability for exclusive-ride service have increased; the operator now concentrates on using exclusive-ride service for more profitable long-haul service while the shared-ride service has absorbed less profitable short-haul trips.

Although the results are preliminary, they are important in several respects. They indicate:

1. Different services attract different markets. The shared-ride fare ($1 to $3 per trip) is significantly more expensive than the bus fare (50¢ per trip—although this fare is frequently significantly lower for riders using a prepaid annual pass), but less expensive then the exclusive-ride taxi service.
2. The new service provides additional options to the automobile, increasing the attractiveness and ridership of existing services.
3. The private provider benefits by having a more profitable overall operation. It was originally anticipated that the exclusive-ride service would be less profitable, but the combination of the two would be more profitable. The increased profitability of exclusive-ride service is a surprise.

New services continue to be introduced in Westport. Several of the Maxytaxi vans are equipped with a wheelchair lift so that areawide service to the physically handicapped is now available. A package-delivery service was recently begun as part of the Maxytaxi service. Small retail establishments which previously bought their own vehicles and utilized part-time drivers are now contracting with the Maxytaxi to provide a similar service at lower costs. The taxi company is also providing supplemental fixed-route service during the peak hours. The transit district is, therefore, able to avoid peaking problems characteristic of most transit operations.

Major problems that have constrained the development of demand-responsive transportation are system reliability and performance. The reliability of small vehicles utilized for demand-responsive service generally has been poor. Vehicle reliability problems have a negative impact on customers, since many systems have not been able to put an adequate number of vehicles on the road, greatly degrading the level of service provided.

The level of service has also suffered as a result of inefficient manual dispatching techniques. The actual wait time and ride time provided customers is often quite different than the promised times. As the size and complexity of the service increases, the ability of a manually dispatched system to provide reliable service decreases. Even when reliable service is provided the total travel time is much greater than with direct automobile service.

Improved system reliability and performance for larger demand-responsive systems should result from the introduction of automated dispatching. The use of an advanced communication system and computer-assisted dispatching is being tested in an Urban Mass Transportation Administration-sponsored demonstration project in Rochester, New York. Preliminary results indicate that the computer system has a major impact on system reliability (as reflected by measures of variance of wait and in-vehicle travel

Figure 8-1 *Small buses. Samples of small buses used for demand-responsive services with moderate to high passengers per hour per vehicle. Vans and taxicabs are usually used for systems with less ridership. (courtesy of American Public Transit Association)*

Figure 8-2 *Small bus of the type used for demand-responsive service. (courtesy of American Public Transit Association)*

time) and that the computer is more efficient than manual dispatching by as much as 30%. These level-of-service and efficiency improvements suggest that automation can have significantly positive impacts on both the quality and cost-effectiveness of

Figure 8-3 *Sample of small buses used for demand-responsive service. (courtesy of American Public Transit Association)*

demand-responsive transit services. The advent of very inexpensive minicomputers make automated dispatching economically feasible for even modest-size systems.

FUTURE DIRECTIONS

Escalating operating deficits associated with public transportation have greatly constrained system expansions and the introduction of new services in metropolitan areas. Many urban areas are questioning whether they should introduce new services in low- and medium-density areas when it is difficult to support ongoing services in higher-density areas. On the other hand, lower-density suburban areas are frequently making significant contributions to a regional funding base for public transportation and are expecting service in return. Providing service to these lower-density areas will be expensive regardless of whether it is fixed-route, demand-responsive, or a combination of the two. Several basic issues must be resolved. First is a resource allocation question—how much money should be spent on public transportation as opposed to other public services? Next is the question of where and how that money should be spent (suburbs or inner city, specialized markets or generalized service, fixed-route or demand-responsive service, etc.). Each urban area must set its own goals and objectives in order to resolve these complex issues.

Since the demand for public transportation in suburban areas is low in comparison with higher-density areas, extensive geographic coverage can be provided in a suburban area with a small-scale demand-responsive service. This approach implies an acceptance of high unit trip costs; however, the per capita trip costs are relatively low.

Thus, all people in the area are provided with some public transportation alternative.

Experience with demand-responsive service during the past decade indicates that it is certainly not a panacea for all our urban transportation problems. It has not been able to produce significant diversion of existing automobile travel to public modes. It does, however, serve certain important needs. In particular, it can provide a public transportation alternative for lower-density markets and serve as a necessary public service for the mobility-disadvantaged markets, particularly the elderly and handicapped.

With the exception of exclusive-ride taxi service, demand-responsive services are relatively new services. As such, we are still learning to design, implement, and operate them. Each year, improvements are being made so that operational reliability and cost effectiveness should improve.

SELECTED BIBLIOGRAPHY

MICHIGAN DEPARTMENT OF STATE HIGHWAYS AND TRANSPORTATION, *Dial-A-Ride Transportation*. Lansing, Mich.: Michigan Department of State Highways and Transportation, October 1975.

POPPER, R. J., AND M. D. BENT, "Simulation Modeling of Demand Responsive Rural Public Transportation Services," in *Modeling and Simulation 7*, Part I, pp. 439–44. Pittsburgh, Pa.: Instrument Society of America, 1976.

TRANSPORTATION RESEARCH BOARD, *Demand-Responsive Transportation*, Special Report 147. Washington, D.C.: Transportation Research Board, 1974.

———, *Demand-Responsive Transportation Systems*, Special Report 136. Washington, D.C.: Transportation Research Board, 1973.

———, *Demand-Responsive Transportation Systems and Services*, Special Report 154. Washington, D.C.: Transportation Research Board, 1975.

TRANSPORTATION SYSTEMS CENTER, *Demand-Reponsive Transportation: State of the Art Overview*, Technology Sharing. Cambridge, Mass.: Transportation Systems Center, August 1974.

Also see the bibliographies of Chapters 7 and 24.

Chapter 9

COMMUTER RIDESHARING

LEW PRATSCH, *U. S. Department of Energy*

A good motto to describe the basis for the success of commuter ridesharing might read—Commuter Pooling Is Better Than Driving Alone. When all is considered, the individual has a better way to get to work. Pooling program sponsors, whether employers, private entrepreneurs, or citizens' groups, are usually pleasantly surprised by the degree of participation (market penetration). Often, it is much higher than was anticipated when the programs were conceived.

Traditional thinking has held that the commuter was in love with his privately driven automobile. In increasing numbers commuters have left their cars at home and switched to the fast, convenient alternatives painstakingly arranged by employers and home-based groups. Notable employer-sponsored carpool-matching programs in the 1960s, often combined with priority parking privileges, were able to more than double automobile occupancy at major employment sites. In the late 1960s, determined residential-based organizations labored within obstructive regulations to establish viable commuter bus groups. In the early 1970s, the commuter bus and carpool modes were strengthened by a new midsized vehicle—the van—which was offered with driver incentives and door-to-door service at an unsubsidized price the commuter would accept. The trends emerging in the mid-1970s are the employer-based multimodal (carpool, vanpool, and buspool) programs; the third-party approach, where vans are provided and vanpools organized by other than the employer or employee; and the individually owned and operated approach, where a commuter provides the van and organizes the vanpool. Each of these three vanpool options have demonstrated their ability to best serve specific commuter markets. These well-developed programs, often designed by the commuters, have achieved continuous growth, usually over a period of 2 or 3 years, as commuters become familiar with pooling modes. Designing a pooling program, however, is not necessarily straightforward and easy. Very few, if any, programs could be considered identical, as all were designed to accommodate local needs.

Shortly before and during the oil embargo of 1973–1974, urbanwide carpool-matching programs were sponsored by a few radio and television stations as a public service. Soliciting commuters to submit data forms by mail for computer carpool matching was found to be inadequate for establishing the sufficiently large data base needed to provide good matching opportunities. As a result of these public service programs and subsequent government-funded urbanwide programs, less than 1% of the auto commuters were provided with viable matches for carpools. Only a handful of these programs continued to exist 3 years after the oil embargo.

Most commuters must resort to hit-or-miss tactics to find a convenient carpool. The major exceptions have been well-organized, and voluntary, employer-sponsored commuter ridesharing programs where vehicle-miles of travel (VMT) have been reduced as much as 50%. The challenge of developing and administering a viable urbanwide pooling program which reduces traffic congestion and vehicular travel by at least 5% is still the dream of many environmentalists, conservationists, and commuters. In fact, it is still a dream for the promoters of any mode or combination of modes. However, a survey conducted in 1974 of employer-sponsored carpool programs shows a 23% reduction in commuter VMT among 197,000 employees from a wide range of companies and cities as well as from both white- and blue-collar professions.[1] A strong indication that such programs do work, and that the concepts are sound, is derived from the fact that well-managed programs have continued to grow regardless of oil availability.

Even though 47% of the nation's automobile commuters are already in private multioccupant cars carrying about 2.5 persons/car,[2] little research has been conducted to substantially increase this base of commuter ridesharing. While successful commuter ridesharing programs continue to expand, the nation has just started up the long learning and growth curve. Far more innovation and determination is required to bring commuter pooling to its maximum usage.

CONCEPTUAL OVERVIEW

The U. S. Environmental Protection Agency (EPA), Department of Transportation (DOT), and Department of Energy (DOE) place commuter pooling among the most powerful tools available to achieve their respective goals of pollution abatement, traffic reduction, and energy conservation. Commuter pooling, consisting largely of

---

[1] LEW PRATSCH, *Carpool and Buspool Matching Guide* (4th ed.). (Washington, D.C.: U.S. Department of Transportation, Federal Highway Administration, January 1975), p. 1.

[2] U.S. DEPARTMENT OF TRANSPORTATION, *Carpool Incentives and Opportunities*, Report of the Secretary of Transportation to the United States Congress pursuant to Section 3(e), Public Law 93-239, Emergency Highway Energy Conservation Act. (Washington, D.C.: U.S. Government Printing Office, February 1975). Now available as PB 241 823.

car- and vanpools combined with elimination of zoning, insurance, and regulatory barriers, not only offers potential for rapid and inexpensive reductions in traffic congestion, air pollution, and energy consumption, but is the most likely option available within the next 10 years capable of substantially reducing commuter VMT.

The vast majority of carpooling and vanpooling potential is derived from markets with little or no conventional bus or fixed-rail service. This potential exists in essentially two major markets: (1) the urban areas of less than 500,000 in population comprising one-half the nation's population with little if any transit service, and (2) the urban areas in excess of 500,000 population with fast-growing suburban-to-suburban markets which now constitute nearly one-half of typical urban area employment or one-fourth of the nation's population. This market has negligible transit service. Thus, about three-fourths of the nation's population is without viable transit alternatives.

Serving at least 10% of this market would be extremely difficult for any mode except cars and vans, owing to low residenital densities and ubiquitous travel patterns. Obviously, there are plenty of empty automobile seats, as only about one-fourth are in use as commuters travel to work. With van production around 600,000 units per year, availability of vans is hardly questionable. This contrasts with buses and fixed rail, which are virtually saturated at rush hour. In addition, the annual production of 5000 buses and 150 rail vehicles per year represents mostly replacement vehicles.[3]

The most significant market for potentially reducing VMT is the 27% of automobile commuters traveling over 16 km (10 mi) to work. This group accounts for 68% of the VMT. (See Table 9-1.) Only about 20% of this group would have to start vanpooling to reduce commuter VMT by 10%. This group is also the most likely to car- and vanpool due to the cost, boredom, and time involved in longer trips and the inability of buses to serve this widely dispersed market. The average vanpool travels 40 km (25 mi) one way and serves this long-distance market with ease. This is a clear-cut distinction between the vanpool market and the typical transit market. The vast majority of the transit users travel less than 16 km (10 mi) one way.

Comprehensive pooling programs have the potential to reduce commuter VMT by an average of 10% throughout the nation by 1985, and this will cause reduction in traffic congestion, air pollution, and energy consumption by even greater percentages.

To provide additional insight into the relationship between VMT and three dependent variables (traffic congestion, air pollution, and energy consumption) a cursory review is in order. It is well known that speeds over 88 km/h (55 mi/h) consume increasing amounts of energy. What is not well known is the relationships of these variables at lower speeds. An example best demonstrates these relationships. The Washington, D.C., Council of Governments reported that 35% of peak-hour travel is on congested arterial streets operating at level-of-service F or under 24 km/h (15

---

[3]AMERICAN PUBLIC TRANSIT ASSOCIATION, *Transit Fact Book*, 1975–76 ed. (Washington, D.C.: American Public Transit Association, 1976), p. 40.

TABLE 9-1
Characteristics of the Nation's Commuter

One-Way Trip Length	Percent of Workers	Percent of Home to Work VMT*	Projected Travel Time (minutes)
5 miles or less	52.1	13.9	15 and less
6-10 miles	20.9	17.8	16-25
11 miles and over	27	68.3	26 and over

*Metric conversion 1 mi = 1.6 km..

Source: Paul V. Svercl and Ruth H. Asin, *Nationwide Personal Transportation Survey (Study): Home-to-Work Trips and Travel,* Report no. 8, prepared for FHWA (Washington, D.C.: U.S. Department of Transportation, August 1973). Data based on unpublished table T-5 from the Nationwide Personal Transportation Survey conducted by the Bureau of Census for the FHWA, 1969-70. Report now available as PB 242 892.

mi/h).[4] Level-of-service F is essentially equal to a volume/capacity (v/c) ratio of 1.0 (see Fig. 9-1). If a pooling program reduces arterial VMT 10%, equivalent to a v/c ratio of 0.9, the average speed jumps 53% from 24 to 37 km/h (15 to 23 mi/h) on curve I. Similar relationships exist for freeways. Such speed increases have favorable impacts on both air pollution and energy consumption. Two major auto-related pollutants, carbon monoxide (CO) and hydrocarbon (HC), decrease significantly as speed increases. (See Figs. 9-2 and 9-3.)

Nitrogen oxide (NO_x) increases slightly as speed increases (Fig. 9-4). In the 1972 case for CO emissions, as speed increases from 24 to 37 km/h (15 to 23 mi/h) the emissions drop 36% from 24 to 16 g/km (39 to 25 g/mi). When combining the 10% drop in VMT with the resultant drop in emissions of 36% an overall reduction of 46% has occurred. While this drop in CO emissions will be most effective in critical central business district (CBD) locations, it may not be representative of an entire highway network.

Table 9-2 shows how fuel economy is effected by variation in the steady cruise speed and urban driving. Three things can be seen from this information. The best fuel economy occurs at a steady speed of between 48 and 80 km/h (30 and 50 mi/h), and there is a substantial penalty for stop-and-go driving and slower speeds in urban areas. Unfortunately, little documentation is available for speeds under 32 km/h (20 mi/h).

The existing automobile fleet represents an enormous underutilized resource at rush hour. In 1970 the average commuter automobile carried only 1.4 persons/car, equivalent to a 28% occupancy rate (assuming 5 seats/car).[5] In many cities, such as

---

[4]RONALD SARROS, *Existing Transportation Systems in the Washington, D.C., Metropolitan Area: A Findings Report* (Washington, D.C.: Metropolitan Washington Council of Governments, June 1972), p. 69.
[5]HARRY E. STRATE, *Nationwide Personal Transportation Survey (Study), Report no. 1: Automobile Occupancy* (Washington, D.C.: U.S. Department of Transportation, Federal Highway Administration, April 1972), p. 7. Now available as PB 242 885.

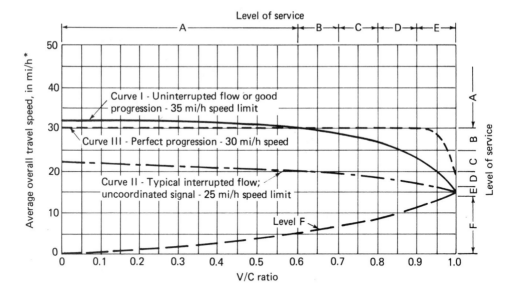

Typical relationships between v/c ratio and average overall travel speed in one direction. A is a condition of free flow; B denotes stable flow with slight delays; C is stable flow with acceptable delay and average speed of about 20 mi/h; D approaches unstable flow; E means unstable flow with intolerable delay; and F means forced flow, jammed traffic with an average speed of less than 15 mi/h.

*Metric conversion: 1 mi = 1.6 km.

Figure 9-1   *Highway levels of service. [Source: Highway Research Board, Highway Capacity Manual: 1965 (Washington, D.C.: Highway Research Board, 1965), p. 320.]*

Dallas, Minneapolis, and Los Angeles, the average is even lower at 1.2 persons/car. For a 0.1 upward shift in the national occupancy rate (persons/car), the consumers save about $1.0 billlion in annual gasoline costs. In addition, reduced expenditures for new commuter facilities and the benefits of an improved environment are incalculable.

To achieve such an upward shift, new marketing approaches including commercialization of third-party approaches and encouraging individually owned and operated vanpools in addition to employer-sponsored pooling programs are necessary. This is true because the majority of commuters work for employers too small to sustain viable independent programs.

While major employers with at least 500 employees per site are the current leaders in pooling, the fact remains that this market constitutes only 25% of all employees. The remaining 75% must be served through a mechanism which brings smaller employers or residential groups together to form large enough bases for viable programs. One innovative concept which can serve all types of highway-related markets, including commuters, is the "transportation broker." The transportation broker, similar to the insurance, real estate, or stock broker, would bring buyers and sellers of

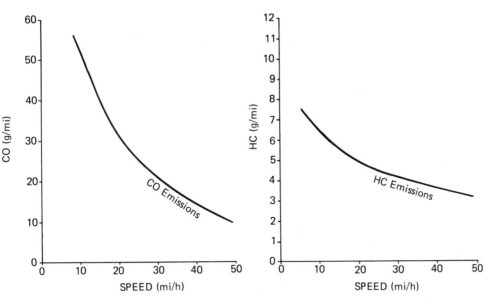

Figure 9-2* *Air pollutant (CO) emission factors as a function of speed*

Figure 9-3* *Air pollutant (HC) emission factors as a function of speed*

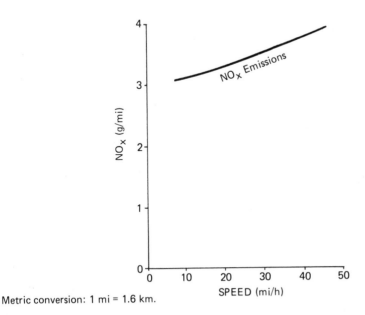

Metric conversion: 1 mi = 1.6 km.

Figure 9-4* *Air pollutant (NO$_x$) emission factors as a function of speed*

*Source: U.S. Environmental Protection Agency, *Supplement no. 2 for Compilation of Air Pollutant Emission Factors*, 2nd ed. (Washington, D.C.: Environmental Protection Agency, April, 1973), p. 3.1.

TABLE 9-2
Fuel Economy vs. Vehicle Speed[a]

	Speed (mi/h)	Fuel Economy (mi/gal)
Urban driving	20	10.0
Cruise	20	16.5
	30	22.0
	40	22.5
	50	21.5
	60	19.5
	70	17.3

[a]Metric conversion: 1 mi = 1.6 km; 1 gal = 3.8 l.

Source: U.S. Environmental Protection Agency, *A Report on Automobile (Automotive) Fuel Economy* (Washington, D.C.: Environmental Protection Agency, October 1973), p. 26

transportation services together by packaging services acceptable to both. The broker's responsibility would be to assist buyers in identifying their specific needs and then seeking the lowest-cost provider (i.e., transit operator, carpool and vanpool operators, taxi or limousine operators) to service those needs. The providers could be fellow commuters willing to share driving. The city of Knoxville, Tennessee, was the first to suggest and implement the brokerage concept. They established a problem-solving orientation and are concentrating on starting, operating, and managing a multimodal, multiownership system.

Another innovative approach could be modeled after the Pentagon's new means of arms procurement designed to cut costs (i.e., broad performance specifications rather than detailed specifications). The Pentagon describes to potential contractors the job that a proposed weapon must accomplish and then lets the companies compete to design the best weapon to do the job. It is up to the contractors to decide whether to use guns, missiles, or bows and arrows. The Pentagon reviews the responses, and a number of design contracts are awarded. Later a few of the companies are picked to produce competitive prototypes. Also included in the analysis are the operation and maintenance costs over the life of the weapons system. These costs can amount to three times the purchase price. After testing the prototypes, the Pentagon awards a production contract to a firm. Likewise, in reducing urban VMT a government agency could fund design contracts for reducing commuter VMT by 5% in each of 10 cities. The apparent best—most cost-effective—approaches could be funded. For those successful contractors, additional contracts would be awarded for additional cities.

The complexity of developing and successfully implementing diverse pooling programs such as the 3M Company Vanpool, Reston Commuter Bus, Inc., or multiemployer programs leads one to believe that one organization cannot fill all the demands. Citizen groups, employers, government agencies, and private operators have all been instrumental in the successful approaches developed to date.

Claims that "voluntary carpooling isn't working," however, simply reflect the fact that there have been no comprehensive, well-funded national or local marketing programs similar to ones used in the automobile or appliance industries. Even without such marketing and promotion programs, spontaneous carpooling captures over one-third of the commuter market. The programs implemented by Hallmark Cards, 3M Company, Reston Commuter Bus, Inc., Colonial Transit, Inc., CONOCO, GEICO, Southern New England Telephone, the Pentagon, Speciality Transit, Inc., Texas Instruments, Cenex, and Polisar are not stereotyped programs, but unique programs serving unique situations. A national marketing program would not only be supportive of such efforts, but would furnish an incentive to similar endeavors.

RIDESHARING SYSTEM DESIGN

Typical commuters want the best possible service they can afford. The vast majority have access to cars and view the cost of commuting by car as either negligible or affordable. Commuters demand a high level of service modeled largely after the "number 1" commuter mode, the privately driven automobile. Any alternative must be convenient, fast, door-to-door service competitive with the automobile. The service must be tailored to their working hours, be reasonably priced, provide a guaranteed comfortable seat, avoid the problems of inclement weather, minimize transfers, and limit their responsibilities to others (i.e., many commuters would rather ride than drive).

To cater to these commuter needs and desires, virtually all successful pooling programs include in varying degrees four essential ingredients: matching, promotion, incentives, and permanence.

To provide these services, two major approaches have emerged, employer-based and urbanwide systems. Well-managed employer-sponsored programs have achieved the greatest market penetration. Employers participating in urbanwide programs have been responsible for a substantial portion of the success in these programs, as working with employers remains the leading means of obtaining commuter involvement. It is also a "natural," as employee starting times and work site are the same and the employer is often in a position to provide encouragement and priority parking.

MATCHING

The cornerstone of any pooling program is the matching of the commuter's time–origin–destination (TOD) needs. Often the only assistance a commuter needs is knowledge of with whom to carpool conveniently. One individual was known to search a telephone book for nearby residences and call a few each night until forming a carpool, but this is a tedious process indeed. To form convenient carpools, the potential matching service must extend beyond friends and associates to virtually all employees at a specific location. By enlarging the universe of prospects, the probability of locating partners within reasonable proximity is greatly enhanced. While the large employers can operate a matching system independently, the smaller employers must have access to a multiemployer matching system for good matches.

Commonly used matching systems are either manual or computerized. Manual systems typically use a large wall map located in a central location at a facility. Referring to a grid or zip code overlay, employees fill in a small card with name, address, phone number, and desired starting time and place the card in a pigeonhole numbered to correspond to their grid number on the map. While these systems are better than nothing, it is rare to find 30 % of the employees maintaining a card on file even if they carpool—it's just too much bother. Often companies with more than a few hundred employees start with a manual system and, after initial successes, switch to a computer system. It is much easier to update computerized information on new or moving employees.

While a number of companies have designed in-house computer-matching systems, the most widely used is the Federal Highway Administration (FHWA) computerized ridesharing-matching system. Techniques include grid-based or automatic address coding. The automatic address coding eliminates the necessity of the applicants locating their residential locations on a grid map and entering them on the data form. The FHWA program streamlines the process of locating potential vanpools and buspools and has a transit information option which allows the commuter to obtain carpool and transit information simultaneously.

The actual matching is relatively routine once the data are collected. The biggest challenge is obtaining a high rate of participation for matching. Matching by zip codes, available through personnel files, has been used for initial vanpool potential surveys, but it is rarely used for carpool matching. While better than nothing for carpool matching, they are often irregular in area size and shape, making matches which are often less than desirable.

PROMOTION

Only limited use has been made of professional marketing or advertising techniques for the promotion of ridesharing. The best single source is often corporate or union endorsement of the concepts via a letter and/or brochures signed by respected officials. This correspondence often identifies priority parking, if any, savings to the commuter, and community benefits. Limited public service advertising has been provided, but it is ineffective to provide considerable advertising without a complete program package, including bona fide matching, to support the advertised concepts. Professionally designed advertising is an important component of any comprehensive ridesharing program.

INCENTIVES

Incentives to implement a ridesharing program exist not only for the commuter but also for the employer and the government. Ridesharing will increase the productivity (efficient usage) of the facilities that would be provided for commuter automobiles. At large facilities where parking is at a premium or long walks are required, priority commuter parking is an excellent incentive. Other employers have provided floating working hours which allow the employee the option of permanently shifting hours to adjust to a bus or carpool schedule. (*Note*: No conclusion can yet be made as to the impact of Flextime[6] on an employee's willingness to share a ride. Some feel it would destroy the bonds that hold a carpool together.) Some employers have agreed to pay part of a vanpool fare in lieu of free parking. This is especially promising where parking costs are high. The savings to the commuter is significant, and if the service is acceptable, he will take advantage of this opportunity.

Employers have an excellent opportunity to save money by reducing the size of the parking facilities needed. Already millions of dollars have been saved by eliminating thousands of parking spaces. Zoning ordinances that formerly required a minimum number of parking spaces per x square feet of work space are now being abandoned as a result of the concern for the environment. Other benefits to employers include reduced absenteeism and tardiness, increased labor market, more-relaxed employees arriving at work, and improved company image. Likewise, government at all levels is beginning to recognize the incentives which can be provided to the commuter in the form of priority ramps, freeway lanes, and park-and-pool lots.

PERMANENCE

Assurance of continued operation of a ridesharing program is an important aspect of a comprehensive program. Commuters do not want their life-styles to be changed by the pooling program going out of existence. Also, the program must assure continued operations to accommodate new or moving employees and those who decide to switch after observing fellow employees' satisfaction. Some form of periodic resurvey directly from the employee or automatic information from the personnel office must supply constantly updated data for matching. Procedures for feedback from the commuters, regularly scheduled review of the program design, and revision of the program operations are also essential.

Most successful ridesharing programs so far have been employer-based. Not enough information is available to provide experienced guidance on the establishment of urbanwide programs operated by government or transportation authorities. The most advisable approach at present seems to consist of government agencies contracting with researchers, marketers, and operators to develop demonstration ridesharing projects, and learning what mechanisms and methods are successful. To translate corporate pooling approaches into successful urbanwide pooling programs, it is suggested that a number of urban-area contractors be given performance or incentive contracts to see what can be accomplished.

FINANCIAL ANALYSIS

Commuting costs are substantial. An individual commuter may pay $2000 per year to drive alone. An employer/business manager may pay $6000 to build each new parking space. A major metropolitan area may pay over $5 billion for a fixed-rail

---

[6]Flextime—a work-hour schedule in which an employee's starting hours can vary from day to day provided that the employee works a core time of 3 to 6 hours each day and a required number of minimum hours per week.

system. Virtually everyone has an economic incentive to improve the productivity of existing facilities, thus increasing the return on our investments. The decision makers should consider increasing ridesharing where it is more cost effective than constructing new highways and parking facilities or increasing transit subsidies.

A comprehensive analysis of commuting costs shows that the automobile driven alone to work is often the most expensive commuter mode, while carpools or vanpools are the least expensive (see Table 9-3). In order to compare the costs of all major modes on an equitable basis it is necessary to consider a downtown-oriented work trip in an urban area in excess of 1 million in population. Even though the U.S. Bureau

TABLE 9-3
Economic Cost of One-Way Urban CBD Commuter Trips,
Combined Modes[a] (urban areas greater than 1,000,000 population), 1975

Travel Mode	Economic Cost per Person 5- to 20-Mile Trips[b]				
	5 mi	10 mi	15 mi	20 mi	Route
Automobile—1 occupant	$2.53	$3.71	$4.90	$6.08	c
Rail transit, kiss-and-ride access[d]	1.64	3.29	4.93	6.57	e
Busway, kiss-and-ride access[d]	1.48	2.95	4.43	5.90	g
Rail transit, walk access	1.37	2.73	4.09	5.46	f
Automobile—1.4 average occupancy	1.81	2.65	3.50	4.34	c
Rail transit, park-and-ride access	1.42	2.62	3.75	4.91	e
Busway, park-and-ride access	1.26	2.28	3.24	4.24	g
Rail transit, bus access	1.12	2.25	3.37	4.49	e
Busway, bus access	0.96	1.91	2.87	3.83	g
Automobile—2 occupants	1.26	1.86	2.45	3.04	c
Bus—conventional	0.88	1.76	2.64	3.52	h
Automobile—3 occupants	0.84	1.24	1.63	2.03	c
Automobile—4 occupants	0.63	0.93	1.22	1.52	c
Automobile—6 occupants	0.42	0.62	0.82	1.01	c
Van—8 occupants	0.36	0.54	0.73	0.92	c

[a] Modes are listed in rank order according to the costs for 10-mile trip.
[b] Metric conversion: 1 mi = 1.6 km.
[c] Half on arterial streets, half on freeways.
[d] Automobile and driver make round trip to rail station.
[e] Half on arterial streets, half on rail.
[f] All rail.
[g] Half on arterial streets, half on busway.
[h] All arterial streets.

Source: Marshall F. Reed, Jr., *The Economic Cost of Commuting,* Technical Study Memorandum no. 13 (Washington, D.C.: Highway Users Federation for Safety and Mobility, July 1975).

of Census indicates that such downtown work trips represent only 9% of total daily work trips, this is the only market where all modes, including fixed rail, are considered. Owing essentially to the high cost of land, these are the most expensive commuter trips.

The costs used in Table 9-3 are the direct costs of the transportation facilities and equipment. The automobile trip includes the capital and operating costs of the automobile, the capital and operating costs of providing downtown parking facilities, and the prorated cost to build, maintain, and operate the highway traversed. The bus trip includes the capital and operating cost of the bus and the prorated cost to build, maintain, and operate the highway traversed. The rail trip includes the capital and operating costs of the rail line, cars, equipment, and stations. Often the commuter perceives only the out-of-pocket costs in comparing commuter costs. Substantial public subsidies on buses and fixed rail make these costs seem smaller; and the private auto costs seem less by assuming that the capital and fixed automobile costs are "unavoidable" if the car is the family car used for other purposes.

The breakdown of the 16-km (10-mi) automobile trip costs shows that only 22%, or 82 cents, of the total costs ($3.71) are clearly out-of-pocket costs (see Table 9-4). Parking costs are largely paid by the businesses, which in 76% of the situations provide free parking to commuters, according to the National Personal Transportation Study. In small cities and most suburban settings with lower residential and employment densities, the costs to provide bus and fixed-rail service often increase substantially while the carpool and vanpool costs drop, as a result of lower parking costs.

TABLE 9-4
Automobile Trip Costs

Cost Element	Economic Cost	Percent
Auto capital	$0.55	15
Auto operating	0.82	22
Highway capital	0.97	26
Highway maintenance and operation	0.03	1
Parking capital	0.91	24
Parking operating	0.43	12
	$3.71	100

Source: Marshall F. Reed, Jr., *The Economic Cost of Commuting,* Technical Study Memorandum no. 13 (Washington, D.C.: Highway Users Federation for Safety and Mobility, July 1975).

With the exception of savings for parking facilities, little documentation exists as to the economic benefits to businesses of sponsoring ridesharing programs. Nevertheless, significant benefits to the company include:

• Reduced absenteeism and tardiness.
• Increased labor markets.

- Increased employee discretionary income (sometimes equivalent to a 5% increase in take-home pay).
- Improved community relations.

While employers indicate the unmeasurable benefits are often substantial, the parking savings alone usually more than justify their investment.

Most employers report relatively low out-of-pocket expenses to establish a pooling program. Companies that have established vanpool programs, considered more expensive than carpool programs, estimate that their one-time total start-up costs range between $10,000 and $30,000. These costs, including out-of-pocket costs, cover the time spent by pertinent groups, such as legal, insurance, personnel, transportation, and service departments, in designing and approving the corporate vanpool policy. Annual operating costs for continuing the programs are much lower but vary considerably based on the size of the program and the type of administration established. Companies report that the additional costs to administer a vanpool program are in the range of $25 per month per van.

Currently, there are no significant federal incentives which favor more efficient utilization of the existing highway system over subsidies for capital investment in transportation facilities and for transit operating costs. The substantial savings which could accrue, however, should be adequate encouragement for local pooling initiatives. In Knoxville, Tennessee, studies have shown that if their urbanwide program was one-half as successful as that achieved at the Tennessee Valley Authority, improvements in critical interstate highway segments could be delayed by as much as 15 years.[7] Dollars for highway expansion due largely to commuter travel loads could be diverted to other urgent transportation needs.

From another perspective, what is it worth to reduce commuter highway VMT by 1%, 2%, or 10% or increase the people-moving capacity of the highway investment by 10%? At one end of the spectrum is a fixed-rail approach. In the Washington, D.C., metropolitan area, a $2.9 billion capital investment for a new fixed-rail system was designed to attract about 10% of the auto commuters to a combined bus and fixed-rail transit system. Serious questions are being raised as to whether the system is worth the revised $5.2 billion price tag. In addition, annual operating costs range between $100 and $200 million. Whether the citizenry can afford, or is willing to pay, the increased tax levy to support the increased price tag is an on-going issue.

In contrast, let us analyze the value of saving 1% of commuter VMT at 10 cents/km (17 cents/mi), a conservative total cost of automobile operation. In the Washington, D.C., area there are roughly 1,000,000 commuters, with about 16% (or 160,000) commuting to work by bus. Assume that the remaining 840,000 commuters average 26 km (16 mi) per day at 1.4 persons/car. This uses 600,000 cars. At 10 cents/km (17 cents/mi) and 250 days/year, the total commuting cost is $408,000,000 per year. Each percent of VMT savings is worth $4.08 million. Thus, an urban area such as Washington, D.C.,

[7]Frank W. Davis, Jr., and others, *Ridesharing and the Knoxville Commuter* (Knoxville, Tenn.: University of Tennessee Transportation Center, August 1975), p. 127. Now available as PB 247 146.

could spend $1 million in tax dollars per year for each 1% of VMT reduction and obtain a benefit–cost ratio in 1 year of 4:1.

Not one city has ever invested in commuter pooling at such a rate, although voluntary employer-sponsored programs have been extremely successful in reducing VMT. Unfortunately, no serious attempts have yet been made to apply the successful principles behind employer-sponsored programs to urbanwide programs.

SUCCESSFUL PROGRAMS

The corporate climate is the most conducive to fostering successful pooling programs, and it represents the largest and fastest-growing segment of the pooling market. Corporate decisions to proceed on such programs usually come from top management. An executive is assigned to oversee the start-up phase and the establishment of a simple straightforward administration system. In the 4 years since the "invention" of the corporate-sponsored vanpool concept, vanpooling has doubled each year, and in late 1977 included 2000 vanpools at 150 sites. A brief summary of a few leading employer-sponsored programs and a citizens-sponsored bus system follow.

TENNESSEE VALLEY AUTHORITY

One of the nation's best pooling efforts is the Tennessee Valley Authority (TVA) program in downtown Knoxville, Tennessee. Overcoming the obstacles of a medium-size city with little traffic congestion and shorter commuter distances than to a major city, this employer of 3000 has reduced commuter VMT by 50% in less than 3 years (see Table 9-5). Development started before the oil embargo, and the program was launched in December 1973, with the first bus carrying four standees. To cover the costs associated with the express bus, the fares were nearly double their former rate. In January 1975, after the number of buses grew to 15, TVA offered an incentive plan with a one-third discount on commuter tickets. In January 1976, ridership was up 800%, and all extra public and private buses (22 in all) available were in service.

With all buses arriving 10 minutes before work, it looks like Grand Central Station on the street outside the TVA headquarters. In an effort to reduce congestion in this vicinity, some buses were scheduled to arrive 5 minutes earlier. Immediately, ridership started declining. The buses were again scheduled as before, and ridership was restored. This testifies to the value of travel time.

Based on the initial success of the TVA pooling program, management and the unions agreed to a continuation of the comprehensive pooling program in lieu of parking spaces at the new Knoxville headquarters, which was completed in 1976. An estimated $5 million in construction costs was saved. In addition to the headquarters pooling program, vanpools were established at a number of other sites. At one site, a four-lane access road to a nuclear power plant construction site was deferred. Since the road was only needed for a few years while over 5000 construction workers would

TABLE 9-5

Modal Shift of TVA Employees in Knoxville

Mode of Transport to Work	November 1973	December 1974	January 1975	June 1975	January 1976
Drive alone (%)	65	42	30	23	19
Ride bus (%)	3½	14	23	29	31
Carpool (%)	30	40	42	43	43
Van, bike, walk (%)	1½	4	5	5	7
Work force	2950	3000	3100	3200	3200

Source: Stanley R. Stokey and others, "An Employer-Based Commuter Ride-Share Program in a Medium Size Urban Area," *Traffice Engineering*, 47, no. 1 (January 1977), 20.

be commuting, the decision was made to increase the average construction worker vehicle occupancy to five persons per vehicle by using hundreds of vans and buses. This was estimated to have saved $7 million in construction costs.

THE 3M COMPANY

The 3M Company in Minneapolis, Minnesota, launched the nation's first commuter vanpool program in April 1973, before the oil embargo. While employment at the company's headquarters site was expected to double, access to the site was limited by the capacity of nearby highway facilities. Assurances were not forthcoming from government officials that adequate highways would be constructed. On-site parking ramps were also inadequate for the anticipated growth. After about 6 months of research and planning, the company agreed to try a six-van pilot program for 6 months. The vanpool was designed to break even with eight paying passengers; the ninth was the driver, who rode free and had private use of the van during the evenings and weekends for a mileage charge. The extra fares for the tenth, eleventh, and twelfth passengers went into the driver's pocket. Within a couple of months after the pilot program started, the company considered it successful and decided to add more vans to meet the growing demand.

Three years later, 91 vans, including 12 privately owned vans, were in operation, carrying over 10% of the employees. A survey found that 49% of the vanpoolers were former automobile drivers and 50% former carpoolers. Overall, 82% considered vanpooling more convenient than their previous mode.[8] A little-noticed part of the 3M program was the increase from 1000 to 2000 in the number of carpoolers. As a result, the number of vehicles arriving at the corporate headquarters actually declined while employment was up 23%, to over 9000 employees. The reduced demand for new parking facilities saved 3M over $2.5 million.

THE CONTINENTAL OIL COMPANY

The Continental Oil Company (CONOCO) in Houston, Texas, recognized the severity of the long-term oil shortage and decided to assist their employees in establishing commuter car- and vanpools in March 1975. Starting with 25% of the 1450 Houston employees in carpools, the company set a goal of 65% pooling. Within a year, the pooling population increased to 16% in vanpools and 36% in carpools. Vanpooling is becoming so popular at CONOCO that employees now ask before buying a house, "Does a van serve this development?" Consequently, realtors are using the availability of van service as a selling aid.

Recognizing an excellent concept, CONOCO management decided to expand vanpooling to as many CONOCO sites throughout the nation as possible. After corporate policy and administrative systems were established for the first site, it was relatively easy to expand to new sites. A number of minor changes were necessary to comply with some state regulations. In one state, the driver was not allowed to pocket

---

[8]ROBERT D. OWENS AND HELEN L. SEVER, *The 3M Commute-A-Van Program: Status Report no. 2* (St. Paul, Minn.: 3M Company, January 1977), p. 51.

the extra fare, so a revised fare and incentive scheme was developed. The driver continues to ride free and has use of the van in the evenings and weekends and is required to accept all riders within a reasonable time and distance variance. The fare is based on a minimum of eight fares, equivalent to a given monthly rate. If, for example, the van was full with 12 people, including the driver, the paying riders would divide the monthly rate by 11, thus automatically reducing each fare. By the middle of 1976, CONOCO had vans in nine states, with sites in other states under development. The nation's smallest known corporate vanpooling site is an oil field with 12 employees and one van.

RESTON COMMUTER BUS, INC.

The Reston Commuter Bus, Inc. (RCB), a nonprofit volunteer commuter group, was established in 1969 to provide an express bus between Reston, Virginia, and Washington, D.C., 40 km (25 mi) away. When a private bus operator was approached about providing the service, the response was "not interested." The operator theorized that affluent suburbanites with two and three cars in the driveway were not interested in buses. Furthermore, the operator commented that if service was started and did fail he would be stuck with a loser which the regulatory body would not allow him to drop. Determined to find a way, Reston residents discovered that a bus could be chartered, but they had to collect fares, determine the routes, and guarantee payment. Unfortunately, the volunteer group had no assets. However, the Reston developer and the bus operator agreed to split the possible losses for a few months. RCB never collected on the guarantee, and the service grew to 23 buses each way in 3 years.

Actually, the bus company's refusal to provide scheduled service was a blessing in disguise, as it led to a flexible user-controlled contract or "buspool" operation. Routes can be improved at will, without the time-consuming scrutiny of a regulatory body; payments from riders are generally made by check; and the routes to and from Reston can be varied en route, allowing the bus to adapt to traffic conditions.

When the public transit authority took over the private bus companies, including the one serving RCB in January 1973, the public agency soon established a no-subsidy policy for RCB, since they received special service. At the time of the public takeover, RCB was paying $40 per one-way bus trip, and after a series of rate increases, the rate was increased to $66.91 in December 1974.[9] To accommodate increased charter rates, the fares were raised to $1.50 one way and a 20 cents subsidy was obtained from Fairfax County. Also, the load factors were raised, often requiring standing. This was unacceptable for a 45-minute commuting trip. After a lengthy and hard-fought battle, RCB dumped the public operator in favor of a private owner-company using part-time drivers and commuters to drive the buses. The cost dropped to $42 per trip, and RCB could once again start expanding service to serve the growing community needs. By 1976, there were 34 buses each way.

---

[9]Washington Metropolitan Area Transit Commission Order 1454, September 5, 1975, Application 861 Docket No. 287, p. 5.

A myriad of institutional obstacles have beset all forms of commuter ridesharing for years. These institutional barriers emerged when public policy was based on past rather than current needs. The post-World War II growth of low-density suburbs, industrial and office parks, shopping malls, and satellite communities presents demand patterns that are vastly different from those of the late 1940s. As travel patterns become more dispersed, the need for flexible, ubiquitous commuter service emerges. With these changes in living patterns, the commuter simply took the path of least resistance and drove alone.

If the nation hopes to encourage massive commuter pooling, regulations must be modernized and the question of legality, which tends to suppress innovation, resolved. Simple solutions must be found to such questions as:

- What can a carpool or vanpool driver charge a rider without risking loss of insurance?
- Are transportation brokers legal?
- How does a citizens' group readily obtain commuter bus service?
- What is a legal carpool?

Fortunately, a precedent has been established for updating laws and working toward a systematic resolution of institutional issues impacting ridesharing. For example, states have passed new laws classifying vanpools as carpools, permitting churches to donate parking facilities for park-and-ride lots without risking their tax-exempt status, and requiring parking garages to provide the height needed for commuter vans.

Concerned citizens in many states will not charge a pool rider because they believe it is illegal or that their insurance will be voided. In many states, carpool drivers are restricted to sharing driving responsibilities or, if fares are collected, only sharing operating costs, such as gasoline, parking, and tolls proportionately with riders. Such a regulation clearly acts as an economic disincentive to carpooling if the driver wants to be fully insured while carrying paying passengers. For example, the total out-of-pocket costs for a typical round trip of 32 km (20 mi) to work in a car that gets 4 km/l (10 mi/gal) would be approximately $1.70—8 l (2 gal) of gas at $0.65, 1 cent/km (2 cents/mi) for tires and oil, no parking fee since 90% of commuters park free. Splitting the $1.70 among five people per week equates to 17 cents per trip, not worth collecting at today's prices. However, if you charged 50 cents per trip, comparable to the transit fare, you would be operating illegally, and would run the risk of voiding your insurance. A risk not worth taking.

In some states, simply sharing driving responsibilities may put the driver in a precarious liability position. Where guest statutes are not in effect, carpool riders may be considered paying passengers, not guests, significantly increasing the liability of the driver. Where the guest statute applies, a person injured while riding in an automobile cannot recover from the driver unless the driver's conduct amounted to willful and wanton misconduct. Where the protection of the guest statute is removed, the driver may be sued for injuries to the passenger arising out of simple negligence. In Ohio, sharing driving responsibilities has been viewed as compensation, removing the guest statute protection. Where the protection of guest statute is removed, coverage provisions of the automobile insurance may be impacted, depending, of course, upon its particular provisions. When carpoolers are uncertain on such legal issues, they will simply avoid getting involved.

The emergence of vanpools, requiring a greater degree of formal organization and the exchange of money, magnified the problems addressed on carpools. Vanpools raised the additional question of driver compensation, insurance costs largely dependent on the way the van is classified, and public utilities regulations. Driver compensation became an issue when it was questioned by a prospective vanpool employer. The employees were to drive commuter vans owned by their employer under a voluntary vanpooling program. The question arose as to whether the time spent driving would be compensable hours of work under the Fair Labor Standards Act. This issue was resolved in an opinion issued by the Wage and Hour Division of the U.S. Department of Labor, which states "that the time spent by employees driving the commuter vans would not constitute compensable hours of work within the meaning of the Act."

The cost of vanpool insurance is dependent on whether the vanpool, or even carpool, is classed as a "for-hire vehicle" or a private carrier. Privately owned vans can obtain insurance for around $500 per year, while groups have had to pay $1400 per year. This difference can easily mean an increase in the fare of nearly $10 per month per person. In general, the for-hire carriers have virtually unlimited liability while a private carrier, such as the private automobile, is generally required to be liable for damage done to occupants of another vehicle and for the occupants of his vehicle where guest statutes are not in effect. This seemingly minor difference can have a substantial impact on the cost of insurance settlements, hence the diffence in the cost of insurance. Fortunately, the major vanpooling employers are either self-insuring or can add, at reasonable cost, vanpool "riders" to their multi-million-dollar corporate insurance policies. This is not true with smaller organizations.

As a result of Minnesota legislation passed April 9, 1976, commuter vans are no longer to be treated as commercial vehicles under the Minnesota no-fault law but as private passenger autos. This means that the passengers in a commuter van who otherwise have auto insurance will initially seek damages from their own insurance company in the event of an accident, and only if they pass the no-fault threshold of $2000 can they seek damages from insurance on the van. Insurance on the commuter van will continue to provide primary coverage for the driver and any passengers without auto insurance. The net effect of this change should be to lower the annual premium on the van insurance, as the initial coverage on most passengers will be spread over the regular auto policies covered by passengers rather than rest entirely on the van insurance.

In early 1975, the California State Public Utilities Commission ruled that a privately owned vanpool was an illegal bus line. The commission also set up new guidelines which stated that vans could operate as carpools with a maximum of nine seats, and only proportionate sharing of out-of-pocket expenses between driver and passengers was allowed. To overcome these guidelines, new legislation was passed which excludes vans from economic regulation as a bus line, provided that the vehicle has less than 15 passenger seats and the driver is on the way to or from his place of employment. By summer 1977, 16 states including Tennessee, Minnesota, North Carolina, and Connecticut made similar changes in their laws.

In Minnesota, commuter vans are exempted from regulation by the Public Service Commission. Additionally, the driver or owners of a commuter van are not held to the standard of care applicable to common carriers nor to the ordinances or regulations that relate exclusively to the regulation of drivers or owners of automobiles for hire (taxis) or other common carriers. Commuter vans remain subject to the motor vehicle regulation, licensing, and taxation of the state, such as those requiring a separate written and driver's test for a Class B license (chauffeur license).

At present, adequate private capital to promote and capitalize on commuter ridesharing may be severely impacted by regulations that limit legal operations. Additional issues center on workmen's compensation, insurance, comparable federal–interstate questions of regulation of vanpooling, tax treatment of in-kind driver compensation, driver liability, classification of commuter services, and zoning regulations which require a minimum number of parking spaces per employee population. If the nation is sincere about substantially reducing commuter VMT, new policies that allow all modes to best serve the markets for which they are best suited must be developed.

SELECTED BIBLIOGRAPHY

Many citations are no longer available from their original source. These citations are often available from the National Technical Information Service, U.S. Department of Commerce, 5285 Port Royal Road, Springfield, Va. 22161. We have verified the order numbers for many of these citations, and they are found at the end of the citation. Prices are available through NTIS at the address above.

DAVIS, FRANK W., JR., AND OTHERS, *Ridesharing and the Knoxville Commuter*. Knoxville, Tenn.: University of Tennessee Transportation Center, August 1975. Now available as PB 247 146.

OWENS, ROBERT D., AND HELEN L. SEVER, *The 3M Commute-A-Van Program: Status Report no. 2.* St. Paul, Minn.: 3M Company, January 1977.

PRATSCH, LEW, *Carpool and Buspool Matching Guide* (4th ed.). Washington D.C.: U.S. Department of Transportation, Federal Highway Administration, January 1975.

REED, MARSHALL F., JR., *The Economic Cost of Commuting*, Technical Study Memorandum no. 13. Washington, D.C.: Highway Users Federation for Safety and Mobility, July 1975.

STOKEY, STANLEY R., AND OTHERS, "An Employer-Based Commuter Ride-Share Program in a Medium Size Urban Area," *Traffic Engineering*, 47, no. 1 (January 1977), 19–24.

Chapter 10

PEDESTRIAN TRANSPORTATION*

JOHN J. FRUIN, *Research Engineer, Port Authority of New York and New Jersey*

> What a piece of work is a man! How
> noble in reason! how infinite in faculty!
> in form, in moving, how express and
> admirable! in action how like an angel!
> in apprehension how like a god! the beauty
> of the world! the paragon of animals!
>
> *Hamlet,* Act Two, Scene Two

Walking is not generally considered a transportation mode. Perhaps this is because it does not employ vehicles, or because it is such a fundamental means of movement. But walking is actually the most vital means of transportation, the one upon which all the activities of society ultimately depend. Upright human locomotion has been recognized as man's most significant evolutionary accomplishment, a unique physical skill that has advanced him eventually to the "walk" on the moon. Walking has been interwoven into all aspects of man's development. It has been said that the first cities were invented to avoid cumbersome and hazardous transportation by collecting the means of survival and prosperity within convenient walking distance. Even in the mechanized society of today, walking is the primary means of internal movement

---

*Much of the material in this chapter has been presented in different form in JOHN J. FRUIN, "Pedway Systems in Urban Centers," *Civil Engineering*, 43, no. 9 (September 1973), 63–66; JOHN J. FRUIN, "Passenger Terminal Design," *Transp. Eng. Journal of ASCE*, 100, no. TE3 (August 1974), 675–86; and JOHN J. FRUIN, "Service and Capacity of People Mover Systems," *Transp. Eng. Journal of ASCE*, 99, no. TE3 (August 1973), 489–97.

within cities, the only means of attaining the necessary face-to-face interaction involved in all the commercial and cultural activities comprising the urban milieu. With the exception of cycling, walking is the only means of human movement by which we can dramatically experience the sensory gradients of sight, sound, and smell that define a "place."

As a means of transportation, walking has many important attributes, most relating directly to the quality of life. Walking provides a versatile linkage between transportation modes which would be impossible to duplicate by other means. The practical range of human walking distances determines the effective service area, convenience, and utility of transit systems. As a transportation mode, walking is continuously available, travel times are predictable, its routes ubiquitous and easily maintainable, service is reliable, free, nonpolluting, non-energy-consuming, and for many, walking provides a healthful, relaxing exercise. The pedestrian mode is gaining recognition as a basic building block in urban system design. Increasing attention is being given to developing vehicle-free zones to reduce urban pollution and return the inner city to its former role as a place for personal interaction. Attempts are being made to improve the walking experience, to make it more safe, convenient, and attractive.

PEDESTRIAN TRANSPORTATION IMPROVEMENT OBJECTIVES

Safety heads the list of improvement objectives for pedestrian transportation because of the annual toll of more than 300,000 pedestrian accidents and 8000 fatalities, about 17% of the total highway casualties in the United States. Because the pedestrian is forced to share the roadway with the automobile, he is particularly vulnerable to serious injury and death. Although pedestrian accidents occur on virtually every type of roadway, 85% of all pedestrian accidents and two-thirds of the fatalities take place on the urban and suburban streets. Twenty-five percent of the pedestrian fatalities are children under age 15, and a widely disproportionate 50% of the fatalities are adults of 40 years or more. While each pedestrian accident has its own particular causes, all have certain factors in common. These center on behavioral error of drivers and pedestrians, the design of the vehicle and its performance, and environmental factors at the accident scene. Pedestrian accident studies indicate that we do not fully understand the complex man–vehicle–environment interaction contributing to pedestrian accidents. For example, one study of accidents in marked and unmarked crosswalks showed a much greater accident experience in the marked crosswalk, perhaps because the pedestrian viewed it as his refuge, whereas the motorist did not. One thing is clear: the only positive pedestrian accident countermeasure is the separation of the pedestrian from the vehicle by providing separate movement systems for both, an idea suggested 500 years ago by Leonardo da Vinci.

The term *pedestrian system* is being increasingly used in recognition that the approach to pedestrian pathway ("pedway") development must be just as systematic as the techniques that have been applied to highway design and development. The primary goals and objects of pedestrian system development are safety, as previously discussed, and the improvement of the physical features of the system to enhance its comfort, security, convenience, continuity, coherence, imageability, and attractiveness. Pedestrian system development not only requires a basic understanding of pedestrian traffic flow characteristics similar to that developed for vehicular flow, but also requires a greater understanding of human behavioral factors.

The comfort of pedestrians is often given little consideration. Even in the worst weather, pedestrians must wait patiently while comfortably enclosed drivers pass by in preemptive traffic priority. Opportunities for weather-protected access systems for pedestrians are sometimes overlooked. For example, from the standpoint of the pedestrian, there is a significant difference between a suburban transit station built on an embankment versus one built on an elevated structure. The elevated station provides a covered, linear "spine," giving the pedestrian a long, weather-protected pathway for access to parking or other transfer modes. Additionally, because cars may be parked beneath an elevated structure, the average walking distance from parked vehicles to the station platform is short. The embankment station provides no covered pathway, and the greater land coverage created by the filled area forces the location of parking away from platform entrances.

Security, convenience, continuity, coherence, imageability, and attractiveness are all related to the utility and spatial configuration of the pedestrian environment. The security of pedestrian systems is enhanced by providing clear lines of sight, good lighting, and where necessary, police presence, either by means of on-site surveillance or remote TV monitoring. If the use of a pedestrian pathway system is inconvenient, involving circuitous routings and grade discontinuities, it will be avoided. The ideal system should connect all major traffic generators with direct linkages in a coherent and easily identifiable configuration. Imageability requires that all the descriptive elements that comprise a space, its edges, paths, nodes, and landmarks, be logically organized to clearly express the image of "place"—a definitive human environment. Attractiveness is related to imageability, but it means more than just aesthetic design. The use of a pedestrian space should be an experience by itself, through the application of well-planned sensory gradients of color, light, sound, surface texture, ground slope, and other interest features.

HUMAN FACTORS AND BEHAVIORAL ASPECTS

Human body dimensions, locomotion characteristics, and behavioral preferences all provide insight into the needs of pedestrians. Normal human locomotion involves many complex skills of balance, timing, and sight which are often taken for granted by all but the physically handicapped. Natural, unimpeded walking requires suitable surface conditions and adequate clear space laterally for the width of the body and the sway characteristic of human locomotion, and longitudinally, or in front of the pedestrian, for perception and reaction to avoid conflicts. Vision plays an important role in human locomotion to determine the condition of walking surfaces, to avoid obstacles or tripping hazards, and for the complex sensory task of judging and tracking the velocity and rate of closure of moving obstacles. The pedestrian's ability to avoid collisions with other pedestrians and moving objects by constantly changing pace, speed, and direction is a most remarkable human skill.

Stair locomotion is a distinctively different activity than level walking because the vertical riser and horizontal tread configuration of the stairs tends to limit many of the aspects of human locomotion that the pedestrian may freely choose when walking. The pacing distance is determined by the length of the stair tread. The height of the riser directly affects the rate of human energy expenditure, and this, coupled with increased concerns about tripping and falling, tends to produce a slower and much more stylized form of locomotion. It has been found that human energy consumption for climbing stairs may vary from 10 to 15 times that needed for walking the equivalent horizontal distance. Surprisingly, descending stairs consumes about three times as much energy as the level. Safety problems, increased energy requirements, and the added complexities of stair locomotion make the use of stairs more difficult for the handicapped. Locomotion on ramped surfaces with slopes up to approximately 3% is practically the equivalent of level walking for most pedestrians, including the handicapped, but as slopes approach 8% locomotion becomes more labored and speed is reduced.

Human body dimensions as well as psychological aspects governing the use of personal space are also important in understanding pedestrian requirements. The plan view of the human body can be viewed approximately as an ellipse with the body depth as its narrowest dimension and shoulder breadth as its widest. A compilation of body dimensions from a number of human factors studies shows that the fully clothed dimensions of the 95th percentile of the population (95% are less than this) are 33 cm (13 in) of body depth and 58 cm (23 in) shoulder breadth. The plan view area of the average male human body occupies an area of approximately 0.14 m^2 (1.5 ft^2). A 46×61 cm (18×24 in) body ellipse equivalent to a standing area of 0.21 m^2 (2.3 ft^2) per person [i.e., SMP (SFP)] has been used by the New York City Transit Authority (NYCTA) to determine the practical capacity of its subway cars. However, psychological research has shown that pedestrians prefer to avoid physical contact and will generally select much larger personal areas where freedom of choice exists. Observations of pedestrian occupancy in elevators indicate that unavoidable physical contact begins at personal areas of 0.26 SMP (2.75 SFP) but that the preferred human buffer zones in psychological experiments range between 0.5 and 1 SMP (5 and 10 SFP). As a point of reference, an opened 76-cm (30-in)-diameter women's umbrella covers an area of about 0.5 m^2 (5 ft^2). The larger personal area preferences of 0.5 to 1 SMP are generally observed in crowded, but free-standing queues at crosswalks, bus stops, and other similar locations; whereas the smaller personal area occupancies, involving physical contact, are usually acceptable only in the most crowded elevators and transit vehicles.

The basic body dimensions, human locomotion characteristics, and psychological preferences are useful for understanding the space required for normal human locomotion and the pedestrian traffic relationships developed in the next section. For example, given the width of the human shoulders, the fact that the human body sways back and forth several inches during locomotion, and the desires to avoid personal contact, it can be seen that a pedestrian requires a lateral space of at least 60 to 90 cm (2 to 3 ft) width for comfortable locomotion. His longitudinal spacing, which includes space for pacing and avoiding conflicts, ranges between 2 to 3 m (8 to 10 ft), giving a minimum area for comfortable human locomotion on level surfaces of about 2 to 3 SMP (20 to 30 SFP). This compares with the very small areas observed in queues and other crowded situations where normal locomotion becomes significantly restricted. The minimum space required for normal locomotion on stairs where pacing is limited by tread width and the sensory zone may only extend two to three treads ahead and is, therefore, considerably reduced, averaging about 1 to 2 SMP (10 to 20 SFP). These minimum areas for normal locomotion, developed on the basis of an evaluation of human factors considerations, are useful for comparison with actual personal areas observed in photographic studies of pedestrians.

PEDESTRIAN CHARACTERISTICS

The primary pedestrian transportation characteristics are speed, walking distance, and traffic capacity. Walking speeds of pedestrians have been found to vary over a wide range depending on personal physical condition, age, sex, and many other variables, including such factors as trip purpose, environmental conditions, and traffic density. Normal walking speeds unrestrained by pedestrian crowding vary between 46 and 107 m/min (150 and 350 ft/min) with the average at about 82 m/min (270 ft/min). As a point of comparison, running the 4-minute mile of competitive track athletics is the equivalent of 402 m/min (1320 ft/min) or about five times the normal average locomotion speed. Average human walking speeds are known to decline with age, particularly after 65, but even healthy oldsters are capable of increasing their average walking speeds by 40%, so as to outdistance the casual younger stroller. Dense pedestrian traffic flow has the effect of reducing the speed of all persons in a traffic stream by reducing effective pacing distance and the ability to bypass other, slower-moving pedestrians.

Photographic studies of pedestrian traffic flow have shown that average individual area occupancies of at least 3 m² (35 ft²)/person are required for pedestrians to attain their normal walking speed and to avoid conflicts with others. Interestingly, the maximum pedestrian-flow volume on a walkway is attained at average individual area occupancies of only about 0.5 SMP (5 SFP). In these crowded conditions, the pedestrian is limited to an uncomfortable shuffling gait of less than half of his normal walking speed. At individual space occupancies under 0.2 SMP (2 SFP), approaching the area of the human body, virtually all movement is stopped, a condition that may become potentially unsafe in confined circumstances, particularly in large crowds subjected to the stress of some perceived emergency. Standards have been developed for pedestrian volumes on walkways and stairways based on individual average pedestrian area occupancies and such qualitative factors as the ability to choose individual locomotion speeds and to avoid conflicts with others. These standards have been classified into various "levels of service" with the higher service levels providing larger personal areas and, therefore, greater pedestrian comfort and convenience. Traffic-flow volumes are necessarily lower at higher levels of service, as illustrated by the graphic relationship of pedestrian area and flow shown in Fig. 10-1. Care must be taken in applying these standards since they represent statistical samples of continuous flow of platoons of pedestrians. Pedestrian flow will often be intermittent, owing to the arrival of passengers off a transit system, or the interruptions of pedestrian traffic flow that may occur on a sidewalk as a result of traffic signals. In these situations, careful analysis of pedestrian arrival patterns and platoon formation is necessary.

LEVEL-OF-SERVICE STANDARDS FOR WALKWAYS
VOLUME VS. MODULE

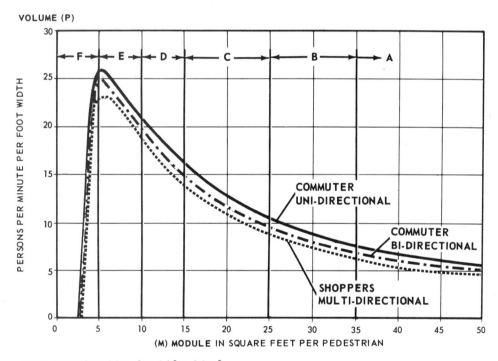

metric conversion: 1 ft = .3m, 1 ft² = .0 9 m².

Figure 10-1 *Level-of-service standards for walkways*

Walkway level-of-service A in Fig. 10-1 provides sufficient space for pedestrians to freely select their own walkway speed, to bypass slower pedestrians, and to avoid crossing conflicts with others; at B, speeds are nearly normal, but conflicts with reverse and cross movements begin to occur; at C, the freedom to freely select individual walking speed or bypass other pedestrians is restricted, and reverse or cross movements result in multiple conflicts; at D, the majority of pedestrians find that locomotion is restricted, with reverse and cross movements extremely difficult and with multiple conflicts occurring throughout the traffic stream; at E, the maximum capacity of the walkway is approached, with locomotion being significantly restricted for all; walkway level-of-service F represents a breakdown in the traffic stream with sporadic flow, frequent contact between pedestrians, multiple conflicts, and psychological discomfort.

The stylized locomotion on stairways imposed by concerns for safety, added exertion, and restraints of the stair treads and risers leads to quite different speed and volume relationships than those observed on walkways. Stair locomotion speeds vary from 15 to 91 m/min (50 to 300 ft/min) with the average at about 30.5 m/min (100 ft/ min), or almost one-third that of level walking. Descending speeds are about 10% faster than ascending due to the assist of gravity. A much wider range of individual speeds exists on stairways, because handicaps, including relatively minor visual impairments, can cause locomotion difficulties. For this reason, stair design requires greater attention to human factors and safety features. Considering human shoulder-width dimensions, body sway, and the fact that many pedestrians have hand-carried articles, 76 cm (30 in) width is required for a convenient individual traffic lane on stairs in heavy-use situations. However, many building codes use a 56-cm (22-in)-width lane for the purposes of building evacuation, and many engineers and architects have adopted this inadequate standard.

Another stair design detail apparently misunderstood is the dimensioning of risers and treads. Structural engineers sometimes detail very steep stairs with high risers and narrow treads to simplify structural framing. While this may save on initial construction costs, it penalizes all future users of the stair for the practical life of the building. Designers are using much lower riser heights and wider treads than in the past, with risers as low as 13 cm (5 in) and tread widths of 36 cm (14 in). The combination of low riser height and wider tread provides a more comfortable and safer stair with greater lifting tolerence for foot movement and a wider platform for foot placement. This benefits the general user population, but is especially appreciated by those whose locomotion is restricted by age or other impairments. The serviceability of more gently sloped stairs has been amply proved by a 15-cm (6-in) riser and 36-cm (14-in) tread stair that has been in constant heavy use for many years on one of the platforms of the New York Pennsylvania Railroad Station.

Other safety considerations in stair design include high lighting levels, at least 270 lux (25 foot-candles), and provision of proper height handrailings extended beyond the stair landings. Additionally, the traffic characteristics of stairs require provision of sufficient width for total traffic in both directions and adequate clear spaces at landings for circulation and queuing.

The level-of-service/flow relationship of pedestrian area occupancy and traffic volumes for stairs is illustrated in Fig. 10-2. Note that the flow capacity of the equivalent width of stairways is less than that of walkways, requiring special consideration where the two interface. A particularly difficult pedestrian system design problem related to this interface capacity difference occurs in design of transit station platforms. A 10-car subway train opening as many as 20 wide doors simultaneously will deliver a batch of arriving passengers at the platform which is virtually impossible to match

LEVEL-OF-SERVICE STANDARDS FOR STAIRWAYS
VOLUME VS. MODULE

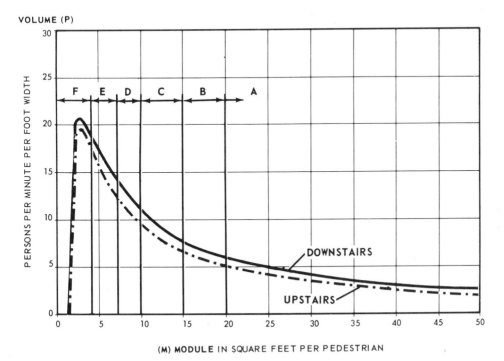

metric conversion: 1 ft = .3m, 1 ft² = .0 9 m².

Figure 10-2 *Level-of-service standards for stairways*

with vertical stair and escalator capacity. This causes delay and pedestrian queuing, forcing the transit station designer to balance vertical capacity and passenger delay against other requirements for pedestrian circulation and standing space on the platform. Since delay perception is a subjective variable dependent on a number of psychological factors, it is a difficult problem. Computer simulations of pedestrian processing on transit platforms are available to aid the analysis process.

At stairway level-of-service A shown in Fig. 10-2, sufficient area is provided to select individual stair locomotion speed and to bypass others, and reverse flows experience little difficulty; at B, speeds are nearly normal for all, but reverse flow conflicts begin; at C, stair locomotion speeds are slightly restricted, bypassing slower pedestrians becomes difficult, and reverse flow conflicts more likely; at D, stair locomotion speeds are restricted for the majority, slower pedestrians cannot be bypassed, reducing stairway speeds, reverse flows encounter extreme difficulties; level-of-service E represents the capacity of the stairway; and F, a breakdown in the traffic stream, sporadic flow, conflicts and contacts between pedestrians, and psychological discomfort.

Queuing is a pedestrian system design consideration which can cause problems ranging from discomfort and inconvenience to danger in confined space. Queuing often occurs in transportation systems on transit platforms and at escalators, stairs, turnstiles, doors, ticket dispensing machines, and similar locations where pedestrians may be delayed, even if momentarily. Queues may be classified into two general types, the linear or ordered queue, in which pedestrians line up in order of their arrival, and the batch queue, where no queuing discipline exists. The spacing between pedestrians in linear queues has been observed to be surprisingly consistent at about 51 cm (20 in). Design elements causing linear queues should be located so that the expected queue length does not extend into pedestrian pathways, interrupting circulation. Bulk queues may be rated at the degree of mobility that they afford, that is, the extent to which moving pedestrians may circulate through the group of standees. This combination of space for standing and mobility is important on transit platforms, where space is required for both waiting and circulation along the platform. Service standards have been developed for queues on the basis of their degrees of mobility, with personal area occupancies averaging 1.2 SMP (13 SFP) or more, allowing free circulation without disturbing others (A); 1 SMP (10 SFP), allowing restricted circulation without disturbance (B); 0.7 SMP (7 SFP), allowing restricted circulation on an "excuse me" basis (C); 0.5 SMP (5 SFP), allowing movement only as a group or with the shifting of several persons (D); 0.3 SMP (3 SFP), allowing no circulation and bordering on unavoidable physical contact (E); and 0.2 SMP (2 SFP), with frequent contact and approaching the area of the human body, allowable on only the most crowded elevators and transit vehicles and potentially dangerous in confined stress situations (F).

Walking distance is of great significance to transportation planners because it determines the effective service area of transportation systems. As with many other aspects of pedestrian behavior, the range of acceptable human walking distances is extremely variable and dependent upon the system context and environmental setting. Numerous surveys of automobile parkers show that the car user prefers to park within 152 m (500 ft) of his destination, but then the auto provides a means of bringing the driver closer to that destination. It is generally believed in transportation planning that about 0.4 km or 0.25 mi (1320 ft) is the limit of acceptable walking distance to a transit stop, and that beyond that distance an additional feeder mode is required, or public transit will not be used for the trip. There is evidence that much longer walking distances are accepted, particularly in large cities. In a study conducted in downtown Boston, 60% of the walking trips were beyond 0.4 km (0.25 mi) and 18% beyond 0.8 km (0.5 mi). Average walking trip distances in midtown Manhattan were found by the New York Regional Planning Association to be 524 m (1720 ft), with a median at 326 m (1070 ft). An interesting walking distance relationship was discovered for users of New York's Port Authority Bus Terminal, the largest facility of its type in the United States. An origin-and-destination survey of passengers departing from the terminal disclosed that one-third of the passengers using the terminal walked from their origins, and that the average walking distance for these persons was about 1067 m (3500 ft). This high average walking distance can be attributed to a number of factors, including (1) that the survey was conducted during fair weather; (2) that the long, rectangular grid pattern of Manhattan streets increases path lengths; (3) that walking is free; and (4) that walking times are more predictable than the combined total of waiting, transfer, and trip times of Manhattan bus, taxi, and transit facilities.

The origin-and-destination survey results provided the data for developing a relationship between walking distance and the proportion of Bus Terminal passengers who walk or use other transportation modes. The data showed that zones with poor transit service were found to have a higher proportion of walkers, and that up to about 305 m (1000 ft) from the terminal, virtually all persons walked; up to 1.6 km (1 mi), almost 50% walked; and 3.2 km (2 mi) was the practical walking limit. The persons in the survey were almost all commuters, representing more of the healthy, nonhandicapped segments of the general population. It is known that some of these persons will also walk in pleasant weather, as a means of exercise.

These rather long walking distances compare with the shorter, but severely criticized, maximum walking distances at major airports. Maximum walking distances from curbside to planeside have been reported to be 527 m (1730 ft) at Chicago O'Hare and Atlanta airports, 503 m (1650 ft) at Dallas; 396 m (1300 ft) at San Francisco International; and approximately 335 m (1100 ft) at the Los Angeles International, John F. Kennedy International, Miami, and Detroit airports. Interterminal distances at these airports were found to vary from 610 to 2438 m (2000 to 8000 ft).

There are indications that the tolerable limit of human walking distance is more situation-related than energy-related. The maximum curb-to-plane walk distances represent a normal 5- to 7-minute walk for most persons, but the anxiety connected with meeting schedules, making the trip, and negotiating an unfamiliar building tend to make these distances appear to be much longer. The tolerable walking distance for a given situation is related to such factors as the trip purpose of the individual, available time, and the walking environment, rather than energy consumption. This strongly suggests that improvement of the design environment to reduce negative psychological factors may be as important as reducing pedestrian walking distances.

MECHANICAL AIDS TO PEDESTRIANS

Escalators and moving walks can be viewed as part of the pedestrian system because they enhance human convenience and extend the pedestrians' effective range. Unlike vehicular systems which require batch loading and unloading, and result in physical intrusion of the place environment because of their size, escalators and moving walks provide continuously available service and can be more readily integrated into the scale of the pedestrian environment. Escalator and moving-walk technology has evolved over a period of more than 100 years, with the first applicable patents being granted prior to the Civil War, and the first operating systems installed before 1900. Observation of the use of these devices shows that their capacities and traffic characteristics are related closely to human factors such as shoulder breadth and the psychological space preferences discussed previously. Even under heavy pedestrian queue situations, escalators and moving walks operate at considerably less than the theoretical capacity developed from the number of step positions delivered per minute, multiplied by the maximum assumed step occupancy. Escalators operating at 27.4 m/min (90 ft/min) deliver 68 steps per minute, and at 36.6 m/min (120 ft/min), 89 steps per minute. Although two persons will frequently occupy one step, average step occupancy in most heavy-use situations is about one person. The theoretical capacity of moving walks is determined by the square-foot area that the walk delivers per minute, divided by an assumed personal area occupancy, usually 0.2 SMP (2 SFP). But this type of crowding is usually not acceptable to pedestrians, so actual use is less under heavy traffic conditions. It has been suggested that if pedestrians walk on moving walkways, the capacity is increased. This is not true, because although walking results in a threefold increase in the relative walkway speed, more than three times this area is required for normal locomotion.

Moving walks were originally intended to speed up pedestrians by increasing their walking speed by one-half. But this has not proved to be the case, particularly in airport applications, where pedestrians may be carrying baggage. Most pedestrians will stand on a moving walk, thus reducing their average speed by more than half that of the walking. Because of this, airline personnel have been observed to bypass crowded moving walks at airports, using them only when they are unoccupied, to obtain the benefit of the walking-time advantage. The fact that pedestrians actually lose time by standing on a moving walk, relative to walking, has led to the development of accelerating moving walks, which would speed up to about 4 to 5 times the normal boarding speeds, or about double the typical walking speed. Accelerating moving walkways are based on concepts involving changes in the treadway surface to increase speeds after boarding and decelerate prior to discharge. The development of an acceptable accelerating moving-walk system, which would most likely be deployed in lengths of 152 to 457 m (500 to 1500 ft), is expected to extend the pedestrian trip range, improve pedestrian convenience, and create new opportunities for developing auto-free zones and other pedestrian-oriented systems.

"People movers," or group rapid transit systems, may also be considered aids to pedestrians under certain circumstances. These systems generally use small to medium-size vehicles operating on close headways in the capacity range of up to a volume of about 10,000 passengers per hour, approximately the maximum capacity of a single escalator. People-mover systems are most applicable where there are uniform traffic demands without extreme peaks, where there are linear trip desire lines concentrated at definitive nodal points, and where there are sufficient trade-offs in human energy, time, and convenience to offset the reliability and freedom of the walking alternative. Except for specific trip corridors, group rapid transit systems cannot accommodate the majority of trip demands in most central business districts, which typically consist of many short, dispersed multipurpose trips. Trip patterns of this type are best served by a well-designed pedestrian network connecting all points of the compass, rather than a linear system. The corridor service characteristic of group rapid transit systems make them well suited to airport and activity center use and, to justify the significant installation and operating costs, in central business districts where a sufficient percentage of the total trip demand is concentrated between two or more points.

PLANNED PEDESTRIAN SYSTEMS

There is much evidence of a growing awareness of the needs of pedestrians. This is because the benefits of pedestrianization, including the reduced spatial intrusion of vehicles with the concomitant reduction in air, noise, and visual pollution, reduced pedestrian accidents, and resulting improvements in human interaction and the quality of life are being recognized. The trend of urban pedestrianization has taken on the form of pedestrian malls and auto-free zones within existing city street systems; the vehicle-free activity center, which would include a number of buildings integrated into a pedestrian precinct; elevated pedestrian "skyway" systems, which have been built in such cities as London, Minneapolis, and Cincinnati; and the underground pedestrian subways in Montreal, Tokyo, and New York. The planning of pedestrian systems is based on consideration of the improvement objectives and pedestrian characteristics developed in this chapter.

Figure 10-3 *Nicollet Mall skyway, Minneapolis. The Minneapolis skyway system consists of an elevated network of connecting bridges and passageways serving many of the major buildings in the downtown area. (courtesy of Greater Minneapolis Chamber of Commerce)*

The classic approach to pedestrian improvements is the separation of the pedestrian from the vehicle either by space or time. Traffic signalization represents an example of separation of pedestrians and vehicles in time, but pedestrians are still exposed to turning vehicles. Traffic signalization also has the disadvantages of causing pedestrian delay, queuing at crosswalks, and the creation of denser platoons of pedestrians than would normally òccur in uninterrupted free flow. The spatial separation of pedestrians and vehicles, either horizontally by pedestrian malls or vertically through elevated or underground pedestrian convenience networks, represents the ultimate improvement objective, but more modest improvements can be quickly and inexpensively attained.

The higher pedestrian accident exposure resulting from vehicles turning into crossing pedestrians suggests that turning movements should be eliminated in high-density pedestrian areas. Many cities already have extensive turn restrictions in downtown areas, but not planned on a systemwide basis. This may not cause as much hardship to motorists as might be thought, since the predominant downtown vehicular movement is the through one.

Figure 10-4 *Pedestrian/transit mall and skyway—Nicollet Mall, Minneapolis. (courtesy of Greater Minneapolis Chamber of Commerce)*

Low-capital improvements include upgrading pedestrian circulation, better street lighting, and standardization of street furniture and signs. Improved circulation is attained by special pedestrian signal cycles and vehicular turn restrictions, sidewalk widenings through the use of building setbacks and arcades, better location of street furniture, and shortening of walking distances by means of midblock connectors where possible. The control of street furniture location is necessary to provide maximum clear width on sidewalks, and also to eliminate obstructions in the vicinity of crosswalks, particularly those that can obscure the turning driver's view of pedestrians. Street lighting improvements upgrade area image and significantly reduce pedestrian accidents and street crime. Many cities have found that lighting improvement programs receive quick popular support and even supplementary private financing on a voluntary basis. Additionally, the change to more efficient modern luminaires often results in reductions in total energy use.

Building setbacks, arcades, pedestrian plazas, and other such amenities can be obtained by bonus zoning amendments which allow building space bonuses to developers who provide them. When pedestrian plazas are provided by private developers, care must be taken that the improvement is carefully integrated into the pedestrian system. Above- or below-grade building plazas do not add to sidewalk capacity, and may actually isolate and inconvenience some pedestrians.

The pedestrian mall is becoming a common improvement, but it must be carefully planned to be successful. The requirements for a viable mall program include complete exclusion of all but emergency vehicles; development of adequate perimeter street capacity to replace that eliminated by the mall; provision of adequate transit and highway access and sufficient parking; upgraded street lighting; and the development of an active and cooperative promotional program based on aesthetic improvements, special events, and coordinated advertising.

The ultimate pedestrian improvement program is the grade-separated pedestrian convenience network. These networks are being built above or below street level, depending on local requirements. The network aspect, particularly the need for continuity within these systems, must be emphasized. New York City has several miles of underground passages serving individual buildings and subway stations. Because these are not interconnected, their use is limited except in the most inclement weather. This is in sharp contrast to the well-planned and heavily utilized 6-km (3.6-mi) underground system in Montreal, Canada.

Underground systems need only be about 3 m (10 ft) below street level, provide full weather protection, and more efficient climate control. They can be easily connected to subway transit stations. Disadvantages of underground systems include their high construction costs, possible conflicts with subsurface utilities, and loss of visual identity with the cityscape above. Aboveground pedestrian convenience networks have the advantage of lower construction costs and greater opportunities for integration and identification with the cityscape. The primary disadvantage of aboveground networks is that their greater height above street level, required to provide vehicle clearances, makes them difficult to relate to belowground transit. Both systems provide the developer or owner with added valuable commercial space.

Pedestrian system planning in transportation terminals and stations follows the same basic pedestrian improvement objectives but requires greater consideration of the heavy pedestrian traffic movements typically occurring in these facilities, the magnified

Figure 10-5 *Montreal, Canada, underground pedestrian network. The system connects major transportation lines and many of the hotels and major retail establishments in the downtown area. (courtesy of Montreal Urban Community Transit Commission)*

value that the traveler is likely to place on time and delay, and the increased need for information and orientation. Also, transportation planners rarely examine the effectiveness of the external walkway network surrounding a transportation terminal or station. The service area of transit, and therefore its potential utilization, could be

Figure 10-6 *Place Bonaventure, Montreal, Canada. Smart shops line three levels of corridors in giant merchandising mart in the heart of the city. (courtesy of City of Montreal)*

increased by more effective planning of this external pedestrian system. Passenger-arrival processes require greater consideration in transit terminal planning since pedestrians may be delivered to downtown stations in train-load batches as high as 1800 passengers within 60 seconds, whereas on the return trip the passengers arrive at the station more gradually. This changes the focus of the pedestrian design since the batch-arrival situation requires concentration on the impacts of heavy short-term demands on stairs, escalators, and other similar pedestrian facilities, whereas the departure situation involves examination of pedestrian standing capacity and circulation on platforms. Pedestrian processing times through transportation terminals should be minimized because of the tendency of the passenger to magnify this time over the equivalent time spent in transit. This human tendency for exaggeration of time spent making inter-modal transfers has been noted by transportation system analysts, with some applying a factor of 2.5: 1 for time spent in a station. Some deep subway systems have been built on the basis of construction cost savings without consideration of the value of pedestrian time that is spent, over the life of the system, traveling to and from the surface and platform level. In some deep stations this can involve an escalator ride of more than 2 minutes. Orientation and information in transportation terminal design is gained by application of the principles of continuity, coherence, and imageability described previously.

The handicapped also deserve consideration in the design of all pedestrian systems. Surveys in the United States indicate there are at least 20 million Americans with disabilities severe enough to restrict or discourage their use of public transportation or the finding of employment commensurate with their qualifications. There are many others with what might be termed minor sight, locomotion, or other impairments that are inconvenienced daily by design features that do not consider these common disabilities.

The ranks of the physically disadvantaged are also expanding at a rate faster than the growth of the general population because medical advances are continually increasing survival rates from accidents and illness and extending life spans of the aged. The very heavy automobile accident rate in this country is a contributor to the ranks, with the added reminder that anyone, despite present physical and mental capabilities, can become disabled at any time, and possibly rendered inoperable in a society ordered only for the most physically fit.

There are other types of impairments that designers sometimes overlook. Passengers in transportation terminals are likely to be physically encumbered by baggage, and subway users by parcels and even heavy winter clothing, a factor that should be considered in designing doorways, turnstiles, stairs, and other similar human interface features. This means that the proportion of physically disadvantaged users in most transportation and building systems constitute a larger population than is generally realized.

While some may believe designing systems with consideration of the physically impaired is a highly idealized, impractical, and costly philosophy, it is not true. The needs of those persons are only a magnification of the problems that face all system users. By recognizing these needs designers can project themselves more easily into the problems of all users, creating designs with greater general utility. On the other hand, design-imposed dysfunctions can limit the economic life and viability of building and transportation systems by continual daily inconvenience. Consideration of the needs of the disadvantaged users of a system is not an idealistic design objective, but a pragmatic approach to producing more utilitarian systems for all.

SELECTED BIBLIOGRAPHY

BREINES, SIMON, AND WILLIAM J. DEAN, *The Pedestrian Revolution: Streets Without Cars.* New York: Random House, Inc., 1975.

FRUIN, JOHN J., *Pedestrian Planning and Design.* New York: Metropolitan Association of Urban Designers and Environmental Planners, Inc., 1971.

NATIONAL COMMISSION ON ARCHITECTURAL BARRIERS, *Design for All Americans.* Washington, D.C.: U.S. Government Printing Office, 1968.

PUSHKAREV, BORIS S., AND JEFFREY M. ZUPAN, *Urban Space for Pedestrians.* Cambridge, Mass.: The M.I.T. Press, 1975.

RUDOFSKY, BERNARD, *Streets for People: A Primer for Americans.* Garden City, N.Y.: Doubleday & Company, Inc., 1970.

Chapter 11

SYSTEM INTEGRATION

Roberta Remak,* *Urban Systems Analysis*

The *transportation resources* of an urban area consist of roads, rails, transit vehicles, automobiles, parking accommodations, bikeways, and pedestrian facilities. These resources offer a broad spectrum of options in mode of urban travel: rail and bus mass transit; ridesharing and demand-responsive paratransit; vehicular and pedestrian private transportation. Figure 11-1 shows the full range of urban transportation modes arranged to reflect their relative passenger-carrying capacity and responsiveness to users' varying travel needs and desires.

We are coming to recognize that all of these various transportation resources and the modal options they offer are interdependent components of the total urban transportation system. However, authority for managing transportation facilities and services is commonly dispersed among a number of public agencies and private businesses that operate, in large part, independently of each other.

The degree of separation of transportation functions varies among urban areas; some have made significant progress toward system integration. Federal transportation assistance programs have encouraged regionwide multimodal transportation planning and coordination of local transportation improvement and management activities. Many states have combined highway and public transit functions within the

*The author wishes to recognize the important contribution of Roman Krzyczkowski, who, prior to his death in April 1975, drew the attention of the transportation community to the need for intermodal integration in creating a successful urban transit system. He was among the first to recognize that European approaches to transit integration might be adapted to U.S. cities and was instrumental in stimulating interest within the Urban Mass Transportation Administration in this concept. As the head of INTERPLAN Corporation, he subsequently directed the UMTA-sponsored study, *Integration of Transit Systems*, that is still today the single most important source of our current knowledge of the subject. The author is proud to have had the opportunity of working with him on this study.

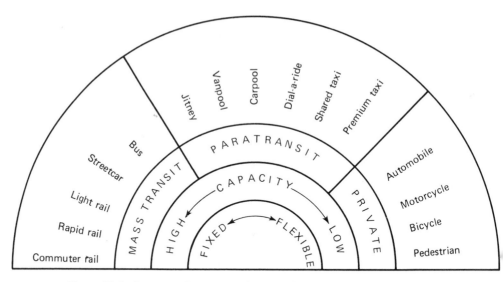

Figure 11-1 *Spectrum of options in urban transportation modes.* [*Source : Developed from graphics presented in Roman Krzyczkowski and others,* Integration of Transit Systems, Summary, *prepared for UMTA (Santa Barbara, Calif. : INTERPLAN Corporation, October 1973) and INTERPLAN Corporation's proposal,* Future Paratransit Requirements, *July 1975.*]

same agencies and extended the scope of their activities to include bikeways, parking facilities and controls, and pedestrian environments.

The long-range goal of system integration is to incorporate all components of urban transportation into a single coordinated planning and operations program that can make the most efficient use of available transportation resources to ensure urban mobility within a wide range of modal options to better serve the users.

CONCEPTS OF INTEGRATION

THE SYSTEM

System integration is essentially a management technique applied to a group of functions that are currently being administered independently, but are, in fact, highly interdependent and could be managed more effectively by being treated as interrelated parts of a single system. The system conceived of as the objective of an integration program will vary. It may be limited to interface between two modes of mass transportation, extend to all mass transit and paratransit operations within a metropolitan area or all modes of both public and private transportation, or it may even encompass the larger urban setting, involving not only transportation, but also land utilization, local economic and social conditions, and the environment.

Inasmuch as this book is focused on public transportation services, the system we will be considering here will be all of the mass transit and paratransit resources for moving people within an urban area. The objectives of this transit integration process are to:

- Operate all the diverse publicly and privately owned services as though they were parts of a single, areawide transit system.
- Eliminate wasteful duplications and extend the availability of service.
- Benefit from combined planning, purchasing, and marketing efforts and joint use of facilities.
- Enable the transit user to travel anywhere in the community on a single fare, transferring efficiently and comfortably between different modes and services.

LEVELS OF INTEGRATION

System integration occurs at three levels: institutional, operational, and physical. *Institutional integration* refers to the creation of an organizational framework within which joint planning and operation of transit services can be carried out. *Operational integration* involves the application of management techniques to optimize the allocation of transit resources and coordinate services. *Physical integration* refers to the provision of jointly used facilities and equipment.

Institutional integration. Four types of organizational arrangements for implementing transit integration were defined by Homburger and Vuchic[1]:

1. *Tariff associations*, limited to contracts on joint tariffs and the distribution of jointly collected revenues. Associations are suitable only in situations where the partners do not compete and share no territory but rather make end-to-end connections. For instance, the airline industry is an example of interurban transport: a passenger can purchase a single ticket covering several flight segments on aircraft of different companies and pays no penalty for using more than one line.
2. *Transit communities*, which not only bind themselves to a common tariff but coordinate routes and schedules and, if appropriate, pool or exchange some rolling stock. The railroads in the United States have long operated under such an arrangement.
3. *Transit federations*, which establish a formal federated agency and delegate to it certain powers related to planning, tariffs, revenue distribution, and so on. The Munich (Germany) Transit Federation is an example.
4. *Mergers*, in which portions of companies or entire companies are merged into one firm, within which the companies either operate as subsidiaries or lose their identity altogther. Examples are transit services in London and Paris.

Of the several organizational alternatives, mergers appear to be the most effective in achieving a high degree of transit integration. A single authority is able to function more efficiently and with greater flexibility than are associations of essentially indepen-

---

[1]WOLFGANG S. HOMBURGER AND VUKAN R. VUCHIC, "Federation of Transit Agencies as a Solution for Service Integration," *Traffic Quarterly*, 24, no. 3 (July 1970), 379.

dent public and private transit operators. In cases where merger is difficult because of state or national ownership of transit or local public and private operators' strong desires to maintain their independent status, federation would be the next best institutional arrangement. It provides for long-term commitments to a broad range of cooperative activities that can serve existing needs for transit integration, and it can also serve as an interim arrangement leading to eventual merger of its members. Transit communities, such as practiced by railroads, and tariff associations, as represented by airlines, are not broad enough in scope to satisfy the diverse purposes of integrating urban transit systems. They can, however, be of use in taking an initial step toward integration.

Some sort of institutional agreements must be reached before operational and physical integration can take place, but it is not necessary to complete a merger of all the transit services in an urban area before any integration is attempted. On the contrary, independent transit operators who might initially oppose the concept of total integration can slowly be brought to recognize the advantages of cooperative efforts by experiencing these in areas that do not appear threatening to them. A first step might be the joint publication of an areawide guide to transit routes, schedules, and fares, followed by a centralized telephone information service. This can, in turn, lead to readjustment of schedules to facilitate intersystem transfers, arrangements to honor each other's transfers, and eventually the entire spectrum of operational and physical integration.

Operational integration. The techniques of operational integration include:

1. *Rationalization of redundant services.* Wasteful duplication of transit service by competing systems is eliminated and resources are redeployed to reduce headways on existing routes and extend services into new areas.
2. *Matching modes to service requirements.* High-capacity, long-haul modes, such as commuter rail and rail rapid and express bus transit, are utilized on major high-density travel corridors, while demand-responsive services and park-and-ride facilities are provided in low-density areas. Circulation systems are operated in high-density, short-haul situations, such as in city centers. Chapter 13 provides a detailed comparison of types of transit services available and the functions within the total system each serves best.
3. *Unification of the fare structure.* A single, areawide fare structure is established that permits riders to purchase one ticket at the beginning of the trip and transfer freely between all modes or lines of service within the system. Most often a graduated fare structure is provided so that each passenger pays according to the length of his total trip.
4. *Fare discounts.* Reduced fares are offered to accomplish three objectives: (a) subsidize travel for selected socioeconomic groups, such as the elderly, handicapped, low-income, or those under driving age; (b) encourage off-peak use of transit through discounts for travel before or after commuter hours; (c) simplify

fare purchasing procedures for regular transit users through weekly or monthly passes.

5. *Honor payment fare systems.* Barriers and turnstiles are removed and ticket collecting or punching is eliminated under the honor system. Inspectors board a small percentage of transit vehicles at random and any passenger found without a valid ticket or pass is subject to a heavy fine. Authorities in Hamburg, Göteborg (Sweden), Munich, and Copenhagen, where such systems are in operation, estimate that no more than 2 to 3% of riders are violators. Advantages of the honor system are savings in operating costs by eliminating ticket takers and conductors and more efficient boarding of transit vehicles by multiple entrances rather than through a single controlled point.

6. *Coordinated public information systems.* Information on routes, schedules, fares, and transfer points for all transit modes and services throughout the urban area is provided by a centralized source. Information services include published route maps, timetables, fare schedules, and promotion materials; uniform street signs and vehicle identification; display material at stops, transfer points, and major stations; and telephone inquiry answering service. Facilities at major stations may include direct-line free telephone connections to an information switchboard and/or automatic locater maps in which paths or points of light indicate desired routes or destinations.

7. *Reserved bus lanes and streets.* Restricting use of designated lanes and streets to buses serves a dual purpose in promoting transit ridership. First, it inhibits automobile travel along freeways and in the central business district (CBD) by limiting the amount of roadway private vehicles are permitted to use; traffic congestion on nonexempt lanes is increased; and direct access to downtown locations on exempt streets is denied. Second, the reliability and speed of bus transit is significantly improved along separate rights-of-way, making public transit a relatively more attractive mode for urban travel.

8. *Parking controls.* Transit ridership can also be promoted by controls that reduce the number of available parking spaces or increase costs of parking. Eliminating on-street parking along heavily traveled CBD streets will permit all vehicles, including transit, to move more freely, or the space formerly occupied by parked vehicles can be designated as a reserved bus lane. Raising costs of parking presents the automobile user with an immediately recognizable increase in driving costs; this is considered a more effective deterrent than raising gasoline taxes or vehicle registration fees. Variable systems of parking restrictions and rates can be employed to achieve specific changes in travel mode. Commuting to work by car can be discouraged by prohibiting on-street parking during morning rush hours and by a graduated rate structure that penalizes all-day parking. Shoppers and other users of downtown businesses, however, are not discouraged from short-term, off-peak use of available parking space.

9. *Changes of work schedules.* Techniques of spreading peak demands for both roadway and transit resources include staggering work hours or introducing

"Flextime." In the former case, employees start and end their working days at prescribed intervals, usually of 15 minutes throughout a 1- to 1.5-hour period. Flextime, on the other hand, permits each employee to select his own working schedule so that he may travel to and from work at off-peak times.

Physical integration. Techniques of physical transit integration include:

1. *Intermodal terminals.* Transfer between modes of transit service is facilitated by intermodal terminals, often described as "transportation centers." The most highly developed of these facilities accommodate commuter rail lines, rail rapid transit lines, light rail and streetcar lines, and bus services, with facilities for transfer from dial-a-ride or circulation feeder services, taxis, or private vehicles. Parking accommodations are provided to encourage park-and-ride travel, and loading areas permit passengers to be dropped off by car (kiss-and-ride). Secure bicycle storage is available to those who use this mode to reach the terminal, and protected pedestrian accommodations are provided for those who live or work close enough to walk. Often some of the costs of operating the terminal are offset by leasing commercial space to shops, restaurants, and personal services, such as barbers and shoe repair, that cater to commuter needs. Where single-fare systems for all transit modes have been established, passengers move freely between the different services without being stopped by barriers or turnstiles.

2. *Transit shelters.* These range from simple weather-protection structures on surface transit routes to "miniterminals" at important stops and transfer points. The more complex facilities may provide automatic ticket vending machines, free direct-line telephone connections to a centralized information service, locater maps, posted routes and schedules, and promotional material on reduced-fare multiride passes or special excursions. Refreshments and newspapers may also be provided, either by vending machines or by a stand operated by an individual under a lease arrangement.

3. *Route, schedule, and vehicle identification.* Standardized identification symbols and display techniques are adopted by all modes and services. Stops are clearly marked with the route numbers of transit vehicles that can be boarded at those points, and departure times are indicated. Where possible, route maps are posted and all transit vehicles are clearly marked, front, loading side, and rear with the number of the routes each vehicle is currently serving.

4. *Park-and-ride facilities.* Drivers are encouraged to leave their cars and complete their trips on public transit by providing parking accommodations at outlying transit stops. Parking may be free or at a minimal charge included in the system-wide transit fare at suburban locations in order to reduce the number of private vehicles using freeway and arterial systems as well as driving into the CBD. In other cases, park-and-ride lots may be provided just outside of the CBD, perhaps with rates set to defray some of the costs of constructing and operating the facility, but with free transfer to the CBD transit circulation system. The objec-

tive of this approach is to discourage automobiles from entering only the CBD or to provide essential mobility within an auto-restricted zone (ARZ).

5. *Pedestrian facilities.* Comfort and safety of pedestrian movement to and from transit is vital to the successful functioning of public transportation systems. Walking is encouraged by grade-separated "skyways" or underground passageways, escalators, and moving sidewalks that protect the pedestrian from direct contact with moving vehicles. In some systems, pedestrians are directed through downtown office buildings and department stores that have been rearranged or designed to accommodate heavy pass-through foot traffic. Pedestrian routes are clearly marked and coordinated with the buildings' own escalators and elevators, with retail store displays, and other customer services oriented to the pedestrian routes. Attractive pedestrian environments can also be developed within auto-restricted zones. If transit circulation is permitted, planting, street furniture, and grade separation are all employed to direct those on foot away from the path of transit vehicles.

TRANSIT INTEGRATION IN EUROPEAN CITIES

Integration of urban transit systems occurred in Europe before the concept was fully recognized in the United States. Institutional integration appeared first in London (1933) and Paris (1949) and more recently in Hamburg (1965) and Munich (1971). Other European efforts toward transit integration have been carried out in such cities as Copenhagen, Stockholm, Göteborg, Oslo, Newcastle (England), and Edinburgh (Scotland). A review of some of the major characteristics of these systems and a more detailed look at one of the most advanced, Munich, can be useful in suggesting approaches to transit integration applicable to urban areas in this country.

MAJOR CHARACTERISTICS OF EUROPEAN INTEGRATED SYSTEMS

INTERPLAN's study of transit integration[2] examined 10 European integrated systems and summarized their findings in a table reproduced here as Table 11-1. The systems are grouped according to whether public transit ridership had increased (Munich, Hamburg, Stockholm), remained stable (Paris, Copenhagen, Oslo), or had declined (Göteborg, London, Newcastle, Edinburgh), and describe selected characteristics of institutional, operational, and physical integration.

One of the most surprising situations observed was that the systems successful in increasing or maintaining their ridership did so in the face of greater growth in automobile ownership than those showing losses in ridership. Whatever the causes—increased traffic congestion, strong promotion of transit—that can only be speculated

---

[2]Roman Krzyczkowski and others, *Integration of Transit Systems, Summary*, prepared for UMTA (Santa Barbara, Calif.: INTERPLAN Corporation, October 1973). Now available as PB 241 273.

TABLE 11-1

Selected Integration Characteristics of 10 European Public Transit Systems

	Increasing Public Transit Ridership				Stable Public Transit Ridership		Decreasing Public Transit Ridership			
	Munich	Hamburg	Stockholm	Paris	Copenhagen	Oslo	Göteborg	London	Newcastle	Edinburgh
City characteristics										
Population (millions)	2.1	2.5	1.5	10.0	1.4	0.7	0.7	7.5	0.9	0.7
Persons per car	3.2	3.8	3.8	4.6	5.2	4.4	3.5	4.7	9.1	5.9
Transit ridership										
Annual trips (millions)	289	645	326	1690	285	175	98	2200	387	168
Trend (annual % change)	+3.3	+1.7	+1.1	cyclic	cyclic	cyclic	−1.0	−1.7	−1.7	−2.0
Rail rapid transit[a]										
System name or type	U-Bahn	U&S-Bahn	T-Bana	Metro	None	T-Bane	Lt. rail	Underground	None	None
Annual ridership (millions)	7	344	137	1076	N/A[b]	30	N/A[b]	700	N/A[b]	N/A[b]
Ridership trend	+	+	+	stable	N/A[b]		N/A[b]	stable	N/A[b]	N/A[b]
Financial status										
Buses	Deficit	Mixed mostly surplus	Planned deficit	Planned deficit	Deficit	Deficit on city-owned op.	Deficit	Deficit	Surplus	Surplus
Rail rapid transit	Deficit				N/A[b]		N/A[b]	Surplus	N/A[b]	N/A[b]
Commuter rail	Deficit				—		N/A[b]	—	Deficit	Deficit
Institutional integration										
Transit planning and operator coordination										
Single regional transport and land-use planning agency			SCC							
Single transit planning organization, several operators	MVV	HVV						GLC		
Single areawide transit operator/transit planner				RATP			GS		PTA	
Multiple planning agencies and operators					KS et al.	OS et al.				ECT, SBG, BR
Degree of operator coordination	Federation control	Federation control	One operator	One operator	Some agreements	None	One operator	Legal requirements	PTA control	None
Operational integration										
Fare-structure characteristics										
Coordinated systemwide inter-modal fares	Yes	Yes	Yes	Yes	No	No	GS system	No	No	No
Coordinated bus mode fares	Yes	Yes	Yes	Yes	Some routes	OS system	GS system	No	No	No
Zonal fares	Yes	No	In city	No	No	OS system	No	Some routes	No	No
Flat fares	No	No	No	Metro	KS system	Central zone	No			
Distance graduated or staged	No	Yes	Suburban	Buses and RER	No	Other systems	Yes	Yes	Yes	Yes
Seasonal passes for zones or routes	Yes	Yes	No	No	KS system	OS system	No	Yes	—	—
Seasonal passes for whole system	Yes	No	Yes	Yes	KS system	No	Yes	Yes	—	ECT system
Special rates for socioeconomic groups	Yes	Yes	Yes	Yes	Yes	No	Yes	Yes	Yes	Yes

TABLE 11-1 Continued

	Increasing Public Transit Ridership			Stable Public Transit Ridership				Decreasing Public Transit Ridership		
	Munich	Hamburg	Stockholm	Paris	Copenhagen	Oslo	Göteborg	London	Newcastle	Edinburgh
Free return trips under time limitations	No	No	Yes	No	No	–	Yes	Some BR routes	No	No
Modal transfer, individual fares available	No	No	No	RATP SNCF	KS-DSB	OS system	No	LTE-BR	No	No
Modal transfer, seasonal passes available	No	No	No	RATP SNCF	No	OS system	No	Yes	–	No
Free transfers within mode	Yes	Yes	Yes	Metro	KS system	Central zone	Yes	Underground	No	No
Free transfers for whole system	Yes	Yes	Yes	No	KS system	Central zone	Yes	No	No	No
Honor system	Yes	Yes	–	Partial	Partial	No	Yes	No	No	No
Automated ticket sales	Yes	Yes	–	Yes	Yes	–	–	Yes	No	No
Emphasis on buses as feeders to rapid transit	Yes	Yes	Yes	Yes	N/A[b]	Within agencies	Most routes	Yes	N/A[b]	N/A[b]
Bus/tram-only lanes and streets	Some	Yes	Yes	Yes	Some	Some	Yes	Some	No	Planned
Controls on automobile traffic										
Parking controls	–	Yes	Yes	Yes	Yes	Yes	Yes	Yes	–	No
Pedestrian malls and streets	Yes	Yes	Yes	Yes	Yes	Yes	Yes	Yes	–	–
Comments			No significant impact	Policy of benign neglect			Traffic restraint scheme	Auto system favored		
Network rationalization (removal of redundant services)	In progress	Complete	Yes	Yes	No	No	Yes	Some	Yes	No
Integrated public information system	Yes	Yes	Yes	Yes	–	–	Yes	Yes	–	–
Physical integration										
Park-and-ride facilities	Yes	Yes	Yes	Yes	No	–	N/A[b]	Yes	No	No
Commuter rail	Some	Yes	Yes	No	N/A[b]	–	Planned	Yes	N/A[b]	N/A[b]
Rail rapid transit	Yes	Some	–	Yes	N/A[b]	No	N/A[b]	Yes	N/A[b]	N/A[b]
Rights-of-way and stations shared by rapid transit and commuter rail	Yes	Yes	Yes	Yes	Some	–	Yes	Some	No	No
Emphasis on pedestrian facilities and services	Yes	Yes	Yes	Yes	Some	Some; more planned	Yes	Some	No	No
Airport-city rail connection	No	Streetcar	No	Planned	No	–	No	Under construction	No	No

[a] Rail systems providing primarily commuter service are not included (e.g., RER in Paris, S-Bahn in Munich).

[b] N/A, not applicable; not available.

Source: Roman Krzyczkowski and others, *Integration of Transit Systems, Summary,* prepared for UMTA (Santa Barbara, Calif.: INTERPLAN Corporation, October 1973), p. 31.

213

upon, this phenomenon is an encouraging sign to U.S. urban areas, indicating that successful transit systems may be developed in spite of our present dependence on private transportation.

The report summarizes its study of European systems with the following observations:

Urban transportation policy

- Land planning and transportation planning are closely coordinated; agencies are empowered to implement plans.
- In most metropolitan areas, transit operations are unified under public ownership.
- Private motoring is not favored to the extent of destroying public transit. Tax revenues from motorists are often used to support rail and bus transit.
- Pedestrians are recognized as an important part of urban traffic.
- Public transit is well supplemented by paratransit; the taxi industry and the public benefit from enlightened legislation, reasonably free entry, and mostly reasonable fare levels.
- The operational management of transit systems is independent from political pressures. Transit operations are competently managed by professionals with appropriate practical and academic backgrounds.
- Transit systems are not expected to be self-supporting; their nonrevenue benefits are well recognized.

Transit financing

1. No rail and bus transit operator covers his *capital* costs from revenue. National and local subsidies range from 50 to 100%.
2. Only a few operators cover *operating* costs from revenues. Cross-subsidization between rail and bus is common. For most systems, the national and local subsidies vary between 60 and 70%. These levels of subsidy enable European transit systems to maintain service at operational levels generally much superior to those in the United States.
3. Up to 7% of transit revenue is earned by nontransportation activities (e.g., rental of space and advertising).

Transit operations

1. All European transit systems have adequate and often superb public information systems.
2. Large metropolitan areas rely on rail and bus systems. Buses are primarily used to provide feeder service on rail networks. In general, the ridership on rail systems is stable or increasing; on buses, decreasing.

Urban environment

1. Riding the transit system and walking are part of the urban way of life for most Europeans. Wide sidewalks, underground passages equipped with escalators, and relative lack of street crime encourage walking. Adequate or good public transportation results in per capita ridership considerably higher than in the United States.
2. While automobile ownership is quickly increasing in Europe (10 million cars manufactured per year in Western Europe versus 7 million in the United States), motorization has not reached American levels (4 to 5 compared to 2.3 persons per car).
3. European highway systems are grossly inadequate and old-fashioned street patterns in urban areas create even greater traffic congestion than in U.S. cities.
4. The cost of motoring is considerably greater than in the United States. Gas costs well over 40 cents/l ($1.50/gallon); insurance and financing are more costly; and the cost of a new automobile is equivalent to one year's earnings for most European urban residents.

THE MUNICH TRANSIT FEDERATION

Munich, the third largest city in West Germany, with a population of over 2.5 million, found itself in the early 1960s with rapidly growing automobile traffic that could not be accommodated in spite of recent widening of city streets, modernizing of traffic controls, and construction of new high-capacity beltways around the city. It became apparent that major improvement of its public transit facilities was essential to the city's further development, and a transportation plan was drawn up that called for an areawide, urban-oriented transit system.

Two of the major elements in this plan were the construction of a new underground rapid transit system (U-Bahn) and the development and improvement of regional railway services (S-Bahn). A special company was founded in 1964, the Tunnel-baugesellschaft, whose sole function was the construction of the rapid transit and railway tunnels. The four partners of this company were the Federal Republic, the State of Bavaria, the City of Munich, and the German Federal Railways. By 1976 the new U-Bahn system covered 20 km (12.4 mi) linked to 401 km (249 mi) of improved lines of 11 suburban railway lines and 480 rte.-km (298 rte.-mi) of light rail and bus service.

The Joint Transportation Agency. The Munich Transit Federation was formed in 1971, after three years of negotiation, by the signing of three contracts: the basic contract signed by the four government partners of the tunnel construction company agreeing to basic transportation development goals and policies; the federation contract signed by the two transit operating authorities, the city and Federal Railways; and the revenue distribution contract signed by the same authorities.

Each of the two federation partners retains ownership over its own facilities and vehicles and is bound by the rights and duties prescribed for each by laws, regulations, and other contractual obligations. Each partner is specifically obliged to carry out the following functions:

- Maintain transit facilities and vehicles.
- Work out detailed operational schedules based on the general guidelines developed by the federation.
- Provide and supervise transit service.
- Make a continuous effort to modernize and improve facilities and procedures.

The functions of the joint agency are:

- Develop operational guidelines for timetables, frequency, and system capacity.
- General planning of the total system network.
- Administer the joint fare system and distribution of revenues.

Specific achievements in transit integration. Since its formation in 1972 the Joint Transportation Agency has carried out the following operational and physical integration:

1. *Rationalization of service.* Train and bus connections parallel to new railway lines were discontinued and the remaining outer sections were converted into feeder services. Schedules are coordinated to facilitate transfers.
2. *Systemwide fare structure and automated fare collections.* The service area is divided into zones, and six different levels of fare are determined by the number of zones through which the passenger travels. A single ticket permits the rider to transfer throughout the system. Reduced fares are available with multiple-ride tickets or weekly and monthly passes. Vending machines are installed in all S-Bahn, U-Bahn, and major surface transit stations and offer both single and multiple tickets. Ticket-canceling devices that stamp the date, time, and location of the machine are placed at all gates and on all surface vehicles. Inspectors examine tickets at random, finding an average of 2% violations.
3. *Public information program.* In addition to a systemwide timetable, the agency publishes several brochures describing the federation concept, the operation of the system, transfer procedures, and even a dictionary of terms. These brochures are illustrated, easy to read, and available in several languages.
4. *Segregation of automobiles and transit vehicles and automobile restraints.* Surface routes on congested roads are segregated from private transport by various means. In the central hub of the city, Marienplatz, vehicular traffic is prohibited and the area transformed into a pedestrian zone.
5. *Multimodal transportation centers.* The Marienplatz underground station is the hub of the transit system. Automatic destination indicators and signs direct passengers to S-Bahn services at the two upper transit levels and the mainline

railroad services at the third level. Entrances at the four corners of the Marien-platz lead into a concourse of several acres, most of which is leased to retailers. In addition to newstands, tobacconists, florists, and snack bars are a large department store and a supermarket. Most U-Bahn and S-Bahn stations are constructed on two levels. At the mezzanine level the passenger finds three large signs: I, indicating the location of the information center with city and transit maps and schedules; F, showing the location of ticket vending machines; and E, locating the ticket-canceling machines and gates leading to the platform. Special ramps permit buses and streetcars to transfer passengers at these stations.

TRANSIT INTEGRATION IN THE UNITED STATES

System integration of public transit in the United States is not yet so highly developed as in Europe. However, the value of integration as a means of improving urban transit services is widely recognized, and important advances toward this objective have been achieved in several metropolitan areas.

FEDERAL TRANSPORTATION POLICIES PROMOTING SYSTEM INTEGRATION

The major impetus toward integration of urban transportation systems has been federal policy. Since the passage of the Urban Mass Transportation Act in 1964, cities have been guided in the direction of public ownership of transit, regionwide transportation planning, and systemwide transportation management improvement.

Public ownership of transit services. From 1964 to 1974, when the Urban Mass Transportation Act was amended, federal aid for local transit improvement was directed exclusively to publicly owned services. During this period local government acquired a great number of ailing privately operated transit systems in order to qualify them for federal assistance. Institutional integration of formerly independent transit services took place in many cities by placing the newly acquired properties under the authority of a single public agency.

Regional transportation planning. Next, local government was required to develop long-range regional transportation plans in order to qualify for federal aid for specific transit improvements. All elements of regional transportation had to be considered— road systems, airports, harbors, pipelines, bikeways, and pedestrian facilities, as well as transit. The plan had also to meet the approval of the several local units of government within the region. This process reinforced local recognition of the interrelationships between elements of the transportation system and needs to coordinate city and suburban transit services.

Systems management and transportation improvement programs. In 1975, metropolitan areas were asked to examine their existing urban transportation needs and resources and develop a coordinated plan of short-term, low-cost transportation management techniques that would improve the effectiveness of the total system. Integration of transit was one of the techniques to be considered by the metropolitan planning organizations (MPOs).

The combination of the long-range regional plan and the short-range transportation management plan provided the basis for drawing up annual plan elements and budgets for transportation improvements. Joint approval of these documents by the Urban Mass Transportation Administration (UMTA) and the Federal Highway Administration (FHWA) was necessary before either agency would allocate funds for any local transportation activity.

EXAMPLES OF SYSTEM INTEGRATION IN U.S. URBAN AREAS

Transit integration efforts throughout the United States exhibit a wide range of approaches and levels of achievement. All types of institutional arrangements have been attempted, and a variety of operational and physical integration techniques have been implemented. The following examples were selected to illustrate how cities in this country are moving toward system integration of urban transportation resources.

Seattle—Merger under a metropolitan authority. Until 1972 the residents of Seattle, Washington, and surrounding King County were served by two transit systems. Within the city limits, the Department of Transportation of the City of Seattle operated buses and the 1.6-km (1-mi) route of the Seattle monorail, constructed in the early 1960s to carry visitors from the CBD to the site of the World's Fair. In the remainder of the county, service was provided by the Metropolitan Transit Corporation, a wholly owned subsidiary of Chromalloy American Corporation. Buses were operated in the suburban areas around Seattle and in small outlying communities. Prohibited from offering intracity services, Metropolitan Transit was permitted to bring suburban passengers into the city only under a "closed-door" operation. The city-owned system was markedly superior to the privately owned suburban system in headways, hours of operation, condition of vehicles, and low fare. It had also recently instituted an express service from North Seattle to the CBD, the "Blue-Streak," and park-and-ride facilities.

An association of cities, special sewer districts, and the government of King County had created a countywide agency, called the Municipality of Metropolitan Seattle (Metro), to plan and administer the area's sewer system. The long-range purpose of this agency was gradually to acquire additional operating functions and become a true metropolitan government. Under the joint sponsorship of Metro and the regional planning organization, and with the informal agreement of both transit operators, measures were presented to the state legislature and voters in King County to fund, through a special sales tax, the operation of a countywide transit system. These measures were approved and the two services were combined under Metro authority.

Under the new administration routes were realigned and extended, park-and-ride lots and bus shelters were constructed, additional vehicles were acquired, express services expanded, exclusive bus lanes designated, and an areawide graduated fare system established.

San Francisco—The federation approach. In 1973 transit services in the nine-county San Francisco Bay area were provided by 20 major operators, including both public agencies and privately owned companies. Merger of these operations under a single, areawide transit authority was generally recognized as impossible within the immediate future because of the vested interests of several large, long-established services. Merger was made even more difficult by the fact that the agency whose service area was the most extensive and might have served as the central authority was the Bay Area Rapid Transit District (BARTD), the most recently created agency and not yet in operation.

Prior to initating rapid rail service in October 1972, BARTD negotiated with the Alameda–Contra Costa Transit District (AC Transit) to eliminate some of that agency's competing bus routes in the East Bay and to provide feeder service to BART stations. Agreements were eventually reached to implement not only these changes, but to reduce fares for passengers transferring from rail to bus. A similar reduction for passengers changing from BART to the San Francisco Municipal Railway (Muni) was subsequently negotiated.

Early in 1974 the formation of a transit federation was announced, to be made up of the five largest publicly owned services in the area: BARTD, AC Transit, Muni, the Golden Gate Bridge, Highway, and Transportation District (GGBHTD), and the Transit District of Santa Clara County (SCCTD). By 1976 they had been joined by four more publicly owned systems and had instituted a regionwide system of transit discount identification cards for handicapped persons and senior citizens.

Interagency transit integration has progressed slowly in the Bay area, but modal integration within agencies is well developed. Muni operates buses, trolleybuses, streetcars, and cable cars under a system of free transfers throughout the city. The GGBHTD operates buses, ferries, and park-and-ride lots in addition to administering a variable toll system for automobiles using the Golden Gate Bridge and planning and developing roads and bikeways in its service area. Weekly and monthly commuter tickets are valid for all modes—ferry, bus, or auto toll.

Chicago—Limited agreements. The Regional Transportation Authority (RTA) in 1976 approved universal transfer policy and a new regional fare structure for city buses operated by the Chicago Transit Authority (CTA), independently operated suburban buses, and commuter railroads. The "RTA Transfer" permits transit users to change between buses of different companies without paying a second fare. The bus systems need not be adjacent; a passenger may ride one suburban bus, board a commuter train into Chicago, and use the transfer on the downtown bus.

Base fares and transfer surcharges have been balanced so as to offset differences in fares charged by city and suburban lines, equalizing the cost of RTA transfers for inbound and outbound passengers. The fare structure for the commuter rail systems is based on 8-km (5-mi) zones with incremental charges for each additional zone.

San Diego—Public contracting for privately operated transit. Two suburban cities within commuting distance of San Diego, La Mesa and El Cajon, contracted with the Yellow Cab Company of San Diego to provide publicly subsidized demand-responsive transit services within their communities. In La Mesa, six-passenger taxi vehicles were purchased by the city under a state capital grants program available only to local government, and leased to the cab company. In El Cajon, the city used local funds to subsidize the use of taxis. The cities set the fares, administered ticket sales, and handled promotion and public information. The taxi company supplied drivers, dispatching services, vehicle maintenance, and system administration for an agreed-upon fee per "live" mile (i.e., one or more passengers in the vehicle). The cities made up the difference between fares paid by users and operating fees charged by the taxi company.

The taxis on duty in the area operated in both regular taxi and subsidized demand-responsive modes. The subsidized ride could be obtained only by presenting a ticket purchased previously at city hall or at one of the local banks. If the user had no ticket, the taxi meter was activated and he was charged at the regular taxi rates. If he wished, the ticket holder could ask to be taken beyond the subsidized service area, in which case the taxi meter was activated at the city limits and the user paid the normal taxi fare for that additional portion of his trip.

Users of the demand-responsive service were taken to points at which they could board buses operated by the San Diego Transit Corporation, but a second fare had to be paid. However, a similar taxi-operated subsidized system in Huntington Park (California) and the Southern California Rapid Transit District serving the Los Angeles area have initiated intersystem transfer privileges.

Westport, Connecticut—The "transportation broker" approach. The Westport Transit District functions as a transportation broker, contracting with bus and taxi operators to provide a variety of services to meet the community's transportation needs—fixed-route circulation, feeder services to commuter rail stations, and special services on subscription for selected user groups, such as the elderly and handicapped, and day-care centers.

Contracts with local taxi operators permit them to offer premium and shared taxi and small package delivery services in addition to subsidized transit services. Twelve-passenger vans are utilized to carry special user groups and complement bus service at low-demand times such as evenings and weekends.

An additional transportation-broker function of the Westport Transit District is to promote carpooling and vanpooling in the area.

Ann Arbor, Michigan—Demand-responsive interface with line-haul transit. Since 1973 the Ann Arbor Transportation Authority has operated a highly successful integrated system of demand-responsive and fixed-route bus service, known as

Teltran. During normal weekday operation dial-a-ride vans collect and distribute passengers in neighborhoods where scheduled bus service does not penetrate. Coordinated schedules of vans and buses provide for efficient free transfer between the two modes at nine points throughout the city. In the evenings and on weekends dial-a-ride provides direct service to the downtown area.

The system was implemented incrementally in one neighborhood at a time. In 1976 service was extended into the last area, completing the citywide system. During this three-year period transit ridership has tripled. Fares are maintained at a low level, and special vans equipped with wheelchair lifts are available to the handicapped at the same fare.

New York—Intermodal transportation centers. The Port Authority Trans-Hudson (PATH) transportation center at Journal Square in Jersey City provides for the arrival and departure of 30,000 passengers per day. Since nearly 45% of PATH riders complete their trips by bus, the facility has extensive bus-loading facilities that permit passengers to transfer easily between modes. Parking facilities are available on two levels for over 600 cars. The center also provides for bicycle, taxi, and kiss-and-ride users. Shops, newsstands, and restaurants are located in the building and rent of these spaces helps to defray operating costs.

Since access to PATH's World Trade Center facility in Manhattan is 75% by foot, 24% by subway, and only 1% by bus, this transportation center emphasizes facilities for pedestrians and convenient transfer between subway lines. Connections to the IRT and Independent 8th Avenue lines are located within the center, and the BMT East Side Broadway line is directly outside the entrance.

The transit center at the Great Neck station of the Long Island Rail Road facilitates transfer of rail commuters to the buses of the Metropolitan Suburban Bus Authority (MSBA). Bus schedules are coordinated with train arrivals and departures, and passengers transfer from one mode to another with a combined bus and rail "UniTicket" issued by the Metropolitan Transportation Authority (MTA).[3] The ticket is also valid at the other end of the rail trip on the Manhattan and Bronx Surface Transit Operating (MABSTOA) buses in Manhattan.

SUMMING UP

System integration is widely recognized as an effective means of improving public transit services in urban areas. Transit integration is more advanced in Europe than in the United States and offers us many examples of institutional arrangements,

---

[3]The constituent agencies of the MTA are the Long Island Rail Road Company, Triborough Bridge and Tunnel Authority, Manhattan and Bronx Surface Transit Operating Authority, Staten Island Rapid Transit Operating Authority, Stewart Airport Land Authority, Metropolitan Suburban Bus Authority, and the New York City Transit Authority, which includes the IRT, BMT, and Independent lines. It provides the New Haven, Erie Lackawanna, and Harlem and Hudson commuter rail services.

operating techniques, and design of intermodal facilities that can be applied in U.S. cities.

Federal transportation policies are promoting system integration in this country not only of transit services but of all urban transportation resources. Examples of successful local experiments in system integration can be found which indicate that U.S. cities are moving toward the goal of totally integrated urban transportation systems.

SELECTED BIBLIOGRAPHY

Many citations are no longer available from their original source. These citations are often available from the National Technical Information Service, U.S. Department of Commerce, 5285 Port Royal Road, Springfield, Va. 22161. We have verified the order numbers for many of these citations, and they are found at the end of the citation. Prices are available through NTIS at the address above.

COLCORD, FRANK C., *Urban Transportation Decision Making 3: The San Francisco Case Study*, prepared for UMTA. Cambridge, Mass.: Massachusetts Institute of Technology, Urban Systems Laboratory, May 1971. Now available as PB 204 954.

HOMBURGER, WOLFGANG S., AND VUKAN R. VUCHIC, "Federation of Transit Agencies as a Solution for Service Integration," *Traffic Quarterly*, 24, no. 3 (July 1970), 379–91.

"Integrated Transport System Is Key to Mobility in Munich, Germany," *Transportation Research News*, no. 66 (September–October 1976), pp. 24–26.

KRZYCZKOWSKI, ROMAN, AND OTHERS, *Integration of Transit Systems; Volume I: Concepts, Status, and Criteria; Volume II: Integrated European Transit Systems; Volume III: Transit Integration in U.S. Urban Areas; and Summary*. Santa Barbara, Calif.: INTERPLAN Corporation, May–October 1973. Now available as PB 241 270, 241 271, 241 272, 241 273.

MYERS, EDWARD T., "Matching the Modes," *MODERN RAILROADS*, 31, no. 3 (March 1976), 62–65.

PUGET SOUND GOVERNMENTAL CONFERENCE, *A Transit Plan for the Metropolitan Area: Seattle and King County*, prepared for the Municipality of Metropolitan Seattle. Seattle, Wash.: Municipality of Metropolitan Seattle, May 1972. Now available as PB 213 558.

PART III

Comparing Transit Modes

INTRODUCTION TO PART III

The purpose of this section is to describe the information necessary and procedures to follow in order to compare one transit mode with another. Comparisons of transit technology based upon cost factors alone are usually misleading because the services provided by each mode may be quite different. Theoretical studies that attempt to determine the passenger volume for which rail or bus is cheapest have reported such a wide range of values at the break-even point as to render the results of little practical use.

Cost data for public transit are essential for computing trends in system operations, in planning extensions and modifications to existing service, and in estimating the likely financial investment of plans for capital investment. Every level of government is concerned with the rising cost of providing transit services, and a careful evaluation of the cost implications inherent in any proposed change is always necessary.

The two components of expenditures for transit are capital and operating costs. Funds for rolling stock and fixed facilities are furnished primarily by the federal and state government through the capital grant program, whereas operating funds are largely from local sources. Operating expenses vary considerably, although labor-related costs will comprise 60 to 75% of the total. Formulas to estimate annual operating costs have been developed based on variables such as vehicle-miles, vehicle-hours, vehicles used in the peak hour, and system revenue. These formulas are useful tools for estimating expected operating expenses for specific system changes. Capital costs involve purchase of vehicles, maintenance facilities, stations, and roadway. Of pressing concern is the rapid escalation of capital costs that has been occurring for vehicles and fixed facilities. Vehicle costs have increased from $40,000 per bus to $60,000 from 1971 to 1977, and from $400,000 per rail car to $700,000 during the same period. Similar increases in construction costs have also taken place.

A comparison of transit modes can be made only within the context of a specific urban setting. The steps to follow are: establish goals for the system; define conditions to be served; define requirements (criteria) and standards; select right-of-way, technology, and type of operations; develop functional designs; evaluate the results; and compare with other alternatives. The criteria for evaluation should examine system performance from the viewpoint of the user, operator, and community. Although one system will be cheapest, it may not be the one selected because other alternatives may have desired features. The process of selection is a complex one and will involve many considerations beyond initial cost.

The most heated controversies have occurred over the selection of technology for rapid transit service. There are many factors behind a community's decision to build a large-scale rapid transit system and a variety of issues to be considered in selecting the appropriate transit technology from among those available. The arguments posed by bus and rail advocates indicate that the controversy will probably not abate. Since the differences in cost between bus and rail may not be that great, the selection will be made on the basis of public perception of each mode's performance.

LESTER A. HOEL, Professor and Chairman,
Department of Civil Engineering,
University of Virginia

Chapter 12

COMPARATIVE COSTS OF TRANSIT MODES

Michael G. Ferreri, *President, Simpson & Curtin Division, Booz, Allen & Hamilton Inc.*

   Discussions of the importance of continuing and enhancing existing transit service, proposals for development of new systems, and plans for capital investment in existing transit systems are supported by any number of concerns which hold out promise for solution to many urban "ills." Public transit has been put forth as part of the solution to:

- Handicapped persons' mobility.
- Economically disadvantaged persons' mobility.
- Cleanup of the environment.
- Urban traffic problems.
- Travel-time savings.
- A tool for shaping urban development.
- A means of saving energy.

Notwithstanding each of those valid considerations, in the final analysis, urban agencies charged with providing and improving transit service confront an economic resource allocation problem which manifests itself in the estimation of the capital and operating expenses (and resulting deficits) necessary to provide those services. To a substantial degree, transit management has been placed in a position of trying to meet increased costs and requests for service within an environment largely determined by forces beyond its control. One such exogenous factor—the density of development—has impaired the productivity of public transportation, while simultaneously contributing to an escalation in the costs necessary to serve potential travel markets. As indicated in Fig. 12-1, service effectiveness, or the number of passengers generated per

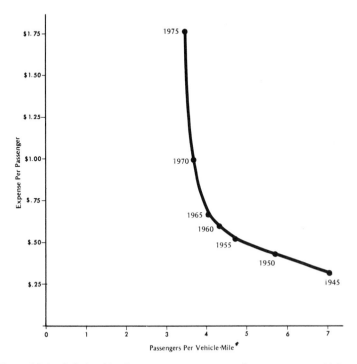

RELATIONSHIP OF EXPENSE PER PASSENGER

AND

PASSENGERS PER VEHICLE·MILE

U.S. TRANSIT SYSTEMS · 1945 — 1975

Figure 12-1 *Relationship of expense per passenger and passengers per vehicle-mile.* [*Source: American Public Transit Association,* Transit Fact Book, *1975–76 ed. (Washington, D.C.: American Public Transit Association, March 1976).*]

vehicle-mile operated, has declined precipitiously since World War II, while the cost of serving the transit rider has increased greatly. Although some escalation in costs may certainly be attributed to inflation and price increases for labor and materials, the growth of automobile ownership and its consequent impact on the location and distribution of urban activities has resulted in lower system effectiveness. Similar to many other collective goods and services, urban sprawl has had a deleterious impact on mass transportation.

In response to the economic resource allocation problem, several sound approaches have been developed to analyze comparative costs of alternative solutions for three basic purposes:

1. Urban areas with fully developed multimodal transit systems coincidentally are almost universally faced with financial problems which have caused a dilemma of maintaining or improving existing operations while trying to contain deficits, leading to a search for methods of productivity improvement.

2. Considerations for short-term service expansions require comparative operating cost analysis to ensure the most cost-effective method of expansion.
3. Longer-range planning for capital improvements to existing systems and/or for installation of completely new systems requires detailed estimates of comparative capital and operating expenses so that the most cost-effective solution is assured.

All of these concerns are driven by the resource allocation question addressed earlier. This question is at issue at all levels of government—federal down to local. The concern has separated itself into the two basic cost areas which comprise capital and operating costs. Historically, capital expenses have involved the replacement of rolling stock and renovation of fixed facilities with substantial assistance of federal grants (at least since 1964). However, financial requirements for capital assistance have constituted a relatively minor portion of the total financial problem. The scale of this

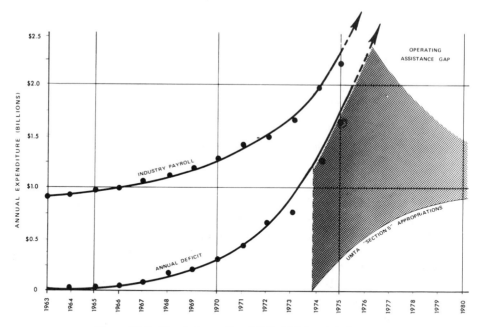

Figure 12-2   *Trend of operating deficit—U.S. transit industry*

approached $2 billion. Further, the trend of operating losses indicates an aggravation of this disparity in the future. Figure 12-2 illustrates this trend and further shows the potential widening of the gap between federal operating assistance under Section 5 of the Urban Mass Transportation Act and the industry deficit. The figure also demonstrates the labor-intensive nature of public transit wherein the deficit curve is almost in parallel with the industry payroll. This chapter concerns itself with an exploration of these costs and the derivation of methods of estimating their magnitude so that comparative costs can be prepared for use in situations in the three categories enumerated. The chapter is organized into a discussion of operating costs—their component composition, their variance by mode, and methods of calculation—and then capital costs which are similarly addressed.

OPERATING COSTS

Figure 12-3 provides an overview of the composition of operating expenses for the U.S. transit industry. These major categories include transportation expense, which is basically the cost of providing the service in the form of drivers, supervisory personnel, and fuel, and constitutes almost half of the total costs (47.5%); and maintenance and garage expenses, which involve primarily repairs to rolling stock, including the labor associated with that function—this category constitutes 20.6% on the average. The next largest category involves administrative and general expenses, including manpower costs, insurance, and safety, which constitute 19.7% of expenses. The balance of all other categories are slightly over 12%. In total, labor-related expenses in the form of wages, salaries, and fringe benefits vary by system but generally constitute 60 to 75% of total cost.

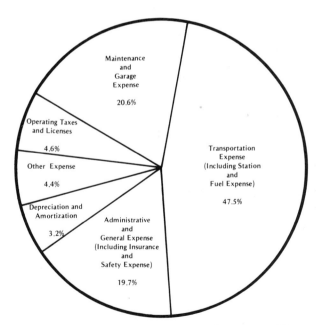

Figure 12-3 *Distribution of nationwide transit operating expenses. [Source: American Public Transit Association, Transit Fact Book, 1975–76 ed. (Washington, D.C.: American Public Transit Association, March, 1976), p. 27.*

These expenses do vary significantly by the mode of operation. The comparative costs can be examined retrospectively for existing transit modes, namely, heavy rail (rail rapid transit), light rail, trolley coach, and bus, and prospectively for new modes, such as automated guideway transit (AGT), including group rapid transit (GRT) and personal rapid transit (PRT). For comparative purposes, it is useful to examine these statistics on unit bases in terms of the cost of providing the service per unit of service provided (which in this case is measured by vehicle-miles operated annually) and per passenger carried. Table 12-1 illustrates the range of unit costs for a variety of existing services and a PRT proposal. It is evident from the table that there are wide variations not only between modes but within modes for unit prices. For example, heavy rail costs vary from $0.65 per vehicle-kilometer ($1.05 per vehicle-mile) in Toronto to $2.90 per vehicle-kilometer ($4.67 per vehicle-mile) for the Bay Area Rapid Transit District (BARTD) operation in San Francisco. Historical light rail costs likewise show system-to-system variations which range from $1.14 per vehicle-kilometer ($1.83 per vehicle-mile) for the Newark City subway (operated by Transport of New Jersey) to $1.63 per vehicle-kilometer ($2.63 per vehicle-mile) for the streetcar system operated by the New Orleans Public Service, Inc. Bus operations indicate ranges as wide as the heavy rail numbers quoted previously. The Twin Cities Area Metropolitan Transit Commission (TCAMTC) in Minneapolis–St. Paul experienced costs of $0.71 per bus-kilometer ($1.15 per bus-mile) in 1975 while the Manhattan and Bronx Surface Transit Operating Authority (MABSTOA) in New York experienced costs of $1.99 per bus-kilometer ($3.21 per bus-mile). Dial-a-ride experience exhibits costs per vehicle-kilometer that are within reason at $0.66 ($1.06 per vehicle-mile). However, cost per passenger is highest of any bus system at $1.13 ($1.82). It is important to note in reviewing these expenses that there are differences which, in some cases, result from the methods of allocating expenses where a system operates more than one mode and also in the policies of providing service, since unit prices can be lowered either by decreasing the numerator or increasing the denominator. The operating expense list is topped off by the inclined plane in Chattanooga, which costs $9.32 per vehicle-kilometer ($15.00 per vehicle-mile).

Examination of operating expense per passenger carried indicates similar wide swings in unit costs. In this case, heavy rail statistics vary from a low of $0.15 per passenger in Montreal to $3.60 per passenger on the Bay Area Rapid Transit District system. It is notable that expense per passenger statistics for bus operations exhibit much more consistency, ranging from $0.24 to $0.49 per passenger.

These statistics are presented for overview purposes; caution is advised in using this kind of simplified unit pricing for cost estimation. Two reasons for caution were previously pointed out; an additional one is the fact that many operating expenses do not vary by vehicle-mile. For instance, wage-related expenses conform more closely to vehicle hours of operation, with speed being an obviously important variable to examine. Further, costs related to maintenance of fixed facilities (e.g., garages) are a function of the size of the fleet required to operate peak service. For these reasons, methods of calculating operating expense for these modes have been developed utilizing multivariable cost allocation models which are calibrated for the expense

TABLE 12-1
Representative Operating Costs—Existing Transit Modes

City/System	Operating Expense (millions)	Vehicle-Miles[a] (millions)	Total Passengers (millions)	Expense/mile[a]	Passenger/Mile[a]	Expense/Passenger
Heavy rail						
New York/NYCTA	$593.3	320.5	1096.0	$ 1.85	3.42	$0.54
Chicago/CTA	90.5	48.8	128.2	1.85	2.63	0.71
Montreal/MUCTC	17.9	14.3	116.4	1.25	8.14	0.15
New York/PATH	35.7	10.5	37.8	3.40	3.60	0.94
Philadelphia/PATCO	12.4	4.3	11.1	2.88	2.58	1.12
Toronto/TTC	31.3	29.7	174.9	1.05	5.89	0.18
San Francisco/BARTD	50.4	10.8	14.0	4.67	1.30	3.60
Intermediate rail (proposed)						
Miami[b]	19.5	30.0	122.0	0.65	4.07	0.16
Twin Cities[c]	16.2	27.9	154.8	0.58	5.55	0.10
Light rail						
New Orleans/NOPSI	2.1	0.8	7.8	2.63	9.75	0.27
Shaker Heights/GCRTA	2.2	1.0	3.7	2.20	3.70	0.59
Newark/TNJ	1.1	0.6	2.5	1.83	4.17	0.44
Toronto/TTC	18.4	10.0	116.1	1.84	11.61	0.16
Personal rapid (proposed)						
Las Vegas[d]	5.9	19.0	17.4	0.31	0.92	0.34
Dial-a-ride						
Average of eight systems[e]	N.A.[f]	N.A.[f]	N.A.[f]	1.06	0.57	1.82
Trolley coach						
Philadelphia/SEPTA	4.4	2.1	14.1	2.09	6.71	0.31
Toronto/TTC	5.1	3.4	32.4	1.50	9.53	0.16
Bus						
New York/NYCTA	182.6	68.6	388.8	2.66	5.67	0.47
New York/MABSTOA	140.2	43.6	339.4	3.21	7.78	0.41
Chicago/CTA	182.7	88.2	497.2	2.07	5.64	0.37
Montreal/MUCTC	95.6	48.0	292.3	1.99	6.09	0.33
Toronto/TTC	59.2	40.5	251.8	1.46	6.22	0.24
Los Angeles/SCRTD	92.8	67.5	204.8	1.37	3.03	0.45
Baltimore/MTA	34.9	25.8	129.1	1.35	5.00	0.27
St. Louis/BSTS	31.6	22.9	63.9	1.38	2.79	0.49
Twin Cities/TCAMTC	26.8	23.3	56.5	1.15	2.42	0.47
Inclined plane						
Chattanooga/CARTA	0.3	0.02	0.5	15.00	25.00	0.60

[a] Metric conversion: 1 mi = 1.6 km.

[b] Simpson & Curtin, *Staging and Financial Plans,* Interim Report, prepared for Metropolitan Dade County Department of Traffic and Transportation (Philadelphia: Simpson & Curtin, January 1972).

[c] Daniel, Mann, Johnson, and Mendenhall, *Cost Estimates and Operating Economics,* Interim Report 8, prepared for Twin Cities Area Metropolitan Transit Commission (Minneapolis, Minn.: Simpson & Curtin/Midwest Planning & Research, Inc., September 11, 1972).

[d] Simpson & Curtin, *Las Vegas PRT Financial Study,* prepared for Monocab, Inc. (Philadelphia: Simpson & Curtin, March 1974).

[e] Boris S. Pushkarev and Jeffrey M. Zupan, *Urban Densities for Public Transportation,* prepared for UMTA by Regional Plan Association (New York: Tri-State Regional Planning Commission, 1976). Now available as PB 256 636.

[f] Not available.

Other Source: American Public Transit Association, *Transit Operating Report for Calendar/Fiscal Year 1974* (Washington, D.C.: American Public Transit Association, November 1975).

conditions of the existing or proposed transit system being analyzed. Another operating-expense estimation technique (more appropriate to situations where no existing system is in place) is to "build up" expenses by estimating numbers of personnel and materials for each functional department. Examples of both techniques follow. A cost-allocation-model derivation for Chicago is described followed by a cost buildup for the planned automated system in Dade County, Florida.

OPERATING-COST-ALLOCATION-MODEL DERIVATION

The preferred technique in developing multivariable cost allocation models is illustrated and derived here through use of the Chicago urban area as an example.[1] The reason for choosing Chicago being that a number of different transit modes are operated in that area and provide for an understanding of differences among bus, commuter rail, and rail rapid transit cost accounting. The technique is valid for and can be applied to any urban area with proper unit data.

Transit operations can be viewed as an economic input–output model. Money is supplied to the system, and transit resources (e.g., vehicle-hours, vehicle-miles, and peak vehicles) are output by the transit system. Mathematically, this economic relationship can be stated as shown in Eq. (12-1):

$$C_t = f(R_1, R_2, R_3, \ldots, R_n) \tag{12-1}$$

where C_t = total cost of transit services (input)
R = transit resources provided (output)
n = number of resources provided

Normally, the cost of providing transit services is presented in a standard list of expense accounts. The cost of each expense account can be denoted C_i, which is the cost of expense account i. The total cost of operations, C_t, for all m expense accounts can be mathematically defined as shown in Eq. (12-2):

$$C_t = \sum_{i=1}^{m} C_i \tag{12-2}$$

where C_i = cost of expense account i
C_t = total cost
m = number of expense accounts

Equation (12-2) represents the input side of transit operations in terms of total cost and the individual cost components. From Eqs. (12-1) and (12-2), it is clear that the input–output relationship for costs and resources can be stated for individual expense accounts as shown in Eq. (12-3):

$$C_i = f(R_1, R_2, R_3, \ldots, R_n) \tag{12-3}$$

The primary assumption of the cost allocation model is that each expense account can be attributed to one or more resources. Thus, for each expense account i, a proportion

---

[1]WALTER CHERWONY AND BRIAN MCCOLLOM, "Development of Multi-Modal Cost Allocation Models," in *The Proceedings of the Fourth Intersociety Conference on Transportation* (Los Angeles: The American Society of Mechanical Engineers, July 1976), pp. 1–9.

of cost allocated to each resource can be specified. For the most part, this assignment or allocation is a subjective process; however, other research has demonstrated the relationship between certain cost accounts and resource levels. For example, fuel cost for a bus operation would logically be allocated entirely to vehicle-miles. Mathematically, the assumption regarding assignment of cost to one or more resources can be stated as shown in Eq. (12-4):

$$\sum_{j=1}^{n} P_{ij} = 1 \qquad (12\text{-}4)$$

where P_{ij} = proportion of cost for expense account i allocated to resource j

Based on Eq. (12-4), cost for each expense account can be allocated to each resource as shown in Eq. (12-5):

$$C_{ij} = C_i P_{ij} \qquad (12\text{-}5)$$

where C_{ij} = cost allocated to resource j for expense account i

By summing all the expense account amounts by resource, the total cost can be stratified by resource as shown in Eq. (12-6):

$$C_j = \sum_{i=1}^{m} C_{ij} \qquad (12\text{-}6)$$

where C_j = cost allocated to resource j

Thus, the sum of cost allocated to each resource is a rearrangement of cost by resources provided rather than expense accounts and will equal the total system cost, as shown in Eq. (12-7):

$$C_t = \sum_{j=1}^{n} C_j \qquad (12\text{-}7)$$

The development of the cost allocation model is the computation of unit cost factor as shown in Eq. (12-8):

$$U_j = \frac{C_j}{R_j} \qquad (12\text{-}8)$$

where U_j = unit cost for resource j

The multivariable cost allocation model can be defined as shown in Eq. (12-9):

$$C_t = U_1 R_1 + U_2 R_2 + U_3 R_3 + \cdots + U_n R_n \qquad (12\text{-}9)$$

Given a set of resource levels for a particular transit route or line, the unit cost can be applied to compute the cost of particular transit service comprising the transit system. Thus, the cost allocation model is quantified from overall system statistics but is applied on individual components that comprise the system.

OPERATING-COST-MODEL EXAMPLE

Having defined the theoretical framework of the cost allocation model, the next step is to apply this approach to the transit operators in the Chicago metropolitan area. A total of five resources were identified as influencing transit operating costs of any mode to be examined and are listed below:

- Vehicle (car)-miles.
- Vehicle-hours.
- Track-miles.
- Peak vehicles (cars).
- System revenue.

Closer scrutiny of the operations of rail and bus carriers suggested that vehicle-miles, peak vehicles, and system revenue should be included in the development of both rail and bus cost allocation models. Although system revenue is not a resource provided by the operator, it was included as a parameter influencing costs, since certain expenditures such as advertising and liability insurance premiums are based on revenue generated. Track-miles were not included in the development of the bus-cost-allocation model, since they operate over public highways and not on an exclusive right-of-way. Vehicle-hours of operation was deleted from the rail-cost model since a considerable portion of the payroll structure is related to vehicle-miles of operation. Also, maintenance charges that are related to use are a function of miles of operation rather than vehicle-hours. In addition, rail carriers compile operating statistics by vehicle-mile rather than vehicle-hour.

COMMUTER-RAILROAD-COST MODELS

For each of the eight railroads, the carrier's expenses were allocated to one of four resources or variables—car-miles, peak car needs, track-miles, and system revenue.

Car-miles. A number of costs are related directly to miles of operation. Expenses such as fuel and maintenance of cars and engines are a direct function of the number of miles operated. Train enginemen's wages are also assigned to the category of car-miles.

Peak car needs. The cost resulting from providing storage, operation, and maintenance facilities for cars is a function of the number of cars required to operate the service rather than the number of miles of service provided. Another significant cost item which varies with the number of peak cars is depreciation. Additionally, salaries of general office personnel and trainmen's wages are assigned to the category of peak car needs.

Track-miles. There are several classes of operating expenses in rail service which are a function of the number of miles of track. Such costs include, for example, road property depreciation and maintenance of office buildings. The cost of these items is a function of the number of units, rather than volume of service operated.

System revenue. Traffic and certain insurance expenses are assigned to the system revenue category, as they are a function of passenger volume, which is proportional to system revenue.

The classification of each operating expense item into one of the four allocation resources is reflected in Table 12-2. This table presents all the operating expense

TABLE 12-2
Allocation of Expense Accounts—Commuter Railroad

Expense Classification	Basis for Allocation			
	Car-Miles[a]	Peak Car Needs	Track-Miles[a]	System Revenue
Maintenance of way and structures				
Superintendence			100%	
Roadway maintenance	50%		50%	
Bridges, trestles, and culverts				
Ties	100%			
Rails	100%			
Other track material	50%		50%	
Ballast	50%		50%	
Track laying and surfacing	50%		50%	
Fences, snowsheds, and signs			100%	
Station and office buildings			100%	
Roadway buildings			100%	
Water stations			100%	
Fuel stations			100%	
Shops and engine houses		100%		
Communications systems	100%			
Signals and interlockers		100%		
Power plants			100%	
Power transmission			100%	
Road property—depreciation			100%	
Roadway machines	100%			
Dismantling road machinery			100%	
Small tools and supplies	100%			
Removing snow, ice, and sand			100%	
Public improvements—maintenance			100%	
Injuries to persons	50%		50%	
Insurance	50%		50%	
Stationery and printing		50%	50%	
Employees' health and welfare benefits	50%		50%	
Maintaining joint tracks, yards, and other facilities—net	50%		50%	
Other expenses	50%		50%	
Maintenance of equipment				
Superintendence		100%		
Shop machinery		100%		
Power-plant machinery		100%		
Diesel locomotives—Repairs—Road	100%			
Diesel locomotives—Repairs—Yard	100%			
Passenger train cars—Repairs	100%			
Work equipment—Repairs		100%		
Miscellaneous equipment repairs		100%		
Equipment depreciation—diesel locomotives		100%		
Equipment depreciation—passenger train cars		100%		
Injuries to persons		100%		
Insurance		100%		
Stationery and printing	50%	50%		
Other expenses	50%	50%		
Equipment depreciation—work equipment		100%		
Equipment depreciation—miscellaneous equipment		100%		
Traffic				
Superintendence				100%
Advertising				100%
Stationery and printing				100%
Employees' health and welfare benefits				100%
Other expenses				100%

TABLE 12-2 Continued

Expense Classification	Basis for Allocation			
	Car-Miles[a]	Peak Car Needs	Track-Miles[a]	System Revenue
Transportation				
Superintendence		100%		
Dispatching trains		100%		
Station employees				100%
Station supplies and expenses;				100%
Yard masters and yard clerks		100%		
Yard conductors and brakemen		100%		
Yard switch and signal tenders		100%		
Yard enginemen		100%		
Yard supplies and expenses		100%		
Train enginemen	100%			
Train fuel	100%			
Servicing train locomotives	100%			
Trainmen		100%		
Train supplies and expenses	50%	50%		
Signal and interlocker operation	100%			
Crossing protection			100%	
Drawbridge operation		100%		
Communication system	100%			
Employees' health and welfare benefits	50%	50%		
Stationery and printing				100%
Other expenses	100%			
Operating joint facilities and tracks—net	50%		50%	
Insurance				100%
Damage to property				100%
Injuries to persons				100%
Damage to livestock on right-of-way			100%	
Miscellaneous				
Dining and buffet service			100%	
Employees' health and welfare benefits[b]				
General				
Salaries and expenses of general officers		100%		
Salaries and expenses of clerks and attendants		100%		
General office supplies and expenses		100%		
Law expenses				100%
Insurance				100%
Employees' health and welfare benefits[b]				
Pensions[b]				
Stationery and printing		100%		
Other expenses		100%		
Taxes				
Payroll taxes[b]				
Property taxes		50%	50%	
Rents payable				
Equipment rentals		100%		
Fixed charges				
Interest on equipment obligations		100%		

[a] Metric conversion: 1 mi = 1.6 km.

[b] Allocated on the basis of total employee compensation by major employment categories (e.g., maintenance of way and structures, traffic, transportation, etc.).

Source: Walter Cherwony and Brian McCollom, "Development of Multi-Modal Cost Allocation Models," in *The Proceedings of the Fourth Intersociety Conference on Transportation* (Los Angeles: The American Society of Mechanical Engineers, July 1976), pp. 1-9.

accounts to which charges were made. To permit fair and unbiased comparisons between carriers, the percent allocations were the same for all commuter railroads.

For example, the cost-allocation-model development for the Chicago and North Western Transportation Company resulted in the apportionment of 39.14% of aggregate cost on the basis of car-miles, 46.11% on the basis of peak car needs, 5.23% allocated on a track-mile basis, and the remaining 9.52% as a function of system revenue. Table 12-3 reflects these apportionments and also indicates the relative weight of each resource variable on a unit cost basis.

TABLE 12-3
Operating-Cost-Allocation-Model Development—
Chicago and North Western Transportation Company

Basis of Allocation	Total Units	Total Cost Allocated	% of Total Cost	Unit Cost
Car-miles[a]	11,104,691	$ 9,272,264	39.14	$0.83/car-mile
Peak car needs	256	10,923,612	46.11	$42,670.36/peak car
Track-miles[a]	358.9	1,239,684	5.23	$3454.12/track-mile
System revenue	$24,278,000	2,254,440	9.52	$0.09/$1 of system revenue
Total		$23,690,000	100.00	

Metric conversion: 1 mi = 1.6 km.
Source: Walter Cherwony and Brian McCollom, "Development of Multi-Modal Cost Allocation Models," in *The Proceedings of the Fourth Intersociety Conference on Transportation* (Los Angeles: The American Society of Mechanical Engineers, July 1976), pp. 1-9.

For the Chicago and North Western Transportation Company, the "four-variable" analysis resulted in the following formula of cost allocation:

$$C = 0.83M + 42{,}670.36V + 3454.12L + 0.09R$$

where C = annual cost of system operation
M = annual car-miles of service
V = peak car needs
L = track-miles
R = annual system revenue

The results of the cost-allocation-model development for the eight railroads in the six-county metropolitan area are presented in Table 12-4. Most of the unit cost factors show wider variability than might be expected among operators in the same geographical region.

It should be noted that a cost allocation model was developed for the Chicago Transit Authority rapid transit operations. Since no other comparable system exists in the Chicago urban area to compare model results, further discussion of this mode is not included here. However, for completeness, the cost model is presented below:

$$C = 0.64M + 27{,}152.17V + 34{,}119.80L + 0.36R$$

TABLE 12-4
Operating-Cost-Allocation-Model Results—Commuter Railroads

Carrier	Power Source	Unit Cost Factors				
		Car-Miles[a] ($/car-mile)	Peak Car Needs ($/peak car)	Track-Miles[a] ($/track-mile)	System Revenue ($/$)
Burlington Northern (BN)	Diesel	1.25	46,265	6,066	0.08
Chicago and North Western (CNW)	Diesel	0.83	42,670	3,454	0.09
Chicago, Milwaukee, St. Paul, and Pacific (MR)	Diesel	1.19	67,522	3,162	0.10
Chicago, Rock Island, and Pacific (RI)	Diesel	1.29	28,409	4,957	0.17
Norfolk and Western (NW)	Diesel	2.31	13,383	235	0.0003
Penn Central (PC)	Diesel	1.23	39,079	839	0.02
Illinois Central Gulf (ICG)	Electric	1.40	35,829	27,222	0.29
Chicago South Shore and South Bend (SS)	Electric	0.98	53,058	3,132	0.17

[a]Metric conversion: 1 mi = 1.6 km.

Source: Walter Cherwony and Brian McCollom, "Development of Multi-Modal Cost Allocation Models," in *The Proceedings of the Fourth Inter-society Conference on Transportation* (Los Angeles: The American Society of Mechanical Engineers, July 1976), pp. 1-9.

BUS-COST MODELS

In a similar fashion to that used for the region's rail carriers, expense accounts for the 10 major bus operators were allocated to one of four resources or variables: vehicle-hours, vehicle-miles, peak vehicle needs, and system revenue.

Vehicle-hours. Operating employees' wages represent by far the largest single element of cost in most transit properties. Employees engaged in operating vehicles are paid on an hourly basis; hence, the allocation of wage expense is most properly made on the basis of hours of service on the system. Similarly, supervision of transportation operations is directly related to the number of hours of service provided, and this item is also properly allocated to the vehicle-hours catgegory.

Vehicle-miles. Many costs are related directly to the miles a bus system operates. Expenses such as fuel, tires, and equipment maintenance are a direct function of miles operated. Material expenses for vehicle bodies, brakes, engines, chassis, and transmissions are also a function of exposure in terms of miles of service. Consequently, these costs, together with the cost of motor fuel, taxes, and certain other miscellaneous expenses, are assigned to the category of vehicle-miles.

Peak vehicle needs. Many individual expense items do not vary as functions of either of the foregoing parameters (i.e., vehicle-hours or vehicle-miles). For example, the cost of providing operating and maintenance facilities for vehicles is determined by the number of vehicles required rather than the number of hours or miles of service provided. Various material expenses are also related to peak vehicle needs. These expenses include the maintenance of building, fixtures, shop and garage, service car equipment, and other miscellaneous shop items. A number of broad overhead expenses will vary with the number of vehicles required to operate the system, including depreciation of equipment, general office costs, and the salaries of general office clerks and officials.

System revenue. Operating costs resulting from injuries and damages are logically assigned to the system revenue category. Traffic promotion, station expenses, and federal income and other taxes are also assigned to this category because they relate primarily to system revenue.

The classification of each operating expense item into one of four allocation variables is presented in Table 12-5. This table aggregates all the operating expense accounts to which charges were made. To facilitate bus operator comparisons, the percent allocations were the same for all bus systems.

As an example, the development of the cost allocation model for the Chicago Transit Authority bus operations resulted in the apportionment of 14.69% of aggregate costs on the basis of vehicle-miles, 54.62% on the basis of vehicle-hours, 25.60% allocated on peak vehicle needs basis, and the remaining 5.09% as a function of system revenue (Table 12-6). For the Chicago Transit Authority, the resultant bus operations cost allocation formula follows:

TABLE 12-5
Allocation of Expense Accounts—Bus Operations

Expense Classification	Basis for Allocation			
	Vehicle-Hours	Vehicle-Miles[a]	Peak Vehicles	System Revenue
Maintenance expense				
Supervision			100%	
Motor buses—repairs		100%		
Tires and tubes		100%		
Miscellaneous shop expenses			100%	
Other maintenance expenses			100%	
Transportation expense				
Supervision	100%			
Bus drivers	100%			
Fuel		100%		
Lubricants		100%		
Service equipment operation				
Other transportation expenses	100%			100%
General and miscellaneous expenses				
Salaries and expenses of general officers			100%	
Salaries and expenses of general office clerks			100%	
General office rent			100%	
General office supplies and expenses			100%	
Traffic promotion				100%
Other general expenses			100%	
Insurance				
Fire, theft, collision			100%	
Public liability and property damage				100%
Workmen's compensation[b]				
Taxes				
General state and local			100%	
State franchise tax on capital stock				100%
Licenses			100%	
Other local			100%	
U.S. motor fuel and oil		100%		
Payroll[b]				
Depreciation				
Building and fixtures			100%	
Motor buses			100%	
Service equipment			100%	
Garage equipment			100%	
Office furniture and equipment			100%	
Miscellaneous equipment			100%	

[a] Metric conversion: 1 mi = 1.6 km.

[b] Allocated on the basis of total employee compensation by major employment categories (e.g., maintenance, transportation, general office, etc.).

Source: Walter Cherwony and Brian McCollom, "Development of Multi-Modal Cost Allocation Models," in *The Proceedings of the Fourth Intersociety Conference on Transportation* (Los Angeles: The American Society of Mechanical Engineers, July 1976), pp. 1-9.

TABLE 12-6
Operating-Cost-Allocation-Model Development—
Chicago Transit Authority—Bus

Basis of Allocation	Total Units	Total Cost Allocated	% of Total Cost	Unit Cost
Vehicle-miles[a]	90,701,804	$ 25,431,448	14.69	$0.28/vehicle-mile
Vehicle-hours	8,500,071	94,572,897	54.62	$11.13/vehicle-hour
Peak vehicles	2,210	44,330,511	25.60	$20,059.22/peak vehicle
System revenue	$138,832,579	8,806,063	5.09	$0.06/$1 of system revenue
Total		$173,140,919	100.00	

[a]Metric conversion: 1 mi = 1.6 km.

Source: Walter Cherwony and Brian McCollom, "Development of Multi-Modal Cost Allocation Models," in *The Proceedings of the Fourth Intersociety Conference on Transportation* (Los Angeles: The American Society of Mechanical Engineers, July 1976), pp. 1-9.

$$C = 11.13H + 0.28M + 20,059.22V + 0.06R$$

where C = annual cost of system operation
 H = annual vehicle-hours of service
 M = annual vehicle-miles of service
 V = peak vehicle needs
 R = annual system revenue

The results of the development of the cost allocation model for the 10 major bus operators in the Chicago metropolitan area are presented in Table 12-7.

OPERATING-COST-BUILDUP EXAMPLE

The preparation of operating expense estimates under this method requires a functional definition of the type of service to be provided and the methods of providing such service. In this example, costs are estimated for a 71.9-km (44.7-mi) AGT system with 48 stations. The functional methods of operation are described as follows.

Automatic train operation (ATO). The rapid transit system will be fully automatically controlled from a central "tower." It is estimated that ATO will require an average of 10 operators per shift, on a three-shift-per-day basis. One "spare" shift will be required to cover holidays, vacations, sickness, and so on, producing a total staff requirement of 40 operators. At peak periods, the 10 console operators would be distributed as follows: four train controllers, four station surveillance, and two power controllers. This operator requirement would be reduced in off-peak periods.

Station operation. Station operations will be automated to the extent possible. Ticket vending machines, automatic turnstiles, and bill changers will be available at each station. While the reliability of these is being improved by the manufacturers,

TABLE 12-7
Operating-Cost-Allocation-Model Results—Bus Operators

Carrier	Ownership	Unit Cost Factors			
		Vehicle-Hours ($/vehicle-hour)	Vehicle-Miles[a] ($/vehicle-mile)	Peak Vehicle Needs ($/peak vehicle)	System Revenue ($/$)
Urban/suburban[b]					
Chicago Transit Authority (CTA)	Public	11.13	0.28	20,059	0.06
South Suburban Safeways (SSS)	Private	6.21	0.18	11,174	0.11
Suburban Transit System (STS)	Private	4.44	0.21	7,645	0.07
United Motor Coach (UMC)	Private	5.08	0.21	5,681	0.08
West Towns (WT)	Private	8.31	0.17	6,533	0.07
Suburban/local[c]					
Aurora Transit System (ATS)	Public	6.03	0.11	13,831	0.11
Elgin Department of Transportation (ELG)	Public	4.54	0.18	5,964	0.07
Joliet Mass Transit District (JMTD)	Public	4.49	0.11	3,161	0.12
Waukegan North Chicago (WNC)	Private	5.17	0.11	4,164	0.06
Village of Wilmette (WIL)	Public	5.23	0.26	5,358	0.21

[a] Metric conversion: 1 mi = 1.6 km.
[b] Provides service between downtown Chicago and nearby suburban communities.
[c] Provides service within outlying satellite communities.

Source: Walter Cherwony and Brian McCollom, "Development of Multi-Modal Cost Allocation Models," in *The Proceedings of the Fourth Intersociety Conference on Transportation* (Los Angeles: The American Society of Mechanical Engineers, July 1976), pp. 1-9.

failures are apt to occur. When such failures occur, it is necessary to (1) operate affected items manually to afford minimum delay to passengers, and (2) repair the failed appliance as rapidly as possible. It is estimated that approximately one man per station, or a staff of 50, will be able to oversee operations and perform ticket-collecting functions in event of failures.

In order to provide for repair of vending machine failures, service of escalators, structural repairs, lighting replacements, air conditioning, and plant servicing, a staff of 50 maintenance engineers will be required. Again, these will be allocated among appropriate shifts with cover for holidays, and so on.

Other station staff will include the security force. Each station will have closed-circuit television surveillance. However, if vandalism or a disturbance is detected, the security force must respond quickly. Road patrols will visit stations on a random roving basis and be in radio communication with the control center at all times. An additional function of the security staff is to empty the cash from the vending and change machines. It is estimated that a security staff of 50 will be required.

One additional category of station staff required will be cleaners. These will normally work second and third shifts and not be required in peak periods in the day. It is expected that part-time labor will be used extensively for this category. However, for cost-estimating purposes, 50 full-time cleaners are included.

Maintenance and yard operation. In the maintenance shops at two facilities, maintenance engineers in the categories of mechanical, electrical, and electronic will be required. These will be supported by laborers and clerical staff. Yard operations personnel will include 30 hostlers and 40 cleaners, and those categories will both work three-shift operations.

Two categories of maintenance engineers will be concerned with guideway maintenance—the track and power crew, and the ways crew. The track and power crew will maintain the running surface, the power system, the communications system, and the trackside units of the control system. The ways crew will maintain and repair the track structure, including support columns.

Other operating costs. Other operating costs will be incurred in the form of replacement parts for vehicles and structures, power purchased, and general accident and other insurance for the system.

The cost of electric power for the entire system, including traction, lighting, heating, console operations, and communication is estimated at 6 cents per vehicle-kilometer per year (9¢ per vehicle-mile per year). Annual mileage of 30 million vehicle-miles (48 million vehicle-kilometers) produces a total power cost of $2.7 million per year.

These estimates result in a buildup of direct salaries of all operating personnel, including allocations for supervisory personnel and employee benefits. These personnel costs when added to operating expenses for materials, spares, power, and insurance produce the overall operating expense estimates indicated in Table 12-8.

Depending upon the problem at hand (i.e., estimating operating expenses for

TABLE 12-8
Summary of AGT Operating Costs

		Total (1970 dollars × 1000)
Wages and salaries		
Automatic train operation		
Console operators	40 @ $10,000/year	$ 400
Station operations		
Custodian/ticket collectors	50 @ $ 8,000/year	400
Appliance maintenance	25 @ $10,000/year	250
General maintenance	25 @ $10,000/year	250
Security force	50 @ $ 9,000/year	450
Cleaners	50 @ $ 6,000/year	300
Vehicle maintenance		
Mechanical	80 @ $10,000/year	800
Electrical	40 @ $12,000/year	480
Electronic	25 @ $15,000/year	375
Laborers	30 @ $ 6,000/year	180
Clerical	20 @ $ 8,000/year	160
Yard operators		
Hostlers	30 @ $ 8,000/year	240
Cleaners	40 @ $ 6,000/year	240
Roadway maintenance		
Track and power crew	20 @ $12,000/year	240
Ways crew	20 @ $10,000/year	200
		$ 4,965
Employee benefits, pension, etc.	(30%)	$1,490
Administration/supervision	(25%)	1,241
		2,731
Total wages and salaries		$ 7,696
Maintenance materials and spares		
Station materials	@ $10,000/station	$ 480
Roadway materials	@ $20,000/operating-mile of road[a]	900
Vehicle materials and spares	@ $ 2,500/vehicle	950
		$ 2,330
Power		2,700
Insurance		500
Estimated annual costs		$13,226
Contingency	(5%)	661
Total		$13,887

[a]Metric conversion: 1 mi = 1.6 km.

Source: Simpson & Curtin, *Staging and Financial Plans,* Interim Report 7, prepared for Metropolitan Dade County Department of Traffic and Transportation (Philadelphia: Simpson & Curtin, January 1972).

changes to an existing system versus installation of a totally new system), either of the preceding two techniques can provide reasonable estimates of operating costs for any mode being analyzed. The advantage of the cost allocation model approach is that it permits not only systemwide cost estimates but also operating expense estimates for individual elements of a system, such as a bus route or a single line of a rail rapid transit/AGT proposal.

CAPITAL COSTS

Figure 12-4 provides a distribution of capital investment for the national transit industry which is a companion to the operating cost distribution presented earlier. The largest national investment is in way and structures for systems currently operating, and comprises 52.4% of the total replacement cost in 1975. The next largest segment is vehicles at almost one-third of the total investment with fixed facilities (i.e., stations, maintenance, and storage) totaling 15.6%. This historical distribution does not differ substantially from the investment distribution that would be associated with any new system that contemplated a mix of transit modes. In this section of the chapter, capital expenses will first be treated by transit mode, including their associated component parts; second, examined by unit prices; and third, reviewed in a comparative total cost summary indicating cost of modal options for application to a corridor.

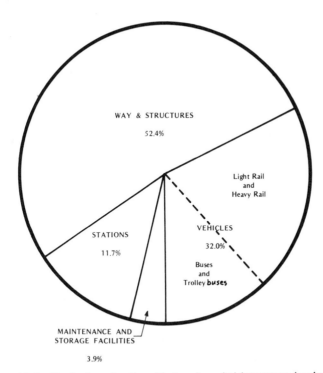

Figure 12-4 *Distribution of nationwide transit capital investment (replacement cost). [Source: American Public Transit Association,* Transit Fact Book, *1975–76 ed. (Washington, D.C.: American Public Transit Association, March 1976), and various reference materials maintained by Simpson & Curtin.]*

Capital expenses of a bus system essentially comprise vehicles and maintenance facilities. Related street furniture, such as shelters and informational signs, are a relatively minor part of the total. In early 1977, significant changes occurred in bus technology (present and future) and methods of procurement. It is useful to examine the trend in vehicle costs relative to this change. Figures 12-5 and 12-6 present trend data for 12-m (40-ft) buses (the standard U.S. coach) and 11-m (35-ft) buses through 1976. The figures are derived from examination of low bids accepted for delivery in that time period.

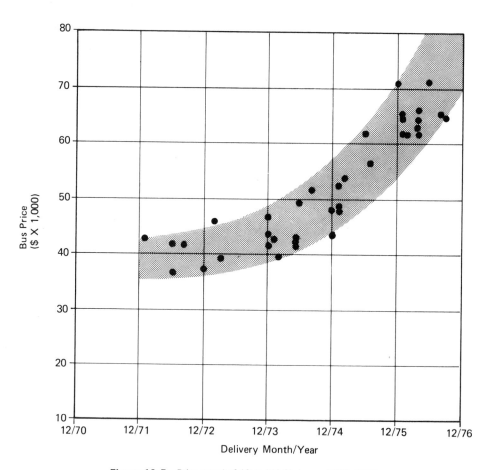

Figure 12-5 *Price trend of 12 m (40 ft) buses 1971–1976*

It is evident from Fig. 12-5 that substantial escalation has occurred in the standard U.S. bus going from an approximate $40,000 per bus average in 1971 to the high $60,000s in 1976—almost a 70% increase in 5 years. The trend of prices for 11-m

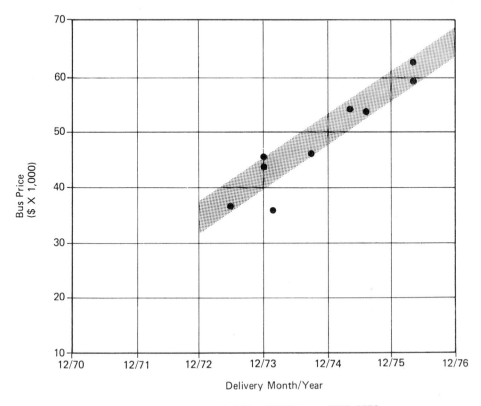

Figure 12-6 *Price trend of 11 m (35 ft) buses 1972–1976*

(35-ft) buses has exhibited almost the same increase, although the change from 1975 to 1976 has not been nearly as dramatic, and the trend has exhibited more of a straight-line projection.

In 1977, the Secretary of Transportation issued policy statements regarding the method of procurement and the type of bus to be procured in instances where Urban Mass Transportation Administration funds are to be used. The significant part of these changes is that they permit the acquisition of advanced design buses (ADBs, in some cases referred to as the intermediate bus) and mandate that by 1979 a composite U.S. Department of Transportation specification be used to procure low-floor buses (referred to as the Transbus) which provide for easy access, particularly to elderly and handicapped riders. It is estimated that this mandate will define a bus that will probably cost approximately $100,000 per unit in 1976 dollars.

The other major element of the system capital expense involves maintenance and storage facilities. A sample of 1975 costs for 17 such facilities indicates a range from less than $0.5 million to almost $10 million. The most appropriate way to examine these costs is on a unit basis by two measures—construction cost per square foot and construction cost per bus. Further, there are differences in these unit prices by functional definition of the facility. Table 12-9 provides representative capital costs for the three main types of facilities. In the case of storage facilities, the six facility sites in Table 12-9 display a cost of $172/m^2$ ($16/ft^2$) to $301/m^2$ ($28/ft^2$) with an average of $248 ($23$). The matching average cost per bus is $10,940. Similar statistics are arrayed in the table for inspection garages which have a cost of $301/m^2$ ($28/ft^2$) average and an average cost per bus of $19,680. Main maintenance facilities average $441/m^2$ ($41/ft^2$) and $650 per bus.

TABLE 12-9
Typical 1975 Capital Cost—Bus Garages

	Cost per Square Foot[a]	Cost per Bus
1. Storage facilities		
Akron, Ohio	$16	$ 5,250
Rochester, N.Y.	22	10,680
Rochester, N.Y.	24	11,490
Kansas City, Mo.	22	11,790
Minneapolis/St. Paul, Minn.	28	15,000
Milwaukee, Wisc.	27	11,440
Average	$23	$10,940
2. Inspection garages		
Pittsburgh, Pa.	$23	$13,050
Pittsburgh, Pa.	29	22,780
Pittsburgh, Pa.	27	19,510
Pittsburgh, Pa.	31	20,560
Pittsburgh, Pa.	29	19,760
Rochester, N.Y.	27	14,300
Minneapolis/St. Paul, Minn.	33	27,800
Average	$28	$19,680
3. Main maintenance facilities		
Dallas, Tex.	$48	$ 8,500
Rochester, N.Y.	44	7,000
Pittsburgh, Pa.	39	5,700
Kansas City, Mo.	32	5,400
Average	$41	$ 6,650
Average all facilities	$29	$13,530

[a]Metric conversion: 1 ft^2 = 0.09 m^2.

Source: Virgil S. Thurlow, John A. Bachman, and C. Denver Lovett, *Bus Maintenance Facilities: A Transit Management Handbook,* prepared for UMTA by The Mitre Corporation (Washington, D.C.: U.S. Government Printing Office, November 1975).

RAIL TRANSIT COSTS

Rail transit costs contain two of the same elements as bus costs (i.e., vehicles and maintenance facilities), but also include guideway, track, stations, power, and other capital expenses. Further, there are differences in each of these elements for different types of rail systems, such as light rail, rail rapid transit, and commuter rail. Escalation of rail transit cars has been more than double the experience with buses over the same time period (i.e., 1971–1976). Rapid transit car costs have increased almost 170%, while commuter rail car costs have escalated almost 200%. The cost of the two vehicle types are approaching each other, and in 1977 both approximated $700,000 per vehicle.

Trend data for light rail vehicles are not available, inasmuch as only one major order has been placed in the same time period. The price per car for light rail vehicles being constructed for Boston and San Francisco between 1975 and 1977 is $300,000 and $315,000, respectively (Boeing would argue that the cost is substantially higher). Variations on rail systems involving new technology, fixed-guideway operations have ranged from very small personal rapid transit (PRT) systems through intermediate-scale group rapid transit (GRT) systems. Vehicle costs for these types of systems have ranged from $100,000 to $500,000 per vehicle.

COMPARATIVE UNIT COSTS

Other elements of capital expense, such as guideways and power, do not lend themselves to gross cost examination in a comparative sense. They must be viewed in unit terms. Table 12-10 provides summary statistics for five modes, showing representative unit prices of guideways and stations. Guideway costs range from a low of $1 million/km ($1.6 million/mi) for light rail to as high as $26 million/km ($42 million/mi) for a busway in subway. These costs are typical, but experience outside these ranges can be found. For example, in a 1976 rail transit system cost study, guideway costs for light rail at-grade in suburban situations have been estimated as low as $466,000/km

TABLE 12-10
Representative Capital Costs by Mode (millions of dollars)

System	Per Mile of Guideway[a]			Stations
	Subway	Elevated	At-Grade	
Heavy rail	$40	$20	$10	$3-15
Intermediate rail	30	15	5	2-6
Light rail	35	15	2	2-6
Busway	42	10	3	2-6
Personal rapid	—	5	—	0.8

[a]Metric conversion: 1 mi = 1.6 km.

Sources: Simpson & Curtin, *Implementation Plan*, Interim Report 6, prepared for the Broward County Transportation Authority (Philadelphia: Simpson & Curtin, September 1973).

Transportation Research Board, *Light Rail Transit*, Special Report 161 (Washington, D.C.: Transportation Research Board, 1975).

Daniel, Mann, Johnson, & Mendenhall, *Cost Estimates and Operating Economics*, Interim Report 8, prepared for the Twin Cities Area Metropolitan Transit Commission (Minneapolis, Minn.: Simpson & Curtin/Midwest Planning & Research, Inc., September 11, 1972).

Vukan R. Vuchic, F. Brian Day, and Richard M. Stanger, *Rail Transit: Characteristics, Innovations and Trends* (Philadelphia: University of Pennsylvania, January 1975).

D. B. Sanders, T. A. Reynen, and K. Bhatt, *Characteristics of Urban Transportation Systems: A Handbook for Transportation Planners*, prepared for U.S. DOT (Chicago: De Leuw, Cather & Co., May 1974).

($750,000/mi).[2] In special instances, such as subway construction in the core of a major city, guideway costs have exceeded $44 to $50 million/km ($70 to $80 million/mi).

Station costs vary substantially with particular local design considerations. A "bare bones" station which is functionally adequate can be built for $1 million or less. On the other hand, urban-area goals for architectural treatments, provision of other service, and enhancement of station environment can drive prices to virtually unlimited costs. The examples in Table 12-10 show a range from less than $1 million to $15 million per station.

Unlike the operating expense example, there is no "formula" approach to capital cost. Each component of a planned new system or for renovation of an existing system should be subjected to a careful engineering analysis which flows from the functional characteristics of the proposed system and estimates of demand for that system. For example, the typical planning process produces modal-split data assigning trips to a projected alternative. These trips, in turn, determine the number of vehicles required on the system, the optimum spacing of stations, fixed-facility type, and other elements. While gross unit statistics can be used for very preliminary estimates of the magnitude of expenditure, decisions on implementation of a system require careful engineering analysis.

As this engineering analysis proceeds, typically alternative systems will be examined so that the planned improvement, expansion, or new system construction can be assessed in light of cost effectiveness and other criteria. This analysis is performed by postulating modal options for a given corridor, costing those options, comparing that to the resultant demand and other impacts on the community, and combining all statistics in a benefit–cost or other type of comparative analysis to decide on the appropriate mode. An example of such a comparison for four different modes is presented in Table 12-11. The bottom line of the table indicates the total capital costs and the unit capital costs for these options in a similar functional deployment. It can be noted that the bus alternative emerges as the lowest capital cost option due in large part to lack of guideway expense because of at-grade operation for a portion of the route. Further in the example, AGT costs are higher than rail rapid transit (shown as RRT) by approximately $3 million/km ($5 million/mi). This table illustrates one part of the comparative analysis. To truly judge the cost of these systems, obviously operating expense must be added and both sets of costs placed on an annual expenditure basis by amortizing capital costs. Further, comparative analysis should examine the present worth of future total investment (capital and operating) by, in effect, "capitalizing future operating expenses." In this way, through the use of operating-cost-allocation models and capital-cost engineering estimates, a complete cost analysis can be prepared for utilization in an alternatives analysis to select the approriate transit mode.

---

[2]T. K. DYER, *Rail Transit System Cost Study*, Final Report, prepared for UMTA (Lexington, Mass.: Thomas K. Dyer, Inc., January 1976). Now available as PB 254 627.

TABLE 12-11

Capital-Costs Comparisons (millions of constant 1975 dollars)

Cost Elements	AGT (8.55 route-miles)		RRT (8.54 route-miles)		LRT (7.84 route-miles)		Bus (7.66 route-miles)	
	Total	$/Route-Mile	Total	$/Route-Mile	Total	$/Route-Mile	Total	$/Route-Mile
Guideway	70.0	8.19	59.5	6.97	22.5	2.87	26.1	3.41
Trackwork	1.8	0.21	7.5	0.88	7.5	0.96	–	–
Landscaping (guideway only)	0.3	0.04	0.3	0.04	0.0	0.00	–	–
Stations and parking lots	22.4	2.62	21.2	2.48	6.9	0.88	3.9	0.51
Rights-of-way costs	13.8	1.61	13.8	1.62	5.6	0.71	5.6	0.73
Ice and snow control	0.7	0.08	0.04	0.00	0.1	0.01	–	–
Yards and shops	15.1	1.77	9.6	1.12	7.6	0.97	7.0	0.91
Power collection and distribution	15.8	1.85	14.2	1.66	5.9	0.75	–	–
Control and crossing protection	9.8	1.15	9.0	1.05	2.0	0.26	0.7	0.09
Feeder busway facilities	13.3	1.56	13.3	1.56	13.3	1.70	13.3	1.74
Subtotal	163.0	19.06	148.44	17.38	71.4	9.11	56.6	7.39
Engineering and administration (15%)	24.5	2.87	22.3	2.61	10.7	1.36	8.5	1.11
Contingencies (25%)	40.8	4.77	37.1	4.34	17.9	2.28	14.2	1.85
Guideway vehicles	83.7	9.79	60.3	7.06	50.4	6.43	–	–
Feeder vehicles	37.3	4.36	37.3	4.37	24.2	3.09	55.0	7.18
Total capital costs	349.3	40.85	305.44	35.76	174.6	22.27	134.3	17.53

aMetric conversion: 1 mi = 1.6 km.

Source: E. S. Diamant and others, *Light Rail Transit: (A) State of the Art Review*, prepared for UMTA (Chicago: De Leuw, Cather & Company, Spring 1976), p. 273. Now available as PB 256 821.

SELECTED BIBLIOGRAPHY

Many citations are no longer available from their original source. These citations are often available from the National Technical Information Service, U.S. Department of Commerce, 5285 Port Royal Road, Springfield, Va. 22161. We have verified the order numbers for many of these citations, and they are found at the end of the citation. Prices are available through NTIS at the address above.

BOOZ, ALLEN APPLIED RESEARCH, *Projection of the Probable Future Development of Urban Transportation Modes*, Final Report, prepared for Rohr Industries, Inc. Bethesda, Md.: Booz, Allen Applied Research, December 1974.

CHERWONY, WALTER, AND BRIAN MCCOLLOM, "Development of Multi-Modal Cost Allocation Models," in *The Proceedings of the Fourth Intersociety Conference on Transportation*, pp. 1–9. Los Angeles: The American Society of Mechanical Engineers, July 1976.

DANIEL, MANN, JOHNSON, AND MENDENHALL, *Cost Estimates and Operating Economics*, Interim Report 8, prepared for Twin Cities Area Metropolitan Transit Commission. Minneapolis, Minn.: Simpson & Curtin/Midwest Planning & Research, Inc., September 1972.

DE LEUW, CATHER & COMPANY, with contributions from The Urban Institute, *Characteristics of Urban Transportation Systems: A Handbook for Transportation Planners*, prepared for UMTA. Chicago: De Leuw, Cather & Company, May 1975. Now available as PB 245 809.

DIAMANT, E. S., AND OTHERS, *Light Rail Transit: (A) State of the Art Review*, prepared for UMTA. Chicago: De Leuw, Cather & Company, Spring 1976. Now available as PB 256 821.

INTERNATIONAL UNION OF PUBLIC TRANSPORT, *International Statistical Handbook of Urban Public Transit*, ed. Lee H. Rogers, 2 vols. Brussels, Belgium: J. Goemaere, 1975.

METROPOLITAN TRANSIT AUTHORITY, *Phase I Plan: Baltimore Region Rapid Transit System*. Baltimore, Md.: Metropolitan Transit Authority, January 1971.

POLIN, LEWIS, AND GEORGE T. MAURO, "Toward the Development of an Accommodation Service Policy," in *The Proceedings of the Fourth Intersociety Conference on Transportation*. Los Angeles: The American Society of Mechanical Engineers, July 1976.

PUSHKAREV, BORIS S., AND JEFFREY M. ZUPAN, *Urban Densities for Public Transportation*, prepared for UMTA by Regional Plan Association. New York: Tri-State Regional Planning Commission, 1976. Now available as PB 256 636. Also available as *Public Transportation and Land Use Policy*. Bloomington, Ind.: Indiana University Press, 1977.

SIMPSON & CURTIN, *Implementation Plan*, Interim Report 6, prepared for Broward County Transportation Authority. Philadelphia: Simpson & Curtin, September 1973.

———, *Las Vegas PRT Financial Feasibility Study*, prepared for Rohr Industries, Inc. Philadelphia: Simpson & Curtin, March 1974.

———, *Staging and Financial Plans*, Interim Report 7, prepared for Metropolitan Dade County Department of Traffic and Transportation. Philadelphia: Simpson & Curtin, January 1972.

SOUTHERN CALIFORNIA ASSOCIATION OF GOVERNMENTS, *Rail Transit Car Costs: A Review, Analysis and Projections*. Los Angeles: Southern California Association of Governments, May 1975. Now available as PB 225 835.

THURLOW, VIRGIL S., JOHN A. BACHMAN, AND C. DENVER LOVETT, *Bus Maintenance Facilities: A Transit Management Handbook*, prepared for UMTA by The Mitre Corporation. Washington, D.C.: U.S. Government Printing Office, November 1975. Now available as PB 250 475.

TRANSPORTATION RESEARCH BOARD, *Light Rail Transit*, Special Report 161. Washington, D.C.: Transportation Research Board, 1975.

VUCHIC, VUKAN R., F. BRIAN DAY, AND RICHARD M. STANGER, *Rail Transit: Characteristics, Innovations and Trends*. Philadelphia: University of Pennsylvania, College of Engineering and Applied Science, January 1975.

WELLS, JOHN D., AND OTHERS, *Economic Characteristics of the Urban Public Transportation Industry*, prepared for U.S. DOT by Institute for Defense Analyses. Washington, D.C.: U.S. Government Printing Office, February 1972.

Chapter 13

COMPARATIVE ANALYSIS AND SELECTION OF TRANSIT MODES

VUKAN R. VUCHIC, *Professor of Transportation Engineering, University of Pennsylvania*

Selection of the best combination of transit modes is the central decision in planning new or expanding existing transit systems. This decision is very important because it not only determines technological, operational, and network characteristics of the planned system, but through these elements it has a major influence on the role the system will assume in the city's physical, economic, social, and environmental conditions and development. Because of their interdependence, all these factors must be considered in the mode selection, making it a very complex task.

It will be shown that some elements of mode comparison and selection can be quantified and thus compared exactly. However, many other elements are qualitative, so their evaluation must include considerable experience and value judgments. The procedure, therefore, cannot be defined by a quantitative model nor can the results of the comparative analysis be expressed by a single quantitative value. The desire to devise a fully "mechanized" comparative analysis and base it on a single criterion (cost) has often been utilized, but it usually produced erroneous results, contrary to real-world conditions and experience. Particularly misleading have been the studies based on average values and models of hypothetical situations.

Following a brief review of previous works on transit mode comparison, including its theoretical basis and applications, this chapter defines requirements for transit service, including the three major interested parties and characteristics of different transit modes. Utilizing these concepts, a general methodology of comprehensive transit system evaluation is presented. An example of application of this methodology is also included.

The studies involving comparison of transit modes vary considerably in their approach and purpose, as well as in quality. The most common types of these studies are briefly reviewed here.

An extensive conceptual framework for comparison of different transit modes was developed by Kuhn.[1] He showed the deficiencies of comparisons based on costs only and emphasized the importance of including not only direct quantitative factors, but also indirect and qualitative ones. He illustrated the methodology by a framework for comparison of a freeway and a rapid transit line. Hill[2] further developed the concepts for transportation plan evaluation, emphasizing the need to consider different affected groups. He proposed a method for systematic handling of nonquantifiable factors which is comprehensive, but extremely complicated for application. Morlok,[3] Manheim,[4] and several other authors emphasized the need to include all major characteristics ("dimensions") of transit modes into their analysis and evaluation.

Another set of studies focused on comparisons of actual characteristics of different transit modes. Vuchic[5] analyzed components of different modes, such as types of rights-of-way, technology (guided vs. steered), and vehicle size, and on the basis of their characteristics compared light rail transit (LRT) with several other modes for different sets of conditions (network types, passenger volumes, etc.). Deen and James[6] compared costs of buses and rapid transit for different types of right-of-way (R/W). Other mode characteristics (comfort, speed, environmental impacts, etc.) were intentionally not included. Lehner[7] presented a comprehensive comparison of all major features of light rail transit and rapid transit, utilizing actual data from many operating systems. Another comprehensive comparison of two actual systems involving different modes (commuter buses on a busway and rail rapid transit) which operate under similar conditions but with different types of service was made by Vuchic and Stanger.[8]

[1]Tillo E. Kuhn, *Public Enterprise Economics and Transport Problems* (Berkeley, Calif.: University of California Press, 1962).

[2]Morris Hill, "A Method for the Evaluation of Transportation Plans," in *Transportation System Analysis and Evaluation of Alternate Plans*, Highway Research Record 180 (Washington, D.C.: Highway Research Board, 1967), pp. 21–34.

[3]Edward K. Morlok, "The Comparison of Transport Technologies," in *Transportation System Evaluation*, Highway Research Record 238 (Washington, D.C.: Highway Research Board, 1968), pp. 1–22.

[4]Marvin L. Manheim, "Principles of Transport Systems Analysis," in *Transportation System Analysis and Evaluation of Alternate Plans*, Highway Research Record 180 (Washington, D.C.: Highway Research Board, 1967), pp. 11–20.

[5]Vukan R. Vuchic, "Place of Light Rail in the Family of Transit Modes," in *Light Rail Transit*, Special Report 161 (Washington, D.C.: Transportation Research Board, 1975), pp. 62–76.

[6]Thomas B. Deen and Donald H. James, "Relative Cost of Bus and Rail Transit Systems," in *Transportation Systems Planning*, Highway Research Record 293 (Washington, D.C.: Highway Research Board, 1969), pp. 33–53.

[7]Friedrich Lehner, "Light Rail and Rapid Transit," in *Light Rail Transit*, Special Report 161 (Washington, D.C.: Transportation Research Board, 1975), pp. 37–49.

[8]V. R. Vuchic and R. M. Stanger, "Lindenwold Rail Line and Shirley Busway: A Comparison," in *Evaluation of Bus Transit Strategies*, Highway Research Record 459 (Washington, D.C.: Highway Research Board, 1973), pp. 13–28.

A third group of studies are those performed for actual planning of new transit systems in individual cities. The comprehensiveness of these studies varies greatly. The study for San Francisco Bay Area Rapid Transit (BART) was a relatively simple task since the performance specifications mandated by the legislature were such that only modes operating on exclusive R/W could meet them. The choice of rail technology was logical. A similar study for Manchester, England,[9] analyzed environmental impacts of alternative technologies in great detail. Alternative modes analyzed for Frankfurt, Germany,[10] had some variations in types of service caused by different characteristics of the compared technologies (monorail, LRT, and rapid transit). Transit mode selections for Baltimore, Rochester (New York), Los Angeles, Denver, Edmonton (Canada), Miami (Florida), Pittsburgh (Pennsylvania), and other cities have been increasingly more comprehensive and detailed. One of the most comprehensive studies was done for Buffalo, New York.[11] It produced a number of excellent conceptual definitions and comparisons of modal characteristics.

Finally, several economic studies of mode comparisons have been performed for hypothetical urban corridors, utilizing average costs from different cities or from one specific metropolitan area. Started by Meyer, Kain, and Wohl,[12] this type of study has been followed by several groups of economists, the most recent one being the University of California group headed by Keeler.[13]

The assumptions and models used in most economic comparisons of modes are so unrealistic that their findings are, in most cases, in sharp variance with the studies of transit in actual cities, mentioned earlier. However, their simplistic approach and seemingly clear results give these studies a totally unjustified credibility among laymen. It is therefore necessary to discuss briefly the major deficiencies inherent in their methodology.

The economic studies are intended to find optimal domains for individual modes defined by the number of passengers they carry during the peak hour. Actually, choice of mode must be based on a number of factors, such as local conditions, alternative means of travel, service quality throughout the day, and short- and long-term impacts on the served area. Optimal domains of modes in terms of passenger volumes, therefore, overlap each other considerably.

The sole criterion used for determining the "optimal mode" is the minimum cost per passenger-trip. This criterion is valid only in the rare cases when modes with

---

[9]DE LEUW, CATHER & COMPANY, WITH HENNESY, CHADWICH, O'HEACHA AND PARTNERS, *Manchester Rapid Transit Study, Volume II: Study of Rapid Transit Systems and Concepts* (Manchester, England: De Leuw, Cather & Company, August 1967).

[10]WOLFGANG S. HOMBURGER, "An Analysis of Different Forms of Rapid Transit," in *Urban Mass Transit Planning* (Berkeley, Calif.: University of California, Institute of Transportation and Traffic Engineering, 1967), pp. 197–203. A summary of a report by K. Leibbrand for Frankfurt, Germany.

[11]NIAGARA FRONTIER TRANSPORTATION AUTHORITY, *Niagara Frontier Mass Transit Study: A Transit Development Program for the Niagara Frontier Region*, prepared for UMTA and New York DOT (Buffalo, N.Y.: Niagara Frontier Transportation Authority, 1971).

[12]J. R. MEYER, J. F. KAIN, AND M. WOHL, *The Urban Transportation Problem* (Cambridge, Mass.: Harvard University Press, 1966).

[13]THEODORE E. KEELER AND OTHERS, *The Full Costs of Urban Transport*, a series of monographs (Berkeley, Calif.: University of California, Institute of Urban and Regional Development, 1974–1975).

identical level of service (L/S) are compared. In most cases each mode has a different L/S–cost combination. Thus, if mode I has a lower cost, but also lower L/S than mode II under given conditions, it would be incorrect to conclude that mode I is better because it is cheaper. If the difference in L/S of mode II is worth its additional cost, mode II is the better one.

A number of important mode characteristics cannot be converted into dollars. But the problem of including these characteristics into mode comparison cannot be solved by elimination of all nonmonetary elements. For example, economic studies often assume that there is sufficient space in central business districts (CBDs) to accommodate freeways and parking facilities for 10,000 or even 30,000 automobiles per hour from a single corridor. Even if this assumption is accepted, the impact of this traffic volume cannot be ignored without making the analysis highly unrealistic.

The computational analysis and the diagrams used by the economic comparisons also have conceptual deficiencies. The basic diagram used presents average cost per trip as a function of passenger volume for different modes, such as in Fig. 13-1. However, each mode has a different L/S and therefore attracts, under any given set of conditions, a different number of passengers. Rail rapid transit attracts more passengers

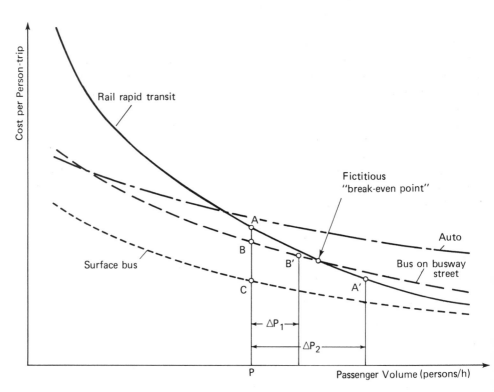

Figure 13-1 *Comparison of modes based on their costs, disregarding differences in level of service and passenger attraction*

than does a bus system using busway and streets. Such a bus system, in turn, has a stronger attraction than does a surface bus system. All three systems are so different from the automobile in type of service and potential user groups that their plots on the same diagram have no meaning.

More specifically, the diagram implies that it presents costs of different modes for any given passenger volume; thus, in Fig. 13-1, cost per trip C for a surface bus appears to compare with cost B for a bus on a busway and street and cost A for rail rapid transit. The fact is that there cannot be a served area in the real world in which these three modes would have the respective unit costs. If a surface bus line would attract P passengers in a given area, then a bus on busway and street would attract a volume $P + \Delta P_1$, and rail rapid transit would attract a volume of $P + \Delta P_2$. Unit cost C therefore should not be compared with costs B or A, but with B' or A'. Moreover, the criterion is not whether, for example, C is lower or higher than B', but whether the cost difference B' $-$ C is worth the attraction of ΔP_1 passengers. Incidentally, this cost difference may sometimes be negative, which makes the higher-quality mode clearly superior even for volumes below the "break-even point." The "break-even point" is actually a fictitious concept: the curves are on different L/S "surfaces" and they do not intersect.

Another problem is that this type of diagram is highly unreliable when it is applied to hypothetical "typical" conditions because of the extreme sensitivity of the curves to the assumptions of the analyst. To change relative positions of curves for different modes by manipulating assumptions of the model is easy. Accordingly, Deen points out in his discussion of the study by Miller et al. that the break-even point varies among different studies from the 2000 and 5000 trips/h range to 50,000 trips/h, which is a difference of some 1000%.[14] This characteristic allows use of this methodology to argue in favor of or against any mode.

The economic studies confuse technologies with modes (see Chapter 4). Since costs of modes are mostly dependent on their type of R/W, the curves in Fig. 13-1 refer more to types of R/W than to bus and rail technologies. A bus on exclusive busway may involve a higher investment and operating cost than light rail transit in a street median.

An example of application of the same methodology to comparison of different vehicles illustrates its inherent shortcomings. Suppose that a Cadillac, a Volkswagen, and a motorcycle are compared on the basis of their costs; travel times are included as cost elements, but different riding qualities, safety, and the fact that many people do not want to ride a motorcycle are ignored. Clearly, the motorcycle would come out as greatly superior to the Volkswagen, which would in turn be far superior to the Cadillac.

Because of these deficiencies, results of the economic studies have little realistic value. Since such important factors as reliability and high frequency of service, comfort, and safety enter the economic models only as cost items, while their major

---

[14]D. R. MILLER AND OTHERS, "Cost Comparison of Busway and Railway Rapid Transit," with discussions, in *Evaluation of Bus Transit Strategies*, Highway Research Record 459 (Washington, D.C.: Highway Research Board, 1973), pp. 1–10.

influence on passenger attraction is disregarded, these studies greatly distort the relationships among modes in favor of low-investment/low-performance systems. Yet, those results, implied to be correct, have often been used to argue against improvements of public transportation infrastructure, and particularly rail transit, although they are contradicted by numerous studies for real cities which have found that rail transit is the best alternative in many major corridors. Examples are the studies for Baltimore, Miami, Rochester, Dayton (Ohio), as well as those quoted previously.[9-11]

The diversity of studies comparing transit systems and modes with respect to their assumptions and results is often confusing. For an excellent review of the state of the art in this field, with a detailed critical analysis of methodologies used by different authors, the reader is referred to the study by Mitric.[15] This study analyzes correctness of both conceptual basis and methodologies employed by various authors, as well as the validity of their findings. Following a detailed documentation of their shortcomings, Mitric suggests abandonment of economic modal comparisons and presents the basic guidelines which comparisons of modes should follow.

CONCEPTUAL ANALYSIS OF URBAN TRANSPORTATION MODES

To facilitate an understanding of the individual operating and technical features of urban passenger transportation systems, a growing urban area can be analyzed. The initial condition is a small human settlement with a few dispersed activities and a basic network of paths among them. For this condition an ideal system of transportation would consist of small vehicles which individual persons or groups would use to travel between different points at the time they desire. The system would be satisfactory in all respects provided that all persons own vehicles and can drive them.

If it is supposed that the settlement grows into a small town, then to a city, and finally into a large urbanized area (see Fig. 13-2), it can be shown that due to increasing volumes of travel its transportation system would be gradually improved through a sequence of the following steps:

- Introduction of large vehicles as common carriers along the main directions of travel.
- Reconstruction of some paths into higher-capacity arterials to accommodate increased traffic volumes.
- Placement of common carriers on separated ways (first partially, then fully controlled rights-of-way).
- Construction of physical guideways along the controlled R/W, allowing operation of trains with much higher line capacity.

---

[15]SLOBODAN MITRIC, *Comparison of Modes in Urban Transport: A Methodological Analysis*, Technical Report (Columbus, Ohio: Ohio State University, Department of Civil Engineering, July 1976). A summary entitled "Comparing Modes in Urban Transportation" appears in *Transportation Evaluation Techniques*, Transportation Research Record 639 (Washington, D.C.: Transportation Research Board, 1977), pp. 19–24.

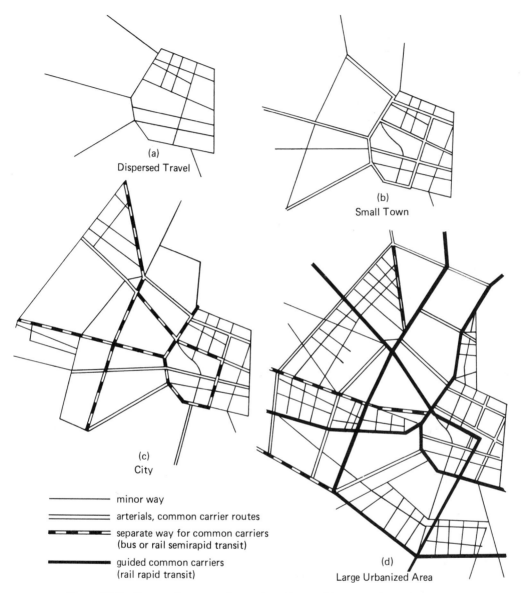

minor way

arterials, common carrier routes

separate way for common carriers
(bus or rail semirapid transit)

guided common carriers
(rail rapid transit)

Figure 13-2 *Change of transportation modes with size of human agglomeration*

- Introduction of fully automatic operation of common-carrier vehicles on guideways.

Each of these steps would require a certain capital investment, but each would also result in higher capacity, improved service quality, or in lower operating cost per passenger than the preceding systems.

It should be noted that the introduction of higher-performance systems would not necessarily result in elimination of the lower-performance systems; the new systems would only take a high volume of travel with higher efficiency than the preceding systems and would allow those systems to resume the high efficiency of operation they have in their primary domain (i.e., at a somewhat lower volume of travel).

Owing to the investment required for individual improvements, each successive system tends to have a more limited network than the preceding system. To allow functioning of all modes in a coordinated manner, transfer facilities must be provided at various contact points.

This conceptual analysis corresponds very closely to actual systems. Urban transportation modes ordered by capacity and performance include private automobiles on local streets, buses, construction of arterials (or freeways), introduction of transit lanes, rail systems with partially controlled R/W (LRT), then with fully controlled R/W (RRT), and finally fully automated intermediate capacity or rapid transit systems which will become operational in the near future. The analysis of individual steps in system improvement can clearly show the trade-offs involved in each upgrading. It can also show that each transportation mode has an optimum domain of operation and no single mode could satisfactorily serve all types of travel: the use of each mode outside its "natural" domain results in high cost, low service quality, and undesirable external effects.

METHODOLOGY FOR MODE COMPARISON AND SELECTION

Each city, area, or corridor to be served by a new transit mode has a unique set of characteristics. For selection of the optimal transit mode it is necessary to define all the site-specific conditions, requirements, and constraints designated as a "conditions set." This set may be considered as the demand side of the selection process. On the supply side are the transit modes, from which the optimal one should be selected for the specific application. The selection procedure includes the following major phases: the definition of the conditions set, preliminary design of alternative modes for comparison, and the comparative evaluation and selection of the optimal mode.

DEFINITION OF THE CONDITIONS SET

Based on the overall transportation policy for the city or individual area and the defined goals for the planned system, specific requirements and standards are developed. To ensure a systematic and comprehensive accounting of all system characteristics, requirements for transit systems are classified into three groups by "interested parties": passengers, operator, and community. A definition of requirements must be done with great care, since some of them are rather difficult to define precisely or to distinguish from others. Also, some of them may be either somewhat differently defined, expanded, or omitted in specific cases. However, the framework of this type of analysis has a general validity for virtually all modes of transportation. The more similar the compared modes and their studied applications are, the more precise their comparative analysis can and should be.

The various requirements are shown in Table 13-1 and will be defined briefly. Those requirements which are generally common to different interested parties are defined only once, since they differ only for specific cases.

TABLE 13-1
Transit System Requirements

Passenger	Operator	Community
Availability	Area coverage	Level of service/passenger attraction
Punctuality	Frequency	Long-range impact
Speed/travel time	Speed	Environmental/energy aspects
User cost	Reliability	Economic efficiency
Comfort	Cost	Social objectives
Convenience	Capacity	
Safety and security	Safety	
	Side effects	
	Passenger attraction	

PASSENGER REQUIREMENTS

Availability. This requirement, without which the population cannot use a transit system, has two facets: *locational*, closeness to a system's terminals, and *temporal*, expressed as frequency of service. For good availability, users must have both reasonably close terminals and adequate frequency of service. Because of cost constraints, trade-offs between the two must often be made. At one extreme is a dense route network with low frequency of service. At the other extreme is frequent service on few routes; users far from terminals do not have the service unless they use feeders. Most urban transit lines utilize a compromise solution: they provide a certain network density and frequency of service. Naturally, with higher demand both can be increased.

Punctuality. Punctuality is defined as schedule adherence. The variance from scheduled travel times may result from traffic delays, vehicle breakdowns, or adverse weather conditions. Since traffic delays and interference dominate as causes, by far the most significant factor for securing punctuality is control over the system (i.e., separation of transit R/W from other traffic).

Speed/travel time. The total door-to-door travel time can be composed of five parts: access, waiting, transfer, travel, and departure times. Relative weights of these time intervals vary, since passengers perceive them differently. Therefore, based on various studies reported in literature, a factor of 2.0 to 2.5 can be used for waiting and transfer times to obtain perceived travel times. The relative weight of walking time depends heavily on the attractiveness of the area.

User cost. The price of transportation is another important factor for travelers. Transit fare is the most significant portion of it, but other out-of-pocket costs are also included, particularly by commuters. In a broader sense, cost of access by automobile and even its fixed costs (if an auto is owned only for that purpose) should also be considered.

Comfort. Comfort is a difficult concept to define because it encompasses many qualitative factors. Paramount are the availability of a seat and the quality of ride (affecting users' ability to read and write). The physical comfort of the seat itself naturally enters in, as does the geometry of the vehicle entrances/exits, width of aisles, presence of air conditioning, jerk and noise levels, image of passengers relative to one's self-image, and the degree of privacy offered, to name a few.

Convenience. While comfort is related to the vehicle, convenience refers to the overall system. Lack of the necessity to transfer is a convenience. Good off-peak service, clear system information, well-designed and protected waiting facilities, and sufficient, close parking (if required) are all user conveniences. By nature, evaluation of conveniences is predominantly qualitative.

Safety and security. Passenger safety in terms of accident prevention is very important, but this aspect is sometimes less important for passengers than protection from crime. Security is measured by statistical records of crime incidents on the system.

OPERATOR REQUIREMENTS

Area coverage. Area "covered" or served by transit is defined as the area within 5 or 10 minutes' walking distance from transit stations. Area coverage by a transit system can be expressed as percent of the urban area which is the transit service area. In examining area coverage, however, network extensiveness, provision of and for access modes, and central business district (CBD) coverage should be considered.

Frequency. Frequency is expressed by the number of vehicle departures per unit time (hour). It is often incorrectly believed that frequency is not important for commuters. While its significance is greater for off-peak hours, it also seriously affects regular riders. For example, there are no residential areas in which only two or three departures during the whole 2-hour peak period would be convenient for all potential users. Short, regular headways are an essential element of attracting all categories of passenger trips.

Speed. While passengers are more sensitive to transfer and waiting than travel times, they also prefer high running speed on the line; the operator is particularly concerned with high commercial speeds on the lines, since they affect his fleet size, labor costs, fuel, maintenance, and above all, attraction of passengers. Several speeds are used in transit systems analysis:

- Travel speed—one-way average speed of vehicle, including stops.
- Commercial speed—average speed, including terminal times.
- Platform speed—overall average speed, including travel to/from garages.
- Paytime speed—average speed based on driver's paid time.

Cost. Although cost is often given an unjustifiably high relative weight (even used as a single evaluation criterion for different systems), it does represent the most important single factor to the operator. In most cases, three aspects of costs are analyzed: investment cost, operating cost, and revenue. All three vary greatly with local conditions and system characteristics, as well as with time (because of inflation). In evaluation, unit costs rather than total costs of individual modes should be compared.

Capacity. Two different capacities can be defined for a system: way capacity and station capacity. The latter, capacity of stations along the line, governs line capacity since it is smaller in all cases except when vehicles from a line-haul section branch out into several terminals; such cases have few applications at present.

Safety. The operator must pay great attention not only to passenger security, but also to operational safety of the system. Modes with inherently high safety (separate R/W, guidance, and fail-safe signal systems are the major factors), therefore, have a major advantage over manually controlled vehicles operated on streets.

Side effects. System effects on the nonusers and the environment for which the operator is responsible include such physical impacts as aesthetics, noise, and air pollution.

Passenger attraction. The number of passengers a transit line carries is usually the most important indicator of its success and its role in urban transportation. The attraction is obviously a function of the type and level of service, but there is also an additional factor, probably best described as *system image*, which can be very important. This image is difficult to define, but it is composed of such aspects as the simplicity of the system, reliability of service, frequency, and regularity, as well as physical characteristics of facilities, primary fixed-line facilities (wires for trolleybuses, tracks for rail modes, or separate R/W for any technology), which give it clear visibility and presence in the eyes of users.

COMMUNITY REQUIREMENTS

Items included in this category, listed in Table 13-1, are self-explanatory. In each specific case they must be carefully defined and analyzed, since they vary more due to local conditions than do such quantitative items as speed or frequency.

As was explained in Chapter 4, transit modes are defined by three characteristics: (1) right-of-way category, (2) technology, and (3) type of service.

RIGHT-OF-WAY CATEGORIES

It is reemphasized here that it is the R/W category which most strongly influences the performance/cost "package" and thus also the level of service/cost characteristics of modes. Transit modes sharing the same facilities with other traffic (R/W category C) can *never* be competitive with the private automobile, either in speed or in overall L/S, since they are subject to all traffic delays and, in addition, must stop for passengers along their way. This is true for streetcars, trolleybuses, or buses (i.e., regardless of technology). Modes with category B R/W, often designated as semirapid transit (e.g., light rail), have a considerably higher speed, reliability, capacity, and so on, than those with category C. The highest L/S in all respects is provided by category A, but at the highest investment cost. This factor usually limits the extent of the network of this category, requiring that it be supplemented by other modes as feeders.

Often the alternatives considered are a smaller network of a higher performance system with feeders, or a larger network of a lower performance system. Many factors influence this choice, but the basic trade-off from the passenger's point of view is between higher L/S (speed, safety, comfort, etc.) on the former and lack of transfer on the latter. Better area coverage is advantageous, but only if the overall L/S remains above a certain acceptable level. If not, passenger attraction may be drastically reduced. The possibility of later system upgrading into a higher performance one is also an important consideration in planning. The most important characteristic of the three R/W categories of transit modes are presented in condensed form in Table 13-2.

A particularly important factor in selecting the category is passenger attraction, which is a direct function of L/S, that is, of competitiveness of the transit system with private automobile. The three categories present different investment cost/level of service combinations, as Fig. 13-3 conceptually shows. This diagram is closely related

TABLE 13-2
Characteristics of the Three Right-of-Way Categories

Characteristics \ R/W Categories	A	B	C
System performance	Very high	High	Low
Service quality	Very high	High	Low
Passenger attraction	Very high	High	Low
Image identification	Very good	Good	Poor
Impact on urban form	Very strong	Strong	Weak
Investment cost	Very high	High	Very low
Automation possibility	Full	Partial	None

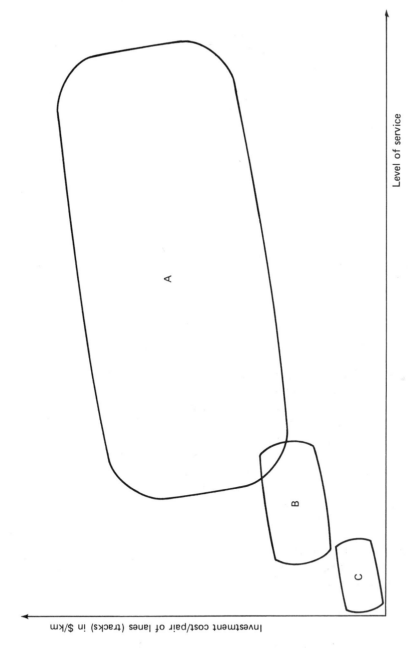

Level of service

Investment cost/pair of lanes (tracks) in $/km

Figure 13-3 *Level of service/investment cost relationship for transit modes with different right-of-way categories*

to Fig. 4-4: L/S shown here is a direct function of system performance shown in Fig. 4-4.

The relationship between L/S and passenger attraction is presented in Figs. 13-4 and 13-5. Figure 13-4 is the conventional diversion curve showing modal split (or distribution of traffic between two highways) as a function of ratio (or difference) of their travel times (or costs). Figure 13-5 shows the same type of diversion curve as a

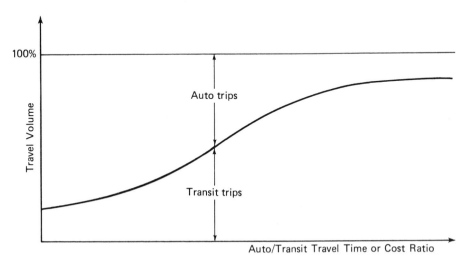

Figure 13-4 *Standard auto/transit modal split or diversion curve*

function of transit L/S, which includes such elements as reliability, comfort, and convenience, in addition to travel time and cost. An increase in the total volume of travel with increasing L/S is also shown. Assuming that auto travel has a certain fixed L/S for the given direction of travel, the share of transit travel increases with its L/S. Since L/S is strongly dependent on the R/W category, domains of each category can be plotted along the abscissa with some mutual overlap, as shown. Thus, the diagram shows conceptually the different volumes of passengers attracted by each category of transit modes, the phenomenon always observed in cities with buses and rapid transit, or other types of modes with different R/W categories.

The selection of the R/W category is more closely related to the overall characteristics of the transit system, its anticipated relationship with other modes and economic, social, and other goals of the city, than to specific technology and operating characteristics of modes. It is therefore not only a technical, but also a high-level planning and political decision.

TECHNOLOGY AND TYPE OF SERVICE

The next step in comparison and selection of modes focuses on determination of technologies and types of service for candidate modes. Two groups of technology are most commonly used: highway and rail. Other systems can be classified into a category of rubber-tired guided or semiguided technologies, which includes trolleybus and

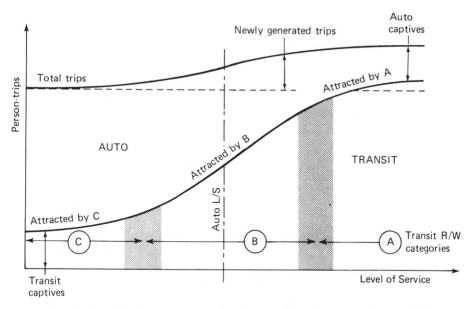

Figure 13-5 *Travel volume and modal split as functions of level of service and R/W categories of transit*

rubber-tired transit; and a special category, including ferryboats, inclines, and several other technologies, as shown in Table 4-2. On the basis of the established requirements for the specific case, several modes are selected as combinations of technologies and types of service for the adopted R/W category. Technologies and types of service are closely related, although not identical. For example, skip-stop service is used mostly on rapid transit systems, but it could be used on any other technology.

Comparative analysis of different technologies within the same R/W category is based primarily on a deeper analysis of specific technical and operating system characteristics, and somewhat less on the overall system impact. The analysis is therefore predominantly technical. It is better defined and more quantitative than the one of R/W categories, and yet it is far from simple: it must include a great number of factors, quantitative and qualitative ones, and evaluate all of them.

SELECTION AND FUNCTIONAL DESIGN OF CANDIDATE MODES

In each specific case of transit mode selection, the engineers-planners must select candidate modes on the basis of an examination of the "conditions set" for the planned system and a knowledge of characteristics of different R/W types, transit technologies, and operations. Planners select those modes which may conceivably satisfy the defined requirements. The more expertise and experience planners have, the more precise their choice, and the fewer candidate modes they will select. Accordingly, in no case will an experienced transit planner compare such drastically different modes as buses on streets and rapid transit, automated guided transit and minibuses, or dial-a-ride and light rail: the conditions sets making the application of the former modes likely will clearly not be suitable for the use of the latter ones.

Once these candidate modes are selected, a functional design must be developed for each one. The network, specific technology, and operation must be determined so that they are compatible with the given conditions. This preliminary design is necessary since different characteristics of modes make their optimal employments different. For example, rapid transit, light rail, and buses on busways would each have its own optimal station locations, connections with other modes, and so on.

THE EVALUATION PROCEDURE

Each candidate mode must now be evaluated with respect to each requirement. The type and depth of evaluation should be determined which are reasonable and practical by the data availability and objectivity of evaluation of qualitative aspects. The evaluation of each parameter can be expressed in one of three basic ways: (1) dollars as measure units, (2) other quantifiable units, or (3) qualitative evaluation.

To derive an overall evaluation of different modes expressed by a single quantitative criterion, two highly subjective and consequently controversial steps would have to be made. First, all parameter evaluations would have to be quantified; and second, their relative weights would have to be assumed. While in some rather simple cases this can be done with reasonably satisfactory results, in transit system evaluations this is seldom the case. The reader, analyst, or decision maker will usually get a better picture of compared modes through a complete list of evaluated items than if presented with a single number based on numerous subjective values which often cannot be tracked down.

AN EXAMPLE

An example of this type of comparative analysis is presented in an abbreviated form in a complex comparison of a rapid transit line (Lindenwold) with express bus service (Shirley Express)—modes with different R/W categories, different technologies, and, related to these, different types of service. Although extensive quantitative analyses were made, it was considered that the numbers could sometimes be misleading because the lines operate under similar, but not identical, conditions sets. Therefore, the final comparative evaluations were made in qualitative terms. The results of the comparison are summarized in Table 13-3. This evaluation was supplemented by a description of analysis of each parameter supported by all important data relevant to it. The findings show more clearly the causes of a 70% higher passenger attraction by the Lindenwold rail line than a comparison limited to cost and travel time only could explain. The study separated differences caused by different local conditions from those caused by inherent characteristics of rail and bus technologies, R/W categories, and types of operations.

TABLE 13-3
Summary of Comparative Analysis:
Lindenwold Rail Line and Shirley Busway

Requirement	Lindenwold	Shirley	Higher-Rated System
Passenger			
Availability	Good	Poor	Lindenwold
Speed-travel time	Good	Very good	Shirley
Reliability	Very good	Poor	Lindenwold
User cost	Good	Very good	Shirley
Comfort	Good	Poor	Lindenwold
Convenience	Good	Fair	Lindenwold
Safety and security	Very good	Good	Lindenwold
Operator			
Area coverage	Good	Very good	Shirley
Frequency	Very good	Very poor	Lindenwold
Speed	Very good	Poor	Lindenwold
Cost: investment	Very poor	Fair	Shirley
Cost: operating	Good	Fair	Lindenwold
Capacity	Good	Poor	Lindenwold
Side effects	Good	Fair	Lindenwold
Passenger attraction	Very good	Good	Lindenwold
Community			
System impact	Very good	Good	Lindenwold

Source: V. R. Vuchic and R. M. Stanger, "Lindenwold Rail Line and Shirley Busway: A Comparison," *Evaluation of Bus Transit Strategies,* Highway Research Record 459 (Washington, D.C.: Highway Research Board), pp. 13-28.

SUMMARY AND CONCLUSIONS

In summary, the procedure for comparative analysis and selection of transportation modes follows these major steps.

- *Step 1:* Based on urban transportation *policy*, develop goals for the transit system.
- *Step 2:* Define *conditions* for the area to be served.
- *Step 3:* Utilizing results from preceding steps, define specific *requirements and standards* for the planned system.
- *Step 4:* Select *R/W type* for candidate modes.
- *Step 5:* Select *technologies* and *type of operation* for candidate modes.
- *Step 6:* Develop *functional designs* for candidate modes.
- *Step 7:* *Evaluate* candidate modes.
- *Step 8:* *Compare* evaluation results and *select* the optimal mode.

In conclusion, it must be stated that a comparative analysis of transit modes is a very complex problem. There is often a strong tendency to simplify this process, even to the extent that only a single item (usually cost) of peak-hour operation is used as the only evaluation criterion. Considerable literature exists on "thresholds" of individual technologies, often not recognizing the importance of R/W types and of a great number of performance and L/S characteristics. This tendency for simplification has, in combination with pursuit of a wrong objective in transit system planning (to provide the minimum cost system), led to many incorrect decisions.

Different transit modes must be compared in a systematic manner and on a comprehensive basis, utilizing many different factors. The methodology presented here facilitates the comparison by classifying transit systems first by their R/W type, affecting strongly their L/S, then by technology, and by type of operation. Although the methodology is not exact due to certain subjective elements, it is greatly superior to the simplistic comparisons based on system costs only. It should be expected that further work and experience with this methodology will bring additional improvements. However, these improvements should not be expected in quantification of individual parameters and mechanization of the evaluation procedure, which is usually accompanied by a reduction of understanding of systems. Rather, the improvements should be made in further formalization of a systematic methodology and comprehensive approach, which will require a much better understanding of transit systems, their operations, and their role in urban transportation than is presently the case.

SELECTED BIBLIOGRAPHY

DE LEUW, CATHER & COMPANY, WITH HENNESY, CHADWICH, O'HEACHA AND PARTNERS, *Manchester Rapid Transit Study, Volume II: Study of Rapid Transit Systems and Concepts.* Manchester, England: De Leuw, Cather & Company, August 1967.

KUHN, TILLO E., *Public Enterprise Economics and Transport Problems* (reprint of 1962 ed.). Westport, Conn.: Greenwood Press, Inc., 1976.

LEE, DOUGLASS B., JR., *A Cost-Oriented Methodology for Short-Range Transportation Planning*, Technical Report no. 66. Iowa City, Iowa: University of Iowa, Center for Urban Transportation Studies, Institute of Urban and Regional Research, January 1976.

——, *Costs of Urban and Suburban Passenger Transportation Modes*, Working Paper Series no. 14. Iowa City, Iowa: University of Iowa, Center for Urban Transportation Studies, Institute of Urban and Regional Research, April 1975.

MITRIC, SLOBODAN, *Comparison of Modes in Urban Transport: A Methodological Analysis*, Technical Report. Columbus, Ohio: Ohio State University, Department of Civil Engineering, July 1976. A summary entitled "Comparing Modes in Urban Transportation" appears in *Transportation Evaluation Techniques*, Transportation Research Record 639, pp. 19–24. Washington, D.C.: Transportation Research Board, 1977.

NIAGARA FRONTIER TRANSPORTATION AUTHORITY, *Niagara Frontier Mass Transit Study: A Transit Development Program for the Niagara Frontier Region*, prepared for UMTA and New York DOT. Buffalo, N.Y.: Niagara Frontier Transportation Authority, 1971.

VUCHIC, VUKAN R., "Place of Light Rail in the Family of Transit Modes," in *Light Rail Transit*, Special Report 161, pp. 62–76. Washington, D.C.: Transportation Research Board, 1975.

——, AND R. M. STANGER, "Lindenwold Rail Line and Shirley Busway: A Comparison," in *Evaluation of Bus Transit Strategies*, Highway Research Record 459, pp. 13–28. Washington, D.C.: Highway Research Board, 1973.

Chapter 14

RAPID TRANSIT MODE SELECTION

THOMAS B. DEEN, *Chairman of the Board, Alan M. Voorhees & Associates, Inc.*

For most cities throughout the world, mass transit can adequately be served by local fixed-route bus service operating on streets, mixed with other traffic, and constrained, due to its required stops and delays from other traffic, to average scheduled speeds of 16 to 19 km/h (10 to 12 mi/h). While not competitive with the automobile, such speeds are adequate as long as trip lengths in corridors served tend to be 8 km (5 mi) or less (or about a 30-minute trip at 12 mi/h) and maximum hourly passenger volumes in one direction are 5000 to 7000 or less.

Many corridors in larger cities do not fit these limitations, however, and ways must be found to devise transit service which operates at higher speeds and with higher capacity than local bus service can provide. Provision of express bus service on freeways can sometimes meet the speed requirements, and if no stops for loading are necessary, higher capacity can also be achieved in this manner. On the other hand, freeways are often congested during peak periods and do not even exist in some corridors. Reserving lanes for exclusive bus use is often publicly unacceptable, and in such situations, strong consideration is often given to construction of rapid transit.

Rapid transit is defined for purposes of this discussion as express, limited-stop transit service provided on exclusive rights-of-way. Vehicles can be steered by drivers or by a guideway, suspended on steel wheels or rubber tires, and propelled by electric motors or petroleum engines. In other words, the choice is between rail or bus systems.

Development costs for rapid transit are always several orders of magnitude greater than for local transit. Moreover, the large costs associated with the guideways, stations, and maintenance facilities are fixed, and thus very careful consideration must be given to their location, since they must effectively serve the community for many decades in order to amortize the large investment. All of this means that the planning and decision-making process for rapid-transit development is much more rigorous, expensive, time consuming, and generally frustrating than for local transit. In addition to system location, questions of financing, phasing, performance, environment and social impacts, and extent of the system must be resolved. Two of the most difficult decisions, however, have to do with

- Whether rapid-transit development should be undertaken at all.
- Which rapid transit mode would be most cost effective in the local environment.

WHETHER TO BUILD

In the United States three major influences can be identified as having major impacts on the decision of whether to embark on rapid-transit development.

1. Financial and institutional factors—those institutional arrangements that dictate the constraints within which the system is to be financed.
2. Attitudinal factors—those predispositions of the community that exist independent of the plan and planning process associated with rapid-transit development.
3. Physical factors—those analytical factors involving the physical layout of the system, its costs, performance, patronage, analysis of benefits, and interaction with other elements of the transportation system.

FINANCIAL AND INSTITUTIONAL FACTORS

To understand the factors influencing the decision to build or not build a project of the monumental proportions normally included in a rapid transit system, one must have some concept of the motivational context of the agency charged with implementation. More often than not, the substantive beginning of the project will have come from another agency, for example, the council of governments' transportation plan, or the comprehensive transportation planning process. This agency will have made a recommendation for rapid transit construction as part of a long-range transportation plan for the area and for the formation of an agency to begin work on it. Often the question of when the plan is to be completed, what type of rapid transit (rail or bus), and locational details are included only in schematic form. The legislature acts on the strength of this general recommendation to enact legislation for the formation of "an Authority to plan, design, build, and operate a rapid transit system," and it often does so without much fanfare or debate, since usually it leaves the question of money for implementation unresolved—contingent upon a successful bond referendum or enactment of additional legislation.

The newly formed transit authority very quickly perceives that its success will be judged by how quickly they get a system planned, financed, designed, and under way. They also intuitively comprehend that getting anything built at all will require a successful bond referendum, which, in turn, is much more easily achieved with a system that is big, bold, glamorous, fast, extensive, and, above all, which appears to serve as much of the affected area as possible from the day the system first opens. Since even a small start on one short line will likely be the biggest public works project in the history of the area, it is much easier to sell the full system if it appears to serve more people. In short, in major urban areas it is easier to sell a $1 billion project than a $100 million project.

At this point the authority must simultaneously court the favor of two masters, each with different tastes: the local one desiring or requiring, if it is to be stimulated at all, an *extensive* system; and the other one, which includes the senior governments being called on to finance much of the project, a truncated, less costly project. The senior government knows it cannot get enough money to fund all of the system being planned, and suspects that good transport planning, economic analysis, and horse sense would dictate a plan which begins small and develops over time. These two masters spend much time during the planning period picking at the authority and demanding changes to the plan to better conform to its individual constraints and wondering why the authority—which, after all, is only trying to resolve conflicts between two divided masters with a compromise plan—is so obtuse. An understanding of this decision-making environment is essential if one is to comprehend how planning for rapid transit is conducted.

The dominance of this financial influence on planning decisions can be seen from actual cases. Toronto began their rapid transit with some surplus money which required no referendum, and the first section was only 6 km (4 mi) long. Baltimore has obtained financing for its system through state legislation, again requiring no popular referendum. They are beginning with one line. Buffalo is moving with a single line under similar circumstances; whereas Washington, San Francisco, Atlanta, Seattle, and Los Angeles all required referenda, and all proposed multiple-line, total systems, to be completed as a package so that all areas would receive service almost simultaneously. Los Angeles, having failed on the referendum, is now proposing the incremental approach.

ATTITUDINAL FACTORS

Decisions relating to the building of rapid transit, as well as the type of system being planned, are heavily influenced by local attitudes and preconceived notions about the importance of transit improvements quite apart from the analytical presentations of the feasibility study. All the larger cities of the United States had comprehensive transportation studies performed as part of the requirements of the 1956 Federal-Aid Highway Act, and most of these recommended a much more modest role for transit than is often now proposed. Basically the same analytical techniques are now being applied; the differences are related to the value systems of the citizenry. Major concerns with the urban environment, energy consumption, and social issues have all surfaced since that time and the assumptions going into the analysis and the analytical processes itself have bent in response toward more transit.

Often the attitude is not necessarily pro-transit so much as it is antihighway or anti-automobile. San Francisco passed their successful transit bond issue in 1962 in the heat of the their freeway revolt. Washington, Baltimore, Boston, and other cities have also experienced freeway revolt symptoms that have helped promote the cause of transit. Concern for the environment was perhaps the factor that was uppermost in the minds of the voters in the Denver area in 1975 when they approved the development of a system to cost more than $1 billion before being presented with details of the system's hardware, performance, or required time for development.

Sometimes civic boosterism is a motivating factor, especially when two cities which have a tradition of rivalry within the same state consider transit development.

For years the federal government has explicitly promoted the concept of transportation planning being carried out at the local level with local planning officials responsible for the outcome. It is therefore inevitable, and perhaps even desirable, for each community to develop its own criteria responsive to its unique values and aspirations. The problem comes when these predispositions fly in the face of physical or economic reality. It makes no economic sense to build a $100 million rapid transit system to carry 5000 passengers/day no matter what one's aspirations, especially if one is asking for financial assistance from some other agency or level of government.

PHYSICAL FACTORS

Regardless of attitudes or institutional arrangements in a community, the physical relationships of activities and topography either lend themselves to the type of service that rapid transit provides or they do not. These physical factors dominate the ultimate cost of constructing the system and how many riders over whom this cost can be distributed.

There have been numerous efforts to measure city attributes in ways that will quickly identify those which can justify rapid transit. Table 14-1 lists several of these. Most are directly related to measures of potential passenger demand, and many could be accepted as valid for most cases. However, criteria related to corridor flows, central-city density, or central business district (CBD) size have limited value since the definition of a corridor, or what constitutes a CBD, or the boundaries of the central city vary between urban areas. Besides, there are "exceptions," and most local decision makers like to think of themselves and their community as exceptional.

One major factor often neglected in lists of aggregate criteria is city configuration. Figure 14-1 shows four typical city configurations. 1B is a typical community with a CBD in the center and the urban area spread in a 360° pattern around it. A rapid transit system serving such an area might require eight spokes, with 45° angles between each one. Examples are Denver, Washington, and Baltimore. 1C has the same population but would require only five spokes to provide the same service, with each spoke carrying heavier volumes (examples: Toronto and Chicago). 1D, again with the same population, can be served with only two spokes, each carrying very heavy volumes (examples: Honolulu and Caracas, Venezuela). The proposed Honolulu system is projected to carry peak line volumes upward of 15,000 passengers/hour, even though the area population is expected to be only about 500,000 persons. The worst situation is shown in 1A, where 16 spokes would be required to serve the area (examples: Min-

TABLE 14-1
Criteria Used in Selected Studies[a]

Criterion	Threshold Value	
	Desired	Minimum
Central city population density (pers./mi^2)	14,000-15,000	10,000-12,000
Passenger flow/corridor (pers./h)	30,000-40,000	
Urban area population	2,000,000	1,000,000
Central city population	700,000	500,000
CBD floor space (ft^2)	50,000,000	25,000,000
CBD destinations/mi^2	300,000	150,000
Peak hour, CBD persons cordon count	100,000	70,000
Daily CBD destinations/corridor	70,000	40,000

[a]Metric conversions: 1 mi = 1.6 km; 1 ft^2 = 0.09 m^2; 1 mi^2 = 2.6 km^2.

Source: Adapted from report by Wilbur Smith and Associates, *Transportation and Parking for Tomorrow's Cities,* prepared for the Automobile Manufacturers Association (New Haven, Conn.: Wilbur Smith and Associates, 1966), p. 1209.

neapolis–St. Paul, Dallas–Ft. Worth). Clearly, the systems shown for each area not only decrease in price from 1A to 1D, but the level of service goes up since requirements for passenger transfers go down (in 1C no one would have to transfer within the rapid portion of the system) and the number of passengers for a given line goes up. The capacity and congestion problems of auto transportation increase also as you go from 1A to 1D, since all travel is concentrated into fewer corridors. The configuration factor is one of the big reasons why Honolulu is seriously considering rapid transit with a population of 0.5 million while Twin Cities with 2.5 million is vacillating. It also suggests that aggregate criteria which do not recognize the configuration factor will find itself faced with many "exceptions."

The other big factor which causes "exceptions" is the availability of cheap right-of-way. If the rapid transit can be built on the surface (and thus avoid subway or elevated construction), say in the median strip of a highway, construction costs (including right-of-way) might typically run $3 million per rte.-km ($5 million per rte.-mi), while, if the line is required to run in a tunnel, costs for subway construction might easily be 10 times this amount. Cleveland, Ohio, built their modest but effective rail system even though patronage is only 3000 to 4000 persons/hour on one of their lines. Such a low patronage on rail makes sense only because of the very low $2.5 million per rte.-km ($4 million per rte.-mi) for the system when built in 1955. Such low costs were possible only because of the availability of an inexpensive right-of-way along existing railroad lines so that no tunneling and very little elevated construction were required.

Figure 14-2 shows the importance of construction costs in determing the total cost of transporting people. It must be observed that costs per passenger-km (mi) exceeding .09 to .12 (15 to 20) cents are probably in excess of the costs of transporting people in cars or buses. From Fig. 14-2 it can be seen that 15,000 passengers/day might be

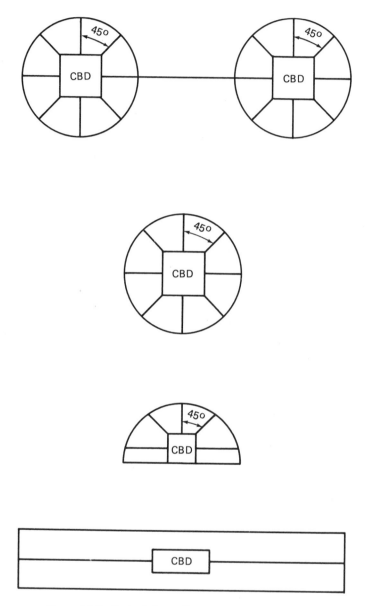

Figure 14-1 *Typical city configurations. (equal population.)*

all that is required to maintain 12 (20) cents/passenger-km (mi) if it can be built for $3 million per km ($5 million per mi); whereas if costs reach $9 million per km ($15 million per mi), patronage must be more than 45,000 per day, and if costs are $22 million per km ($35 million per mi), patronage must be above 100,000 per day.

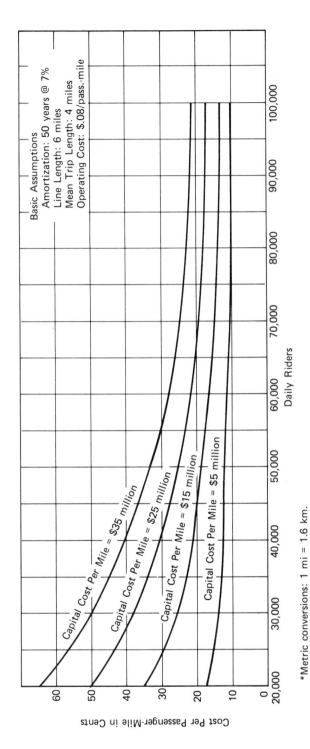

Figure 14-2 *Cost per passenger-mile versus daily patronage* [*Source: Adapted from report by Alan M. Voorhees & Associates, Inc., A Long Range View of Transit in Nashville,* (Mc Lean, Va.: *Alan M. Voorhees & Associates, Inc., September 1970, rev. September 1971*).]

*Metric conversions: 1 mi = 1.6 km.

The major issue concerning physical factors finally boils down to the bottom-line question of what it is going to cost per passenger-kilometer (mile) to transport people. If this cost exceeds the costs of other modes by significant amounts, then justification, if any, in terms of overall community benefits, must be examined more critically before an affirmative decision is made. On the other hand, if the cost is equal to or less than other existing modes, then the "go" decision can be made more easily. Unfortunately, the question of the cost effectiveness of proposed U.S. transit systems, both rail and bus, in terms of its ultimate product, a "passenger-kilometer (mile)," is often not presented. Table 14-2, nevertheless, shows the projected costs of several rail systems as of 1967–1969.

ECONOMIC ANALYSIS

Economic analysis has often been an important component of determining the feasibility of large capital intensive projects and has been made a precondition for the financing of high-cost transportation projects by such institutions as the World Bank and the Department of Environment of the United Kingdom. Such examinations, often called benefit–cost analyses, attempt to measure the magnitude of total benefits expected to accrue over the entire life cycle of the project compared to its total costs. Both benefits and costs expected in the more distant future are heavily discounted compared to short-term effects. In the case of a rapid transit project, the costs include the one-time cost of land acquisition and system construction as well as the continuing costs of system operation. Benefits include operating cost savings and time savings of passengers who otherwise would have used private cars, buses, or other modes of travel; included also are time savings from those choosing to remain in their cars but experiencing less congestion.

Economic analysis is an effective way to compute and compare those costs and benefits that can reasonably be translated into monetary terms. Urban goals of the late 1960s and 1970s, however, have been increasingly oriented toward values that are difficult if not impossible to measure monetarily. For example, determining the dollar value of increasing the mobility of the poor, or of encouraging particular land-use patterns, or of reducing air pollution is a complex task. The lack of comprehensiveness of economic analysis, thus, is an acknowledged shortcoming.

However, serious economic analysis for U.S. rapid transit proposals is often brushed off for two other reasons:

1. Officials responsible for building the system must get voter support from the entire area if they are to build anything. The amount of investment then is a function of what it costs to cover the area—investment analysis becomes irrelevant in such an environment.
2. Economic analysis of benefits and costs is in disrepute in the United States, partly because it must necessarily depend on some heroic and less than totally agreed on assumptions, and partly because it has been bent unsuccessfully by authorities who used it as a tool for justifying actions they fervently desired to take for other reasons.

TABLE 14-2
Costs for Several U.S. Rapid Transit Systems

Item	Twin Cities	Atlanta	Washington, D.C.	Baltimore	Los Angeles	San Francisco
Annual patronage (millions)	101	102	327	141	236	202
Capital costs ($million)	923	475	1828	1117	1788	1200
Annual capital costs ($ million)	61.3	31.6	121.5	74.5	119.2	79.8
Annual operating costs ($ million)	34.6	44.9	90.0	43.2	103.0	74.2
Total annual costs ($ million)	95.9	76.5	211.5	117.4	222.2	154.0
Costs per passenger-trip ($)	0.95	0.75	0.65	0.83	0.94	0.76
Average trip length km (mi)	8.9 (5.5)	12.1 (7.5)	11.4 (7.1)	9.2 (5.7)	13.7 (8.5)	12.9 (8.0)
Costs per passenger-km (mi) ($)	0.11 (0.17)	0.06 (0.10)	0.06 (0.09)	0.09 (0.15)	0.07 (0.11)	0.06 (0.10)

Sources: Alan M. Voorhees & Associates, Inc., Twin Cities: In-House Working Papers (System A) (McLean, Va.: Alan M. Voorhees & Associates, Inc., October 1970).

Alan M. Voorhees & Associates, Inc., Atlanta: Draft Technical Report (Recommended System) (McLean, Va.: Alan M. Voorhees & Associates, Inc., April 1969).

W. C. Gilman & Co., Inc., and Alan M. Voorhees & Associates, Inc., Washington, D.C.: Traffic, Revenue and Operating Costs (McLean, Va.: Alan M. Voorhees & Associates, Inc., February 1969).

Daniel, Mann, Johnson and Kaiser Engineers, Baltimore Region Rapid Transit System, Feasibility and Preliminary Engineering (Baltimore: Daniel, Mann, Johnson & Mendenhall, July 1968).

Southern California Rapid Transit District, Los Angeles: A Final Report, and Appendix B (Los Angeles: Southern California Rapid Transit District, May 1968).

Simpson & Curtin, 1975 Operating Costs, Coordinated Transit for the San Francisco Bay Area, (Philadelphia: Simpson & Curtin, October 1967), p. 107.

Alan M. Voorhees & Associates, Inc., Development of a Long Range Transit Improvement Program for the Twin Cities Area, Technical Report 3 (McLean, Va.: Alan M. Voorhees & Associates, Inc., November 1969).

The lack of standardized methodologies for such studies has further deteriorated the repute of benefit–cost (B/C) analysis because the need for system justification motivates the analyst to add benefits from as many sources as his imagination can produce. If some categories are simply alternative ways of counting the same benefits—no matter—no one is really serious about it anyway.

Table 14-3 shows a comparison of benefits estimated for several selected rapid transit proposals. The table has grouped all benefits into three categories as follows:

1. *Transportation* (*direct*) *benefits*. Include travel-time and operating cost savings for various classes of users of the transport system (all modes).
2. *Community* (*indirect*) *benefits*. Include those other benefits deemed by the analyst to be quantifiable but stemming from secondary effects of the transportation improvement.
3. *Miscellaneous benefits*. Include items not conveniently classed into the other two categories.

The direct benefits included for various studies seem the most uniform in concept. Most components of direct benefits were included by most studies. Some seem to be guilty of double counting by including both accident and insurance cost reductions.

Indirect benefits, on the other hand, seem to vary widely with little agreement as to what items to include, and values included seeming to vary surprisingly. Little is known about estimating secondary benefits, and analysts used widely differing methodologies. Many of the benefit categories included under "indirect benefits" are probably different ways of measuring the same benefit, and, even if accurately measured, may simply be an exercise in double, triple, or other multiple counting, especially if the direct benefits have already been tallied.

The miscellaneous benefits may represent further departures from rigorous benefit–cost methodologies. For example, the inclusion of "savings from transport investments no longer needed" implies that one is comparing the improved situation (if the rapid transit is built) with something other than a null system (i.e., one where only committed additional investments will be made in transportation improvements). "Savings in fare expenditures" are also a questionable benefit, since such savings to riders must mean an added cost to taxpayers in a time when most systems operate at a deficit. Beyond that, they are simply revenue reductions, and system revenue has no place in the analysis since it is neither a benefit nor a cost but a component of system financing. "Savings in bus system operation costs" should, for uniformity, be regarded as a reduction in system cost (to be found in the denominator of the B/C ratio) instead of as a benefit (in the numerator).

Table 14-4 is similar to Table 14-3 except that all the values are normalized by dividing the benefits by the number of transit system riders in the design year. Since almost all transit system benefits are highly correlated with the number of riders it carries (more precisely, most benefits are related to the number of "additional riders" the system attracts above the "null" system), one would expect to see some similarity in benefits per rider obtained in different categories. Unfortunately, this is not the

TABLE 14-3
Benefits Estimated for Selected Rapid Transit Proposals
(millions of 1973 dollars after discounting to net present value)

Metro Area	Trips Diverted from Autos — Operating Cost Savings	Parking Cost Savings	Auto Insurance Cost Savings	Additional Vehicle Savings	Reduction in Accident Costs	Continuing Transit Trips — Time Savings	Trips Continuing to Use Autos — Time Savings	Trips Continuing to Use Autos — Operating Cost Savings	Savings to Trucking Industry	Employee Parking Cost Savings to Suburban Employers	Increased Construction Employment Throughout Projected Construction	Greater Economic Output	Increased Business Productivity	Decrease in Government Expenditures	Increase in Government Tax Receipts	Increase in Number of Destination Opportunities	Additional Transit Services Included in Transit Plan	Savings in Transit Fare Expenditures	Savings from Transport Investments no Longer Required	Savings in Bus System Operating Costs	Total Benefit-Cost Ratio Estimated for System
Buffalo	39	52	10	55	X	← 100 →	X	X	X	X	X	X	X	X	X	X	X	-90	X	50	1.15
Atlanta	120	114	25	177	818	241	1365	353	752	29	X	X	X	X	X	X	X	X	X	64	2.79
Baltimore	539	155	26	169	132	235	43	117	182	X	109	44	X	40	136	X	X	X	2553	X	1.31
Honolulu	699	317	29	580	60	175	1629	354	X	X	272	22	X	X	X	X	X	-743	X	X	3.80
Los Angeles	956	516	X	78	107	941	697	102	28	X	545	682	341	341	X	568	X	-798	X	X	1.87
Washington	246	324	46	376	X	211	1753	205	88	73	X	X	X	X	X	X	X	X	X	X	3.17
Cleveland	← 333 →					← 618 →		X	X	X	X	X	X	156	X	X	110	341	X	X	1.23

Sources: Regional Planning Council, *Baltimore Region Rapid Transit System, Feasibility and Preliminary Engineering* (Baltimore: Regional Planning Council, July 1968). Metropolitan Transit Authority, *Baltimore Region Rapid Transit System, Phase I Plan* (Baltimore: Metropolitan Transit Authority, January 1971). Department of Transportation Services, City and County of Honolulu, *Honolulu Rapid Transit System, Preliminary Engineering Evaluation Program, Final Report* (Honolulu, Hawaii: Department of Transportation Services, December 1972). Niagara Frontier Transportation Authority, *Niagara Frontier Mass Transit Study, Technical Report* (Buffalo, N.Y.: Niagara Frontier Transportation Authority, September 1971). Metropolitan Atlanta Rapid Transit Authority, *Rapid Transit for Metro Atlanta* (Atlanta, Ga.: Metropolitan Atlanta Rapid Transit Authority, September 1971). Southern California Rapid Transit District, *Southern California Rapid Transit District, Final Report* (Los Angeles: Southern California Rapid Transit District, May 1968). Washington Metropolitan Area Transit Authority, *Technical Appendix, Benefits to the Washington Area from the Adopted Regional Transit System* (Washington, D.C.: Washington Metropolitan Area Transit Authority, October 1968). Alan M. Voorhees & Associates, Inc., *Ten-Year Transit Development Program (Cleveland, Ohio)* (McLean, Va.: Alan M. Voorhees & Associates, Inc., August 1974).

TABLE 14-4
Benefits per Design-Year Rider for Selected Rapid Transit Proposals
(net present value or benefits in 1973 dollars divided by design-year riders)

Metro Area	Design Year	Annual Patronage in Design Year (millions)	Trips Diverted from Autos: Operating Cost Savings	Trips Diverted: Parking Cost Savings	Trips Diverted: Auto Insurance Cost Savings	Trips Diverted: Additional Vehicle Savings	Trips Diverted: Reduction in Accident Costs	Trips Diverted: Time Savings	Continuing Transit Trips: Time Savings	Continuing Transit Trips: Operating Cost Savings	Trips Continuing to Use Autos: Savings to Trucking Industry	Trips Continuing to Use Autos: Employee Parking Cost Savings to Suburban Employers	Increased Construction Employment Throughout Project Construction	Greater Economic Output	Increased Business Productivity	Decrease in Government Expenditures	Increase in Government Tax Receipts	Increase in Number of Destination Opportunities	Additional Transit Services Included in Transit Plan	Savings in Transit Fare Expenditures	Savings from Transport Investments no Longer Required	Savings in Bus System Operating Costs	Total Benefits
Buffalo	1995	44	0.88	1.16	0.23	1.24	X	←— 2.25 —→	→	X	X	X	X	X	X	X	X	X	X	−2.04	X	1.14	4.86
Atlanta	1995	163	0.74	0.70	0.15	1.08	5.01	1.48	8.36	2.16	4.61	0.17	X	X	X	X	X	X	X	X	X	0.30	24.85
Baltimore	1985	107	5.03	1.45	0.24	1.58	X	1.23	2.20	1.10	1.70	0.40	1.01	0.41	X	0.38	1.27	X	X	X	23.84	X	41.84
Honolulu	1995	101	6.93	3.14	0.28	5.75	0.59	1.74	16.14	3.51	X	X	2.70	0.21	X	X	X	X	X	−7.36	X	X	33.63
Los Angeles	1980	138	6.91	3.73	X	0.56	0.78	6.81	2.38	0.74	0.20	X	X	4.93	2.47	2.47	X	X	X	X	X	X	31.88
Washington	1990	293	0.84	1.11	0.16	1.28	X	0.72	5.99	X	0.30	0.25	3.94	X	X	X	X	4.11	X	−5.77	X	X	13.03
Cleveland	1985	128	←— 2.61 —→	→	→	→	X	←— 4.85 —→	1.61	X	X	X	X	X	X	1.22	X	X	0.86	2.67	X	X	13.82

Sources: Regional Planning Council, *Baltimore Region Rapid Transit System, Feasibility and Preliminary Engineering* (Baltimore: Regional Planning Council, July 1968). Metropolitan Transit Authority, *Baltimore Region Rapid Transit System, Phase I Plan* (Baltimore: Metropolitan Transit Authority, January 1971). Department of Transportation Services, City and County of Honolulu, *Honolulu Rapid Transit System, Preliminary Engineering Evaluation Program, Final Report* (Honolulu, Hawaii: Department of Transportation Services, December 1972). Niagara Frontier Transportation Authority, *Niagara Frontier Mass Transit Study, Technical Report* (Buffalo, N.Y.: Niagara Frontier Transportation Authority, September 1971). Metropolitan Atlanta Rapid Transit Authority, *Rapid Transit for Metro Atlanta* (Atlanta, Ga.: Metropolitan Atlanta Rapid Transit Authority, September 1971). Southern California Rapid Transit District, *Southern California Rapid Transit District, Final Report* (Los Angeles: Southern California Rapid Transit District, May 1968). Washington Metropolitan Area Transit Authority, *Technical Appendix, Benefits to the Washington Area from the Adopted Regional Transit System* (Washington, D.C.: Washington Metropolitan Area Transit Authority, October 1968). Alan M. Voorhees & Associates, Inc., *Ten-Year Transit Development Program (Cleveland, Ohio)* (McLean, Va.: Alan M. Voorhees & Associates, Inc., August 1974).

case. Here even the "direct benefits" vary widely in value. Operating cost savings per person diverted to the improved transit system vary from over $6.90 for Honolulu and Los Angeles to only $0.74 in Atlanta. Time savings for trips which continue to use cars after transit improvement (due to reduction in highway congestion) vary from Honolulu's $16.14 down to Baltimore's $0.40.

Figure 14-3 summarizes the values and distributions of direct, indirect, and miscellaneous benefits for different cities. The absolute value of total benefits per design-year rider varies from Baltimore's $41.34 down to Buffalo's $4.86. It is difficult to explain why there should be a tenfold difference. The proportion of all benefits which are related to direct transportation benefits varies even more, from more than 100% in Buffalo and Honolulu to only 36% in Baltimore.

Table 14-5 suggests some of the reasons for such wide variations. The *discount rate*—the presumed time value of money used to discount the value of future benefits and costs back to present worth—is a critical assumption used in B/C analysis and

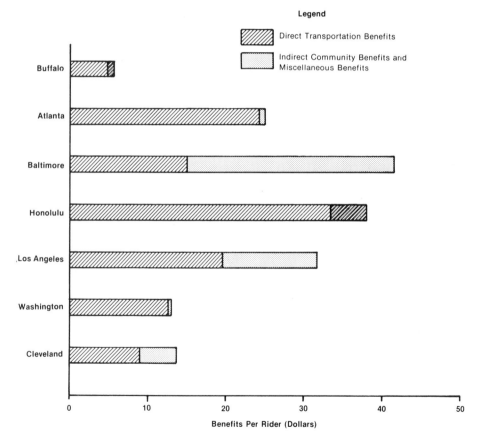

Figure 14-3 *Benefits per design-year rider. (Net present value of benefits in 1973 dollars divided by design-year riders.)*

can make a big difference in the results when comparing systems with different degrees of capital intensiveness. As shown in Table 14-5, this value varies from 4% in Buffalo to 6% in Atlanta. The value of travel-time savings has varied from $0.60 to $3.60 per hour. Figure 14-3 graphically shows the proportional effect on total benefits of the direct transportation benefits as estimated in various studies. Clearly, the relative value of such systems cannot even be hinted at when the input assumptions are so variant.

TABLE 14-5
Selected Differences in Benefit/Cost Assumptions

Metro Area	Discount Rate (%)	Value of Time ($/hour)	Direct Benefits as % of Total
Buffalo	4	1.72	119
Atlanta	6	3.00	98
Baltimore	4	0.60	36
Honolulu	5	3.19	113
Los Angeles	6	3.60	62
Washington	4	2.95	98
Cleveland	6	2.80	66

It is believed that studies could be much improved and find much greater utility if certain aspects were prescribed and standardized. The U.S. Department of Transportation (DOT) should require studies of rapid transit feasibility to meet such standards prior to applications for federal funds. Development of standards for the transportation (direct) benefits should be a simple matter. Standards for community (indirect) benefits will be more difficult, but separate identification of these will at least allow the reviewer to see the extent to which system justification depends on these less precise measures.

Such a specification would include a definition of the categories of benefits which can be quantified, a consistent range of values to assume for the value of time, a range of values to be used for the value of money (the discount rate), a requirement to conduct the analysis in constant (noninflating) dollars, a cut off in the acceptance of benefits not expected until the distant future, an explicit statement of land-use assumptions, and specification of the economic measures to be presented. The latter should, as a minimum, include the benefit–cost ratio, the net present value of the project, and the first-year benefits.

Clearly, benefit–cost analysis is not a substitute for good sense; other nonquantifiable, but none the less important, factors are also at work and must be evaluated. It would seem, however, that consistent measuring of those elements which are measurable would be of assistance and would, in the case of a very low benefit–cost ratio, serve as a warning that other nonmeasurable factors must be weighted very heavily in the final evaluation if such a system is to be justified.

Technology provides the planner with five transit modes which have at least the potential for supplying rapid transit services. These are:

1. *Rail rapid transit* (*RRT*), which may be defined as steel-wheeled, electric-powered vehicles capable of operation in trains of two or more cars, on entirely grade-separated rights-of-way, generally loading and unloading passengers from stations with platforms at floor level permitting rapid entry and exit.
2. *Light rail transit* (*LRT*), which is basically the same as rail rapid transit except that it has the flexibility of operating mixed with other traffic for segments of a line and loading may take place from low or medium-height platforms. Under these conditions electric power must be obtained from overhead wires instead of a low-level third rail.
3. *Bus rapid transit* (*BRT*), which is a system utilizing buses operating, at least in part, on exclusive rights-of-way with stops at least 0.8 km (0.5 mi) apart, permitting high-speed operation.
4. *Commuter railroad*, the use of rail passenger trains, generally on an existing railroad which usually is used for freight as well as for passenger service, moving within a single metropolitan area.
5. *Personal rapid transit* (*PRT*), the use of small electrically powered vehicles on an exclusive guideway, automated to allow system operation without operators on the vehicles.

Commuter railroads are a special case, since the availability of an active rail line appropriately situated is a prerequisite for this type of service. Most commuter railroads in operation in the 1970s were begun many decades ago by the private railroad companies looking for ways to expand their profitable passenger service. The profits have long since disappeared, but the need for the service has not, and in several of our major cities, especially New York, Chicago, Philadelphia, and Boston, they continue to perform a vital transportation role, albeit now with large public subsidy. Although there have been many studies of the potential for such service in other cities, generally the benefit–cost trade-off looks unfavorable except for the occasional expansion of existing service. Rarely has completely new service been justified (e.g., Toronto), and this only in those cities where (1) the track is already in good condition, (2) the tracks penetrate deep into the CBD and good distribution is available from the central terminal to other destinations, and (3) significant residential areas can be serviced by the outlying track locations. In no case have the analyses looked favorable where any significant new track, terminals, or other fixed facilities had to be built in order to inaugurate the service. Thus, a city either has well-located high-quality track or it

---

[1]For further definition of modes, see Chapter 4.

does not. Most do not, and commuter railroads in such cases must remain a non-option.

Personal rapid transit (PRT) is an emerging technology which, because of its potential capability of producing more frequent service and fewer stops en route, many have felt could produce the higher service levels needed in American cities to compete for our largely auto-oriented mobility patterns. So far the technology has advanced only as far as group rapid transit, which, with its larger vehicles and longer headways, is restricted to the relatively slow, short trip movements found in major activity centers (e.g., airports, university campuses). The higher speeds, instant switching, very close headways, and reliability characteristics required to produce the capacity and service needs for metropolitan-wide service will require a very large investment in research over a number of years. Most transportation specialists concede that such PRT service is not currently at a stage of development where it can be implemented with confidence by local authorities. The Urban Mass Transportation Administration (UMTA), by its hesitance to finance the local development of such systems, has implicitly agreed. UMTA's program to demonstrate four or more downtown "people-mover" systems is based on known technology and is not expected to further the development of the mode significantly.

As a practical matter, then, a city has three choices: RRT, LRT, and BRT. In area after area, the choice is an agonizing one, being made only after years of debate, delays, and great frustration. The record suggests that in some cases the choice gets confused and is used by those who prefer no system to delay the process altogether. In many cases the arguments are waged at a superficial level and often overlook the fact that the choice of technology is only one of a number of choices necessary, some of which can affect costs and service more than the technology issue.

Several studies have been made which try to compare the relative costs of the systems (particularly RRT and BRT), with widely varying results. For example, Miller[2] found that RRT was almost always cheaper, whereas the Institute for Defense Analysis[3] found that BRT is always cheaper. Deen[4] found that either could be cheaper, depending on the volume to be carried and on the extent of the subway segments required. Reasons for such variance among responsible investigators are many, but there are two that dominate the confusion. They are:

1. A failure to recognize the huge differences in costs associated with alternative vertical alignment configurations. Underground construction costs 3 to 5 times that of elevated; and elevated construction costs 3 to 5 times that of surface construction. Finally, surface systems (or segments) themselves can vary by a

[2]D. R. MILLER AND OTHERS, "Cost Comparison of Busway and Railway Rapid Transit," in *Evaluation of Bus Transit Strategies*, Highway Research Record 459 (Washington, D.C.: Highway Research Board, 1973), pp. 1–10.

[3]J. HAYDEN BOYD, NORMAN J. ASHER, AND ELLIOT S. WETZLER, *Evaluation of Rail Rapid Transit & Express Bus Service in the Urban Commuter Market*, prepared for U.S. DOT (Arlington, Va.: Institute for Defense Analyses, October 1973). Now available as PB 265 236.

[4]THOMAS B. DEEN AND DONALD H. JAMES, "Relative Costs of Bus and Rail Transit Systems," in *Transportation Systems Planning*, Highway Research Record 293 (Washington, D.C.: Highway Research Board, 1969), pp. 33–53.

factor of 3 to 5, depending on whether they can be located on streets mixed with other traffic, or must be located on an exclusive right-of-way (R/W). These ratios tend to hold true for all technologies, and their sheer magnitude guarantees that any analysis that does not explicitly account for them is probably going to get unreliable answers. Figure 14-4 shows the very large differences in cost in rail transit construction, depending on whether surface, elevated, underground, or some combination is built.

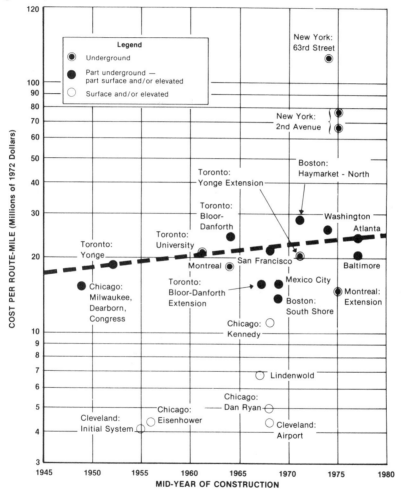

*Metric conversion: 1 ft = .3 m; 1 mi = 1.6 km.

Figure 14-4 *Rail transit system costs versus mid-year construction: including right-of-way.**[*Source: Adapted from J. Hayden Boyd, Norman J. Asher, and Elliot S. Wetzler,* Evaluation of Rail Rapid Transit and Express Bus Service in the Urban Commuter Market, *prepared for Assistant Secretary for Policy Plans and International Affairs, U.S. DOT (Arlington, Va.: Institute for Defense Analyses, October 1973).*]

2. A failure to recognize the complexities intrinsic to the decision to select subway vs. elevated vs. surface (exclusive R/W) vs. surface (mixed traffic).

It is fair to say that the decisions made on vertical configuration are the fundamental ones with respect to the ultimate costs of the system, and that they can transcend by an order of magnitude the related, but often separate, question of technology selection. The lack of understanding of these relationships have caused no end of confusion where system costs are compared. For example, a number of the early research studies of the potentials for PRT concluded that very large cost savings would be possible because it was assumed that they could be built elevated or in some instances on the surface; whereas they were compared to conventional RRT systems which normally had a portion underground. The reasons for the RRT being underground were not recognized; had they been, there would have been less optimism about locating PRTs universally anywhere in an elevated configuration, and cost differences would have been much less dramatic.

RELATIONSHIP OF PLANNING ELEMENTS

Figure 14-5 depicts some basic relationships in the planning process that shape decision on the vertical configuration-technology issue. As noted, the process begins with a recognition of the planning–design goals: to maximize benefits (which are always very closely related to ridership: e.g., air pollution reduction is directly related to the number of people attracted from their cars), to minimize costs, to minimize any adverse social or environmental impacts, and to design a system to attract the public support to generate the financing required to build it. The designer-planner must do this with available technology with its constraints of space requirements, costs, and performance. He or she also must do it allowing for the topography and physical shape and dimensions of the city, which, in turn, influence the horizontal and vertical configuration of the system. The combination of the elements produce a system design with attributes such as speed, service frequency, capacity, and costs, which satisfy, in part, the goals. The designer-planner can develop alternative systems which make different trade-offs between costs–service–technology configuration and produce different system attributes which satisfy, in different ways, the original goals. This process of trying and testing alternatives produces results which are never entirely conclusive or compelling since no system will service all the goals; and the choices between the realistic alternatives available must be resolved through political compromises achieved by the many varied interests involved. The main point from Fig. 14-5 is that the attributes of the selected system are influenced by goals, configuration, *and* technology constraints, not by the latter alone.

One of the fundamental trade-offs which must be made in system planning is among

- The system's total mileage.
- The ease of access of the system to the high-activity centers of the city.
- The selection of vertical configuration.

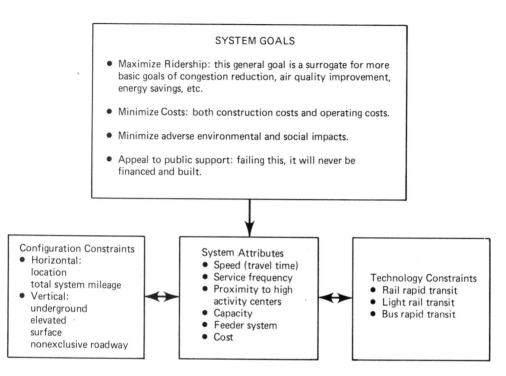

Figure 14-5 *Relationship between elements influencing system planning*

One of the first difficulties faced by the transit planner in developing alternative system plans for evaluation is that no system can provide much of a service boost unless it can provide service within a convenient walking distance of the traveler's ultimate destination or origin. Secondary feeder services can often be used at one end of the trip (thus inducing one mode transfer), but rarely can the traveler be induced to make two transfers. This puts a large priority on locating stations very close to the centers of the highest-density areas of the city, the very locations where land costs are at a premium, where existing rights-of-way are least likely to exist, where elevated segments are most likely to meet strong resistance, and where the demolition associated with any construction on the surface is difficult, disruptive, and expensive. Because of the cost multiples in going underground, it is safe to say that the choice of underground would almost never be made were it not for these factors. In many instances, if underground is not possible, then the area simply will go unserved.

Planners can reach more activities through use of more underground (for a system with a given mileage). In so doing they increase potential ridership and benefits to be derived from the system. Unfortunately, by so doing they also increase the costs. Whether the underground is worth the extra costs depends on how much is required, how many passengers will be obtained, and how noxious the alternatives are. Clearly, these are complicated issues that can only be determined by a detailed study of the specific site in question, and even then can be reasonably debated.

While generally all of the foregoing tends to hold true for any of the technologies, it is nevertheless true that some technologies lend themselves to some situations better than others. For example, if one is certain that a given line must be underground for its entire 19-km (12-mi) length and must carry 30,000 passengers per hour in one direction, then the choice is clearly RRT. High costs of ventilation and large stations required for the high volume of required buses eliminate BRT from contention. The high-capacity need eliminates LRT. Other scenarios could be developed which would favor BRT or LRT in a compelling fashion. Unfortunately, the more typical situation is not so clear.

Table 14-6 shows in tabular form some of the more typical relationships between system goals, which can be translated into design objectives and finally into design methods and technology attributes. For example, to meet the goal of high ridership, the designer might choose the objective of locating stations as close to as many high-activity centers as possible and, in selected instances, go underground to make this possible. In this case RRT might be the favored technology, with a second choice of LRT, and the poorest BRT. The achievement of other goals, however, requires other objectives and methods, often in conflict with each other, and completely alters the ranking of the alternative technology choices.

RAIL SYSTEMS VS. BUS SYSTEMS

While the choice between RRT and LRT is confusing and often difficult, the really intense controversies seem to be generated in making the choice between rail (whether RRT or LRT) and bus systems. Understanding these controversies requires a recognition that very large economic interests are influenced by the final choice since highway–automobile interest groups favor and tend to support bus systems while a different set of interest groups support the rail equipment industry.

Perhaps the greatest factor against the use of buses is related to the public's attitude. Existing local transit has a tarnished image with most urbanites, and those with cars tend not to use them. New rapid transit systems, on the other hand, have a very favorable image in the public mind. Thus, the agency proposing a bus system, particularly one which will require a large capital investment, must make an uncommonly convincing case to obtain voter approval. Transit authorities sense this public sentiment and, partly as a result, have yet to go to a bond referendum to build an extensive bus system which includes significant mileage of new busways in any city.

Institutional arrangements also tend to conspire against buses since the existing bus system is often operated by a different agency than the one charged with rapid-transit development. How can the transit development agency propose to build busways, stations, and other facilities when it cannot ensure that service will be operated on them once built? Even consultants have been known to give pause before recommending busways, especially if working for the transit development agency; whereas busways might be designed and built by the highway agency.

TABLE 14-6
Some Relationships Between Technology Attributes and Design Goals

Goal	Design Objective	Design Method	Technology Suitability Rank		
			RRT	LRT	BRT
Maximize ridership	Locate stations within easy walk of many major centers	Locate system underground so as to avoid demolition of existing development in high-density areas and to avoid poor environment of elevated stations	1	2	3
		Use many stations and high line mileage	1	1	1
	Provide high-frequency service	Use short trains or single-vehicle trains with short headways	2	2	1
	Maximize scheduled speed	Provide grade separation for entire system	1	2	3
		Provide skip-stop and express service	2	2	1
Minimize construction cost	Maximize use of existing rights-of-way to avoid heavy underground and elevated construction	Use freeway medians, railroads, power-line rights-of-way even though these may be distant from activity centers	1	1	1
		In lower-density areas, let system run on streets or highways mixed with other traffic	3	2	1
	Reduce total construction required	Reduce system mileage, number of stations	1	1	1
		Use short trains to reduce station length	2	2	1
		Use simpler stations, low platforms, etc.	2	1	1
	Reduce system complexity	Eliminate power distribution and control systems	2	2	1
Minimize operating cost	Reduce operating personnel	Use long trains to reduce personnel/passenger ratio	1	2	3
		Use more complex systems with more automation	1	2	3
		Use short trains in off-peak	3	2	1
Maximize public support	Provide service to widest possible area	Use low cost/mile systems: maximum use of at-grade nonexclusive R/W	3	2	1
	Provide systems which fit predispositions of public	Use rail systems; avoid bus systems	1	2	3

INTRINSIC DIFFERENCES

Aside from attitudinal and institutional factors, there are inherent physical features that distinguish the performance and cost characteristics of bus and rail systems. Comparison of the features in any definitive way has thus far not been accomplished, however, and the arguments about the relative efficiency of the two modes continue to escalate as fast as transit construction costs. Both bus and rail systems have advocates that present their arguments in superficial terms that tend to obscure the real differences that are already sufficiently complex. Bus advocates argue that buses are more flexible and therefore capable of change as the city changes; that they can offer more nontransfer service between different points where trips are not aligned into a high-density corridor; and that rail systems are just too expensive anyway. Rail advocates argue, in response, that rail systems have more capacity; that rail operating costs are lower, offsetting higher construction costs of rail; and that they are faster, safer, and have greater acceleration.

It is useful to examine some of the various claims as a way of highlighting the real differences between systems.

Bus advocates claim that:

1. *Buses are more flexible and are more appropriate for diffuse trip patterns, since individual routes can be set up for different groups of trips.* There is little doubt that bus routes can be more easily changed than rail routes. Yet, if special busways are built, they are as fixed as a railway. Flexibility is also a disadvantage if one of the purposes of building a transit system is to encourage denser land development patterns. As to providing nontransfer rides by bus between many points in an urban area, this can only be done by sacrificing service frequency. An analysis for the Los Angeles area showed that providing for direct service between all potential bus collection areas would result in an average of two bus trips per day per route, clearly an unacceptable frequency. Buses have some ability to provide direct service compared to rail, but it is limited in practice.

2. *Buses can provide higher speeds than rail when used on a busway, since they can provide nonstop service.* This is probably true, but its effects are marginal. Buses can travel at nonstop speeds of 64 to 80 km/h (40 to 50 mi/h) on an urban busway (the San Bernadino busway completed in 1974 in Los Angeles was soon operating under a speed limit imposed by the operating agency). Rail systems run at schedule speeds of 48 to 72 km/h (30 to 45 mi/h), depending on station spacing. Frequency of service at individual points along the line suffers when buses are skipping stops, however; service between points on the same line is made circuitous also. In addition, the extra station bypassing lanes necessary for the buses under these conditions require more space than is sometimes possible to find in a dense urban environment.

3. *Buses are cheaper than rail.* No doubt the cheapest transit system possible is through use of buses on existing streets and freeways. Such service is often slow and unreliable, however, since it is subject to traffic delays and congestion. In other words, you can pay less and get less. The real issue between systems concerns whether comparable service can be provided at a lower cost. Buses using specially constructed busways may or may not be cheaper, depending primarily on passenger volume and whether the transit route must operate partially or wholly in tunnel. Estimated costs of busway construction (not including right-of-way) for most of the U.S. busway proposals from 1969 through 1974 (virtually all of which have called for surface systems) have averaged about $1.6 million per

km ($2.5 million per mi). These may be compared to costs of $2.5 to 6.2 million per km ($4.0 to 10.0 million per mi), including R/W, for surface rail systems in Fig. 14-4. Either busways or rail systems require land, grading, drainage, structures, and roadway preparation. Comparison of right-of-way needs show that bus and rail have similar requirements. The most significant differences result from the need for rail for power distribution and control systems which are not normally required for bus systems, but can represent from 12 to 18% of rail costs. Rail construction costs then will tend to be somewhat higher than for busways as long as passenger volumes are low (and large bus stations are thus not required) and subways are only a small part of the system.

4. *If buses are given priority treatment on existing roads and streets, then buses can provide high-level service at much lower cost than rail.* This is probably true, at least in those corridors where freeways exist and where lanes can be reserved for buses.

Rail advocates claim that:

1. *Rail systems have more capacity.* This is true. However, many of the existing and proposed rail systems actually have capacities that are well within the range of bus systems and well below ultimate rail capacity; thus, capacity is irrelevant to the argument in many instances. Rail systems can carry 30,000 passengers/hour per track (and more if properly designed); bus systems can carry a similar number per lane *as long as the buses do not stop on the roadway.* If passenger pickup along the way is required (as at rail stations), then the bus lane can carry only about 7500 passengers/hour or else multilane bus stations are necessary, requiring much more space (which might not be available in a crowded urban environment) than rail stations.
2. *Rail systems are more energy efficient.* This may or may not be true in particular instances, depending largely on the average occupancy of the vehicles. Research has shown that buses in large cities can be as energy efficient as the San Francisco Bay Area Rapid Transit (BART) system, for example.[5]
3. *Rail systems do not cause as much air pollution as buses.* This may well be true in areas where electrical power generation is nonpolluting (e.g., hydroelectric generation). Even if it is polluting, the problem out near the power generation plant often is not as acute as it is inside the city. Besides, the issue may be irrelevant, since both bus or rail with reasonable patronage cause so little pollution per passenger-mile compared to autos that the one providing the greatest service, and therefore the greatest diversion from autos, might prove to be the most nonpolluting.
4. *Rail systems have lower operating costs than bus systems.* This may be true, at least as long as passenger volume is large enough to take advantage of the multiple-car per operator capacity of rail systems.

---

[5]ALAN M. VOORHEES & ASSOCIATES, INC., *Energy Efficiencies of Urban Passenger Transportation*, Technical Study Memorandum no. 9 (Washington, D.C.: Highway Users Federation for Safety and Mobility, May 1974).

Some of these potential rail system efficiencies are lost on some of the older U.S. rail networks (e.g., Boston), which operate under labor rules requiring more operating personnel than necessary. The requirement for larger numbers of maintenance personnel, station attendants, and in some cases, special police reduces much of rail potential operating cost efficiencies, however.

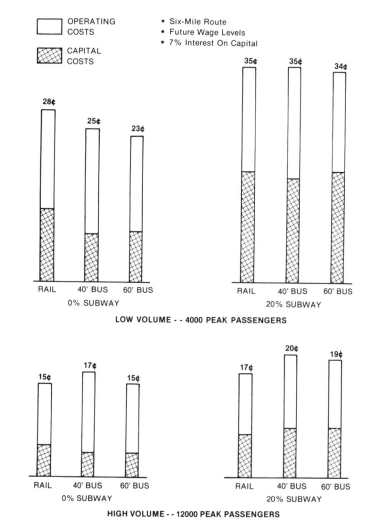

*Metric conversion: 1 ft = .3 m; 1mi = 1.6 km.

Figure 14-6   *Total rail and busway costs (cents/passenger).* *[Source: Thomas B. Deen and Donald H. James, "Relative Costs of Bus and Rail Transit Systems," in Transportation Systems Planning, Highway Research Record 293 (Washington, D.C.: Highway Research Board, 1969), p. 52.]*

ARE BUS SYSTEMS CHEAPER OVERALL?

It is around this question that the greatest controversy is centered. From the foregoing discussion it should be evident that the passenger load, length of the system located in tunnel, and the space available for system facilities will influence the answer. Other factors include the size of bus units to be operated, the ratio of peak to off-peak traffic loads, and the amount of service provided in excess of load requirements during off-peak periods. Figure 14-6 indicates that where volumes exceed 12,000 passengers/hour and/or more than 20% of the line must be in tunnel, rail systems can be cheaper.

CONCLUSIONS

Arguments about the relative costs of rail rapid transit and bus rapid transit are seen to be transcended by the more complex decisions about whether the system—whatever the technology—must be underground, elevated, or on the surface. Public acceptance also leans toward rail systems even when bus systems might serve better for less cost. Even so, the differences between costs of rail and busway systems are not as great as is often supposed, and often the decision will have to be made on factors other than cost.

SELECTED BIBLIOGRAPHY

BHATT, KIRAN, "Comparative Analysis of Urban Transportation Costs," in *Transit Planning*, Transportation Research Record 559, pp. 101–16. Washington, D.C.: Transportation Research Board, 1976.

BOYD, J. HAYDEN, NORMAN J. ASHER, AND ELLIOT S. WETZLER, "Evaluation of Rail Rapid Transit and Express Bus Service in the Urban Commuter Market," abridgement, in *Transit Planning*, Transportation Research Record 559, pp. 44–46. Washington, D.C.: Transportation Research Board, 1976.

DEEN, THOMAS B., AND DONALD H. JAMES, "Relative Costs of Bus and Rail Transit Systems," in *Transportation Systems Planning*, Highway Research Record 293, pp. 33–53. Washington, D.C.: Highway Research Board, 1969.

————, WALTER M. KULASH, AND STEPHEN BAKER, "Critical Decisions in the Rapid Transit Planning Process," in *Transit Planning*, Transportation Research Record 559, pp. 33–43. Washington, D.C.: Transportation Research Board, 1976.

————, AND ROBERT E. SKINNER, JR., "Responses to Alternatives Analysis Requirements," *Transit Journal*, 2, no. 4 (November 1976), 53–71.

MILLER, DAVID R., AND OTHERS, "Cost Comparison of Busway and Railway Rapid Transit," in *Evaluation of Bus Transit Strategies*, Highway Research Record 459, pp. 1–10. Washington, D.C.: Highway Research Board, 1973.

MITRIC, SLOBODAN, *Comparisons of Modes in Urban Transport: A Methological Analysis*, Technical Report. Columbus, Ohio: The Ohio State University, Department of Civil Engineering, July 1976.

VUCHIC, VUKAN R., "Comparative Analysis and Selection of Transit Modes," in *Transit Planning*, Transportation Research Record 559, pp. 51–62. Washington, D.C.: Transportation Research Board, 1976.

PART IV

Planning Public Transportation Systems

INTRODUCTION TO PART IV

The purpose of this section is to provide perspective concerning the context and approaches to planning for public transportation services. Transportation planning has been an evolving process. Beginning with highway planning surveys of the 1940s that were concerned largely with counting traffic and monitoring trends on rural roads, transportation planning in the 1950s and early 1960s became synonomous with home-interview origin–destination surveys and computerized formulas (models) for replicating and forecasting trips on large-scale highway and transit networks.

The comprehensive planning process of the 1960s was inadequate because it failed to include the effect that large-scale systems had on the environment, the impact of energy availability on travel, the responses of citizens to proposed plans, the equity of transport investments in terms of who would benefit and who would pay, and many other factors that could not be incorporated into a computer analysis. The planning process was primarily geared to analyze the travel effects of urban sections of the interstate highway program or extensive rail transit systems such as San Francisco's BART or Washington Metro, for a single 20-year planning horizon, and generally excluded alternatives that did not involve construction of new facilities. More recent planning approaches stress multiyear programming, rather than "one-shot" system plans, that are continually updated and revised, and stress public participation and project review.

The program development process for transportation system management (TSM) strategies, which by definition implies short-range, low-capital improvements, will likely involve a cycle consisting of initiating the planning process by a coordinating agency; reviewing priorities; establishing goals, criteria, and system performance measures; selecting candidate TSM actions; estimating costs and impacts; and preparing project priorities for funding and implementation. The process is a flexible one that may utilize different elements of the cycle, depending upon the TSM action being considered.

Rural transit planning involves a process not dissimilar from that used in urban areas, namely, needs identification and problem definition; establishing goals and objectives for users, operators, and community; defining alternative strategies that are technological, administrative, and operational; estimating demand, assessing community impacts, and computing costs; evaluation, selection, and implementation. The dilemma of serving rural transportation needs by public transit is that demand is low with respect to the cost for providing services and willingness to pay. Furthermore, since rural transportation is often furnished by various social agencies, the organizational structure and the quality of management are primary factors in the level of service and financial integrity of services offered.

Transit planning differs from highway planning because most public transit services involve operational concerns, whereas highway planners have dealt largely with facility construction and design. The factors that influence planning decisions for transit, include length of planning period, consumer attitudes, availability of funds, evaluation, political and regulatory concerns, method of operation, sources of revenue, and labor. Essentially, highway planning has its roots in engineering, whereas transit planning involves management and operations skills as well.

LESTER A. HOEL, Professor and Chairman,
Department of Civil Engineering,
University of Virginia

Chapter 15

EVOLUTION OF URBAN
TRANSPORTATION PLANNING

EDWARD WEINER*, *Manager, Urban Analysis Program, Office of the Secretary, U. S. Department of Transportation*

Urban transportation planning, as it has been practiced in the 1970s, has its roots in highway planning. Over the years, as new concerns were raised and changes in attitudes surfaced, modifications to planning techniques and processes were introduced. These modifications sought to make the planning process more responsive and sensitive to those areas of concern. Early highway planning concentrated on developing a network of all-weather highways and with connecting the various portions of the nation. As this work was being addressed, the problems of serving increased traffic growth surfaced. With the planning of transportation for urban areas came additional problems of land development, disruption and dislocation, environmental degradation, citizen participation, and social concerns such as providing transportation for the disadvantaged. More recently there has been concern about energy consumption.

Modifications to the planning process took a number of years to evolve. Some of these problems are still so new that urban areas are still in the process of developing methods to address them. During such transitional periods, some urban areas which have the resources and technical capability develop new concepts and techniques for dealing with such topics. These new ideas are diffused by various means throughout the nation. The rate at which the new concepts are accepted varies from area to area. Consequently, the quality and depth of planning is highly variant at any point in time.

Current urban transportation planning practice is considerably more sophisticated, complex, and costly than its highway planning precedent. But, it has evolved thus because of the wide range of issues it is forced to deal with.

*The author gratefully acknowledges the valuable comments provided by David S. Gendell of the Federal Highway Administration, Urban Planning Division, and Raymond Weil of the Office of the Secretary, Office of Transportation Economic Analysis, in the preparation of this chapter.

This chapter traces the evolution of urban transportation planning from the early highway planning activities to the 1976 guidelines issued by the federal government for a joint highway–transit planning process.

EARLY HIGHWAY PLANNING ACTIVITIES

In the earlier years of highway construction, the automobile had been regarded as a pleasure vehicle rather than an important means of transportation. Consequently, comparatively short sections of highways were built from the cities into the countryside. During this period, urban roads were considered to be adequate, particularly in comparison to rural roads. Although the concept of a continuous national system of highways was recognized in the Federal-Aid Highway Act of 1925, there were significant gaps in many important through routes. In addition, highway pavements were largely inadequate to carry major traffic loads.

The need for a systematic approach to the planning of highways was recognized in the early 1930s as the rapid growth in automobile ownership and highway travel placed increasing demands on an inadequate highway system. It became clear that these growing problems necessitated the collection and analysis of information on highways and their use on a more comprehensive scale than had ever before been attemped.

FEDERAL-AID HIGHWAY ACT OF 1934

Beginning with the Federal-Aid Highway Act of 1934, the Congress authorized that 1.5% of the amount apportioned to any state annually for construction could be used for surveys, plans, engineering, and economic analyses of projects for future construction. The act created the cooperative arrangement between the Bureau of Public Roads (now the Federal Highway Administration) and the state highway departments known as the statewide highway planning surveys. By 1940, all states were participating in this program.

As an initial activity, these highway planning surveys included a complete inventory and mapping of the highway system and its physical characteristics. Traffic surveys were undertaken to determine the volumes of traffic by vehicle type, weight, and dimensions. Financial studies were made to determine the relationship of highway finances to other financial operations within each state, to assess the ability of the states to finance the construction and operation of the highway system, and to indicate how to allocate highway taxes among the users. Many of these same types of activities are still being performed on a continuing basis by highway agencies.

THE TOLL-ROAD STUDY

By the mid-1930s there was considerable sentiment for a few long-distance, controlled-access highways connecting major cities. Advocates of such a highway system assumed that the public would be willing to finance much of its costs by tolls. The

Bureau of Public Roads was requested by President Roosevelt in 1937 to study this idea, and two years later it published the report, *Toll Roads and Free Roads*.[1]

The study recommended the construction of a highway system to be comprised of direct, interregional highways with all necessary connections through and around cities. It concluded that this nationwide highway system could not be financed solely through tolls, even though certain sections could. It also recommended the creation of a Federal Land Authority empowered to acquire, hold, sell, and lease land. The report emphasized the problem of transportation within major cities and used the city of Baltimore as an example.

THE INTERREGIONAL HIGHWAY REPORT

In April 1941, President Roosevelt appointed the National Interregional Highway Committee to investigate the need for a limited system of national highways to improve the facilities available for interregional transportation. The staff work was done by the Public Roads Administration, and in 1944 the findings of the study were published in the report, *Interregional Highways*.[2] A system of highways, designated the "National System of Interstate and Defense Highways," was recommended and authorized in the Federal-Aid Highway Act of 1944. However, it was not until the Federal-Aid Highway Act of 1956 that any significant work on the system began.

This study was unique in the annals of transportation planning and the implementation of its findings has had profound effects on American life-styles and industry. The study brought planners, engineers, and economists together with the highway officials responsible for implementing highway programs. The final route choices were influenced as much by strategic necessity and such factors as population density, concentrations of manufacturing activity, and agricultural production as by existing and future traffic.

The importance of the system within cities was recognized, but it was not intended that these highways serve urban commuter travel demands in the major cities. As stated in the report, "it is important, both locally and nationally, to recognize the recommended system . . . as that system and those routes which best and most directly join region to region and major city to major city."[3]

The report recognized the need to coordinate with other modes of transporation and for cooperation at all levels of government. It reiterated the need for a Federal Land Authority with the power of excess condemnation and similiar authorities at the state level.

---

[1]U.S. CONGRESS, *Toll Roads and Free Roads*, House Document no. 272, 76th Congress, 1st Session (Washington, D.C.: U.S. Government Printing Office, 1939).

[2]U.S. CONGRESS, *Interregional Highways*, Message from the President of the United States Transmitting a Report of the National Interregional Highway Committee, House Document no. 379, 78th Congress, 2nd Session (Washington, D.C.: U.S. Government Printing Office, 1944).

[3]Ibid.

THE BEGINNINGS OF URBAN TRANSPORTATION PLANNING

EARLY URBAN TRAVEL SURVEYS

Most urban areas did not begin urban travel surveys until 1944. It was during that year that the Federal-Aid Highway Act authorized the expenditure of funds on urban extensions of the federal-aid primary and secondary highway systems. Until that time, there was a lack of information on urban travel which could be used for the planning of highway facilities. In fact, no comprehensive survey methods had been developed which could provide the required information. Because of the complex nature of urban street systems and the shifting of travel from route to route, traffic volumes were not a satisfactory guide to needed improvements. A study of the origin and destination of trips and the basic factors affecting travel was needed.

The method developed to meet this need was the home-interview origin–destination survey. Household members were interviewed to obtain information on the number, purpose, mode, origin, and destination of all trips made on a particular day. These urban travel surveys were used in the planning of highway facilities, particularly expressway systems, and in determining design features. However, these surveys did not produce a plan. It was apparent to planners at this time that if certain relationships between land use and travel could be measured, these relationships could be used as a means to project future travel. It remained for the development of the computer, with its ability to process large masses of data from these surveys, to permit estimation of these relations between travel, land use, and other factors. The first major test using this approach to develop a future highway plan was during the early 1950s in San Juan, Puerto Rico, and in Detroit.

EARLY TRANSIT PLANNING

During this period, transit planning was being carried out by operators as part of the regular activities of operating a transit system. There was no federal assistance for planning or construction and little federal interest. In some urban areas, transit authorities were created to take over and operate the transit system. The Chicago Transit Authority was created in 1945, the Metropolitan Transit Authority in Boston in 1947, and the New York City Transit Authority in 1955.

It was at this time that the San Francisco Bay area began planning for a regional rapid transit system. In 1956, the Rapid Transit Commission proposed a 198-km (123-mi) system in a five-county area. As a result of this study, the Bay Area Rapid Transit District (BARTD) was created within the five counties. BARTD completed the planning for the transit system and conducted preliminary engineering and financial studies. In November 1962 the voters approved a bond issue to build a three-county, 121-km (75-mi) system.

NATIONAL COMMITTEE ON URBAN TRANSPORTATION

While highway departments were placing major emphasis on arterial routes, city street congestion was steadily worsening. It was in this atmosphere that the National Committee on Urban Transportation was created in 1954. Its purpose was "to help cities do a better job of transportation planning through systematic collection of basic facts . . . to afford the public the best possible transportation at the least possible cost and aid in accomplishing desirable goals of urban renewal and sound urban growth."[4]

The committee was composed of experts in a wide range of fields, representing federal, state, and city governments, transit, and other interests. It developed a guidebook, *Better Transportation for Your City*,[5] designed to help local officials establish an orderly program of urban transportation planning. The guide received national recognition and was supplemented by a series of 17 procedure manuals describing techniques for planning highway, transit, and terminal improvements. The two manuals on transit, *Measuring Transit Services* and *Recommended Standards, Warrants, and Objectives for Transit Services and Facilities*,[6] are still in use as references. While the guide and manuals were primarily intended for the attention of local officials, they stressed the need for cooperative action, full communication between professionals and decision makers, and the development of transportation systems in keeping with broad objectives of community development. They provided, for the first time, fully documented procedures for systematic transportation planning.

HOUSING ACT OF 1954

An important cornerstone of the federal policy concerning urban planning was Section 701 of the Housing Act of 1954. The act demonstrated congressional concern with urban problems and recognition of the urban planning process as an appropriate approach to dealing with such problems. Section 701 authorized the provision of federal planning assistance to state planning agencies, cities, and other municipalities having a population of less than 50,000 persons, and after further amendments, to metropolitan and regional planning agencies.

The intent of the act was to encourage an orderly process of urban planning to address the problems associated with urban growth and the formulation of local plans and policies. The act indicated that planning should occur on a regionwide basis within the framework of comprehensive planning.

FEDERAL-AID HIGHWAY ACT OF 1956

During this early development in urban transportation planning came the Federal-Aid Highway Act of 1956. The act authorized the first two years of funding for construction of the 41,000-mi (66,000-km) National System of Interstate and Defense

---

[4]NATIONAL COMMITTEE ON URBAN TRANSPORTATION, *Better Transportation for Your City: A Guide to the Factual Development of Urban Transportation Plans*, including 17 procedure manuals (Chicago: Public Administration Service, 1958).

[5]Ibid.

[6]Ibid.

Highways. The companion Highway Revenue Act of 1956 established the highway trust fund and specified a 90% federal matching share for the interstate program. These two acts were the end result of a report prepared by the President's Advisory Committee on the National Highway Program.

These acts launched the largest single public works program yet undertaken and established the concept of funding highways, through user charges, on a continuing basis. About 20% of the Interstate System mileage was designated as urban, upon request of the state highway departments. The purpose of these routes was to provide alternative interstate service into, through, and around urban areas. The program has had profound impacts on urban areas and caused the development of countervailing forces to balance the urban highway building program.

SAGAMORE CONFERENCE

The availability of large amounts of funds from the 1956 acts brought immediate response to develop action programs. To encourage the cooperative development of highway plans and programs, a conference was held in 1958 in the Sagamore Center of Syracuse University.

The conference focused on the need to conduct planning of urban transportation, including public transportation, on a regionwide comprehensive basis in a manner which supports the orderly development of urban areas. The conference report recognized that urban transportation plans should be evaluated through a grand accounting of benefits and costs which included both user and nonuser impacts.[7]

The conference recommendations were endorsed and their implementation urged, but progress was slow. The larger urban areas were carrying out pioneering urban transportation studies, the most noteworthy being the Chicago Area Transportation Study (CATS). But, few of the smaller urban areas had begun planning studies due to the lack of capable staff to perform urban transportation planning.

To encourage smaller urban areas to begin planning efforts, the American Municipal Association, the American Association of State Highway Officials, and the National Association of County Officials jointly launched a program in early 1962 to describe and explain how to carry out urban transportation planning. This program was initially directed at urban areas under 250,000 population.

HOUSING ACT OF 1961

The first legislation that explicitly dealt with urban mass transportation was the Housing Act of 1961. This act was passed largely as a result of growing financial difficulties with commuter rail services. It inaugurated a small, low-interest program for acquisitions and capital improvements for mass transit systems and a demonstration program.

This act also contained a provision for making federal urban planning assistance available for "preparation of comprehensive urban transportation surveys, studies,

---

[7]*Sagamore Conference on Highways and Urban Development: Guidelines for Action*, October 5–9, 1958, sponsored by American Municipal Association, AASHO, HRB, and Syracuse University (n.p.: n.d.).

and plans to aid in solving problems of traffic congestion, facilitating the circulation of people and goods in metropolitan and other urban areas and reducing transportation needs."[8] The act also permitted federal aid "to facilitate comprehensive planning for urban development, including coordinated transportation systems on a continuing basis."[9] These provisions of the act amended the Section 701 planning programs which were created by the Housing Act of 1954.

URBAN TRANSPORTATION PLANNING COMES OF AGE

JOINT REPORT ON URBAN MASS TRANSPORTATION

In March 1962, a joint report on urban mass transportation was submitted to President Kennedy, at his request, by the Secretary of Commerce and the Housing and Home Finance Administrator.[10] This report integrated the objectives of the highway and mass transit programs, which were comparatively independent up to that point but growing closer through cooperative activities.

The general thrust of this report, as it relates to planning, can be summarized by the following exerpt from the transmittal letter.

> Transportation is one of the key factors in shaping our cities. As our urban communities increasingly undertake deliberate measures to guide their development and renewal, we must be sure that transportation planning and construction are integral parts of general development planning and programming. One of our main recommendations is that Federal aid for urban transportation facilities should be made available only when urban communities have prepared or are actively preparing up-to-date general plans for the entire urban area which relate transportations plans to land-use and development plans.
>
> The major objectives of urban transportation policy are the achievement of sound land-use patterns, the assurance of transportation facilities for all segments of the population, the improvement in overall traffic flow, and the meeting of total urban transportation needs at minimum cost. Only a balanced transportation system can attain these goals—and in many urban areas this means an extensive mass transportation network fully integrated with the highway and street system. But mass transportation has in recent years experienced capital consumption rather than expansion. A cycle of fare increases and service cuts to offset loss of ridership followed by further declines in use points clearly to the need for a substantial contribution of public funds to support needed mass transportation improvements. We therefore recommend a new program of grants and loans for urban mass transportation.[11]

---

[8]WASHINGTON CENTER FOR METROPOLITAN STUDIES, *Comprehensive Planning for Metropolitan Development*, prepared for UMTA (Washington, D.C.: U.S. Department of Transportation, 1970). Now available as PB 200 135.

[9]Ibid.

[10]U.S. SENATE, "Urban Transportation—Joint Report to the President by the Secretary of Commerce and the Housing and Home Finance Administration," *Urban Mass Transportation—1962*, 87th Congress, 2nd Session, pp. 71–81 (Washington, D.C.: U.S. Government Printing Office, 1962).

[11]Ibid.

In April 1962, President Kennedy delivered his first message to Congress on the subject of transportation. Many of the ideas and recommendations related to urban transportation in the message drew upon the previously mentioned joint report.

The President's message recognized the close relationship between transportation and community development and the need to properly balance the use of private automobiles and mass transportation to help shape and service urban areas. It stressed the need to promote the economic efficiency and livability of urban areas. It also recommended continued close cooperation between the Department of Commerce and the Housing and Home Finance Adminstration (HHFA).

This transportation message opened a new era in urban transportation and lead to passage of two landmark pieces of urban legislation: the Federal-Aid Highway Act of 1962 and the Urban Mass Transportation Act of 1964.

FEDERAL-AID HIGHWAY ACT OF 1962

The Federal-Aid Highway Act of 1962 provided a major stimulus to urban transportation planning. Section 9 of the act, which is now Section 134 of Title 23 states:

> It is declared to be in the national interest to encourage and promote the development of transportation systems embracing various modes of transport in a manner that will serve the states and local communities efficiently and effectively.[12]

This statement of policy followed directly from the recommendations of the Sagamore conference and President Kennedy's Transportation Message. Moreover, the section directed the Secretary to cooperate with the states

> in the development of long-range highway plans and programs which are properly coordinated with plans for improvements in other affected forms of transportation and which are formulated with due consideration to their probable effect on the future development of urban areas. . . .[13]

The last sentence of the section, which required that urban highway construction projects be based on a planning process, legislated for the first time a planning requirement:

> After July 1, 1965, the Secretary shall not approve under section 105 of this title any programs for projects in any urban area of more than fifty thousand population unless he finds that such projects are based on a continuing, comprehensive transportation planning process carried out cooperatively by states and local communities in conformance with the objectives stated in this section.[14]

---

[12]FEDERAL HIGHWAY ADMINISTRATION, *Federal Laws and Material Related to the Federal Highway Administration* (Washington, D.C.: U.S. Government Printing Office, November 1976).
[13]Ibid.
[14]Ibid.

Two features of the act are particularly significant with respect to organizational arrangements for carrying out the planning process. First, it called for a planning process in urban areas rather than in cities, which sets the scale at the metropolitan or regional level. Second, it called for the process to be carried on cooperatively by the states and local communities. Because qualified planning agencies to mount such a transportation planning process were lacking in many urban areas, the Bureau of Public Roads (now the Federal Highway Administration) required the creation of planning agencies or organizational arrangements which would be capable of carrying out the required planning process. These planning organizations quickly came into being because of the growing momentum of the highway program and the cooperative financing of the planning process by HHFA and the Bureau of Public Roads.

HERSHEY CONFERENCE

In response to the growing concern about freeway construction in urban areas, the Hershey Conference on Freeways in the Urban Setting was convened in June 1962.[15] The conference recommendations reinforced the need to integrate highway planning and urban development. It recognized that this planning should be done as a team effort which draws upon the skills of engineers, architects, city planners, and other specialists. Further, the planning effort should be carried out in a manner which involves community participation.

RESPONSE TO THE 1962 ACT

The Bureau of Public Roads organized quickly to carry out the planning requirements of the 1962 highway act. Guidelines interpreting the act issued in March 1963 defined the elements of a continuing, comprehensive, cooperative planning process. These guidelines and further refinements and expansions upon them covered all aspects for organizing and carrying out the 3C planning process. Through its Urban Planning Division, the BPR carried out a broad program to develop planning procedures and computer programs, write procedural manuals and guides, give training courses, and provide technical assistance.

This effort to define the "3C planning process," to develop the techniques for carrying out the planning, and to provide technical assistance and training completely transformed the manner in which urban transportation planning was performed. By the legislated deadline of July 1, 1965, all the 224 existing urbanized areas which fell under the 1962 act had an urban transportation planning process underway.

URBAN MASS TRANSPORTATION ACT OF 1964

The first real effort to provide federal assistance for urban mass transportation development was the passage of the Urban Mass Transportation Act of 1964. The

---

[15]*Freeways in the Urban Setting: The Hershey Conference*, June 1962, sponsored by AASHO, American Municipal Association, and National Association of County Officials (Washington, D.C.: Automotive Safety Foundation, n.d.).

objective of the act, still in the spirit of President Kennedy's Transportation Message, was "to encourage the planning and establishment of areawide urban mass transportation systems needed for economical and desirable urban development."[16]

The act required that federal assistance be provided for construction or acquisition of such transit facilities and equipment necessary to carry out a program for a unified or coordinated mass transportation system as part of the "comprehensively planned development of the urban areas."[17]

The act authorized federal capital grants for up to two-thirds of the net project cost of construction, reconstruction, or acquisition of mass transportation facilities and equipment. Net project cost was defined as that portion of the total project cost that could not be readily financed from transit revenues. However, the federal share was to be held to 50% in those areas which had not completed their comprehensive planning process, that is, had not produced a plan. All federal funds dispersed had to be channeled through public agencies. Transit projects were to be initiated locally.

A program of research, development, and demonstrations was also authorized by the 1964 act. The objective of this program was to "assist in the reduction of urban transportation needs, the improvement of mass transportation service, or the contribution of such service toward meeting total urban transportation needs at minimum cost."[18]

However, Congress did not authorize much money to carry this legislation out. No more than $150 million per year was authorized under the 1964 act and the actual appropriations fell short of even that amount.

1966 AMENDMENTS TO THE URBAN MASS TRANSPORTATION ACT OF 1964

To fill several gaps in the 1964 act, several amendments were passed in 1966. One created the technical studies program, which provided federal assistance up to a two-thirds federal matching share for planning, engineering, and designing of urban mass transportation projects or other similiar technical activities leading to application for a capital grant.

Another section authorized grants to be made for management training. A third authorized a project to study and prepare a program of research for developing new systems of urban transportation. This section produced the farsighted report to Congress in 1968, *Tomorrow's Transportation: New Systems for the Urban Future*, which recommended a long-range balanced program of research on hardware, planning, and operational improvements.[19] It was this study that first brought to public attention

---

[16] URBAN MASS TRANSPORTATION ADMINISTRATION, *Urban Mass Transportation Act of 1964 and Related Laws*, as amended through February 5, 1976 (Washington, D.C.: U.S. Government Printing Office, 1976).

[17] Ibid.

[18] Ibid.

[19] LEON MONROE COLE, ed., *Tomorrow's Transportation: New Systems for the Urban Future*, prepared by U.S. Department of Housing and Urban Development (Washington, D.C.: U.S. Government Printing Office, 1968).

many new systems such as dial-a-bus, personal rapid transit, dual mode, pallet systems, and tracked air-cushioned vehicle systems.[20]

WILLIAMSBURG CONFERENCE

By 1965, there was concern that planning processes were not adequately evaluating social and community values. Few planning studies had developed goal-based evaluation methodologies. A conference in Williamsburg, Virginia, was held to discuss this problem. The conference resolves highlighted the need to identify urban goals and objectives which should be used to evaluate urban transportation plans.[21] It emphasized that many values may not be quantifiable but, nonetheless, should not be ignored. The conference also endorsed the concept of making maximum use of existing transportation facilities through traffic management and land-use controls.

IMPROVED GOVERNMENTAL AND PROGRAM COORDINATION

As federal programs proliferated, intergovernmental coordination became more difficult and time consuming. Several actions were directed at alleviating this problem. One result was to encourage broader, multifunctional planning agencies.

HOUSING AND URBAN DEVELOPMENT ACT OF 1965

The Housing and Urban Development Act of 1965 created the Department of Housing and Urban Development (HUD). In addition, the act amended the Section 701 urban planning assistance program established under the Housing Act of 1954 by authorizing grants to be made to "organizations composed of public officials whom he (the Secretary of HUD) finds to be representative of the political jurisdictions within a metropolitan area or urban region . . . "[22] for the purposes of comprehensive planning.

This provision enabled such organizations as councils of governments (COGs) to receive assistance to carry on substantive urban planning functions and thereby gave impetus to the formation of such COGs.

DEPARTMENT OF TRANSPORTATION ACT OF 1966

In 1966, the Department of Transportation (DOT) was created to coordinate transportation programs and to facilitate development and improvement of coordinated transportation service utilizing private enterprise to the maximum extent feasible. DOT was directed to provide leadership in the identification of transportation problems and solutions, stimulate new technological advances, encourage

---

[20]The contents of this report are discussed further in Chapter 34.

[21]*Highways and Urban Development*, report on the Second National Conference, Williamsburg, Virginia, December 12–16, 1965, sponsored by AASHO, National Association of Counties, and National League of Cities (n.p.: n.d.).

[22]WASHINGTON CENTER FOR METROPOLITAN STUDIES, *Comprehensive Planning*.

cooperation among all interested parties, and recommend national policies and programs to accomplish these objectives.

The division of responsibility for urban transportation planning between DOT and HUD, however, was left unclear. It took more than a year for DOT and HUD to come to an agreement on their respective responsibilities. This agreement, known as Reorganization Plan No. 2, took effect in July 1968. Under it, DOT assumed responsibility for the mass transportation capital grant, technical studies, and managerial training grant programs subject to HUD certification of the planning requirements for capital grant applications. Research and development was divided up. DOT assumed responsibility for improving the operation of conventional transit systems and HUD assumed responsibility for urban transportation as it related to comprehensive planning. Joint responsibility was assigned for advanced technological systems. The Reorganization Plan also created the Urban Mass Transportation Administration (UMTA).

DEMONSTRATION CITIES AND METROPOLITAN DEVELOPMENT ACT OF 1966

Section 204 of the Demonstration Cities and Metropolitan Development Act of 1966 was significant in asserting federal interest in improving the coordination of public facility construction projects to obtain maximum effectiveness of federal spending and to relate such projects to areawide development plans. It required that all applications for the planning and construction of facilities must be submitted to an areawide planning agency for review and comment. The object of this section of the act was to encourage the coordination of planning and construction of physical facilities in urban areas. Procedures to implement this act were issued by the Bureau of the Budget in Circular no. 82. In response to these review requirements, many urban areas established new planning agencies or reorganized existing agencies to include elected officials as required by the circular.

INTERGOVERNMENTAL COOPERATION ACT OF 1968

Section 204 of the Demonstration Cities and Metropolitan Development Act was the forerunner of much more extensive legislation, adopted in 1968, designed to coordinate federal grant-in-aid programs at federal and state levels. The Intergovernmental Cooperation Act of 1968 required that federal agencies notify the governors or legislatures of the purpose and amounts of any grants-in-aid to their states. The purpose of this requirement was to make it possible for states to more effectively plan for their overall development.

CIRCULAR NO. A-95

To implement the 1968 Intergovernmental Cooperation Act, the Bureau of the Budget issued Circular no. A-95 in July 1969, which superseded Circular no. A-82. This circular required that the governor of each state designate a "clearinghouse" at the state level and for each metropolitan area. The function of these clearinghouses is to review and comment on projects proposed for federal aid in terms of their compatibility with comprehensive plans and to coordinate among agencies having plans and programs which might be affected by the projects. These clearinghouses had to be empowered under state or local laws to perform comprehensive planning in an area.

The circular established a project notification and review system (PNRS) which specified how the review and coordination process would be carried out and the amount of time for each step in the process. The PNRS contained an "early warning" feature which required that a local applicant for a federal grant or loan notify the state and local clearinghouses at the time it decided to seek assistance. The clearinghouse has 30 days to indicate further interest in the project or to arrange to provide project coordination. This regulation was designed to alleviate the problem many review agencies had of learning of an application only after it had been prepared, and thereby having little opportunity to help shape it.

Circular no. A-95 provided a most definitive federal statement of the process through which planning for urban areas should be accomplished. Its emphasis was not on substance but on process and on the intergovernmental linkages required to carry out the process.

ORGANIZATIONAL CHANGES AT THE STATE AND LOCAL LEVEL

These various acts and regulations to improve intergovernmental program coordination accelerated the creation of broader multifunctional agencies. At the state level, 39 departments of transportation had been created by 1977. Most of the departments have multimodal planning, programming, and coordinating functions. At the local level, there has been a growing trend for transportation planning to be performed by comprehensive planning agencies, generally those designated as the A-95 clearinghouse.

RECOGNITION OF ENVIRONMENTAL ISSUES
AND CITIZEN INVOLVEMENT

By the late 1960s the growing concern for environmental quality, particularly air pollution, and the reaction to public decisions without citizen involvement had put considerable pressures on the planning process and its ability to adapt to change.

CITIZEN PARTICIPATION AND THE TWO-HEARING PROCESS

Citizen reaction to highway projects usually was most vocal at public hearings. It became clear that citizens could not effectively contribute to a highway decision by the time the project had already been designed. Many of the issues related to the basic issue of whether to build the highway project at all and the consideration of alternative modes of transportation. Consequently, in early 1969, Policy and Procedure Memorandum 20-8, which established a two-hearing process, was issued by the Federal Highway Administration (FHWA).

The first "corridor public hearing" was to be held before the route location was made and was designed to afford citizens the opportunity to comment on the need for and location of the highway project. The second "highway design public hearing" was to focus on the specific location and design features. This PPM also required the consideration of social, economic, and environmental effects prior to submission of a project for federal aid.

It was recognized that even a two-hearing process did not provide adequate opportunity for citizen involvement and, worse, provided a difficult atmosphere for dialogue. In late 1969, the basic guidelines for the 3C planning process were amended to require citizen participation in all phases of the planning process from the setting of goals through the analysis of alternatives. Consequently, it became the responsibility of the planning agency to seek out public views.

NATIONAL ENVIRONMENTAL POLICY ACT OF 1969

The federal government's concern for environmental issues dates back to the passage of the Air Quality Control Act of 1955 which directed the Surgeon General to conduct research to abate air pollution. Through a series of acts since that time, the federal government's involvement in environmental matters broadened and deepened.

In 1969, a singularly important piece of environmental legislation was passed, the National Environmental Policy Act of 1969 (NEPA). This act presented a significant departure from prior legislation in that it enunciated for the first time a broad national policy to prevent or eliminate damage to the environment. The act stated that it is national policy to "encourage productive and enjoyable harmony between man and his environment."[23]

Federal agencies were required under the act to use a systematic interdisciplinary approach to the planning and decision making which affected the environment. It also required that an environmental impact statement (EIS) be prepared for all legislation and major federal actions which significantly affect the environment. The EIS was to contain information on the environmental impact of the proposed action, unavoidable impacts, alternatives to the action, the relationship between short-term and long-term impacts, and irretrievable commitments of resources. The federal agency was to seek comments on the action and its impacts from affected jurisdictions and make all information public.

The act also created the Council on Environmental Quality to implement the policy and advise the President on environmental matters.

ENVIRONMENTAL QUALITY IMPROVEMENT ACT OF 1970

The Environmental Quality Improvement Act of 1970 was passed as a companion to the NEPA. It established the Office of Environmental Quality which was charged with assisting federal agencies to evaluate present and proposed programs and with promoting research on the environment.

---

[23]U.S. DEPARTMENT OF TRANSPORTATION, *1974 National Transportation Report: Current Performance and Future Prospects* (Washington, D.C.: U.S. Government Printing Office, July 1975).

These two acts dealing with the environment mark the first reversal in over a decade of the trend to decentralize decision making to the state and local levels of government. It required the federal government to make the final determination on the trade-off between facility improvements and environmental quality. Further, it created a complicated and expensive process in the requirement for preparing an EIS and for seeking comments from all concerned agencies. In this manner, the acts actually created a new planning process in parallel with the urban transportation planning process.

CLEAN AIR ACT AMENDMENTS OF 1970

The Clean Air Act Amendments of 1970 reinforced the central position of the federal government to make final decisions affecting the environment. This act created the Environmental Protection Agency (EPA) and empowered it to set ambient air quality standards. Required reductions in new automobile emissions were specified in the act. It authorized EPA to require states to formulate implementation plans describing how they would achieve and maintain the ambient air quality standards. In 1971, EPA promulgated national ambient air quality standards and proposed regulations on state implementation plans (SIPs) to meet these standards.

The preparation, submission, and review of the state implementation plans occurred outside the traditional urban transportation planning process, and, in many instances, did not involve the planning agencies developing transportation plans. This problem became particularly difficult for urban areas that could not meet the air quality standards even if new automobiles met the air pollution emission standards. In these instances, transportation control plans (TCPs) were required which contained additional measures to reduce automobile emissions. Many of these TCPs contained changes in urban transportation systems and their operation to effect the reduction in emissions. Rarely were these TCPs developed jointly with those agencies developing urban transportation plans. It took several years of dialogue between these air pollution and transportation planning agencies to mediate joint plans and policies for urban transportation and air quality.

Another impact of the environmental legislation, particularly the Clean Air Act Amendments, was the increased emphasis on short-term changes in transportation systems. In that the deadline for meeting the ambient air quality standards was fairly short, EPA was primarily concerned with actions that could affect air quality in that time frame. The actions precluded major construction and generally focused on low-capital and traffic management measures. Up to this time, urban transportation planning had been focused on long-range (20 years or more) planning.

THE BEGINNINGS OF MULTIMODAL URBAN TRANSPORTATION PLANNING

By the late 1960s, the urban transportation planning process was receiving criticism on a number of issues. It was criticized for inadequate treatment of social and environmental impacts. The planning process had still not become multimodal and was not adequately evaluating a wide range of alternatives. Planning was focused almost exclusively on long-range time horizons; and the technical procedures to carry out planning were too cumbersome, time consuming, and rigid to adapt to new issues quickly.

During the 1970s actions were taken to address these criticisms. In some instances legislation was passed to require that something be done. Legislation that increased funds for mass transportation and placed transit on a more equal footing with highways considerably strengthened multimodal planning and implementation.

URBAN MASS TRANSPORTATION ASSISTANCE ACT OF 1970

The Urban Mass Transportation Assistance Act of 1970 was another landmark in federal financing for mass transportation. It provided the first long-term commitment of federal funds. Until the passage of this act, federal funds for mass transportation had been limited. It was difficult to plan and implement a program of mass transportation projects over several years because of the uncertainty of future funding.

The 1970 act implied a federal commitment for the expenditure of at least $10 billion over a 12-year period to permit confident and continuing local planning and greater flexibility in program administration. The act authorized $3.1 billion to finance urban mass transportation beginning in fiscal year 1971. It permitted the use of "contract authority" whereby the Secretary of Transportation was authorized to incur obligations on behalf of the United States with Congress pledged to appropriate the funds required to liquidate the obligations. This provision allowed long-term commitments of funds to be made.

This act also established a strong federal policy on transportation of elderly and handicapped persons:

> ... elderly and handicapped persons have the same right as other persons to utilize mass transportation facilities and services; that special efforts shall be made in the planning and design of mass transportation facilities and services so that the availability to elderly and handicapped persons to mass transportation which they can effectively utilize will be assured....[24]

The act authorized that 2% of the capital grant and 1.5% of the research funds might be set aside and used to finance programs to aid elderly and handicapped persons.

The act also added requirements for public hearings on the economic, social, and environmental impacts of a proposed project and on its consistency with the comprehensive plan for the area. It also required an analysis of the environmental impact of the proposed project and for the Secretary of Transportation to determine that there was no feasible or prudent alternative to any adverse impact that might result.

FEDERAL-AID HIGHWAY ACT OF 1970

The Federal-Aid Highway Act of 1970 established the federal-aid urban highway system. The system in each urban area was to be designed to serve major centers of activity and to best serve local goals and objectives. Routes on the system were to be

---

[24]URBAN MASS TRANSPORTATION ADMINISTRATION, *Urban Mass Transportation Act of 1964.*

selected by local officials and state highway departments cooperatively. This provision significantly increased the influence of local jurisdictions in urban highway decisions. The influence of local officials in urban areas was further strengthened by an amendment to Section 134 on urban transportation planning:

> No highway project may be constructed in any urban area of fifty thousand population or more unless the responsible local officials of such urban area . . . have been consulted and their views considered with respect to the corridor, the location and the design of the project.[25]

Funds for the federal-aid urban system were to be allocated on the basis of total urbanized area population within the state. The act also authorized the expenditure of highway funds on exclusive or preferential bus lanes and related facilities. This could only be done if the bus project reduced the need for additional highway construction or if no other highway project could provide the person-carrying capacity of the bus project. There had to be assurances, as well, that the transit operator would utilize the facility. An additional provision of the act authorized expenditures of highway funds on fringe and corridor parking facilities adjacent to the federal-aid urban system which were designed in conjunction with public transportation services.

This act also incorporated a number of requirements related to the environment. One required the issuance of guidelines for full consideration of economic, social, and environmental impacts of highway projects. A second related to the promulgation of guidelines for assuring that highway projects were consistent with SIPs developed under the Clean Air Act.

As a result of the 1970 highway and transit acts, projects for both modes would have to meet similiar criteria related to impact assessment and public hearings. The highway act also increased the federal matching share to 70% for all noninterstate highways, making it comparable to the 66.67% federal share for mass transportation. In addition, the highway act legally required consistency between SIPs and urban highway plans.

MT. POCONO CONFERENCE

In recognition of the widespread awareness that urban transportation planning had not kept pace with changing conditions, a conference on Organization for Continuing Urban Transportation Planning was held at Mt. Pocono, Pennsylvania, in 1971. The focus of this conference was on multimodal transportation planning evolving from the earlier conferences which focused on highway planning and the separation between planning and implementation.

The conference recommended close coordination of planning efforts as a means of achieving orderly development of urban areas and relating the planning process more closely to decision-making processes at all levels of government. It urged that urban planning be strengthened through state enabling legislation and bolstered by equitable local representation. Further, citizen participation should occur continually throughout the planning process but should not be considered as a substitute for decision making by elected officials.

---

[25]FEDERAL HIGHWAY ADMINISTRATION, *Federal Laws and Material.*

All comprehensive and functional planning, including multimodal transportation planning, should be integrated, including the environmental impact assessment process. The planning process should continually refine the long-range regional transportation plan at the subarea scale and focus on a 5- to 15-year time frame so that planning would be more relevant to programming and project implementation.

Transportation planning should consider service levels consistent with local goals, and a wide range of alternatives should be evaluated. The impact of changes in the transportation system should be monitored to improve future decision-making and planning efforts.

The conference report went on to urge that this more inclusive kind of planning be supported by flexible funding from the federal level to avoid a preference for any mode so as to not unbalance specific urban transportation decisions contrary to local goals and priorities. The conference also supported additional resources for planning, research, and training.

DOT INITIATIVES TOWARD PLANNING UNIFICATION

The U.S. Department of Transportation had been working for several years on integrating the individual modal planning programs. In 1971, DOT established a trial program of intermodal planning in the field. The overall objective of the program was to integrate the modal planning programs at the urban-area level rather than at the federal level. With the successful completion of the trial program, the DOT implemented the program on a permanent basis by establishing intermodal planning groups (IPGs) in each of the 10 DOT regions. The IPGs were charged with responsibility for obtaining and reviewing an annual unified work program for all planning activities in an urban area; for obtaining agreement on a single recipient agency for areawide transportation planning grants in each urban area; and, for obtaining a short-term (3- to 5-year) transportation capital improvement program, updated annually, from each recipient agency.

Also in 1971, a departmental transportation planning committee was established to promote a coordinated department-wide process for urban-area and statewide transportation planning and for unified funding of such planning. As a result of the efforts of the committee, a DOT order was issued in 1973 which required that all urbanized areas submit annual unified work programs for all transportation planning activities as a condition for receiving any DOT planning funds. These work programs must include all transportation-related planning activities, identification of the agency responsible for each activity, and the proposed funding sources. The work programs are used to rationalize planning activities and joint funding under the DOT planning assistance programs.

FEDERAL-AID HIGHWAY ACT OF 1973

The Federal-Aid Highway Act of 1973 contained two provisions which increased the flexibility in the use of highway funds for urban mass transportation in the spirit of the Mt. Pocono conference. First, federal-aid urban system funds can be used for capital expenditures on urban mass transportation projects. This provision took effect gradually, but was unrestricted starting in fiscal year 1976. Second, funds for interstate highway projects can be relinquished and replaced by an equivalent amount from the general fund and spent on mass transportation projects in a particular state. The relinquished funds revert back to the highway trust fund.

This opening up of the highway trust fund for urban mass transportation was a significant breakthrough sought for many years by transit supporters. These changes provided completely new avenues of federal assistance for funding urban mass transportation.

The 1973 act had other provisions related to urban mass transportation. First, it raised the federal matching share for urban mass transportation projects from 66.67% to 80%, except for urban system substitutions, which remain at 70%. Second, it raised the level of funds under the UMTA capital grant program by $3 billion, to $6.1 billion. Third, it permitted expenditure of highway funds for bus-related public transportation facilities, including fringe parking on all federal-aid highway systems.

The act called for realigning of all federal-aid systems based on functional usage. It authorized expenditures on the new federal-aid urban system and modified several provisions related to it. *Urban* was defined as any area of 5000 or more in population. Apportioned funds for the system were earmarked for urban areas of 200,000 or more population. Most important, it changed the relationship between the state and local officials in designating routes for the system. It authorized local officials in urbanized areas to choose routes with the concurrence of state highway departments.

Two additional provisions related directly to planning. For the first time urban transportation planning was funded separately. One-half of 1% of all federal-aid funds were designated for this purpose and apportioned to the states on the basis of urbanized area population. These funds were to be made available to the metropolitan planning organizations (MPOs) responsible for comprehensive transportation planning in urban areas.

The 1973 Federal-Aid Highway Act took a significant step toward integrating and balancing the highway and mass transportation programs. It increased the decision-making role of areawide MPOs and broadened the scope of planning.

1972 AND 1974 NATIONAL TRANSPORTATION STUDIES

Although urban transportation planning had been legislatively required for over a decade, the results had not been used in the development of national transportation policy. Beyond that, a composite national picture of these urban transportation plans did not exist even though they were the basis for capital expenditure decisions by the federal government. In the early 1970s, the Department of Transportation conducted two national transportation studies to inventory and assess the current and planned transportation system as viewed by the states and urban areas.

The two studies differed in their emphasis. The 1972 National Transportation Study obtained information on the existing transportation system as of 1970, the transportation needs for the 1970–1990 period, and short-range (1974–1978) and long-range (1979–1990) capital improvement programs under three federal funding assumptions. The study showed that the total transportation needs of the states and urban areas exceeded the financial resources of the nation to implement them and discussed the use of low-capital alternatives to improve the productivity of the existing transportation system, particularly in urban areas.

The 1974 National Transportation Study related more closely to the ongoing urban transportation planning processes. It obtained information on the 1972 inventories, long-range plans (1972–1990), and short-range programs (1972–1980) for the transportation system in a more comprehensive manner than did the 1972 study. The transportation system for all three time periods was described in terms of the supply of facilities, equipment, and services, travel demand, system performance, social and environmental impacts, and capital and operating costs. Information on low-capital alternatives and new technological systems was also included. The 1972–1980 program was based on a forecast of federal funds that could reasonably be expected to be available and an estimate of state and local funds for the period. This study again demonstrated that the long-range plans were overly ambitious in terms of the financial resources that might be available for transportation. Further, it showed that even after the expenditure of vast amounts of money for urban transportation, urban transportation systems would differ little in character in the foreseeable future.

The National Transportation Study process introduced the concept of tying state and urban transportation planning into national transportation planning and policy formulation. It stressed multimodal analysis, assessment of a wide range of measures of the transportation system, budget limitations on plans and programs, and increasing the productivity of the existing transportation system. Although these concepts were not new, it was the first time that they had been incorporated into such a vast national planning effort.

NATIONAL MASS TRANSPORTATION ASSISTANCE ACT OF 1974

The National Mass Transportation Assistance Act of 1974 authorized for the first time the use of federal funds for transit operating assistance. It thus continued the trend to broaden the use of federal urban transportation funds. The act authorized $11.8 billion over a 6-year period. Almost $4 billion was to be allocated to urban areas by a formula based on population and population density. The funds could be used for either capital projects or operating assistance. Of the remaining $7.8 billion, $7.3 billion was made available for capital assistance at the discretion of the Secretary of Transportation and the remainder was for rural mass transportation.

JOINT HIGHWAY—TRANSIT PLANNING REGULATIONS

UMTA and FHWA had worked for several years on joint regulations to guide urban transportation planning. Final regulations were issued to take effect in October 1975. They superseded all previous guidelines, policies, and regulations issued on urban transportation planning by UMTA and FHWA.

The regulations provided for the joint designation of MPOs to carry out planning and required agreements on the division of responsibility where the MPOs and A-95 agencies were different. A multiyear prospectus and annual unified work program had to be submitted specifying all transportation-related planning activities for an urban area as a condition for receiving federal planning funds.

The urban transportation planning process was required to produce a long-range transportation plan, which had to be reviewed annually to confirm its validity. The transportation plan had to contain a long-range element and a shorter-range "transportation systems management" element (TSME) for improving the operation of existing transportation systems without new facilities.

A multiyear "transportation improvement program" (TIP) also had to be developed consistent with the transportation plan. It had to contain an annual element that would be the basis for the federal funding of projects in an urban area.

The regulations provided for a joint annual certification of the planning process. This certification was required as a condition for receiving federal funds for projects. The regulations incorporated previously legislated requirements related to social, economic, and environmental impact analysis, air quality planning, and the elderly and handicapped.

These joint regulations applied to all urban highway and transit programs including those for transit operating assistance. They represented the most important action up to that time to bring about multimodal urban transportation planning and programming of projects. These regulations were another turning point in the evolution of urban transportation planning and are likely to set the tone for the next few years.

MAJOR URBAN MASS TRANSPORTATION INVESTMENT CRITERIA

The level of federal funds for urban mass transportation has increased dramatically since 1970. However, the requests for federal funds from urban areas have outpaced this increase. Consequently, the need to assure that these funds be used effectively and productively became apparent.

To fill this need, UMTA developed a draft policy statement to guide future decisions regarding federal assistance in the funding of major mass transportation investment projects. The policy embodied a number of principles.

First, areawide transportation improvement plans should be multimodal and include regionwide and community-level transit services. Second, major mass transportation investment projects should be planned and implemented in stages to avoid premature investment in costly fixed facilities and to preserve maximum flexibility to respond to future unknowns. Third, full consideration should be given to improving the management and operation of existing transportation systems. Fourth, the analysis of alternatives should include a determination of which alternative meets the local area's social, environmental, and transportation goals most cost effectively. And fifth, full opportunity should be provided for involvement of the public and local officials in all phases of the planning and evaluation process.

UMTA has stated that the level of federal funding would be based on a cost-effective alternative which meets the urban area's needs and goals in a 5- to 15-year time frame and which is consistent with the long-range transportation plan.

A conference on Evaluation of Urban Transportation Alternatives was held at Airlie House, Virginia, in February 1975 to review these draft guidelines. The conference was attended by a broad spectrum of persons from all levels of government, the transit industry, consultants, universities, and private citizens. The conference report indicated a number of concerns with the policy which were transmitted to UMTA to aid in revising it. The final policy was published in the *Federal Register* in September 1976.

THE ENERGY CRISIS

In the fall of 1973, the Arab states embargoed oil shipments to the United States and in doing so began a new era in transportation planning. The importance of oil is so paramount to the economy and, in particular, the transportation sector that oil shortages and price increases significantly impact transportation plans.

Greater emphasis is being given to the management of transportation systems, to overall reductions in travel, and to increasing the efficiency of travel in terms of the amount of energy that is required. Although many of these ideas were advanced in relation to improving air quality, the energy crisis gave them added impetus.

Although it is too early to speculate on the eventual effect of incorporating energy concerns into the planning process, it is likely that they will dominate future planning activities at least through the 1970s.

SUMMARY OBSERVATIONS

The urban transportation planning process has undergone considerable change since 1945. It has evolved from an urban highway planning process, which was an extension of rural highway planning activities into urban areas. Gradually, as improved survey techniques were developed, the understanding of the complexities of urban areas grew. The relationship between land development and transportation was recognized in early urban transportation planning studies and conferences, although this relationship is still not well understood.

In the 1960s, pressures from outside the planning process raised new issues which planners were forced to address. Issues of dislocation and disruption, environmental impacts, citizen participation, social concerns such as transportation for the disadvantaged, and, more recently, energy shortages were added to the range of concerns for the planning process. New issues were being identified at a rate faster than many urban transportation planning processes were able to respond to them.

Early transit planning developed in a different institutional environment than early urban highway planning. Until 1966, when the technical studies program was created, transit planning was a local matter carried out largely by transit operators. It took a decade to bring highway and transit planning under a common set of guidelines and regulations. The impact of these joint highway-transit planning regulations is yet to be seen.

It is clear that the early urban transportation planning processes were structured too rigidly and had little flexibility to adapt to changing conditions. This observation is easy to make in retrospect. But the process has always been fashioned to respond to the issues of the day and it was difficult to see how these issues would change. There is little doubt that new problems will arise, in the years to come, which are now unforeseen. If there is a lesson to be learned, it is that planning processes should be more open and receptive to new ideas and concerns and should evolve in a manner that would facilitate treating these new issues.

As the urban transportation planning process has embraced a wider range of issues, impacts, and alternatives, and has involved a larger number and greater diversity of participants, it has become more complex and time consuming. Considerable effort in the future will have to be expended to develop approaches for addressing these problems and for keeping urban transportation planning a manageable and relevant activity. The planning process has come a long way but there are still challenges ahead, many of them presently unknown.

SELECTED BIBLIOGRAPHY

Many citations are no longer available from their original source. These citations are often available from the National Technical Information Service, U.S. Department of Commerce, 5285 Port Royal Road, Springfield, Va. 22161. We have verified the order numbers for many of these citations, and they are found at the end of the citation. Prices are available through NTIS at the address above.

ADVISORY COMMISSION ON INTERGOVERNMENTAL RELATIONS, *Toward More Balanced Transportation: New Intergovernmental Proposals*, Report A-49. Washington, D.C.: U.S. Government Printing Office, 1974.

COLE, LEON MONROE, ed., *Tomorrow's Transportation: New Systems for the Urban Future*, prepared by U.S. Department of Housing and Urban Development. Washington, D.C.: U.S. Government Printing Office, 1968.

CRON, FREDERICK W., "Highway Design for Motor Vehicles—A Historical Review, Part 2: The Beginnings of Traffic Research," *Public Roads*, 38, no. 4 (March 1975), 163–74.

FEDERAL HIGHWAY ADMINISTRATION, *Stewardship Report on Administration of the Federal-Aid Highway Program 1956–1970*. Washington, D.C.: U.S. Department of Transportation, April 1970.

Freeways in the Urban Setting: The Hershey Conference, June 1962, sponsored by AASHO, American Municipal Association, and National Association of County Officials. Washington, D.C.: Automotive Safety Foundation, n.d.

HIGHWAY RESEARCH BOARD, *Organization for Continuing Urban Transportation Planning*, Special Report 139. Washington, D.C.: Highway Research Board, 1973.

Highways and Urban Development, report on the Second National Conference, Williamsburg, Virginia, December 12–16, 1965, sponsored by AASHO, National Association of Counties, and National League of Cities. n.p.: n.d.

HOLMES, E. H., "Highway Planning in the United States" (unpublished, presented at the IV World Meeting, International Road Federation, Madrid, Spain, 1962).

———, "The State-of-the-Art in Urban Transportation Planning or How We Got Here," *Transportation*, 1, no. 4 (March 1973), 379–401.

———, AND J. T. LYNCH, "Highway Planning: Past, Present, and Future," *Journal of the Highway Division*, Proceedings of the ASCE, 83, no. HW3 (July 1957), 1298–1 to 1298–13.

HOMBURGER, WOLFGANG S., ed., *Urban Mass Transit Planning*. Berkeley, Calif.: University of California Institute of Transportation and Traffic Engineering, 1967.

MARPLE, GARLAND E., "Urban Areas Make Transportation Plans" (unpublished paper presented at the 1969 American Society of Civil Engineers Meeting on Transportation Engineering).

MILLER, DAVID R., ed., *Urban Transportation Policy: New Perspectives*. Lexington, Mass.: Lexington Books, 1972.

NATIONAL COMMITTEE ON URBAN TRANSPORTATION, *Better Transportation for Your City: A Guide to the Factual Development of Urban Transportation Plans*, including 17 procedure manuals. Chicago: Public Administration Service, 1958.

POLICY COMMITTEE DETROIT METROPOLITAN AREA TRAFFIC STUDY, *Report on the Detroit Metropolitan Area Traffic Study, Part I: Data Summary and Interpretation* and *Part II: Future Traffic and a Long Range Expressway Plan*. Lansing, Mich.: Speaker-Hines and Thomas, Inc., State Printers, July 1955 and March 1956.

Sagamore Conference on Highways and Urban Development: Guidelines for Action, October 5–9, 1958, sponsored by American Municipal Association, AASHO, HRB, and Syracuse University. n.p.: n.d.

SMERK, GEORGE M., ed., *Readings in Urban Transportation*. Bloomington, Ind.: Indiana University Press, 1968.

TAX FOUNDATION, INC., *Urban Mass Transportation in Perspective*, Research Publication no. 14. New York: Tax Foundation, Inc., 1968.

U.S. CONGRESS, *Interregional Highways*, Message from the President of the United States Transmitting a Report of the National Interregional Highway Committee, House Document no. 379, 78th Congress, 2nd Session. Washington, D.C.: U.S. Government Printing Office, 1944.

———, *Toll Roads and Free Roads*, House Document no. 272, 76th Congress, 1st Session. Washington, D.C.: U.S. Government Printing Office, 1939.

U.S. DEPARTMENT OF COMMERCE, BUREAU OF PUBLIC ROADS, *Highway Progress: 1965*, Annual Report of the Bureau of Public Roads, Fiscal Year 1965. Washington, D.C.: U.S. Government Printing Office, October 1965.

U.S. DEPARTMENT OF TRANSPORTATION, *1974 National Transportation Report: Current Performance and Future Prospects*. Washington, D.C.: U.S. Government Printing Office, July 1975.

———, AND U.S. DEPARTMENT OF HOUSING AND URBAN DEVELOPMENT, *Report to the Congress of the United States on Urban Transportation Policies and Activities*. Washington, D.C.: U.S. Department of Transportation and U.S. Department of Housing and Urban Development, June 1974.

U.S. SENATE, "Urban Transportation—Joint Report to the President by the Secretary of Commerce and the Housing and Home Finance Administration," *Urban Mass Transportation—1962*, 87th Congress, 2nd Session, pp. 71–81. Washington, D.C.: U.S. Government Printing Office, 1962.

WASHINGTON CENTER FOR METROPOLITAN STUDIES, *Comprehensive Planning for Metropolitan Development*, prepared for UMTA. Washington, D.C.: U.S. Department of Transportation, 1970. Now available as PB 200 135.

WEINER, EDWARD, "Workshop 3: The Planner's Role," in *Research Needs for Evaluating Urban Public Transportation*, Special Report 155, pp. 40–44. Washington, D.C.: Transportation Research Board, 1975.

Chapter 16

TOWARD MORE PROGRAMMATIC PLANNING*

Marvin L. Manheim, *Professor, Transportation Systems Division, Department of Civil Engineering, and Center for Transportation Studies, Massachusetts Institute of Technology*

This chapter discusses the present urban transportation planning process. As a consequence of recent federal regulations, profound and far-reaching changes have occurred in this process. A new "model" of planning is emerging, which does not appear to be fully recognized or understood by transportation professionals. The purpose of this chapter is to describe this model.

We will discuss:

- The major features of the new planning model.
- Why this model came about.
- How present federal regulations and other actions reflect this model.
- Some of the issues still remaining in achieving successful implementation of this model.

*This chapter draws on the substantial research effort, since 1968, of the Transportation and Community Values Project, Center for Transportation Studies, Massachusetts Institute of Technology, and the ideas and writings of the many people who contributed to this effort. Specific acknowledgments are reflected in the footnotes. Particularly important contributions to the ideas presented here were made by Wayne M. Pecknold, Lance E. Neumann, Elizabeth Deakin, Arlee T. Reno, and John H. Suhrbier. See especially Marvin L. Manheim and others, *Transportation Decision-Making: A Guide to Social and Environmental Considerations*, NCHRP Report 156 (Washington, D.C.: Transportation Research Board, 1975), and Lance A. Neumann, "Integrating Transportation System Planning and Programming: An Implementation Strategy Approach" (unpublished doctoral dissertation, Department of Civil Engineering, Massachusetts Institute of Technology, 1976) from which documents Figs. 16-1, 16-2, 16-3, and 16-5 were adapted. The author also acknowledges fruitful discussions with many professional colleagues on these ideas. An earlier version of this chapter, "The Emerging Planning Process: Neither Long-Range Nor Short-Range, But Adaptive and (Hopefully) Decisive," was presented at the January 1977 meeting of the Transportation Research Board and will be published in the *Transportation Research Record* series.

A MODEL FOR REALISTIC PLANNING

The new model of the planning process has six major features. It is programmatic, periodic, planning-informed, participatory yet decisive, performance-oriented, and professionally responsible.

PROGRAMMATIC: MULTIYEAR PROGRAM PLAN

The product of planning is a multiyear program plan (MYPP), consisting of a program of actions staged over a multiyear period, from 1 to 25 (more or less) years. The first year of the plan is firm and detailed: it is the set of specific implementable actions which will be taken in the next year (i.e., inclusion of an action in the first year of the MYPP represents a decision to implement that project in the next year). Each succeeding year of the plan is less firm and less detailed. The actions in the first few years (up to year 3 or 5) of the MYPP constitute the "short-range plan"; those in the 6- to 15-year period the "midrange plan"; and those in the 16- to 25-year period the "long-range plan."

The MYPP contains all significant transportation actions proposed for the region: all modes, and all types of transportation and related options—changes in facilities, in vehicle fleets, in operating policies (routes, schedules, fares, classes of services, restraint and other disincentive policies, etc.), and in organizations and institutions, as well as in transportation-related actions (staggered work hours, land-use controls, sewer and water policies, etc.).

The MYPP also includes "studies" projects—planning and design activities, as well as monitoring, evaluation, and research. These actions are as important as "implementation" actions, because they influence, and sometimes constrain, what "implementation" actions can be considered seriously in future years—you cannot *consider* implementing a major new transit service strategy *next* year if you did not do some homework on it *this* year.

The MYPP logically should have different degrees of detail for different types of action. The MYPP for a region (e.g., a metropolitan area or state) may contain component MYPPs for subregions of the region. Different levels of detail would be appropriate for different levels of geographic aggregation. The MYPP for a county or medium-size city would be more detailed than that for a state. The state MYPP would summarize in a single item what might be 10 to 30 specific actions in a county MYPP. Each subregional MYPP might contain component MYPPs for agencies with different functional responsibilities (e.g., a transit MYPP, a municipal traffic department's MYPP).

The basic concept of a MYPP is outlined in Fig. 16-1. An example, based on a case study, is given in Fig. 16-2.

The MYPP can show where decisions on actions to be taken in future years have not yet been made, or are contingent on alternative outcomes of earlier actions. For

Actions	Year(s)			
	1 "Implement"	2 3 4 5 "Short-Range"	6 . . . . 15 "Mid-Range"	15 . . . . . 25 or 30 "Long-Range"
Implementation				

Facilities
  - New
  - Improvements				

Vehicles				
Operating (Including pricing)				
Management				
Institutional				
Transportation related				
Studies:				
Planning				
Design				
Monitoring				
Evaluation				
Research				
Costs:				
Category A				
. . .				
Category Z				

Figure 16-1 *Transportation multiyear program plan*

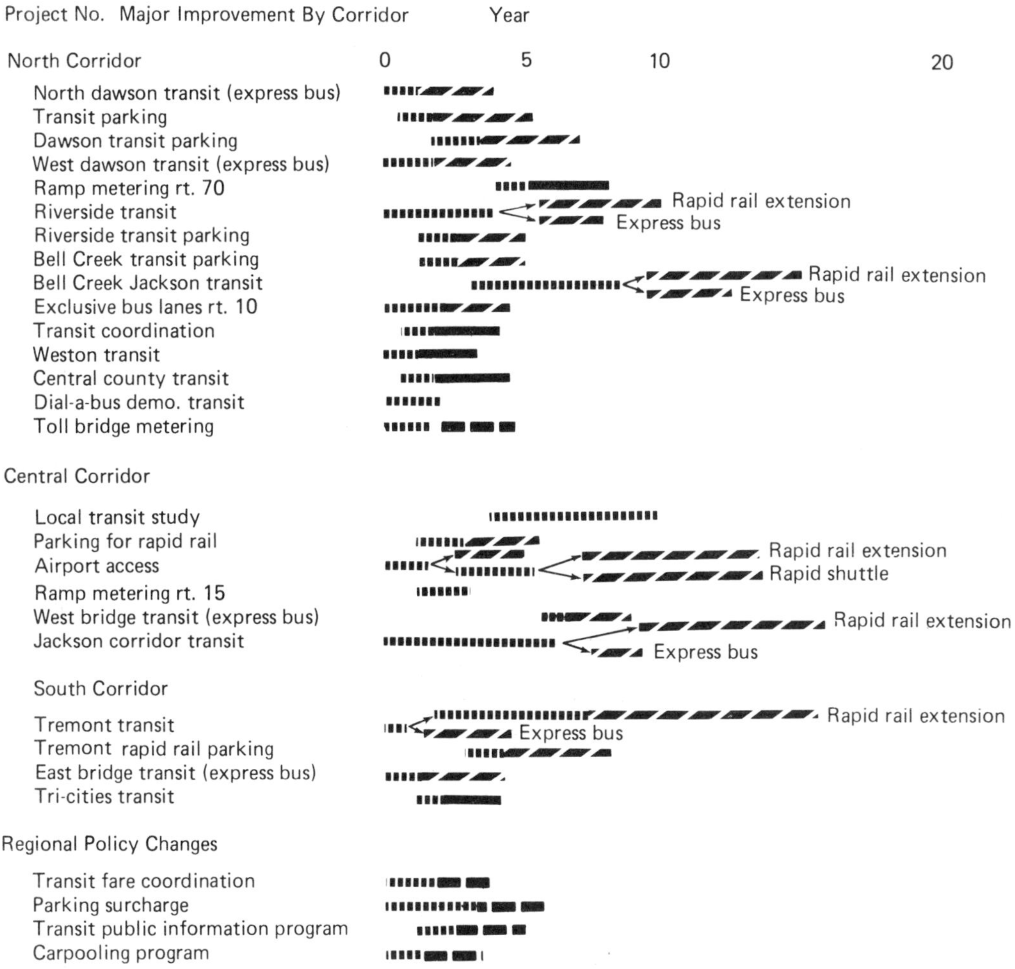

Project No. Major Improvement By Corridor   Year

North Corridor   0   5   10   20

North dawson transit (express bus)
Transit parking
Dawson transit parking
West dawson transit (express bus)
Ramp metering rt. 70
Riverside transit   Rapid rail extension
                                                         Express bus
Riverside transit parking
Bell Creek transit parking
Bell Creek Jackson transit   Rapid rail extension
                                                         Express bus
Exclusive bus lanes rt. 10
Transit coordination
Weston transit
Central county transit
Dial-a-bus demo. transit
Toll bridge metering

Central Corridor

Local transit study
Parking for rapid rail
Airport access   Rapid rail extension
                                                         Rapid shuttle
Ramp metering rt. 15
West bridge transit (express bus)   Rapid rail extension
Jackson corridor transit   Express bus

South Corridor

Tremont transit   Rapid rail extension
                                                         Express bus
Tremont rapid rail parking
East bridge transit (express bus)
Tri-cities transit

Regional Policy Changes

Transit fare coordination
Parking surcharge
Transit public information program
Carpooling program

Cost $ in millions

Study	10	28	57
Highway implementation	19	18	36
Highway operating	—	—	—
Transit implementation	72	239	477
Transit operating	300	520	1077
TOTAL	401	805	1647

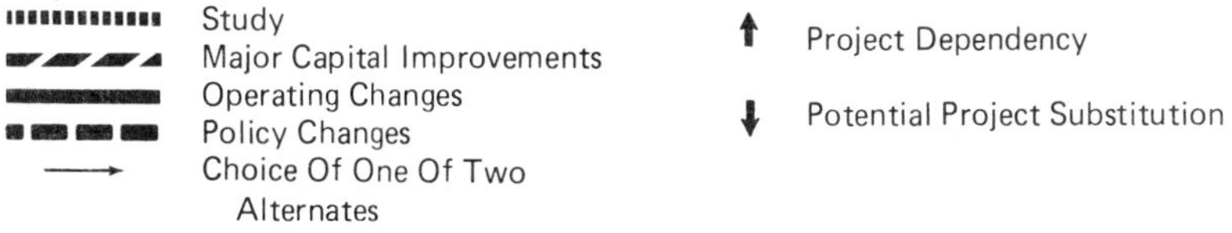

Study
Major Capital Improvements   ↑ Project Dependency
Operating Changes
Policy Changes   ↓ Potential Project Substitution
Choice Of One Of Two
Alternates

Figure 16-2 Example MYPP. [Source: Lance A. Neumann, "Integrating Transportation System Planning and Programming: An Implementation Strategy Approach" (unpublished Ph.D. dissertation, Department of Civil Engineering, Massachusetts Institute of Technology, 1976) and Marvin L. Manheim and others, Transportation Decision Making: A Guide to Social and Environmental Considerations, NHCRP Report 156 (Washington, D.C.: Transportation Research Board, 1975), p. 93.]

327

example, unresolved issues can be included or explicit contingencies shown, as by the arrows in the example in Fig. 16-2.

PERIODIC

The MYPP is reviewed annually and revised, in an explicit decision process. In this process, progress in implementing actions in the first year of the preceding year's MYPP is reviewed.

Obviously, not all elements of the MYPP would be subject to the same degree of scrutiny in each annual cycle. For example, the long-range portion of the MYPP might be revised in a major way only once every 3 or 5 years, or when a major decision is to be taken on implementing a major project in the next year.

PLANNING-INFORMED PROGRAMMING

In the periodic decision process, some of the actions in the second year of the preceding year's MYPP may be advanced into the first year of the new MYPP, reflecting decisions to implement those actions; others, however, may be deferred for implementation or may be discarded altogether. This reflects the fact that while the MYPP lays out planned future actions, in actuality *the only truly firm decision is an implementable one:* how to spend next year's dollars. Since future actions in the MYPP are never certain of implementation until they move into the first year of a then-current MYPP, an important issue in choosing an action for implementation in a given year is its degree of "commitment" versus "flexibility": if this action is implemented, which future options will be foreclosed, and which will still remain open for future implementation?

Traditional long-range (LR) planning thus must play an important role, but executed in a different style than has been traditional. In the past, LR planning developed and analyzed alternative comprehensive plans for a single, future "target" year, 25 or 30 years away, and then produced an "adopted" long-range plan. Once the plan was adopted, the tasks were then seen as, simply, to implement the plan by programming, designing, and constructing the specific projects included in the plan.

While this traditional view is no longer appropriate, long-range planning still has a positive role in the planning process—to inform the annual process of decision making, by

- Assessing the midrange and long-range consequences of near-term actions.
- Assessing which alternative future options are left open, and which foreclosed, by specific actions being considered now for implementation soon.
- Exploring alternative views of the region's future state in the "target year" and alternative staging of actions over the full 25- to 30-year planning period.

Thus, in the new model, system or long-range planning is a continuing activity that provides a context for the periodic decision process.

Shared power. In decisions about urban transportation today, there are many important participants, and power is shared. The major participating agencies include, but are not limited to, metropolitan planning organizations (MPOs), areawide special-purpose agencies, transit operators, state highway and transit agencies, local elected officials, municipal and county public works, traffic, and planning units, and so on. In addition, a large number of interest groups, reflecting a very wide spectrum of views about transportation and related issues, also participate in the decision process. No single agency in any region has complete power to determine alone the region's transportation system. Different agencies have important roles in the process; different agencies have different perspectives, insights and experiences, and constituencies. All can play useful roles in the process of reaching a decision, periodically, on the MYPP.

Timely public involvement. In developing alternative MYPPs and reaching a decision periodically in the annual decision process, there should be

> full opportunity for the timely involvement of the public, local elected officials, and all levels of government. . . . This involvement should be initiated early, so that all affected groups have an opportunity to influence the process in a timely and constructive fashion, particularly as to the alternatives to be considered, measures of effectiveness to be used, actions to be taken to minimize or avoid adverse effects, and priority actions for implementation.[1]

Pressures for decisiveness. In a context of shared power and substantial public involvement, there is a great danger of a failure to make decisions, particularly on the "hard" issues.[2] With an explicit periodic process, and if there is sufficient funding flexibility, there are counterbalancing pressures for decisiveness.

In a periodic process, the primary focus of decision each year is on the actions to be implemented in the next year. Therefore, most effects of many of the actions will be visible within a short period of time. Further, the funds to be utilized in implementing the selected actions are "real" money—they are not potential or possible costs or revenues 20, 10, or even 5 years away, but they are next year's money; next year's money is both a target—something worth fighting for—and a constraint, in that only the funds available can be expended. The immediacy of these effects, especially the fiscal constraint, means the making of decisions on the first years of the MYPP is very serious business.

---

[1]URBAN MASS TRANSPORTATION ADMINISTRATION, "Major Urban Mass Transportation Investments—Statement of Policy," *Federal Register*, 41, no. 185 (September 22, 1976), 41514; also FEDERAL HIGHWAY ADMINISTRATION, *Process Guidelines (Social, Economic, and Environmental Effects on Highway Projects)*, Policy and Procedure Memorandum 90-4 (Washington, D.C.: Federal Highway Administration, June 1, 1973), also published as FEDERAL HIGHWAY ADMINISTRATION, "Process Guidelines (for the Development of Environmental Action Plans)," in *Federal-Aid Highway Program Manual* (Washington, D.C.: Federal Highway Administration, December 30, 1974), vol. 7, chap. 7, sec. 1.

[2]ALAN A. ALTSHULER AND ROBERT W. CURRY, "The Changing Environment of Urban Development Policy—Shared Power or Shared Impotence?" *Urban Law Annual*, 10 (1975), 3–41.

Furthermore, if disbursement of any funds for implementation of any actions at all is contingent upon the approval of the total first year of the MYPP (and of course if the funds are desired), there is intense pressure to reach a decision: to resolve conflicts about which actions get what priority, in order to get some actions funded.

In an era of shared power, the pressure to make a decision in order to be able to spend next year's money is a very important catalyst to constructive resolution of conflicts.

In other words: *programming makes planning relevant.*

Flexibility. Funding flexibility plays a key role in enabling decisiveness. In an ideal world, there should be complete flexibility of funding among all possible actions in a MYPP. Decision makers should be free to use the available funds for capital (infrastructure, vehicle acquisition) or operating (subsidies, organization, and facility maintenance) or other implementation projects, or for studies (planning, design, preliminary engineering, or research) as well as for transportation modes and geographic sub-areas within the region, without constraints. If complete flexibility existed, there would be full opportunity for negotiation of conflicting desires among different interests: short-range versus long-range, operators versus users, and among users in different areas, of different income classes, and with different mobility needs and different trip purposes.

Funding flexibility allows decisions about alternative allocations of funds to be viewed on their merits, rather than because $1 of local money buys $4 of federal money if used in category A but only two if used in category B; or because funds can only be used for category C even if local consensus is for something from category D.

Unfortunately, in the United States, such flexibility only exists in part. Planning and engineering funds are different from capital and operating funds; there still are some modal restrictions, geographic restrictions, and use restrictions on much federal funding for transportation and almost all state and local funds.

PERFORMANCE-ORIENTED

Because of the periodic nature of the process, specific attention can be given to monitoring the performance of the planning process in terms of results actually achieved:

- Specific goals can be established about objectives to be achieved in the next few years—e.g., a 2% increase in transit modal split or a fare reduction of 50% for elderly.
- Specific procedures can be implemented to monitor the actual changes which occur in the transportation system and other urban activities—e.g., travel time, transit schedule adherence, building vacancy rates.
- Actions implemented as a result of past MYPPs can be monitored.
- Using the data from monitoring activities, the observed changes can be analyzed, relative to earlier predictions and statements of objectives, to evaluate the effectiveness of implemented actions and revise programmed future actions.

It is now coming to be widely accepted that there is no rational, objective technical procedure for deciding what course of action is "best" for a complex society such as a metropolitan area or a state. Such a society is composed of many different groups, each group with different values, needs, and objectives. They do not agree on the "values of society," at least not at the detailed operational level required in choosing among alternative transportation projects or programs. In this context, no quantitative method such as economic analysis ("cost–benefit" analysis) or other numerical methods can be used as the sole or even dominant basis for determining which action is "best" in "the overall public interest." Rather, instead of erecting a "smokescreen" of elaborate technical methodology, the analysis of alternatives should seek to catalyze constructive debate about conflicting objectives and priorities.

Thus, the analysis of alternative MYPPs should seek to clarify the key issues which should be debated in the appropriate political process. This is a challenging responsibility for the professionals involved, the staffs of transportation-related agencies.

Specifically, this means that the technical analysis of alternative MYPPs should recognize that:

- A range of alternative MYPPs should be considered, which represent real choices—that is, with significantly different distributions of beneficial and adverse effects.
- Information is needed about a wide range of effects (transportation service, costs and revenues, and economic, social, environmental, etc.) of alternative MYPPs, and the distribution of those effects.
- Evaluation of alternative MYPPs should be oriented to producing summaries, in language and formats understandable to officials and the public, of key issues and trade-offs which should be considered in adopting a MYPP.[4]

WHY THIS MODEL CAME ABOUT

It is useful to review, briefly, how this model came about, both in political and in theoretical terms.

THE "RATIONAL MODEL" ERA

An important event in the evolution of transportation planning was the inclusion of Section 134 in the 1962 Federal-Aid Highway Act, which required "a continuing

---

[3]MARVIN L. MANHEIM, *Fundamentals of Transportation Systems Analysis* (Cambridge, Mass.: The M.I.T. Press, in press), especially chaps. 14, "Choice," and 15, "The Role of the Professional"; MANHEIM AND OTHERS, *Transportation Decision-Making*. Also see FEDERAL HIGHWAY ADMINISTRATION, *Process Guidelines* and URBAN MASS TRANSPORTATION ADMINISTRATION, "Major Urban Mass Transportation Investments."

[4]MANHEIM, *Fundamentals*, chap. 9, "Evaluation"; MANHEIM AND OTHERS, *Transportation Decision-Making*, chap. 3, "Evaluation and Reporting," pp. 36–51.

comprehensive transportation planning process carried on cooperatively by States and local communities . . ." in all urbanized areas of greater than 50,000 population.[5] The resulting "3C" process—for "continuing," "comprehensive," and "cooperative," key words in the legislation—created modern transportation planning, with new institutions, and a new profession complete with new technical tools. The transportation planning process which resulted had an image consonant with that which arises out of a rational or "synoptic" conception of decision making.[6] The image had the following elements.

Rational analysis process. A transportation planning study follows these steps: (1) formulate goals; (2) develop alternatives; (3) predict consequences; (4) evaluate the consequences of the alternatives with respect to the goals; (5) select that plan which is "best" according to the goals. Further, the goals are usually expressed in part in terms of a desired physical land-use pattern in the "target year," 25 to 30 years in the future.

Rational political process. A comprehensive transportation planning organization is established in any one of a variety of forms; and the decisions on adoption of a plan are made by the "policy board" of that organization, composed of elected or appointed officials representative in some sense of the metropolitan area.

Rational implementation of adopted "master plan." The long-range transportation plan which is adopted describes the desired state of the transportation system in the target year; it is a "master plan" to guide future transportation decisions. Once adopted, the plan is then staged, to be implemented step by step in an orderly fashion over the 25- to 30-year period between "now" and the "target year." Periodically, say every 5 to 10 years, it may be useful to review progress made in implementing the plan and, if necessary, make some adjustments. By and large, however, it is expected that the master plan, once adopted, will be implemented.

Sequential flow of work in an orderly fashion. Once the plan is adopted, the major task of the planning organization is finished. The implementation of the plan is now the responsibility of "implementing" agencies such as state or local highway departments and local transit agencies. Within these agencies, the work flows in an orderly, "programmed" sequence: once the planning or "system" studies are completed, the next steps are the successive stages of location studies, design (or preliminary engineering), and construction (in the case of highway or new transit facilities), shown in Fig. 16-3.

---

[5]FEDERAL HIGHWAY ADMINISTRATION, *Federal Laws and Material Relating to the Federal Highway Administration* (Washington, D.C.: U.S. Government Printing Office, November 1976), Title 23, chap. 1, sec. 134, p. II-54.

[6]DAVID BRAYBROOKE AND CHARLES E. LINDBLOM, *A Strategy of Decision: Policy Evaluation as a Social Process* (Glencoe, Ill.: Free Press, 1963); MARVIN L. MANHEIM, EARL R. RUITER, AND KIRAN U. BHATT, *Search and Choice in Transport Systems Planning: Summary Report*, Research Report R68-40 (Cambridge, Mass.: Massachusetts Institute of Technology, Department of Civil Engineering, 1968).

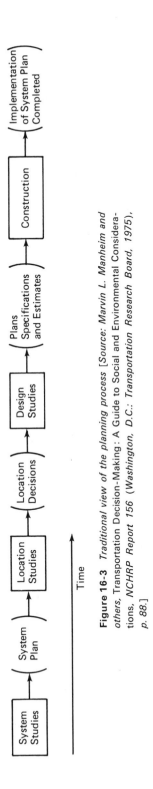

Figure 16-3 *Traditional view of the planning process [Source: Marvin L. Manheim and others, Transportation Decision-Making: A Guide to Social and Environmental Considerations, NCHRP Report 156 (Washington, D.C.: Transportation Research Board, 1975), p. 88.]*

This "rational" era of transportation planning was, of course, short-lived in many metropolitan areas. As implementation began to proceed on the adopted plans, serious political controversies erupted, bringing about "the freeway revolt" of the late 1960s.[7] The actual construction of major freeway projects in urban areas, together with the displacement of significant numbers of homes and jobs, and in the context of changing national and local political awareness and abilities, caused significant and far-reaching changes in the transportation planning process.

At first, changes were focused on the process of planning and designing specific transportation facilities, primarily highway projects. The changes were:

1. Consideration of nontransportation options coordinated with transportation facility plans, such as "joint development," replacement housing, and similar elements of comprehensive "corridor" policies produced by "multidisciplinary design teams."[8]
2. Consideration of broader impacts than simply user travel costs and transportation facility costs.[9]
3. Recognition of the legitimacy—and practical political importance—of involvement of not only local officials, but also the public in the project planning and design process.[10]

These evolutions in political perspectives on transportation facility planning and design found reflection in the related growth of the environmental movement. This was expressed in new laws, such as the National Environmental Policy Act (NEPA) of 1969 and the Clean Air Act Amendments of 1970, in new levels of political activism, and in new judicial interpretations. As a result, state highway and transportation agencies began making significant changes in their approaches to project implementation—

---

[7]LYN SHEPARD, "The Freeway Revolt," a series of 10 articles in *The Christian Science Monitor* (Boston, 1968); FRANK C. COLCORD, *Urban Transportation Decision Making*, series of monographs, see the Chapter 30 bibliography.

[8]LOWELL K. BRIDWELL, "Freeways in the Urban Environment," in *Joint Development and Multiple Use of Transportation Rights-of-Way*, Special Report 104 (Washington, D.C.: Highway Research Board, 1969), pp. 88–100; EDWARD J. DEVINE, *Multi-Discipline Design Teams for Transportation Facilities: A Study of the Administrative, Planning and Community Participation Aspects of Design Teams*, prepared for U.S. DOT (n.p.: State of Washington Planning and Community Affairs Agency, August 1971).

[9]FEDERAL HIGHWAY ADMINISTRATION, *Environmental Impact and Related Statements*, Policy and Procedure Memorandum 90-1 (Washington, D.C.: Federal Highway Administration, September 7, 1972), revision of FEDERAL HIGHWAY ADMINISTRATION, *Guidelines for Implementing Section 102(2)(C) of the National Environmental Policy Act of 1969, Section 1653(f) of 49 U.S.C., Section 470f of U.S.C., and Section 309 of the Clean Air Act of 1970* (Washington, D.C.: Federal Highway Administration, August 24, 1971).

[10]STUART L. HILL, "Century Freeway (Watts)," in *Joint Development and Multiple Use of Transportation Rights-of-Way*, Special Report 104 (Washington, D.C.: Highway Research Board, 1969), pp. 68–74; J. A. LEGARRA AND T. R. LAMMERS, "The Highway Administrator Looks at Values," in *Transportation and Community Values*, Special Report 105 (Washington, D.C.: Highway Research Board, 1969), pp. 109–16; HIGHWAY RESEARCH BOARD, *Citizen Participation in Transportation Planning*, Special Report 142 (Washington, D.C.: Highway Research Board, 1973).

location and design studies, primarily for highways (i.e., project implementation as distinct from system studies).

In response to a provision of the Federal-Aid Highway Act of 1970, the Federal Highway Administration (FHWA) moved to accelerate and institutionalize these changes. In PPM 90-4, FHWA established a requirement for each state transportation agency to review its own organization and procedures, make necessary changes, and document the revised processes in "action plans."[11]

In their action plans, each state transportation agency was required to include in its standard procedures and assignments of responsibility provisions for

- Consideration of a range of alternatives.
- Identification of social, economic, and environmental effects.
- Timely and constructive involvement of other agencies and the public.
- Use of a systematic interdisciplinary approach.
- Documentation of the process of reaching decisions.
- Interrelation of system and project decisions.

This last provision is the one most relevant to our discussion here. Let us examine this issue more closely.

PROJECT VERSUS SYSTEM: THE ISSUES[12]

The forces for change, and actions taken, as previously described, had significant impact on the process of implementation planning, design, and construction of specific highway facilities and, in many cases, major transit facilities. For example, the need for public involvement and for identification of a range of impacts came to be widely recognized (and reinforced by the environmental impact statement requirement of NEPA and the action plans); on the other hand, the range of alternatives considered was not always as extensive as some would have desired.

However, the degree of change at the level of systems planning was far less significant than that at the project level. Some innovations *were* developed.

1. A complete restudy was done of a major metropolitan area's transportation system plan: the Boston Transportation Planning Review demonstrated the application of the principles described earlier (range of alternatives, timely public involvement, identification of social, economic, and environmental effects) in a comprehensive metropolitan planning context.[13] Although highly innovative in its approach, this was a one-time study to resolve a particular set of crisis issues (although the style is being perpetuated to some extent by a continu-

---

[11]FEDERAL HIGHWAY ADMINISTRATION, *Process Guidelines*.

[12]This and the following section draw heavily on collaborative work with John H. Suhrbier, Wayne M. Pecknold, and Lance A. Neumann.

[13]RALPH GAKENHEIMER, *Transportation Planning as Response to Controversy: The Boston Case* (Cambridge, Mass.: The M.I.T. Press, 1976).

ing organization in the Boston region), and has been repeated in only one other metropolitan area in North America.[14]

2. Innovative policies were adopted in several states, such as the California Department of Transportation's "corridor study policy," which required agreement by local officials on a study *and* the program of work for any type of transportation project.[15]

3. And, in response to the action plan's requirement for interrelating system and project planning, in some states explicit approaches to subarea transportation studies and to system-level environmental reports were formulated.[16]

While these innovations were important, they were somewhat isolated advances by progressive agencies and officials. Still lacking was a coherent national (federal, state, and local) approach which adjusted the system-planning process from the "rational model" era to the changed realities of transportation politics, in the same depth to which changes had been accomplished at the project level.

The problem can be summarized as follows.[17] As noted, transportation system and project planning traditionally have been viewed as sequential activities, as shown in Fig. 16-3. This sequential approach encountered serious problems in the context of the forces for change described previously.

Existence of system-level environmental effects. There are environmental effects implied by a system plan that cannot be analyzed on a project-by-project basis. Land-use impacts, regional economic development, housing, air quality, and changes in traffic patterns are examples of issues that must be handled on a systemwide basis.

System constraints on project decisions. Decisions that are made during system planning studies may predetermine significantly some of the social, economic, and environmental effects of a proposed project. Thus, the staffs, when doing location and design studies, often felt constrained in their ability to take actions to alleviate or avoid adverse economic, social, or environmental effects if these actions would disrupt prior system planning decisions. Generally, the development of a system plan included the choice of technology, service characteristics, and general location of a particular

---

[14]RICHARD M. SOBERMAN, "Developing Transportation and Land Use Alternatives in Toronto," in *Transportation and Land Use Planning Abroad*, Special Report 168 (Washington, D.C.: Transportation Research Board, 1976), pp. 23–34; WHIPPLE STEINKRAUSS, "Public Participation in the Metropolitan Toronto Transportation Plan Review," in *Transportation and Land Use Planning Abroad*, Special Report 168 (Washington, D.C.: Transportation Research Board, 1976), pp. 35–40.

[15]CALIFORNIA DIVISION OF HIGHWAYS, *Transportation Corridor/Route Location Study Procedures*, Circular Letter 72-10 (Sacramento, Calif.: California Division of Highways, January 28, 1972).

[16]JACK KINSTLINGER, "Relationships of Areawide, Subarea, and Project Planning in the Urban Transportation Planning Process" (unpublished paper presented to the Subcommittee on Urban Affairs and Socio-Economic Factors, American Association of State Highway Officials, Phoenix, Ariz., 1972); CALIFORNIA DEPARTMENT OF TRANSPORTATION, *State of California Action Plan for Transportation Planning and Development* (n.p.: California Business and Transportation Agency, June 1973); PENNSYLVANIA DEPARTMENT OF TRANSPORTATION, *Action Plan* (Harrisburg, Pa.: Pennsylvania Department of Transportation, September 1973).

[17]MANHEIM AND OTHERS, *Transportation Decision-Making*.

link in the network. Thus, these choices were seen as fixed and unchangeable in project planning studies, no matter how serious the issues raised by particular interests. In particular, the project design team was usually not free to question the "need" for a facility, as that supposedly had been clearly established by system planning studies— even though project studies might have developed information on possible adverse effects or sources of increased costs which called that "need" into question.

Little system-level environmental analysis. Since careful environmental impact analysis usually was not undertaken until project studies, significant resources might be expended for the design of projects which later might be delayed, extensively revised, or even dropped from further study, as a result of discovery of adverse environmental effects not anticipated in system-level planning. Such changes in project concepts or schedules created the need to revise implementation programs and system plans. While such delays or changes are never totally avoidable, anticipating project environmental impacts in system studies might have resulted in fewer delays and disruptions to implementation programs.

There are, however, several reasons why it has been difficult to anticipate significant social, environmental, and economic effects during system planning studies:

1. Many impacts of system decisions are long-term and are diffused over wide areas of a region.
2. The impacts are difficult to predict because of poor knowledge of cause-and-effect relationships (e.g., land-use changes).
3. Some impacts are unknown because they are not really fixed until specific project planning, location, and perhaps even design decisions have been made.
4. Public involvement is useful in obtaining the views of different interests as to what impacts are important. However, often it has been difficult to achieve effective public involvement in system planning studies because of the remoteness of most system planning decisions, in that they concern actions to be implemented 15 or more years in the future.

Yet even with these difficulties in anticipating many social, economic, and environmental effects during system planning, it is still necessary to make key system planning decisions. Clearly, serious consideration of these effects is necessary at both the system and project levels.

Failure to recognize the existence of significant uncertainties. The system master plan gave a precise picture of what the future transportation system was intended to be in some target year (e.g., 1995). Sometimes the master plan also included a staging of the proposed implementation of the plan; often this was left open. When the master plan failed to include specification of the staged implementation program that would be followed in bringing about the master plan, the master plan usually represented an unrealistic goal, because it did not take into account the problems and uncertainties in implementing the system on a step-by-step basis. Because completion of the plan (or completion on time) was assumed, year-by-year decisions on specific projects were distorted; if a more realistic perspective on completion of the system were taken, different project decisions would have been made in many cases.[18]

More important, by focusing on only one future system, the master planning approach loses flexibility to revise plans. The implementation program is geared toward the construction of one plan for one "target year." Since it is assumed that all projects in the plan will be built, projects may be selected that will operate effectively only when other interdependent projects are completed.[19] Then, if community and environmental impacts discovered during project studies bring into question the need for one project or several links in the system, it is both technically and psychologically difficult to respond positively by considering new projects or new system concepts. Because no provision has been made in system studies for a range of project designs, or the potential deletion of a particular link, a large amount of resources are required to revise the plan later.

Uncertainties in funding, community preferences, and the impacts of a particular action place severe limitations on a master plan approach. Transportation options must be developed with the knowledge that today's decisions are based on an imperfect understanding of the future of a region. Unforeseen changes may require new responses and adaptations that are impossible to fully anticipate.

Institutional barriers. The traditional sequential approach also had unfortunate implications institutionally, because different personnel and organizations played different roles in the process. Personnel involved in system studies and in project planning typically had, and still have, very different perspectives on transportation problems. At the system level, areawide issues are addressed and the transportation planning profession is predominant; at the project level, more detailed design work and local issues are emphasized and traditional engineering skills play a much larger role.

Even more important than the difference in disciplines is the fact that system and project studies are generally carried on in different units within an agency, or most often, in different agencies, compounding communication problems. System planning in a metropolitan area has usually been done by the staff of a metropolitan planning organization or a planning unit in a statewide transportation agency. Project implementation—location and design studies and construction supervision—has generally been done by "implementing" agencies—state highway agency personnel for major highway projects, county or municipal personnel for arterial street and many traffic engineering projects, and transit agency staff for transit projects.

---

[18]LANCE A. NEUMANN AND WAYNE M. PECKNOLD, "Application of the Time-Staged Strategic Approach to System Planning," in *Transportation Systems Planning and Analysis*, Highway Research Record 435 (Washington, D.C.: Highway Research Board, 1973), pp. 20–31.

[19]A classic example is the Boston-area highway system, which required completion of the inner belt circular distributor to function effectively—but that facility will never be built, and the Boston area must live with the results.

These "cultural" and "institutional" gaps created significant conflicts and differences of views, especially when coupled with differences in political constituencies.

INTEGRATING SYSTEM AND PROJECT DECISIONS THROUGH PROGRAMMING

The discussion in the preceding section shows how the traditional view of planning has had great difficulty dealing with the changed context of transportation. The resolution of these problems lay in recognizing that *the important decisions are the programming choices—the annual decisions on how to spend money in the next year.* Programming decisions are the decisions that commit resources to projects or to studies. Historically, the world of programming was a "third world," separate from either system planning or project implementation. Yet, this was where the real action was.

In 1973, as part of the process of assisting FHWA in developing and implementing the *Process Guidelines* (PPM 90–4), one research team examined opportunities to improve the interrelationship of urban system and project planning. Based upon extensive field research, they concluded that

> The single highest priority action is to open the programming process to timely input from more directions. . . .
>
> There are several reasons for the emphasis on programming. The goal of the programming recommendations is to foster knowledge about and constructive debate on a region's proposed program of transportation improvements. Programming is an important political decision as well as a technical decision and should be a very open process. In addition, community interaction at the system level is difficult to catalyze, and to do so requires tying together short run and long run considerations. Project decisions do have system effects, and it is essential that the long run consequences of short run decisions about projects be made clear. Programming provides the most general activity area for considering the short and long run actions together in one open forum. Thus it represents an opportunity to achieve more effective community interaction in system planning by tying together issues of immediate concern to local officials and interest groups with considerations about long term directions. Opening up the process of programming to debate and negotiation provides added pressures and incentives to implement more appropriate technical procedures as well. . . .
>
> The programming "forum" to be created would provide a link between system and project planning in *each* 3-C area. This basic forum could then be supplemented by other more specific links, such as "sub-area" or other intermediate level studies, as a local option.
>
> The basic thrust of FHWA policy should be to *require* strengthening of the programming forum. Where states and regions desire, FHWA should also allow and encourage the use of sub-area or other studies which serve to better integrate system and project planning decisions.[20]

These views were apparently shared by other professionals both inside and outside of government. In a panel discussion on the same subject, similar views were

---

[20]ARLEE RENO, BEN SCHNEIDEMAN, AND MARVIN L. MANHEIM, *Opportunities to Improve the Interrelationship of Urban System and Project Planning,* report for FHWA, Report USL73-1 (Cambridge, Mass.: Massachusetts Institute of Technology, Urban Systems Laboratory, 1973), pp. 6–7.

expressed. Particularly important was the significant leverage from the 1973 Federal-Aid Highway Act:

> Several panel members felt that provisions of [The Act] would significantly shift the orientation of transportation planning and program implementation by placing increased emphasis on short-range "low capital" actions and operating policies.[21]

As a consequence of this orientation shift, the Urban Mass Transportation Administration and Federal Highway Administration had already begun moving to focus on the programming process as a part of an overall effort to unify their previously separate planning requirements.[22] The result of these shared perceptions surfaced into public view with the promulgation of the regulations on the transportation improvement program.[23]

Thus was set in motion the evolution of the urban transportation planning process toward the realization of the "new model" described previously. At the same time, it should be noted, several metropolitan areas had been shifting, for various reasons, toward a transportation plan format with a heavy emphasis on the short-range, and toward an annual updating process.[24]

CURRENT FEDERAL URBAN TRANSPORTATION POLICIES IN RELATION TO THE MODEL

THE PRESENT REGULATIONS

The current joint regulations of the Federal Highway Administration (FHWA) and Urban Mass Transportation Administration (UMTA) of the U.S. Department of Transportation reflect this model in many important respects.[25] The regulations require that the metropolitan area planning process produce these elements:

1. A "transportation plan consisting of a transportation systems management element and a long-range element."[26]
   a. The long-range plan provides "for the long-range transportation needs of the urbanized area . . ." identifies "new transportation policies and transportation facilities or major changes in existing facilities . . ." and "shall be

---

[21]JOHN H. SUHRBIER AND ELIZABETH BENNETT, eds., *Proceedings of a Panel Discussion on the Interrelation of Transportation Systems and Project Decisions* (Washington, D.C.: Office of Environmental Policy, Federal Highway Administration, November 1, 1973), unpaged Summary.

[22]Ibid.

[23]FEDERAL HIGHWAY ADMINISTRATION AND URBAN MASS TRANSPORTATION ADMINISTRATION, "Transportation Improvement Program," *Federal Register*, 40, no. 181 (September 17, 1975), Part II. Promulgates Title 23, Code of Federal Regulations (CFR) 450, hereafter referred to as 23 CFR 450; FEDERAL HIGHWAY ADMINISTRATION AND URBAN MASS TRANSPORTATION ADMINISTRATION, "Notice of Proposed Rule-Making: Transportation Improvement Program," *Federal Register*, 39, no. 217 (November 8, 1974), Part II.

[24]METROPOLITAN TRANSPORTATION COMMISSION, *Regional Transportation Plan for the San Francisco Bay Area* (Berkeley, Calif.: Metropolitan Transportation Commission, 1974); SOUTHERN CALIFORNIA ASSOCIATION OF GOVERNMENTS, *1975, Regional Transportation Plan* (Los Angeles: Southern California Association of Governments, 1975). In California, this process was accelerated by AB 69 (1972) which established an annual, multilevel (regions and state) planning process.

[25]23 CFR 450, pp. 42976–84.

[26]23 CFR 450.116, p. 42978.

consistent with the area's comprehensive long-range land use plan, urban development objectives, and the area's overall social, economic, environmental, system performance and energy conservation goals and objectives."[27] Thus, the long-range plan corresponds to the long-range portion of the MYPP.

b. The transportation systems management element (TSME) provides "for the short-range transportation needs of the urbanized area by making efficient use of existing transportation resources and providing for the movement of people in an efficient manner . . ." and identifies "traffic engineering, public transportation, regulatory, pricing, management, operational and other improvements to the existing urban transportation system *not including new transportation facilities or major changes in existing facilities* [emphasis added]."[28]

2. A transportation improvement program (TIP) and annual element (AE):

a. The TIP is "a staged multiyear program of transportation improvements . . ."[29] which are "recommended from the transportation systems management and long-range elements of the transportation plan. . . ."[30] The TIP covers a period of not less than 3 years and may cover up to 5 or more years.[31] The TIP "shall: (a) Identify transportation improvements recommended for advancement during the program period; (b) Indicate the area's priorities; (c) Group improvements of similar urgency and anticipated staging into appropriate staging periods; (d) Include realistic estimates of total costs and revenues for the program period; and (e) Include a discussion of how improvements recommended from the long-range element and the transportation systems management element . . . were merged into the program."[32]

b. The annual element of the TIP is "a list of transportation improvement projects proposed for implementation during the first program year,"[33] including all federally funded projects and some nonfederally funded ones. "Federally funded projects shall be initiated for inclusion in the annual element at all stages in the development of the transportation improvement for which program action is proposed."[34] "For informational purposes, all nonfederally funded projects recommended from the transportation systems management element," shall be included.[35] "The annual element shall be reasonably consistent with the amount of Federal funds expected to be available to the area."[36]

[27]Ibid.
[28]Ibid.
[29]23 CFR 450.304, p. 42982.
[30]23 CFR 450.306, p. 42982.
[31]Ibid.
[32]23 CFR 450.308, p. 42982.
[33]23 CFR 450.304, p. 42982.
[34]23 CFR 450.310, p. 42982.
[35]23 CFR 450.312, p. 42983.
[36]Ibid.

c. The types of actions to be included in the TIP include, but are not necessarily limited to

engineering related to the acquisition or construction of transportation facilities; acquisition of rights-of-way, construction, and reconstruction of highways, busways, and fixed guideways; fringe parking facilities; major street improvements; transit rolling stock acquisitions; TOPICS projects; bicycle and pedestrian facilities; major revisions in levels of transit service and transit route structures; initiation of exclusive and preferential bus and carpool lanes; staggered work hours; measures to encourage carpooling; regulation of parking supply and costs; and projects to meet the special needs of the elderly and handicapped.[37]

3. A planning work program, including a prospectus and a unified planning work program (UPWP):
   a. The prospectus establishes "a multiyear framework within which the unified planning work program is accomplished . . ." which includes "A summary of the planning program including discussion of the important transportation issues facing the area . . ." and provides "A general description of the status and anticipated accomplishments . . ." of the various technical and planning activities, and "A description of the functional responsibilities of each participating agency. . . ."[38]
   b. The unified planning work program shall "Annually describe all urban transportation and transportation-related planning activities anticipated within the area during the next 1- or 2-year period regardless of funding sources. . . ."[39]
   c. The prospectus and UPWP may be combined in a single document.
4. In addition to these planning and programming requirements, present procedures require project-specific documents:
   a. Project applications—For each transportation improvement project for which federal funding is sought, from discretionary funds, submittal of a project application is required, requesting funding approval for the project, with details of the proposed project and with certifications of compliance with numerous legislatively mandated requirements (e.g., civil rights, public hearing, environmental impact statement). Such applications can cover requests for a grant for preliminary engineering or for a capital grant for construction.
   b. Technical documents—Supporting and preceding these project applications are various technical documents, such as technical studies of project alternatives and draft and final environmental impact statements.
   c. Alternatives analysis—For major mass transportation investment projects which involve "new construction or extension of a fixed guideway system (rapid rail, light rail, commuter rail, automated guideway transit) or a busway . . ." (except under specified conditions), an "analysis of alterna-

---

[37]23 CFR 450, "Transportation Improvement Program," Preamble to Subpart C, p. 42981.
[38]23 CFR 450.114, p. 42983.
[39]Ibid.

tives" of particular scope and form is required which culminates in a project application combined with an environmental impact statement (EIS) prior to the award of a grant for preliminary engineering.[40] (In principle, of course, an analysis of alternatives is required for all projects as a consequence of the National Environmental Policy Act of 1969.)

RELATION TO THE CONCEPTUAL MODEL

The federal regulations clearly embody many significant features of the model described previously.

Programmatic. The MYPP is represented by the two plan documents—the long-range plan and the transportation systems management element; the programming document—the TIP and its annual element (AE); and the two planning activities documents—the prospectus and the UPWP.

However, instead of the conceptual simplicity of a single MYPP document, the components are scattered over five separate documents (treating the AE as an integral part of the TIP). (See Fig. 16-4.) Further, there are some voids: since the TSME *excludes* new transportation facilities or major changes in existing facilities, proposed actions of this type in the period beyond the TIP (5 years) and before the LR plan horizon (25 or 30 years) are *not* described anywhere. Thus, it is unclear where the staging of the LR plan would be shown.

Finally, there may still be confusion between the idea that "plans" are statements of needs or desires unconstrained by resources, while "programs" are realistic, resource-constrained implementable actions, so the TIP is essentially different from the plan-. ning documents. This is already evident as most of the TSM elements submitted in the first cycle appear not to have included the realism of appraising the proposed actions against available resources. We disagree with this view and this separation.

It should be noted that the TSM element does, indeed, emphasize certain types of actions to promote transportation system efficiency, while the MYPP concept is only procedural; it does not highlight particular types of actions. (Since national priorities can be expected to change from time to time, we believe the MYPP concept should be separated from current policies to promote specific types of actions, such as TSM. The extent to which current national policies are reflected in the actions of the MYPP should be highlighted in the content of the MYPP.)

Periodic. The regulations require that the TIP and UPWP be updated annually; and that the transportation plan—both the TSM and LR elements—"be reviewed annually to confirm its validity and its consistency with current transportation and land use conditions."[41] Administratively, however, the present procedures are that the UPWP, TSM, and TIP are submitted for review at different times in the annual cycle.

---

[40]URBAN MASS TRANSPORTATION ADMINISTRATION, "Major Urban Mass Transportation Investments," pp. 41512–14.

[41]23 CFR 450.116(a), p. 42978.

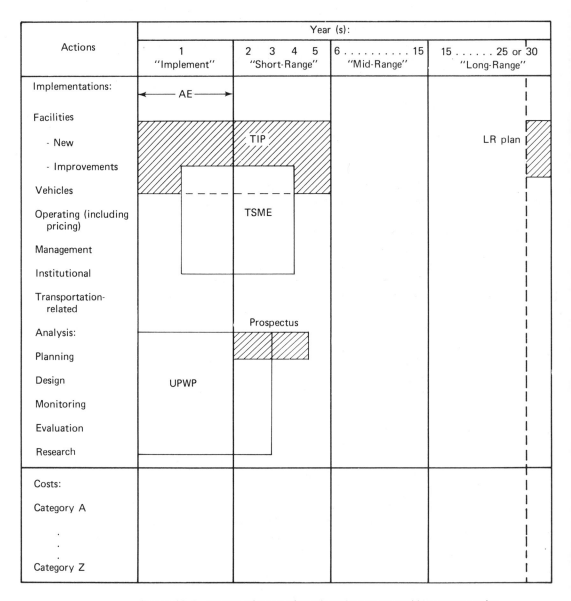

Figure 16-4 *Relation of present federal requirements to multiyear program plan*

This seems more a question of spreading out the bureaucratic workload evenly than well-thought-through organization of federal and local roles in a coherent annual decision cycle.

Planning-informed. The LR plan plays an important role in developing the TIP. However, it is not clear to what extent the TIP must be consistent with the LR plan, or, put another way, just how divergent the two can be without necessitating major revision of the LR plan. Further, the details of the relationship between the LR plan and the other elements is sufficiently unclear that many practitioners have raised questions about it.

Participatory yet decisive. The regulations reflect very clearly the shared power among the several transportation agencies—the MPO, publicly owned operators of mass transportation, state highway or transportation agencies, and local elected officials (acting through the MPO). These regulations do not spell out what the process working arrangements are to be (except that the MPO has certain "lead" responsibilities), as this must be determined in the unique political structure of each urban area. It is unclear yet how this is working from a national perspective; initially, there was significant resistance precisely because transit and highway agencies recognized the importance of the programming lever on the implementation of projects and many agencies and officials did not feel that the MPO should play even a lead role in this process.

It is also not clear how well the limited but important funding flexibility is working, or the pressure for reaching a decision in order to have an approved program. One hypothesis would be that, even though there is funding flexibility in the apportioned programs (the urban system funds provided under the Federal-Aid Highway laws, Title 23,[42] and the federal Urban Mass Transportation Act, Title 49[43]), there are significant constraints on the ability to shift funds (for example, limits on the local matching share's use and significant differences in the federal–local splits) so that significantly different alternative allocations of funds to alternative mixes of projects are not yet being explored in most urban areas. That is, the issues of alternative TIPs are not yet being crystallized; what is happening is that the TIPs—and TSMs—which have been developed so far seem to be mostly assemblages of projects proposed by lower-level jurisdictions (counties, incorporated areas of greater than 200,000 population) and transit agencies and state highway agencies.

This may also be related to the apparent lack of substantial public involvement in the programming process to this point.

Performance-oriented. Little obvious effort is being manifested on explicit statements of goals and monitoring of the degree of goal achievement. The regulations do not require this; the closest is the requirement that the annual element include some projects from the TSM, but that requires only implementation, not monitoring and evaluation.

Professionally responsible. Here the regulations are silent, except in the case of the UPWP, for which the original DOT order included requirements similar to those

---

[42]FEDERAL HIGHWAY ADMINISTRATION, *Federal Laws*, Title 23, USC 104(b)(6), pp. II-19 and 20.

[43]URBAN MASS TRANSPORTATION ADMINISTRATION, *Urban Mass Transportation Act of 1964 and Related Laws*, as amended through February 5, 1976, Title, 49, USC 1604, sec. 5 (Washington, D.C.: U.S. Government Printing Office, 1976), pp. 10–14.

of the *Process Guidelines*; and in the "Analysis of Alternatives Policy,"[44] which applies only to UMTA-funded major fixed-guideway projects. Nothing, however, in the new FHWA–UMTA regulations requires consideration of a range of alternatives, identification of social, economic, and environmental effects, or timely public involvement, in developing the TIP and its annual element or the TSME.

This is a very important omission. For example, the substantive thrust of the TSM requirement could be negated if initial steps to implement, say, an auto-restricted zone, were undertaken without a carefully executed program of public involvement and thoughtful analysis of alternatives and their effects.[45]

UNRESOLVED ISSUES

APPRAISAL

From the preceding section it appears that the general conceptual structure of the planning process described previously is present in part in the process created by the new regulations. Unfortunately, the implementation of the process as promulgated in the regulations does not communicate this clarity.

1. There are still too many "paperwork" requirements—too many separate documents.
2. The role of long-range planning in what appears to be a short-run-oriented process seems unclear, especially to the individuals and organizations which have invested much effort in long-range planning.
3. As often with major new federal initiatives, there are those who see this as just another bureaucratic requirement for a piece of paper, while there are others who see it as a major opportunity for change.
4. The depth of change required to make this process work is greater than many people realize: the new regulations must be supported by follow-through on a number of fronts—strengthened institutions and institutional interrelationships; shifts of staff priorities; provision of technical information and methods, and training to encourage personnel to adapt to new responsibilities and challenges; and others.
5. Follow-through is needed at the local level to make the new process work more effectively.

Perhaps the most significant issues lie in the area of ensuring that the new process created by these regulations does have the desired features described under "Partici-

---

[44]URBAN MASS TRANSPORTATION ADMINISTRATION, "Major Urban Mass Transportation Investments," pp. 41512–14.

[45]GARY HAWTHORN AND MARVIN L. MANHEIM, "Guidelines for Implementing a Comprehensive Policy of Traffic Restraints" (unpublished paper for the Organisation for Economic Co-operation and Development Conference, "Better Towns with Less Traffic," April 1975).

patory Yet Decisive" and "Professionally Responsible." These are essential to achieving the full promise of the new process.

SPECIFIC ISSUES

It is possible to suggest some specific issues, and approaches to these issues, which can overcome the weaknesses in the present process.

Consolidate planning documents. While the present federal requirements make significant progress toward implementing the new model, they do not go far enough. There are still too many separate documents required for local submittal to the feds.

One important consolidation step is in process of being implemented.[46] UMTA is consolidating the requirements for project applications for discretionary-funded capital projects with the TIP, so that appropriate documentation will be submitted either on a one-time basis or annually with the TIP. Thus, approval of the TIP then will constitute approval of each project in the annual element of the TIP—except where there may be unresolved questions such as delay for 13(c) certification. However, it is unclear what FHWA's policy will be in this respect.

A second important step would be to combine the three presently separate requirements for a TSM, long-range plan, and TIP into a single document in the format of a MYPP. The reasons are both theoretical and practical. All time frames of planning should include both capital and noncapital projects: even in a long-range plan, non-capital actions should be specified, such as the general shape of any auto-disincentive policies anticipated 25 years from now; and while it is current policy to emphasize TSM-type policies, the short-range portion of the planning document should include *both* capital and TSM-type policies so as to focus local decisions on trade-offs between the two classes of actions. [It is especially important that alternative transit service programs (routes, schedules, fares) be presented so that trade-offs among alternative distributions of transit service improvements are debated.]

Further, fiscal constraints should be explicitly operative in the early years of the plan, so there is no difference between a TIP—a "program"—and the short-range portion of the MYPP—a "plan": *the first year of the program must be implementable within available resources*. Where efforts are proposed to bring about alternative levels of funding in future years, the MYPP should show explicitly alternative options in future years corresponding to whether the funding level changes.

Finally, pulling these three pieces together into a single submittal would reduce the required preparation time at the local level, and review time at the federal level.

One objection could be the present federal policy to promote TSM-type projects (i.e., to improve efficiency). This objective could be met equally well by simply requiring a summary statement in the MYPP indicating which projects in the annual element are TSM-type projects, summarizing their costs, and so on. In fact, if TSM projects are considered separately, as at present, it may be *more* difficult to get serious commit-

---

[46]"Policy," and "UMTA Cuts Red Tape," *MASS TRANSIT*, 3, no. 9 (October 1976), pp. 18–21, 24, 28.

ments than if there is more explicit focus on local trade-offs between TSM and capital projects, and on consideration of realistic budget constraints.

There is the possibility of going an additional step: combine the prospectus—UPWP with the TSM–LR plan–TIP document.[47] The result would then be a "true" MYPP, in that both implementation projects and studies would be in the same document. The argument for this is that decisions on studies should be made concurrently with decisions on projects, because the results of next year's studies influence what options are realistically available in future years. The argument against is that the MYPP might now be too complex for local preparation and consideration for adoption, or for federal review. This objection can be answered by a well-articulated set of procedures in the annual adoption cycle, so that the focus is on the "studies" portion of the MYPP at one point, and on the "action" projects at a later point, but there is still explicit opportunity for interactions.

Articulate and demonstrate the role of long-range planning. The general relationship of long-range planning to the programming process was suggested earlier. Figure 16-5 shows how system-level studies, with long-range, midrange, and even short-range perspectives, is an on-going activity in which a variety of system concepts are explored as background for specific project implementation studies.[48] (Compare this with Fig. 16-3.)

IMPROVE THE QUALITY OF THE PLANNING–PROGRAMMING PROCESS

This area deals with the concerns discussed under "Participatory Yet Decisive" and "Professionally Responsible."

Range of realistic alternatives. It is essential that real alternatives be developed and discussed openly in the annual programming cycle. Even in regions where there is substantial agreement on the general direction of transport policy, there inevitably will still be some differences of opinion about priorities for implementation in the next year, especially within fixed fiscal resources: what levels of transit service improvements for whom; whether to accelerate or defer particular action; whether to implement the second year of last year's TIP as adopted or make changes; and so on. In regions where there are unresolved issues, there clearly should be alternative TIPs on the table for discussion: major incentives for transit use, major disincentives for

---

[47]RENO, SCHNEIDEMAN, AND MANHEIM, *Opportunities to Improve.*

[48]The metaphor of statistical decision theory is a useful one and has influenced the development of this image of the planning process. See further: MANHEIM, RUITER, AND BHATT, *Search and Choice;* NEUMANN AND PECKNOLD, "Application of Time-Staged"; ORGANISATION FOR ECONOMIC CO-OPERATION AND DEVELOPMENT, *The Urban Transportation Planning Process*, report of a panel of experts (Paris: Organisation for Economic Co-operation and Development, 1971); W. M. PECKNOLD, "Evolution of Transport Systems: An Analysis of Time-Staged Investment Strategies under Uncertainty" (unpublished Ph.D. thesis, Department of Civil Engineering, Massachusetts Institute of Technology, 1970); URBAN MASS TRANSPORTATION ADMINISTRATION, "Major Urban Mass Transportation Investments." For a practical application, see JOHN R. LAWSON, MARVIN L. MANHEIM, AND DARWIN G. STUART, "Guideway Transit for Southern California: A Policy Analysis," in *Personal Rapid Transit III*, eds. Dennis A. Gary, William L. Garrard, and Alain L. Kornhauser (Minneapolis, Minn.: University of Minnesota, 1976), pp. 137–54.

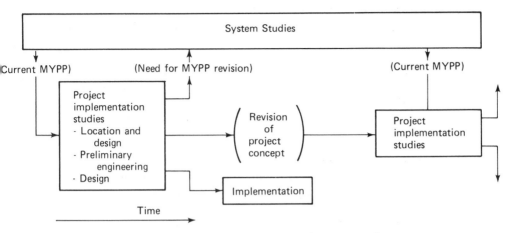

Figure 16-5 *System studies as a context for project studies*

single-occupancy auto use, whether to upgrade an existing highway facility, whether to advance a major transit capital project, alternative subregional allocations of resources. Issues such as these call for the development and discussion of alternative TIPs which reflect the alternative choices.

These alternatives should be realistic. In particular, the appropriate constraints to available funds should be met. The only exception to this requirement is when the program alternative includes specific action proposals to *change* the level of funding.

It is particularly important, in response to current national policy, that alternative TSM actions, and alternative levels of commitment to TSM-type actions, be explicitly explored.

Identification of effects and discussion of trade-offs. It is also important that, to provide a basis for informed choice among alternative TIPs, adequate and timely information should be available on the likely effects of the alternatives across the full range of travel, economic, social, and environmental effects. The level of detail and degree of accuracy should be consistent with the significance of the impacts, the available time and other resources, and the state of the technical art (simplified planning methods will usually be more appropriate than complete regional models, and pencil-and-paper methods will often be more useful than computer methods).[49]

This information should be presented and discussed in ways that clarify the issues, by bringing out the key trade-offs among alternatives in the style mandated by NEPA for the EIS.[50]

---

[49]CAMBRIDGE SYSTEMATICS, INC., *Final Report: Dual Mode Transit Planning Case Study, Vol. III: Transit Sketch Planning Methodology* (Washington, D.C.: U.S. Department of Transportation, Urban Mass Transportation Administration, 1976); MARVIN L. MANHEIM, PETER FURTH, AND ILAN SALOMAN, *Responsive Analysis Methods: A Compendium of Programs for Pocket Calculators* (Cambridge, Mass.: Massachusetts Institute of Technology, Department of Civil Engineering, in press); MANHEIM, *Fundamentals*, chap. 3.

[50]MANHEIM, *Fundamentals*, chap. 9; MANHEIM AND OTHERS, *Transportation Decision-Making*, chap. 3, "Evaluation and Reporting," pp. 36–51.

A key secondary element here is the need to develop and disseminate rapidly technical tools more appropriate for the analysis of alternative TIPs than the traditional LR planning tools.

Public involvement. It is not clear that there has been sufficient timely public involvement in the development and adoption of the TIP/AE. In each metropolitan area it is essential that maximum effort be made to raise the public awareness of the importance of influencing the annual programming decision and to make available adequate and timely opportunities for the public to do so.

Make the annual cycle explicit. As a summary of the preceding points, it is imperative that the participating agencies define the steps and procedures which will be followed each year in developing and adopting the TIP. Particularly important are the major milestones in that cycle, such as the major points for public participation, the points at which a draft TIP/EIS is circulated, the point at which a final program adoption decision will be made. Procedures should be described for ensuring that significant alternatives are developed early in the process, that adequate and timely information is developed on the likely effects of alternative programs, that there is timely and constructive public involvement, that a systematic interdisciplinary approach is utilized, that system and project decisions are fully integrated, and that the locus and process of decision making is clearly described. It will also be important to structure separate, but interrelated, processes at the local, subregional, and regional levels.[51]

One way of implementing this would be to expand and update the state transportation agency's action plan by incorporating regional action plans developed for each urbanized area by the MPO, transit operators, local officials, and other interested parties in each area.[52] (Or alternatively require urban-area action plans explicitly.)

Make the process more performance-oriented. A performance-oriented process is one in which participants are held responsible this year for whether or not they achieved what they said they would achieve in past decision making. (This is especially critical for TSM-type actions.) Several steps can be taken to increase the degree of performance orientation in the process:

1. The annually submitted MYPP should include, in the discussion of the effects of alternative actions, specific estimates of the effects of the adopted actions. At a minimum, these should include estimates of changes in demand (highway volumes, transit ridership, auto occupancy, elderly and handicapped usage,

---

[51]Kirtland C. Mead, Marvin L. Manheim, and Arlee T. Reno, "Basic Issues in Incorporating Community and Environmental Factors in the Transport System Planning Process," in *Proceedings— Twelfth Annual Meeting, Changing Times and Keeping Up*, Transportation Research Forum, 12, no. 1 (Philadelphia) (Oxford, Ind.: The Richard B. Cross Company, 1971), pp. 323–37; Kirtland C. Mead, "Design of a Statewide Transportation Planning Process: An Application to California" (unpublished Ph.D. thesis, Department of Civil Engineering, Massachusetts Institute of Technology, June 1973).

[52]This would appear to have been the intent of Congress, since Section 5(2) of the Urban Mass Transportation Act as amended by Section 103(a) of PL 93-503 has the same language as Section 109(h) of Title 23 added by Section 136(b) of PL 91-605.

etc.), in service levels (travel times, fares), in costs and revenues, and in legally required effects (e.g., air quality levels); to the extent practicable, other effects should be stated explicitly, too.

2. The annually submitted MYPP should report observations on what changes occurred in the past year, comparisons of these changes with those that were predicted in previous year's MYPP submittals, and discussions of reasons for significant discrepancies (for example, why did exclusive bus lanes fail to achieve transit travel-time reductions initially predicted; why was transit ridership on a new express line 20% greater than predicted?).

3. The "studies" portion of the MYPP should include specific actions to collect and analyze data on actual system performance to provide these inputs.

Potential expandability. Our previous comments indicate the effectiveness of the new model in dealing with the realities of urban transportation politics today: shared power and uncertainty. Why shouldn't the same approach work for other aspects of metropolitan, state, and national planning? For example:

1. Bring more reality into metropolitan comprehensive planning: at the metropolitan level include in the MYPP *all* projects for which federal funds will be requested in the next year, including housing, sewers and water, and education. Thus, the A-95 clearinghouse would be brought into a more visible role, although we hasten to add not necessarily *the* sole decision-making role, as major programs would still lie largely within the province of the program-oriented agencies (e.g., the MPO and other transportation agencies for the transportation sector).

2. Bring more coordination into state-level transportation planning: at the state level, expand the state MYPP to include all modes of transportation, and both passenger and freight (e.g., the statewide rail plan, state aviation plan).

3. Strengthen the national transportation planning process: a multimodal transportation MYPP should be utilized at the national level as the format for federal statement of national transportation objectives and programs. The level of detail or aggregation would be that appropriate to a national perspective. All federal transportation funds should be included, both apportioned and discretionary. The annual development and adoption of an updated national MYPP should be conducted in interaction with the annual cycles for state and metropolitan area MYPPs; the working out of the dynamics of these interrelationships is not trivial, since realistic funding levels must be incorporated in the decisions at each level.

4. Fold in present separate requirements: for example, the requirements for meeting air quality standards now reflected in transportation control plans, at the metropolitan level,[53] and for state energy conservation plans, could be met by appropriate statements in the MYPP summary referencing those sections of the

---

[53] ELIZABETH DEAKIN, GREIG HARVEY, AND ANN RAPPAPORT, *Air Quality Considerations in Transportation Planning—Recommendations for an Improved Process*, CTS Report 77-15 (Cambridge, Mass.: Massachusetts Institute of Technology, Center for Transportation Studies, June 1977).

MYPP which describe to what extent specific air quality, conservation, or other objectives are met.

CONCLUSIONS

A new view of the planning process is now being implemented. This new process is programmatic, periodic, planning-informed, participatory yet decisive, performance-oriented, and professionally responsible. This is a politically realistic process, in that it recognizes and utilizes the natural focus on here and now, and the realities of shared power. Through this process, planning can become politically relevant; this process should lead to implementable, and implemented, decisions.

In this process, the historical separation of long-range and short-range planning becomes irrelevant: they are two different facets of the annual process of updating the multiyear program plan.

While progress has been made toward implementing this new model, there are still significant challenges facing the professional community to get this new planning process to work more effectively:

1. The need to increase the effectiveness of the decision-making process by working to improve interagency coordination in a shared decision-making process and to develop, document, and disseminate the procedures to be followed by all parties in the annual decision cycle.
2. The need to increase the responsibility of the process by working to see that the really important issues get surfaced for open debate; and that a program of timely public involvement provides a mechanism for expression of views on these issues.
3. The need to do more effective analyses (e.g., travel predictions, environmental effects) which are relevant to the more open, more political, more "real" decision process in this new model.
4. The need to improve and institutionalize this new process.
5. The need at the same time to push for the program goals enunciated in the TSM requirement, elderly and handicapped requirements, and other current national policy objectives.

Above all, we must find ways

> to simplify procedures, accelerate the decision process, and enable democratically elected officials to make more of the key balancing decisions.[54]

We believe the path to achieving this objective is to completely implement the planning model described here.

---

[54]ALTSHULER AND CURRY, "The Changing Environment," p. 36.

SELECTED BIBLIOGRAPHY

ALTSHULER, ALAN A., AND ROBERT W. CURRY, "The Changing Environment of Urban Development Policy —Shared Power or Shared Impotence?" *Urban Law Annual*, 10 (1975), 3–41.

BRAYBROOKE, DAVID, AND CHARLES E. LINDBLOM, *A Strategy of Decision: Policy Evaluation as a Social Process*. Glencoe, Ill.: Free Press, 1963.

BRIDWELL, LOWELL K., "Freeways in the Urban Environment," in *Joint Development and Multiple Use of Transportation Rights-of-Way*, Special Report 104, pp. 88–100. Washington, D.C.: Highway Research Board, 1969.

COLCORD, FRANK C., *Urban Transportation Decision Making*, a series of monographs, see the Chapter 30 bibliography.

DEAKIN, ELIZABETH, GREIG HARVEY, AND ANN RAPPAPORT, *Air Quality Considerations in Transportation Planning—Recommendations for an Improved Process*, CTS Report 77-15. Cambridge, Mass.: Massachusetts Institute of Technology, Center for Transportation Studies, June 1977.

DEVINE, EDWARD J., *Multi-Discipline Design Teams for Transportation Facilities: A Study of the Administrative, Planning and Community Participation Aspects of Design Teams*, prepared for U.S. DOT. n.p.: State of Washington Planning and Community Affairs Agency, August 1971.

GAKENHEIMER, RALPH, *Transportation Planning as Response to Controversy: The Boston Case*. Cambridge, Mass.: The M.I.T. Press, 1976.

HIGHWAY RESEARCH BOARD, *Citizen Participation in Transportation Planning*, Special Report 142. Washington, D.C.: Highway Research Board, 1973.

HILL, STUART L., "Century Freeway (Watts)," in *Joint Development and Multiple Use of Transportation Rights-of-Way*, Special Report 104, pp. 68–74. Washington, D.C.: Highway Research Board, 1969.

LAWSON, JOHN R., MARVIN L. MANHEIM, AND DARWIN G. STUART, "Guideway Transit for Southern California: A Policy Analysis," in *Personal Rapid Transit III*, eds. Dennis A. Gary, William L. Garrard, and Alain L. Kornhauser, pp. 137–54. Minneapolis, Minn.: University of Minnesota, 1976.

LEGARRA, J. A., AND T. R. LAMMERS, "The Highway Administrator Looks at Values," in *Transportation and Community Values*, Special Report 105, pp. 109–16. Washington, D.C.: Highway Research Board, 1969.

MANHEIM, MARVIN L., *Fundamentals of Transportation Systems Analysis*. Cambridge, Mass.: The M.I.T. Press, in press.

———, EARL R. RUITER, AND KIRAN U. BHATT, *Search and Choice in Transport Systems Planning: Summary Report*, Research Report R68-40. Cambridge, Mass.: Massachusetts Institute of Technology, Department of Civil Engineering, 1968.

———, AND OTHERS, *Transportation Decision-Making: A Guide to Social and Environmental Considerations*, NCHRP Report 156. Washington, D.C.: Transportation Research Board, 1975.

MEAD, KIRTLAND C., MARVIN L. MANHEIM, AND ARLEE T. RENO, "Basic Issues in Incorporating Community and Environmental Factors in the Transport System Planning Process," in *Proceedings—Twelfth Annual Meeting, Changing Times and Keeping Up*. Transportation Research Forum, 12, no. 1 (Philadelphia), pp. 323–37. Oxford, Ind.: The Richard B. Cross Company, 1971.

NEUMANN, LANCE A., "Integrating System Planning and Programming: An Implementation Strategy Approach" (unpublished Ph.D. dissertation. Department of Civil Engineering, Massachusetts Institute of Technology, 1976).

———, AND WAYNE M. PECKNOLD, "Application of the Time-Staged Strategic Approach to System Planning," in *Transportation Systems Planning and Analysis*, Highway Research Record 435, pp. 20–31. Washington, D.C.: Highway Research Board, 1973.

ORGANISATION FOR ECONOMIC CO-OPERATION AND DEVELOPMENT, *The Urban Transportation Planning Process*, report of a panel of experts. Paris: Organisation for Economic Co-operation and Development, 1971.

RENO, ARLEE, BEN SCHNEIDEMAN, AND MARVIN L. MANHEIM, *Opportunities to Improve the Interrelationship of Urban System and Project Planning*, report for FHWA, Report USL73-1. Cambridge, Mass.: Massachusetts Institute of Technology, Urban Systems Laboratory, 1973.

SOBERMAN, RICHARD M., "Developing Transportation and Land Use Alternatives in Toronto," in *Transportation and Land Use Planning Abroad*, Special Report 168, pp. 23–34. Washington, D.C.: Transportation Research Board, 1976.

STEINKRAUSS, WHIPPLE, "Public Participation in the Metropolitan Toronto Transportation Plan Review," in *Transportation and Land Use Planning Abroad*, Special Report 168, pp. 35–40. Washington, D.C.: Transportation Research Board, 1976.

SUHRBIER, JOHN H., AND ELIZABETH BENNETT, eds., *Proceedings of a Panel Discussion on the Interrelation of Transportation Systems and Project Decisions*. Washington, D.C.: Office of Environmental Policy, Federal Highway Administration, November 1, 1973.

Chapter 17

TSM PLANNING—AN EMERGING PROCESS*

Stephen C. Lockwood,† *Vice President, Alan M. Voorhees & Associates, Inc.*

The transition from bulldozer to control tower represents a radical reorientation for transportation planning. Resource constraints, recognition of negative impacts, and changes in social priorities have combined to end the heroic era of transportation system expansion—leaving most of urban America with a mature transportation infrastructure. There is a growing recognition that these existing facilities and users represent a man–machine system which can be managed. In the future, service improvements will increasingly result not just from capital-intensive system additions designed to accommodate increasing demand, but from information-intensive operation of the existing system oriented toward a mix of transport and nontransport objectives.

Transportation systems management (TSM)[1] encompasses a broad range of potential improvement strategies whose common distinguishing characteristic is a nonfacility, low-capital-cost operations orientation. TSM strategies mobilize both demand management and supply optimization to more effectively capitalize on existing highway and transit facilities and achieve a broad range of transportation-related goals. Under this broad definition, TSM planning is now the required focus for the short-range transportation element of the transportation improvement program required by the U.S. Department of Transportation from metropolitan areas.[2] It will

---

*An earlier version of this chapter was published as Stephen C. Lockwood and Frederick A. Wagner, "Methodological Framework for the TSM Planning Process," in *Transportation System Management*, Special Report 172 (Washington, D.C.: Transportation Research Board, 1977), pp. 100–118.

†This chapter has benefited from discussions with Thomas B. Deen and Keith Gilbert of Alan M. Voorhees & Associates; Frederick A. Wagner; David Jones of the University of California at Berkeley; and John J. Roark and Garrison P. Smith of North Central Texas Council of Governments.

[1]The terms "system" and "systems" are currently used interchangeably in discussing TSM. In the Code of Federal Regulations, Title 23 (Chapter I), Subpart A, Part 450 uses "systems" and Title 49 (Chapter VI), Subpart B, Part 613 uses "system."

[2]Federal Highway Administration and Urban Mass Transportation Administration, "Transportation Improvement Program," *Federal Register*, vol. 40, no. 181 (September 17, 1975).

increasingly become the dominant focus of all urban transportation service improvement strategies.

THE INEVITABILITY OF TSM

The changes in the context for urban transporation improvements which have
converged in this shift toward TSM are complex and interrelated. An appreciation of
them clarifies both the logic and potential of a comprehensive approach to TSM
strategy making. These changes include:

1. *Escalating costs of major projects.* Construction costs have risen at rates of from
   10 to 15% annually, consistently exceeding estimates. In addition, an aging
   highway system requires that an increasing proportion of available budgets be
   devoted to maintenance while transit labor and energy-related operating cost
   increases are forcing service cutbacks in many areas.
2. *Increasing competition for public funds.* Competition is taking place both
   among the expanding programs within the transportation sector and between
   transport and other high-priority social and economic needs. New funding is not
   lightly granted by the political process. As inflation challenges the ability of
   local government to continue to deliver traditional public services, transportation budgets are constrained and scrutinized. The burden of proof is increasingly
   on any proposal for new system construction.
3. *Demographic and land-use changes.* Overall population growth has slowed
   considerably forcing urban transportation planners to deflate earlier forecasts.
   Urban/rural differentiation has diminished and density curves have flattened as
   small and moderate-size cities have grown at the expense of large ones. These
   trends have undercut the forecasts of dramatic increases in demand in large cities
   and focused attention on the more modest problems of smaller urban areas.
4. *A closer examination of efficiency and equity.* The cost effectiveness of major
   urban transportation investments are, for the first time, being openly and widely
   argued within the transportation planning/engineering profession. The productivity of existing public transit is being evaluated. Transit plans are also being
   questioned for their equity implications with respect to inner-city/suburban and
   rich/poor benefits. In many urban areas, it is difficult to demonstrate substantial
   user benefits from new transit systems. Accepted highway engineering standards,
   painfully developed over three decades, are also being reviewed for their cost
   effectiveness.
5. *Public resistance to new construction.* The public continues to evidence a
   heightened sensitivity to the mixed blessings of major system additions. Environmental and community-disruption impacts sparked a highway revolt that
   evolved into a conventional wisdom which has spread to transit construction as
   well. It is apparent that many of the short- and long-range environmental,
   social, and economic consequences of construction are neither desirable nor
   avoidable within acceptable costs.

6. *The need for flexible system response.* The volatility of energy supplies, tightened environmental standards, and organized demands of special user groups require increased responsiveness from the transportation system. The short lead-time requirements of these successive "crises" render capital-intensive improvements irrelevant and emphasize the importance of exercising operational control over the existing transportation systems—both supply and demand.

THE INSTITUTIONAL RESISTANCE TO TSM

The reactions of transportation institutions to these context changes is a continued demonstration of the American penchant for a "technology fix." In response to public disenchantment with highway construction, planners have produced a parade of successive transit technologies—rapid transit, light rail transit, "people movers," paratransit, etc.—currently built at a rate of expenditure approaching the highway program itself. A "build"-oriented transportation industry continues to focus on system additions and problems for them to solve, while generalizing the merits of each new technology far beyond its reasonable applicability.

In such an institutional environment, TSM has been seen as an unappealing last resort—"TSM means *T*oo *S*mall to *M*atter." It lacks the hard-hat glamour of something new and expensive and focuses on a return to boring fundamentals.

Moreover, the formalization of TSM as a required planning activity at the metropolitan level has been surrounded by confusion relating to the preconceptions of the professional audience. To traffic engineers, it has neo-TOPICS[3] overtones; to transit operators, it is business as usual; to environmentalists, it is reminiscent of the transportation control plan experience; to social welfare advocates, it appears as a tool for service equity; to city planners, it is transportation supporting urban revitalization.

While all these associations are relevant, they have tended to obscure the distinctive identity of TSM as a coherent generic improvement strategy appropriately responsive to a new era for transportation. This new era is forcing certain requirements on the nature of acceptable and effective urban transportation improvements:

- They must be cheap—with respect to both capital and operating costs—through privatizing operating costs and capitalizing on sunk investments.
- They must concentrate on matching existing supply to demand through flexible operation using incentives, disincentives, and user information systems.
- They must only add new supply which is truly an "infrastructure for management."
- They must differentiate among users, targeting socially agreed upon groups and purposes for priority treatment or specialized service, and they may restrict access by others to certain places at certain times.
- They must incorporate true cost and benefit allocations both for equity reasons and to reduce uncompensated external impacts and system inefficiencies.

---

[3]TOPICS was a late 1960s FHWA program to increase highway capacity and safety.

- They must coordinate people and goods movement through rationalizing competing or uncoordinated institutional arrangements.
- They must be responsive to a broad range of mobility and competing nontransportation objectives and constraints requiring trade-offs and "second-best" solutions.

AN AGENDA FOR ACTION

This striving for comprehensiveness implies an ambitious agenda for innovative transportation strategy development—both technically and institutionally. For the unique aspect of TSM is not the component parts—separate TSM actions, many of which in isolation are well understood—but the process of combining them into coherent, mutually reinforcing strategies using the full range of actions in pursuit of specific objectives.

Realization of the synergistic potential of TSM, therefore, requires development of a clearer concept of how TSM strategies can be developed and implemented. Current barriers to implementation include the requirement of instituting an administrative and organization-intensive reorientation, and the need for an effective TSM planning process. This reorientation involves threatening excursions into encouraging new forms of interprofessional collaboration, fostering new institutional arrangements, forging new political alliances, redirecting existing funding, and developing innovative planning methods. Indeed, many transportation institutions which grew up during the "build" era now see TSM as a threat to their traditional professional competency, their raison d'être, and their current sources of political support.

Over time, however, the traditional transportation planning preoccupation with long-range, capital-intensive improvements will inevitably appear more and more irrelevant and the logic of TSM will become more compelling. The development of a structured TSM planning process model will help dilute the current tendency to view TSM planning as a top-down imposed requirement and encourage a more widespread recognition of its logic as the increasingly relevant transportation improvement strategy for an ever-growing proportion of urban America. The remainder of the chapter develops the outlines of such a process.

TSM IN THE TRANSPORTATION PLANNING PROCESS

Chapter 16 has discussed the evolution of the overall metropolitan transportation planning process. It has seen halting progress toward systematic strategy making which shows a balanced regard for both immediate and long-range needs and a healthy respect for the options required by uncertainty. Current requirements focus on short- and long-range elements without a clearly defined concern for the relationship between them. But while the long-range element and short-range element (TSM) differ in fundamental ways, there are significant relationships:

1. Long-range planning deals with capital-intensive improvements requiring years to plan and implement. TSM encompasses low-budget actions which, by definition, seldom require more than a year to plan and implement and may be recycled several times during one cycle of long-range planning, thereby changing the context for the long range.
2. Capital-intensive projects may require TSM support for full cost effectiveness or rely on TSM as an interim substitute or stage for many years.
3. TSM strategies are, by definition, non-capital-intensive and in many cases may be seen as alternatives to the capital-intensive components of long-range plans.
4. Middle-range planning, identified by Manheim as an important gap in contemporary planning, is precisely that time frame where "major" TSM projects and "minor" capital-intensive projects might be expected.
5. TSM planning should be experimental. It offers short-term opportunities to monitor and modify; whereas long-range planning is oriented toward elaborate alternatives analysis, prediction under long-range uncertainties, large-scale engineering, and living with the results.
6. Although it is convenient to look at TSM program preparation as a repetitive annual process, in fact, the TSM program development process does not appear each year as a new and different activity. The more routine TSM-type actions are implemented on a regular basis, and quantification of system performance is generally a continuing function.

A GENERALIZED TSM PLANNING CYCLE

The TSM program development process is likely to be found in many sizes and shapes and can be blurred in the time dimension. However, it is convenient and useful to define a normative process in terms of a single interrelated series of steps as though those steps were going to be operated in sequence from start to finish as a complete exercise. Whether the preparation of a TSM element of an annual program is undertaken by a single individual in a single agency or jointly by a multimodal study team assembled from several agencies, the technical steps in the process will remain essentially the same (see Fig. 17-1). In general, these steps cover initiation, diagnosis of existing performance, project selection, cost and impact estimation, consideration of priority in the light of fund availability and implementation constraints, and preparation of the recommended program of projects.

The initiation of the process is an institutional matter. A coordinated annual start, led by the metropolitan planning organization (MPO), can assist by permitting government assessment of budgets, current-year program status, carry-over projects, potential of interagency and interjurisdictional cooperation, and identification of regional versus local roles.

The technical cycle conventionally begins by reviewing current priorities—official goals and objectives or unofficial political reality—as a guide to ensuring program relevance to current concerns. Related performance measures or measures of effectiveness can be identified to determine current system performance in relationship to current priorities.

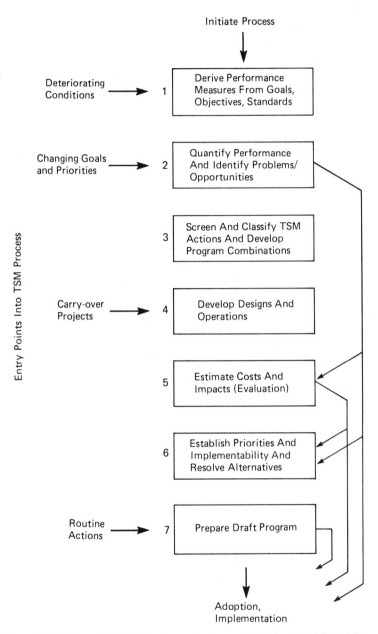

Figure 17-1 *Overall TSM planning cycle (normative)* [*Source: Adapted from Donald G. Capelle, Frederick A. Wagner, and Stephen C. Lockwood, "Transportation Systems Management,"* AMV T ch Notes, *4, No. 2 (July 15, 1976).*]

System performance measures are used to select data to compare the actual state of the system with standards, or among areas, or with previously set targets. Standardized records and surveys must be maintained on a continuing basis for this purpose.

Candidate TSM actions and action combinations are determined by reference to their characteristics and potential impacts on performance measures, singly or in combination. Warrants and handbooks, now in development, as well as professional experience, will provide guidance. Single-mode or single-jurisdiction actions are developed by the appropriate agency. Multimodal actions are analyzed on a jurisdictional or regional basis. This step ends with an interagency joint examination to identify conflicts, potential trade-offs, and intermodal impacts among the range of candidate actions.

Design and cost estimates are carried out by the appropriate agency using agreed-upon project limits. Impacts may be determined on a local, agency, or regional level. Both manual and automated techniques are being developed to estimate performance measure changes as actual experience accumulates. Computer-based analyses or those relating to regional data bases may be performed by the MPO. This step ends with a joint intermodal, interagency review of impact estimates, including possible recycling of estimates to account for synergism or to develop a more comprehensive strategy.

The integration of actions into an overall program includes the estimation of comparative changes in the performance measures which are caused by each action. A simple cost-effectiveness index for actions can assist in determining priorities, with MPO technical committees acting as a forum for this process. Funding constraints by jurisdiction and modes are introduced and conflicts identified. A priority list provides guidance for local-jurisdiction budget and program decisions, state departments of transportation (DOTs) and regional transit agency decisions on interjurisdictional projects, and federal agencies.

The material developed is formated by agencies according to their individual needs; submitted for jurisdictional approval; and routed to the MPO for integration into the overall transportation improvement program.

FLEXIBILITY IN THE PROCESS

This type of planning process has considerable flexibility in the "who," "how," and "when" of its operation. This flexibility must be recognized in the development of more formalized TSM procedures. The formal procedures, and accompanying improved methodologies, must be designed to create opportunities and to motivate the comprehensive exercise of the TSM process in a coordinated, intermodal manner. Three important characteristics lend the normative process the flexibility required by the nature of TSM.

First, the variety of actions falling under the TSM heading suggest that the planning cycle will differ depending on the nature of specific actions included. Little or no analysis and planning is required for "routine" TSM actions—simple and inexpensive actions whose impact is well understood and where repeated experience has shown such actions to be beneficial and effective. These are usually single-mode/single-jurisdiction actions. Such actions are often conceived and implemented within a very short time—days or weeks—because of their well-recognized characteristics and consequences. This group may comprise 70 to 80% of TSM actions. On the other hand, there are projects with unknown impacts, often multimodal with interjurisdictional scope or regional influence, that require special consideration. These projects, the other 20 to 30%, would likely be cycled through all the technical steps of Fig. 17-1 and may require the attention of a regional-level TSM team.

Second, the normative process cycles can and should be entered at a number of points. At least four events outside the format process might trigger a TSM project:

- Obviously deteriorating conditions requiring an early remedy.
- Imposition of a new local goal or a goal imposed by a higher jurisdiction or a change in political priorities.
- Carry-over projects not implemented from previous year evaluations.
- "Routine" actions, typically taken by local operations on a day-to-day basis.

These situations lead to the varying entry points identified by the arrows on the left-hand side of Fig. 17-1. Not every step of the technical process need be exercised each time the process is utilized. Further, the bypass loops on the right-hand side of the diagram attempt to show how steps might be skipped, depending upon the complexity of the project and the particular needs of the agency involved.

Third, not only are the technical steps in the TSM process likely to be used in different combinations, but the process itself is likely to be applied in different ways under various institutional arrangements. The political jurisdiction must now be accepted as the basic level at which the process is exercised, because they have the largest measure of budget control and operational authority over most of the physical components of TSM. The jurisdictional levels envisioned include cities, counties, special-purpose authorities, and districts of the state department of highways and public transportation. TSM programs developed at the subarea or corridor level by separate jurisdictional departments can be combined into a jurisdictional program and such programs or components thereof combined into regional programs. Capitalizing on the full breadth and depth of TSM will require an increased degree of cooperation among participating agencies and departments. The degree and nature of intermodal and interjurisdictional collaboration will depend on the size of the target area, the complexity of the problems being considered, and the customary method of operation for the agencies involved. However, since TSM planning is intended to be multimodal and areawide in scope, formalization of the TSM process—the development of methods to prepare and evaluate a merged intermodal program—is vital. In the future, jurisdictional distinctions may become blurred by the impact of regional authorities or by an increase in the share of budget moneys that might be allocated among modes or jurisdictions at the regional level.

TSM-RELATED PLANNING METHODOLOGIES

While the rationale for TSM as the primary focus of future transportation planning is compelling, efforts to understand, much less exploit, its full potential are just beginning. Institutional experience and previous habits with the components of TSM may tend to inhibit a comprehensive approach. The role of the MPO and other local institutional actors in developing a coordinated TSM program is unclear, although the potential is apparent.

The issues that have supported the logic of TSM may even require a major shift in the "model" of the planning process to incorporate increased bargaining among the institutions involved in implementation. This could result in formalizing a hybrid planning process at the metropolitan level, incorporating elements of both "top-down," systematic, goals-achieved-oriented planning and "bottoms-up," ad hoc, negotiation-based planning.

Regardless of the appropriate institutional context which may evolve, the technical problems remain. For each planning activity—goal formation, problem identification, formulation and evaluation of strategies, monitoring, and modification—there remain substantial gaps in methodologies and techniques. To the degree to which TSM planning in metropolitan areas is to achieve its full systemwide potential and be more than an uncoordinated" happening," these gaps must be filled.

PROBLEM DIAGNOSIS AND PROGRAM FORMATION

A unique aspect of TSM as a comprehensive program is its ability to specifically target a large number of distinct (and potentially conflicting) objectives or problems. This is a result of the disaggregate small-scale nature of most TSM actions and the many ways in which they can be combined. The possible range of program objectives for TSM strategies includes mobility, energy conservation, environmental and community preservation, and economic efficiency. These may be imposed by a higher level of government, adopted by local jurisdictions as part of a formal goal set, derived from the planner's knowledge of local political priorities, or based simply on a widespread view of local problems. Program formation requires an understanding of TSM actions and how they relate to various conditions perceived as objective-related "problems."

A systematic process must be developed for formulating TSM strategies in response to existing problems if TSM is to become an effective program in the hands of local engineers and planners. The broad range of problems and opportunities encompassed by the TSM concept suggests that no *single* method for identifying specific primary TSM actions is appropriate. Rather, a collection of techniques can be employed which differ in their rigor, cost, and data requirements. While many basic local transportation problems may be easy to identify, rigorous techniques are needed to locate those conditions amenable to TSM solutions on a regionwide basis.

OBJECTIVE-BASED APPROACH

The conventional goal-based "forward-seeking" approach—often characterized as an obsolete appendage to planning—can be valuable in ordering the priorities and trade-offs inherent in the broader purposes of TSM. This technique of problem identification requires a set of performance measures, either derived from local transportation and transportation-related goals and objectives or from performance standards required by an external (federal) program to meet transportation service and related nontransportation targets. The existence of a "problem" is detected when system performance measures indicate that some aspect of the system is "below standard." The system performance data is derived from ad hoc field measurements, continuing surveillance (or diagnostic simulation), and presented in terms of performance measures which reflect system conditions for comparison with the performance standard. TSM solutions are then designed to favorably impact the appropriate performance measures.

POINTS OF VIEW AND OBJECTIVE CONFLICTS

Since TSM actions will have varying incidences with respect to impacts, it is also not surprising that any single objective can have a substantially different interpretation —depending on point of view. Seldom will the objectives of all points of view be simultaneously favorably impacted. The determination of what constitutes a "good" versus "bad" strategy is becoming increasingly complex. Any transportation objective, if narrowly defined, may have counterproductive effects on other objectives. One example is the implicit conflict between the desire to improve flow (and thus increase mobility) without inducing new trips or increasing overall vehicle-miles of travel (with attendant negative environmental and energy consequences).

The broad range of potential objectives or problem areas constituting targets for TSM actions suggests that trade-offs will be implicit in any strategy—trade-offs among different types of transportation impacts, between transportation and nontransportation impacts, between users and nonusers, and among geographic areas or groups of persons affected. Therefore, within any given goal area, the objectives can usefully be broken down by point of view, indicating in the objectives statement the intended incidence-target group. Figure 17-2 indicates a characteristic set of goals, objectives, and points of view.

OBJECTIVES AND PERFORMANCE MEASURES

Any given strategy composed of one or more specific TSM action will have a differing impact on the performance measure which reflect the program objectives. Given a priori general knowledge about the impact of specific TSM actions on each performance measure, preliminary selections can be made of the most promising actions for subsequent evaluation—at the local level for comparing the relative effectiveness of various potential TSM strategies and at the regional level where TSM strategies can be composed into an overall program. More systematic impact estimation and evaluation can then follow for the nonroutine TSM actions.

While the conventional measures of transportation level of service will remain an important measure of program benefits, broader performance measures must be designed to evaluate the ability of TSM strategies to produce positive impacts on objectives other than transportation service. Safety, air pollution, energy use, environmental and community disruption, and impacts on the public and private economies

Key:
● = Direct beneficiary
○ = Indirect beneficiary
■ = Instrumental

GOALS	GOAL-DERIVED OBJECTIVE	System User	System Manager	System Abutters	Public (Community)	Other
Improve Personal Mobility	Reduce total travel time spent in satisfying travel demands	●	■			○
	Improve individual trip time reliability (work trips)	●	■			○
	Provide higher occupancy, vehicle opportunities alternatives to private auto	●	■	○		○
	Provide good quality transportation service to transit dependents	■			●	●
	Provide improved facilities for nonmotorized modes	●		●	●	●
	Be responsive to changing consumer needs	●				
Improve Public Safety and Health	Reduce occurrence of traffic accidents	●	■		○	
	Reduce personal injuries and deaths resulting from accidents	●	■		○	
	Reduce emotional stress encountered by highway users and nonusers	●	○		●	
	Reduce automotive emissions	○	○	●	●	●
Enhance Environmental and Community Quality	Reduce noise and vibration generated by transportation operation	■	●	●	●	
	Minimize ecological impacts of traffic	■		●	●	
	Complement long-range urban land-use goals	■		●	●	
	Minimize community disruption and relocation	■	●	●	○	
	Enhance the aesthetic quality of the urban environment	■	●	●	○	
Conserve Natural Resources	Reduce fuel consumed in satisfying travel demands	●	○	●	●	
Improve Economic Efficiency	Increase the person and goods movement capacity of existing streets and highways	○	■		●	
	Reduce the personal costs of satisfying urban travel demands	●	■		●	
	Reduce the total public costs of urban transportation	○	■		●	
	Provide economically efficient urban goods movement				■	●
	Reduce the economic damages resulting from traffic accidents	●	■		●	
	Reduce the cost of providing given levels of transportation service	●	■		●	
	Minimize adverse economic impacts caused by urban traffic	●	●		■	

POINTS OF VIEW

Figure 17-2 *Objectives and points of view* [*Source: Adapted from Donald G. Capelle, Frederick A. Wagner, and Stephen C. Lockwood, "Transportation Systems Management," AMV Tech Notes, 4, No. 2 (July 15, 1976).*]

may be relevant. A comprehensive but efficient set of objective- or problem-related performance measures must be developed so that the TSM action with the highest potential can be quickly identified for further evaluation.

Performance measures will play a critical role as measures of effectiveness in evaluation of TSM plans as well as in post-operation reconfiguration of strategies to improve their effectiveness. Indeed, usable performance measures will provide the basis for the development of a structured TSM information system on a continuing basis, which is the foundation on which an evolving program of TSM improvements must be built. In addition, considering the relatively crude state of knowledge about many TSM actions, it is especially important to develop continuous monitoring and surveillance of key performance measures to provide the feedback needed to increase program effectiveness and, simultaneously, advance the state of the art.

Relevance criteria. Performance measures must be carefully designed to provide data to determine strategy effectiveness across a broad range of objective-related categories. They must also be carefully targeted on specific traffic and travel behavior variables which are the best indicators of effects. To do so, they must be selected with both strategy dimensions (how strategies work) and objective indicators (what is affected) in mind. Good performance measures represent a compromise between these two concepts and must:

- Be defined as to target (type of traveler, trip, vehicle type, etc.).
- Be responsive to the incidence of impact, user and nonuser.
- Be characterized by geographic area of both application and influence.
- Be oriented to specific time periods and to specific finite lengths of time—these may vary and can include an all-day, peak-hour, weekly, or other basis.
- Be directly or indirectly related to the objective—performance measures must be indicative of the primary or secondary travel behavior effects which they are designed to induce.
- Be formulated at a proper level of detail for type of analysis being performed.

Technical feasibility criteria. In addition to criteria for evaluating the substantive relationship of performance measures to impacts and impacts to objectives, a set of technical feasibility criteria must also be used to ensure that performance measures are practically useful in both simulation and in the field. Feasible performance measures must:

- Be quantifiable.
- Be measurable in simulation and in the field.
- Be based on sensitive indicators.
- Be statistically efficient.
- Avoid redundancy.

Effectiveness in respect to demand. No set of performance measures can be properly understood unless they are accompanied by a fundamental measure of travel demand. In the case of personal travel, demand is probably best measured as person-miles of travel within given time and space boundaries. Even if the main emphasis of TSM is to maximize effectiveness for a *given* set of person trip origins and destinations (i.e., fixed person-miles of travel demand), it is essential to formulate an evaluation framework in which demand can be different for two or more data sets being compared. This is essential because due to external forces, travel demand changes over time and space and it is sensitive to improvements or degradations in system supply.

Performance measures for mobility user costs, safety. Performance measures must be developed for each objective of interest. A partial listing of typical objectives and examples of associated performance measures are given in Table 17-1. The few example measures shown give an indication of the definitional character of the measures.

TABLE 17-1
Example Objectives and Performance Measures

Example TSM Objective	Example Performance Measures
Improve level of service of urban travel	• Total travel time or delay in person-hours • Weighted average speed for person travel
Provide attractive alternatives to driving private autos	• Mode split percentages • Percentage of population within x miles (walking distance) of scheduled transit service at home and at work • Average occupancy per vehicle-trip
Provide good quality, affordable transportation services to the elderly, handicapped, poor, and very young	• Percentage of special groups population to whom any specialized transportation services are available • Percentage of special groups disposable income expended on transportation
Improve facilities for nonmotorized travel modes (pedestrian, bicycle)	• Total miles of improved bicycle or pedestrian pathways • Total person-miles of travel by pedestrians or bicyclists
Reduce the occurrence of traffic accidents	• Total number of motor vehicle accidents • Number of accidents per million vehicle-miles
Reduce automotive emissions and impacts	• Grams of carbon monoxide, hydrocarbons, and nitrogen oxides emitted • Grams of emittants per person-mile
Reduce noise impacts	• Noise levels in decibels at different distances from transportation facilities • Percentage of residents subjected to noise levels exceeding specified tolerance limits
Reduce fuel consumed in satisfying urban travel	• Gallons of gasoline and diesel fuel consumed • Average fuel economy in person-miles per gallon
Reduce public cost of urban transportation systems	• Net annual cost of ownership and operation of transportation facilities by mode (total cost less direct fares, toll revenues, and parking charges) • Net annual cost per capita for urban area

Performance measures for transportation-related impacts. The available methods for measuring environmental and energy factors associated with traffic characteristics can be broken down into the two broad categories of direct and indirect methods. Direct methods refer to those requiring field measurement by using instrument or other devices, data analysis, and interpretation of measurement results. However, the general approach taken in most studies of transportation-related impacts is to use the indirect methods. This is done by determining the fundamental traffic flow characteristic impacts, such as traffic volumes, modal composition, and travel times directly and then computing other impacts indirectly from the traffic data by using statistical estimating relationships, computer simulation models, nomographs, table look-ups, and so on. Such an approach appears to be a valid way to estimate performance measures indicative of impacts such as emissions, energy consumption, and noise.

RELIANCE ON KNOWLEDGE OF ROUTINE ACTIONS

Since the described methodology involves system performance data (including possible field measurements) and systematic comparison with standards, it is not appropriate for relatively simple and extremely inexpensive TSM actions. In many cases, such as minor operational changes where little capital investment is involved, experiments can be based on a less rigorous definition of problems.

Simple problem inventories can be made based on the existing technical knowledge. Certain routine actions are already typically undertaken by action agencies without study. Examples include known areas of arterial friction suggesting new parking regulations, bus-loading problems suggesting service changes, and management adjustments to improve efficiency and marketing. Other TSM actions can be based on existing successful examples without carrying out any problem analysis. Innovative services and fare adjustments are examples.

Further TSM experience will support the development of warrants for generic circumstances. Warrants indicating the most promising approaches can simplify program development and still permit the modification of actions to local circumstances.

IMPACT-BASED PROGRAM DEFINITION

For an efficient TSM program definition, the characteristics of a broad range of potential actions must be understood before they can be composed into strategies to meet local objectives and solve local problems. While several lists of TSM strategies have been compiled, none represent a systematic functional classification of the complete range of relevant traffic operations and control, transit operations, and transportation management actions. Table 17-2 illustrates TSM actions grouped into strategy categories under six basic classes of strategy:

- Mandatory usage controls.
- User information/assistance.
- Economic controls (pricing).
- Transit operations modifications.
- Minor supply additions.
- Demand modification.

TABLE 17-2
Classification of Strategy Categories and Action Elements

	Category	Action Element
Mandatory usage controls	Crossing control	Bus priority signal systems Signal timing optimization Signal installation or removal Pedestrian grade-separation provisions Computerized signal control systems
	Entry control	One-way streets Right-turn-on-red Reversible streets Turning-movement restrictions Area restrictions (ARZs) Ramp metering Preferential entrance ramps Entrance-ramp closures Through-traffic restrictions on residential streets
	Lane usage control	Reversible lanes Preferential lanes for high-occupancy vehicles Lane-use/turning-movement restrictions Intersection channelization Bicycle lanes
	Curb control	Parking restrictions Bus-stop relocations Loading zones establishment Sidewalk widening Truck delivery restrictions
	Speed control	Speed limits (maximum/minimum)
	Parking control	Preferential parking for high-occupancy vehicles Parking duration restrictions More stringent enforcement of parking controls
User information/assistance	Education	Broadening of driver education to "transportation education"
	Pre-trip assistance	Pre-trip traffice condition information Ridesharing matching information Truck routing and scheduling optimization Transit route/schedule information Paratransit services information
	En route assistance	System condition broadcasts Traffic-flow condition signs Progression speed advisory signs Route advisory signs Incident detection and management Motorist aid
Pricing	Road pricing	Facility tolls Area tolls or licenses Vehicle ownership taxation Vehicle usage taxation (fuel or mileage) Congestion pricing Differential tolls
	Parking pricing	Parking duration pricing Elimination of parking subsidies Differential parking pricing for high-occupancy vehicles Parking taxes
	Transit/paratransit pricing	General fare reduction Peak-period/midday fare differentials Free transit Paratransit subsidies Elderly and youth fares Commuter farebook discounts

TABLE 17-2 continued

Category	Action Element
Transit operating modification	
Operational improvements	Bus route modifications Bus schedule modifications Increased passenger loading efficiency Simplified fare collection Fare collection elimination Substitution of demand-responsive service in place of fixed-route/ fixed-schedule service in selected time periods
Mode transfer	Bus-stop relocating Park-and-ride facilities Submodal integration Station/stop amenity improvements Feeder/distribution improvements Simplified transfers
Management efficiency	Technical cooperation (traffic/transit) Marketing improvements Programming improvements Accounting improvements Maintenance improvements Monitoring and surveillance Transit automated vehicle identification Improved security
Supply Augmentation	
Transit	Shuttle bus service Express bus service Subscription bus service
Street/highway	Selective street and intersection widening New lanes for high-occupancy vehicles Special freeway ramp additions Bus-loading bays Freeway bus stops (bus parks)
Paratransit operation	Ridesharing incentives Ridesharing brokerage Taxi deregulation/rule changes Jitney operation Demand-responsive transit Vanpool programs (employer)
Nonmotorized	Pedestrian malls Bicycle paths Sidewalk widening
Parking	Parking supply reduction or restraint CBD fringe parking Suburban park-and-ride facilities
Goods	Terminal consolidation Increase in truck lot sizes Off-street loading facilities

TABLE 17-2 continued

	Category	Action Element
Demand modification	Modification of time distribution of demand	Staggered hours Flextime Shortened workweek Expanded evening hours for shopping and service establishments Expanded weekend opening of shopping and service establishments

	Modification of frequency of demand	Expansion of home delivery of goods/services
		Substitution of communications for transportation
		   Written communications (e.g., bank by mail)
		   Telecommunications

	Modification of spatial location	Land-use change

Source: Adapted from Donald G. Capelle, Frederick A. Wagner, and Stephen C. Lockwood, "Transportation Systems Management," *AMV Tech Notes,* 4, no. 2 (July 15, 1976), 4.

Travel behavior and response time. TSM focuses attention on the potential inherent in the complete range of behavior modification, ranging far beyond the typical domains of the traffic engineer and transit operator. The enlarged palette of TSM includes actions to both improve supply and to manage demand. The fundamental management concepts can be stated in terms of the basic traffic/travel behavior targets:

- Improve traffic flow characteristics.
- Redistribute traffic spatially (path).
- Redistribute traffic temporally (timing).
- Redistribute traffic modally (mode choice).
- Modify trip distribution/length.
- Modify trip frequency (total demand).

Target. Each TSM action can be developed to affect specific people and goods who make up system users. These include:

- Auto drivers.
- Auto passengers.
- Transit passengers.
- Pedestrians.
- Bicycle riders.
- Goods movement (trucks).

Many strategies affect more than one mode, but large numbers of concepts can be focused on high-occupancy vehicles or other specific groups.

Other TSM action characteristics which will be relevant in strategy composition include:

- Scale of application.
- Zone of influence.
- Implementation difficulty.
- Response time.

Relative effectiveness. Which TSM action should be selected for program formulation will depend, in large measure, on preliminary estimates of their relative effectiveness prior to actual evaluations.

For many potential TSM actions, the potential range of impacts with respect to any given measure of effectiveness can be judged a priori by investigating dimensions of the strategy as revealed in taxonomies about the scale and timing of impacts or through knowledge of hypothesized or known impact mechanisms. Matrices can be used to determine the relation of certain actions to performance measures of interest as a crude first cut. The separation of preliminary proposals into "routine" versus "special" actions will permit concentration on the latter.

STRATEGY DEVELOPMENT—COMBINING ACTIONS

The full range of TSM tools including information, restraints, and demand management must be considered in developing comprehensive strategies. The goal of making more efficient use of the existing urban transportation system will, therefore, require drawing together the fragmented components of traffic engineering, transit operations, and overall transportation management. Within such a framework, the narrow focus of traditional traffic engineering or transit operations is no longer appropriate.

To exploit the full potential of TSM, individual actions must be combined into program packages. With an understanding of the characteristics of potential TSM action elements and a knowledge of the priority objectives and problem areas, the potential of combinations can be investigated. The combinatory process requires knowledge of their interactions as well as their independent impacts. A wide range of interrelationships can be shown, including synergistic, independent, overlapping, equivalent, and counterproductive.

Other rules of action combination useful in strategy making include:

1. *Repetition of successful (or promising) actions on a regionwide basis.* Many of the smaller scale TSM actions can have a maximum effect if they are applied in many similar locations. Signalization and parking strategies are typical examples.

2. *Combinations of mutually supporting TSM actions.* To be fully effective, some TSM actions require other related and coordinated actions. Area restrictions or parking programs may require compensating transit service. Curb control measures may require a special goods delivery program. Dynamic routing requires supporting information systems. Pooling programs may benefit from priority treatment.

3. *Combinations to offset negative impact.* Certain TSM actions may have a positive impact on one group or area and a negative impact on another without compensating actions. For example, a TSM program diverting traffic from residential streets onto an arterial system may require a pedestrian safety program on the arterial system to compensate for increased traffic.

STRATEGY COMPREHENSIVENESS

The enormous flexibility implied by the range of potential tools which have been characterized highlights the importance of a creative approach to selecting and combining TSM actions into an overall program. This potential suggests the following guides toward comprehensiveness:

- Focus on people and goods—not vehicles.
- Determine primary and secondary impacts.
- Review options for all modes.
- Use demand as well as supply management.
- Include service and infrastructure strategies as well as facility-oriented strategies.
- Review potential for upgrading existing TSM actions.
- Employ preferential treatment approach.
- Use real-time supply modifications.
- Employ incentives and disincentives.
- Form spatial hierarchies of action.
- Integrate long- and short-range actions.

INSTITUTIONAL CONSTRAINTS

Annual TSM program development must necessarily consider those strategies and projects which appear to be most meritorious on objective-fulfillment grounds within real-world limitations. These may include:

1. *Funding constraints.* The absolute limits on funds available will sometimes limit TSM strategy selection. Just as often, the timing of funds coming from different jurisdictions or functional agencies will delay implementation. Similarly, administration of funding from various senior government (including the federal government) categorical grant and formula assistance programs will sometimes prohibit or delay implementation.

2. *Manpower restraints.* The nature of certain TSM strategies is that they often require a high level of planning and design activity compared to their total cost.

This means that some of the more complex projects may often have to be delayed in order to provide the necessary planning and design input. Similar limitations may be observed with respect to manpower needed for public relations, enforcement, and so on.

3. *Institutional approval and coordination.* The more complex TSM strategies often involve numerous local and state government agencies. Such strategies are often necessarily costly in terms of the efforts and time required for approval and coordination.

IMPACT ESTIMATION AND EVALUATION

The complexity of the challenge facing TSM arises out of the large number of potential strategies and the substantial gaps in the state-of-the-art knowledge about their characteristics and effectiveness with respect to a broadened range of goals. Cost-effective application depends on an increased understanding of the relative impacts of various strategies in different combinations in terms of a sensitive (and efficient) number of performance measures. The available knowledge about the relative effectiveness of various TSM actions varies widely.

Program design requires some estimate of likely impacts. However, the level of rigor required in evaluation must be appropriate to the cost of the action and the scale of expected impacts. The need for systematic evaluation will be much less for cheaper strategies for which the cost of not knowing is less than the cost of finding out. For the more simple TSM actions, analytical procedures are being developed to permit either manual or automated determination of the impacts of specific TSM actions.[4]

Such procedures, in turn, specify methods to be followed to estimate impacts using the appropriate tables, formulas, graphs, rules of thumbs, etc., or existing computer-based routines to predict the magnitude and type of impact on each selected performance measure. These techniques can produce useful order-of-magnitude impacts on performance measures in the context of a reasonable system data base. Combined with cost estimates, this approach yields cost-effectiveness measures which can be used to evaluate various alternative TSM actions. The choice between manual and automated procedure will depend on time and cost considerations as well as the accuracy desired. The development and modification of warrants for specific TSM actions and the design of handbooks will substantially simplify the formation, evaluation, and implementation of comprehensive TSM programs.

SIMULATION

In cases where a proposed TSM strategy is costly, complex in application (such as strategy combinations), pervasive in expected impact (regional and/or multimodal), or

---

[4]ALAN M. VOORHEES & ASSOCIATES, INC., *A Handbook for Transportation System Management Planning: An Analytical Approach to the Development and Evaluation of Transit-Related TSM Projects and Alternatives,* 2 vols., prepared for the North Central Texas Council of Governments (draft, August 1977).

simply not well understood, more rigorous analysis, including systematic impact prediction and alternatives analysis, will be useful. In larger cities and regions where there are significant potentials for the complete range of TSM strategies, considerable economies can be achieved through evaluation and screening of strategies via computer-based simulation prior to implementation.

Any impact prediction process must replicate, as closely as possible, the actual impact of the strategy on system performance and travel behavior. Travel paths, time of day, mode, and traffic flow characteristics are the primary travel behavior attributes that are affected in the short term by TSM actions. Trip distribution and frequency are attributes that will be impacted as TSM actions are implemented on a sustained basis. Given that these six aspects of travel will be modified by TSM strategies and simulation, models used to produce quantitative performance measures values must be structured to simulate these travel behavioral characteristics.

In assembling a model set from existing tools to estimate the impact of TSM strategies, it is useful to note that current practice tends to treat these travel characteristics by different concepts. Trip frequency, destination, mode, and, in part, time-of-day choices are dealt with in the generic group *travel demand models*. Path and flow are considered from a different viewpoint and fall into a generic grouping of *traffic flow and path models*. Full simulation requirements can be met by combining travel demand and traffic flow models which have the appropriate characteristics into a framework that can flexibly respond to various TSM strategy impacts. These models and networks must be carefully interfaced to simulate the results in time and space of various strategy combinations so that derived measures of effectiveness will provide a meaningful evaluation of strategy impacts for each major objective.

Since transportation is an equilibrium process, the feedback between supply and demand over the network must also be accommodated in the simulation. A particular TSM policy may cause link volume changes, which in turn impact travel conditions and consequently demand itself. Depending on the TSM strategy to be tested, flow and demand models may be used separately or in combination.

TSM INFORMATION SYSTEM

As indicated in the introduction, an essential element of a comprehensive TSM program is its continuing, iterative, flexible, incremental, modifiable character. These characteristics depend heavily on information—information on TSM strategy impacts as a basis for program formation and later modification and information on TSM action effectiveness as a basis for state-of-the-art development. The need for a systematic TSM information system is especially important given the marginal nature of many TSM impacts and their synergistic character.

The development of a TSM information system as an integral part of the TSM planning process deserves special attention. In contrast to traditional transportation planning, which places a premium on one-time impact prediction for design, TSM planning places a premium on continuous impact monitoring for both design and operation. Data requirements for field monitoring must be identified and collection feasibility and cost determined so that trade-offs between the sensitivity of performance measures and their cost and accuracy can be assessed. The data collection methodologies must be subjected to real-world tests in order to verify analytic approaches and revise performance measures as necessary.

Areawide data collection methodology. Only a few of the TSM strategies need to be applied in a total metropolitan context (e.g., vehicle and gas taxes, transit fare changes, public information). Such areawide-type actions tend to be ones that are aimed at changing total vehicular travel demand. These can best be evaluated using behavioral travel demand forecasting models as previously discussed, rather than measuring system performance in the field.

Several approaches to *direct* areawide measurement can also be considered. Most of these involve random or quasi-random selection of locations or entities to survey repeatedly:

- Random survey links.
- Random test sections.
- Instrumentation in private cars.
- Randomly selected household surveys.
- Randomly selected parking facilities surveys.

Subarea or corridor data collection methodology. Most TSM strategies are currently planned and implemented for a subarea, corridor, or subcomponents thereof rather than for a total urban area. Subarea or corridor TSM evaluations will often necessitate direct measurements of changes in traffic-flow quality on given paths, changes in distribution of demand on paths and time of day, and changes in mode. More detailed data will be needed to evaluate all these elements of performance.

Solutions to problems of maintaining a continuing TSM information system are still in their infancy. There are a large number of manual and automated techniques available with various practical advantages and disadvantages. Table 17-3 characterizes alternative techniques for collecting level-of-service data.

In addition to the practical aspects of surveillance, however, there are theoretical issues in developing a sampling scheme. Location issues related to TSM action, area of application, and zone of influence, must be considered. After these considerations, the important question of how many locations to sample must be faced. The sample size-precision interrelationship can be estimated theoretically if reasonably valid assumptions can be made about the underlying distribution of the traffic variables of interest across all locations. Similarly, time boundaries can be established by considering factors such as response time; seasonal variations; whether general levels of areawide transportation system effectiveness are of concern or impacts of specific TSM actions are being measured; and whether traffic only during certain hours of the day is of interest (e.g., peak hours) or if consideration should be given to total daily travel for all trip purposes. After these general time boundaries have been defined, the alternative sampling plans within these boundaries can be defined.

TABLE 17-3
Data Collection Techniques

Technique	Advantages	Disadvantages	Comments
Manual data collection	• Does not require purchase of sophisticated hardware. • All traffic engineering organizations are familiar with the technique.	• Expensive. • Difficult to cover large area accurately. • Only restricted set of variables can be measured. • Not practically used over long time period.	
Floating car	• Better coverage than manual techniques. • Can measure flow, fuel consumption, and emissions with proper instrumentation. • Hardware is readily adaptable to this technique.	• Small sample size. • Expensive. • Not practical for long time period.	
Fixed locations for automated sensors	• Data can easily be acquired and processed. • Large sample size and good wide-area coverage possible. • Technology is within the state of the art. • Simultaneous measurements can be made over entire area of interest.	• Initial installation expensive. • Cannot readily measure fuel consumption.	• Best suited to cities using computer-control signal system. • EPA research for emissions measurements has produced devices applicable to this technique.
Rooftop and aerial photography	• Wide-area coverage possible. • Simultaneous measurements over the entire area possible. • Large spatial sample sizes possible.	• Extremely expensive. • Only limited temporal samples are possible. • Only useful for measuring traffice flow variables.	• Experiments with automated processing of this data have not been successful.
Instrumentation of private vehicles	• Large sample sizes in time and space possible. • All variables can be measured. • Automated processing of data is possible.	• Instrumentation is expensive. • Location-specific data cannot be obtained. • Administration of experiment could be complex.	• OST planning development of device to perform this function.

TABLE 17-3 continued

Technique	Advantages	Disadvantages	Comments
Portable automatic sensors	• Data easily acquired. • Large-scale sample size; lane-specific counts, speed, composition. • State-of-the-art equipment.	• Large-scale manual or automated data reduction. • Possible software needs. • Limited spatial distribution.	• Simple counts or TDC equipment (cassettes).
TV surveillance	• Wide range of MOEs. • Relatively inexpensive.	• Poor nighttime resolution. • Manual data reduction.	• Reusable video tapes. • Data reduction in parallel.
Data logging	• Wide-area coverage. • May be used with floating car.	• Expensive. • Manual data reduction.	• Permanent record.

In some larger cities, automated capabilities for surveillance and control systems already exist and could be used to test new and additional TSM measures in prototype application. A basic deficiency in all these existing networks is that performance measures have been stated in *vehicle* units rather than in *person* units or some other vehicle "value" units. For the near term, however, reliance on manual observation of bus travel times, loads, schedule adherence, and so on, will continue.

EVALUATION

The essence of evaluation is the comparison of objective-related costs and impacts, positive and negative, of each potential TSM alternative in a way which illustrates significant differences and similarities. The mix of impacts will vary by the alternatives and affect different groups (users and nonusers) and areas, leaving some losers and others gainers.

During evaluation, the individual estimates of impact are compared and, if necessary, combined. In many cases it would be expected that the impact generated by one mode on another will necessitate a recycling back to impact estimation to revise estimates. Also, impacts generated by regional projects would be introduced into the local assessment.

Relative effectiveness for each proposed TSM action would be calculated as the percentage point change that an estimated impact could cause in existing performance, or as a ratio of one impact to others in the same class, or by some other method of estimation. In this way, impact could be reduced to a dimensionless figure of merit. This can be done on a regional or local jurisdiction basis.

The calculated effectiveness would be related to cost. A weighting factor could be introduced at this point in order to establish the relative importance of different impacts since some impacts will undoubtedly be considered more important than others by different individuals or groups. This factor (one for each impact) could be arbitrarily selected or could reflect results of policy-maker concerns.

When the list of all TSM projects in the region is put in order, using regionally based cost effectiveness, a type of priority list is produced independent of mode or location. Similarly, a cost-effectiveness listing under jurisdictional effectiveness measures (or optionally a simple abstract of the regional listing) would produce a priority ranking list for the use of the local agencies. The cost-effectiveness ranking is used (with other input, if desired) to select from among alternatives. This selection can be from among single-mode alternative actions (perhaps ranked only within the single-mode system), or from among intermodal trade-off alternatives (ranked by cost effectiveness in the total, multimodal system), or from among choices of independent projects (different modes in different locations), where such projects are competing for the same funds. This latter choice probably could be based on regionally calculated cost effectiveness (among other factors).

The relationship between the selected TSM actions and capital projects can be investigated through time and location comparisons. This step rechecks the influence of capital projects that will either substitute for or terminate TSM actions. Also, cases where TSM actions can lead to a postponement of capital projects would be identified. The cutoff point on the lists of priorities is determined by using fund availability estimates for jurisdiction and mode.

THE NEED FOR TRADE-OFFS

For some TSM projects and in some contexts, comparative evaluation can be a relatively simple process. As long as one TSM alternative action dominates others across all measures of effectiveness, the decision as to "best" is obvious—it is the alternative with more service and benefits and less negative impact for a given investment. Very often, however, a more costly alternative has both more positive impacts and more negative impacts than other cheaper alternatives; this is further complicated when certain types of impacts occur in one alternative but not in another. Then dominance of one alternative is not at all clear and selection of a "best" alternative depends on the relative importance given by the evaluator to one impact category versus another. Determining relative importance becomes particularly problematic when both monetary and nonquantifiable issues are involved.

Since the relative importance of impact categories and groups depends on values, such evaluation is ultimately a political act; that is, selection of a "best" alternative depends on the evaluator's view of the relative importance of different cost and impact categories and his/her concept of an "equitable" distribution of impacts in society.

Evaluating becomes more complex when such trade-offs are implicit in selecting a "best" alternative. Many otherwise useful evaluation techniques lose their utility. At the regional level, the transit and highway technical committees which exist in most MPOs could provide the principal forum for the evaluation of alternatives.

SUMMARY

The improvement of the state of the art in TSM planning will be gradual—as has been the development of the "modal" long-range planning process. To improve the technical capability to carry out continuing TSM planning, several state-of-the-art improvements are needed. First, more efficient use of the existing urban transportation system implies combinations of traffic engineering, transit operations, and transportation management into TSM strategies; the narrow focus of traditional traffic engineering/transit operations is no longer appropriate. A comprehensive and systematic strategy must focus on moving people and goods—not just vehicles. Research and field experience is needed to characterize the broad range of possible TSM strategies and combinations in the sense of both transportation as well as nontransportation objectives.

Second, hypotheses about the impact of combined TSM strategies must be carefully refined through actual application and analysis so that resources can be directed toward those actions which demonstrate substantial effectiveness with respect to transportation and related objectives. While traffic flow will remain an important measure of mobility, a comprehensive but efficient set of performance measures must be designed to evaluate the ability of TSM strategies to produce positive benefits in the areas of safety, air pollution, energy use, environmental and community disruption, and the public and private economies.

Third, combined strategies and performance measures must be tested in demonstration contexts so that reliable and valid performance data are produced and the most promising strategies are identified for use at the local level. Cost-effective application depends on an increased understanding of the relative impacts of various strategies in different combinations in terms of a sensitive (and efficient) number of measures of effectiveness. For simple TSM actions, analysis of current experience for its transferability and the development of generalized warrants for TSM strategy application may be possible. In the case of more complex strategies, considerable economies may be achieved through evaluation and screening via simulation prior to implementation. A very wide range of methods and techniques, both computer-assisted and non-computer-based, currently exist which appear to be applicable to TSM planning activities. This is so because the concept of TSM itself is so broad, cutting across many specialized transportation disciplines, including transportation planning, transit operations, traffic engineering, transport service regulation, finance and pricing policy, and so forth. The methods and techniques in use and under development by all these types of specialists, individually, are considered pertinent to the diverse aspects of TSM planning. One of the challenges of TSM planning is to achieve cross fertilization among the various speciality disciplines, and integration of their analytical techniques to more effectively meet the practical requirements of the TSM planning process.

Fourth, research findings on both relative strategy effectiveness and performance measures' robustness must be continually subjected to the test of transferability to real-world conditions, with appropriate attention to data collection requirements, strategy feasibility, and local capabilities. Results of this process can then be translated into usable guidelines for local planners, operators, and engineers as well as into an agenda for continuing research and development activities.

The transition from the preoccupation with constuction to systems management may be one of such fundamental proportions that it will not take place quickly. It may take a decade or more, with the shift being more evolutional than revolutionary. The coordination of many small-scale actions toward objectives agreed upon in a multi-institutional context poses a far greater challenge than did the implementation of large-scale capital-intensive projects. But this is the challenge of the future of transportation planning.

SELECTED BIBLIOGRAPHY

Many citations are no longer available from their original source. These citations are often available from the National Technical Information Service, U.S. Department of Commerce, 5285 Port Royal Road, Springfield, Va. 22161. We have verified the order numbers for many of these citations, and they are found at the end of the citation. Prices are available through NTIS at the address above.

HEATON, CARLA, CHESTER MCCALL, AND ROBERT WAKSMAN, *Evaluation Guidelines for Service and Methods Demonstration Projects*, prepared for UMTA by the Transportation Systems Center and CACI, Inc. Cambridge, Mass.: Transportation Systems Center, February 1976. Now available as PB 251 891.

JHK & ASSOCIATES, *A Selected Bibliography and Reference Document in Transportation System Management*, prepared for FHWA (draft, May 1977).

KENDALL, DONALD, AND OTHERS, *Service and Methods Demonstration Program Annual Report*, prepared for UMTA. Cambridge, Mass.: Transportation Systems Center, April 1977.

KEYANI, BARBARA IBARRA, AND EVELYN S. PUTNAM, *Transportation System Management: State of the Art*, February 1977, prepared for UMTA by INTERPLAN Corporation. Washington, D.C.: U.S. Government Printing Office, n.d.—report date September 1976. Now available as PB 266 953.

ORAM, RICHARD L., *Transportation System Management: (A) Bibliography of Technical Reports*, prepared for UMTA and FHWA by UMTA. Washington, D.C.: Urban Mass Transportation Administration, May 1976. Now available as PB 257 273.

PRATT, R. H. ASSOCIATES, INC., *Low Cost Urban Transportation Alternatives: A Study of Ways to Increase the Effectiveness of Existing Transportation Facilities, Vol. I: Results of a Survey and Analysis of Twenty-One Low Cost Techniques, Vol. II: Results of Case Studies and Analysis of Busway Applications in the United States*, and *Executive Summary*, prepared for U.S. DOT, Office of Urban Transportation Systems. Kensington, Md.: R. H. Pratt Associates, Inc., January 1973. Now available as PB 223 197, 223 922, and 223 926.

REMAK, ROBERTA, AND SANDRA ROSENBLOOM, *Peak-Period Traffic Congestion: Options for Current Programs*, NCHRP Report 169. Washington, D.C.: Transportation Research Board, 1976.

SLAVIN, H., D. KENDALL, AND C. HEATON, *Service and Methods Demonstration Program Annual Report—Executive Summary*, prepared for UMTA. Cambridge, Mass.: Transportation Systems Center, April 1977.

TRANSPORTATION RESEARCH BOARD, *Better Use of Existing Transportation Facilities*, Special Report 153. Washington, D.C.: Transportation Research Board, 1975.

———, *Transportation System Management*, Special Report 172. Washington, D.C.: Transportation Research Board, 1977.

TRANSPORTATION SYSTEMS CENTER, *Priority Techniques for High Occupancy Vehicles: State-of-the-Art Overview*, November 1975, Technology Sharing, prepared for U.S. DOT Office of the Secretary, UMTA, and FHWA. Washington, D.C.: U.S. Government Printing Office, 1975.

URBAN MASS TRANSPORTATION ADMINISTRATION, *A Directory of Research Development and Demonstration Projects (Innovation in Public Transportation)*, Fiscal Year 1975. Washington, D.C.: U.S. Government Printing Office, 1976. Now available as PB 213 228.

———, AND FEDERAL HIGHWAY ADMINISTRATION, "Transportation System Management: Supplementary Information on Development and Implementation of TSM Plans" (unpublished paper, December 1975).

VOORHEES, ALAN M. & ASSOCIATES, INC., *A Handbook for Transportation System Management Planning: An Analytical Approach to the Development and Evaluation of Transit-Related TSM Projects and Alternatives*, 2 vols., prepared for the North Central Texas Council of Governments (draft, August 1977).

Also see the bibliographies of Chapters 7, 8, 9, 10, 32, and 33.

Chapter 18

RURAL PUBLIC TRANSPORTATION

ROBERT JAY POPPER,* *Department of Civil Engineering,*
Virginia Polytechnic Institute and State University, and
JOHN W. DICKEY, *Environmental and Urban Studies,*
Virginia Polytechnic Institute and State University

There has been a recent flurry of interest in the development and implementation of public transportation systems in rural environments. The interest has been stimulated in part by the current availability of federal funds to support such services, and also by the recognition of the severe mobility deficiencies commonly found in rural areas. The typical scenario in a rural county is one of a geographically scattered population which desires to travel to a limited number of destinations, usually in a nearby town or the county seat. Trip lengths are longer than those provided by urban transit systems and population densities are generally not sufficient to support conventional fixed-route services. In addition, rural road networks may not be highly connective, resulting in circuitous and costly transportation service.

The needs and alternative strategies for solving the transportation problems of the more than 54 million rural residents have been analyzed in numerous state and federally supported studies. These studies have illustrated what must be considered the basic paradox of rural public transportation. The dilemma is that by any of several analysis methods, the need for rural public transportation appears to be self-evident, if not critical. However, the actual economic demand is low, and there appears little chance of maintaining self-supporting rural public transportation systems. This position is concisely stated as a warning to rural transit planners in a recent federal publication providing guidelines for system operation and management.

> [A] planner should begin by recognizing one fundamental reality; the demand for rural
> transit service is very low. Regardless of how much hardship may be created by the lack of

---

*Deceased April 1978.

such service, there are few people, especially the potential riders, who are willing and able to pay for it.[1]

Perhaps, a corollary to this warning should also be issued. While the need for public passenger transportation may be clearly established, it should not be assumed that there are not any existing resources within the community that could be used for providing rural transportation. The school bus system is an example of one of the most widespread forms of such potential transportation. In addition, many rural areas are served by taxi companies and, in a few cases, by actual mass transit systems (particularly in areas close to larger cities or sources of employment). Nor has funding necessarily been lacking. In Virginia, for instance, approximately $33 million was spent in 1972 for rural transportation by various service agencies, although 93% of this was for school busing.[2] One must question, then, the sudden interest in rural transportation problems. How crucial are the needs?

DEFINING AND ESTIMATING RURAL TRAVEL NEEDS

It is extremely difficult to provide complete answers to the question of the magnitude of rural public transportation needs. Nonetheless, it is not difficult to establish the critical need for adequate transportation services to rural residents. The energy crisis and recent inflation have both focused attention on the singular dependence of the rural population on the automobile. Few economical alternatives to private automobile travel exist. Particularly acute problems face the transportation disadvantaged sector of the population, including the elderly, handicapped, youth, and those limited by single auto ownership. Difficulties are also particularly evident for those elderly and poor who desire to travel to points of human services delivery in nearby town centers.

On a national scale, data from the Nationwide Personal Transportation Survey (conducted by the Bureau of the Census for the Federal Highway Administration, 1969–1970) help to illustrate the magnitude of rural travel problems and needs.[3] The data confirm that those living in unincorporated areas travel more frequently and generally take longer trips than average. Public transportation is used for work trips by only 2.6% of the people in unincorporated areas, and 3.1% of those in towns with less than 5000 population. In addition, it can be seen in Table 18-1 that only 12.4% of all households in unincorporated areas do not own cars (mostly the poor and elderly).

While these data are only nationwide averages, they suggest some definite trends in rural travel. For one, there is an overwhelming reliance on automobile travel.

---

[1]U.S. DEPARTMENT OF TRANSPORTATION, OFFICE OF POLICY AND PLANS DEVELOPMENT, *Rural Transit Operations and Management* (Washington, D.C.: U.S. Department of Transportation, n.d.), p. 3.

[2]JOHN W. DICKEY, *Rural Public Transportation Needs and Recommendations* (Blacksburg, Va.: Virginia Polytechnic Institute and State University, Center for Urban and Regional Studies, November 1973), p. 38.

[3]Ibid., pp. 8–22.

TABLE 18-1
Percent of Households by Automobile Ownership and Place of Residence

Number of Automobiles Owned	Unincorporated Areas	Incorporated Place, Population						All Incorporated Places	All Areas and Places
		Less than 5000	5000–24,999	25,000–49,999	50,000–99,999	100,000–999,999	1,000,000 and over		
One car	52.8	48.4	45.9	49.8	46.8	47.5	40.8	46.4	48.4
Two cars	29.5	29.3	30.4	30.1	27.9	22.6	10.5	25.0	26.4
Three or more cars	5.3	4.4	6.5	6.2	5.5	2.9	1.1	4.3	4.6
Total with cars	87.6	82.1	82.8	86.1	80.2	73.0	52.4	75.7	79.4
Having no cars	12.4	17.9	17.2	13.9	19.8	27.0	47.6	24.3	20.6
Total	100.0	100.0	100.0	100.0	100.0	100.0	100.0	100.0	100.0
Number of household (000)	19,116	6142	10,421	4124	4124	11,661	6,031	43,388	62,504

Source: Data based on unpublished Table H-18 from the Nationwide Personal Transportation Survey conducted by the Bureau of the Census for the FHWA, 1969-1970.

Second, those rural households in reasonably stable and comfortable financial positions are willing to drive more often and longer. These households may not perceive any pressing travel needs or problems. Third, the small fraction of those rural families who are "transportation disadvantaged" have urgent travel needs. Thus, in many cases the problem breaks down to one of whether or not a privileged majority is willing to subsidize the transportation costs for a dependent minority.

Since rural transportation problems and needs are so closely correlated with auto availability, several analysts have measured needs in terms of automobile accessibility. In a report to the U.S. Senate, Ira Kaye suggested that "transportation-deprived" households are those which do not own an automobile and "transportation-handicapped" households are those which own no more than one automobile.[4] The latter definition recognizes the fact that the breadwinner is expected to utilize the only car available for work trips. A survey indicated that in at least 28 states, over two-thirds of the rural population could be classified as transportation-handicapped, and that in 12 states at least 20% of the households were transportation-deprived.

Burkhardt and Eby produced a refined algorithm for assessing rural transportation needs.[5] They recognize that need must include both the factors of transportation availability (e.g., car, taxi, shared rides, walking, bus service) and the concomitant factors of transportation affordability (e.g., level of income/household). A numerical rating scheme is devised to produce composite levels of need based on the degree of modal accessibility plus the level of income. However, the authors recognize the arbitrary nature of the needs estimation process and suggest a probing of consumer behavior through demand analyses.

Unfortunately, since the concept of need for rural transportation services is not rigidly defined, it is difficult to measure. Various analysts have taken different approaches to judge needs, and there is not a clear uniformity of opinion. Basically three broad approaches are available. Perhaps the most common approach is for experts, such as engineers, planners, sociologists, and/or transportation managers, to assess relative needs based on various social indicators and their best judgments. Second, need may be gauged from a survey of potential users, developed through a home-interview questionnaire. Finally, need may be estimated by comparing the travel behavior of a target group against a standard taken from local or national travel surveys.

For example, need is assessed to exist in the health services field when a board of competent observers indicates that enough services are not available to maintain minimum quality-of-life standards. It is difficult to establish a comparable minimum amount of transportation which must be provided to a rural household so that it would have enough transportation accessibility to maintain a minimum standard of living.

---

[4]U.S. SENATE, COMMITTEE ON AGRICULTURE AND FORESTRY, *Prelude to Legislation to Solve the Growing Crisis in Rural Transportation, Part II: Meeting Rural Transportation Needs* (Washington, D.C.: U.S. Government Printing Office, February 10, 1975), p. 281.

[5]JON E. BURKHARDT AND CHARLES L. EBY, "Need as a Criterion for Transportation Planning," in *Transportation Systems Planning and Analysis*, Highway Research Record 435 (Washington, D.C.: Highway Research Board, 1973), p. 37.

Yet, an analysis of rural trip-making characteristics relative to a set of established norms appears to be the most objective way to project needs.

The distinction between rural transportation needs and rural travel demands is most crucial to the eventual development and implementation of transit services and should be recognized. Unlike need, demand is based on the economic willingness-to-pay concept, and is measured by the quantity of travel occurring relative to a precise set of environmental circumstances (e.g., the price of travel). Demands are registered in a market and are, therefore, related to the user's income level. Those with low incomes, or no automobiles available, are less likely to demand travel.

This contrasts sharply with the social concept of need. Travel needs are a fixed amount of travel that is deemed necessary to provide an adequate standard of living. This quantity is not affected by the price of travel. That is, one may be assessed to have a need to travel independent of the ability or willingness to pay. In this context, need is an equity criterion, indicating a deviation from an established norm which should be corrected.

Each technique that could be used to estimate the magnitude of rural transportation needs is somewhat arbitrary, and the corresponding limitations should be recognized by planning agencies developing a need estimate. For example, solely using the judgments of experts is completely devoid of community participation in a project that is pertinent to the community's welfare.

The second methodology, an opinion poll of area residents, poses severe measurement problems. Home interviews by both Burkhardt and Robertson failed to identify significant need when respondents were asked what trips they would like to make that they currently were not making.[6] In both studies, the "desired" trips were found to be less than 6.0% of the existing ones, although the investigators commented that many of the respondents somehow could not grasp the idea of "desired trips" and thus probably substantially underestimated them. In any case, the major point is that it is exceedingly difficult to find any major unserved demand in this manner.

The third technique probably is the most realistic, although it also suffers some serious drawbacks. If comparisons are made to travel in urban areas, for example, one must remember that rural households are usually more self-sufficient. However, when there is the desire to travel, the distances involved are generally longer. Thus, we would expect different needs for trip making when compared to the average urbanite.

Another difficulty in making comparisons is that in most states the rural population tends to be older and poorer.[7] These are precisely the types of people that make fewer trips, even in urban areas. Any comparison, therefore, should be with population groups of similar characteristics. Even then we may find that older people in rural areas "need" to make fewer trips because of the locational self-sufficiency and because

[6]JOHN W. DICKEY AND CHARLES B. NOTESS, "Rural Public Transportation Problems and Needs," in *Toward a Unification of National and State Policy (and Action) on the Transportation Disadvantaged, Part II: Rural Perspectives*, Proceedings of the Fourth Annual Conference on the Transportation Disadvantaged, December 3, 4, 5, 1974, eds. William G. Bell and William T. Olsen (Tallahassee, Fla.: Florida State University, n.d.), pp. 1–33.

[7]WILLIAM LERNER, ed., *County and City Data Book 1972: A Statistical Abstract Supplement*, U.S. Department of Commerce (Washington, D.C.: U.S. Government Printing Office, 1973).

of the traditional helpfulness of nearby relatives and neighbors in providing transportation.

This third technique has been utilized in several consultants' studies.[8] In general,
this approach is known as gap analysis, and it is based on the hypothesis that a difference in trip-making rates (e.g., the gap) is a direct indicator of transportation need.
To apply this procedure a minimum trip-making rate is set as the standard amount of
transportation to be supplied. Usually, an areawide average volume of trips generated
per household per day is used for the standard.

There are immediate problems in choosing the average. In a study of Raleigh
County, West Virginia, it was noted that a national average, a statewide average, a
county average, or averages of rural and poor populations might be used.[9] In fact, it
would appear that the choice of an average is so crucial to the magnitude of the needs
estimate that the transportation analyst should be certain to make all assumptions
clear to decision makers.

Trip-making rates may be cross-classified to attain a more realistic estimate of
transportation needs. This approach is dependent only on the detail of the data collected. One strategy is to cross-classify the travel data by target groups and by trip
purpose. A target group is an identifiable unit of rural trip makers such as the elderly
or the handicapped. A cross classification of average travel rates to be used in a gap
analysis estimate of rural travel needs in North Georgia is shown in Table 18-2. Needs
estimates, specific to this area only, are then developed for the individual target groups
isolated in the study.

A continuing problem to those required to establish rural public transportation

TABLE 18-2
Trip-Generation Rates

Trip Purpose	Rural Elderly		Rural Handicapped	
	% of Trips	Trips/Week	% of Trips	Trips/Week
Grocery shopping	33.7	1.8	26.2	1.4
Other shopping	15.3	0.8	8.7	0.5
Health care	3.8	0.2	13.0	0.7
Personal business	20.1	1.1	13.0	0.7
Socio-recreational	26.3	1.4	17.4	0.9
Other	0.8	0.1	21.7	1.2

Source: Robert L. Martin and others, *Summary Report: Planning and Development Program for Mass
Transportation Services and Facilities for the Elderly and Handicapped in the State of Georgia* (Raleigh,
N.C.: Kimley-Horn and Associates, Inc., April 1975), p. 54.

---

[8]ROBERT L. MARTIN AND OTHERS, *Summary Report: Planning and Development Program for Mass Transportation Services and Facilities for the Elderly and Handicapped in the State of Georgia* (Raleigh, N.C.:
Kimley-Horn and Associates, Inc., April 1975).

[9]JON E. BURKHARDT AND OTHERS, *The Transportation Needs of the Rural Poor*, prepared for Office of
Research and Development, U.S. DOT (Bethesda, Md.: Resource Management Corporation, July 1969),
p. 14.

needs has been the lack of a comprehensive data base. While urban transportation studies rank second only to the Bureau of the Census in terms of data collection efforts, rural areas have been almost completely ignored. One reason for this, of course, is the large expanse of rural territory in this country and the resultant prohibitive cost of conducting home-interview origin–destination surveys similar to those done in metropolitan areas. Another reason is the comparative lack of congestion and related problems such as air pollution and accidents. Even census data are less helpful in rural areas, since the smallest geographic unit usually is the enumeration district—about 104 km² (40 mi²) in size in Virginia—and since much valuable information (e.g., income and trip-to-work) is not collected. Without such basic transportation and census data, it is obviously difficult to make a determination of the exact level of rural transportation needs.

PLANNING RURAL PUBLIC TRANSPORTATION SYSTEMS

The procedures for preliminary planning of rural public transportation systems are not unlike those adhered to in urban studies. These procedures are outlined in Fig. 18-1. Differences exist in the types of techniques commonly utilized within the various component tasks of the planning process, such as demand estimation or community impact evaluation. A number of simplified procedures are usually incorporated, reflecting two important differences between urban and rural planning studies. For one, few rural data are available and costs of extensive on-site data collection are usually too burdensome for planning staffs. Second, rural studies may be performed by a small staff and without extensive technical data analysis capabilities.

The needs study and problem definition phases of the process are crucial to the development of operational objectives and the eventual system design. For most rural systems, the costs of the service are kept as low as possible, and therefore routes must be carefully tailored to serve only the desired trip purposes, users, and geographic areas as identified in the needs study.

Careful decisions must be made to determine the types of trip purposes to be served. Work trips are only included in a relatively small percentage of the rural systems examined by the U.S. Department of Transportation.[10] Many systems are tailored to the delivery of rural human services, such as Head Start and adult training programs. Other systems give preference to the elderly or the handicapped. A representative list of recently operated rural transportation systems is shown in Table 18-3.

In the planning process, a number of candidate systems are postulated and evaluated and a best choice alternative is selected. Evaluation of alternatives, usually considers three parties: the users, the operators, and the community (e.g., affected nonusers). Each candidate system is evaluated in terms of its impact upon these parties. For example, operators are interested in the projected operating deficit (or

---

[10]U.S. Department of Transportation, *Rural Transit*.

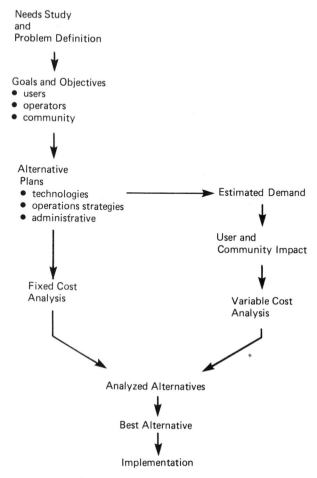

Figure 18-1 *A planning methodology for rural public transportation*

profit), users are concerned with the levels of service provided, and various local groups are interested in such factors as business impact, employment generated, and community image.

DEFINING ALTERNATIVES

A variety of vehicle types and operating strategies have been suggested as applicable to rural public transportation. In general, it is expected that vehicles would be selected on a cost-effective basis, but this may not always be the case. For example, some agencies may choose to provide fewer vehicles with expensive equipment (e.g., lifts for handicapped), although the actual demand for these facilities is extremely limited.

TABLE 18-3

Summary of Information on 75 Selected Rural Transportation Projects in the United States

	Number of Projects[a]		Number of Projects[a]
Target group (or groups) served by the projects		Geographical area served	
Elderly	58	One county	43
Poor	26	Multicounty	28
Head Start pupils	12	Statewide	3
General public	6	Reservation	1
Handicapped	6	Sponsoring agency	
Members of a transportation cooperative	3	Community Action Agency (CAA)	36
Other (workers, university students, etc.)	13	Area Agency on Aging (AOA)	14
Trip purpose (or purposes) served by the projects		Local government	9
Medical services	29	Transportation agency	8
Shopping	25	Private, profit-making	2
General	24	Other (state agencies, human services agencies, etc.)	6
Social services	22	Fare structure	
Head Start	10	No fare	24
Nutrition programs	7	Set fare	29
Services provided by sponsoring agency	4	Voluntary donation	15
Education and job training	4	Combination of the above	3
Work/specific purposes	3	Unknown	4
Other, (recreation, etc.)	5	Financial support	
Type of service		Office of Economic Opportunity (OEO)	35
Demand-responsive	27	Federal funds for the elderly (AOA, HEW)	23
Fixed-route, fixed-schedule	29	Other federal funds (Department of Labor, Department of Transportation)	13
Combination of above	19		
Frequency of operation		State	18
Daily (at least 6 days per week)	8	Local	17
Monday through Friday	50	Contractors	5
Two/three times per week	8	Contributions (foundations, businesses, etc.)	4
Once a week	4	Appalachian Regional Commission	2
Bimonthly	2		2
Monthly	2		1
Unknown	1		

[a]Numbers do not, in some cases, add to 75 because of the duplication of categories when described in a particular project.

Source: Transportation Systems Center, *Rural Passenger Transportation: State-of-the-Art Overview* (Draft Copy, May 1976).

Most rural transit systems have chosen to purchase either van-type vehicles or small transit buses. In general, they also tend to buy new vehicles rather than used ones. The reasons for new vehicles are twofold. For one, the purchase of older vehicles involves a trade-off of depreciation for maintenance costs. Maintenance costs for older vehicles may prove to be unacceptably high, especially when the purchase price of new vehicles is fully or partially subsidized from outside sources. Second, operators are especially cognizant of the impact of a clean and reliable vehicle on ridership. They prefer the positive community impact of shiny new vehicles.

Rural transportation planners are encouraged to consider many vehicle choice options and operating strategies in developing prospective systems. In addition, they are expected to survey all existing providers and supply options and to consider other usually neglected alternatives for improving rural mobility. These include carpools, community volunteer groups, and mobile delivery of human services. A representative list of technological alternatives for transit service follows.

1. *Conventional bus system.* A conventional bus system would have 30- to 60-seat passenger buses operating on fixed routes and fixed schedules. One variation that seems to be more feasible for low-density rural areas is periodic scheduling, where, instead of daily service, buses serve different areas on different days of the week. Every citizen is offered a dependable means of transportation at least once a week to the local town or closest urbanized area. In this manner capital and maintenance costs are kept low.

2. *Minibuses.* The minibus, having a capacity ranging from 8 passengers in some vans to 20 in the larger models, is more popular for meeting the transportation needs of the rural areas where demand does not warrant the use of larger vehicles. Because of their low capital and operating costs, minibuses may be able to run routes that were considered economically infeasible with the conventional buses. Also, they can be more easily maneuvered on the substandard roads often found in rural areas. Another potential use for minibuses is as a feeder system. They would collect passengers on the back roads and drop them off at waiting stations on the main routes where the larger buses operate.

   Perhaps, the most extensively described rural transportation project utilizing small vans on fixed routes occurred in Raleigh County, West Virginia.[11] An in-depth evaluation of these services was performed by Resource Management Corporation for the Federal Highway Administration. When funding from the Office of Economic Opportunity (OEO) was terminated, the free bus service in Raleigh County was discontinued and the system eventually failed. It was noted that while operating, the system maintained extremely high vehicle load factors. However, no major protests occurred after it was disbanded.

3. *Dial-a-ride* (*Dial-a-bus*). No matter how small and economical the bus, the demand in many rural areas usually is too small and too scattered to warrant fixed schedules and routes. Demand-responsive or demand-activated systems are more feasible. Dial-a-ride is one such system, using minibuses or vans and

---

[11]BURKHARDT, *Transportation Needs.*

offering door-to-door service on a telephoned demand-scheduled basis. In many situations an advance sign-up system for citizens is more practical, such as those found in rural Michigan counties. This option is termed "planned demand" and usually requires 24-hour advance notice to a dispatcher. A similar type of planned demand service has been suggested for rural Pennsylvania counties. This type of service is particularly attractive to elderly and handicapped segments of the population who would have difficulty obtaining access to fixed-route service.

4. *Mail-a-bus.* If the rural area is characterized by low telephone ownership, it may be more effective to use the postal system as a means of transmitting information concerning desired rides. Requests put in the mailbox during the day would be collected that night by a dispatcher at the post office, who would then schedule his buses for pickups and deliveries the following day. In some situations it may even be possible to have the mail truck itself serve as a passenger conveyance.

5. *Jitneys.* The jitney is analogous to dial-a-ride in that it is partially demand-responsive, but it differs in that instead of being a bus or van it is usually a private passenger car or station wagon that travels along a semifixed route. These vehicles travel basically one route, but vary somewhat to offer door-to-door service. The jitney driver may offer reserved seating, but more often he cruises along until waved down by an individual desiring a ride. In urban areas no strict schedules are adhered to, but in rural areas a somewhat fixed schedule would be necessary because of the probable few number of jitneys traveling on the back roads. Jitneys have not been extensively used in rural transport systems, but could be applicable to areas with well-defined travel corridors, such as the mountain valleys of Appalachia.

6. *School buses.* Most rural areas are served by a central school system which usually requires an extensive fleet of school buses. These buses generally are idle most of the day and could be used for other needed transportation functions. However, in many states there are legal restrictions on their use. Another difficulty is that of scheduling, as school buses are available for nonschool purposes in the late morning and early afternoon, thereby eliminating their use for work trips. Part-time drivers for the short nonschool use period would have to be found, and use during the off-peak periods might hinder maintenance operations in the bus garages. Despite these problems, some state legislatures have passed laws allowing counties to use school buses for purposes other than the transportation of children.

7. *Taxis.* This solution, unlike the jitney, is completely demand-responsive. One problem with the taxi is that the usual practice of servicing only one request at a time forces up the cost of using this mode, and makes it prohibitive to many rural families. Yet, if subsidized or coordinated with other modes, the taxi could become valuable in solving the rural transportation problem. Situations where the taxi might be used include:

   a. Where dispatching ensures filling the taxi to capacity with the cost being split between all the parties (known as shared-ride services).

b. Where, by pooling resources and hiring the taxi by the day, service organizations find they save money in the long run by not having to purchase and maintain their own vehicle. Also they do not waste valuable employee time by sending them out in departmental cars to pick up patients or other service recipients.

c. As the final link in a trip. For example, once an intercity bus passenger is left off in town, he could rely upon the taxi to complete his journey.

The basic objections to utilizing existing taxi companies for provision of rural transportation are the regulations eliminating the possibility of shared rides, and also the difficulty that aged or handicapped persons have using small vehicles. However, financially sound taxi companies generally have smoothed out the types of operational and administrative start-up problems that may plague newly formed rural systems (e.g., maintenance, dispatching, management). Such companies would be logical choices to operate rural public transportation systems.

A comparison of costs typical of various vehicle technologies operating in rural environments is presented in Table 18-4. While small vehicles are cheaper to run than large ones, the total cost of transportation/seat-mile decreases markedly with increasing vehicle capacity. However, for most rural systems, capacity is not a problem, as most vehicle load factors are low. In fact, vehicle selection should not be made solely on the basis of these costs, but must also consider the degree of capital subsidization, user level of service provided, and the type of demand to be satisfied.

It should be noted that one of the largest components of the total operating costs is the drivers' wages. Rural transit systems, just as their urban counterparts, are highly labor intensive. Some economies may be achieved by providing demand-responsive services that minimize vehicle-miles and vehicle-hours of service, yet still provide a minimum acceptable level of service to the users.

A number of operating strategies are feasible for rural localities. The alternatives may be analyzed by considering different types of routing and headways. Many operating systems provide both fixed-route/fixed-schedule and demand-responsive services, or innovative service that features aspects of all the alternatives. The fixed routes generally serve work trips, are used as connectors between town centers, or are closely tied in to a human services delivery system (such as a senior-citizen lunch program). Occasionally, the topography of a rural county is ideally suited for fixed routes, such as the Appalachian corridors in Raleigh County, West Virginia.

Partially demand-responsive systems include those using route-deviation or point-deviation systems. These services have been operated in small-town environments, and provide more flexibility than the fixed-route/fixed-schedule system.

Fully demand-responsive services, with dynamic routing, have generally not been applied in rural scenarios, especially if the system is to cover an entire county, since demand densities are too low.

However, the door-to-door service properties of these systems are highly desirable. Therefore, some rural counties have provided door-to-door transportation services on a scheduled (e.g., planned-demand) basis. Often the same vehicles that carry peak-hour work trips will operate in the planned-demand mode between the peak hours. To

TABLE 18-4
Typical Total Costs per Seat-Mile in a Rural Environment[a]

	Car	Van	Small Transit Bus	Medium Transit Bus	Large Transit Bus	School Bus
Capacity (seats)	5	10	20	30	50	44
Speed	30	25	18	18	15	15
Fuel consumption km/l (mi/gal)	5.5 (13)	4.3 (10)	2.9 (7)	2.6 (6)	2.1 (5)	2.9 (7)
Fuel type (cost/gal)	Gas $0.50	Gas $0.50	Gas $0.50	Diesel $0.38	Diesel $0.38	Gas $0.50
Fuel	0.039	0.050	0.072	0.064	0.076	0.072
Maintenance rolling stock	0.045	0.090	0.125	0.125	0.150	0.140
Injury and damages	0.025	0.030	0.042	0.042	0.050	0.050
General and misc.	0.050	0.060	0.083	0.083	0.100	0.100
Administrative	0.035	0.042	0.058	0.058	0.070	0.070
Wage ($3/h)	0.100	0.120	0.167	0.167	0.200	0.200
Total operating cost	0.294	0.392	0.547	0.539	0.646	0.632
Capital cost	0.037	0.069	0.125	0.115	0.167	0.054
Total cost/vehicle-mile	0.331	0.461	0.672	0.654	0.761	0.686
Total cost/seat-mile	0.066	0.046	0.034	0.022	0.015	0.016

[a]Metric conversion: 1 mi = 1.6 km; 1 gal = 3.8 l.

Source: Pennsylvania Governor's Task Force on Rural Transportation, *Rural Transportation in Pennsylvania: Problems and Prospects* (Harrisburg, Pa.: Governor's Task Force on Rural Transportation, May 1974), vol. I.

increase the economic efficiency of these systems, the county is often divided into sectors, with service in a sector only being offered on specific days of the week.

There are numerous routing and scheduling options for rural transit systems. However, very few guidelines exist to aid in the development of routes or schedules for a new rural service. Operating experience, which is gradually mounting, is perhaps the best source for current guidelines. Experience with rural transit systems in North and South Carolina led to the following conclusions about scheduling.[12]

[12]EXPANDED METRO MOBILITY TASK FORCE, *Rural Transportation in the Southeast*, prepared for Office of the Secretarial Representative, U.S. DOT (Atlanta, Ga.: Southeastern Federal Regional Council, November 1974). Now available as PB 238 880.

1. Rural worker schedules should rarely exceed 1.5 hours total run time from origin to destination. Workers tend to resist trip time which is more than double car-trip time.
2. Rural social delivery schedules can be somewhat longer in overall duration (about 2 hours is maximum). As a rule, trip needs in this category have less urgency, and passenger demands on the schedule are less critical.
3. Rural social delivery schedules should allow 2 hours between arrival time and return time for general business and shopping needs.
4. Rural demand-route schedules should have generous time allowances built in for passengers enbarking with groceries and for elderly passengers, who are slower to board and discharge. Stop allowances should be roughly estimated at 2 to 3 minutes apiece. This is more difficult to achieve on fixed-route schedules.
5. Fixed-route schedules should be geared for an average open road speed of 64 to 72 km/h (40 to 45 mi/h) with a time insertion of about 2 to 5 minutes at each mainline stopping point. Very little allowance is required (at first) for flag-stop possibilities. These will usually be rare during the first year of operation.
6. All schedules should consider allowing at least 5 to 10 minutes' delay at each end of a long—about 40 km (25 mi)—run. This scheduled slack time permits drivers to catch up on any unplanned delays on the prior leg.
7. Worker buses should always have at least a 10-minute prior arrival time at the factory gate to allow time for workers to check in. Less than that will produce a drastic and immediate drop in worker ridership, since they are by far the most critical riders in the system.

ROUTING RULES

Routing rules have been gained as a product of operating experiences. Most are stated as rules of thumb that should not be blindly adhered to in all cases. Typically the following rules are worthy of attention.

1. From experience, most studies have illustrated the reluctance of rural passengers to walk as much as 0.4 km (0.25 mi) to a fixed-route bus stop. A rider survey of the users of the Raleigh County bus system provided the following data[13]:

distance to point of boarding bus	percentage of riders
At home	73
< 0.4 km (0.25 mi)	11
0.4–0.8 km (0.25–0.5 mi)	7
0.8–1.6 km (0.5–1 mi)	5
> 1.6 km (1 mi)	3
No reply	1

---

[13]BURKHARDT, *Transportation Needs.*

2. For many-to-one demand-responsive services, loop routes radiating about a central destination are desirable. Passengers are returned home as the vehicle leaves the central destination and picked up on the return to town. This procedure shortens the average passenger's in-vehicle travel time.
3. Routes should not be modified to accommodate only one or two people.
4. The consequences of variable and irregular scheduling typical of route-deviation bus systems place severe restrictions on the reliability, and hence feasibility, of that alternative. Riders have more confidence in a fixed-route system or an advance reservation door-to-door service.

In summary, the design of a successful rural transportation system (including vehicle selection, routing, and scheduling) is currently more of an art than a science. Many guidelines are available, but one cannot assess the exact impact of changing any of the design variables without actually operating a system. It is anticipated that the experiences of the rural transportation demonstration projects, funded through Section 147 of the Federal-Aid Highway Act of 1973, will aid in developing insights concerning the selection, routing, and scheduling of vehicles.

ESTIMATING DEMAND

Although the estimation of potential ridership is a difficult task, it is an essential component to the planning and design of a rural transportation system. The inefficiencies associated with an underutilized vehicle fleet may eventually result in the premature demise of rural transit services. A demand projection should, therefore, serve as the primary basis for the system's design.

A number of techniques have been suggested as being relevant to demand projection. However, recent experience has shown that some of these methods are not reliable and should be avoided. Those considered, at the present time, to be unacceptable are:

- A local "would-you-ride" survey.
- Gap analysis.
- Professional opinions.

For example, a common approach to demand estimation has involved door-to-door attitude surveys prior to the development of the transportation service. Such surveys generally include questions about the number and types of transit trips that would be made under various environmental conditions (e.g., quality of service, automobile availability, frequency). There are two serious flaws with this method of demand projection. The first difficulty is that multipurpose journeys are often not measured properly by the questionnaire. Generally, respondents are asked to indicate how many trips they would make on the service, if it existed, for each trip purpose. In doing so, they often neglect to consider multipurpose trips and provide an overestimate of the actual number of person trips. Second, and of critical importance, the demand forecast on the basis of attitude surveys of this type generally are not verified by actual travel behavior. In a survey of prospective travel frequencies in a small town in New York (Oneonta), public response indicated that a demand-activated bus service would generate 33,700 trips/week when an actual service in a comparable nearby small town (Batavia, New York) only generated 1500 trips/week.[14] The clear absurdity of this estimate of demand illustrates the fact that public opinion surveys cannot be directly translated into actual vehicle trips.

Both gap analysis and the use of professional opinion (such as the Delphi technique) are also fraught with difficulties. Gap analysis is better suited as a needs estimation tool. The use of experts' opinions, as incorporated into a "goals attainment" procedure, has not been tested enough to be recommended.

It is evident that demand forecasts for a particular area should be tempered by a knowledge of the existing levels of demand for like transportation services in other similar localities. That is, a knowledge of the "ballpark" demand observed in currently operating transit systems is a necessary precursor to more exacting estimates. Table 18-5 presents a summary of some existing rural transportation systems and their service characteristics.[15] Some of these programs include special service to the elderly, while others have a broader ridership base. Trip-generation rates in Table 18-5 are presented in terms of annual transit trips (one-way) per capita. Note that most systems are servicing less than 1.0 transit trip per resident per year. This rate of travel might be used as a liberal rule of thumb for maximum anticipated ridership, in the absence of better data. Many systems will not even produce this level of ridership. In a study

TABLE 18-5
Observed Rates of Transit Use

Trip-Generation Rate (Annual trips per capita)	Location
4.00-10.00	Batavia, N.Y. (dial-a-ride)
3.00-4.00	High estimate, small urban areas (Pa.)
2.00-3.00	High estimate, rural (Pa.)
1.00-2.00	Mid-Delta (Ark.)
0.50-1.00	Raleigh County (W. Va.)
	Low estimate, small urban areas (Pa.)
0.25-0.50	Venango Action Corp. (Pa.)
	Low estimate, rural (Pa.)
0.00-0.25	Kingsport, Tenn.
	Potter County (Pa.)
	McKean County (Pa.)

[14]D. T. HARTGEN AND C. A. KECK, *Forecasting Dial-A-Bus Ridership in Small Urban Areas*, Preliminary Research Report 50 (Albany, N.Y.: New York State Department of Transportation, Planning Research Unit, April 1974).

[15]ROBERT J. POPPER, CHARLES B. NOTESS, AND RICARDO N. ZAPATA, "Demand for Special Transit Systems to Serve the Rural Elderly," in *Transportation Issues: The Disadvantaged, the Elderly, and Citizen Involvement*, Transportation Research Record 618 (Washington, D.C.: Transportation Research Board, 1976), pp. 1-6.

for the State of Pennsylvania, a range of travel rates between 0.3 and 2.4 annual trips per capita was used to develop a forecast of statewide potential rural transit demand.[16] This is quite an expansive range (the highest estimate being eight times the lowest), and may prove to be of little aid to a planner trying to decide on a realistic demand level to use for a particular county or planning district.

Generally, three approaches to estimating demand may be feasible:

- A trip-generation-rate model.
- A regression model.
- A participation-rate model.

At present, only the trip-generation model has been utilized to any extent, and it is the obvious choice for preliminary planning. However, a functional-demand equation developed by Burkhardt and Lago through statistical analysis of fixed-route and demand-responsive systems may prove quite useful.[17] As yet, it has not been applied to rural planning efforts. A third methodology analyzes the demand for rural transit to social services in terms of the participation rate of those utilizing social services and the likelihood of transit use for travel to the services. This technique may be well suited for those rural transit systems designed to act primarily as a human services delivery system for the elderly.

The trip-generation-rate model is an aggregate approach. That is, trip rates are assumed to hold for an entire population. However, by detailing exact target groups that are expected to utilize the system, a more refined travel estimate is produced.

To compute demand by means of the trip-generation-rate model, the following formula is used:

$$D = \sum_{i=1}^{n} d_i(\text{POP}_i)$$

where
$D =$ total annual demand for transit trips
$d_i =$ annual trips per person in the ith target group
$(\text{POP}_i) =$ population of the ith target group
$n =$ number of target groups

In Pennsylvania studies, planners selected two target groups, the elderly and the nonelderly poor, which were expected to comprise 80% of the public transportation system ridership. Therefore, the demand equation becomes

$$D = \frac{12(\text{POP}_{\text{elderly}}) + 19(\text{POP}_{\text{poor}})}{0.80}$$

where the annual trip-making rates for the two groups were projected to be 12 and 19 annual trips, respectively. Subsequent demand studies with Wisconsin data have

---

[16]JON E. BURKHARDT AND WILLIAM W. MILLAR, "Estimating Cost of Providing Rural Transportation Service," in *Transportation for Elderly, Disadvantaged, and Handicapped People in Rural Areas*, Transportation Research Record 578, (Washington, D.C.: Transportation Research Board, 1976), pp. 8–15.

[17]JON E. BURKHARDT AND ARMANDO M. LAGO, "The Demand for Rural Public Transportation Routes," in *Proceedings—Seventeenth Annual Meeting, Beyond the Bicentennial: The Transportation Challenge*, Transportation Research Forum, 17, no. 1 (Boston) (Oxford, Ind.: The Richard B. Cross Company, 1976), pp. 449–503.

shown that use of a "no-auto-available" target group produced more accurate demand projections.

COSTS OF RURAL TRANSIT SERVICE

The costs of providing rural transit have been documented and analyzed in several reports. A relatively clear picture is emerging from which rough cost estimates can be based. However, each locality must prepare individual cost analyses that reflect the local variations in labor wage rates, vehicle operating costs, and administrative overhead. A survey of cost studies illustrates the typical cost structure for a rural system.[18]

1. In Pennsylvania, the Governor's Task Force on Rural Transportation estimated the average total cost to vary between 33 and 76 cents/vehicle-mile (20 to 47 cents/vehicle-km), depending on the type of vehicle selected.
2. The U.S. Department of Transportation's survey of rural systems shows a cost range of 33 to 60 cents/vehicle-mile (20 to 37 cents/vehicle-km), with most projects costing about 45 cents/vehicle-mile (28 cents/vehicle-km).
3. A survey of rural transport systems to serve the rural elderly stated that costs ranged between 50 and 70 cents/vehicle-mile (31 to 43 cents/vehicle-km).
4. Another survey conducted by the Transportation Institute at North Carolina A & T State University revealed a cost range between 58 and 92 cents/vehicle-mile (36 to 57 cents/vehicle-km).

Data used in the North Carolina survey yields the following breakdown of component costs: administrative overhead, 41%; driver compensation, 28%; vehicle operating costs, 25%; vehicle depreciation, 6%. These data were generated from an analysis of 10 separate projects. By sorting the cost data according to the seating capacity of the system, a more detailed cost breakdown is developed (Table 18-6). The results suggest that there may be some economies of scale for larger-capacity systems.

Administrative overhead is typically the largest component of cost facing a rural system. It is a function of the size of the staff, which may include a director, a dispatcher, a secretary, and assistants. Systems run by community action agencies often utilize existing personnel to fulfill these tasks. Several sources have indicated the importance of a good director to the success of a system. This is one area where additional salary compensation may prove to be quite cost-effective.

Vehicle operating costs include fuel, maintenance and repairs, and insurance. A wide variation in insurance costs (between $500 and $5000 per vehicle per year) was noted in a federal survey.[19] Apparently, insurance companies do not have much experience with rural carriers, and it is suggested that a rural transit director should investigate several prospective sellers.

Variations in maintenance costs reflect the degree of vehicle utilization and also whether the maintenance is performed in-house or on a contracted basis. Fuel-cost

---

[18]TRANSPORTATION SYSTEMS CENTER, *Rural Passenger Transportation: State-of-the-Art Overview*, Technology Sharing Series (Washington, D.C.: U.S. Department of Transportation, October 1976), pp. 35–36.
[19]U.S. DEPARTMENT OF TRANSPORTATION, *Rural Transit*, p. 16.

TABLE 18-6
Summary of Average/Vehicle Annual Operating Costs
of Rural Public Transportation Systems by Seating Capacity, 1974

Cost Items	Systems by Seating Capacity				
	Under 100	100-200	200-300	Over 300	All Systems
Total fixed cost	$ 9,101	$2,809	$2,330	$ 8,878	$ 5,511
Administrative					
Salary and fringe benefits	6,799	1,461	1,069	6,151	3,578
Consultants	0	28	25	0	15
Travel	151	90	28	0	53
Telephone	620	52	47	657	322
Supplies	110	92	40	390	184
Equipment	96	6	15	185	79
Miscellaneous	385	30	36	638	279
Rolling stock					
Depreciation	550	722	759	548	670
License	21	74	67	27	52
Insurance	368	254	244	282	279
Total variable cost	4,038	6,289	4,141	8,482	6,349
Driver's compensation	2,390	3,551	1,264	4,960	3,370
Rolling stock					
Gasoline	882	2,076	2,027	2,660	2,173
Oil and lubrication	103	133	102	282	175
Maintenance and repairs	664	529	748	580	631
Total cost	$13,139	$9,098	$6,471	$17,360	$11,860

Source: David Chen and others, *A Cost Analysis of Rural Public Transportation Systems* (Greensboro, N.C.: North Carolina A & T State University, Transportation Institute, April 1975).

savings may be realized by achieving nonprofit status and purchasing from local public agencies.

Drivers' wage rates may also vary considerably. Typical prevailing hourly wages for professionals in 1972–1973 ranged between $2 and $3.50 per hour. These expenses are markedly reduced if nonprofessional drivers or volunteers are used. But often, a rural transportation system obtaining federal funds must satisfy the requirements of Section 13(c) of the Urban Mass Transportation Act, as amended. It ensures that a protective labor agreement is made before the capital grants covered are approved, and may result in a transportation agency being required to use unionized drivers.

IMPACT ANALYSIS

Most rural transportation systems have been small and generally are not expected to produce a marked impact on the local area's economy. A study of the impact of a rural transit system in Raleigh County, West Virginia, resulted in the classification scheme shown in Table 18-7. Two factors that may be crucial to continued community

TABLE 18-7
Impact Groups and Possible Effects of a Program
to Provide Transportation for the Rural Poor

Impact Group	Type of Effect	Direct Effect	Indirect Effect
Transportation system users	Changes in cash income from:		
	productivity increase	X	X
	transportation savings	X	X
	use of government programs	X	X
	increased shopping opportunities	X	X
	Market value of goods and services received:		
	transportation	X	
	government services	X	
	Intangible benefits	X	
Transportation service providers: employees of the system for the poor	Salaries	X	X
Transport service providers: suppliers of the system for the poor	Profit and wages on vehicles sold	X	X
	Material value added on vehicles	X	X
	Profits and wages for transport infrastructure	X	X
	Material value added for transport infrastructure		X
	Profits and wages for maintenance services	X	X
	Material value added for maintenance		X
Transport service providers: competitors	Loss of profit from poor who switch to new system	X	X
	Loss of wages	X	X
	Loss of material value added		X
Other county entrepreneurs	Change in income as a result of accessibility changes for the users of the new system	X	X
	Change in income as a result of income effects in users of the new system	X	X
	Change in material value added		X

Source: Jon E. Burkhardt and others, *The Transportation Needs of the Rural Poor,* prepared for Office of Research and Development, U.S. DOT (Bethesda, Md.: Resource Management Corporation, July 1969).

acceptance of the system are the effects of competing transportation providers and the effects on other county entrepreneurs. For example, in Raleigh County, transit patrons reported significant savings in grocery expenses by being able to use the chain stores in the City of Beckley rather than the local markets. While this benefit was clearly evident to the transit users, it appears as a disbenefit to the local grocery store entrepreneurs. The effect of the transit system is a distributional one, benefiting the transit users and Beckley entrepreneurs at the expense of the local market owners (and their patrons). It is not clear whether such a redistribution might produce additional long-run social or cultural impacts on the lives of the rural poor. Nonetheless, the possibility of such impact should be considered.

ANALYZING ALTERNATIVES

Few rural transportation systems are rigidly evaluated in terms of economic benefits and costs. Yet, evaluations are necessary in the preliminary planning phases to isolate the most feasible plans. In addition, a continuing program evaluation provides valuable data and insights for improving existing transit services.

Evaluations should be constructed to measure the level of transportation service provided to users and also the efficiency of operator resource utilization. Sets of these measures may be combined into productivity matrices or indices for system evaluation. The general form of a productivity matrix relates input factors (labor hours, seat-miles, etc.) to transportation output levels as typically measured by passenger-miles, passenger trips, and revenue.

This matrix may be expanded substantially to reflect the situation involving rural public transportation. For example, transportation outputs may be viewed by a rider in terms of the user level-of-service factors shown in Table 18-8, such as frequency, multipurpose trip capability, and seating comfort. That is, from a planning perspective the system should be designed to produce output that is measured by more than just passenger-miles of transportation. Additional factors affecting the operators and the community are also listed in Table 18-8. Input factors to the transportation service include the vehicles, the labor, the energy utilized in producing transportation outputs, and the associated costs.

Initial evaluations of alternatives are carried out to identify important trade-offs that are available to the planner. User level-of-service measures, operator resource utilization levels, and community impact factors are assessed for each alternative. These data are then placed into a decision array format for further evaluation.

For example, in a simulation study of demand-responsive transportation in rural Virginia, alternatives were defined by the service-area size (called a sector) and the number of vehicles assigned to a sector.[20] Sector size was defined as either the entire county or one of five wedge-shaped fractions of the county. Level-of-service (L/S) factors and system resource utilization and cost factors were then determined for each combination of service area and number of vehicles. From these data, an analyst is able to evaluate three possible demand-responsive service options.

- *Option A:* Purchase enough vehicles to meet the target demand and run them over the entire county.

[20]R. J. POPPER AND M. D. BENT, "Simulation Modeling of Demand Responsive Rural Public Transportation Services," in *Modeling and Simulation 7* (Pittsburgh, Pa.: Instrument Society of America, 1976), Part I, pp. 439–44.

TABLE 18-8
Evaluation Measures for Rural Public Transportation

I. Transportation service to users

  A. Quality

    1. Convenience
      Travel time
      Pickup/delivery proximity
      Frequency
      Reservation requirements
      Compatability of schedule

    2. Comfort
      Seating
      Delay at stops
      Others

    3. Privacy
      Traveler mix
      Information requirements

    4. Fare

    5. Dependability

    6. Safety

  B. Quantity

    1. Outreach

    2. Service area

    3. Demand generation
      Urgent
      Target group
      Total

    4. Demand satisfaction
      Urgent
      Target group
      Total

II. Operator efficiency

    1. Revenue

    2. Cost factors
      Capital
      Operational

    3. Resource utilization
      Vehicle load factor
      Personnel utilization
      Route deadhead mileage
      Energy consumption

III. Community/area impact

    1. Economic
      Employment
      Business

    2. Social
      Service utilization
      Others

    3. Political

Source: Adapted from Charles B. Notess, Robert Jay Popper, and Ricardo N. Zapata, *Transportation of Elderly to Rural Social Services* (Blacksburg, Va.: Virginia Polytechnic Institute and State University, Center for Urban and Regional Studies, 1975).

- *Option B:* Purchase enough vehicles to meet the target demand and run the entire fleet within a sector. Alternate sectors according to the day of the week.
- *Option C:* Confine service to sectors, but operate vehicles simultaneously in all sectors. Purchase enough vehicles to meet demand or provide at least daily service in each sector.

These options are compared in Table 18-9. The major differences in the alternatives are the number of vehicles required, the time level-of-service measure, the daily route mileage, the number of passengers per mile, and the fuel efficiency. These differences lead to some interesting cost-based comparisons for the particular study area. By restricting service to one sector per day, the fleet size can be reduced by one vehicle, and the route mileage can be reduced by 25% from a countywide service. Also, daily operating costs (including fuel, insurance, licenses, maintenance, repair, labor, and vehicle depreciation, but not administrative costs) can be reduced by approximately 20%. However, once-a-week service may not provide an acceptable level of service. By purchasing a fifth vehicle, one vehicle may be assigned to each of five sectors, with all vehicles operating simultaneously. This may be an acceptable alternative, although daily operating costs will increase to a level comparable to the costs of option A. Option C, with simultaneous service to all sectors, is slightly preferable to the unrestricted countywide service from an operations standpoint.

IMPLEMENTATION

Once a rural public transportation system has been adequately planned, the complex task of implementation begins. Three problem areas that are viewed as crucial by existing operators are:

- The organizational structure of the transportation service.
- The institutional constraints typically facing a rural transit system.
- The sources of funding available to support rural transportation services.

The development of an organizational structure to provide transportation services is perhaps one of the more difficult problems to be faced at this time. There is no present example in this country of an organization in which there is a coordination of all agencies providing transportation (such as health, welfare, education, extension, aged, and highways, not to mention taxi companies, churches, and manufacturing plants). Of course, to reconcile the rules, guidelines, policies, and legal constraints of all these groups would be extremely difficult. Some are federal agencies; others are state, regional, and/or local; still others are private (profit and nonprofit). Some can pay only the travel costs of their own personnel; others can pay for their clients also. Some can pay only capital costs; others can only reimburse operating costs. In many cases, "transportation" does not even show up as a line item in their budgets. Add to all this

TABLE 18-9

Evaluative Measures for Alternative Operating Configurations

Option	Target Capacity	Required Buses	System Capacity	Time[a] L/S	Total Rte.-Miles[b]	Passengers per Mile[b]	Fuel Ratio[c]	Daily Operating Cost
A: Countywide unrestricted	50/day	5	63	1.66	761	2.06	0.93	$225
B: One sector per day	50/day	4	64	1.82	571	2.88	0.68	$176
C: Simultaneous sector service	50/day	5	68	1.62	673	2.30	0.78	$222

[a] The ratio of travel time over the road (bus/private auto).

[b] Metric conversion: 1 mi = 1.6 km.

[c] The ratio of gallons of gas consumed by the bus system to that used by a taxi system with no deadhead mileage.

the fact that volunteer services probably will be needed to make the organization even close to feasible financially, and the situation becomes even more complex.

A desired characteristic of any such rural public transportation organization would be flexibility in response to the uncertainties of funding sources and potentials. One year there may be funds available for transporting low-income people to job training programs; the next, for older people to activities; and the next, for any people living in small urban areas with a population from 5000 to 50,000. In the future we might expect even more idiosyncrasies depending on fuel availability, work relief programs for the unemployed, guaranteed incomes, and other program possibilities.

Rural transportation cooperatives (RTCs) have been proposed (and implemented) as being a particularly suitable organizational structure to provide rural transportation. The typical RTC is a private nonprofit firm incorporated under the rules and regulations of the state. In this capacity, it has the capability of contracting with various private and public agencies for transportation services.

However, to qualify for the maximum available federal funding, it is advantageous for the cooperative to be organized as an arm of a transportation district or similar state agency. This facilitates the cooperative's ability to win federal funds, particularly those from the U.S. Department of Transportation, which must pass through a state agency. The arrangement might also let the RTC receive planning and technical assistance from the state agency.

Perhaps the main organizational benefit of this structure, as seen by rural transportation managers, is the ability to obtain exemptions from state transportation regulation. The RTC could, therefore, set its own routes, schedules, and fares. It also could utilize volunteer labor and seek contributions in a similar manner to the rural electrification and farm cooperatives that have preceded it.

Whatever the organizational structure, it appears that quality of management is the key to survival. The manager must be aggressive and properly trained to pursue all possible sources of funding. Furthermore, he or she must be adept at communicating with local policy and decision makers concerning the need for rural transportation services, and marketing and consumer-oriented approaches are also needed to sell the services to the various community and user groups.

Next to securing adequate funding, the most serious implementation task facing a rural transportation service is that of coping with state legal and regulatory requirements. State economic regulation generally requires the transportation service to acquire an operating certificate from the state regulatory board (usually called the public utilities commission, or PUC). While PUC regulation may provide significant advantages (e.g., restricting competition, rider safety standards), it also limits the flexibility of services that can be offered. Usually, fares, routes, and schedules can only be changed with prior PUC approval, which may be a slow process. Agencies have also reported higher insurance costs under PUC regulation.[21] Some agencies avoid PUC interference by not charging a fare. However, this may restrict a valuable source of revenue and is generally not recommended.

---

[21]TRANSPORTATION SYSTEMS CENTER, *Rural Passenger Transportation*, p. 33.

Funding, as noted, is subject to many uncertainties. It is difficult, moreover, to envision any system that will be self-sufficient, and federal and local subsidization will certainly play a critical role. One hope is that the transportation services of various social agencies can be consolidated in some fashion, thereby saving money already being spent (or possibly freeing it to be used for other purposes, including more transportation). In addition, passage of the National Mass Transportation Assistance Act of 1974 appears to provide a stable base of funds for rural transportation systems. Funding difficulties, then, are not insurmountable but still represent the principal problem facing rural public transportation.

The following sources have been used to partially finance rural transportation systems:[22]

1. *Fares.* Fares are a substantial source of revenue for rural systems, and usually average between 1 and 3 cents/passenger-km (2 and 5 cents/passenger-mi).
2. *Membership dues.* Rural transportation cooperatives, such as OATS (Older Adult Transportation System) in Missouri, charge a fixed membership fee.
3. *Contracts with human services agencies.* This is a preferred source of funding for at least two reasons. For one, it provides a stable base of funds for the contract period. Second, the problems associated with the many overlapping and fragmented transportation services currently provided by these agencies is avoided. In addition, it provides an excellent method of estimating demands and vehicle requirements.
4. *Other private sources.* Funds may be generated by using vehicles for charter services, by providing advertising space, and by seeking local business contributions.
5. *Federal grants.* Several sources of federal funding are applicable to rural transportation. Unfortunately, some are available for capital purchases, some for operating expenses, others to reimburse travel expenses, and still others are limited to specific user groups.
6. *State grants.* Presently, little coordination exists between the many state and local human resource agencies providing transportation services. These programs often parallel federal HEW (Department of Health, Education, and Welfare) programs.

SUMMARY

Rural public transportation is one of a set of feasible options for improving the mobility of rural residents. Several funding sources are currently available to subsidize these services, making rural public transit a near-reality.

The planning of these systems is undertaken without a comprehensive understanding or data base to gauge rural travel needs and behaviors. Therefore, designers

---

[22]Ibid., pp. 36–38.

and operators of rural systems must be cautious to tailor the system to the anticipated needs without wasting limited resources. Preliminary experiences with existing systems have provided limited information to use in estimating demands, projecting costs, and evaluating impacts.

The future of rural public transportation will depend largely on its financial stability. If the federal government, along with state and local sources, supports the systems, we may see a marked improvement in the quality of life for the rural-transportation-disadvantaged. At present, however, much has been written about the plight of these people, but little has been accomplished to improve their lot.

SELECTED BIBLIOGRAPHY

Many citations are no longer available from their original source. These citations are often available from the National Technical Information Service, U.S. Department of Commerce, 5285 Port Royal Road, Springfield, Va. 22161. We have verified the order numbers for many of these citations, and they are found at the end of the citation. Prices are available through NTIS at the address above.

BELL, WILLIAM G., AND WILLIAM T. OLSEN, eds., *Toward a Unification of National and State Policy (and Action) on the Transportation Disadvantaged, Part II: Rural Perspectives*, Proceedings of the Fourth Annual Conference on the Transportation Disadvantaged, December 3, 4, 5, 1974. Tallahassee, Fla.: Florida State University, n.d.

BRIGGS, RONALD, "Designing Transportation Systems for Low Density Rural Regions" (unpublished paper presented at the Annual Meeting of the Association of American Geographers, April 1975).

BROOKS, SUANNE, *Transportation Authorities in Federal Human Services Programs*. Atlanta, Ga.: U.S. Department of Health, Education, and Welfare, Office of the Regional Director, January 1976. Now available as SHR-0000739.

BURKHARDT, JON E., AND CHARLES L. EBY, "Need as a Criterion for Transportation Planning," in *Transportation Systems Planning and Analysis*, Highway Research Record 435, pp. 32–41. Washington, D.C.: Highway Research Board, 1973.

————, AND ARMANDO M. LAGO, "The Demand for Rural Public Transportation Routes," in *Proceedings— Seventeenth Annual Meeting, Beyond the Bicentennial: The Transportation Challenge*, Transportation Research Forum, 17, no. 1 (Boston), pp, 449–503. Oxford, Ind.: The Richard B. Cross Company, 1976.

————, AND WILLIAM W. MILLAR, "Estimating Cost of Providing Rural Transportation Service," in *Transportation for Elderly, Disadvantaged, and Handicapped People in Rural Areas*, Transportation Research Record 578, pp. 8–15. Washington, D.C.: Transportation Research Board, 1976.

————, AND OTHERS, *A Study of the Transportation Problems of the Rural Poor*, in 2 vols., prepared for Office of Economic Development. Bethesda, Md.: Resource Management Corporation, January 1972. Reprinted by FHWA. Now available as PB 208 158 and 210 187.

————, AND OTHERS, *The Transportation Needs of the Rural Poor*, prepared for Office of Research and Development, U.S. DOT. Bethesda, Md.: Resource Management Corporation, July 1969.

CHEN, DAVID, AND OTHERS, *A Cost Analysis of Rural Public Transportation Systems*. Greensboro, N.C.: North Carolina A & T State University, Transportation Institute, April 1975.

DICKEY, JOHN, AND CHARLES V. S. MIX, "Rural Public Transportation in Virginia," in *Public Transportation Planning Issues*, Transportation Research Record 519, pp. 56–65. Washington, D.C.: Transportation Research Board, 1974.

EXPANDED METRO MOBILITY TASK FORCE, *Rural Transportation in the Southeast*, prepared for Office of the Secretarial Representative, U.S. DOT. Atlanta, Ga.: Southeastern Federal Regional Council, November 1974. Now available as PB 238 880.

FLUSBERG, MARTIN, "An Innovative Public Transportation System for a Small City: The Merrill, Wisconsin Case Study," in *Bus Transportation Strategies*, Transportation Research Record 606, pp. 54–59. Washington, D.C.: Transportation Research Board, 1977.

HARTGEN, D. T., AND C. A. KECK, *Forecasting Dial-A-Bus Ridership in Small Urban Areas*, Preliminary Research Report 50. Albany, N.Y.: New York State Department of Transportation, Planning Research Unit, April 1974.

HAUSER, EDWIN W., *A Goals Attainment Approach for Estimating Demands for Rural Public Transportation.* Raleigh, N.C.: Kimley-Horn and Associates, Inc., January 1976.

————, AND OTHERS, *The Use of Existing Facilities for Transporting Disadvantaged Residents of Rural Areas,* in 2 vols., prepared for FHWA. Raleigh, N.C.: Kimley-Horn and Associates, Inc., January 1975. Now available as PB 248 746 and 248 747.

INSTITUTE OF PUBLIC ADMINISTRATION, *Transportation for Older Americans: A State-of-the-Art Report,* prepared for Administration on Aging, U.S. Department of Health, Education, and Welfare. Washington, D.C.: Institute of Public Administration, April 1975. Now available as PB 243 441.

KIDDER, ALICE E., "Economics of Rural Public Transportation Programs," in *Transportation for Elderly, Disadvantaged, and Handicapped People in Rural Areas,* Transportation Research Record 578, pp. 1–7. Washington, D.C.: Transportation Research Board, 1976.

MCKELVEY, DOUGLAS, *Considerations in Planning and Operating Transportation Systems for Older Americans and Public Systems in Rural Areas.* Iowa City, Iowa: University of Iowa, May 1975. Now available as PB 254 756.

MARTIN, ROBERT L., AND OTHERS, *Summary Report: Planning and Development Program for Mass Transportation Services and Facilities for the Elderly and Handicapped in the State of Georgia.* Raleigh, N.C.: Kimley-Horn and Associates, Inc., April 1975.

MICHIGAN DEPARTMENT OF STATE HIGHWAYS AND TRANSPORTATION, *Dial-A-Ride Transportation.* Lansing, Mich.: Michigan Department of State Highways and Transportation, October 1975.

MIX, CHARLES V. S., AND JOHN W. DICKEY, *The Need for and Design of a Rural Transportation System for Madison County, Virginia.* Blacksburg, Va.: Virginia Polytechnic Institute and State University, Center for Urban and Regional Studies, May 1974. Now available as PB 239 852.

NOTESS, CHARLES B., ROBERT JAY POPPER, AND RICARDO N. ZAPATA, *Transportation of Elderly to Rural Social Services.* Blacksburg, Va.: Virginia Polytechnic Institute and State University, Center for Urban and Regional Studies, 1975.

PENNSYLVANIA DEPARTMENT OF TRANSPORTATION, *Pennsylvania Mass Transit Statistical Report: 1974–1975.* Harrisburg, Pa.: Pennsylvania Department of Transportation, 1976.

PENNSYLVANIA GOVERNOR'S TASK FORCE ON RURAL TRANSPORTATION, *Rural Transportation in Pennsylvania: Problems and Prospects,* vols. I and II. Harrisburg, Pa.: Governor's Task Force on Rural Transportation, May 1974.

PETERSON, E. J., AND R. L. SMITH, "An Evaluation of the Accuracy of Three Rural Public Transportation Demand Models," in *Proceedings of the First National Conference on Rural Public Transportation,* June 7–9, 1976, ed. Douglas J. McKelvey, prepared for U.S. DOT. Greensboro, N.C.: North Carolina A & T State University, Transportation Institute, October 27, 1976. Now available as PB 262 808.

POPPER, R. J., AND M. D. BENT, "Simulation Modeling of Demand Responsive Rural Public Transportation Services," in *Modeling and Simulation 7,* Part I, pp. 439–44. Pittsburgh, Pa.: Instrument Society of America, 1976.

————, CHARLES B. NOTESS, AND RICARDO N. ZAPATA, "The Demand for Special Transit Systems to Serve the Rural Elderly," in *Transportation Issues: The Disadvantaged, the Elderly, and Citizen Involvement,* Transportation Research Record 618. Washington, D.C.: Transportation Research Board, in preparation.

ROBERTSON, R. N., *A Methodology for Determining Rural Public Transportation Needs in Virginia.* Charlottesville, Va.: Virginia Highway Research Council, March 1974.

SALTZMAN, ARTHUR, "Rural Transit Needs and Feasibility Techniques," in *Proceedings—Seventeenth Annual Meeting, Beyond the Bicentennial: The Transportation Challenge,* Transportation Research Forum, 17, no. 1 (Boston), pp. 491–98. Oxford, Ind.: The Richard B. Cross Company, 1976.

TRANSPORTATION SYSTEMS CENTER, *Rural Passenger Transportation.* Washington, D.C.: U.S. Government Printing Office, May 1976.

U.S. DEPARTMENT OF TRANSPORTATION, OFFICE OF POLICY AND PLANS DEVELOPMENT, *Rural Transit Operations and Management.* Washington, D.C.: U.S. Government Printing Office, n.d.

————, OFFICE OF THE SECRETARY, *Travel Barriers.* Washington, D.C.: U.S. Government Printing Office, May 1970. Full report by Abt Associates, Cambridge, Mass. Now available as PB 187 327.

U.S. SENATE, COMMITTEE ON AGRICULTURE AND FORESTRY, *Prelude to Legislation to Solve the Growing Crisis in Rural Transportation, Part I: Transportation in Rural America, Part II: Meeting Rural Transportation Needs.* Washington, D.C.: U.S. Government Printing Office, February 10, 1975.

Chapter 19

PERSPECTIVES OF TRANSIT
AND HIGHWAY PLANNING

KENNETH W. HEATHINGTON, *Director, Transportation Center,*
The University of Tennessee

Highway planning has a long history within the United States. The first highway planning was oriented more toward traffic engineering and dealt with simple volume counts and other activities related to traffic engineering improvements on rural highways. In the 1930s the federal government began to provide a source of funding for conducting planning studies with state highway department personnel. At this time the planning consisted of such activities as the planning of bypasses around cities or towns to relieve the traffic congestion within the intracity area.

In 1944 the first origin and destination study was conducted in Memphis, Tennessee. This origin and destination study was concerned with the collection of data on trips made by private automobile. The more comprehensive urban transportation planning process began in the early 1950s. Very sophisticated models were developed requiring a great need for computer capabilities to carry out the analyses. In the 1950s and 1960s, many millions of dollars were spent to refine and update these large and complex transportation planning models, which typically included trip generation, distribution, assignment, and modal split.

Even though the transportation planning process did include a modal split analysis, little attention was given to transit planning. A basic reason for so little attention being given to transit planning, especially in the early years, was that public transportation was in the private sector rather than the public sector. In the mid-1960s when public transportation began to fall under public ownership, more attention began to be given to transit planning. In many areas this growing interest was taken over by those individuals engaged in the highway planning field, usually because there simply was no one else to take on the task. Many of the techniques that had been utilized in the highway planning field for years were also utilized in transit planning. Attempts

410

were made to incorporate into transit planning such concepts as levels of service, long-range forecasting of capital expenditures, and other items that had been used in the highway field. However, the methodologies utilized in highway planning were not necessarily transferable to the transit field.

In addition to the highway field, other public works programs have been directed toward construction of facilities. Construction programs for sewers, public buildings, parking garages, dams, and other projects have been oriented toward the design and construction of permanent facilities that do not necessarily require a continuing management function. Once the facility was constructed, there was little need, if any, for a continual monitoring of the facility. In addition, once the funds were approved for construction, there was not a yearly request for more funds to reconstruct the same facility. Public bodies became accustomed to allocating funds almost on a one-time basis for each facility.

Transit services, of course, are considered for funding on a recurring basis. Management becomes a critical element and determines the effectiveness of the services provided from both financial and level-of-service aspects. Some public bodies have had difficulty in adjusting to non-facility-oriented programs requiring continual evaluation. Recent emphasis in the transit and highway field on transportation system management (TSM) requires that an analysis be made of methods of managing resources rather than remain oriented toward construction of new facilities. This increased emphasis on management should lead to a more effective utilization of resources. However, this approach of TSM will require planners, environmentalists, engineers, citizen groups, public works directors, and others to develop an understanding of the difference between planning and designing for facilities and operations. This chapter addresses some of the major differences in planning and designing for highways and transit operations. The examples used are oriented toward bus or van services of a fixed-route, fixed-schedule and/or paratransit nature rather than toward permanent facilities such as rail.

DIFFERENCES BETWEEN HIGHWAY AND TRANSIT PLANNING

PLANNING FOR FACILITIES

Highway planning is oriented toward the construction of fixed facilities such as freeways, rural highways, arterial streets, and/or collectors. The facility is fixed, immobile, and will not move with time. The facility does not have to be continuously redesigned or reconstructed. However, transit systems (with the exception of fixed-guideway systems) are not fixed facilities. The vast majority of transit systems are composed of buses or similar vehicles operating over a network of streets and roads. Routes and schedules change in some instances almost daily or weekly and thus bear qualities quite different from those of a fixed facility. There is a constant need for reevaluation and redesign to meet the changing needs of the consumer. One design or schedule of service normally will not be adequate over long periods of time.

DESIGN ORIENTATION

Traditionally, highway planning has been oriented toward engineering concepts. Standards were developed for the design and construction of these fixed facilities. Certain characteristics were involved in the design of highways, and an engineering background was required to successfully accomplish the design.

Transit operations are more business-oriented than engineering-oriented. There are few standards that actually can be adopted and applied as uniformly as one applies a standard to the construction of a bridge. Changes must be made almost on a daily basis, as with any business operation, if a system is to be successful. Flexibility is a necessity that is often lacking in highway planning.

PLANNING ORIENTATION

Highway planning normally has been concerned with a long-range plan of 20 or more years. Traffic volumes are forecast for 20 to 25 years, and facilities are planned to accommodate the expected traffic in that long-range period. Some consideration is given to the present facilities, but most of the attention is given to the highway system that should exist sometime in the future.

Transit is not oriented nearly as much to long-range planning. It is readily admitted that it does take a substantial amount of time to plan and design rail or fixed-guideway facilities. However, the majority of transit operations involve buses and similar vehicles that provide service over existing street systems. In actual operations one finds a transit system similar to a business, where the planning horizon is normally in the range of 1 to 3 years, with a maximum of about 5 to 7 years. Few, if any, businesses make strong commitments to long-range plans covering 20 years or longer. Transit operations must be flexible and, except for fixed-guideway systems, normally should not be committed to a plan that covers more than 3 to 5 years.

PROVISION OF NEW FACILITIES

It has been always understood and generally accepted that one could not build a new highway tomorrow, the week after, or even next year. It was expected that new highway facilities would involve long-range planning activities and that the actual construction of the facility would require many years.

Because most transit systems, particularly bus systems, do not require dedicated rights-of-way (R/W), the public often expects services to be provided tomorrow or at least the day after. Therefore, those responsible for transit services often are not afforded the luxury of promising to provide facilities and services that may not be available for 20 years or more.

CHANGING CONSUMER BEHAVIOR

The highway planner or designer has never been expected to modify the behavior of the user of the facility (i.e., product). Once the highway was built, normally there was sufficient traffic available to justify the facility. One did not have to encourage vehicles to use new facilities. In fact, in most traffic forecasting there is a "generated" traffic factor utilized which indicates that there will be more trips made than normally would be made if the new facility did not exist.

This simply is not the case in the transit field. The transit manager is expected to change consumer behavior and thus attract people to the transit system. The general public has not desired to see their transit vehicles traversing city streets without passengers. Therefore, the transit planner must look toward concepts that can modify the travel behavior of people to get them out of the auto and into the bus.

AVAILABILITY OF FUNDS

Since 1956, the highway trust fund has provided available resources for the planning, design, and construction of highways. In reality, there was little concern over funding because funds would be available each year for continuing the highway program. Many individuals felt that more funds should be available; however, there was little fear that the programs would have to be stopped or severely curtailed because of the unavailability of funds.

Most transit funding has been almost on a year-to-year basis. As of late 1978, there had been no trust funds established that would provide a long-range funding base for transit services. Many times, the next year's level of service depends upon the budget of a city council. This budget is reevaluated completely each year. In the operation of any transit service, a need for funding beyond a 12-month period is necessary to ensure appropriate planning. However, the transit planner must realize that the funding procedures for transit require a different approach to the planning process.

EVALUATION OF FACILITIES

Once a highway facility has been constructed, one does not usually make an evaluation to see if the traffic actually does justify the construction of the facility in terms of cost or services provided. Generally, there is more traffic on the facility than is forecast for any given year. Normally, no evaluation is made of the level of service provided unless congestion becomes extremely severe and improvements in the facility are needed. Overdesigned highway facilities do not receive critical comment. There are thousands of miles of interstate rural highways that will perhaps never become congested. Generally, there is less criticism of an overdesigned (more capacity than is needed) highway than one that is underdesigned. This concept, of course, is not true for the transit area.

Transit is evaluated almost daily because of the deficits that are incurred in the system operations. This is particularly true at budget time, when the amount of subsidy must be provided in the budgets of municipalities or authorities. Overdesigned transit systems receive much criticism. While it is readily agreed that the evaluation process for transit leaves something to be desired, nevertheless, the operations are reviewed, particularly if a deficit will exist. The manager of the transit system must justify the deficit on a regularly scheduled basis.

CROSSING POLITICAL BOUNDARIES

It is generally not difficult to cross political boundaries with highways. Most political divisions in the past have desired new highway facilities in their areas. The establishment of major routes usually lay at the state level of government, which provided an easier method of crossing most political boundaries.

Transit, often being a localized form of operation, finds itself with much difficulty in serving different political jurisdictions. Because of regulatory constraints at local and state levels, transit operations are often limited in scope and the ability to serve a wide-area market. This can lead to many inefficiencies in planning for and providing transit services, and it complicates coordination between systems. In the San Francisco Bay area, for instance, there are eight major service providers, each of which has constraints on its allowed service area.

REGULATORY AGENCIES

The majority of major highway facilities are planned and built by state agencies, such as a highway department, with no other agencies, such as public service commissions, regulating the particular facility. Of course, one sees variations, such as with toll roads and other specialized facilities. However, there has been very little impact of any type of regulations on the operations of highway facilities, except in isolated cases.

The regulators of public services at the state and local levels have had a direct impact and, in many instances, a great constraining impact on the provision of services, particularly paratransit services. Many of these regulatory agencies simply have prohibited innovative services from being provided. The regulatory issues become a very important input to the planning process and have a definite bearing upon innovative approaches for the provision of services.

CAPITAL COSTS

The operational or maintenance costs of a highway to government are small when compared to the total capital outlays required for constructing a highway facility. With the exception of the construction of dedicated R/W facilities such as rail rapid transit systems, the annual operating costs are a large portion of the total annual cost of a transit system, and the annual operational costs continue to be a burden upon the transit system. The more vehicles needed in the system, the more funds needed to operate them. It is much easier to obtain the capital for transit vehicles than it is to obtain the annual operational and maintenance funds needed to provide services with those vehicles.

SERVING PEAK-PERIOD VOLUMES

Highway facilities are considered successful if they adequately serve peak-period traffic. Very few complaints are made if the highway facilities successfully carry the peak volumes but have little traffic in the off-peak period. In many instances, highway facilities have been designed to serve a peak period of only 5 to 15 minutes each day.

This was possible since there were adequate resources from the highway trust fund to construct facilities based on such short peak-period volumes.

The transit system normally is able to handle the peak-period volumes. However, it is the shortage of passengers in the off-peak periods that becomes detrimental to transit operations and arouses criticism. The transit system is expected to carry large volumes at all times because the unused capacity in the off-peak periods is obvious and generates deficits. The criteria for success are vastly different for transit services than for highway facilities.

DEMAND FORECASTS

When the traffic forecasts have been made for highway facilities and the facilities are constructed, there is little concern about how close the forecast for the traffic is to the actual traffic on the facility. This is due, of course, to the fact that in many instances the traffic recorded actually exceeded the amount forecast. Also, it is understood that the facility is built and there is not much that can be done if the traffic is different. In the transit field the forecast for transit ridership is compared with the actual ridership almost daily, and certainly yearly. Any discrepancies found are generally highlighted, to the chagrin of the transit planner.

AVAILABILITY OF A FACILITY

The marginal costs of keeping a highway facility open to traffic for 24 hours a day, 7 days a week, are relatively minor when compared to operating the facility on a limited hourly basis. Most likely the costs would be greater for intermittent operations. Thus, the highway facility is available at all times for any potential user of the system.

The marginal cost of providing transit services for any additional time period is high. In most systems, service is not provided on a 24-hour basis and, therefore, because of the ratio of marginal cost to marginal revenue, a user of a transit system can only travel at specified hours of the day. It becomes difficult when an individual is totally dependent on transit for all travel needs.

THE CONCEPT OF LARGENESS

The concept of "more of the same is better" has prevailed in highway planning (e.g., four lanes are better than two and six better than four for serving the traveling public). Of course, there have been some limits to this idea (as there are limits to the number of lanes that one would desire for a highway).

Some planners have applied the concept "more is better" to the transit field. However, in this field the idea is totally false. Two buses operating over the same route are not necessarily better than one. Headways of 15 minutes are not necessarily better than 30 minutes. More of the same in the transit field does not in any way ensure that it will be better than that which exists. Providing more of that which is already unacceptable will not lead to improvements in ridership or financial standing. As an example, there have been transit systems that have expanded route-miles, decreased headways, and broadened the area of coverage; and the reported results may show an increase in total daily patronage. However, the number of revenue passengers per mile (which is a more efficient indicator) has remained about the same, and in some instances has been reduced.

REVENUE PRODUCERS

The concept of a given highway facility having to generate revenue has not been accepted universally. It is true that some toll roads have been financially successful; however, many toll roads have not been. Past surveys seem to indicate that much of the traveling public is not receptive to paying user charges to travel on a highway facility. The resistance to toll charges by the traveling motorist may, in part, be due to the erroneous perception that gasoline taxes are used to build all highways. Of course, money from bond issues is normally used to construct toll facilities. The toll charges are used to retire the bonds. However, the traveling public may feel that they are paying "twice" for the ability to travel on a toll facility.

Free transit has never been accepted universally as a means of increasing patronage on transit systems. In fact, some limited experiments have indicated that free or fare-reduced services do not necessarily have a large impact upon an increase in ridership (i.e., Rome experiment and Atlanta). Generally, it is desired that the farebox will provide a substantial amount of the total cost of operation. The amount that the farebox can actually provide, of course, has been decreasing each year as costs escalate. Most political groups, be they transit authority, local government, or any other organization that has control over a transit operation, certainly expect this mode of travel to be revenue-producing.

LABOR CONSTRAINTS

The operation and maintenance of a highway facility is generally not affected by labor unions or labor constraints. A labor strike usually would not close a highway, nor are there labor contracts to negotiate in order to keep the majority of highway facilities open. In the transit field, labor has a very definite impact on the operations. It has an impact not only on the cost of operations, but on the type of innovativeness that one can introduce into the transit field.

THE UTILIZATION OF MATHEMATICAL MODELS

Mathematical models, such as with the traffic assignment package, are used to test various highway systems that could be proposed for building. Various schemes of design can be tested through large-scale computer models to see how well they would serve particular traffic demands. These models are a substitute for product testing. Mathematical models are not truly behavioral in structure, which limits their effectiveness as a substitute for product testing. In highway planning, many of the mathematical models that have been developed have been based on trend analysis and have not been behavioral models in the traditional sense.

With transit, particularly with buses and similar vehicles, product testing can be utilized. *Product testing* simply means that a product is provided and tested as to the consumer acceptance of the service. In the transit field, one needs to change or modify human behavior. If models are used in transit planning, they must be truly behavioral in nature for forecasting the demand for particular types of service innovation.

MARKET ORIENTATION

Very few highway operations have developed a marketing program to attract vehicles to the system. This has never been needed. Generally, there has always been a sufficient demand for the facility. Thus, marketing has been completely absent from the highway planning field. Marketing is an absolute necessity in the transit field. Without marketing one can never achieve success in providing transit services. The highway planner generally is not trained in marketing and so cannot make substantial contributions in this area.

MANAGEMENT ORIENTATION

A highway facility, after it is constructed, has little attention paid to it from a management point of view. Of course, in certain instances, as with toll roads and implementation of TSM techniques, management does play a part; but generally, one can say that management does not play a major role in the operation of normal highway facilities.

Management is the key to providing successful public transportation services. Without proper management, there will not be successful transit systems.

CONCLUSION

Most public facility planners have not been trained in appropriate management techniques. The whole concept of planning for transit services is so different from highway planning that there must be a realignment of thinking. Highway planners may have difficulty moving into transit planning positions and performing as they should and may have little impact on improving transit services if the planning for transit services is incorporated into the traditional highway planning activities. There is a need to view transit planning in its proper perspective and to separate it, to a certain extent, from the techniques used in highway planning. This does not mean that there should not be an integration of transit services with highway facilities. However, it does mean that the methods and tools used for the planning of transit services are different from those required for highway facilities.

SELECTED BIBLIOGRAPHY

HEATHINGTON, KENNETH W., *Evaluation Procedures for Public Transportation Services*, prepared for Tennessee Bureau of Mass Transit. Nashville, Tenn.: Tennessee Department of Transportation, 1975.
———, "A Planning Perspective on Evaluating Urban Public Transportation," in *Research Needs for Evaluating Urban Public Transportation*, Special Report 155, pp. 14–23. Washington, D.C.: Transportation Research Board, 1975.

PART V

Managing and Operating Public Transit Systems

INTRODUCTION TO PART V

The purpose of this section is to describe the elements in managing and operating a public transportation system. Transit management has not had the tradition and experience common in the private sector, nor has the role of marketing and consumer behavior been recognized until recently. Rather, transit management has focused principally on its equipment: servicing, maintenance, scheduling, dispatching, and operations. Most transit properties are small, and there has been little incentive for young managers to select transit employment as a career.

Transit management should begin with establishment of goals and objectives to be achieved by the operation. These should be developed in cooperation with a board of directors who work with management in allocating resources for public transportation. Consumer behavior should be understood and a marketing strategy developed that recognizes different needs and then develops services directed at specific target groups. The marketing mix includes the product (type, quality, and access to service), the price, and promotion.

The transit manager must devote attention to many tasks and establish priorities for the efforts expended by the agency. The basic characteristics of transit define the manager's role. Transit is a competitive retail enterprise generally operating on a cash basis, is highly labor-intensive, and is regulated by outside government agencies. These constraints place a boundary on the transit manager's responsibilities and help to define those activities that will require major effort.

Marketing involves both selling of the agencies' existing products and planning new products for future demand. To effectively market public transportation, five basic questions must be answered: What are the communities' goals and objectives? What market segments must be served to meet these goals? What combinations of services, price, and promotion must be offered to accomplish community objectives? When should services be terminated? How should the transit authority be organized to ensure that community objectives are achieved? Thus, many aspects of public transit management are similar to those of the private firm, especially in product planning, development, and retaining flexibility in adjusting services to meet changing needs.

Product marketing targeted to the needs of specific groups will attract patrons to use public transportation, but the system will ultimately be judged on its operational performance. A key attribute in retaining patronage is that the passengers travel safely without bodily harm or accident. Transit security on buses and trains involves a variety of approaches that attempt to deter, thwart, or apprehend a criminal. For example, crimes on buses were reduced markedly when exact-fare lock boxes were installed, and the use of police decoys in high-crime areas has proved to be an effective means of reducing crimes in subways. The transit industry programs for maintaining an excellent safety record include driver training, vehicle maintenance, accident records, and standards.

The role of private industry in furnishing public transportation services has been severely limited due to regulatory constraints placed upon new firms that desire to enter the market. These are being lifted somewhat, as witnessed by laws in many states exempting vanpools with 15 or fewer riders from state regulations. The brokerage concept is a means for enlarging the role of private industry by matching supply and demand, in ways similar to that used by an insurance company or real estate agency.

Finally, despite management efforts to identify transit markets, operating expenses are not recovered from the farebox. Accordingly, the sources of transit subsidy (federal, state, and local) and the merits of furnishing subsidies to the provider of services or to the user directly are important management concerns.

Lester A. Hoel, Professor and Chairman,
Department of Civil Engineering,
University of Virginia

Chapter 20

THE MANAGEMENT OF PUBLIC TRANSIT*

GEORGE M. SMERK, *Professor of Transportation, Graduate School of Business, Indiana University*

Much of the interest and improvement in urban mass transportation has come as a result of efforts by the national government, spurred on by vigorous lobbying by urban interest groups, including the transit industry. Public policy toward urban mass transportation on the federal level began in 1961 with a small-scale program of demonstrations and loans. After a slow start, the programs established by the federal government picked up momentum; by 1970, federal aid was available through the Urban Mass Transportation Administration (UMTA) for a variety of program purposes, including capital improvements; research, development, and demonstration; planning; and management training. In 1973 certain moneys of the highway trust fund were made available for mass transportation purposes. In 1974 Congress adopted legislation that gave federal transit funds to *urbanized areas* (cities above 50,000 population) on a formula basis.

Much of the research sponsored by UMTA in the past was devoted to the development of hardware, in the apparent hope that there would be a breakthrough in technology that would somehow help solve the problems of mass transportation. Through 1972, there was little emphasis on research and development for the purpose of helping to upgrade management or to develop new concepts and new approaches to the management of urban mass transit. Happily, beginning in the early part of 1973, UMTA began to turn more of its attention and funds toward the improvement of transit management. This change in attitude by UMTA reflects a growing concern with the quality of management in transit and recognition of its importance in making transit more useful and attractive to the urban traveler.

---

*Some of the ideas in this chapter originally appeared in: GEORGE M. SMERK, "Mass Transit Management," *Business Horizons*, 14, no. 6 (December 1971), 5, 8–16.

UMTA's recognition of the importance of transit management is testimony of an often-overlooked fact of life in public transportation. Obviously, technology and its improvement is important in any enterprise, but the tools of technology are merely resources and can be only as effective as management skill permits them to be. With major capital improvements made or under way in all parts of the nation, it is only good sense to examine carefully the concepts and approaches to transit management that will permit the assets of a transit firm—both human and material—to be utilized most effectively.

THE ROOTS OF THE TRANSIT MANAGEMENT PROBLEM

Transit was traditionally managed as a privately owned, monopolistic public utility; long ago, the growth in the use of private automobiles largely whittled away this monopoly of mass transportation. Now that most of the transit industry is publicly owned, the management problem is even more clouded in terms of a rationale to guide managers along the proper pathway. The management of publicly owned enterprises poses a major difficulty in the United States, since the country does not have a long history or well-developed ethic of public enterprise management. Whatever tradition exists is based mainly on the management of truly monopolistic undertakings, such as city-owned water utilities. The lessons learned in the management of the only water company in town provide few clues for management of a mass transportation agency that must operate in direct competition with the private automobile. Modern business management techniques could have a revolutionary impact on traditional transit management. As an example, the transit industry and its management has almost always been operations-oriented. This means that the conventionally well-managed transit property is adept at servicing and maintaining equipment; scheduling, dispatching, and otherwise seeing to it that equipment is on the street and rolling; and utilizing vehicles and personnel in what is hoped to be the least costly manner. What traditional management lacks is a feel for the consumer and, perhaps even more important, the potential consumer of public transportation services. On the other hand, modern business management techniques and strategies are generally aimed primarily at serving the consumer. Similar techniques and strategies are applicable to the transit industry, especially in its role as a competitor to the automobile or—in view of environmental and energy problems—as an alternative to the private car. The purpose of this chapter is to examine some of the reasons behind the typical management rubric in public transportation, and to sketch out the kind of approach that would be most practical in establishing a framework of managerial practice appropriate to today's transit situation.

Transit management has traditionally been consumed with interest in the operations of transit, rather than concerned with the consumers who use it. Transit is not unique in this orientation; it is common in the transportation industries. One very good reason for this attitude is that transportation firms, transit included, usually possess very complex operation problems that tend to overshadow other proper concerns of management. In the developmental stages of most modes of transport, the problems of scheduling men and equipment, fighting the elements, and overcoming the limitations of equipment and facilities were matters of paramount urgency.

Finding and retaining good management people is a problem for any enterprise, but transit has had even more difficulty because it has been in the unenviable position of being a declining industry for more than half a century. Low managerial pay is one aspect of such an industry. Perhaps even worse, conservatism of approach is inherent in such declining situations; innovation is avoided and the practices of the past become embalmed in the actions of the present. The painful contraction of service and inevitable decline in prestige of working in such an industry presents little that is attractive to new blood.

Unfortunately, even before the automotive revolution was under way, the transit industry had been seriously weakened by financial peccadillos, stock jobbing, unscrupulous promoters, and a host of other practices that left the viability of large segments of the transit industry in a financially embarrassed and weakened state. The skyrocketing cost increases of the World War I period and interest due on overinflated capitalization, together with limitations on the amount of fare that might be charged and other statutory obligations connected with operating franchises, led to the bankruptcy of a major portion of the transit industry by 1918.

Forced to meet the challenge of the automobile while near bankruptcy, the transit industry developed a strong and understandable concern with cost cutting. At the same time, vigor was diminished and innovation suppressed because of the state of the industry. Some management talent, and capital, was available from the electrical utility industry, of which many transit firms were a part in the 1920s; however, declining ridership, which was due to the increasing availability of dependable automobiles at reasonable prices, cut revenues and made transit less and less attractive to the parent utility companies, especially after the start of the Great Depression. On top of that, the Holding Company Act of 1934 caused the divorce of many transit firms from their electric utility parents; this effectively diverted the transit industry from major currents of managerial talent and removed many transit firms from any hope of receiving major transfusions of capital from their erstwhile parent firms.

In the wake of the pullout of electric utilities from the transit business, transit holding companies—some controlling a score or more properties—arrived on the scene to fill the vacuum. Many of these holding companies were organized in conjunction with major motorbus equipment manufacturers and suppliers bent on the substitution of buses for streetcars in the transit industry. The focus of attention in this period was generally not one of great concern with the mass transportation consumer or with the development of consumer-oriented management. Rather, it was the superintendence of disinvestment in electric railways and mastering the art of operating buses as nearly like streetcars as possible.

Perhaps even more of a problem in recruiting and retaining the type of management needed in transit was the fact that since the 1920s the industry had not been part of the conventional mainstream of American business, which tended to be dominated by growing national firms that required the services of large numbers of professionally trained, middle-management personnel. The challenges and rewards of working with a major national firm are substantial for persons of managerial talent. Transit firms, with the exceptions of a few giants in the largest cities, are relatively small enterprises, and the possibilities of promotion and economic reward appear to be slim to young people looking for a career with real opportunity. In addition, the financial weakness of the transit industry, especially since the end of World War II, has usually made it sadly uncompetitive in salaries. This is not to say that there are not many persons of real skill in the transit industry; there are. But these people generally stumbled into their positions; they did not arrrive there as a result of careful recruitment or an early decision to seek out transit as an interesting and rewarding career area. In all truth, because of the lack of "outside" interest in transit, promoting from within has often been the only option open to the industry. Obviously, this cuts down the field of choice. Moreover, for a person of talent within the transit field, other industry is likely to beckon with higher pay and better working conditions.

TRANSIT AND THE EXAMPLE OF THE MODERN BUSINESS FIRM

The new interest of state, local, and federal governments toward public transportation improvements has enhanced the transit industry's importance. The industry is being asked to cope with the nation's need for improved mobility and overall quality of life in U.S. cities, and for reduced automobile use in order to protect the environment and cut the demands of transportation on scarce energy resources. In short, there is a vital need to strengthen transit management and to bring transit into line with modern concepts of management in order for it to meet new and important roles into which it has been cast.

There are lessons for the management of public transportation in the approach used by the modern business firm. Such firms usually focus on carefully defined objectives (share of the market, return on investment, return on sales, etc.) and the thoughtful manipulation of human and material resources to reach the objective. Marketing thus becomes a matter of major importance and a central part of the structure of the institution. The market is carefully researched, the pulse of the consumer is taken, not only to determine total demand but also to discover the particular mix of price and service that will appeal to given segments of the market. In the modern business firm different varieties of product or service are tailor-made for different market segments, along with price and promotional activities aimed at different pocketbooks, life-styles, and viewpoints.

The canny modern firm, after getting a handle on the market potential, turns loose its production experts, product design engineers, and product development staff to see if it can profitably produce what it has determined that the public wants. The physical supply and distribution staff smooth the flow and cut the costs of collecting the elements of production and, after the production process, of distributing goods to the market. The financial staff analyzes the potential profit of various products and seeks the funds to do the job from internal and external sources. Accountants, electronic data processing experts, and information system developers devise information systems and cost controls, both to provide for a flow of necessary information for management and to prevent waste and inefficiency. Promotion, sales, and advertising personnel work up competitive strategies and plan programs to bring the product to the attention of the public. If, after a careful and complete analysis is made, the firm can, indeed, produce a product and sell it in line with its objectives, the final decision will be made to go ahead. Much the same approach can be used in the management of public transportation enterprise.

There is an obvious need for a modern approach to transit management and a new breed of manager with a professional education in business, adept at applying a systematic approach to transit operations and marketing similar to that utilized by most modern business firms. The proper type of management for today's public transportation firm should concentrate on clear-cut, consumer-oriented objectives, organizing the firm to meet these objectives, and utilizing the marketing management concept as a means of turning transit into an industry responsive to consumers.

GOAL SETTING

The value of striving toward defined goals is related to what Samuel Johnson found in the possibility of being hanged—it does wonders in focusing the attention of the mind. What this means in practice is that transit managers and public officials must be specific about what transit is supposed to accomplish. The organizational structure can then be tailored to help meet the goals.

Transit objectives have to be precise and workable, not vague, general hopes. Simply "making transit service better" will not suffice. Goals must be concrete and sufficiently practical to enable them to be used in the process of setting realistic objectives such as providing transit service to meet the needs of the bulk of the members of the community or bringing the operating deficit within reasonable bounds. Such goals can be reasonably translated into objectives.

The rule for formulating practical objectives demands that the goals be clear and definite, attainable, measurable, and reached by a given target date. A good example of such an objective would be "to provide transit service at least every 20 minutes during the major portion of the day, within two blocks of every residence in the city by January 1, 1985." Such an objective must, naturally, fit into the overall plans and goals for urban development within the city. Whole sets of detailed minor objectives and priorities may be established to help in achieving the principal objective.

A multiplicity of objectives of major and minor consequence are no impediment to the fulfillment of major objectives, as long as all the objectives are in concord with the primary thrust of action. A program of vehicle replacement to cut the average age of the transit fleet and reduce maintenance problems and costs would be in accord with the objectives of service on a dependable 20-minute headway. On the other hand, objectives of minimizing maintenance effort and maximizing reliability of service would clearly be in conflict with one another.

Private operators must, of course, focus on profit if they are to remain in business. In a narrow but certainly not improper sense, the private firm can conclude that it is on the right track if, over time, it is profitable. The publicly owned firm must have service as a primary goal; its clue to success in the short run will most likely be an increase in the number of riders. In the long run, the success of the public firm will be in its approach to the realization of the goals and objectives established for it, which may have little or nothing to do with profit.

THE BOARD OF DIRECTORS AND MANAGEMENT

The business of setting goals and objectives and translating them into action involves interplay between transit management and those who govern the transit entity. This may be a board of directors of a transit authority; where transit is operated as a city department, the governing body of a transit property may be the city council. If transit is operated as a city utility, direction may come from a board of public works or a city utility board. Generally, in larger communities the governing body is most apt to be the board of a transit authority or a transit district, the latter usually having taxing authority. In larger urban places the transit authority may be metropolitan in nature to cover the whole of the urbanized area. Whatever the particular arrangement, the directors of a publicly owned transit agency can be a source of aid or trouble for those engaged in the day-to-day management of the transit property. A board is usually trouble because the directors do not understand their proper role.

The proper function of directors is to set the broad goals of the organization, to provide policy guidelines, and, in conjunction with management, to help establish priorities and objectives. In a public enterprise the directors are representatives of the public; in some cases the directors may be elected, and in other instances the directors may be chosen by elected officials. The chairman of the modern transit board of directors usually has the chores of keeping political fences well mended and, in company with the other directors and elected officials, of seeing to it that the general thrust of mass transportation is in line with the overall goals and objectives of the municipality served.

Directors should, of course, be concerned with the overall direction in which the transit agency is moving; indeed, they should help set that direction. They should also be involved in helping to obtain and to allocate, in a general way, resources for public transportation. However, directors should not be involved in detailed resource allocation.

Where directors do not understand their proper role, they are likely to hinder the day-to-day affairs of operating transit. Interference in management prerogatives by directors can demolish managerial morale, especially when directors insist on having their way in matters that are unsafe, unwise, uneconomical, or may cause managerial performance to appear unprofessional. Directors have been known to attempt to write schedules, force transit routes into hopeless territories, serve favored shopping centers, order special services, and even commandeer vehicles for private use. Insisting on schedules, routes, and services that are not warranted is probably the worst offense.

One of the problems that has appeared in the switchover of transit from private to public enterprise is the evolution of the board of directors. In the initial stages of public ownership, strong and active members of the community—the so-called "movers and shakers"—apparently can be attracted to serve. Once the enterprise is on its feet, the movers and shakers tend to move on to other undertakings of a more challenging nature; over time, more political individuals or weaker persons with less stature in the community may become directors. It is often at this stage that management is most bothered; being unsure of their role, later generations of directors often meddle in the business of day-to-day management. Part of the problem is simply one of the directors learning what their job really is. It takes time for directors to develop knowledge of transit. For this reason, perhaps the tenure of office should be rather lengthy with staggered terms, with the more senior directors the only ones eligible for the chairmanship. Above all, of course, those who name directors must choose wisely.

CONSUMER BEHAVIOR

Regardless of the form of ownership, the key to effective goal setting in transit today has to be consumer orientation. This is so because it is not very likely that any city would choose to force its citizens to use mass transportation.

However, in these days of concern with pollution of the environment and shortage of energy, it is appropriate for local government—perhaps at the behest of state and national government—to apply incentives to encourage use of public transportation along with disincentives to help discourage use of the private automobile. Low transit fares and a surtax on parking may become common features of U.S. urban life. In any event, the public cannot be expected to utilize transit merely as an expression of civic concern; there must be something in it for the consumer if transit is to attract patronage. It should be noted that the philosophy of the federal government in the future will be to discourage the use of the automobile in urban settings. At long last, it has dawned on the U.S. Department of Transportation (DOT) that continuing to provide highway facilities to meet the apparently limitless demands of the private motorist is a losing battle; it is a classic example of supply tending to create its own demand.

Federal policy requires that urban areas provide plans and programs to ensure that transit equipment functions as efficiently as possible. Successful transit operation is mainly a function of marketing, in the broadest sense of the term, as it relates to consumers and potential consumers of transit service. Specific goals will differ from place to place, as well as the organizational structure needed to meet the goals; in all cases, however, it is necessary that the goals, objectives, organization, and action be grounded in an understanding of consumer behavior and translation of that understanding into appropriate marketing effort.

It may not appear, at first blush, that consumers act rationally. However, there is both motivation and logic behind consumers' actions, no matter how erratic it may appear to the outside observer. The point is illustrated in the simple model of consumer behavior illustrated in Fig. 20-1. The elements of the model are as follows:

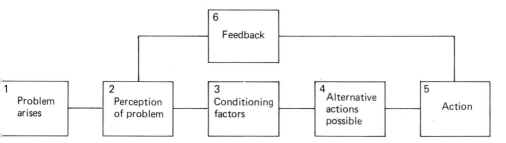

Figure 20-1 *Simple model of consumer behavior.* [*Source: George M. Smerk, "Mass Transit Management,"* Business Horizons, *14, no. 6 (December 1971), 11.*]

1. *A problem arises.* Behavior is problem-solving in nature; consumers will act to solve their problems through purchase and/or use of a product or service.
2. *Perception.* The realization that there is a problem and the nature of that problem is communicated to the brain by the senses.
3. *Conditioning.* Conditioning is comprised of the factors that act as a filter or a preprogramming to consumers' attitudes and approaches to the problem they perceive. The most important of the conditioning factors are imposed by society. For example, natives or longtime residents of the United States would be affected and conditioned by Western civilization in general. More specifically, they would be affected by the society of the nation as a whole and the region in which they live, together with the general class in those regions of which they are a part. Also important are the immediate groups of which they are members and the groups with which they identify and which they attempt to copy. All human beings grow hungry, but in the United States hungry persons would be unlikely to eat candied ants or grasshoppers in cream sauce as a supper repast at 3 o'clock, nor would they eat their breakfast cornflakes and milk with their fingers. Nature may tell us that we are hungry, but our society determines what we will eat, and when and how it will be consumed.
4. *Alternatives.* Consumers must evaluate and select among the various alternatives that are open, acceptable, and known to them. It should be understood that, to the consumer, an option that is unknown does not exist in any meaningful way. In deciding among alternatives, consumers perform rough mental calculations of the time, energy, and money that must be expended on each of the alternatives.
5. *Action.* Consumers act in accordance with the acceptable alternative that meets whatever constraints they face in terms of time, energy, and money. In short,

consumers will choose the least "costly" acceptable alternative that is open to them.

6. *Feedback.* Feedback is the means by which consumers determine whether or not their problems have been solved by the choices they have made and the actions they have taken. If not satisfied that the problem has been solved, consumers will select alternatives.

For transit management that is trying to attract more patronage, perhaps the most fertile fields for imaginative and useful marketing work are the conditioning factors in conjunction with the alternatives open to the consumer. For example, management might take action in a program that would attempt to affect conditioning so that mass transportation was accepted by an increasing number of sectors of society. To carry this out, objectives and policies should be shaped with improvements of transit's image and acceptability by the public kept in mind. The image of transit as a service for the losers of society has to be changed, or those who identify with winners will not be attracted. By means of good, reliable transit performance, along with careful advertising and community relations work, a more positive attitude toward mass transportation may be developed among middle-class consumers and potential consumers.

Promotion of transit as a reasonable alternative to the private automobile is one approach that might be taken in the marketing area. Apart from social stigmas that may be attached to transit, it is fair to say that transit is usually not considered to be an adequate substitute for the automobile. In light of the behavioral model discussed earlier, transit may be more expensive in time, effort, and money than the private auto. Transit may also be *perceived* as more time- and energy-consuming and more costly in pecuniary terms even if, in reality, it is not. Consumers will, of course, behave in terms of what they believe to be true.

Under these circumstances, the proper marketing ploy for management is to take steps to reduce the actual and perceived time, energy, and money costs of transit. To effect a real reduction of time and effort, careful rethinking and restructuring of transit routes and schedules is needed. It might also mean fare reduction or restructuring of fares to make the price–service package attractive to consumers. Figure 20-2 provides a graphic presentation of a trip and possible sites of the cost involved. Assuming that the fare for a transit ride is lower in money cost than the total cost of using an automobile, it is still important to cut other costs. Lengthy walks to transit stops, long running time of vehicles, unattractive equipment or facilities, inconvenient transfers, and grumpy employees all add to the cost of energy and time needed by transit consumers. By reviewing all the segments of a trip, management can make cost reductions where needed; for instance, better coordination of schedules may cut transfer time drastically. Better integration of routes may reduce the need for transit patrons to transfer between routes.

Fare reductions may appear to be the easiest way of making transit more attractive, since it is a direct and obvious action. Even so, the traveling public may not be convinced that transit is much of a bargain if travel time is lengthy. Cutting down on travel time and the other impediments to consumer attraction are not easy. For

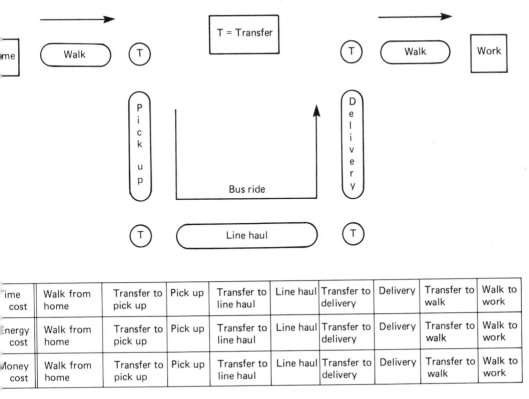

Figure 20-2 *Journey analysis: time, energy, and money cost*

Time cost	Walk from home	Transfer to pick up	Pick up	Transfer to line haul	Line haul	Transfer to delivery	Delivery	Transfer to walk	Walk to work
Energy cost	Walk from home	Transfer to pick up	Pick up	Transfer to line haul	Line haul	Transfer to delivery	Delivery	Transfer to walk	Walk to work
Money cost	Walk from home	Transfer to pick up	Pick up	Transfer to line haul	Line haul	Transfer to delivery	Delivery	Transfer to walk	Walk to work

example, most transit managers—except on grade-separated rapid transit systems—have little or no control over the right-of-way their vehicles must utilize. The typical street shared by automobiles, trucks, transit vehicles, and pedestrians offers many opportunities for delay to the transit service. In such a situation, reserved transit lanes are necessary to speed the movement of transit vehicles.

If the general national impression of transit is largely negative, image improvement will need far more than mere cosmetic treatment. Overcoming a bad image is probably a tougher job than creating a new public impression from scratch. The real proof of the pudding lies in the quality of the service–price package that is offered to the public.

ENVIRONMENTS OF THE TRANSIT MANAGER

Transit managers operate within several environments; some of these are not within their control. As an example, the manager of a given transit property must, by and large, live with national and state situations much as they are found. Any impact on the national environment will probably be nil. Over time, and in concert with other transit managers, they may have some impact on state policy, but it will probably not be easy or immediate. The general local situation is also somewhat out of control, but not totally so. Transit management may be able to work with public officials to ensure that, say, parking bans at bus stops will be enforced. Again, a local manager may be able to gain use of reserved lanes for transit through careful negotiations with the local government.

On the other hand, within the transit firm itself, management may exercise a considerable degree of regulation. Transit management holds the reins of a fairly large number of variables; through the manipulation of those variables, it can provide a variety of service packages with differing degrees of appeal to the public. If the consumer-oriented marketing–management approach is to be used, recognition must be given to all the elements of the transit firm that may effectively be commanded by management. Moreover, great care must be taken to see that those elements are considered in a systematic fashion, with careful attention paid to their interrelationships.

Some of the principal aspects of transit firms are:

- The organization of the firm to meet stated goals, as well as input on goal formulation.
- The information collected by the firm and how it is used for management purposes, including accounting and ridership data and other information needed for effective managerial control, reporting to regulatory or control bodies, financial records, and decision making.
- The personnel selected by the firm, how it is recruited and trained, and the methods used in supervision of personnel and negotiation with organized labor.
- The selection of equipment.
- The maintenance program for equipment and facilities.
- Routing.
- Schedules.
- Communication for efficient, effective, and dependable operation, especially between operators and supervisors.
- The overall marketing program.
- The advertising program.
- The public information program, including maps, schedules, and information signs and graphics.
- Community relations programs.

In keeping with the operations-oriented philosophy, the organization chart of the typical transit firm naturally treats operations as the central function with maintenance, clerical work, and administration functions as adjuncts. Marketing is and has been totally neglected in most transit firms. In some cases, transit may mistake an advertising program for a real marketing program. If a transit organization is to be geared to carry out the objectives of a truly consumer-oriented service, marketing must be the core element about which the organization structure is built. A modern organization structure for transit is illustrated in Fig. 20-3.

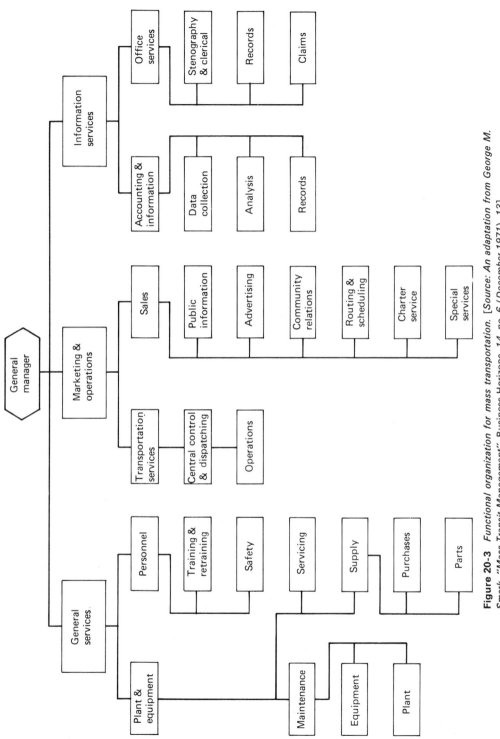

Figure 20-3 *Functional organization for mass transportation. [Source: An adaptation from George M. Smerk, "Mass Transit Management", Business Horizons 14, no. 6 (December 1971), 13]*

In examining Fig. 20-3, it should be recognized that this is a functional organization chart, showing tasks to be performed—not a detailed chart that provides slots for individuals. "Marketing and Operations" covers the various jobs related to selling and running the service. "Information Services" includes the office and accounting functions as well as the gathering of statistics for managerial decision-making and planning purposes. "General Services" involves the hardware and personnel functions, safety, servicing and maintenance of equipment and facilities, and the purchasing and control of supplies. The precise details of an organization and the number of positions would naturally depend upon the size of the transit property and the degree of specialization possible with a larger firm.

THE MARKETING PROGRAM

Marketing is far more than a stepped-up sales effort. The marketing program of a transit firm must be positively directed to the task of discovering opportunities to serve the public. A private firm will, of course, analyze the results of its services and continue those operations that, in the long run, appear to be most profitable. The publicly owned firm should continue to offer certain needed and desired services, regardless of their profitability, within the context of its stated objectives. At the same time, the publicly owned firm should take steps to increase patronage and revenues so that income is maximized to the greatest extent possible without causing the service to suffer. Obviously, the greater the income, the better the overall level of service that might be provided.

A transit property must adopt a marketing strategy that is appropriate to its situation in a competitive transportation market. Since resources are inevitably limited, to avoid waste, the marketing effort must be focused as finely as possible. The best scheme is to direct marketing effort toward particular segments of the overall market rather than to try to reach everyone at the same time. In addition to meeting the needs of obvious patronage groups, marketing should direct a careful promotional effort toward those nonusers who can reasonably be judged as potential transit riders.

One truism: the market for public transportation does not consist of a homogeneous mass of consumers, sometimes dubbed "human freight" by insensitive transit management. A single-service approach will not suffice in a real, heterogeneous market because the market is divided into segments of consumers with different needs and desires that require different packages of service. The market segment, in strategic terms, is the smallest unit for which it is worth tailoring a separate marketing program. The concept of the marketing mix is useful in dealing with the segments of the transit market. It includes product, price, and promotion, and transit managers must try to reach the segments with various combinations of these elements. The job of the transit marketer is to pick out the worthwhile segments from the mass of travel demand and discover means to serve those for which transit can play an effective and useful role.

The most natural and easy approach to marketing transit is to appeal initially, through a general service offering, to the most accessible segments of the market. In the first stages of the marketing program, these would probably consist of those patrons without an alternative means of travel regularly available to them. The early work would involve approaches pointed at the improvement of the quality, status, and general image of mass transportation.

Through concentration on reliability, convenience, comfort, value for money, speed, and other quality factors, the initially served segments should be held and used as a base upon which to build the transit market. Quality improvements and higher standards of service should be promoted through relevant media. Over time, word-of-mouth comments by satisfied customers will help to reinforce and strengthen the transit image. After the potential of the initial segments are tapped, the next best segment should be sought, held, and so on. Figure 20-4 illustrates the procedure.

The service should be directed toward reducing the time, energy, and money cost of travel, and at improving public acceptance. This may be achieved by emphasizing reliable, on-time performance, new and comfortable equipment, and reasonable prices. Once patrons have become accustomed to the service offering, market research should be utilized to derive a cross section of who is using the service. Next, further research into the market should be utilized to determine who is not using transit, and the reason

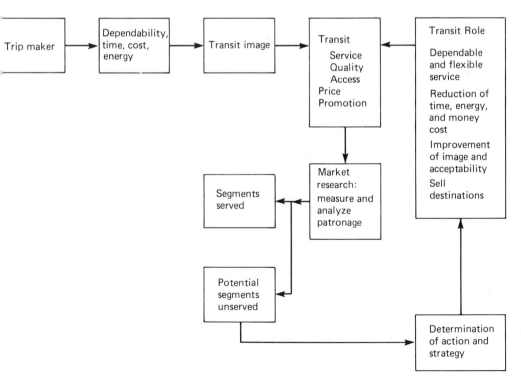

Figure 20-4 *Market segmentation model*

for the nonuse. Certain additional segments may be revealed that have promise if some slight adjustment is made to the marketing mix. For example, offering fast express bus service from the outskirts of the city to the downtown area may prove to be attractive to those currently using automobiles.

Some segments will be ruled out as inaccessible to transit. The salesperson who must carry bulky sample cases on his or her visits to customers is an example; shoppers lugging home 2 weeks' worth of groceries is another. Only those segments large enough and accessible enough to warrant cultivation should be pursued.

THE MARKETING MIX

The concept of the marketing mix, as adopted from consumer product industries, is a key element in the process of tapping and holding a given segment of a transit market. The mix consists of all product, price, and promotion activities under the control of management that may be varied to meet the needs of the different transit market segments.

In transit, the first element of the marketing mix—the product—includes the types of service, the quality of service, and the customer's access to it. Transit service types may be divided into several categories: regular route, special, and charter services. In regular-route service, the configuration of the routes and time schedules are the principal variables. Special services are those not following regular routes; such services may be offered to a sporting event or to particular points in a city for special affairs. Subscription services offering customers door-to-door transit service on a monthly basis would also fall into this category. Demand-responsive service—or dial-a-ride, as it is often called—is a flexible, door-to-door type of service that increases the number of options available to management in serving various market segments where regular bus service would not meet the needs. Charters, which involve a private service under contract to a given group, are another variation.

The quality of the service is also important in the product element of the mix. Such factors as air-conditioned equipment, comfortable seating, cheerful decor, reliability, shelters for waiting passengers, courtesy of personnel, transfer requirements, travel time, and *access* (distance from origin or destination point to the transit route) are all important. Subscription bus service or demand-initiated bus service, both previously mentioned, are other ways of improving access. The latter service is initiated by a telephone call from the consumer, and the bus is dispatched to the consumer by means of two-way radio; the buses travel an irregular route connecting the origin and destination points of several consumers as directly as possible.

Pricing is the second major ingredient in the mix. It cannot be considered in total isolation from the rest of the package of product and promotion. It is a matter of providing value for money. Poor service, regardless of price, is still poor service and may not even yield value for money at a substandard fare. High-quality service is far more likely to be perceived as giving good value even at a relatively high price.

Promotion is the third part of the mix. It includes advertising in various media, ranging from radio and television through newspapers and circulars. Promotion also includes public information such as maps, schedules, and graphics to inform the public of the service and how to use it. Community relations are also part of the promotional package; this is the process of both directly meeting the public and of keeping the public informed of transit activities. Community relations should be a two-way street of communication and feedback; it is another way that management can find out how the public feels about the service and what the public wishes to have in the way of service changes and improvements. The various means of promotion should be brought into play to inform the public of what is offered and to help build an image of vigor and interest in meeting public needs.

The concept of market segmentation and the marketing mix can be joined together in an operational program.[1] Five customer segments are selected for consideration, and a profile of each of them is developed, as shown in Table 20-1. The groups selected include manager/professional, clerical or office workers, inner city, elderly, and suburban housewife. Each of these segments appears to be large enough to make the efforts of a transit company to attract patronage worthwhile economically. The chosen requirements also provide a cross section of users who have different destinations, different needs, and who receive a different mix of benefits from the service.

The manager/professional segment includes persons in the higher-income brackets, who probably tend to place a higher value on their time; travel time and quick and easy access to the service are more important to this segment than are some of the other factors, as shown in the benefits section of Table 20-1. This segment of the market should be appealed to mainly with service improvements rather than with cost savings.

The clerical segment is similar in many ways to the manager/professional segment; the major difference is the lower income level and the increased importance of cost savings as a factor of appeal. Both the manager/professional and clerical segments need transportation between suburban areas and the central city.

Inner-city residents require a different transit service because they not only have travel patterns related to movement within the central city but also between central-city residences and outlying job locations in the suburbs. The need for dependable, low-cost mass transportation service is highly important to the inner-city segment, since many in this group are in the low-income bracket and do not own automobiles. Travel-time savings and ease of access are probably of lesser importance to this segment because of relative dependence upon transit.

The elderly make up another segment. This is already a large portion of the population and one that is growing rapidly in the United States as life spans slowly increase. Since most persons considered as elderly are retired, their transit needs are not for the journey to work, which is of major importance to the manager/professional, clerical, and inner-city segments. Rather, the elderly are looking for service that will provide

---

[1]This very interesting approach was presented in an important article: NORMAN KANGUN AND WILLIAM A. STAPLES, "Selling Urban Transit," *Business Horizons*, 18, no. 1 (February 1975), 57–66.

TABLE 20-1
Profiles of Existing and Potential Customers

Segmentation Base	Customer Segment				
	Manager/ Professional	Clerical	Inner City	Elderly	Suburban Housewife
Benefits[a]					
Travel-time savings	H	H	M	L	M
Dependability	M	M	H	M	M
Cost savings	L	M	H	H	L
Accessibility	H	H	L	H	H
Travel-time options	H	H	M	M	M
Purpose of trip[b]	Work/recreation	Work/shopping	Work/shopping	Shopping/medical	Shopping/recreation
Geography[c]					
Origin	Suburb/CC	Suburb/CC	CC	CC	Suburb
Destination	CBD	CBD	Suburb	CC/CBD	Suburb
Potential frequency of weekly use					
Heavy (5 or more trips)	X	X			
Medium (2-4 trips)			X	X	
Light (1 trip)					X
Nonuser (0 trips)					
Usage time[d]	Peak	Peak	Peak	Off-peak	Off-peak
Demographics[e]					
Income (in thousands)	$15-20	$7-9	$3-5	$3-6	$12-16
Age	35-54	25-34	35-64	65+	35-54
Years of education	13-16	12-15	8-12	5-12	13-16
Availability of car	Yes	Yes	No	No	Yes

[a] Travel-time savings—the reduction in the amount of time required for the user to travel from origin to destination.
Dependability—the increase in the likelihood that the user's expected departure and arrival times coincide with the actual service provided.
Cost savings—the monetary savings to the user from using transit service.
Accessibility—the minimization of user effort required in getting to and from the the transit stations.
Travel-time options—the number of alternative travel times available to the user for a given transit trip.
Level of importance—H, high; M, medium; L, low.

[b] Refers to primary trip of each customer segment.

[c] CC (urban area other than central business district); CBD (central business district).

[d] Peak: 7:30 to 9:30 a.m. and 4:30 to 6:30 p.m.; off-peak: 9:30 a.m. to 4:30 p.m. and 6:30 p.m. to 5:30 a.m.

[e] Based on 1970 *U.S. Census of Population.*

Source: Norman Kangun and William A. Staples, "Selling Urban Transit," *Business Horizons,* 18, no. 1 (February 1975), 61.

mobility for shopping, personal business, and medical visits. Cost savings and accessibility are apt to rank very highly in the list of transit factors, with time savings and travel time of less importance.

The final customer segment is that of suburban housewife. This segment resembles the manager/professional group in income and car ownership, although travel probably takes place most often during the off-peak times of the day. This is a tough segment to go after because of relatively high income and automobile ownership.

Table 20-1 analyzes the five segments in terms of the benefits that each might receive from transit, the trip purpose, geography (in the sense of origin and destination points), the frequency of use, the time of the transit trip, plus certain demographic factors.

In Table 20-2 the marketing strategy is laid out in a summary format. Here the marketing mix elements are shown with the variations necessary to serve each of the segments. Contrast the service mix elements for each of the segments: for example, on the item of the characteristics of the vehicles. The manager/professional segment, which will most likely be attracted by service quality, should be wooed by a standard bus that is fitted with a fairly plush interior, including carpet, to lend a bit of eye appeal. Less fancy standard buses (probably air-conditioned in this day and age) are supplied for the clerical and inner-city segments of the market. To meet the needs of the elderly and suburban housewife segments, small buses or vans are indicated for a demand-responsive or dial-a-ride service.

Again, the coverage of the services offered to the manager/professional, clerical, and inner-city segments is for the total metropolitan area; the elderly segment is offered a service that covers selected central-city locations, while the suburban housewife is offered a service to selected suburban locations.

In the area of pricing, note that the manager/professional and clerical segments are expected to pay full fare, while discount or promotional fares are offered the other segments, reflecting both the lower income of the inner-city and elderly persons, and the difficulty of attracting the suburban housewife away from the automobile.

In the matter of promotion, the benefits of the service are stressed for the manager/professional segment; low price—as well as other factors—is stressed for clerical, inner-city, and elderly segments; and flexibility is stressed for the elderly and suburban housewife segments. The media utilized are also varied for each segment, as is the type of transit information offered.

The plan of attack outlined in the tables is not expected to be the be-all and end-all. However, it does provide a conceptual picture of the starting point in developing a marketing strategy and in putting together different parts of the marketing mix in an operational fashion. In other words, transit management can use this approach to focus on the segments named, or other segments of its choosing, and lay out an operating plan. Based on this, a transit firm could make an initial offering of service. Then the process described graphically in Fig. 20-4 should be implemented; that is, research should be aimed at determining if the desired segments were being reached. Various parts of the operational strategy laid out in Table 20-2 could then be tinkered with in order to improve performance.

TABLE 20-2

Conceptual Format for Marketing Strategies

Marketing Mix Element	Customer Segment				
	Manager/ Professional	Clerical	Inner City	Elderly	Suburban Housewife
Service					
Vehicle characteristics	Standard capacity 40-60; air-conditioned; carpeted	Standard	Standard	Bus/van capacity 10-25; air-conditioned; carpeted	Bus/van
Routes					
Hours	Fixed 6 a.m.-7 p.m.	Fixed 6 a.m.-7 p.m.	Fixed 6 a.m.-7 p.m.	Variable 9 a.m.-9 p.m.	Variable 9 a.m.-9 p.m.
Direct/transfer	Direct	Primarily direct, except at major interchange points	Transfer	Direct	Primarily direct, except with interzone transfer
Arrival and departure times	Fixed	Fixed	Fixed	Flexible	Flexible
Interval time (per route)	Peak: 3/hour	Peak: 3/hour	Peak: 2/hour	2/hour	2/hour
Coverage	Total metropolitan area	Total metropolitan area	Total metropolitan area	Selected central city locations	Selected suburban locations
Shelter/station density	High	High	Moderate	Low	Low
Origin Designation	Moderate	Moderate	Moderate	Low	Low
Availability of station parking	Some	Limited	Unnecessary	Unnecessary	Unnecessary
Pricing					
Fares	Full	Full	Discount	Discount	Promotional
Volume purchase discounts	Yes	Yes	No	No	No
Promotion					
Theme	Service benefits, work activities	Service, low price, socializing	Low price, dependability	Low price, time flexibility, peer group interaction	Time flexibility, trip flexibility, reduced auto use
Media	Spot television, business papers, local radio	Spot television, local radio	Local radio, direct mail	Direct mail, spot television	Spot television, local radio, suburban newspapers
Transit information	Central metropolitan area information center	Multiple ticket locations	Mobile information centers	Special operator	Special operator

Source: Adapted from Norman Kangun and William A. Staples, "Selling Urban Transit," *Business Horizons*, 18, no. 1 (February 1975), 63.

While much time and effort must be devoted to the marketing of mass transportation if modern business management methods are to be adapted to the transit industry, there are obviously other aspects of management that also require major attention.

Personnel and labor relations are a prime problem area in mass transportation. The mass transportation industry of the United States has perhaps been most guilty of lack of careful selection in the personnel area. Recruiting has been virtually unknown in the industry, and the industry's long decline has made it difficult to attract or retain as many first-rate people for management and nonmanagement positions as would otherwise be the case. The need to assess manpower needs carefully and recruit personnel with equal care, based on the best criteria available, is an important formula in any progressive business enterprise. Once the desired people are hired, careful training should be provided, which must go beyond just how to operate or maintain vehicles. It must also include an effort to give rank-and-file personnel a good feel for the overall direction in which the transit agency is moving, with stress upon the importance of the individual employee to the success of the enterprise.

The operators of vehicles are especially important since they are virtually the only transit personnel who come in contact with the public; in effect, they are the salespersons of the mass transportation industry. Operators, and others who deal directly with the public, must be carefully trained in the sales function as well as operations. A good personnel program includes issuing job standards, monitoring job performance, and retraining personnel as necessary.

Good personnel relations, which include programs of benefits and sincere and honest dealings with employees and their problems, are probably the best way to prevent labor difficulties in public transportation. This is especially true for public enterprises receiving federal aid covered by Section 13(c) of the Urban Mass Transportation Act of 1964, as amended. Labor must be no worse off as a result of such a grant than it was before the grant was made. Since the local union, in effect, is one of the parties who must sign off on the application for these federal funds, good management–labor relations are a necessity; grants may otherwise be jeopardized by refusal of the local union to give its acquiescence.

Another critical element that management must deal with realistically is maintenance. Preventive maintenance is indispensable for reliable service; unfortunately, this type of maintenance often falls by the wayside in lean times. Preventive maintenance is very simply the process of finding a problem before it becomes a breakdown or the cause of an accident. It is for this reason, as an example, that power-steering-fluid hoses are inspected or replaced on a regular basis rather than waiting until a hose breaks and the power steering on a bus becomes inoperable. Moreover, in these days of high equipment costs, a good preventive maintenance program can reduce the number of pieces of equipment that must be held out of service as a backup to cover breakdowns and other problems that arise in operations. As a result, major savings can be made in capital investment, and greater reliability of service can be offered.

All of the various elements related to the management of transit—personnel, maintenance, routing and scheduling, equipment selection, communications, marketing, and organization—must be related in a systematic fashion by management. None of these elements stand alone; they must be woven together into a total managerial fabric. Understanding the relationship and knowing how best to take advantage of the various resources within a firm is the manager's prime job and must be fully understood in order to provide quality transit service.

The transit manager of today is faced with both opportunities and problems that are unlike those of his predecessor in the times long gone by, when transit had a virtual monopoly of transportation in American cities. The great opportunity facing transit management is the adoption of modern business practices, which will result in smooth and effective operation of the transit service, with concomitant benefits to the community. Transit problems are most likely to arise from the industry's poor public image and poor quality of service, especially at the time of public takeover.

As director of a public enterprise, the transit manager exists in a new relationship with public officials. This often means that transit is called upon to perform social functions undreamed of in times past. The provision of special lower fares and special services for elderly and handicapped citizens is now required of all transit properties that accept federal funds. Those involved in transit management must constantly arm themselves with facts and figures to make sure that public officials realize the implications of decisions made in regard to public services.

Management opportunities in the public transit field have probably never been more interesting or more exciting than at the present time. What lies ahead is equally as fascinating as the great challenges that faced the transit managers a century ago who mastered the problems of operating horse-railway systems and then were involved in the adventure of the changeover to electric traction. Whether or not the transit industry can meet its new challenges will largely lie in the hands of the coming generation of transit managers.

CONCLUSION

Management is a critical but often overlooked element in a successful urban mass transportation service. The use of modern business management concepts and techniques makes sense in the process of improving transit service. The important thing is to focus on consumers and how best to serve them. Only in this way can public transportation meet the reality of today's competitive market for transit service, and the need to help improve life in U.S. urban areas.

Chapter 21

TRANSIT OPERATIONS—
THE MANAGER'S PERSPECTIVE

Philip J. Ringo, *President, ATE Management and Service Co., Inc.*

Today's public transit manager faces a management challenge that is matched in few if any enterprises, public or private. Whether the system managed is a five-vehicle demand-responsive system in a small town, or a fixed-route, multimode system in a large metropolitan area, the successful transit manager must be knowledgeable in a wide range of traditional technical areas, including maintenance, transportation, marketing, planning, finance and accounting, insurance and safety, personnel, training, and labor relations. Additionally, he or she, in most cases, must communicate with and respond to an appointed or elected board of directors as well as establish lines of communication with numerous local and regional elected officials. Add to this the requirement to communicate with and relate to other interest groups, the metropolitan planning organization (MPO), state department of transportation, the Urban Mass Transportation Administration (UMTA), and many others, not the least of which is the riding public, and the total management task becomes staggering.

This chapter attempts to define the major aspects of the management task as confronted by the general manager of a contemporary public transit system. The focus of the chapter is on conventional fixed-route transit, although many of the problems and approaches described are applicable to paratransit operations as well.

The successful transit manager is one who establishes and maintains management priorities, but above all masters the basic elements of transit operations. Large or small systems, fixed-route or variable, all transit operations have basic characteristics which prescribe the management task. These basic characteristics show that transit is

- A retail enterprise, and therefore competitive and marketable.
- Labor-intensive.

- A cash business.
- Regulated.

Implicit in each of these characteristics is the premise that transit is a consumer business in the public retail enterprise sense, and therefore subject to wide variation in terms of efficiency of operation. Unfortunately, this point is often overlooked by newcomers to transit, because a well-run transit operation often seems to "run itself." However, those who have seen a poorly run transit operation will attest to the fact that tremendous inefficiency and waste can develop and become institutionalized in a transit operation.

If the foregoing is a reasonable outline of the basic characteristics of urban transit, how should the potential or aspiring transit manager begin to make some sense of the management task? The first step in the management of any organization is identification of operating goals and objectives and of available resources. In simple terms this translates to "defining the objectives of your organization and fitting available resources to the efficient accomplishment of those objectives." Other authors in this volume will speak in much greater detail regarding the goal formulation and resource allocation process. For the purposes of this chapter we will assume that the organizational, institutional, financial, and other related questions, such as type of service to be provided, have been resolved. We will not attempt to define the universe of all the technical aspects of transit operations, but rather relate the four basic characteristics of transit to a management approach to transit operations.

A RETAIL ENTERPRISE, COMPETITIVE AND MARKETABLE

The first characteristic of transit to a great extent determines the operating task. The words "retail," "competitive," and "marketable" all point to an operating emphasis on the product (transit service) and the consumer (the transit rider). Each element of transit operations should relate back to the product and reflect a basic consumer orientation.

The first aspect of transit operations to be addressed by the manager is service design. The definition of the transit product and the manner in which it is presented to potential users is the beginning point for any transit operation. Unlike other consumer products, transit service has no "shelf life." It is placed on the street before the consumer and is either utilized or ignored. There is no second chance, or mark down, to recover from a poor choice of service. On the other hand, skillful service design can produce a product which is competitive with other modes of transportation and which is utilized to capacity. Unfortunately, service design often is the last operating area to receive attention from management. If there is any one "must" that a transit manager should hold to, it is the need for placing service design at the top of the list of operating priorities.

It has been said that the process of constructing a transit route structure and defining service levels is as much of an art as it is a science. Even with the much welcomed advent to transit of modern market research, operations research, and other sophisticated management approaches, the process of service design does remain very much of an imprecise science. Such terms as sketch planning, transit screens, computerized transit-demand models, and many other approaches to service design will be thrust upon and bewilder the transit manager. Rather than try to explore each of these techniques, or to attempt a theoretical exercise in service design, the following are conceptual elements which have proven to be extremely important in the practical design of competitive transit service:

1. Successful service design is skillful aggregation of a number of individual travel needs. The concept of a "mass" movement of people only exists in the largest metropolitan areas. A successful transit service is built based on the complete understanding that the product must be designed to meet individual travel needs. Accordingly, service must be timed to accommodate specific user desires. Commuter service that arrives downtown 5 minutes after work start-time is totally worthless to a prospective rider making a competitive choice.
2. Fixed-route service which repeats in standard time segments is more understandable and attractive to the consumer. "Clock headways" which repeat each 15, 30, or 60 minutes, as an example, are much preferable to those with variable pickup times.
3. Service frequency must be realistic in terms of traffic condition and running times. The ideal service design will allow running time that makes the passenger feel that the vehicle is moving safely and expeditiously.
4. Transfers should be avoided whenever possible. When transfers are inevitable, waiting time should be kept to a minimum. Through routing or "spoking" of fixed-route systems can eliminate many transfer situations and should be utilized whenever possible.
5. Major activity centers should be identified and attempts made to tailor service specifically to their start and end times. Additionally, early contact with such centers can result in modification of start and end times to better correspond with peak requirements and vehicle availability.
6. Newly initiated service requires at least 90 days, and preferably 180 days, to demonstrate actual potential. Shorter periods of time do not allow for accurate measures of demand and use.
7. Public input is often the most valuable single factor in designing new service.

These are some, but by no means all, of the basic considerations that go into successful service design.

Of equal importance to the transit manager is the realization that the service design activity cannot be approached from a parochial viewpoint. Whether the system is fixed-route, vanpool, demand-responsive, or some variation, it must take its place within the total tranportation structure of the area being served. This requires an awareness of highway and street planning and projects, a participation in major activity generators before final traffic design has been made, and a general sensitivity for the broad transportation requirements of the area. The much welcomed emphasis being placed by the federal government on coordination between traditional highway and transit activities supports this. Regardless of external pressures in this area, it is in the best interests of the transit manager to pursue actively avenues which lead to better coordination of the total area transportation system.

Careful attention to the service design concepts described earlier is only the beginning in the detailed process of the successful placing of the transit product before the user. Consequently, the transit manager's task does not end after the layout of a reasonable service plan. Following logically from the service design function is the task of determining the manner in which the transit product is to be placed and delivered.

The availability of federal, state, and local funding for capital purchases has provided most transit systems with the ability to upgrade rolling stock, operating facilities, and other capital items, such as shelters and signs, for the first time in many years. As a result, most transit managers are faced with a myriad of decisions regarding vehicle size, site location, passenger amenities, bid documents, architect and engineer selection criteria, and many other facets of a capital expansion program. However, working from the context of a consumer orientation, there are certain basic concepts that the transit operator should follow in preparing a capital program.

In beginning to shape the delivery of the transit product, the manager must remember that transit is competing for riders with one of the most persuasive and sophisticated influences on American life in the twentieth century, the private automobile. Even with the recent emphasis on smaller cars and more economic operation, the passenger automobile of the 1970s is a luxurious, attractive mode of transportation. For the transit operator to be successful in his competitive quest, the product offered by transit must attempt to meet this competitive challenge as completely as possible. This means presenting a transit vehicle which is comfortable: clean; cool in the summer; warm in the winter; with safe, convenient entrances/exits; and adequate space to sit or stand. The concept of padded seats and "first-class leg room" should not be confined strictly to automakers and the airline industry.

At the same time that the transit manager strives for a competitive delivery package, it is important to remember that capital purchases must be evaluated in light of their total impact on the transit organization. Sophisticated data processing equipment may be very glamourous, yet totally inappropriate for a small to medium-size system, where a bookkeeping machine or computer service bureau would perform the job with complete adequacy. The transit manager also must be realistic in terms of the capabilities of the staff to absorb and utilize new capital items, as well as the ability of the budget to absorb the ongoing cost of maintenance and use of capital items. Passenger shelters, for example, may appear to be a one-time cost item, but they require significant ongoing maintenance and cleanup if they are to serve a useful purpose and be a credit to the operation. A graffiti-covered shelter surrounded by trash can reduce patronage rather than attract it.

Once the delivery package has been determined, the color scheme chosen, the vehicles bid and ordered, the transit manager must devise a marketing plan to communicate the availability of the transit product. Marketing of any consumer product is a complicated affair, with a tremendous array of sophisticated tools and techniques available to the manager. However, successful marketing of transit maintains the simple goal of selling seats (rides) to individuals. Broad-based goals of "improving transit's image" are admirable in the abstract and can have an important place in a comprehensive marketing program. Nonetheless, the transit manager must never lose sight of the fact that the only acceptable result of consumer marketing is increased use of the product.

In developing the basic marketing plan, the transit manager should focus first on techniques designed to make information about the product available to prospective users. This means the basic information items such as timetables, route maps, and, above all, the telephone information number. If these three marketing tools are well designed and executed, the basis for a sound marketing program is established.

Depending on the size of the system and the availability of resources, the transit manager then will broaden his marketing program to include the traditional media (newspaper, television, radio, direct mail) available to reach the consumer. Again, the emphasis should be placed on a specific targeting of potential riders, either through the choice of media ("drive-time" radio if the target is the work-trip commuter) or choice of message (advertisement of new service to a particular area). In devising a marketing plan the transit manager should also take advantage of the many techniques developed by successful consumer marketers. If the goal is to attract totally new riders to the system, the use of introductory free rides (or free samples in the consumer product parlance) is an effective way to introduce the product to the consumer.

One of the positive aspects of public transit as it relates to marketing is the availability of a tremendous amount of low-cost or no-cost marketing and promotional assistance. Because of its public impact, transit receives a considerable amount of coverage from the broadcast and print media. An aggressive manager will utilize this attention to the utmost, continually informing the media of events on the transit system that will have an effect on current and future riders. In addition, merchant-sponsored transit activities, public service radio and television time, civic group assistance, all are available to an alert transit manager. Again, however, the marketing function will succeed only if the basic goal of selling rides to people is followed.

LABOR-INTENSIVE

To this point we have talked about items which, although essential to the operation of any transit system, are ones that can be dealt with in the abstract. Service design ultimately manifests itself in a route structure on a system map or public timetable; a successful capital program results in a series of gleaming vehicles with a new paint scheme, operating out of a modern maintenance and operating facility. With the product ready for presentation to the consumer, the "people equation" takes hold and the management task begins in earnest.

Usually over 70% of all transit operating expenses come from those costs associated with personnel. In the hectic process of government grants, planning meetings, marketing plans, and all of the very necessary tasks which accompany the management of a modern transit system, it is often easy to forget that the burden of preparing the product for delivery to the prospective user and the actual presentation of the product is in the hands of the rank-and-file workers of the transit system—the mechanic, the cleaner, and most important, the vehicle operator. The successful transit manager will make the understanding of the problems, challenges, and motivations of these employees a basic part of the management function. Even more important he or she will structure the organization so that the consumer orientation is imparted to each individual employee. When this is accomplished successfully, that orientation will be reflected in the contact, direct or indirect, that each employee has with the public.

An example of indirect employee contact with the consumer is the maintenance function. In a transit system the consumer theoretically never comes face to face with a maintenance employee other than through an equipment breakdown. Nevertheless, the effectiveness of the maintenance organization is an integral part of a consumer-oriented transit operation. Very simply this means a clean vehicle which performs in a manner satisfactory to meet its scheduled run (or demand-responsive series of trips) without disruption for mechanical purposes.

Attainment of this simple goal requires a very sophisticated maintenance management plan which balances labor, tools, and equipment within the context of an operating environment where the vehicle is usually available for necessary repair only at night. Although the generally accepted industry standard of vehicle spares of 10% provides some flexibility in this regard, the transit operator must anticipate inevitable mechanical problems through a realistic preventive maintenance program. In addition, the maintenance function must allow for necessary servicing activities (washing, cleaning, minor maintenance, and other "running repairs"), while at the same time having the capability to perform major unit overhauls and rebuilds.

The maintenance function is one of the few areas in transit operations where effective management can have a direct impact on the monthly operating statement and the capital budget. It is not unusual to see well-maintained 20-year-old transit buses in daily operation after having logged over 1 million miles of revenue service. Sturdier rail and light rail vehicles often double this performance. Unfortunately, too often the maintenance function is viewed as an operating function which mysteriously works by itself. On systems with this operating attitude there is a constant refrain regarding poorly designed vehicles and the lack of trained personnel. In most of these cases the actual flaw is the lack of any coordinated approach to maintenance management. In avoiding this management failure the transit manager should go through the following checklist as it pertains to the maintenance function:

- Is the importance of good vehicle maintenance as it relates directly to the success of the entire transit system understood by management and is this understanding communicated to the rest of the organization?
- Does the maintenance function have adequate working space and equipment to accomplish its tasks in an efficient manner?
- Have realistic standards and procedures for maintenance performance been established and communicated to the organization?

• Is adequate training and retraining a part of maintenance manpower planning?

A positive answer to these questions will not ensure a transit operation free of maintenance problems. It will, however, provide the basis for making the successful link between the maintenance function and the consumer.

The transit manager is now at the moment of truth. The service level has been determined, the public has been informed, the product has been packaged, and the ability to maintain the delivery of the package has been assured. Each of these functions can be performed flawlessly and yet the entire operation will fail without the final ingredient, the transit operator. The transit operator in a well-managed transit system assures that the product is placed before the user as advertised, when advertised.

It is difficult to overemphasize the importance of the transportation function. The execution of the many facets of this aspect of transit operations is absolutely essential to a successful system. As in all skilled-labor situations (and driving a transit vehicle is a skill), the task begins with the recruitment and training of qualified personnel. This means not only a solid grounding in the basics of the operation of the vehicle, but an immediate awareness of the importance of the manner in which the product is placed before the user. It is a worn-out cliche that one surly driver can do more harm than an expensive marketing campaign can offset. It seems more appropriate to say that a courteous, friendly transit driver forms the solid foundation for a transit system that can grow and attract new riders.

With all the emphasis on the new techniques in transit, it becomes easy to ignore the importance of the transit operator. In dealing with this aspect of transit operations the transit manager must maintain three broad objectives:

1. The maximum utilization of human resources must be obtained within the constraints of work rules, schedules, and other operating conditions.
2. Operators must be provided a working environment that is clean, comfortable, and as safe as possible.
3. There must be an established framework for performance of the transportation function. This must be clearly communicated to the operators. On-street supervision should be provided, and an understood mechanism for dealing with failure to perform must be maintained.

In simple terms, this means that the transit manager must attempt to assign labor and equipment in the most efficient manner possible. The ultimate goal is a 100% correlation between hours in revenue service and payroll hours. Even though this is almost impossible to attain, a productivity goal of this type should be set. Driver comfort and safety, both during and after actual operation of the vehicle, is another management goal. Finally, the development of a consistent system of supervision and discipline is essential in a well-managed transportation department.

Above all, the transit driver, dispatcher, street supervisor, and all those who come into daily contact with the riding public must understand the consumer orientation of the transit enterprise and recognize their individual roles in supporting that orientation. This can be done through supportive management activities such as driver-of-the-month awards, safety dinners, courtesy awards, and the old-fashioned, but no less effective, morale stimulants provided by such employee activities as bowling leagues and employee newspapers. In the final analysis, there is no substitute for the transit manager who believes in the consumer orientation and communicates that belief to the entire organization.

A CASH BUSINESS

Having successfully negotiated the management hurdles of service design, marketing, maintenance, and transportation, the transit manager might appear to have completed the management task. However, if the operation is successful, the manager must ensure that the results of that success are adequately protected. The transit manager must always understand the basic fact that transit is by nature a cash business. With some exceptions as they relate to passes and other bulk purchases of transit rides, the consumer pays for each ride as the ride is utilized. This places the transit manager in the position of having to account for and process a significant amount of cash on a daily basis. Without belaboring the point or making any other comments regarding basic human nature, it is imperative that the transit manager understand that with the presence of significant amounts of cash comes the possibility of a certain amount of that cash not reaching its ultimate intended destination (which is the depository of the transit system's bank). This requires the institution of specific and comprehensive safeguards to assure that all cash collected remains within the control of the transit system. Fortunately, modern farebox collection equipment removes a great deal of the temptation and problems that were associated with earlier fare collection equipment and counting paraphernalia. Still, it is a basic operating requirement that safeguards and checks and balances be instituted in regard to cash handling and processing.

In addition to basic cash or token fare, there are many other methods of handling the mechanics of the fare structure. Weekly, monthly, and annual passes; multiple-strip and single tickets; even credit cards are used as methods to provide incentives to transit use. Each method has its proponents and detractors. Many transit systems, for example, find passes an extremely attractive fare-structure mechanism, while others contend that they are subject to significant abuse and even counterfeiting. In any case, a management decision to expand the mechanics of fare collection does not lead to an elimination of the need for safeguards. Any device that can be exchanged or used for the transit product can be abused and must be subject to control.

REGULATED

Since the horse-drawn trolley days, transit has been a regulated industry. Under private ownership, the Interstate Commerce Commission, the Public Utilities Commission, or the Public Services Commission acted to control fare and service levels and often dictated the rate of return on investor capital. With the advent of public transit these regulatory agencies have, to a great extent, passed from direct involvement on the transit scene. However, the transit manager is by no means able to operate in an autonomous fashion. In most cases, the rate hearings of the past have been replaced by the Urban Mass Transportation Administration (UMTA) required public hearing, the metropolitan planning organization (MPO) required transit development plan (TDP), the transportation improvement program (TIP), the development and implementation of transportation system management elements (TSMEs), the A-95 review, and many other local, regional, and federal requirements. While the terms may have changed from "regulation" to "coordinated planning," the result is the same.

The regulatory function as it pertains to transit means that the transit manager cannot operate in a vacuum. There are many and varied institutions who have a stake in transit and who will rightfully assert that stake as it relates to daily operations. If transit managers are to participate in the varied programs that offer capital and operating assistance, they immediately become subject to regulatory requirements relating to application for and control of such funds. This involves the transit manager not only in the application for capital and operating assistance, but in the coordinated planning process as defined by the federal government and as implemented by the MPO. Unfortunately, all too often transit managers feel that this activity is a nuisance and one that can be ignored with impunity and without any detrimental effect on the ability to manage. This could not be further from the truth. The requirement for transit managers to participate in the planning process is a real and continuing one. Ultimately, if transit managers do not become involved, the process may cause them to alter their concept of service drastically and may dictate the shape of the management function.

This concept of public involvement or regulation of transit brings the manager full circle to the consumer orientation of transit. The impact of a citizen governing board or a user advisory group is directly tied to the fact that transit is made available to the public at large and, in most cases, is supported by the taxpaying segment of the public. Users and supporters of the enterprise demand involvement in the provision of service, and the manager must respond to that demand.

Transit managers of the 1970s are faced with an unusually broad spectrum of management problems and tasks. Interestingly enough, this management spectrum is as broad on a 5-vehicle system as it is on a 500-vehicle one. Add to this the fishbowl operating environment that comes with a publicly owned consumer enterprise and you have a management challenge that is sometimes frustrating but is never dull. Involvement in transit operations provides the ability to make a direct impact on one of America's most pressing problems: the provision of mobility within the context of limited national resources. The manner in which transit meets this challenge will have a demonstrable impact on the future quality of life in the United States. As the person directly in charge of the development and the presentation of the transit product, transit managers will bear the brunt of transit's failures and will rightfully share in the rewards of its success.

Chapter 22

PUBLIC TRANSPORTATION MARKETING

FRANK W. DAVIS, Jr., *Associate Professor of Marketing and Transportation, University of Tennessee, and* RAY A. MUNDY, *Associate Professor of Marketing and Transportation, University of Tennessee*

"Marketing" is a word currently used quite extensively in public transportation, but generally in the wrong context. Marketing is not just advertising or selling. In the broadest sense, it is the process by which a community allocates resources for the benefit of its citizens.

MARKETING AND RESOURCE ALLOCATION FOR CONSUMERS

An agency or organization, whether public or private, has resources at its disposal. These resources include financial resources which may be budgeted, endowed, or received as a result of sales or taxes; people with various skills and training; and existing facilities including vehicles, buildings, and equipment. The purpose of the agency is to use its resources to generate benefits to society and to the holders of the resources, including employees, stockholders, foundations, renters, and so on.

In the United States there are two ways that society controls the actions of these organizations and agencies to ensure that the nation's resources are used to benefit society as well as workers and owners of facilities. First, consumers are given freedom of choice in the marketplace so that if they do not like the products or services that one agency provides, they do not have to buy them. This stops the flow of resources to that agency. Second, if the agency receives its funds from the political budgeting process instead of the marketplace, the public has the indirect secret ballot process to vote its approval or disapproval of the way funds are budgeted.

Problems occur when institutional issues restrict the consumer's choice in the marketplace or when his vote is ineffective in redirecting the allocation of resources in the political process. Examples of institutional restrictions include limited numbers of supply agencies, lack of consumer information, seller dishonesty, and large bureaucracies that do not change in response to free elections. Long-term commitments of funds that are not responsive to changing voter mandates, and the development of one-sided lobbying efforts are also institutional restrictions. In the long run, the ability of our society to use its resources to meet its changing needs is largely determined by the responsiveness of resource allocations to the voice of the consumer in the free marketplace and the voice of the citizen in free elections. Micro-marketing is the process in which an agency maintains contact with its customers (clients), determines their evolving needs, and directs the agency's allocation of resources to provide the products or services that best meet their needs. The success of the market plan is measured by the number of people that freely choose the product or service as the best option available to them.

The major failing of any firm or agency is to become so enamored with its current product or internal operations that it no longer considers the evolving needs of the consumer; the product or service then loses market share because it does not meet society's needs as well as a competitive product or service. Instead of "receiving the consumer's message," the "product-oriented" company rationalizes that the product is not at fault but that the consumer is becoming increasingly irrational. The "market-oriented" firm, on the other hand, recognizes that the needs of the consumer must be the focal point of the planning process, while the actual product or service that the agency produces is only a short-run manifestation of the way the agency feels it can best meet current consumer needs with existing resources. Tomorrow the product will change as consumer needs change, as the marketing department better understands these needs, and as the agency develops greater flexibility in deploying its resources.

MARKETING MANAGEMENT: LONG RUN VS. SHORT RUN

Today's marketing consists of two major components: selling the agency's existing products or services in the short run so that it can obtain the funds needed to keep the agency viable; and product planning, which redirects the agency's resources to develop new products and services which will better serve society's evolving needs in the long run. The sales area includes advertising, order taking, financing, promotional programs, distribution programs, and associated activities which better inform the consumer about the existing product or service, make it easier for the consumer to obtain and use the product or service, and persuade the consumer to try it. Product planning consists of market research, which determines what products or services consumers will probably want; institutional research to determine the degree to which government contracts, agreements (i.e., labor contracts, supplier contracts, distribution contracts), competitor suppliers, and other factors limit the options available to the agency; and financial research to determine the financial resources that the agency will have to develop new product or service offerings to society. Once this research is completed, the agency develops a master strategy to better meet society's needs and to reap greater financial returns. In public transportation, this could be through the farebox or through politically approved budgets. The goals or objectives of this master strategy could be to benefit the agency through higher salaries to its employees (drivers and managers), higher prices to its suppliers (bus manufacturers, fuel suppliers, etc.), and higher income to its stockholders and/or lower taxes to the public bodies. Thus, a neglect of sales leads to an immediate loss of agency viability, while an emphasis on sales at the expense of product planning simply postpones the loss of viability.

Generally speaking, the generic sales function is well defined and understood by public transportation companies who regularly advertise, print schedules, experiment with fares, and engage in other promotional programs. Therefore, the remainder of this chapter will emphasize product planning activities. Consequently, the emphasis will not be on how to get more people to ride the existing bus or subway, but rather how to identify new public transportation markets that should be served regardless of mode. (For a description of transit company marketing activities, see Chapters 20 and 21.)

PUBLIC TRANSPORTATION MARKETING

An effective public transportation marketing effort must answer five basic questions.

- What is the community trying to do?
- Who must be served to accomplish the community's objectives?
- What combination of service, vehicles, price, and promotion will have to be offered to win the acceptance of those who must be served to accomplish the community's objectives?
- When should the service be terminated?
- How should the community's public transportation agency be organized to ensure that its objectives are accomplished?

Once these questions are answered, the public transportation agency can develop and implement a master strategy to accomplish these objectives.

WHAT IS THE COMMUNITY TRYING TO DO?

Goals and objectives are given frequent "lip service" but are seldom accomplished operationally. In many public transportation agencies, stated goals are so broad that no one could possibly disagree with them; but in daily operations, the mandate is so restrictive that there is virtually no flexibility for change. For example, the goals of the urban transportation plan may be "to provide the highest degree of mobility possible to stimulate economic prosperity or the development of human resources and more efficient land use." In practice, however, the regional transit authority has a mandate to operate a fixed-route, fixed-schedule bus company. Whether the operational goals are limited by public mandate, by the perspective of the operators, or by the "certificate of convenience and necessity" issued by a regulatory body, there is little probability that product planning will ever suggest alternative forms of service much different from the narrow range of services currently in operation. If the giant organizations of today had had such a restrictive mandate, IBM would process only punched cards for the Census Bureau, Standard Oil would sell only kerosene for lamps, Sears would be a mail-order house for farm supplies only, and the March of Dimes would accept funds only for polio research. The reason these giant endeavors have had room to grow is that they utilized broad operational goals which allowed them to use their resources to grow with their consumers.

Accordingly, the broader goals of public transportation must be achieved operationally by the public transportation agency. The authors suggest that the role of the public agency is "to accomplish transportation-dependent urban goals at the lowest possible cost." Some of these transportation-dependent urban goals include:

1. *Increase the efficiency and effectiveness of public investment in transportation facilities and services.* For example, the life of specific facilities may be extended without expending large sums of money for new construction (i.e., people may be channeled into carpools or buses to postpone or substitute for the construction of new bridges or highways). Another example would be to eliminate the need to make long-term capital commitments in areas with rapidly changing land-use patterns which would soon make the expensive infrastructure obsolete (i.e., the use of buses, vans, and carpools to eliminate the need for new highways or rail extensions).
2. *Improve environmental quality, and promote efficient energy use and the development of other resources.* Many urban areas are concerned about improving environmental quality standards, reducing energy use, developing human resources, promoting tourist attractions, and generally developing all resources.
3. *Provide desired mobility to the public transportation dependent.* Most communities feel a social obligation to provide transportation to specific groups, such as the elderly, the handicapped, school children, the young, non-automobile owners, nondrivers, low-income groups, and other special groups.
4. *Support and promote desirable land-use development patterns.* The promotion of central business district activity, control of night or daytime traffic densities in specific areas, or development of regional activity centers (objectives may vary among communities) are a few examples.
5. *Accommodate individuals who desire public transportation services.* Most communities are willing to provide transportation services to those who desire it or have a need for it, as long as it can be provided economically or can satisfy one of the previously stated goals or objectives.

In each case, these operational goals necessitate the identification of a specific clientele that must be transported between specific origins and destinations at specific times if the goals are to be accomplished. Thus, product planning activities can be directed to the level of services required by these specific individuals; and sales can concentrate on selling new service to the specific groups identified.

WHO MUST BE SERVED TO ACCOMPLISH THE COMMUNITY'S OBJECTIVES?

Market segments are groups of individuals who have common identifiable transportation needs. If a transportation agency does not have specific goals, there is a tendency to attempt to serve all people without consciously realizing that each of the many diverse market segments has different transportation needs. Examples of market segments include suburban commuters going to a downtown office complex at 8:30 a.m., the blue-collar worker going from the older residential areas to a suburban industrial park, suburban school children going to swim meets and ball games, senior citizens on shopping excursions, or tourists traveling between airport, hotels, restaurants, and gift shops. An effort to serve all markets with the same type of service ensures that no market is served well.

Once the public transportation agency has identified its goals, it can identify the market segment that must be served to accomplish those goals. For example, if the goal is to relieve congestion on the Golden Gate Bridge between the hours of 7 a.m. and 9 a.m., the market segment that must be served to accomplish the agency's goals are morning commuters who live in Marin County and travel to San Francisco. If, on the other hand, the community is concerned about meeting its perceived social and legal obligations to the handicapped, the product planning activity must locate the handicapped who need service and determine when and where they want and/or need to travel. The results of this step may be a list of individuals, complete with the trip origins, trip destinations, and trip times. In many cases, the list will include names, addresses, and phone numbers.

Frequently, transportation planners concern themselves only with aggregate origin–destination data. They may be appalled at the recommended detail and the smallness of each market segment. This is understandable since transportation planners have been very successful in building a highway system that has been generally well received by a heterogeneous public and are anxious to apply the same proven methodology to mass transit. Unfortunately, they forget that the success of the highway system has been greatly influenced by the product planning effort of private industry which has provided a variety of vehicles, including large trucks, motorcycles, motor homes, pickup trucks, and a large selection of automobiles, to adapt the highway network to the diverse individualized needs of many different market segments. Similarly, in public transportation the market planners must now recognize the existence of many diverse market segments, each with widely differing needs. Then the product planner will develop a wide variety of services, each of which will meet the needs of individual market segments, although they may represent only 1 to 3% of the marketplace. In short, the key component of public transportation product planning is to identify the potential market segments, determine the potential demand of each segment, and develop alternative means of serving the special needs of each segment. Next, the product planner should rank each new market by potential and develop recommendations as to which new markets should be served and the priority with which each service should be initiated.

WHAT COMBINATIONS OF SERVICES WILL WIN ACCEPTANCE OF THOSE WHO MUST BE SERVED TO ACCOMPLISH COMMUNITY OBJECTIVES?

The private firm whose major goals are improving wages and stabilizing employment opportunities for its workers and increasing rates of return for investors is generally free to offer any type of product or service that is legal, acceptable to the public, and within the firm's financial, technical, and managerial capacities. Thus, rail companies have entered such diverse fields as real estate, trucking, bus lines, snack foods, and hotels where they felt they could better accomplish the firm's goals. Public transportation authorities should utilize the same marketing strategy to accomplish their goals. Public agencies, however, are expected to accomplish community goals at the lowest possible costs. (Typical community goals have been presented earlier in this chapter.) Therefore, the public authority should limit activities to solving community goals through various transportation schemes. Although this implies that the public authority should not enter oblique fields such as hotels and food catering, it does indicate that it should ensure that a variety of services, sufficient to meet the individual needs of each market segment, must be offered if urban goals are to be served effectively.

The typical marketing firm realizes that its success in accomplishing its objectives will be determined by how well it provides the final consumer with a product or service the consumer wants. Since the customer does not care which firm actually produces, transports, stores, and finances the product, most firms will make extensive use of many other firms. Sears once tried to manufacture as well as sell their products, but now they buy virtually all their products from independent companies. Likewise, Western Auto relies on independent companies to both produce and sell all their products. Taxi and trucking companies are increasingly relying on private owner-operators to provide the actual transportation, while the firm handles the dispatching, the sales, and product planning functions.

Likewise, the public transportation agency has many options available for the actual delivery of service, and its success will depend upon how well it utilizes all the options available to it. For example:

- The agency can own the equipment and use civil servants to operate all phases of the service.
- The agency can own the equipment and hire one or more contract management firms to provide any or all parts of the service.
- The agency can contract with private companies to provide a wide variety of services on a contractual or bid basis.

- The agency can encourage private operators to enter the marketplace by removing prohibitive restrictions and regulating the private carrier as deemed necessary by the specific situation.

Accordingly, it should be recognized that the primary role of the public transportation agency is not to provide one type of transportation service, but rather to evaluate the needs of the various market segments that must be served to accomplish community goals and ensure that the service to them is provided in the most economical way. This is accomplished by:

- Determining whether individuals within the target market are currently making the trip.
- Determining the level of service to which the target market has become accustomed.
- Predicting the level of service necessary to induce the target market to shift from the current mode to one that will better accomplish urban objectives.
- Developing schemes and strategies to effect this modal shift utilizing appropriate combinations of vehicles, contractors, private operators, public systems, and regulatory policies necessary.
- Selecting the lowest cost scheme available if several alternatives can accomplish the modal shift necessary to accomplish urban objectives.

Once the product planning group has located the target market and developed a strategy for effecting the modal shift necessary to accomplish the urban objectives, it must decide on the most cost-effective method of promoting the service. In general, the publicity should focus on the target market with as little promotion wasted on nonpotential buyers as possible. Presentations to neighborhood groups, in-plant posters, handbills, or billboards on highly traveled corridors may be effective for commuters; but notices in community clubs or health facilities may be more effective for senior citizens, and promotions in schools, YMCAs, and sports areas may better reach school-age children. In essence, specialized services should be promoted to the special groups that will use them.

The fare charged for the service should be low enough to ensure goals are met, but high enough to cover all costs if possible. It should be remembered that a low price alone will not make a service attractive which does not meet the rider's needs. Payment methods are also an integral part of the marketing package. Exact-fare programs expedite loading and reduce robbery potential. Subscription fares and monthly passes provide the same benefit as well as encouraging the rider to make a one-time commitment to continue riding. Use of credit cards, as is being demonstrated in the lower Naugatuck Valley of Connecticut, has benefits in data collection and elimination of coin collection, allows pricing flexibility, and reduces out-of-pocket payment bias. Payroll deduction programs offer the additional advantage of making the purchase of tickets easier to budget. Employer sales of tickets, especially when accompanied by an employer's strong promotional program and partial subsidy, greatly strengthen the incentive for the worker to ride on a regular basis. Shopping centers may be willing to either subsidize a shopper's fare or supply a vehicle and driver to provide the service, if encouraged by the public agency.

Once a service is offered to a specific market segment, it is important to monitor the success of that service to ensure not only that the urban goals are achieved, but also that the service changes to meet the evolving needs of the user. This feedback can best be obtained from someone who is in close contact with the target market. Vanpool programs usually rely on the driver to maintain rider enthusiasm. Company commuter programs may rely on a plant coordinator. Subscription programs often rely on a "busmeister." It does not matter who provides the feedback as long as someone has the responsibility and authority to make changes to keep the consumers satisfied and to relay complaints, problems, and observations to the product planning staff.

WHEN SHOULD THE SERVICE BE TERMINATED?

Public transportation, like all products or services, has a definite product life cycle. The product-life-cycle concept is a recognition that any new service or product when first introduced into the marketplace requires a period of time before it is widely accepted by consumers. During this period, sales increase, slowly at first and then more rapidly, as consumers become aware of the product's benefits. Then, the sales of the product level off as it saturates its intended market segments and ceases to attract new users. Soon the service begins to lose market share to a new product which better meets the new needs of the target market. If the service offering is not modified to keep pace with the changing needs of the consumer, sales will diminish until at some point the agency must decide that it is time to discontinue the product or service. Likewise, public transportation companies should continue to monitor ridership for each individual service offering to determine where it is in the product life cycle; they should have firm guidelines showing when to promote and expand and also when to discontinue service.

Unlike private firms, public agencies have a political and social obligation to continue service whose absence would produce a severe social consequence even though demand is very low. This political pressure to continue highly unproductive runs is at the root of much of the criticism of traditional public transportation. The operating company is criticized if it does not provide the service, but if it does provide the service, it is criticized for operating empty vehicles and incurring large deficits. Thus, it is imperative for the politically astute public transportation agency to develop alternatives which allow lower-cost ways of continuing the service so that the agency can avoid the "all-or-nothing" dilemma, which generates such strong criticism regardless of the decision. For example, a declining market strategy could consist of continuing traditional bus service as long as the route generates two to four passengers per mile of operation. The second stage might be contractual service with a limousine or van operator to provide service if ridership is slightly below this level. A third stage may be a contractual taxi service, with the fourth stage being a voucher system subsidizing a few dependent riders who are free to use any mode they desire and can obtain—including the use of casual carriers, such as neighbors, friends, and relatives.

The key to effective product planning and management is to remember that there is a market (client group) that must be served to accomplish urban objectives and that the role of the market planning group is to manage community resources to ensure that the market is served in the most efficient way. Current public criticism of public transportation is not aimed at the efficiency of the bus or subway system operation but rather at the ineffectiveness of traditional services in meeting the needs of a wide range of market segments that desire service.

HOW SHOULD THE MARKETING MANAGEMENT FUNCTION BE ORGANIZED?

The main consideration for locating the marketing functions in a public transportation agency are:

1. The sales function should be located at a high enough level so that consumer needs are emphasized at least as much as are the operations and finance function of the agency.
2. The product planning function should be located at a level high enough so that it will not be biased by traditional product loyalties. For example, if all product and financial planning for Ford Motor Company were done by the Lincoln-Mercury Division, it is highly unlikely that Ford would ever consider the development of farm machinery, industrial equipment, lawn and garden supplies, home appliances, and computers. Likewise, urban transportation product planning must be done at a high enough level so that it considers all transportation alternatives rather than merely perpetuating the existing establishment.

Considering the traditional orientation of regional transportation authorities (RTAs) and the public takeover of bus and subway companies, the organization shown in Fig. 22-1 is suggested. Under this organization, the public transportation agency would completely divorce itself from any one form of public transportation but would be responsible for promoting whichever combination of services that would best meet public needs. This is extremely important now, as public expectations for service, especially in the low-density suburban areas and during the peak-hour commuter periods, are simply beyond traditional bus and rail companies' ability to serve at a reasonable cost. Unless alternatives are developed to meet these needs, the growing taxpayer rebellion may greatly reduce financial support for the transportation agencies. By publicly acknowledging what traditional systems can and cannot realistically do and by developing the multimodal coordinating role of the agency, unrealistic expectations of the traditional systems can be diffused and new types of services to serve suburban residents and commuters can develop. Under this organization, the authority could have the same relationship with the traditional transit systems as they would with private carriers, vanpools, taxicabs, school buses, church buses, human services agencies, commuter bus clubs, and any other evolving services. The director of marketing would become the focal point of citizen input, research into service-level requirements,

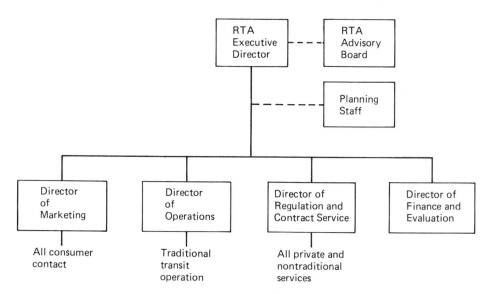

Figure 22-1 *Suggested organizational structure for a market-oriented public transportation agency. This organizational chart is actually a transitional organization that is necessary because of the heavy operational orientation of existing RTAs. Once the potential of the full family of services becomes reality, the director of operations and the director of regulation and contract services could be merged to become the manager of services. While the RTAs are so extremely oriented toward operations, the director of regulation and contract services is needed to serve as an advocate for the other options. Once the RTA can become user oriented, then an advocate for other options is no longer needed since the director of services will promote that combination of services that best meets community needs.*

the sales and promotional function, and all the other activities suggested in this chapter. The director of operations would be responsible for ensuring that required service levels are met by the traditional transportation system. The director of regulation and contract services would be responsible for contracting with private operators to provide service to the authority and for overseeing the regulation and promotion of the private sector. The director of finance and evaluation would be responsible for evaluating the cost effectiveness of all the alternatives currently in operation, for coordinating funding, and for billing and paying the users and suppliers of transportation. In essence, marketing decides what services are needed; operations provides traditional services; regulation and contract services develops and promotes new options; and finance evaluates operations and makes sure the community gets the best value for the expenditure. Jointly, a committee composed of the four directors reporting to and including the executive director is responsible for handling the coordination, budgeting, and planning of all transportation services with the support of the planning staff. The regional transportation board is responsible for setting policy and overseeing the directors. Once a strategy for each problem area is developed by the executive committee, each director carries out his/or her responsibility. Marketing sells the program, operations ensures that traditional service is available, regulation and contract services ensures that new options are developed, and finance makes sure that the region is receiving the most cost-effective service.

This organization will sound unusual to the traditionalist who views government's role in transportation from the highway perspective. Where government's role has been limited to the planning, designing, and construction of fixed facilities, the only function of government was to plan alternative construction projects and to hold coordinating and public meetings (1) to eliminate duplication of projects, (2) to ensure the proper interface between completed facilities, and (3) to rank the proposed projects according to community desires. Now with the continually growing number of vehicles on already congested highways, the completeness of the interstate system, and growing resistance to new highway construction, especially in urban areas, transportation efforts are shifting from a planning role to a marketing-management role. The marketing-management role will consist of increasing vehicle throughput on the highways and increasing the number of people carried in each vehicle. Therefore, the organization needs to be restructured to reflect the new role.

CONCLUSION

If government is going to assume the role of ensuring that public transportation is available, it not only must develop a diversity of different product offerings to meet the specific needs of diverse target markets but, at the same time, it also must accomplish urban goals. In addition, the organization must be designed like that of the private firm which is oriented to "resource management" to accomplish specific objectives as opposed to the facility planning organization which is designed to coordinate planning and to obtain public approval on long-term construction projects. Like a private company, it will want to rely heavily on coordinating activities among all operators, specialists, and contractors instead of operating all service themselves. The challenge of operating in the competitive sphere where the public can choose is great. Product and service offerings of all kinds fail each year and cease to exist, yet this is what public transportation officials must do if they are to successfully accomplish urban goals. There may be a large cost associated with accomplishing changing urban goals in a society with constantly changing needs and life-styles and it is increasingly difficult with diminishing resources. The only alternative, however, is to live in a regimented society that prohibits the freedom of citizens to choose individual life-styles.

If public transportation is to be successful in accomplishing urban goals, it must be allowed to change to match changing conditions. Where restrictive regulation inhibits change, where contracts and franchises eliminate innovative competition, where narrowly defined operating mandates or other factors merely protect and preserve the traditional, there is no role for marketing since the service offering cannot change to keep pace with evolving consumer needs. If, on the other hand, urban goals and citizens' needs become the focus of public transportation, then marketing will become the key element in the management equation for developing a variety of services to meet varying public needs.

SELECTED BIBLIOGRAPHY

Many citations are no longer available from their original source. These citations are often available from the National Technical Information Service, U.S. Department of Commerce, 5285 Port Royal Road, Springfield, Va. 22161. We have verified the order numbers for many of these citations, and they are found at the end of the citation. Prices are available through NTIS at the address above.

CRAVENS, DAVID W., RAY A. MUNDY, AND ROBERT B. WOODRUFF, "Potential for Marketing Management Application in Public Transportation Planning," in *New Marketing for Social and Economic Progress and Marketing Contribution to the Firm and to the Society*, the Combined Proceedings of the American Marketing Association, Series no. 36, ed. Ronald C. Curhan. Portland, Ore.: American Marketing Association, 1974.

DAVIS, FRANK W., JR., "Effective Transit Policy-Making at the Local Level," in *Research Needs for Evaluating Urban Public Transportation*, Special Report 155, pp. 9–13. Washington, D.C.: Transportation Research Board, 1975.

———, "Regulatory Barriers to Innovation and the Knoxville Experience," in *Economic Regulation of Urban Public Transportation*, review draft of conference held September 19–22, at Annapolis, Md., sponsored by U.S. DOT, Office of Secretary, FHWA, UMTA, FEO, and EPA. Washington, D.C.: Transportation Research Board, 1976.

———, AND KRISTEN OEN, *Solving Public Passenger Transportation Problems: A Need for Policy Reorientation*. Washington, D.C.: U.S. Department of Transportation, 1977. Now available through NTIS.

———, AND OTHERS, "Comparison of Privately and Publicly Owned Demand-Responsive Systems," in *Transit Planning*, Transportation Research Record 559, pp. 11–20. Washington, D.C.: Transportation Research Board, 1976.

———, AND OTHERS, *Increased Transportation Efficiency Through Ridesharing: The Brokerage Approach*. Washington, D.C.: U.S. Department of Transportation, 1977. Now available through NTIS.

LEVITT, THEODORE, "Marketing Myopia," *Harvard Business Review*, 38, no. 4 (July-August 1960), 45–56.

LOVELOCK, CHRISTOPHER H., *Consumer Oriented Approaches to Marketing Urban Transit*, Research Report no. 3, prepared for UMTA. Stanford, Calif.: Stanford University Graduate School of Business, March 1973. Now available as PB 220 781.

MUNDY, RAY A., *Marketing Urban Mass Transit—1973*, prepared for UMTA. University Park, Pa.: Pennsylvania State University Transportation and Traffic Center, January 1974. Now available as PB 231 310.

SCHNEIDER, LEWIS M., *Marketing Urban Mass Transit: A Comparative Study of Management Strategies*. Boston: Harvard Graduate School of Business Administration, Division of Research, 1965.

———, "Marketing Urban Transit," in *Mass Transportation*, Highway Research Record 318, pp. 16–19. Washington, D.C.: Highway Research Board, 1970.

STEIN, MARIN M., "Application of Attitude Surveys in Transportation Planning and Impact Studies: A Case Study of Southwest Washington, D.C.," *Traffic Quarterly*, 29, no. 1 (January 1975), 51–63.

WACHS, MARTIN, "Consumer Attitudes Toward Transit Service: An Interpretive Review," *Journal of the American Institute of Planners*, 42, no. 1 (January 1976), 96–104.

Chapter 23

PUBLIC TRANSIT PASSENGER SECURITY AND SAFETY

LESTER A. HOEL, *Professor and Chairman, Department of Civil Engineering, University of Virginia*

The occurrence of crime and vandalism on public transit is part of the larger urban problem of crime on the streets. Crime occurrences in major cities have created fear of walking alone at night and have caused destruction to buildings and property. Similarly, crime on transit systems can create fear of riding the system and cause costly damage to transit vehicles, stations, and property. The use of public transit is based on attributes such as travel time, cost, comfort, convenience, and availability, but if the system is viewed as dangerous it is likely that a patron will select another mode or not make the trip. Although the perception of security may or may not fit reality, patrons will avoid situations where they feel threatened or unsafe.

The extent of crime and vandalism in public transit systems when compared with that occurring within the city as a whole is not fully understood. A study by the American Transit Association (ATA) of 37 U.S. transit systems, accounting for 60% of the annual vehicle-miles and revenue passengers, concluded that the risk of being involved in a criminal incident is at least two times greater when riding on most major transit systems than it is in nontransit circumstances.[1] On the other hand, a survey of transit crime in Chicago indicated that a greater probability exists of crime occurrence on the city streets than on the Chicago Transit Authority system.[2]

---

[1] EDWARD J. THRASHER AND JOHN B. SCHNELL, "Scope of Crime and Vandalism on Urban Transit Systems," in *Crime and Vandalism in Public Transportation*, Transportation Research Record 487 (Washington, D.C.: Transportation Research Board, 1974), p. 40. This conclusion is based on a transit crime index computed as the average number of trips per person multiplied by 15 minutes (duration of an average trip) and then divided by the total number of minutes in a year. These were compared with the FBI crime index.

The American Transit Association and the Institute of Rapid Transit united in 1974 as the American Public Transit Association.

[2] RONALD C. JOHNSON, "Mass Transit Security in Chicago," in *Proceedings—Fifteenth Annual Meeting, Transportation Research Forum*, 15, no. 1 (San Francisco) (Oxford, Ind.: The Richard B. Cross Company, 1974), p. 227. The measures used in Chicago were based on a crime-ridership index, which is the number of crimes per 1,000,000 passengers carried.

The extent of transit crime and its direct cost is difficult to establish because crimes may go unreported, repair to vandalized property may be deferred, or crimes may not have the same definition in every jurisdication. An estimate of the range of national criminal incidents and costs was made by ATA. These are shown in Table 23-1.

TABLE 23-1
Extent of Crime and Vandalism on U.S. Transit Systems, 1971

Transit crimes:	33,194-39,011
Vandalism cost:	$7,743,837-$9,994,600
Liability cost:	$1,849,955-$2,327,892

Source: Edward J. Thrasher and John B. Schnell, "Scope of Crime and Vandalism on Urban Transit Systems," in *Crime and Vandalism in Public Transportation*, Transportation Research Record 487 (Washington, D.C.: Transportation Research Board, 1974), p. 34.

A comparison of transit crimes on buses and rail rapid transit indicates that substantially fewer crimes are committed on buses than rapid transit. Table 23-2 shows the number and types of crimes that occurred on the Chicago Transit Authority system during 1971 and the first 6 months of 1972. The table shows that crimes on rail rapid transit accounted for 84.1% of all transit robberies (armed, strong armed, and attempted strong armed); 53% of transit battery (physical contact, injury with or without a weapon, stabbing, or shooting); and 91.7% of all transit crimes against persons (murder, rape, indecency, etc.). Of total transit crimes, 75% occurred on the rapid transit system, and when compared with the number of riders, there are 7.2 crimes per 1 million persons on the rapid transit system and 0.7 crime per 1 million persons on the bus system, or a factor of 10 to 1.

The much larger incidence of crime on rail rapid transit is based on several factors. Robberies on buses have been significantly reduced as a result of the exact-fare lock box system now used on most buses. Many older rapid transit stations

TABLE 23-2
Number and Types of Crimes on CTA Bus and Rapid Transit

Type of crime	Robbery		Battery		Crimes Against Persons	
	Number	%	Number	%	Number	%
Rapid transit	1204	84.1	334	53.0	110	91.7
Bus	228	15.9	296	47.0	10	8.3
Total	1432	100.0	630	100.0	120	100.0

Source: Adapted from Ronald C. Johnson, "Mass Transit Security in Chicago," in *Proceedings—Fifteenth Annual Meeting, Transportation Research Forum*, 15, No. 1 (San Francisco) (Oxford, Ind.: The Richard B. Cross Company, 1974), p. 228.

furnish an ideal environment for criminal acts, including both places to hide and means of escape. Stations are often located in high-crime areas, thus providing additional opportunity for criminals to ply their trade. During evening and weekend off-peak hours when ridership is low, passengers are especially vulnerable, lacking the safety in numbers that a crowd provides (a paradoxical benefit of the morning and afternoon peak period). Finally, buses travel on surface streets visible both to city patrolmen and the ever-present driver; whereas rail rapid transit is isolated from the city—either in a subway or elevated above ground—and many portions of the station and train are beyond the view of a transit employee or police.

The purpose of this part of the chapter is to review several aspects of security on transit systems, including characterisitcs of crime occurrences, means for controlling crime, attitudes and perceptions about crime on public transit, and transit agency organization for security purposes. These items will be discussed separately for bus and rail transit as their system characteristics and security needs are considerably different.

PASSENGER SECURITY ON BUS NETWORKS

We have noted that reported incidents of crime and vandalism on bus networks are considerably lower than on rapid transit. These results have been further confirmed by surveys of both riders and nonriders on bus systems in Chicago, Milwaukee, and Washington, D.C. One survey compared ridership on an elevated rail rapid transit (el) and a parallel express bus route.[3] The study noted that a large number of bus users live within a short walk of the el station, but elect not to travel by rapid transit. Although cost and travel-time factors were equivalent, the study found that "the variable most frequently chosen as the most important reason for using or not using the bus or el respectively is safety, i.e., freedom from personal attack, harrassment, etc."[4]

Patrons and nonriders in Milwaukee were interviewed along a bus transit route that experienced a high degree (1677 incidents per year) of reported transit crimes and vandalism.[5] Personal security ranked sixth and fifth from a list of eight service characteristics for on-bus and corridor surveys, respectively. This study concluded that personal security on the bus route is not perceived as a critical factor, being consistently ranked lower than frequency of service, fare level, travel time, and convenience. The study also concluded that preference for not riding the bus after dark may be due primarily to fear of walking and waiting on the street corner rather than in riding on the bus itself. In fact, the bus could be perceived as a place of refuge on a dark

---

[3]Neil D. Ferrari and Michael F. Trentacoste, "Personal Security on Public Transit," in *Proceedings—Fifteenth Annual Meeting, Transportation Research Forum*, 15, no. 1 (San Francisco) (Oxford, Ind.: The Richard B. Cross Company, 1974), pp. 214–23.

[4]Ibid., p. 219.

[5]Kumares C. Sinha and Forrest P. Roemer, "Personal Security in Buses and Its Effects on Ridership in Milwaukee," in *Crime and Vandalism in Public Transportation*, Transportation Research Record 487 (Washington, D.C.: Transportation Research Board, 1974), pp. 13–25.

night. Finally, no loss in patronage was noted that could be attributed to crime or vandalism.

A similar study in Washington, D.C., reported probable existence of concern about crime and vandalism large enough to affect ridership patterns.[6] Nearly 30% reported that personal security was a factor in selecting specific times when not to use the bus. They prefer to ride in daylight hours (especially older people). These comparative studies, while not conclusive, appear to indicate that perceptions of security on bus transit will depend heavily upon the direct experience with crime occurrences (e.g., vandalisms, verbal threats) experienced by the rider. Riders tend to feel safe if they have never witnessed serious criminal or rowdy action on a bus.

Finally, a study of passenger volumes on a bus route in Baltimore before and after a holdup of the driver and passengers failed to reveal a significant decrease in ridership.[7] The crime occurred in the afternoon and the four criminals were apprehended within minutes of the crime.

The problem of robbery of bus drivers has been largely eliminated by the exact-fare lock box system now in effect in most transit systems. In 1968 there were over 3600 robberies and 330 injuries to bus drivers nationally (an increase of about 350% in 3 years). Subsequent to instituting exact-fare procedures that year, these incidents were substantially reduced.[8] This simple method removed the major object of the robbery, but the potential for injury to drivers (assault) was not eliminated.

A study by Stanford Research Institute (SRI) to evaluate means to reduce robberies and assaults of bus drivers concluded that the great majority of the robberies (78%) occurred between 6:00 p.m. and 6:00 a.m., 95% of drivers were not suspicious before the event, there was little time for a driver to activate a signal for help, and in a majority of cases the driver was alone.[9] A follow-up study by the director of the SRI report concluded that the problem of assault against bus drivers remains, and vandalism continues to be a constant problem.[10]

Three approaches can be used to reduce assaults against a bus driver and passengers. These are (1) create an environment in which a crime will not be attempted (deterrence), (2) furnish devices to enable the driver to summon help (thwarting), and (3) improve means for capturing the criminal subsequent to the crime (apprehension). Table 23-3 lists various ways that might be used to implement these methods.

Those measures that involve the driver directly, such as being isolated in a booth, carrying firearms or mace, wearing protective clothing, isolating or immobilizing the criminal, and traveling with a security guard, have been found to be unworkable. A more acceptable approach is the use of alarms intended to aid the driver in sum-

---

[6]EDWARD J. THRASHER AND JOHN B. SCHNELL, "Studies of Public Attitudes Toward Transit Crime and Vandalism," in *Crime and Vandalism in Public Transportation*, Transportation Research Record 487 (Washington, D.C.: Transportation Research Board, 1974), pp. 28–30.

[7]Ibid.

[8]PAUL GRAY, "Robbery and Assault of Bus Drivers," *Operations Research*, 19, no. 2 (March–April 1971), 258, 259.

[9]Ibid., p. 262.

[10]PAUL GRAY, "Robbery and Assault of Bus Drivers Revisited," in *Proceedings—Fifteenth Annual Meeting, Transportation Research Forum*, 15, no. 1 (San Francisco) (Oxford, Ind.: The Richard B. Cross Company, 1974), p. 245.

TABLE 23-3
Methods for Reducing Robberies and Assaults on Buses

Deterrence
    Eliminate or reduce cash availability
    Isolate driver in separate booth
    Furnish extra personnel on buses
    Furnish police or security guards
    Publicize security measures

Thwarting
    Furnish alarms on buses
    Use impregnable strongboxes
    Furnish means to isolate the criminal
    Immobilize criminal with chemical (mace) or mechanical means
    Furnish protective clothing for drivers

Apprehension
    Two-way radio
    Covert alarms
    Bus-locator systems
    Marking of stolen property
    Marking of criminal with dyes or radioactive particles
    Closed-circuit television
    Picture taking
    Voice prints

Source: Adapted from Paul Gray, "Robbery and Assault of Bus Drivers," *Operations Research,* 19, no. 2 (March-April 1971), 261.

moning help. Types of alarms include (1) a flashing light to signal nearby police, (2) two-way radios, and (3) silent alarms sent to police headquarters (similar to devices used in banks). Coupled with the alarm system could be the use of automatic vehicle monitoring (AVM) systems. AVM, which has been used successfully in rerouting of buses, is based on coded identification located on the sides of the vehicle that is "read" electronically by posts located along the route.

There is some doubt that alarm systems can be effective in thwarting a crime in progress, unless police help happens to be nearby. This is so because of the time required to transmit the alarm, process the information, dispatch aid, and proceed to the site of the crime. Even if alarms or two-way communication were effective in thwarting assaults, they would not likely be used as drivers tend to forget to activate the alarm or are instructed by the criminal (who is generally aware of the system) not to move. The possibility that the alarm will be accidentally or falsely triggered always exists, further limiting the credibility of the devices. Despite the general ineffectiveness of alarms and vehicle monitoring systems to stop a crime in progress, they do furnish some reassurance to the driver and passengers. For example, the two-way radio is especially useful as a means of communicating with the dispatcher's office, and while not effective as a crime deterrent, it is used to report a crime, notify the police of disturbances on the bus (vandals, rowdys, sudden illness, etc.), report traffic accidents, breakdowns, bottlenecks, and other emergencies.

The use of photography, perhaps during high-crime periods, has been suggested as a means of identifying criminals active on buses. Although every person would be photographed, the film is processed only when a crime occurs. This method would assist in pursuing the criminal and could be a deterrent. Although widely used by banks to record holdups in process, it is not deemed cost effective for transit buses, nor has the acceptance by the riding public been determined.

Some cities have resorted to special transit crime task forces during periods when assault on drivers and passengers became a highly visible problem. These crisis periods occur following a highly publicized assault (e.g., a murder) or a series of assaults either on a specific bus route or within a high-crime area of the city. The usual response has been to furnish a police detail that is assigned to that problem. For example, following a series of assaults on bus drivers in Los Angeles, a special roving unit of the Los Angeles Police Department was given the problem. Their approach was to be highly visible to the riding public, to follow buses and board them at random times, and to respond rapidly to calls for help. Similar techniques have been used in other cities when public outcry demanded immediate attention. In Los Angeles, the program was discontinued after the problem was "solved." The technique of assigned police protection, highly visible and randomly applied, is extremely effective, as it provides an element of surprise. The uncertainty in the criminal's mind as to the likelihood of capture severely reduces illegal activities, and criminals move elsewhere. This method, however, is costly and has been used primarily when special problems arise and not during periods when relative calm prevails.

PASSENGER SECURITY ON RAIL RAPID TRANSIT SYSTEMS

As noted earlier, transit crimes on rail rapid transit are significantly greater than on bus systems and citizens' perception of this difference is consistent with reality. The most comprehensive evaluation of the extent of criminal activity on a rapid transit system was a study of crime occurrences and citizen interviews for the city of Chicago. Significant findings included the following[11]:

1. Crime in rapid transit occurs largely in stations: 70% of crimes occurred in station areas, of which 63% were committed on platforms.
2. The character of the neighborhood in which the station is located has a strong effect on crime occurrence. Stations where the crime rate was highest are located in areas of high street-crime rates and high unemployment.
3. Crime tends to be committed by groups of individuals in a familiar neighborhood. Criminals tend to escape on foot through a station exit rather than by train. In Chicago, offenders were predominately young, male, and black (50% under age 21 and 91% under age 31).
4. Rapid transit crimes tend to occur during off-peak periods. The highest risk day for robberies is Sunday and the next highest is Saturday. The highest risk

---

[11]Robert Shellow and others, *Improvement of Mass Transit Security in Chicago: A Report to the City of Chicago Department of Public Works Recommending Specific Security Measures for Demonstration on Chicago Transit Authority Facilities,* prepared for UMTA (Pittsburgh, Pa.: Carnegie-Mellon University, June 30, 1973).

period is 8:00 p.m. to 5:00 a.m., and the peak risk time is between 1:00 and 4:00 a.m. Assault and battery tends to occur during more heavily traveled periods.

5. For robberies only, the annual transit crime rate is 332 per 100,000 persons; whereas the on-street robbery crime rate is 954 per 100,000 persons. Nationally, the comparable robbery crime rate is 187 per 100,000 persons. These figures indicate that rapid transit crime rates tend to be lower than crime rates for the city in which the system is located.

6. Citizens consider security a factor in not riding transit, but auto ownership, time, cost, and convenience are the predominant factors. Most citizens' perception of crime is confirmed in fact. Of nonriders, 25% cited security as a factor for not riding transit, but 80% of this group cited ownership of an auto as their principal reason.

7. More low-income people say they are insecure on transit than do higher-income people, but high-income people more often cite insecurity as the reason for not riding. It is well known that in Chicago poorer people predominate the group that uses transit, and these persons, while exposed to unsafe conditions, can do little to change their situation. When possible, however, riders tend to avoid traveling at night.

8. Many rapid transit riders are not willing to use the system between 6:00 p.m. and 6:00 a.m. (80%), and very few indicate that they would ride after midnight. The fear of riding transit after dark reflects not only the dangers within the system but also the risk of personal injury when walking to and from the rapid transit station.

9. Perceptions of safety for individual transit modes or elements of the trip are (in decreasing levels of safety) riding the bus, waiting for the bus, walking to the station, riding the train, waiting at the rapid transit station, and (least secure) stairs, ramps, or tunnels.

Transit security measures for rapid transit systems are directed primarily at station areas, as these are the points of highest crime occurrence and greatest passenger vulnerability, although security on transit vehicles is also an important concern. The principal objective of station-related security countermeasures is that passengers be visible to transit personnel, police, and other passengers so that criminal acts are prevented or help summoned quickly. Accordingly, architectural design of transit station areas should include consideration of the following features:

- Clear lines of sight unobscured by columns and concessions.
- Ticket collection booth centrally located for greatest visibility.
- Straight corridors and passageways, with ample width and good lighting.
- Closed-circuit TV monitors on platform areas and other hidden locations.
- High levels of illumination.
- Clearly defined station and circulation areas no larger than needed for passenger boarding and alighting.

- Provision of variable-size areas for peak and off-peak periods.
- Minimum number of exit and entry points.
- Locked and supervised toilet facilities.
- Clearly defined corridors and waiting areas partitioned from storage and non-public spaces.
- Fences, one-way gates, and other directional devices to control passenger flow.

Rapid transit stations and vehicles can also be made more secure by the provision of communications aids to summon help if a crime occurs. Two types are available: alarms and closed-circuit television.[12]

A simple warning alarm could be used to attract attention or summon police. Silent alarms, for example, are sometimes used by transit ticket agents to alert police of a problem in the station. As with alarms on buses, these devices suffer from the fact that response time is usually too long, passengers may be fearful of attracting attention and not activate the alarm, little information is transmitted by an alarm, and many calls will prove to be false. Telephones can also act as alarm devices, and these have been installed in some transit systems, with a direct line to the security office. Telephones can serve to reassure passengers and furnish information as well as assist in calling for help.

Continuous closed-circuit television monitoring is an effective means of visually inspecting station areas from a central control point. Cameras directed at various places, such as passageways, stairs, platforms, telephone locations, and so on, can be called up on a central monitor, when desired, to furnish information about activity anywhere in the station. These devices may also be used to verify a telephone request for help or information. The benefits of continuous television monitoring of transit station areas could suffer from the effects of boredom or fatigue on the observer's ability to detect and report a crime in progress. The likelihood that a crime will be observed at all is further dependent on the presence of an active television scan at the time.

To counteract the disadvantages of simple alarms and continuous television monitoring, while utilizing their benefits, a system has been proposed for Chicago that combines the alarm, telephone, and television monitor into a single unit.[13] The system known as teleview alert (TVA) includes the following elements:

1. *Movable gates or barriers* that limit the accessible platform area to the space required by a reduced train length during off-peak hours.
2. *Emergency telephones.* These are located in the restricted area and activated by a push button. The call is automatically placed to a central security area.
3. *Closed-circuit TV cameras.* These are activitated by the telephone or push bars

---

[12]ROBERT SHELLOW, JAMES P. ROMUALDI, AND EUGENE W. BARTEL, "Crime in Rapid Transit Systems: An Analysis and a Recommended Security and Surveillance System," in *Crime and Vandalism in Public Transportation*, Transportation Research Record 487 (Washington, D.C.: Transportation Research Board, 1974), p. 7.
[13]Ibid., pp. 8–11.

spaced 6 to 9 m (20 to 30 ft) apart on the station platform, stairway, ramp, and turnstile areas. Five cameras, facing away from the exit, are actuated simultaneously when a passenger presses a bar. Central monitors observe the activity or can turn the cameras on remotely if desired.

4. *Public-address systems* would be available for use by persons observing the television monitors for the purpose of reassuring passengers, calling to vandals, or providing information.

The effect of special police forces on crime in the New York City subways was analyzed subsequent to the deployment of uniformed patrols on rapid transit lines, between the hours of 8:00 p.m. and 4:00 a.m.[14] The study concluded that in spite of stepped-up police activities, the rate of serious crime increased steadily from year to year although the addition of uniformed patrol officers in the subway system effected a decrease in the amount of serious crime committed at the times and places where officers were used. The study noted a temporary decrease in crime during hours when no special patrols were in force and attributed this "phantom effect" to the mistaken belief by criminals that police might be on duty. After this effect wore off, crime during these hours increased most rapidly during the hours with fewest patrolmen.

The New York study confirmed other findings that high-crime stations are located in high-crime areas, and recommended that police be redeployed to current high-crime-rate locations rather than to be continually stationed uniformly throughout the system. This element of surprise would capitalize on the phantom effect previously noted by withholding knowledge about the likelihood that police officers would be in the area. Another related police strategy is the use of decoys, police disguised in such a way as to trigger a criminal act. For example, if a police officer disguised as a sleeping drunk is robbed, the criminal will be quickly apprehended by other officers who had been kept hidden from view. Finally, the use of special K-9 patrols is seen not only as a deterrent but also as an effective means for restoring order on a train and in pursuing and interrogating a suspect.

VANDALISM

Vandalism, the willful destruction of property, is a constant problem for transit agencies. Vandals are usually school-age children, and the crime is viewed as an aspect of juvenile delinquincy. The types of destruction to transit property include breaking windows, ripping seats, graffiti, and stoning moving vehicles.

The short-term goal of transit agencies is to protect its property, to apprehend and prosecute those who vandalize, to protect its patrons, and to minimize adverse effects on ridership. The long-term goal is to modify the behavior of juveniles in such a manner that they will not choose to destroy transit property. Thus, techniques used by

---

[14]JAN M. CHAIKEN, MICHAEL W. LAWLESS, AND KEITH A. STEVENSON, *The Impact of Police Activity on Subway Crime*, The Rand Paper Series, P-5203 (Santa Monica, Calif.: The Rand Corporation, March 1974). Now available as AD 786 863.

transit agencies to combat vandalism include (1) the use of vandalproof materials for seats and windows, (2) the use of easy-to-clean surfaces to facilitate removal of graffiti, (3) eliminating or making it difficult to purchase spray paint, (4) the use of police-alarm systems, (5) the use of helicopter patrols, (6) the establishment of education programs in schools, and (7) cooperation with judicial and school authorities.[15]

Broken windows on buses comprise the largest single replacement cost item. Some transit systems, where problems are minor, are installing low-cost tempered safety glass. In higher-crime areas, more costly break-resistant materials are often used, such as coated acrylic or polycarbonate. Damaged seats are the second largest cost item, and transit systems have resorted to fiberglass seats that resist the vandal's knife. Hard seats, while puncture-proof, are less comfortable and furnish inviting surfaces for graffiti. Graffiti is an act of vandalism difficult to counteract. Use of strong cleaning compounds, working with suppliers to withhold sales of spray paint, and use of surface materials that can be cleaned easily, have all been tried but with little success, especially in larger cities.

The Southeastern Pennsylvania Transportation Authority (SEPTA) has taken direct action against "graffiti artists" through the use of special police units that patrol high-graffiti areas. Through arrests and subsequent convictions, as well as the always possible presence of security officers, the extent of graffiti has been significantly reduced. SEPTA's proposed ordinance to ban the sale of spray paint to juveniles was defeated by the Philadelphia City Council, but paint and hardware dealers have cooperated by placing these items in less accessible locations.

A serious problem is the stoning or derailing of trains by youths. These acts cause extensive damage to moving trains and buses, and have killed or injured drivers and passengers. The use of helicopters to spot trespassers and vandals has been successfully demonstrated by SEPTA.[16] Youths walking on railroad property are in personal danger (in one year 14 persons were killed crossing tracks in the Philadelphia area), and stonings of trains have been costly to the railroads. A demonstration program by SEPTA of helicopter surveillance and ground patrol contact has resulted in the capture and arrest of several youths observed stoning trains or trespassing.

Several transit agencies have worked directly with schools by presenting talks about the problems of vandalism. The effectiveness of this approach depends on the ability of the speaker to communicate to the students the seriousness of the problem, the extent of cooperation by school authorities, and the follow-up of the talks with other types of reinforcement. A program sponsored by SEPTA for schools located along a rail line where stonings were a serious problem contributed to reducing the number of incidents. Washington, D.C., Metro (WMATA) has effectively used two football players as role models to make presentations in schools about the problems of vandalism of the buses and to explain the students' responsibility as good citizens.

---

[15]Edward J. Thrasher and John B. Schnell, "Summary Report on Vandalism and Passenger Security in the Transit Industry," in *Crime and Vandalism in Public Transportation*, Transportation Research Record 487 (Washington, D.C.: Transportation Research Board, 1974), pp. 46–54.

[16]Theodore A. Beadle, "Vandalism: Combating Transportation's Blight," *Metropolitan*, 70, no. 3 (May–June 1974), 28–29.

When transit networks cross political boundaries the question of police jurisdiction over control of the system can become an issue. The matter is especially relevant for large rapid transit systems because of their physical isolation from the city and the many communities that these systems serve.

The viewpoint of public transit managers is that crime on transit is but a part of the overall urban crime problem and, therefore, is the responsibility of the local law enforcement agency. They contend further that the existence of a rapid transit line does not create new crime and, in fact, the existence of public transit could assist police on foot in moving about the city. Management is also concerned that the additional burden of a separate police force will further strain its budget, and with rising deficits, the prospect of additional public transit employees added as civil servants is viewed with great concern. Furthermore, transit management has contended that it is the obligation of local law enforcement agencies to protect citizens in their jurisdiction and that they are better trained and qualified to undertake this mission.

Local law enforcement agencies often regard large-scale rapid transit as a special problem beyond their means to address. This is not true in small and medium-size cities where buses are the only form of public transit and are handled simply as any vehicle (truck, taxi, or auto) that operates on public streets. Local police in large cities view large transit systems as a separate governmental agency with resources and responsibility to furnish their own security forces or to reimburse local police for this protection. Legally, local police agencies have the responsibility for protection and enforcement of laws within their jurisdiction, but added personnel are required to adequately protect stations, trains in motion, and transit property.[17]

A study of policing intercommunity mass transit systems outlined the major problems created by relying solely on a local police force comprised of officers from various communities.[18] These are:

1. *Jurisdicational confusion* (which community takes responsibility for the crime, how to handle crimes on trains, what happens when a crime occurring in one community is reported to police in another).
2. *Reporting of and response to crime.* Lack of centralized control of crime reports and standardized procedures could cause delays and inconsistency in response. The lack of coordination, ill-defined chain of command, and lack of accountability could lead to loss of confidence by the riding public.
3. *Police patrol coverage.* The number of police assigned to patrol transit properties could vary considerably, especially between inner cities and suburbs.

---

[17]KEITH BERNARD, "Planning and Development of the BART Police Services Department," in *Proceedings—Fifteenth Annual Meeting, Transportation Research Forum*, 15, no. 1 (San Francisco) (Oxford, Ind.: The Richard B. Cross Company, 1974), pp. 240–44.

[18]P. S. WALLACE AND R. M. BUREN, *Policing Inter-community Mass Transit Systems: Proposed Legislation for Chicago with a Consideration of Other Cities*, prepared for UMTA (Chicago: University of Illinois at Chicago Circle, March 1974). Now available as PB 235 677.

4. *Crime recording.* Owing to lack of coordination, methods of recording crimes will vary considerably, and compilation of systemwide data would be extremely difficult.
5. *Specialized training required by transit police.* Policing of mass transit systems requires unique skills and understanding, including characteristics of transit riders, crime types, system elements, and special problems. On the other hand, a single police force accountable to one jurisdiction would be more effective by furnishing a central location for reporting crimes, specialized patrol procedures, accurate crime reports, and a police force specially trained for transit problems.

Specially trained police are not uncommon and are used by industry, apartment complexes, city and regional parks, department stores, shopping centers, etc., where special problems cannot be adequately handled locally. Transit systems also operate under varying arrangements. For example, the Chicago Transit Authority (CTA) shares responsibility with the Chicago Police Department. The CTA is responsible for protecting transit property and the Police Department for protecting transit employees and riders. The transit authority police department in New York is responsible for security on the New York subway system. Transit police are financed from tax revenue, and they are intended to complement the activities of the New York City police. Transit security in the San Francisco Bay Area Rapid Transit System (BART) is the responsibility of a specially created BART Police Services Department. That force was required because of the reluctance by local police agencies to furnish the necessary security forces. Separate but limited transit security forces are also in effect in Boston, whereas Cleveland transit security is the responsibility of local police.

The type of police organization available to serve transit systems will affect the level of security that is furnished to its riders. If their services are scattered and without coordination and leadership, then the effectiveness of other countermeasures, which are intended to secure police help quickly, might be limited. Planning for new transit systems and resolving the problems of crime on older ones may require a comprehensive assessment of the organizational and fiscal responsibilities of the transit agency and the local community for security matters.

TRANSIT SAFETY

Bus and rail transit are the safest modes of transportation in the United States.[19] According to data supplied by the National Safety Council and the American Public Transit Association, the average number of fatalities per 100 million passenger-kilometers (miles) in a 20-year period is only 0.06 (0.09) for public transit; whereas

---

[19]HIGHWAY RESEARCH BOARD TASK FORCE ON URBAN MASS TRANSPORTATION SAFETY STANDARDS, *Safety in Urban Mass Transportation: The State of the Art* (Washington, D.C.: National Academy of Sciences, National Research Council, and National Academy of Engineering, Division of Engineering, April 1973).

the corresponding figure for passenger cars and taxis is 1.4 (2.2); domestic air, 0.2 (0.3); and railroads, 0.08 (0.13).[20]

The elements of a transit safety program involve employee training, equipment and facility maintenance, vehicle operations, public information, accident record keeping and analysis, and establishment of clearly stated safety goals. The active participation of transit management and concern for safety aspects of the operation are essential.

The experience of one bus property serves to illustrate several desirable features of a comprehensive safety management program.[21] These are:

1. Careful prescreening of applicants for employment to select bus operators that are likely to be safe and courteous drivers. Over 40 applicants may be screened to fill each position. Attributes such as character, lack of police record or driver citations, and attitudes are determined prior to employment.
2. Training period for bus operators. The training program includes written tests on regulations and traveling the route under supervision.
3. Reporting of defects at the end of each run. Operators are required to turn in a "defect or o.k." report after making a thorough check of the bus.
4. Maintain 24-hour garage operation. Periodic and special maintenance of buses in a modern fully equipped garage ensures that buses are in excellent running condition.
5. Goal setting for transit safety. Each year the goal is last year's record minus 5%. Pride in achieving this goal is reflected in the excellent condition of the buses that are repaired (or bumpers replaced) soon after being damaged.
6. Self insurance. Owing to its record of transit safety and confidence, the system can be self-insured.
7. Complete accident reporting, including details about the accident and responsibility.
8. Communications with employees. Through safety committees, suggestions are made concerning ways in which safety procedures can be improved.
9. Recognition of employee contributions to the safety program and individual safe-driving records.
10. Refresher courses for drivers when needed.
11. Participation by the safety office in vehicle modifications and preparation of specifications for new buses.

Safety for bus transit also involves vehicle designs that improve the likelihood that an accident will not occur. Features added to improve safety are turn signals on the sides of buses, energy-absorbing (water) bumpers, nonskid floors, adequate lighting, adequate clearance for doors, and visibility of doors and windshields. Bus-stop locations; avoidance of dangerous corners or intersections; adequate bus-stop distances

---

[20]B. R. STOKES, "A Record of Transit Safety," *Transit Journal*, 2, no. 3 (August 1976), p. 5.
[21]HIGHWAY RESEARCH BOARD, *Safety*, pp. 88–98.

for boarding, alighting, and merging with traffic; avoiding railroad crossings; and adherence to traffic controls are examples of operational measures taken to minimize accidents.

Safety for rail transit involves considerations of both operations and equipment and facilities. The safety guidelines for urban rapid transit systems are contained in the report, *Moving People Safely*, prepared by the Institute of Rapid Transit. This report furnishes guidelines and standards for the inspection of facilities (track and stations), cars, and communications. The report recommends procedures for maintenance testing and inspection of electrical power systems and a uniform code of operating rules for the rapid transit industry. Finally, the report suggests procedures to follow in emergency situations, such as equipment or power failures, fire, derailments or collisions, bomb threats, persons in contact with the third rail, and flooding.[22]

In summary, the transit industry has maintained its safety record by directing attention toward areas of personnel, technology, operations, and management. Each of these areas requires an overall strategy and goal setting buttressed by thorough accident reporting and analysis. The commitment of the industry was expressed by B. R. Stokes, Executive Director of the American Public Transit Association,[23] "The transit industry has a special consciousness of safety and accident prevention because of the very nature of the business. Transit carries people—there is no more precious cargo."

SELECTED BIBLIOGRAPHY

Many citations are no longer available from their original source. These citations are often available from the National Technical Information Service, U.S. Department of Commerce, 5285 Port Royal Road, Springfield, Va. 22161. We have verified the order numbers for many of these citations, and they are found at the end of the citation. Prices are available through NTIS at the address above.

BATTELLE, COLUMBUS LABORATORIES, *Safety in Urban Mass Transportation: Research Report, Summary*, prepared for UMTA under subcontract to Naval Underwater Systems Center. Columbus, Ohio: Battelle, Columbus Laboratories, May 6, 1975.

CHAIKEN, JAN M., MICHAEL W. LAWLESS, AND KEITH A. STEVENSON, *The Impact of Police Activity on Subway Crime*, The Rand Paper Series, P-5203. Santa Monica, Calif.: The Rand Corporation, March 1974. Now available as AD 786 863.

CHEANEY, E. S., AND OTHERS, *Safety in Urban Mass Transportation: Guidelines Manual*, prepared for UMTA under subcontract to Naval Underwater Systems Center. Columbus, Ohio: Battelle, Columbus Laboratories, May 5, 1975. Now available as PB 245 413.

COULTAS, ROBERT, ed., *Moving People Safely: Safety Guidelines for Urban Rapid Transit Systems*, prepared by Passenger Safety Committee. Washington, D.C.: Institute for Rapid Transit, May 1972.

HIGHWAY RESEARCH BOARD TASK FORCE ON URBAN MASS TRANSPORTATION SAFETY STANDARDS, *Safety in Urban Mass Transportation: The State of the Art*. Washington, D.C.: National Academy of Sciences, National Research Council, and National Academy of Engineering, Division of Engineering, April 1973.

SCHNELL, JOHN B., *Vandalism and Passenger Security: A Study of Crime and Vandalism on Urban Mass Transit Systems in the United States and Canada*, prepared for UMTA. Washington, D.C.: American Transit Association, September 1973. Now available as PB 226 854.

---

[22]ROBERT COULTAS, ed., *Moving People Safely: Safety Guidelines for Urban Rapid Transit Systems*, prepared by Passenger Safety Committee (Washington, D.C.: Institute for Rapid Transit, May 1972).

[23]STOKES, "A Record of Transit Safety," p. 12.

SHELLOW, ROBERT, AND OTHERS, *Improvement of Mass Transit Security in Chicago: A Report to the City of Chicago Department of Public Works Recommending Specific Security Measures for Demonstration on Chicago Transit Authority Facilities*, prepared for UMTA. Pittsburgh, Pa.: Carnegie-Mellon University, June 30, 1973.

SIEGEL, L. AND OTHERS, *An Assessment of Crime and Policing Responses in Urban Mass Transit Systems*. McLean, Va.: The MITRE Corporation, April 1977.

STANFORD RESEARCH INSTITUTE AND UNIVERSITY OF CALIFORNIA, *Reduction of Robberies and Assaults of Bus Drivers, Vol. I: Summary, Vol. II: The Scope of the Crime Problem and Its Resolution, Vol. III: Technological and Operational Methods*, prepared for Alameda–Contra Costa Transit District. Menlo Park, Calif.: Stanford Research Institute, December 1970.

TRANSPORTATION RESEARCH BOARD, *Crime and Vandalism in Public Transportation*, Transportation Research Record 487. Washington, D.C.: Transportation Research Board, 1974.

WALLACE, P. S., AND R. M. BUREN, *Policing Inter-community Mass Transit Systems: Proposed Legislation for Chicago with a Consideration of Other Cities*, prepared for UMTA. Chicago: University of Illinois at Chicago Circle, March 1974. Now available as PB 235 677.

Chapter 24

THE ROLE OF PRIVATE INDUSTRY

KENNETH W. HEATHINGTON, *Director, Transportation Center,*
The University of Tennessee

There are many components that comprise the public transportation system in an urban area. There are public transportation services of a traditional fixed-route, fixed-schedule nature; taxi services; airport ground transportation services; special services for the handicapped and elderly; and many other types of services. Some of the systems that provide these services may be publicly owned and operated, others may be privately owned and operated, while others may be publicly owned but privately operated.

For almost three-quarters of a century, private industry provided most, if not all, of these public transportation services in a majority of the urban areas in the United States. Only in a small number of the urban areas, such as San Francisco, Chicago, and New York, did publicly owned systems come into being before the 1960s. From the early part of the century, however, some private operations were in difficult financial condition. In many cases this was alleviated by World War II, but, in general, many systems allowed service to deteriorate steadily as they slowly lost in the mobility battle with the automobile and the dispersion of the population. This decrease in service and ridership became very pronounced following World War II.

In the 1960s the federal government, and many of the people working in the public transportation field, felt that public ownership and operation of public transportation systems was a solution to the problems that confronted these systems. Thus, Congress passed the Urban Mass Transportation Act of 1964, which provided funds for purchasing capital equipment.

Since the 1964 act there has been a large increase in the number of systems that have been purchased and operated by public bodies. The original act gave impetus to the purchasing of private public transportation companies by the public sector. The act was viewed as providing a means of solving the financial plight of the private firms because (1) there would be an elimination of the payment of taxes, (2) the public sector could operate systems more economically, (3) the profit motive would be eliminated, (4) services could be expanded and an increase in ridership would result, and (5) federal support would permit much of the financial burden to be borne at the federal level. The underlying causes of the financial problems of the private systems seemed to be overlooked. The dispersion of the population into low-density areas, the increased availability of the automobile to an ever-increasing number of households, the restrictive nature of regulations at all levels of government, and many other circumstances were often felt to be secondary to a lack of money.

It was found that moneys made available for capital expenditures did not solve the financial problems of the public transportation systems. The Urban Mass Transportation Act of 1964 was then amended to provide for operating subsidies to assist local communities in making service improvements and to reduce the operating costs to local government.

Even with these increased resources, some of the objectives of the Urban Mass Transportation Act are not being met in many urban areas. Possibly sufficient time has not elapsed to see the beginning of a trend toward improved ridership and public acceptance of public transportation. It may be that public transportation was in such a deteriorated condition that it will take years and many billions of dollars to realize sufficient improvements to attract enough patronage to result in a cost-effective system.

Moreover, results from public funds being invested in public transportation services have been less than desirable in many instances. If one uses the figures from the *Transit Fact Book*[1] and divides the changed operating subsidy between 1974 and 1975 (given as an increased operating deficit of $403.8 million) by the increased ridership in these years, the result indicates that the operating subsidy amounted to almost $27 for each of the added rides. Of course, this is a distortion, as it does not consider the improved service given to the millions of other riders, but it does indicate the high cost for the marginal increased ridership during this period. Costs have not been reduced, but have greatly increased with public ownership and operation of public transportation services. Between 1970 and 1976 transit deficits increased over 800%. The ratio of operating revenues to operating costs was reduced from 91% to only 56%. The largest contributor to operating costs, of course, was inflation at about 50%, but the next largest contributor was labor at 20%. Other factors included in the increase in transit costs were additional employment, increased service, fuel, and insurance. However, only about 8% of the increased costs can be attributed to increase in service. All these factors added almost $2 billion to the cost of providing transit services in this six-year period. Most of the $2 billion—about $1.5 billion—went to labor for wages and fringe benefits. In 1976 transit employees had the highest average monthly salaries of any public sector employees. Their annual salary was slightly over $16,000. Labor costs have been rising faster in publicly owned transit systems than in other major industries, such as steel and automotive. In some systems, the increased operating

---

[1] AMERICAN PUBLIC TRANSIT ASSOCIATION, *Transit Fact Book*, 1975–76 ed. (Washington, D.C.: American Public Transit Association, 1976).

funds simply provided higher wages for labor without any increase in service. In some instances, public transportation services have been reduced rather than expanded as a result of public ownership. Many of these systems have been experiencing a rapid increase in costs in concert with a reduction in services. This, of course, is not true for all publicly owned systems, but there has been a trend toward permitting costs to increase without an additional increase in services.

The increased deficits have been partly due to a decrease in fares or a refusal to raise fares as operating costs increased. When public transportation services are taken out from under the private sector, there is often public pressure exerted to decrease fares and provide service in areas with extremely low ridership. Since these decisions are often political with publicly owned systems, the net result of the decision-making process is increased deficits. Political pressure is not as great on the private firms to reduce fares and at the same time to expand service. The public bodies have become so accustomed to deficit spending that the term "unfunded deficit," which is now used to describe that portion of the deficit not covered by local, state, or federal subsidies, causes little alarm.

Because of the rapidly expanding costs and the large increases in operating deficits, urban areas, in general, have not encouraged private industry to provide public transportation services. This attitude may stem from fear of competition and subsequent loss of patronage where public transportation is perceived as a tax-subsidized monopoly. More recently, however, political bodies have begun to realize that public ownership is not in itself a solution to the problems in the public transportation field. There are, of course, many private companies still providing public transportation services, and in some areas, this private involvement is increasing. In almost all areas, taxis are still owned and operated by the private enterprise sector, although some companies are in weak financial condition. Ground transportation services to and from airports are normally provided by private industry. (An exception to this is the SURTRAN system operating out of the Dallas–Fort Worth Airport.) In some urban areas, car rentals are being utilized as a means of providing airport gound transportation services as well as other activities. There are many special services, such as those for the handicapped and elderly, that are currently provided by private companies. In general, these enterprises provide a high level of service at moderately high fares. They are profitable and in demand by particular market segments. In addition, there are new types of services, such as vanpools and carpools, now operated largely by the private sector, which carry a substantial number of people.

Since the mid-1970s, there has been a reevaluation as to the role that private industry should play in providing public transportation services. Much of the change in thinking has come about because of the increasing use of paratransit services. These services, such as priority taxi, shared-ride taxi, dial-a-bus, express bus, and employee vanpools, are often more economically provided by the private sector. The traditional public transportation system (i.e., fixed-route, fixed-schedule service) is not oriented toward providing a variety of services because of a lack of (1) authority, (2) organizational structure, (3) expertise, (4) reasonable cost, and/or (5) financial support. Often, the traditional public transportation systems viewed these other types of services as competition. It has required several years of public operation of traditional transit services before many communities began to realize that no single mode of public transportation could meet the total needs of the community for public transportation services. Communities began to expand the range of public transportation services, and the private sector became an important element in accomplishing this expansion. It would appear that the role of the private sector will increase as the range of public transportation services expands. This will be especially true if the costs of providing services are a major consideration.

REGULATORY ISSUES

Many of the private companies that were engaged in public transportation services ceased operations because of regulatory problems. While it is true that other things contributed to the demise of private companies, regulatory problems probably have been the greatest single contributing factor. Regulatory agencies, such as public service and public utility commissions, have tended to take the position of rigid observance of existing legislation rather than develop and propose legislation that would strengthen the transportation industry. The needs of the transportation industry have changed over the years as the environment in which it has operated has changed. However, the utility regulators tend to view their role as an enforcer rather than as an advocate for needed change. (A parallel example can be taken from the energy field.) Conditions must become extremely critical before changes occur in legislation, thus directing a regulatory body to move toward a more progressive stand. Consequently, a regulator is more often a follower than a leader in guiding the development of appropriate and timely regulations for the industry.

National policy often promotes a specific concept only to have a regulatory agency retard its accomplishment. As an example, Congress and the executive branch have promoted increased utilization of all forms of public transportation to reduce congestion and air pollution and, perhaps most important, to reduce energy consumption. However, regulatory agencies have retarded or stopped carpools, vanpools, school-bus charter services, shared-ride taxi systems, and a host of other services, to ensure strict compliance with existing laws. In few cases, if any, have the regulators been instrumental in leading the way to make needed changes in order to accomplish national policy.

The public service and utility commissions traditionally believed in granting monopolies to transportation systems. The consumer is then supposed to be protected by "regulated and fair" rates established by the commission. By controlling the rates, the regulators then assure that the supplier makes substantial profits in certain areas; conversely, they can require them to subsidize unprofitable services in other areas. The basic assumption, which is false, is that all suppliers incur the same costs in providing a given level of service in a given area. The commissions generally assume that management does not play a strong role in determining the cost of supplying service. Then, based on these assumptions, they often prohibit new suppliers from providing service.

The regulatory agencies place a high value on carrier liability. One of their arguments against entry of small firms into the marketplace is that the liability that can be afforded by the smaller firms will not sufficiently protect the passengers. However, there has been some interest in trying to reduce the liability requirements of suppliers. One state has been discussing a proposal to make the passenger responsible for "first coverage" in case of an accident. This concept places a certain responsiblity on the passengers to take reasonable precautions in riding on public transportation systems. This is similar to certain European laws for liability. If such coverage could be passed on to the passengers, smaller firms would be in a better financial position relative to providing the rapidly escalating liability coverage.

The transportation regulator does not have direct interest or authority in the labor area. However, by prohibiting easy entry into the field, it, in effect, gives labor a monopoly on control of supply costs. Labor, knowing that no one else can enter the field, can negotiate terms that greatly increase the cost of operations. These terms include not only wage rates but also union rules relating to part-time labor, minimum number of hours per week, split shifts, level of bargaining units, job bidding, termination policies, and so on, which may drive the costs of providing services up exponentially. Management knows that, in time, the regulator will normally grant an increase in fares to offset the increased labor costs. (This pattern can be illustrated in various other areas of monopolies, such as telephone companies, electric utilities, and water districts.) Without the expressed intention of doing so, the regulatory agency often tends to assist in the escalation of costs of operation.

The philosopy with which the public service and utility commissions have operated over the years can be summarized in the following five basic assumptions[2]:

1. The transportation industry is basically a natural monopoly with substantial economies of scale (i.e., cost decreases substantially as use increases).
2. The transportation industry is imbued with a broad public interest; consequently, it is strongly in the public interest to make certain that a minimum level of service is provided to all people in a nonprejudicial and nondiscriminatory manner.
3. Since the public, through its regulatory agency, has the authority to determine levels of service and to prohibit discriminatory or prejudicial treatment of unprofitable business, it has an obligation to ensure that the carrier receives an adequate rate of return, given honest and effective management. Therefore, rates are determined not by competitive market forces, but on a regulated rate-of-return basis, if the carrier is providing the prescribed level of service and the management is not found guilty of fraud or gross mismanagement.
4. Since the service levels are prescribed by the regulatory process and since most management is reasonably effective, the economic structure of virtually all carriers is similar. Therefore, there is no public benefit in having a particular carrier provide the service.

---

[2]FRANK W. DAVIS, JR., AND OTHERS, *Increased Transportation Efficiency Through Ridesharing: The Brokerage Approach* (Knoxville, Tenn.: The University of Tennessee Transportation Center, 1976).

5. Since the carrier is providing the service deemed necessary for the public at a price deemed reasonable by the regulatory agency, the sole effect of competition would be to increase the unit cost of the natural monopoly. Competing carriers could lower cost only by serving the profitable routes and by not providing adequate service to the less-profitable areas. Consequently, competition should be prohibited from "skimming the cream" rightfully belonging to the regulated carriers in order to subsidize service needed in the less-profitable areas. This is the principle of cross-subsidization. Strict entry controls are established to protect the carrier (or carriers), who operate according to the requirements of the regulatory bodies. New carriers can operate only if they furnish proof of their fitness, willingness, and ability to serve the public. In addition, they must prove that their operation is necessary for the public's convenience and that existing carriers are unable to meet the specific needs the new carrier will serve.

EXAMPLES OF REGULATORY CONSTRAINT

There are many examples of regulatory constraints that reduce the role of the private sector in providing public transportation services. One such constraint, with a negative impact upon public transportation companies, is the discouraging of diversification by companies into other transportation activities. As an example, a carrier that provides services for passengers cannot necessarily carry goods. It is generally very difficult for a company to diversify into other activities without undergoing numerous hearings and submitting innumerable petitions before regulatory bodies. This pursuit of diversification is time consuming, costly in terms of dollars for legal services, and, in most cases, ends in failure.

Most private companies cannot expand or reduce services without formal interaction with regulatory bodies. Frequently, such requests are denied after much time and thousands of dollars have been spent in legal services. Many companies decide to cease operations rather than continue to address the numerous regulatory problems, as the requested changes are often necessary to keep operations viable. In some cases the regulatory constraints place undue hardships upon the private companies and prohibit them from expansion into activities that would increase their revenue. By not being able to increase revenues, a firm's earnings tend to decrease over time until an overall profitable operation cannot be maintained.

Because of the regulatory structure in many states, newer, smaller firms, which often have excellent potential for providing good service, do not enter into the public transportation field. A newer firm with only a few vehicles might seek to provide certain small portions of public transportation services, but cannot obtain permission (or meet the requirements) to provide these services. These small firms quickly learn that they must meet the same requirements as the large firms, even though the total volume of passengers carried is substantially less. For example, there is little or no difference in insurance rates for school buses providing a limited amount of charter service to football games and for large corporations such as Greyhound or Trailways that provide substantial charter service.

Until recently it was illegal in most states, if not all, for an individual to operate a carpool if the amount of money collected from the riders exceeded the cost of operations. Insurance is also a problem for these individuals. This same regulatory constraint has applied to individuals wanting to operate a van to carry 12 to 15 passengers. All the regulatory problems (insurance, operating permits, etc.) tend to discourage new and innovative ideas from being incorporated into the public transportation field. It is particularly discouraging for the smaller firms, which often do not have a large financial backing, but are willing and capable of providing services that would be useful to particular market segments.

There are many small markets which large companies do not find attractive enough to provide service. Thus, the investment, if it is to be made, must come from the smaller firms. Generally, the regulatory bodies prohibit the smaller firm from entering the marketplace at the insistence of the larger firm; the larger firm feels that the smaller firm might expand its services if given a franchise to operate. As a result, the smaller firm is prohibited from providing the service, the larger firm refuses to provide the service, and the public is the loser. Originally, the regulatory bodies were established to protect the public; it now seems that often they are more interested in protecting the large suppliers whether the service is supplied or not. Unfortunately, in some cases, public agencies then take over the service at public cost.

Many public transportation firms have an exclusive franchise for an area even though a full range of services may not be provided. In some instances, they may not be furnishing an adequate level of service, but since they have an exclusive franchise, all other firms are prohibited from providing service in that area. As an example, a publicly owned system had a franchise to operate in an urban area, and citizens in a low-income portion of the city requested local bus service. Services were supplied for a short period of time, but the ridership was not sufficient to continue at the fares charged. A private firm offered to provide services at the same fares charged by the publicly owned system; however, the publicly owned system argued against permitting the private operator to provide those services because the publicly owned system had an exclusive franchise. As a result, although the franchised public operator would not provide the services, the private operator was not permitted to provide them either.

In another urban area, there were no local private firms that provided charter service. One had to charter from a private operator located some 105 km (65 mi) away and had to pay for the 210 km (130 mi) of deadhead travel. The local public transportation system, which was publicly owned, attempted to develop charter services in the area but was denied the request to provide these services by the regulatory commission. Local residents complained to no avail that they could not afford the charter services provided by the private sector because of the amount of deadhead time that had to be paid. As a result, the consumer was denied services that would have been beneficial to the community as a whole, since it would have helped to pay for the existing system as well as to provide a needed service.

In one local community there was one small airport with very limited air service of one flight per day at undesirable hours. There was a large airport some 97 to 113 km (60 to 70 mi) away that had good service to any portion of the United States. The smaller city had no ground transportation to the major airport. A local travel agency purchased three limousines to provide ground transportation service from the smaller community to the major airport. [In this state a 90-day temporary permit for operation can be obtained with ease. After 90 days, a hearing is held by the Public Service Commission (PSC) to permit or deny further service rights.] Three runs per day were made, and the demand for service was excellent. After the 90-day trial period, a PSC hearing was held. The airline company filed a petition to deny service, indicating that it would substantially hurt their business. The two major bus companies filed a similar petition, even though each had only two runs per day between the smaller community and the center of the larger urban area. It was about 24 km (15 mi) from the center city to the airport, and the bus companies did not provide service to the airport. A railroad filed a similar petition, even though they did not operate any passenger trains.

Needless to say, the PSC denied the travel agency the right to provide service to the major airport. In this particular instance, no one's interest was really served, especially the consumers'. The demand for service did not increase on the other modes nor would it have been decreased. They were serving different markets. The consumer continued to drive an automobile to the airport.

Some states are now changing their regulations to permit easier entry into the public transportation field. As an example, several have recently changed the regulations on carpools and vanpools. In California, for example, a vehicle that has 15 passengers or less will be excluded from the regulatory constraints placed on larger types of vehicles. However, these changes in the regulatory area have come about as an indirect result of the energy shortage rather than a perceived need for improvement in the public transportation field. It is unfortunate that it takes an extraneous crisis to effect a needed change in regulations. On the other hand, the trend seems to be toward more deregulation in many areas of public transportation, which should encourage more entries into the field with more services being provided to the public at a lower cost. Such actions are to be encouraged. Moreover, they really need to be done as a result of an overall assessment of the present regulations.

Regulations have had a direct impact upon the roles that both the public and private sectors have in providing public transportation services. Generally, the greatest impact has been on the private sector, and the impact has been negative. However, it must be pointed out that the larger suppliers do not necessarily subscribe to deregulation or even regulation reform. But without changes in the regulatory area, one can expect increasing costs to the consumer and larger deficits incurred by public bodies providing public transportation services.

BROKERAGE CONCEPT

Undeniably, there is a role for private industry to play in providing public transportation services. In most urban areas, particularly smaller ones, the private industry role should be much larger than the public role. The brokerage concept is being developed to encourage private industry to assume more of the responsibilities in providing public transportation services. The brokerage concept in transportation is similar to the methods employed by an insurance agency. For example, an insurance agency may represent several insurance firms. The insurance agency's responsibility is to find an insurance company to fulfill the needs of the customer. In some instances an individual or a firm may be covered by two, three, or more insurance companies. In the taxi industry, for example, a company may be self-insured up to $25,000. Company A may insure the taxi company from $25,000 to $50,000. Company B may insure the taxi company from $50,000 to $100,000, and company C will provide the coverage in excess of $100,000. The concept of the insurance agency is to match the needs of the consumer with the ability of an insurance company to provide the coverage.

The concept of the brokerage firm operating in the transportation field is to match the supply with the demand. While there is an adequate supply of transportation services in most urban areas, there is also a substantial demand for public transportation services. However, there has been a mismatch of supply and demand for many years. Thus, the demand is not satisfied, and there is an inefficiency incorporated into the supply aspects. The result is that huge operating deficits are being incurred by local urban areas.

The concept of the brokerage firm is that the services needed should be matched with the supply that is most appropriate. Utilization of private industry for some of these services does provide for competition. In a free-enterprise system this should result in a lower cost for the services that are provided. One might employ a contractual arrangement to provide the services in much the same manner as one does with an insurance firm. The contract time period might be a function of the capital required by the private firm to provide the services; that is, the more capital that would be required to provide the equipment, the longer the contract period would be.

If there is a diffusion of companies providing services, this provides the mechanism for diffusing many of the labor issues. In large urban areas, where many of the public transportation systems are publicly owned, one labor strike can curtail or stop all public transportation services. However, in areas where there are many components providing these services, it is difficult for any one union to curtail all public transportation operations.

The brokerage concept, in reality, is an umbrella organization that assists with regulatory issues, marketing, planning, and other aspects but does not necessarily operate or provide any of the services. In fact, it would be more desirable if the brokerage firm did not own any equipment or provide the operation of any of the components. However, in some urban areas, this would be unrealistic, and a portion of the services may have to be provided by the brokerage firm. This alternative should, of course, be utilized as little as possible.

With the proper application of the brokerage concept, firms of various sizes can be utilized effectively. As an example, with a large vanpool program in an urban area, the owning of a single van by an individual or 200 vans by a company could be effectively utilized. The gradation could go from those who would like to operate a carpool on a profitable basis to those individuals who might have one or more large buses. In certain instances, there could be several portions of a fixed-route, fixed-schedule service that could be provided by different private enterprise companies. All the companies might operate under the same color scheme and logo, but would be providing individual portions of the total service. The brokerage firm should have the capabilities to put together a "package" of suppliers that would meet the total service requirements.

SOME EXAMPLES OF PRIVATE ENTERPRISE PROVIDING PUBLIC TRANSPORTATION SERVICE

TRANSPORTATION SERVICES FOR THE ELDERLY

The City of Oak Ridge, Tennessee, desired to provide transportation services at reduced fares to senior citizens 60 years of age and older.[3] Oak Ridge, a small community of approximately 28,000 population without any traditional bus transit services, had two taxi companies operating. During the initial planning discussions of a transportation program for senior citizens, the city thought of purchasing their own vehicles and hiring their own drivers and dispatcher. After reviewing the possible alternatives available to them, the city decided on a program in which services would be provided by the two local taxi companies.

In the program, now in operation, senior citizens can purchase a transportation coupon worth $1 of travel for 25 cents. The city subsidizes 65 cents of the coupon, and the taxi companies receive 90 cents for each coupon redeemed. Thus, 25% of the cost is provided by senior citizens, 65% by the city, and 10% by the private sector. A senior citizen can choose either of the two taxi companies to provide the services needed. If the fare is in excess of $1, a senior citizen must pay the additional cost. If the fare is less than $1, the total coupon still must be remitted to the cab company. From a survey conducted by the city, approximately 10 to 15% of the coupons are redeemed for rides costing less than $1.

By utilizing the taxi companies, senior citizens do not have to make advance reservations for transportation services. They are treated like any other customer of the taxi companies. In the first 18 months of operation, some 550 senior citizens have used this service. Over 45,500 coupons have been sold in this period of operation. Approximately 85% of the riders are female, with most of them being widowed, divorced, or single. The ridership is 83% retired, and 50% have an annual income less than $6000. Fifty-eight percent of the ridership do not have an automobile in their household, and 74% do not hold a valid driver's license. All these figures show that the service is providing needed mobility to those with restricted automobile availability, and the taxi firms benefit from the increased business. In 1976, the cost to the city was approximately $15,000 per year.

---

[3]Information on this program obtained from M. Lyle Lacy III, Assistant to the City Manager, Oak Ridge, Tennessee.

Two examples of shared-ride taxi systems in operation are found in Davenport, Iowa, and Hicksville, New York.[4] These systems are innovative taxi enterprises which, in their manner of operation, resemble many of the publicly owned dial-a-ride systems. Specifically, they provide on-call, door-to-door public transportation on a shared-ride basis, pooling unrelated trips into the same cab, when practicable, by deviating from the direct route. Except for the movement of masses of commuters during rush hours, the shared-ride taxi systems perform most of the functions of their scheduled-bus competitors. Moreover, the composition markets for the bus and shared-ride taxi systems are remarkably similar.

In location, size, population characteristics, and other respects, the study areas of Davenport and Hicksville are dissimilar. Davenport is in a cluster of four incorporated communities collectively known as the "quad cities," a metropolitan area embracing a population of approximately 300,000. With a 1970 population of nearly 98,500, almost 11% more than in 1960, Davenport itself is the largest city of the four communities. Situated along the Mississippi River, this municipality and its neighbors constitute an important Midwestern trade and industrial center.

Hicksville, however, is an unincorporated community located within Nassau County on Long Island. Not only is Hicksville the smaller of the two study areas in terms of population (approximately 48,100 in 1970), but, during the period from 1960 to 1970, it experienced a 4.6% decrease in population. It, too, is the site of a large number of diverse industries; in addition, it is a major transportation hub, with the local Long Island Rail Road station handling the largest number of commuter rail passengers of any station on the island.

During the period from April 1973 to January 1974, the number of passengers carried by the shared-ride taxi system in Davenport on weekdays ranged from 750 to 1530, an average of approximately 1040. In the same period, the Hicksville system transported between 380 and 970 passengers on weekdays, an average of nearly 700 riders. On Saturdays the demand for shared-ride taxi service in Davenport, averaging approximately 1100 customers, was consistent with the mean level of ridership on weekdays; whereas in Hicksville, patronage of the shared-ride taxi system on Saturdays declined to 440 passengers. The demand declined further in Hicksville on Sundays to approximately 250 patrons, and the number of persons taking a taxi in Davenport on Sundays dropped to approximately 650.

In addition to providing shared-ride taxi service, the standard mode of operation, both taxi companies offer direct door-to-door transportation upon request. This results in a higher fare while assuring the customer exclusive use of the cab. In both study areas, however, the demand for each firm's exclusive cab service was virtually nonexistent, averaging one trip per weekday.

---

[4]KENNETH W. HEATHINGTON AND OTHERS, *An Analysis of Two Privately-Owned Shared-Ride Taxi Systems: Executive Summary*, prepared for UMTA (Knoxville, Tenn.: The University of Tennessee Transportation Center, 1975). Now available as PB 245 106.

More persons traveled by bus than by shared-ride cab in Davenport, according to estimates furnished by the local transit authority. The buses typically carried between 2500 and 3000 passengers on weekdays. Between 1967 and 1972, however, annual ridership on the bus system had declined 50%, from 1.5 million to 750,000; whereas annual patronage of the shared-ride taxi system had risen 179%, from 174,000 to 485,000. In Hicksville, the bus system serves all of Nassau County; accurate estimates of the number of bus passengers from Hicksville itself were unavailable. Except for the movement of masses of commuters during the morning and afternoon rush hours, the shared-ride taxi systems perform many of the same functions performed by their bus competitors. To travel to and from work was predominately the most common purpose for using both the bus and shared-ride taxi systems, although in Davenport less than 50% of the taxi trips were work trips, whereas nearly 60% of the bus trips were work trips. In both study areas, trips taken for social, recreation, medical, or personal business purposes constituted a slightly higher fraction of the trips made by taxi than by bus.

JITNEY SERVICE

A jitney system operates in Chattanooga, Tennessee, and is comprised of some 84 jitney cabs.[5,6] These cabs carry people along the line between Patton Parkway and Ducktown for 35 cents. Jitneys will deviate three blocks from their normal route for an extra 10 cents with a charge of 10 cents for each additional block traveled off the regular route. Of course, there has been a substantial amount of dispute concerning the legality of operating jitneys in the Chattanooga area. However, it was estimated that the Chattanooga jitney service carried some 20 million riders in 1972.[7] More comprehensive jitney services are in operation in San Francisco (along Mission Street) and Atlantic City, New Jersey. It will be interesting to observe if the Atlantic City service will be able to accommodate the increased ridership that is expected to result from the visitor boom caused by legalization of gambling in 1976.

COMMUTER BUS SERVICES

Tidewater area, Virginia. For many years, private enterprise has provided transportation services to employees of the military bases in the Norfolk, Virginia Beach, and Hampton Roads, Virginia, area. It is estimated that slightly over 10% of all the commuters are transported by the private carriers. This is about 4 times as many as are transported by traditional bus transit in the area. There are some 180 privately

---

[5]FRANK W. DAVIS, JR., AND STUART SCHLOSSBERG, *Transit Planning for Results: A Consumer Oriented Approach* (Knoxville, Tenn.: The University of Tennessee Transportation Center, 1975).

[6]TELFAIR BROOKE III, *An Analysis of an Urban Jitney System in Chattanooga, Tennessee* (Knoxville, Tenn.: The University of Tennessee Transportation Center, 1976).

[7]WILBUR SMITH AND ASSOCIATES, *Transit Study* (Chattanooga, Tenn.: Wilbur Smith and Associates, 1969).

owned buses operating in the area, as compared to approximately 250 public transit buses.[8]

Table 24-1 lists the breakdown of work trips to all the Tidewater-area military installations. There are some 5500 passengers carried by private commuter buses, whereas the public transit transports only 1500 work-trip passengers. Single-occupancy autos provide services for some 36,000 passengers. Carpools provide services for approximately 10,500.

TABLE 24-1
Work Trips to All Tidewater Military Installations

Mode	Passengers	Percentage
Private commuter buses	5,500	10.3
Public transit	1,500	2.8
Auto (single occupancy)	36,000	67.3
Carpool	10,500	19.6
Total	53,500	100.0

Source: Personal correspondence from Jim Echols, Executive Director, Tidewater Transportation Commission, July 22, 1974.

Colonial Transit. The Colonial Transit Company operates out of Fredericksburg, Virginia. In 1969 the company was very small, having some 13 vehicles and a gross revenue of $65,979 per year.[9] The company mainly provided some traditional transit school bus service and miscellaneous charters. In 1970, after a major effort, Colonial Transit received authority to transport commuters from northern Virginia into the Washington, D.C., area. This transit system uses many employees working full time in the Washington, D.C., area to operate or drive the buses. Since their shift in emphasis to commuter services, the company has grown substantially. In 1974 they reported a total operation revenue for motor-carrier operations of $964,938 and had increased their number of buses to 70.

Table 24-2 indicates the growth of Colonial Transit in providing public transportation services. As of November 1975, the Colonial Transit bus fleet had reached approximately 100, and the annual gross revenue had increased to about $2.4 million.

VANPOOLING

There are many vanpooling programs operated by the private sector—such programs as those of the 3M Company, Tennessee Valley Authority, Atlantic Richfield, and Continental Oil Company. These are discussed in detail in other chapters.

---

[8]Correspondence from James Echols, Executive Director, Tidewater Transportation Commission, July 22, 1974.
[9]Personal conversation with Robert Gibbons, Executive Vice President, Colonial Transit Company.

TABLE 24-2
Colonial Transit Statistics

1974 Income Statement

Income

Total operation revenue from motor
carrier operations $964,938

Expenses

Operations and maintenance expenses	546,912
Depreciation expense	176,508
Operating taxes and licenses	16,619
Total expense of motor carrier operations	$740,039
Net motor carrier operating income	$224,898

Operating Statistics

Year	Buses	Express Commuter Passengers (000's)	Express Commuter Passenger Revenue (000's)	Gross Revenue (000's)
1969	13	0	$ 0	$ 66
1970	17	44	55	177
1971	27	150	139	243
1972	38	a	306	437
1973	45	945	436	622[b]
1974	70	a	633	965

[a] Ridership not given on 1972 report or 1974 report.
[b] The desire of drivers to find additional charter work increased revenue of charter from $9789 in 1969 to $107,963 in 1973.

Source: Annual Report MP-2 to the Interstate Commerce Commission.

However, the point to be made is that the private sector has a strong role to play in many areas of public transportation, with commuter pooling being a very active one.

CONCLUSIONS

There are many forms of services provided by private enterprise in the public transportation field. Many are very innovative and do quite well financially. They also pay taxes, licenses, fees, and so on. Almost without exception, all provide a meaningful contribution to the total number of passengers served by public transportation systems in an urban area. In the past the contribution made by the private-enterprise sector was often overlooked in the urban transportation planning process. If these private-enterprise companies were removed, there would be a substantial reduction in services provided.

A brief survey of the literature indicates that the majority of growth in public transportation ridership may be occurring within the private sector. The private sector must provide services that meet with the consumer's approval; otherwise, in the free-enterprise system, losses will be incurred, and the operation will eventually fail. The private sector does not receive direct capital or operating subsidies and thus must rely on fares or indirect subsidies to cover all costs and provide for a profit incentive. Without this incentive, providers of transportation services may not be as innovative as is necessary to meet the changing needs and desires of the consumers.

There is a role for private industry to play in providing public transportation services in any urban area. This role is a vital one and should increase over the next few years. Private industry has erroneously been pushed aside in the provision of public transportation services in many of our urban areas. It is in the best interest of urban areas to *increase* the role of the private sector in providing these services. Increased utilization of the private sector should ameliorate labor problems, operating deficits, and other issues which are often better handled by the private sector than by the public sector.

For the short run, there will most likely be more emphasis placed upon the private sector being more fully integrated into the public transportation field. This will include better utilization of taxis and airport limousine services, special services for the handicapped and elderly, and so on. With the increase of operating deficits that are occurring, many local communities are making a critical review of the process in which public transportation services are now being provided. It is generally to the benefit of urban areas, the consumer, private industry, and local governments to provide for better integration of private industry into the provision of public transportation services.

SELECTED BIBLIOGRAPHY

Many citations are no longer available from their original source. These citations are often available from the National Technical Information Service, U.S. Department of Commerce, 5285 Port Royal Road, Springfield, Va. 22161. We have verified the order numbers for many of these citations, and they are found at the end of the citation. Prices are available through NTIS at the address above.

BURBANK, C. J., "Transit Financing: Trends and Outlook for the Future" (unpublished paper presented at the Transportation Research Board conference, Government Responsibilities for Financing Efficient Urban Transportation, Ocean City, Md., September 11-14, 1977).

DAVIS, FRANK W., JR., "The Future of Paratransit Regulations," (accepted for publication by State Transportation Specialists).

————, *Intercity Bus Transport: The Tennessee Experience*. Knoxville, Tenn.: The University of Tennessee Center for Business and Economic Research, 1974.

————, "Public Transit," *Tennessee Survey of Business*, 10, no. 1 (September–October 1974), 13.

————, *Regulatory Barriers to Innovation and the Knoxville Experience*. Knoxville, Tenn.: The University of Tennessee Transportation Center, 1977.

————, AND JOHN D. BEESON, *The Brokerage Approach to Public Transportation*. Knoxville, Tenn.: The University of Tennessee Transportation Center, May 1976.

————, AND STUART SCHLOSSBERG, *Transit Planning for Results: A Consumer Oriented Approach*. Knoxville, Tenn.: The University of Tennessee Transportation Center, 1975.

————, AND OTHERS, "Bus and Taxi Package Express—A Major Component of Urban Goods Movement," in *Proceedings—Fifteenth Annual Meeting, Transportation in Focus*, Transportation Research Forum, 15, no. 1 (San Francisco), pp. 145–52. Oxford, Ind.: The Richard B. Cross Company, 1974.

————, AND OTHERS, "Comparison of Privately and Publicly Owned Demand-Responsive Systems," in *Transit Planning*, Transportation Research Record 559, pp. 11–20. Washington, D.C.: Transportation Research Board, 1976.

————, AND OTHERS, *Economic Characteristics of (Privately-Owned) Shared-Ride Taxi Systems*, prepared for UMTA. Knoxville, Tenn.: The University of Tennessee Transportation Center, October 1974. Now available as PB 245 104.

————, AND OTHERS, *Increased Transportation Efficiency Through Ridesharing: The Brokerage Approach*. Knoxville, Tenn.: The University of Tennessee Transportation Center, 1976.

————, AND OTHERS, *A Preliminary Analysis of Two Shared-Ride Taxi Systems*, prepared for UMTA. Knoxville, Tenn.: The University of Tennessee Transportation Center, August 1973. Now available as PB 245 102.

————, AND OTHERS, *Ridesharing and the Knoxville Commuter*. Knoxville, Tenn.: The University of Tennessee Transportation Center, August 1975. Now available as PB 247 146.

————, AND OTHERS, *Summary of Intercity Bus Operation in the State of Tennessee*. Knoxville, Tenn.: The University of Tennessee Transportation Center, 1974.

HEATHINGTON, KENNETH W., "Taxis and Other Private Transportation Services," in *Demand-Responsive Transportation Systems & Services*, Special Report 154, pp. 84–86. Washington, D.C.: Transportation Research Board, 1974.

————, AND JAMES D. BROGAN, *Demand Responsive Transportation Systems*, prepared for Bureau of Mass Transit, Tennessee Department of Transportation. Knoxville, Tenn.: The University of Tennessee Transportation Center, August 1974.

————, AND MARCEL J. ZOBRAK, "An Analysis of Two Privately Owned Demand-Responsive Transportation Systems," in *Proceedings: International Conference on Transportation*, Bruges, Belgium, Transportation Research Forum, pp. 336–42. Oxford, Ind.: The Richard B. Cross Company, June 1973.

————, AND OTHERS, *An Analysis of Two Privately Owned Shared-Ride Taxi Systems: Executive Summary*, prepared for UMTA. Knoxville, Tenn.: The University of Tennessee Transportation Center, 1975. Now available as PB 245 106.

————, AND OTHERS, "Demand-Responsive Transportation Systems in the Private Sector," in *New Transportation Systems*, Transportation Research Record 522, pp. 47–55. Washington, D.C.: Transportation Research Board, 1974.

————, AND OTHERS, *An Organizational and Environmental Review of Two Privately-Owned, Shared-Ride Taxi Systems*, prepared for UMTA. Knoxville, Tenn.: The University of Tennessee Transportation Center, October 1974. Now available as PB 245 103.

————, AND OTHERS, *Shared-Ride Taxi Systems: An Analysis in Summary*, prepared for UMTA. Knoxville, Tenn.: The University of Tennessee Transportation Center, August 1973. Now available as PB 245 101.

————, AND OTHERS, "Summary of Organizational and Environmental Review of 2 Privately Owned, Shared-Ride Taxi Systems," in *Transit Planning*, Transportation Research Record 559, pp. 21–32. Washington, D.C.: Transportation Research Board, 1976.

MIDDENDORF, DAVID P., AND KENNETH W. HEATHINGTON, "Bus and Shared-Ride Taxi Use in Two Small Urban Areas" in *Bus Transportation Strategies*. Transportation Research Record 606, pp. 48–53. Washington, D.C.: Transportation Research Board, 1976.

————, AND OTHERS, *An Analysis of the Demand for Bus and Shared-Ride Taxi Service in Two Smaller Urban Areas*, prepared for UMTA. Knoxville, Tenn.: The University of Tennessee Transportation Center, 1975. Now available as PB 245 105.

WILBUR SMITH, AND ASSOCIATES, *Transit Study*. Chattanooga, Tenn.: Wilbur Smith and Associates, 1969.

Chapter 25

FINANCING PUBLIC TRANSPORTATION

ROBERT G. McGILLIVRAY, *The Urban Institute, and*
RONALD F. KIRBY, *The Urban Institute*

Public policies requiring that certain public transportation services be provided at fares that do not cover costs have been accompanied by substantial governmental expenditure on subsidies for these services. As of 1976, the subsidies have been directed primarily to fixed-route transit services; over the previous two decades, bus and rail transit systems were gradually brought under public ownership and supported with subsidy funds from federal, state, and local levels of government. Recently, there has been interest in subsidizing other public transportation services, such as door-to-door dial-a-ride, for special groups like the elderly and handicapped and, in some communities, for the population at large.

Public transportation includes all those services which are available to the general public: conventional bus and rail transit, commuter rail, and various "paratransit" services, such as taxi, dial-a-ride, and jitney services, rental cars, organized car- and vanpools, and specialized subscription bus services.

The subsidy programs discussed in this chapter are concerned primarily with supporting conventional bus and rail transit services. It will be argued, however, that greater consideration should be given to supporting paratransit services serving certain kinds of travel demand, particularly in low-density areas, and to involving other public transportation providers, such as taxicab and limousine operators, in subsidy programs.

A recent study compared the magnitudes of the transit and taxicab industries for 1973.[1] It was estimated that taxicabs carried 3.4 billion passengers compared to 6.6

---

[1] JOHN WELLS, *An Analysis of Taxicab Operating Characteristics*, prepared by the International Taxicab Association and Wells Research Company for UMTA (Washington, D.C.: U.S. Department of Transportation, August 1975).

billion for rail and bus transit[2] (excluding commuter rail). Passenger revenue was $3.9 billion for taxicabs as against $1.8 billion for transit. Employment was 494,000 for the taxicab industry and 140,000 for transit. Taxicab vehicle-km (vehicle-mi) were estimated at 21.6 (13.4) billion compared to 2.9 (1.8) billion for transit. The estimates for the taxicab industry are probably less accurate than those for the transit industry, since data for the former are more difficult to acquire. Even so, the magnitudes of the estimates suggest that the taxicab industry constitutes a considerable portion of the public transportation business in the United States.

Subsidy funds for public transportation are currently being provided by all levels of government, and by different agencies within those governments: agencies responsible for transportation as well as agencies responsible for a variety of health and welfare programs. Subsidies are provided under numerous different programs which earmark funds for certain kinds of services, for certain transportation providers, for certain types of transportation expenditures, or for certain client groups, with a great deal of variation from program to program. Unfortunately, these earmarking requirements and associated administrative procedures often present major obstacles to the most effective use of the funds at the local level: funds earmarked for capital expenditures and for nonprofit organizations cannot readily be used to subsidize shared-taxi services, for example, even though the latter services might best serve local objectives. This chapter briefly reviews current subsidy programs and assesses their effectiveness in promoting the provision of efficient public transportation services.

REVIEW OF CURRENT SUBSIDY PROGRAMS

Over the period from World War II to the early 1960s, fares for transit services typically increased with costs, and services were cut back as ridership declined. More recently, however, policy makers have elected to stabilize fares and to reverse the trend of service cutbacks. As costs have continued to increase, revenues from fares have covered a decreasing proportion of transit costs. Thus, subsidies have expanded rapidly over the period. Between 1970 and 1975 the total industry operating deficit increased to nearly 6 times its 1970 level and, in 1975, was estimated at more than $1.7 billion per year.[3] (Preliminary figures for 1976 indicate an increase to about $1.86 billion for that year.)[4] The U.S. Department of Transportation has reported that during the 1974 National Transportation Study the responses of the states on questions relating to transit fare policies for 1990 (and presumably for the more near-term as well) indicated plans for small or no fare increases. This suggested a strong trend toward a general fare-stabilization policy around the country.

---

[2]AMERICAN PUBLIC TRANSIT ASSOCIATION, *Transit Fact Book*, 1974–75 ed. (Washington, D.C.: American Public Transit Association, 1975).

[3]Ibid.

[4]American Public Transit Association, *Transit Fact Book*, 1976–77 ed. (Washington, D.C.: American Public Transit Association, 1977).

However, rapidly escalating transit deficits have begun to alarm local decision makers. Since most transit systems have, for a variety of reasons, been brought under public ownership, it is a local government responsibility to decide how to pay for deficits. As competition for public funds has increased, so have pressures to increase fares. There are a number of reasons, both political and economic, for holding fares down. However, pressures on local budgets may dictate fare increases or service cutbacks in areas where transit is a lower priority than other public services.[5] In fact, there have been a few recent cases of fare increases of about 40 to 50%, which appear to indicate the beginning of a new trend toward raising revenue from the farebox rather than the general taxpayer.

In order to provide financial support for growing transit deficits, a number of subsidy programs have been instituted. All levels of government—federal, state, and local—are involved to some degree in transit subsidization. Federal transit subsidies had, until the mid-1970s, been restricted to grants provided to local governmental units for the purposes of capital purchase, technical or planning studies, and demonstration projects. In 1973 and 1974, however, two additional sources of support were introduced. Under certain conditions, federal highway trust fund moneys can now be used for public transportation. And there is now a program for subsidizing operating expenses for public transportation operations.

State aid to public transportation can be broken into three categories: direct subsidies through grants or allocations similar to those from federal sources; state tax relief; and special taxing powers which permit local entities to raise funds. Programs, powers, and relief measures vary considerably among states, with more highly urbanized states typically having more funds and other aids and permitting more local flexibility.

Local bodies have adopted a wide variety of organizational forms and subsidy arrangements. In larger urban areas, private transit operating companies have been replaced by various kinds of governmental agencies which have been set up to facilitate operating transit on a deficit basis. Subsidy mechanisms include those based upon measures of output (such as passenger-miles) or capacity (such as vehicle-miles); those appropriated directly to cover deficits; and those which involve reductions in costs of inputs such as relief from gasoline, property, or sales taxes.

The magnitude of subsidy required for a particular transit operator *for a particular period* is, in principle, approximately the same as the deficit for that period. The American Public Transit Association provides an estimate of the level of the overall deficit for 1972 of $513 million for the transit industry (excluding commuter rail).[6] Another source provides an estimate of $1.2 billion for subsidies by all levels of government for 1972.[7] Even this estimate (which was conservatively low due to under-

[5]MICHAEL A. KEMP AND MELVYN D. CHESLOW, "Transportation," in *The Urban Predicament*, eds. William Gorham and Nathan Glazer (Washington, D.C.: The Urban Institute, 1976), pp. 281–356.

[6]AMERICAN PUBLIC TRANSIT ASSOCIATION, *Transit Fact Book.*

[7]U.S. DEPARTMENT OF TRANSPORTATION, *A Study of Urban Mass Transportation Needs and Financing*, report of the Secretary of Transportation to the U.S. Congress (Washington, D.C.: U.S. Department of Transportation, July 1974).

reporting) of the total outlays of governments for capital purchases, operating subsidies, and reduced fare reimbursements was more than double the level of the deficit. One reason for this is that subsidies for the purpose of making capital purchases extend far beyond the year in which they are made. Expenditures can be added over systems, and equal deficits and profits for different systems may cancel each other. By any accounting, however, both deficits and subsidies for transit are extensive and growing.

There are many fiscal mechanisms through which governments obtain funds for financing transportation deficits. The federal government is financed through a variety of means, including taxation, debt, and expansion of the money supply. The taxes from which the bulk of the revenue is comprised are the individual and corporate income and social security taxes. A variety of other taxes exist, such as the federal excise tax of 4 cents per gallon on gasoline, which has a long history of being earmarked for highways. However, as will be explained later, in 1973 some of these revenues were made available, under certain conditions, for transit purposes.

Since state and local governments do not control the money supply, their ability to finance is limited to debt and taxation. State and local bodies employ a variety of tax and bond mechanisms; the latter of these must be secured by tax or other revenues, such as those from bridge and road tolls.[8] Most of the tax devices are not directly linked to the recipient of the funds, the largest sources of state and local revenues being the property and general sales taxes. It is, therefore, often thought that these taxes are primary sources of transit subsidies. However, there is no necessary connection between the taxes contributing to general funds and the expenditures from those funds. In some cases, of course, property tax and, to a lesser extent, general sales tax revenues are earmarked for transit. Other sources of revenue which have provided earmarked funds for transit subsidies include motor vehicle registration fees, cigarette excise tax revenues, lottery revenues, utility surcharge revenues, parking-lot surcharge revenues, gasoline excise and sales tax revenues, and payroll tax revenues.[9]

The remainder of this section will discuss some of the details of current subsidy programs. The comprehensiveness will necessarily vary with the level of government. All major federal programs will be discussed. A number of state subsidy programs will be included, and some examples of local programs will be presented.

FEDERAL SUBSIDIES

Pressure from large urban areas, particularly those having or contemplating fixed-rail transit systems, resulted in the passage of mass transportation aid bills in 1961 and 1964.[10] In 1961, $50 million was authorized for capital loans and an additional $25

---

[8]JAMES A. MAXWELL, *Financing State and Local Governments* (rev. ed.), Studies of Government Finance Series (Washington, D.C.: The Brookings Institution, 1969).

[9]ANN MAURER DeBEER, *Financing Operating Subsidies for Urban Mass Transit Systems: An Analysis of State and Local Tax Options*, prepared for UMTA (Washington, D.C.: Consortium of Universities, June 1974). Now available as PB 239 634.

[10]ROYCE HANSON, "Congress Copes with Mass Transit, 1960–1964," in *Congress and Urban Problems: A Casebook on the Legislative Process*, eds. Frederic N. Cleaveland and Associates (Washington, D.C.: The Brookings Institution, 1969).

million was authorized for demonstration projects. It soon became clear that the loan program was ineffective, so in 1964 a capital grants program was instituted under the Urban Mass Transportation Act of 1964. The new program was begun at a $375 million level for 3 years. The demonstration program was continued and expanded with $50 million of the $375 million available for research, development, and demonstrations (RD&D). Grants were available on a two-thirds federal, one-third local matching basis once planning requirements were met. Appropriations lagged somewhat behind these authorizations, but since both authorizations and appropriations remained available for succeeding fiscal years, this was not a major problem.

The 1964 act continued to be amended with additional capital grant authorizations for 2 years in 1966 and for 1 year in 1968 and 1969. In 1970 the program was increased to $3.1 billion, and this limit was subsequently increased in 1973 to $6.1 billion and again in 1974 to $10.9 billion. In 1974, the scope of the act was also enlarged to permit part of the funds to be used for operating assistance. It appears that Congress has decided to allow the budgetary process to rule the year-to-year expenditures under the program.[11] (Initially, there was a state limitation which effectively blocked major new rail capital facilities, but this was dropped in 1974.)

The capital assistance program has been available to eligible local public bodies with provision for state review, a requirement for eligibility being an approved transportation plan. Planning funds were also made available under the act. Until 1973 the capital and planning funds were available on a two-thirds federal and one-third local basis. The Federal-Aid Highway Act of 1973 amended the Urban Mass Transportation Act by raising the federal share to a maximum of 80% for capital funds and 100% for planning funds.

The demonstration part of the RD&D funding has been available to local bodies not only through local initiative but also by federal solicitation. Local matching funds are not required by statute but sometimes have been requested as an assurance of local interest. Demonstration funds are, however, not what would normally be considered subsidy.

The Federal-Aid Highway Acts of 1970 and 1973 provided a new source of public transportation funds. They permitted the use of federal-aid highway funds for preferential bus lanes and other bus-oriented facilities and, under conditions having to do with replacement of federal-aid highway system components with transit system facilities, they permitted the use of highway funds to purchase buses and rail transit equipment and facilities.

The National Mass Transportation Assistance Act of 1974, which amended the Urban Mass Transportation Act, authorized certain funds to be apportioned to states for *either* capital *or* operating subsidies; capital grants are provided on a (maximum) 80% federal, 20% local match while operating grants require at least a 50% local match. Authorizations were $300 million for fiscal year 1975, $500 million for fiscal year 1976, $650 million for fiscal year 1977, $775 million for fiscal year 1978, $850 million

[11]Urban Mass Transportation Administration, *Urban Mass Transportation Act of 1964 and Related Laws*, as amended through February 5, 1976 (Washington, D.C.: U.S. Government Printing Office, 1976).

for fiscal year 1979, and $900 million for fiscal year 1980. Apportionments to states remaining unexpended for 2 years must be returned to the federal government. The 1974 act provided that apportionments be made on the basis of a formula weighted one-half by urbanized area population and one-half by urbanized area population density. It required states to submit programs of projects for approval before receiving part or all of their apportionments.

Through September 30, 1976, expenditures under the capital grants program had been heavily oriented to conventional bus and rail services. About 33% of the nearly $5.8 billion spent had been directed to scheduled bus services, about 64% to rail services, and the remainder to ferryboat and other services. Insignificant amounts had gone to paratransit services such as dial-a-ride and subscription bus.

As of February 9, 1977, nearly $886 million had been expended on grants out of the funds available for operating assistance. Less than 6% of this amount was spent on capital grants, with over 94% being used for operating assistance. During 1976, the Ford administration proposed amendments to limit the portion of this assistance which could be used for operating expenses, but the amendments received little support in the Congress. For 1976, a preliminary estimate of total federal operating assistance was $423 million compared to $367 million state operating assistance and $857 million local operating assistance.[12]

Federal subsidy funds are also provided for public transportation services by the Department of Health, Education, and Welfare. A recent study identified over 60 human services programs allowing expenditures for transportation services.[13] However, public transportation is only one among many items of expenditure under these programs, and it is rarely accounted for separately. As a result, it is virtually impossible at present to estimate the level of expenditures on public transportation under human services programs. There is no doubt, however, that these expenditures are substantial and growing.

STATE SUBSIDIES

Certain states with relatively high proportions of urban populations have provided aid to commuter rail operations. For example, New Jersey has assisted such operations by providing funds for meeting operating deficits on an "avoidable-cost" basis. Those expenses which the carrier could avoid if commuter service were abandoned are funded in this way.[14] Another example is a New York State program within metropolitan New York which has provided, *inter alia*, 2 cents per passenger and 25 cents per commuter car-mile for commuter rail services.[15]

---

[12]American Public Transit Association, *Transit Fact Book*, 1976–77 ed.

[13]SUANNE BROOKS, *Transportation Authorities in Federal Human Services Programs* (Atlanta, Ga.: U.S. Department of Health, Education, and Welfare, Office of the Regional Director, March 1976). Now available as SHR-0000739.

[14]DAVID W. JONES, JR., JOHN MOLLENKOPF, AND HILARY ROWEN, *Transit Operating Assistance: Options for a Second-Generation Program of State Aid*, prepared for California Department of Transportation, Division of Transportation Planning (Stanford, Calif.: Stanford University, Stanford Transportation Program and the Center for Interdisciplinary Research, February 1976).

[15]BRENT O. BAIR AND DOUGLAS J. McKELVEY, *Current State Practices in Transit Funding*, Technical Report no. 63, prepared for UMTA (n.p.: University of Iowa, Center for Urban Transportation Studies, Institute of Urban and Regional Research, July 1975).

Many states have special financial provisions relating to conventional transit. According to a 1973 study, there were 27 states with provisions for tax relief pertaining to property, income, or bonds of the local operating agency. In addition, 16 states had laws governing motor fuel tax exemptions or refunds for transit operations. Six states also provided reduced-fare support for school children or elderly persons consisting of direct reimbursement of the difference between the regular and the reduced fare.[16]

Many states, like the federal government, offer assistance for capital purchases. In a 1975 survey, 18 states indicated that they provided a portion of the local share in order to help local jurisdictions obtain federal capital grants. Cost-sharing ratios varied among states. Four states were found to provide all local matching funds, five provided over half the local share, and four more provided half. Some states varied their contributions toward the local share among local recipients.[17]

The same survey indicated that 14 states provided operating assistance to eligible local bodies. Since operating deficits are a pervasive problem for conventional transit in the United States, the states often apply allocation procedures for disbursing such subsidy funds. Allocation has been based upon the amount of the deficit, on demographic criteria, and on measures of the candidate system's performance. In addition, the percentage of subsidy has varied; for example, Connecticut and Rhode Island have paid all operating losses, Connecticut requiring revenues to equal or exceed 60% of operating costs. The intent in New Jersey is to pay 75% of operating losses on buses in addition to all the (avoidable) losses on commuter rail. Massachusetts has paid one-half of *total* costs providing that revenues equal at least one-third of this. Maryland has assumed all the operating losses of the Baltimore system, but one-half elsewhere in the state. Table 25-1 summarizes the data collected by Carstens et al.

At the time of the survey, Michigan and New York State employed performance criteria for allocation. New York, in addition to the commuter rail subsidy previously reported, has provided 2 cents per passenger, 7 cents per bus-mile, and 8 cents per rail rapid transit car-mile. Michigan has provided up to 33% of operating costs, the funds being allocated by a formula: one-half distributed according to percentage of urban population of the state's total urban population and the other half prorated by a similarly based share of annual transit vehicle-miles.

California developed a program for allocating transit funds to areas on the basis of sales tax revenues by county of origin.[18] California's 1971 Transit Development Act (TDA) was quite complex, and will be discussed in somewhat more detail than other state programs for it illustrates a number of options. The TDA applied the California sales tax to the sale of gasoline and made 0.25 cent of the 5 cents sales tax (5% of total such revenues) available for transit development and operation. In general, 85% of TDA revenues could be used for operating purposes provided that local government supplied equal matching funds for operating assistance. TDA funds are collected by

---

[16]WILLIAM D. HART, *Public Financial Support for Transit*, Technical Study Memorandum no. 7 (Washington, D.C.: Highway Users Federation for Safety and Mobility, rev. September 1973).

[17]R. L. CARSTENS, C. R. MERCIER, AND E. J. KANNEL, "Current Status of State Level Support for Transit," in *Urban Transportation Finance*, Transportation Research Record 589 (Washington, D.C.: Transportation Research Board, 1976), pp. 14–19.

[18]JONES, *Transit Operating Assistance*.

TABLE 25-1
Allocation of State Funds to Local Transit, 1975

State	Capital Improvements — Does State Provide Funds?[a]	Capital — All	Capital — Over Half	Capital — Half	Capital — Not Known	Capital — Variable	Operating Assistance — Does State Provide Funds?[a]	Operating — All	Operating — Over Half	Operating — Half	Operating — Variable	Technical Assistance — Specifically Allocated Funds (not including statewide planning)[a]	Special Projects — Reduced Fares—Elderly	Special Projects — Demonstration Grants	Special Projects — Other
Alaska	Y				×		N					Y			
California	Y	×				×	Y				×	Y		×	
Connecticut	Y	×					Y	×				Y		×	
Delaware	Y			×		×	Y		×			Y		×	
Florida	Y			×			N					Y			
Georgia	N						N					Y			
Hawaii	Y		×				N					Y			
Illinois	Y						Y		×			Y			
Kentucky	Y		×				Y					Y			
Maryland	Y					×	Y			×		Y	×	×	
Massachusetts	Y			×		×	Y			×		N	×		
Michigan	N		×				Y		×			N		×	
Minnesota	N						Y					Y		×	
Nebraska	N						N					N			
Nevada	N						N					Y			
New Jersey	Y	×					Y				×	Y	×		
New York	Y						N				×	N	×		
Ohio	Y		×			×	Y				×	N			
Pennsylvania	Y		×				Y		×			Y	×	×	
Rhode Island	Y	×					Y	×				Y	×		
Tennessee	Y		×	×			N					Y			
Virginia	Y		×			×	Y		×			Y			
Washington	Y					×	Y				×	Y			×
Wisconsin	N						Y		×			Y	×	×	

[a]Y, yes; N, no.

Source: R. L. Carstens, C. R. Mercier, and E. J. Kannel, "Current Status of State Level Support for Transit," in *Urban Transportation Finance*, Transportation Research Record 589 (Washington, D.C.: Transportation Research Board, 1976), pp. 14-19.

the state and returned to the county of origin. In certain urban counties, the funds must be used for transit purposes. In other counties they may, at local discretion, be used for street and road purposes, after finding that there are no unmet transit needs in the area which can be reasonably met.

The method for allocating TDA funds within the urban regions has varied. For example, the Metropolitan Transportation Commission (MTC) has had considerable authority for determining allocations in the San Francisco Bay area. With several operators having jurisdictions which cover parts of more than one county and some having overlapping jurisdictions, these allocations can be both sensitive and difficult. MTC has allocated these funds on the basis of services provided. In practice, service levels have been determined by examination of specific areas. If an area is served by a route no more than 0.25 mi (0.4 km) away with headways of 15 to 30 minutes during the peak; if there is relatively frequent service for 10 hours a day, 5 days a week; and if there is some night and weekend service, then the area qualifies for all its allocation. Allocations among operations within the same county have proved to be complex. The Bay Area Rapid Transit District serves three of the MTC counties and has received about 25% of the funds for providing regional services for each of these. Much of the remainder has gone to the two operators—Alameda–Contra Costa Transit District and the San Francisco Municipal Railway—which provide local transit services in their jurisdictions.[19]

Subsidy programs at the state level are constantly changing as new legislation is enacted. The trend is for more state programs primarily to help local jurisdictions qualify for federal funds and secondarily to provide funding or relief in areas less well covered by federal programs.

LOCAL SUBSIDIES

The number of local bodies providing assistance to conventional transit has continued to expand rapidly. Local governments have responded to state and federal programs by creating bodies appropriate to receive grants or to activate powers delegated by states. In 1973, 23 states reportedly permitted cities or other public bodies to tax within their jurisdictions to obtain funds for transit subsidies.[20] Some states permitted the formation of special transit districts or other similar bodies for the purpose of owning, operating, and maintaining transit systems. Frequently, however, the formation of local bodies or levies of special taxes must be approved by a referendum.

A variety of mechanisms are used by local agencies. Most frequently, the funds necessary to cover the deficit are appropriated through special or general property taxation or other local taxes. In a few cities, transit has been operated by utility com-

---

[19]Since federal operating subsidies were required to go to a designated recipient, MTC also has had considerable power to allocate these "Section 5" funds. The procedures for determining service coverage of various operators are similar to those for TDA funds. The resulting proportions were, of course, quite different due to different overall allocation criteria. Nat Gage of MTC was kind enough to explain both TDA and Section 5 allocations in a personal interview.

[20]HART, *Public Financial Support*.

panies which provide indirect transit subsidies from utility revenues. Frequently, profitable charter or school bus operations are a source of indirect transit subsidy.[21] In a few places, facilities or equipment are owned by local government agencies and leased to private operators at below-market rates. Various contract operations have become moderately popular.

New York City in 1975 offered a scenario with an interesting variety of organizational arrangements and subsidies.[22] Transit was provided by the Metropolitan Transportation Authority (MTA), the Port Authority Trans-Hudson Corporation (PATH) under the Port Authority of New York and New Jersey, and by several privately owned bus companies operating in Manhattan and Queens. PATH provides rapid transit commuter service between Manhattan and New Jersey and is organizationally distinct from MTA. MTA operates rail rapid transit and bus transit authorities, commuter rail lines, airports, and a bridge and tunnel authority. MTA finances operation deficits in some of these components from surpluses in others. Additional funds come from the New York State and federal programs which have already been described. Capital funds for MTA have also been provided from state bond issues. The city reimburses some operators for reduced fares for elderly and for free transit for police and firemen. The city and state reimburse operators for reduced and free fares for school children. The city pays the full cost of the New York City Transit Police, owns the property of the two transit authorities, and pays the principal and interest on their debt. These arrangements serve to suggest the complexity of financial and institutional relationships in large urban areas.

In the Seattle, Washington, area, King County residents voted to form a metropolitan municipal corporation, a Washington State option. The resulting Municipality of Metropolitan Seattle (Metro) was established to provide both water pollution control and public transit services within its service area. In has provided some additional transit services outside its area on a contractual basis and some special scheduled services for major sports events in the surrounding area. State law also permitted local transit agencies to levy a 1% motor vehicle excise tax which is really a transfer of funds from an already existing statewide 2% tax. Transit bodies, in order to qualify for the 1% motor vehicle use tax revenues within their boundaries, were required to raise at least as much revenue by any of a list of possible "clearly local" taxes. Metro chose a sales tax of 0.3% as its local funding device. Metro took over the bus system from the city, which then provided funds to pay for some services, most notably a fare-free program in the downtown area. In addition to the local share of federal highway programs, the State Highway Department also pays the local share of certain park-and-ride lots and bus access lanes on state and federal-aid highways.[23]

---

[21]AMERICAN PUBLIC TRANSIT ASSOCIATION, *Transit Financial Assistance, Reported for Calendar/Fiscal Year 1974 and Calendar/Fiscal Year 1973* (Washington, D.C.: American Public Transit Association, May 1976).

[22]URBAN MASS TRANSPORTATION ADMINISTRATION, *Feasibility of Federal Assistance for Urban Mass Transportation Operating Costs* (Washington, D.C.: Urban Mass Transportation Administration, November 1971).

[23]We are indebted to Gayle Rothrock of Metro for helpful information on Metro and Washington State programs.

The City of El Cajon, a California city of 62,000 near San Diego, instituted a program whereby persons desiring point-to-point travel within the city limits could purchase tickets usable for 24-hour-a-day dial-a-ride service provided by a taxicab company. It entails the user paying 50 cents for a ticket to be used to purchase a one-way ride. The program provided for the taxicab operator to be reimbursed by the city at a rate of $0.80 per occupied taxicab-mile of service provided in the dial-a-ride mode. The city considers the subsidy cost of about $1 per rider to compare favorably with the $6 to $8 per rider formerly needed to support certain low-density bus routes.[24] Funding for the program is from the city's general fund.

ASSESSMENT OF CURRENT SUBSIDY PROGRAMS

The subsidy mechanisms already discussed are characterized by being paid directly to transportation providers for offering services at fares which produce revenues insufficient to cover costs. These can be termed *provider-side* subsidies. In contrast, in a few places, special users are permitted to purchase transportation vouchers at prices substantially below the value of the vouchers to providers. The users can exchange these vouchers for transportation services, and the providers can then redeem them with a subsidizing public agency at values agreed upon in advance. Subsidies of this kind can be called *user-side* subsidies. The El Cajon program considered in the previous section is a provider-side subsidy since the subsidy is not based upon the vouchers but on vehicle-miles of service provided. Existing provider-side subsidies have often been criticized for lacking the proper incentives for operators. This section includes a discussion of some of the strengths and weaknesses of the major existing programs and alternatives to them.

The major target for criticism has been the federal capital grants program. It has developed into the most pervasive and best-funded subsidy program for public passenger transportation in existence in the United States. The primary focus of complaints against this program has been its limitation of funds to capital expenditures. A study by Tye suggested that the capital grants mechanism encourages underutilization and/or premature replacement of capital equipment.[25] Tye found that the strongest argument for restricting federal subsidies to capital equipment did not hold true for motorbus equipment in Cleveland, Ohio, and Chicago, Illinois. These systems were not undercapitalized prior to the institution of the capital grants program. Further, after the capital grants program was under way, the stocks of buses in Cleveland and Chicago were underutilized relative to the optimum. Also, older vehicles were underutilized relative to new ones. Tye concluded that the capital grants program led to waste of capital relative to other inputs. While the conclusion appears correct,

[24]RONALD F. KIRBY AND GERALD K. MILLER, "Some Promising Innovations in Taxicab Operations," *Transportation*, 4, no. 4 (December 1975), 369–86.

[25]WILLIAM B. TYE, "The Capital Grant as a Subsidy Device: The Case Study of Urban Mass Transportation," in *The Economics of Federal Subsidy Programs, Part 6: Transportation Subsidies*, U.S. Congress Joint Economic Committee, Joint Committee Print, 93rd Congress, 1st Session, February 26, 1973 (Washington, D.C.: U.S. Government Printing Office, 1973), pp. 796–826.

the evidence is somewhat indirect, and it remains difficult to place an actual, rather than a theoretical, value on the waste due to the program.

It has also been suggested that the limitation of capital grants to publicly owned transit systems has encouraged use of public bus transit for some services which could be provided more efficiently by taxicabs or other private operators.[26] Where services such as dial-a-ride have been made available by public transit systems, costs have been considerably higher than for shared-ride services provided by taxicab systems. Subsidy mechanisms permitting private sector operations such as shared-taxi, jitney, or shuttle services to operate at a small deficit might result in lower costs to the user or the taxpayer than similar services offered by public transit operators. (Stockfisch argued that bureaucracies do not economize on resources.[27] It is worth adding that private firms on contracts covering costs with a percentage of cost as fee for profit have incentives similar to those for bureaucracies.) Such subsidy mechanisms might encourage competition by permitting providers to compete for patronage. The incentive might be to please the user rather than the subsidizing agency. Again, the evidence is indirect; it is difficult to estimate values of cost savings without more evidence on alternative mechanisms.

The federal capital grants program did not rule out public purchase of capital equipment and facilities for operation by the private sector through leasing arrangements. Yet, few localities have chosen this form except with contract management. This may in part be due to the fact that low-capital alternatives such as taxicabs have not been encouraged by the capital subsidy mechanism. Capital costs of taxicab systems are very likely a smaller percentage of total costs than are those for bus systems. Of course, it is also due to institutional rigidity relative to labor. A 1974 study contended that the clauses in the Urban Mass Transportation Act restricting capital grants to public bodies and the preservation of the economic position of existing labor organizations have resulted in higher wage rates, more inflexible work rules, and generally higher operating costs than would have prevailed under less rigid rules on these matters.[28] Although these arguments are probably correct, evidence on the magnitude of added cost is conjectural.

The incentive question can also be raised as regards operating or unrestricted subsidies. The difficulty is to preserve or create incentives for management and labor to seek efficient methods.[29] The most popular method of state and local provision of subsidy has been based upon deficit. Federal operating subsidies have been allocated by a demographic formula, but additional justification has been required from local bodies. Deficit subsidies provide funds only for unprofitable operations. They do not create incentives for improving service, controlling costs, or responding to changing demands. However, they have the advantage of low administrative costs relative to subsidies based upon inputs or outputs.

---

[26]RONALD F. KIRBY AND OTHERS, *Para-Transit: Neglected Options for Urban Mobility* (Washington, D.C.: The Urban Institute, 1975). Also available as PB 234 320.

[27]J. A. STOCKFISCH, *Three Essays on the Economics of Subsidies*, prepared for U.S. DOT (Arlington, Va.: Institute for Defense Analyses, March 1973). Now available as PB 219 078.

[28]GEORGE W. HILTON, *Federal Transit Subsidies: The Urban Mass Transportation Assistance Program* (Washington, D.C.: American Enterprise Institute for Policy Research, 1974).

[29]URBAN MASS TRANSPORTATION ADMINISTRATION, *Feasibility of Federal Assistance.*

Tax relief measures are examples of input subsidies. Such subsidies encourage use of the subsidized cost element relative to other inputs. The argument against this approach is identical to that regarding capital subsidies. There is less incentive to control a subsidized cost than an unsubsidized one; thus, it may be used wastefully. There is no particular incentive to respond to the needs of the users of the services.

Output subsidies can be based upon measures of system capacity or upon measures of use. The latter type can be provider-side or user-side, depending on the mechanism employed. Output subsidies are complicated in that they do not ensure that a given level of deficit will be covered; it is difficult to set the "correct" amount of subsidy. Subsidies paid to operators on the basis of capacity do not ensure responsiveness to desires of users. However, where there is a single operator and the proper service level is defined and agreed upon, it may be more efficient to pay a subsidy based upon total use to the operator rather than the user, since it would probably be less costly administratively. On the other hand, if there is a desire to let demand find its proper level, given some amount of subsidy per user, and there are many providers, it is likely that the user-side subsidy would be more efficient.[30]

More generally, experience to date with user-side subsidies suggests that users will obtain high-quality services from the providers, that the various public transportation alternatives will be used in an efficient manner, and that providers will operate their services efficiently. Some administrative difficulty may be experienced, however, in reimbursing providers and guarding against fraud. Experience with provider-side subsidies suggests that although administration of the subsidy funds is relatively straightforward, competition among providers disappears, and costs of service rise more rapidly than they might have with other subsidy approaches. Further, those providers receiving the subsidies may be overutilized while other providers are underutilized. Although existing evidence supports these hypotheses, the empirical evidence supporting them is fragmented and incomplete. Further empirical analysis is needed to test the hypotheses more completely and to provide a basis for a comprehensive evaluation of different subsidy techniques.

CONCLUSION

Public transportation is currently financed by a variety of government subsidy programs which supplement revenues generated from the farebox and other private sources. Subsidy programs are administered by numerous agencies at all levels of government, and funds available under the programs are subject to earmarking requirements which vary greatly from program to program. Some of these requirements limit subsidy funds to certain types of transportation providers, such as publicly owned or nonprofit agencies, and limit the use of the funds to certain kinds of transportation expenditures, capital as opposed to operating, for example. There is con-

---

[30]RONALD F. KIRBY AND ROBERT G. McGILLIVRAY, "Alternative Subsidy Techniques for Urban Public Transportation," in *Urban Transportation Finance*, Transportation Research Record 589 (Washington, D.C.: Transportation Research Board, 1976), pp. 25–29.

siderable evidence to suggest that such limitations are leading to overuse of the subsidized providers and expenditures and the neglect of more efficient alternatives.

Relaxation of requirements which earmark subsidy funds by provider type and type of transportation expenditure would permit more efficient use of subsidy funds for public transportation. If, in addition, greater cooperation were fostered between the numerous government agencies responsible for administering subsidy programs, more opportunities for improving the efficiency and effectiveness of the programs might be recognized and exploited. Finally, subsidy funds should be made available under conditions that encourage providers to offer high-quality service to eligible users, and to operate efficiently. Subsidy techniques which offer these incentives need to be given greater consideration if subsidy programs are to be effective in achieving policy objectives for public transportation services.

SELECTED BIBLIOGRAPHY

Many citations are no longer available from their original source. These citations are often available from the National Technical Information Service, U.S. Department of Commerce, 5285 Port Royal Road, Springfield, Va. 22161. We have verified the order numbers for many of these citations, and they are found at the end of the citation. Prices are available through NTIS at the address above.

BAIR, BRENT O., AND DOUGLAS J. MCKELVEY, *Current State Practices in Transit Funding*, Technical Report no. 63, prepared for UMTA. n.p.: University of Iowa Center for Urban Transportation Studies, Institute of Urban and Regional Research, July 1975. An abridgement of a paper on this subject, "Analysis of State Transit Funding Methodologies," is found in *Urban Transportation Finance*, Transportation Research Record 589, pp. 33–35. Washington, D.C.: Transportation Research Board, 1976.

BROOKS, SUANNE, *Transportation Authorities in Federal Human Services Programs*. Atlanta, Ga.: U.S. Department of Health, Education, and Welfare, Office of the Regional Director, March 1976. Now available as SHR-0000739.

CARSTENS, R. L., C. R. MERCIER, AND E. J. KANNEL, "Current Status of State Level Support for Transit," in *Urban Transportation Finance*, Transportation Research Record 589, pp. 14–19. Washington, D.C.: Transportation Research Board, 1976.

DEBEER, ANN MAURER, *Financing Operating Subsidies for Urban Mass Transit Systems: An Analysis of State and Local Tax Options*, prepared for UMTA. Washington, D.C.: Consortium of Universities, June 1974. Now available as PB 239 634.

HANSON, ROYCE, "Congress Copes with Mass Transit, 1960–1964," in *Congress and Urban Problems: A Casebook on the Legislative Process*, eds. Frederic N. Cleaveland and Associates. Washington, D.C.: The Brookings Institution, 1969.

HART, WILLIAM D., *Public Financial Support for Transit*, Technical Study Memorandum no. 7. Washington, D.C.: Highway Users Federation for Safety and Mobility, rev. September 1973.

HILTON, GEORGE W., *Federal Transit Subsidies: The Urban Mass Transportation Assistance Program*. Washington, D.C.: American Enterprise Institute for Policy Research, 1974.

JONES, DAVID W., JR., JOHN MOLLENKOPF, AND HILARY ROWEN, *Transit Operating Assistance: Options for a Second-Generation Program of State Aid*, prepared for California Department of Transportation, Division of Transportation Planning. Stanford, Calif.: Stanford University, Stanford Transportation Program and the Center for Interdisciplinary Research, February 1976.

KEMP, MICHAEL A., AND MELVYN D. CHESLOW, "Transportation," in *The Urban Predicament*, eds. William Gorham and Nathan Glazer, pp. 281–356. Washington, D.C.: The Urban Institute, 1976.

KIRBY, RONALD F., AND ROBERT G. MCGILLIVRAY, "Alternative Subsidy Techniques for Urban Public Transportation," in *Urban Transportation Finance*, Transportation Research Record 589, pp. 25–29. Washington, D.C.: Transportation Research Board, 1976.

———, AND GERALD K. MILLER, "Some Promising Innovations in Taxicab Operations," *Transportation*, 4, no. 4 (December 1975), 369–86.

———, AND OTHERS, *Para-Transit: Neglected Options for Urban Mobility*. Washington, D.C.: The Urban Institute, 1975. Also available as PB 234 320.

MAXWELL, JAMES A., *Financing State and Local Governments* (rev. ed.). Studies of Government Finance Series. Washington, D.C.: The Brookings Institution, 1969.

STOCKFISCH, J. A., *Three Essays on the Economics of Subsidies*, prepared for U.S. DOT. Arlington, Va.: Institute for Defense Analyses, March 1973. Now available as PB 219 078.

TYE, WILLIAM B., "The Capital Grant as a Subsidy Device: The Case Study of Urban Mass Transportation," in *The Economics of Federal Subsidy Programs, Part 6: Transportation Subsidies*, U.S. Congress Joint Economic Committee, Joint Committee Print, 93rd Congress, 1st Session, February 26, 1973, pp. 796–826. Washington, D.C.: U.S. Government Printing Office, 1973.

U.S. DEPARTMENT OF TRANSPORTATION, *A Study of Urban Mass Transportation Needs and Financing*, report of the Secretary of Transportation to the U.S. Congress. Washington, D.C.: U.S. Department of Transportation, July 1974.

URBAN MASS TRANSPORTATION ADMINISTRATION, *Feasibility of Federal Assistance for Urban Mass Transportation Operating Costs*. Washington, D.C.: Urban Mass Transportation Administration, November 1971.

WELLS, JOHN, *An Analysis of Taxicab Operating Characteristics*, prepared by the International Taxicab Association and Wells Research Company for UMTA. Washington, D.C.: U.S. Department of Transportation, August 1975.

PART VI

Policy Considerations

INTRODUCTION TO PART VI

The purpose of this section is to show the interrelationship of public transportation services to societal and institutional concerns. Among the current policy areas that influence the choice of public investment in transportation systems are urban land development, environmental impact, energy availability, and social welfare. The effectiveness of the transit industry to meet national goals is related to its political institutions and labor management relations. The value structure of society, as reflected in the political process, is the ultimate determinant of the extent to which public transit is perceived as being responsive to contemporary national issues.

The relationship of transportation and land-use development has been a topic of academic inquiry for over a century. For rural land the linkages have been direct because transportation is a component of production and cheap transportation spurs economic development. For urban areas the relationships are less clear as transportation is but one of many factors influencing location decisions, and the ubiquity of transportation facilities tends to neutralize this factor in determining land-development choices. Large-scale rapid transit systems, such as in Toronto, San Francisco, and Philadelphia, have presented an opportunity to examine these phenomena in a modern urban setting.

Transportation has an effect on the environment, which is the physical surroundings in which people live. The effects of changes in the environment caused by transportation are of concern to society and may influence its selection of transportation systems. For example, freeways in cities became unpopular because their impact was to displace homes and businesses, create noise and air pollution, and increase traffic congestion. Public outcry resulted in requiring that transportation plans assess the environmental impact of proposed actions. Public transportation has been viewed as environmentally benign compared with highways, and impact studies of the San Francisco Bay Area Rapid Transit system have furnished extensive data on specific impacts. The environmental effects of other transit modes are not as well known but appear to be less extensive than highways. The ability to demonstrate greater environmental effects is directly related to the extent that auto trips are diverted to transit. Positive effects would be noted in air and noise pollution; negative effects could occur in and around transit stations.

The realization that petroleum resources are finite was vividly demonstrated during the oil embargo of 1973. Public transportation was strained to capacity as auto commuters looked for alternative transportation, and the continuing effect of energy availability will be to alter the nature and extent of travel in urban areas.

The provision of transportation to persons disadvantaged because they do not have an available automobile has become one of the principal societal motivations for public support of transit. The social welfare aspect of transportation is a policy issue that addresses the extent to which subsidies should be provided in order to furnish transportation services to the poor, elderly, and the handicapped. Among the issues are the extent to which conventional transit or paratransit will supply services; the agencies' responsibility for supplying financial support; and the requirements that transit systems be constructed to accommodate the handicapped.

The manner in which the transit industry functions is influenced by its organizational structure and its relationship with its employees. The institutional arrangements for public transportation have been changing from that of private autonomous corporations with limited territory to public agencies responsible for entire metropolitan areas. The public agencies have been losing autonomy and are being subsumed within larger metropolitan governments. One positive effect of this development is the greater responsiveness of transit authorities to citizen input and public policy. Labor costs represent the largest expenditure of transit service, work rules influence operating procedures, and job security requirements affect proposals for system changes and innovation.

The "bottom line" for public transportation is: does the public perceive that transit can meet changing environmental, energy, and land-use needs, or will the automobile continue to provide private transportation, albeit in modified form? The viewpoints involved in this decision and the principal attributes that will influence the choice of transportation modes in the future are safety, comfort, accessibility, reliability, cost, and efficiency. The words form the acronym SCARCE, an appropriate term to describe the availability of these attributes in many present transit systems. As improvements occur through better service, marketing, management, and equipment, the public should perceive transit in a more dominant role than at present.

LESTER A. HOEL, Professor and Chairman,
Department of Civil Engineering,
University of Virginia

Chapter 26

URBAN TRANSPORTATION AND LAND USE

W. L. GARRISON, *Director, Institute of Transportation Studies,*
University of California, Berkeley

That urban transportation and urban land use are related is not at issue; they are. At issue is the nature and extent of this relationship and how it may be and ought to be recognized and incorporated in urban transportation management and development processes. Several scenarios may be imagined; each makes assumptions about transportation and land use.

Many urban planning professionals and many transit advocates imagine an urban future in which continuing improvements in transit service lead to positive urban land-use rearrangements. As a consequence of transit development, residential land uses will be denser, and activity centers will evolve at interchange points on transit lines. In turn, this changed and neatly arranged pattern of land uses will generate easy-to-serve transit trips. More, the rearrangement of urban land uses and the provision of transportation services by transit will decrease fuel consumption and the consumption of other resources; it will decrease travel times. The city will be a better place to live and more parsimonious in its use of resources. The federal Urban Mass Transportation Administration believes so strongly in this scenario that it promotes "value capture": using the increases in land value from transit investment to help pay for transit investment.

The subtitle for a *Wall Street Journal* roundup on transportation in the year 2000 published on April 1, 1976, was: "Auto Engineers Try to Cut Weight, Fuel Hogging; Transit's Outlook Is Dim." That quotation sums up another scenario: forces dispersing travel patterns and economic activities are so great that there is no hope of straightjacketing land use; there is little hope for increased transit ridership, much less transit-induced changes in land use. The main need for the future is a cleaned-up and more energy-efficient automobile to serve dispersed patterns of urban land uses.

Still another scenario is driven by the energy crisis. The increased cost of energy will make travel more expensive and denser urban populations will result. Additionally, increased cost of energy will encourage transit ridership, and the future will be one of dense populations in urban centers served by transit systems.

An endless list of additional scenarios may be added to these three by combining them in different ways, by considering different developmental time frames, or by adding new ingredients. The puzzle for the analyst and planner is that of which scenario will hold, and some sense of the solution or solutions to the puzzle does matter. Actions taken today may be costly or valuable in the future to the extent that analysts can correctly guess the future.

The discussion to follow will respond to the question of how land-use and transportation matters ought to be viewed by the transportation analyst.

BACKGROUND

Land-use theory is as old as economics. Land, labor, and capital are the primary inputs of production, and as observed years ago by von Thünen and Ricardo, the use of land is determined, in part, by its location. The location of transportation facilities and the technology used specify the relative location of places. Social and economic activities and their use of land are determined by relative locational advantages.

The land-use theory is reflected by history. Water transportation technology and water routes dominated in the early days of the nation; Louisville at the falls of the Ohio River and Cincinnati on the great north bend of the Ohio River are examples of inland cities that drew their comparative advantages from a network of waterways. In addition, numerous cities on the Atlantic seaboard developed at the fall line between the crystalline rock of the Piedmont and the flatter coastal plain with its water access to the Atlantic. Later, the destinies of these places waxed or waned depending on land uses in their hinterlands and their transportation connections to those hinterlands. For example, land-use and trade patterns tied to the Erie Canal gave New York its early advantage over Boston, Baltimore, and Philadelphia.

In the eastern United States, the development of the railroads tended to reinforce, in the main, the fabric of urban development and rural land uses established by waterways, although St. Louis lost its dominance to Chicago, and Atlanta and Indianapolis owe their locational advantages mainly to rail rather than to water. The settlement of the semiarid and arid West and the Pacific states was a somewhat different story; but it, too, was a story where transportation set the major patterns for urban and rural development.

Looking at the way cities were built during these periods, it is also clear that transportation gave a heavy imprint to urban form. Most cities got started during walking, wagon, and buggy days. Transportation was expensive, and the older parts of today's cities have a dense grid of streets reflecting the early need for short transportation routes. Often, those old parts of cities are near waterfronts, for good access to that transportation technology was needed. It is no surprise that the streets in Manhattan providing access to the waterfront are closely spaced relative to those oriented up and down the island, for this grid accommodated the early pattern of movements.

Later, horse-drawn trams, cable cars, suburban rail passenger service, and street-cars all affected the pattern of urban routes and land uses.

Bicyclists also affected the urban route and land-use pattern, and they quite literally paved the way for the automobile, for bicyclists were advocates of improved facilities, which they soon had to share with the automobile. Bicycles, like the automobile, made personal transportation widely available, and its social significance was a precursor to that of the automobile.

Hard on the heels of the bicycle came the automobile, and most of the history of which we need to be reminded begins around the turn of the century, or a little later, as numbers of automobiles attempted to operate in urban areas.

This was a time when cities were truly booming; the greatest rate of urban growth in this country occurred around the turn of the century. Immigration, industrialization, and mechanization of farming were in full swing.

Early in the 1900s several ingredients came together: the automobile, the "city-beautiful" movement, which began several decades earlier, and urban-based, public-spirited organizations. American cities began to engage in an earlier form of transportation and traffic planning intertwined with the broad goals of the city-beautiful movement. Philadelphia developed its parkway from City Hall to Fairmount Park. Chicago and Milwaukee began their lakeside parkways and parks, and leaders in Pittsburgh, Pennsylvania, dreamed of emulating hilly Mediterranean towns. To the extent that American cities have parkways and large parks, they stem in the main from this period. So also do the arterial and local street patterns, local methods of financing, and public works and/or city engineering departments.

Methods developed during the early decades of this century for the provision of local and arterial streets were the context for transportation and land-use interrelations in urban areas from early in the century through to the Great Depression of the 1930s. Excepting large city-beautiful parks, land use was mainly a *laissez-faire* matter. Transportation was put in place to serve the developers.

This period saw debates about automobiles and transit, about regional planning, and about arrangements of residential and industrial areas. But with one exception, these were just debates. The exception was that of the desirability and constitutionality of zoning, an issue that reached the Supreme Court in 1926 in a case involving Euclid, a suburb of Cleveland. The case was settled in favor of zoning.

But this was late in the period that we are describing and land-use control by zoning did not really come into its own until the 1930s and 1940s. When its time did begin to come, the Great Depression and then the preoccupation with World War II left the zoning instrument with but little to do. Typically, existing patterns of land uses were surveyed, and zoning ordinances were adopted to protect existing land uses from new nonconforming uses. But since there was little development, there was little threat from nonconforming land uses.

The post-World War II story is known to all. Two decades of rapid residential suburbanization occurred; urban industrial, commercial, and service activities also grew and shifted spatially with the suburbs. The relative use of automobiles continued to expand; and mass transit systems—which had enjoyed a boom during World War II following depression hard times—were gradually driven to the brink of bankruptcy and beyond. Also, the inner cities did not fair well. Some began to lose population relatively, and in many cases absolutely, and all faced problems of housing, transportation, education, criminal justice, financing, and so on.

The post-World War II story of transportation and land use continued the theme established in earlier decades of the century. Local government mechanisms for the provision of streets and arterials continued to function as urban land uses expanded; transportation was provided to meet urban growth and land-use needs. Such mechanisms also functioned for delivery of other infrastructure activities such as water supply and sewage; too, the suburbs were zoned, and generally developers were required to comply with subdivision standards. Joining these mechanisms, a new powerful element entered the transportation infrastructure: federal funding of freeways.

Planning for freeways began soon after World War II, particularly in the states of California and Washington and in the cities of Detroit and Chicago. The freeway movement leaped ahead with interstate legislation and federal funding in 1956. Finally, early in the 1960s, a continuous transportation planning process was required of cities greater than 50,000 in population.

What was new, and what was not new?

The provision of transportation continued to be steered by development goals. Local streets continued to be intimately tuned to land development. As land was developed, streets were built. The grid of arterials was expanded as land was converted to urban uses, and freeways were also planned and built to serve the expected expansion of urban land uses. Freeway planning procedures estimated the physical expansion of the urban area and then located and sized freeways according to the travel implications of spatially extended land uses. The process was the old process: build facilities to serve development.

The federal and state governments became involved in urban transportation and land development matters. This was new. Although just before World War II federal aid became available for the urban extensions of the state highway systems, this involvement was minor. The new involvement was not minor. The urban portions of the interstate were eligible for federal funding, and federal money also came with transit and other programs. Federal interest in the planning process was felt through the mandating of procedures as well as federal review over those proposed projects where federal money was involved.

The federal interest in urban areas was also manifest in many programs other than transportation. While there had been some depression-era federal interest in housing, federal interest in the general well-being of urban areas expanded in 1948. Federal interest now runs the gamut of schools, sewage, air quality, welfare, and so on.

In the main, then, the two or two-and-one-half decades, say roughly until 1970, after World War II were those when historical transportation and land development themes continued but with an augmented cast of characters, primarily because transportation and land-use planning, financing, and other development processes had increased federal ingredients.

The great freeway revolt began in the late 1960s; it had a land development ingredient. It was marked by neighborhood and community resistance to construction of facilities. But its roots, to the extent that they can be seen, seem to go well beyond that immediate issue. It seemed to stem, in part, from the belief that the continued building of freeways tilted the competitive balance against the inner city versus the suburb and was responsible for a set of urban social problems. The revolt also reflected public concern about converting rural land to urban uses, about air pollution and the environment, and perhaps about the cumbersome and complex transportation planning and decision processes in which citizens had little part. But whatever the roots and concerns of the freeway revolt, we now have a great national debate about urban transportation: transit versus the automobile, transportation and urban form, the use of land resources by transportation, and financing and the incidence of cost and benefits from transportation construction are all current issues of public debate.

These issues as they interact with transportation and land use will be considered later. To conclude this background section, note that in past settings and within past programs, transportation and land-use relations were immediate, and they were straightforward. Given that there were markets for furs, wheat, cotton, and lumber, provision of transportation opened the way for the development of the nation's land and its resources. Given that there was demand for residential, industrial, and other activities in urban areas and that promoters were there to undertake development, transportation enabled development.

PRESENT DEBATES

"Role reversal" perhaps best describes one thrust of the current debates about transportation and land use. In previous decades, transportation served land development. Land developers converted land on the fringe of the city to urban uses, and the transportation system was put in place to provide transportation for the urban fringe. While the present debate ranges widely in its prescriptions of what society ought to be doing, one thing is sure, transportation ought not to be put into place automatically. It ought to be a tool or an instrument of socially prescribed development.

A second thrust of the current debate is that transportation must somehow be more neutral, more balanced. The debate seems to have several parts. One part of the debate observes that the automobile highway system now overly dominates urban movements. Some need other transportation forms; a balance must be restored. This is one argument for the preservation and enhancement of transit.

The neutrality argument also has a land-use content. Transportation is blamed for the decline of the central city vis-à-vis other parts of the metropolitan area; it is blamed for the relative decline of central business districts. Transportation has not been neutral; it has disadvantaged locations in the center of the city versus locations in outlying areas.

Less frequently, but sometimes more convincingly, the debate about neutrality runs to whether or not motorists are paying the full cost for their transportation and, particularly, the cost of externalities—the cost of air pollution and noise pollution especially. While this neutrality debate is very simple in outline, it becomes very complex when specific trips in specific places are analyzed. The commuter's trip on a congested route is one thing from the standpoint of cost and external impacts. The trip on an uncongested arterial in a small town may be quite another.

The notion that transportation should be both neutral and supportive of societal goals is to some extent a contradiction. Certainly, the pursuit of any goal favors some more than it does others, no matter how carefully goals and programs are formulated.

There is also the matter of interpreting the demands of those who seek neutrality. The tradition of public programs is that of responding to claims for rights and the allocation of fair shares. Perhaps when neutrality enters as an issue in public debate it is a clamor for the redressing of the fair-shares balance more than it is a clamor about accounting concepts. It is illuminating, for example, that there is at this time a clamor by rural interests for major new investment programs in rural facilities. This clamor may be driven by a feeling that the urban areas have had more than their fair share in recent decades. And to the extent that the rural clamor may be heard politically and that the funds come from the same pot, perhaps the urban versus rural neutrality or fair-shares issue will have great impact in decades to come.

Note that the historical overview answered a different question from those posed by present debates. Given a condition ripe for development, transportation was one of the enabling factors, and of course, the way in which transportation was made available shaped the nature of developments. As noted, for example, the availability of transportation to the interior of the United States influenced the growth of port cities. Also, streetcar lines, the pre-automobile street grid, and the subsequent location of arterials and freeways shaped the fine detail of urban land development.

In order to clarify the ways in which transportation and land development enter the present debate, it will be useful to identify some issues that are now the subjects of such debate:

1. Preserving and enhancing investments made previously. Examples are numerous —that transportation should preserve and enhance the inner city is one. Another is that of maintaining the viability of numerous medium and small urban centers.
2. Protecting environmentally fragile and/or relatively unique environmental resources. Examples are again numerous: transportation should protect coastal environments and structures with historical value.
3. Preserving resources believed to be scarce. Transportation and land-use arrangements should decrease consumption of energy, land, and materials of many types.
4. Supporting new development or redevelopment. Transportation will be needed if new urban centers are to be built concomitant with development of new coal mining centers; sustaining and increasing agricultural exports will require new transportation investments.
5. Redistributing income. The provision of transportation services for the poor is

seen as a direct surrogate for the redistribution of income, and it is also seen as providing the poor with an instrumentality which will enable them to engage more fully in economic life.

A first matter to be noted is that the current debate issues, of which these are a sample, have content other than land use and transportation. Indeed, in general, transportation and land use are physical expressions of the outcomes of deeper matters. The terms "transportation" and "land use" are surrogates. The actual basic matters that these terms raise are the ways in which individuals and institutions organize and control their activities, make claims on resources, and use resources. For instance, it is said that transportation should decrease its use of resources. A richer statement would call on institutions and individuals to change in ways affecting their use of land and transportation.

The issues of the debate are also problems seeking solutions; they are matters of public debate because they are not being adequately handled. It is useful to ask why they are not being adequately managed; more pointedly, to ask what is missing that is thwarting issue resolution. Some categories of what might be missing are *knowledge*, *instruments*, *consensus*, and *articulation*. The *knowledge* category includes the sufficient understandings of relationships and sufficient data so that issues may be stated crisply and solutions for problems identified and evaluated. *Instruments* include institutions and technologies necessary to problem solving; and *consensus* refers to public agreements with respect to goals, either in political or marketplace formats, and represented by laws, regulations, and/or markets that form instruments for problem solving. Finally, *articulation* refers to coordination of the various instruments necessary to development.

Imagine a table with, say, issues arrayed across the top and "What Is Missing?" categories arrayed down the side. One could then attempt to fill in the table for an issue by asking what is missing to support resolving that issue. A full exploration of a particular issue would include many, many topics, and it is difficult to imagine an issue in which the terms transportation and land use did not enter. Thinking through several issues, which the reader is invited to do, a sense of a role for transportation and land use begins to emerge. Transportation and land use must be considered in issue resolution; what needs to be done tends to focus elsewhere: Reach consensus so that . . . Change funding mechanisms in order to . . . Clarify the nature of investment choices in order to . . . Shift regulation to affect. . . .

The point developed in this section has to do with the contrast between the way transportation and land-use questions enter into public debates about issues and the political, social, and economic processes that must be handled to manage those issues. There is a tendency to put transportation and land use up front when issues are debated. But on thinking hard about those issues, transportation and land use are often not at their core. Transportation and land use are the outcomes of political, social, and economic processes. Consequently, the analyst must guard against assuming that transportation and land-use management are instrumentalities for problem solution, and this is the point of this section.

Having examined the question of the relevance of focusing issue resolution on transportation and land use, the discussion will now address what is known about transportation and land use. One level of observation tells us that urban land uses and transportation are closely linked. For instance, shopping centers are at accessible places on the transportation system, and industrial areas, old and new, have certain kinds of transportation associations. But this is a casual observation; it suggests that transportation and land use are related; it does not establish that point, nor does it specify the nature of transportation and land-use relationships. When observing spatial association, one might be, in short, observing only that land use and transportation are the outcome of a common cause.

So let us consult land-use theory. Beginning with patterns of causality that are taken to be elementary, think through the nature of land and transportation relations. The starting concepts are old; they are simple. The land supply is finite. Man's wants are not finite, so land has value. The values of lands with similar characteristics differ depending upon locational attributes. So land in Iowa City has higher value than land on farms in the tributary area of that city because of its more strategic location; it has a higher location rent.

Von Thünen and Dunn,[1] among others, have dealt with agricultural land uses and Isard[2] and Alonso[3] with urban land uses. How are different kinds of land uses allocated and equilibrium among land uses achieved? How does land use reflect an equilibrium between the supply of what land produces and demands? Dunn's agricultural analysis is instructive; while rural in perspective, it provides an easy route to the urban landscape. Define

$$R_i^c = Y^c P_j^c - Y^c T^c D_{ij}$$

where R_i^c = rent of a unit of land at i producing commodity c
Y^c = yield of commodity c per unit of land
P_j^c = price per unit of commodity c at its market
T^c = transportation cost per unit of commodity c, per unit of distance
D_{ij} = distance to market: the distance from the production point, i, to the market at j

Now imagine a unit of farmland located at some distance, D_{ij}, from the market at j. The rent calculation is simple. Take the price at the market and multiply by the yield per unit of land; this yields rent per unit of land. But this gross rent must be discounted by transportation cost, which involves the amount to be transported per unit of land, Y^c, the transportation cost per unit of commodity per unit of distance, T^c, and the distance, D_{ij}. The calculation yields the net rent at place i.

---

[1]EDGAR S. DUNN, JR., *The Location of Agricultural Production* (Gainesville, Fla.: University of Florida Press, 1954).

[2]WALTER ISARD, *Location and Space-Economy* (Cambridge, Mass.: The M.I.T. Press, 1956).

[3]WILLIAM ALONSO, *Location and Land Use: Toward a General Theory of Land Rents*, Joint Center for Urban Studies Publication Series (Cambridge, Mass.: Harvard University Press, 1964).

The reader might find it useful to sketch declines in rents away from the market at *j*. Note that because different commodities have different yields and transportation costs, as well as different prices, individual rent gradients would intercept at the market differently and slope from the market differently. The rent-gradient explanation for rural land use is that the farmer selects that crop which returns the highest net rent. And this selection depends upon the slopes and intercepts of the functions describing rent gradients for different crops. Equilibrium of production and prices is achieved through the interaction of the market price and the quality of land where a commodity is produced. Try some sketches using functions with different slopes ($Y^k T^k$'s) and market intercepts ($Y^k P_j^k$'s).

It is not hard to stretch one's imagination and bring this thinking to the urban area. In the urban area, there are many, many kinds of land uses, so we must think of there being many, many rent gradients. Most gradients are thought to decrease outward from the center of the urban area. Downtown business activities typically pay the highest rents and thus locate centrally. Residential land uses typically pay lower rents and tend to be nearer the periphery. In Alonso's treatment of urban land uses, users of urban land have bid rent functions which they use to calculate how much they would be willing to rent a piece of land in a particular location. All actors bid against each other, and an equilibrium of land use and land value is achieved.

Although reviewed in a terse way here, the theory is clear: accessibility determines the worth of land for different uses at different locations. If transportation costs are changed, the rent gradients change; since land uses and rents for land are tied each to the other by market processes, land-use potentials are changed. The causality is clear.

The theory is simple; the world is complex. Are the land-use and transportation relationships as they exist in the world of complexity discernible? An extensive record of such relationships exists with respect to the impact of highway transportation on land values and land development and the location of urban activities. The record was particularly stimulated by Section 210 of the Highway Revenue Act of 1956, which required that nonuser benefits from interstate investment be investigated. These 210 studies are summarized in part in the reports to Congress of the Highway Cost Allocation Study; the record is much too vast even to be touched on here.[4] Also, its analysis would be complex. Many relationships were claimed. However, there has been considerable controversy about the validity of the methodologies used, about the extent to which land development was a joint outcome of many forces, and about the extent that net changes in development were involved.

Our interest in the terms of today's debates is concerned with transit, and the record with respect to transit is not nearly so full as it is for highways. Certainly the

---

[4]U.S. CONGRESS, *Progress Report of the Highway Cost Allocation Study;* First—House Document no. 106, 85th Congress, 1st Session, March 4, 1957; Second—House Document no. 344, 85th Congress, 2nd Session, March 3, 1958; Third—House Document no. 91, 86th Congress, 1st Session, 1959; Fourth—House Document no. 355, 86th Congress, 2nd Session, 1960; *Final Report of the Highway Cost Allocation Study*, House Document no. 54, 87th Congress, 1st Session, January 16, 1961; *Final Report of the Highway Cost Allocation Study, Part VI: Studies of the Economic and Social Effects of Highway Improvement*, House Document no. 72, 87th Congress, 1st Session, January 23, 1961 (Washington, D.C.: U.S. Government Printing Office).

centerpiece in the transit and land-use literature is a study, published by E. H. Spengler in 1930, summarizing a set of investigations undertaken to clarify debate in New York City with respect to transit and land values.[5] Spengler undertook a section-by-section analysis of the New York transit system and of developments in the environments of that system. His overall conclusion was that transit was only one of a number of development forces which, if in place, would lead to development. He observed that if factors were such that a neighborhood was declining, it continued to decline regardless of transit investment. Depending on a number of factors, stagnant neighborhoods remained stagnant and developing areas continued to develop. Transit was only one of a number of development forces.

Some work has analyzed more recent North American experiences. Kovach,[6] Libicki,[7] and Heenan[8] have published separate observations on the Toronto experience subsequent to 1954, when the first leg of the subway was completed. Considerable activity-center and dense residential development occurred along the first leg, which Heenan suggests was a spillover from downtown. Subsequent development impacts have been much less sharp. Both Libicki and Kovach point out that high-density residential development has been characteristic of recent change in Canadian cities, and they suggest that Toronto seems to be no different from other cities on that scale.

Developments within Canadian cities illustrate a point made earlier: the analyst should be aware that transportation and land-use matters are outcomes of social and economic processes. E. M. Horwood has pointed out (in conversation) that individuals in Canada do not pay capital gains taxes on their private dwellings. This suggests that families in Canada would purchase private dwellings in order to accumulate capital. However, interest paid on mortgages is not deductible from income prior to taxes, as it is in the United States. So the residential purchase or rent choice is different in Canada than it is in the United States, and perhaps taxation procedures help to explain the development of high-density residential areas in Canada.

Boyce et al.[9] and Gannon and Dear[10] have studied the Lindenwold line rather thoroughly. That line, completed in 1968, extends from Philadelphia into Camden County, New Jersey. Boyce's analysis suggests that major changes in Camden County turned on the availability of land and zoning restrictions. Gannon and Dear judged that the Lindenwold line enhanced the attractiveness of the downtown Philadelphia

---

[5]EDWIN H. SPENGLER, *Land Values in New York in Relation to Transit Facilities* (New York: Columbia University Press, 1930).

[6]CAROL KOVACH, "On Conducting an 'Impact' Study of a Rapid Transit Facility—The Case of Toronto" (unpublished paper presented at the Montreal Joint Transportation Engineering Meeting, preprint MTL-23, 1974).

[7]MARTIN C. LIBICKI, *Land Use Impacts of Major Transit Improvements*, prepared for U.S. DOT, Office of the Secretary by Office of Transportation Planning Analysis (Washington, D.C.: U.S. Department of Transportation, March 1975).

[8]G. W. HEENAN, "The Economic Effect of Rapid Transit on Real Estate Development," *Appraisal Journal*, 36, no. 2 (April 1968), 213–24.

[9]DAVID E. BOYCE AND OTHERS, *Impact of Rapid Transit on Suburban Residential Property Values and Land Development*, prepared for U.S. DOT, Office of the Secretary (Philadelphia: University of Pennsylvania, November 1972). Now available as PB 220 693.

[10]COLIN A. GANNON AND MICHAEL J. DEAR, *The Impact of Rail Rapid Transit Systems on Commercial Office Development: The Case of the Philadelphia–Lindenwold Speedline*, prepared for UMTA (Philadelphia: University of Pennsylvania, June 1972). Now available as PB 212 906.

area, and that several percentage points of the increase in downtown office space might be attributed to its presence.

A major study has been mounted to judge the impacts of the San Francisco Bay Area Rapid Transit (BART) system. The findings from that study are still not in. It is generally agreed that the impacts of BART on the suburbanization process and developments around outlying stations are nil. Webber suggests that there may have been some developmental impacts in downtown San Francisco.[11]

Not to be able to find relationships does not prove that they are absent. Among other things, one could conjecture on the following:

- Transit impacts on land development take a rather long time to work themselves out. The land development process has not been studied over a long enough period of time.
- The transit impact on urban land development is real, although small. Larger transit investments would have great impact.

While there may have been some truth to these conjectures, they rather smack of clutching at straws. Spengler's 1930 publication would seem to deserve the higher confidence; again, his conclusion was that urban land development turns on many factors, of which transportation is one.

SUMMING UP

Let us review the structure of this discussion. It began by puzzling the future of urban transportation and urban land development. Will transit and activity center development tend to reinforce each other? The many relations between transportation and land development that may be observed in history were then noted. Particular attention was given to the expansion of highway transportation and urban development since the turn of the century.

The discussion then examined societal expectations from transportation and land use as those expectations have been expressed in recent years. Transportation and land use are to work together to manage social, economic, and environmental issues. Some issues of current debate were examined, and it was noted that the selection of instruments for issue resolution should not give priority to transportation and land use.

Land-use theory was then briefly consulted; it explains transportation and land-use relationships through location rent. The subsequent examination of empirical studies indicated that the land development process is a highly complex one and that transportation is just one factor bearing on land development.

The message in this essay is thus really very simple. Today, many expect much of the transportation–land development relationship; they tend to view it as the primary

---

[11]Melvin M. Webber, "The BART Experience—What Have We Learned?" reprinted from *The Public Interest*, no. 45 (Fall 1976), pp. 79–108. Copyright © by National Affairs, Inc.

shaper of urban areas and as an instrument for social problem solving. The urban transportation professional should be aware that the situation is much more complex. The problems to be solved are complex; land development is not a simple function of transportation.

SELECTED BIBLIOGRAPHY

Many citations are no longer available from their original source. These citations are often available from the National Technical Information Service, U.S. Department of Commerce, 5285 Port Royal Road, Springfield, Va. 22161. We have verified the order numbers for many of these citations, and they are found at the end of the citation. Prices are available through NTIS at the address above.

ALONSO, WILLIAM, *Location and Land Use: Toward a General Theory of Land Rents*. Joint Center for Urban Studies Publication Series. Cambridge, Mass.: Harvard University Press, 1964.

BOYCE, DAVID E., AND OTHERS, *Impact of Rapid Transit on Suburban Residential Property Values and Land Development*, prepared for U.S. DOT, Office of the Secretary. Philadelphia: University of Pennsylvania, November 1972. Now available as PB 220 693.

DUNN, EDGAR S., JR., *The Location of Agricultural Production*. Gainesville, Fla.: University of Florida Press, 1954.

GANNON, COLIN A., AND MICHAEL J. DEAR, *The Impact of Rail Rapid Transit Systems on Commercial Office Development: The Case of the Philadelphia–Lindenwold Speedline*, prepared for UMTA. Philadelphia: University of Pennsylvania, June 1972. Now available as PB 212 906.

HEENAN, G. W., "The Economic Effect of Rapid Transit on Real Estate Development," *Appraisal Journal*, 36, no. 2 (April 1968), 213–24.

ISARD, WALTER, *Location and Space-Economy*. Cambridge, Mass.: The M.I.T. Press, 1956.

KNIGHT, ROBERT L., AND LISA L. TRYGG, *Land Use Impacts of Rapid Transit: Implications of Recent Experience*, prepared for U.S. DOT, Office of the Secretary. San Francisco: De Leuw, Cather & Company, August 1977.

KOVACH, CAROL, "On Conducting an 'Impact' Study of a Rapid Transit Facility—The Case of Toronto (unpublished paper presented at the Montreal Joint Transportation Engineering Meeting, preprint MTL-23, 1974).

LIBICKI, MARTIN C., *Land Use Impacts of Major Transit Improvements*, prepared for U.S. DOT, Office of the Secretary by Office of Transportation Planning Analysis. Washington, D.C.: U.S. Department of Transportation, March 1975.

SPENGLER, EDWIN H., *Land Values in New York in Relation to Transit Facilities*. New York: Columbia University Press, 1930.

U.S. CONGRESS, *Progress Report of the Highway Cost Allocation Study*; First—House Document no. 106, 85th Congress, 1st Session, March 4, 1957; Second—House Document no. 344, 85th Congress, 2nd Session, March 3, 1958; Third—House Document no. 91, 86th Conqress, 1st Session, 1959; Fourth—House Document no. 355, 86th Congress, 2nd Session, 1960. Washington, D.C.: U.S. Government Printing Office.

————, *Final Report of the Highway Cost Allocation Study*, House Document no. 54, 87th Congress, 1st Session, January 16, 1961. Washington, D.C.: U.S. Government Printing Office.

————, *Final Report of the Highway Cost Allocation Study, Part VI: Studies of the Economic and Social Effects of Highway Improvement*, House Document no. 72, 87th Congress, 1st Session, January 23, 1961. Washington, D.C.: U.S. Government Printing Office.

WEBBER, MELVIN M., "The BART Experience—What Have We Learned?" reprinted from *The Public Interest*, no. 45 (Fall 1976), pp. 79–108. Copyright © by National Affairs, Inc.

Chapter 27

ENVIRONMENTAL IMPACTS OF TRANSIT SYSTEMS

ROBERT L. KNIGHT, *Director of Planning Research, De Leuw,*
Cather & Company, and DONALD APPLEYARD, *Professor, Institute*
of Urban and Regional Development, University
of California, Berkeley

Rationales for the development of rapid transit systems in recent years have been based largely on reducing the adverse effects of overreliance on the automobile. These adverse effects of the auto and its associated roadway facilities have been substantially environmental; they include the destruction of homes, neighborhoods, jobs, and other valued urban places, as well as natural habitats and environments, for the construction of freeways and other large-scale facilities. Further effects of the auto itself include noise, vibration, air pollution, visual blight, and intrusion, as well as excessive energy use. Dependence on the automobile has also been a major force in urban sprawl, with freeway construction encouraging scattered low-density residential development in suburban areas.

Rapid transit, in one form or another, has often been seen as a means of minimizing such environmental consequences. It is reasoned to do so by reducing traffic (particularly commute traffic) generally and avoiding further construction of urban freeways, while at the same time encouraging more intensive activity at transit-oriented nodes. In so doing, it is hoped that transit might particularly help to reduce suburban sprawl and strengthen the centers of older cities, now increasingly congested and difficult to reach by car. Implicit in these objectives is a vision of rapid transit as a contributor to the humane city. This ideal is typically seen as small in scale, with intensely active, pedestrian-oriented public environments.

These hopes may or may not be justified. However, they have been powerful enough to generate widespread and enthusiastic political backing and even considerable public financial support for new transit systems in many cities. This chapter's purpose is to look at some of the facts behind those hopes—the nature and scale of environmental impacts, for good and ill, which seem to occur when a major new transit system or component is provided.

ENVIRONMENTAL IMPACT ASSESSMENT

As hopes and proposed transit solutions have appeared, a methodology of environmental impact assessment has emerged to aid in their evaluation. Much of this methodology has been developed in response to federal environmental protection legislation. Its intent is to assess environmental "benefits" and "costs" of new projects and systems in a systematic, comprehensive way. However, much of the methodology so far available is essentially guesswork, because of the lack of empirical verification. Some empirical analysis efforts have been completed recently or are now under way to assess the environmental impacts of actual freeway, street traffic, and rapid transit systems.[1] This chapter will outline some of the issues, problems, and models involved, as well as empirical evidence and other information currently available on such impacts as a result of these studies and other early efforts.

ISSUES IN IMPACT ASSESSMENT

A number of issues which have been raised over the years provide a general indication of the scope of environmental impact concerns. Some of these deal with definitions of the key concepts involved: What is the "environment"? What is an "impact"? Which impacts should be considered? What criteria should be used in their evaluation? How do "direct" or immediate impacts relate to "indirect" or remote impacts?

Another set of important issues is addressed to the nature of impacts and how they occur: What are the relationships among environmental, land-use, political, and economic impacts? How are impacts likely to change with time? What are the primary causes of impact? How reliably and precisely can impacts and causes be identified?

Finally, other issues focus on the policy implications of environmental impacts. How do the impacts of mass transit systems compare and combine with those of other transportation systems and strategies? How can impacts be ameliorated and controlled by policy and planning decisions? How does current knowledge of impacts affect the selection of recommended policies? How might improved accuracy of assessment affect this?

Most of these issues will be touched upon in the following pages.

KEY CONCEPTS AND DEFINITIONS

IMPACT GENERATION

Environment is a tricky term. Because of its popularization, it is often loosely and inconsistently used. Perhaps its most popular connotation is also its narrowest and most misleading: that of the wild or "natural" flora and fauna or, only slightly more

---

[1]In the Selected Bibliography, see: APPLEYARD, GERSON, AND LINTELL; APPLEYARD AND OTHERS; LANE; GRUEN ASSOCIATES; SKIDMORE, OWINGS & MERRILL; and VOORHEES & ASSOCIATES.

broadly, all natural ecological components, including atmospheric and waterway systems. In dealing with environmental effects of public transit in urban places, such definitions are especially misleading because the "natural" components of the environment tend to be relatively little affected.

A properly relevant definition must center on human survival and advancement. This does not mean that protection of the natural environment is unimportant, but rather that other environmental concerns are more relevant in an urban system. Our current popular concern with even the "natural" environment is for the most part based on a belief in its importance in ensuring a healthy continuation of the human species, rather than simply protecting flora and fauna for their own sake. Thus, for purposes of transit system development, the relevant environment must be defined much more broadly. It must include all the physical components of the world, be they "natural" or man-made, on which people must depend in their everyday functioning. It is this *human* environment, in all its complexity, that is to be protected and advanced.

Environmental *impact* is simply any change (in this case, induced by transit) in this broadly defined environment. Impacts occur in a chainlike manner, with initial impacts leading to others (see Fig. 27-1). An initial change in the environment (e.g., introduction of a transit system) creates a set of *emissions* which lead to some *direct* impacts on various aspects of the physical environment (e.g., changes in community

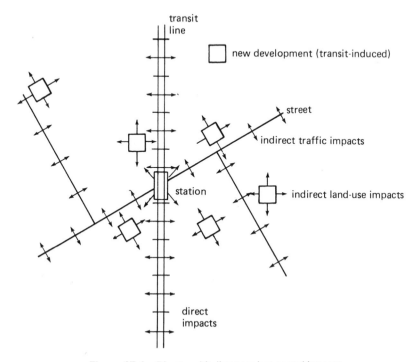

Figure 27-1   *Direct and indirect environmental impacts.*

noise levels), which may in turn generate *indirect* ones (e.g., changes in traffic levels, activity patterns, demographics, or land use). This chain can have many steps. Emissions also can be *magnified* or *mitigated* by intervening features, such as sound barriers, distance, or elevation, which modify the impacts on surrounding populations.

Two parallel sets of conditions, "with transit" and "without transit," must be compared to define an impact. At least one of these scenarios is necessarily hypothetical, and in the case of forecasts for alternative proposed systems, both are. Impacts are, thus, defined as the specific differences between the two. This is especially essential for indirect impacts, which often depend on the estimated difference in land-development rates and patterns with and without the transit system. Current transportation–land use mathematical projection models are not very satisfactory for this purpose. Whether they or some mechanically less complex approach is used, judgmental adjustments must be applied to the results to ensure consideration of important subjective factors.

Transit systems have *internal* impacts on travelers and *external* impacts on the larger environment. Transit's role as an environment for its users is in many ways as important as its influence on its own external environment and the people who depend on that environment. This chapter will concentrate on external impacts; the traveler environment is dealt with in other chapters.

An important aspect of environmental impacts is their often *dynamic* nature. These environmental effects occur not all at once but tend to change as time passes, since a transit system inevitably changes in its impact-causing attributes. Planning and anticipation lead to construction, which culminates in a start-up phase of operations. This may last for several years, with gradual changes, until a stable operational condition is reached. Finally, some impacts, such as demographic or land-use changes, may not be visible for many years after operations have stabilized. Each stage has its own environmental impacts, which can differ dramatically in consequence.

RESPONSE TO IMPACTS

The *perception* and *evaluation* of these impacts and subsequent behavioral *response* by persons who are affected are the culmination of the environmental impact process. These terms are used in the psychological rather than the colloquial sense, to encompass all the reactions of the human organism, including unconscious as well as conscious elements. Thus, an effect on air quality may lead to illness, and noise may cause emotional distress.

Such behavioral responses can lead to further changes in perceptions and evaluations, in a recursive fashion. The degree of behavioral adaptation (such as moving to the back of the house or not allowing the children to play on the street), psychological adaptation (readjusting expectations), environmental modification (building fences or installing soundproof insulation), or public action (political opposition) which the individual finds necessary can profoundly affect perceptions and evaluations of the source of the impacts—in turn possibly leading to other behavioral responses (such as deciding to move).

Many of the concepts and definitions just described can be better understood diagrammatically. Figure 27-2 is one form of such a presentation, indicating linkages between the sources of impact, the impacts themselves, their effects on people, and a variety of actions taken in response. Note that the process is a continuous one involving substantial feedback, rather than a one-time adjustment to impact. Although the figure emphasizes operational impacts, those related to the planning, construction, and all the other different phases of a transit system's life fit equally well.

These environmental impacts may fall on several *population groups*. Adjacent residents are usually of greatest concern, and may themselves differ in exposure or sensitivity. Others include those who work, play, or travel near the system's facilities, and the general population of the region. All must be considered in impact evaluation.

TYPES OF IMPACT

At each stage in the transit development process, from anticipation to the regular operation of the system after many years of service, many *types* of environmental impact occur. Many typologies of environmental impact have been developed, usually as checklists for specific types of studies. Most of these tend to be biased toward a particular facet of the natural or social environment and are often not well suited to comprehensive urban transit impact studies. Ultimately, however, the main criterion for selection must be that of relevance to human activities and preferences, as noted earlier. A sample list of such impacts is given in Appendix A. These are couched in negative terms, but many impacts could be improvements in the factors cited rather than detriments.

One way of categorizing impacts for study is according to the aspect or dimension of the existing environment which is affected by some emission. Relevant dimensions of the environment may be defined in many ways. One possible approach is the way in which they act on the individual: for example, a typology of acoustic, atmospheric, visual, natural-ecologic, interpersonal security, and neighborhood integrity dimensions was used effectively in the BART (San Francisco Bay Area Rapid Transit) Impact Program. Emissions of the transit system, such as sound, physical mass, movement of vehicles, and the flow of patrons, act on these dimensions to produce a wide variety of impacts. Many other approaches are possible. However, the objective of all must be to ensure that no major impact is omitted or misrepresented.

SOME PROBLEMS IN IMPACT ASSESSMENT

The foregoing discussion demonstrated the broad scope of a comprehensive impact analysis. With such a scope, some things must inevitably be treated only lightly or omitted from consideration in practical studies. What to emphasize and what to omit thus becomes a serious question. There is a danger that its solution will be determined primarily by what is most readily measurable or of current popularized concern.

More generally, direct impacts, particularly those occurring only during the stable,

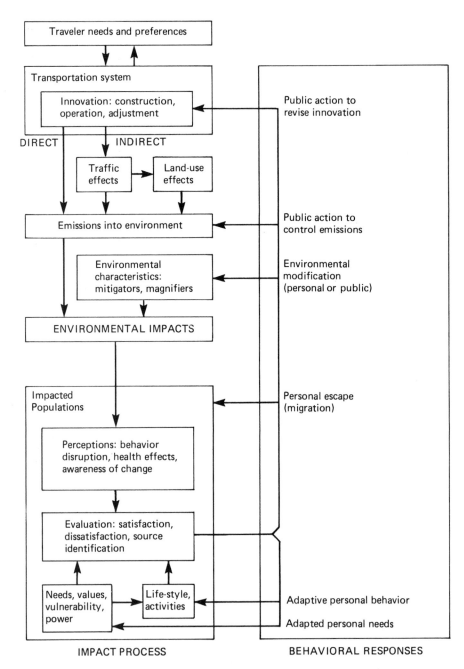

Figure 27-2 *Socio-environmental impacts of transport innovations.*

full-scale period of the system's operational life, are relatively easily assessed but may in some cases actually be less important than some of the indirect impacts arising from the system's long-term effects on land use. Likewise, the disruptive impacts of construction may produce lasting effects more serious than any operational impacts, and start-up and shakedown operations may have impacts more severe than those of later stable service. Consequently, the evaluation of impact should be longitudinal (i.e., over the life of the system) rather than a cross-sectional "snapshot."

IMPACTS OF RAIL RAPID TRANSIT

THE BART CASE STUDY

Largely because of the BART Impact Program, a substantial body of empirical information exists on the environmental impacts of conventional rail rapid transit systems. This section will summarize these effects. A following section will deal with impacts of other transit modes, using the BART data as a point of departure.

In some important ways, the BART system is not representative of other recent conventional rapid rail systems. Its role is primarily that of connecting low-density suburban residential communities in an auto-dependent metropolis to a downtown center, rather than facilitating movement within the densely populated central city. Its lines are therefore radial, and they extend much farther into the suburbs than do other recent systems in cities such as Toronto and Montreal. Its lines and stations are also primarily aboveground (except downtown), in contrast to the nearly all-subway configurations of the Toronto and Montreal systems. These differences have important implications for environmental impact. However, BART's size, variations in design, and diversity of surroundings provide a wealth of specific impact conditions, including many similar to those found on other new transit systems now under construction or proposed elsewhere.

CONSTRUCTION IMPACTS

In an absolute sense, the adverse effects of the rapid transit construction process can be substantial. With BART as well as the Washington, D.C., Metro and other recent systems, the most serious effect appears to be that of the disruption of traffic and trade along streets subjected to long periods of open-cut subway construction. In some recent cases, subway construction on downtown streets was under way for over 5 years, with some indications of large losses in trade for businesses along the right-of-way (see Fig. 27-3). Small businesses were apparently most affected; it has been asserted that many did not survive to enjoy the benefits of the completed subway system, although documentation on this point is sparse. Experiences elsewhere are similar; in Amsterdam, for example, the new metro has been responsible for the demolition of a historic neighborhood, causing serious community conflicts.

Figure 27-3 *Long-term closure of Market Street in downtown San Francisco for BART subway construction. (courtesy of Bay Area Rapid Transit District)*

Housing dislocation is another significant problem. Although the BART system is almost entirely sited along prior transportation rights-of-way such as railroads and freeways, recent research indicates that over 3000 housing units were taken for the construction of the 114-km (71-mi), 34-station system. Many of these were at suburban station parking-lot sites, which are up to 8 acres (32,400 m²) in size and often in residential areas. Others were concentrated along routes in which the existing right-of-way had to be widened to accommodate the trackway (see Fig. 27-4). Even this large number, however, is small when placed in the perspective of the system's length (an average of well under 50 units per mile—31 per kilometer) and in comparison with urban freeway construction requirements (often 200 to 500 or more units per mile—124 to 310 per kilometer).

Construction effects of *aerial and at-grade trackways* are relatively benign, owing to their simplicity and rapid construction. However, even this level of activity is at variance with the quiet character of many residential areas, and led to many complaints during BART's construction. Construction of *tunneled* subway lines, as in

Figure 27-4 *Removal of homes for construction of BART Concord Station and parking lot. (courtesy of Bay Area Rapid Transit District)*

Montreal, is of course least disruptive except at points of access and removal of material. *Open-cut* subway construction, particularly at stations, is most disruptive; other problem areas include suburban station sites, particularly those with parking lots, which tend to be used as staging areas and generate substantial truck traffic and noise.

Major efforts needed to ameliorate such impacts include use of more rapid subway construction techniques, careful planning of interim traffic and transit reroutings, and an intensive program of public relations (such as BART's) to inform nearby residents and others of impending activity as well as to respond to complaints. Finally, it must be recognized that minimization of land acquisition and its attendant dislocation, by doing the construction on narrow rights-of-way, necessarily produces the strongest construction impacts (as well as later operational impacts) on the nearby residences and businesses which might otherwise have been taken in right-of-way acquisition.

EARLY OPERATIONS IMPACTS

The early operations period of some new rail rapid transit systems has been characterized by a variety of difficulties in achieving both reliable system operations and harmony with surroundings. BART's problems with the mechanical reliability of its trains and automatic train control system, for example, have resulted in a lengthy period of environmental impacts of somewhat less intensity than those which will appear later when the system's trains are running at more frequent intervals and on .

weekends. Most important among such impacts is train noise along the system's elevated lines; this is now a moderate problem in the one to two blocks in quiet residential areas nearest the lines but will affect more areas with later full operations.

This initial operations period is also characterized by patronage levels substantially lower than those likely to be reached after service is improved. As a result, impacts related to patronage will increase. The most important of these are related to traffic, parking, and connecting bus service at the suburban stations. In the case of BART, parking now overflows from many of the station lots onto adjacent streets, to such an extent that lot expansions and/or improved feeder bus service will be required as patronage increases. This is similar to experience elsewhere, notably on the Toronto and Montreal systems as well as the Philadelphia area's Lindenwold line.

These change-prone impacts are typically those attributable to the system's *operations*; in contrast, those due to its *facilities* are likely to be relatively stable over time. Included among these are impacts on the visual environment and natural ecology, and neighborhood effects such as closing of streets and paths across the right-of-way. These stable effects as well as other impacts of full operations are discussed in the following section.

IMPACTS UNDER STABLE FULL-SCALE OPERATIONS

The major finding of the BART study of environmental impacts was that the system's effects are generally small and will continue to be so. This applies to regional effects, such as reduction of auto air pollution, as well as localized impacts both at the stations and along the lines. Exceptions are noted in the following paragraphs, along with other details that may be applicable to new systems proposed elsewhere.

BART's effect on the region's air quality and energy use is insignificant, primarily because it is forecast to carry only 3 % of the region's daily vehicular trips. In addition, much of its patronage is drawn from previous bus users rather than auto drivers or passengers. The system, however, is now a prominent part of San Francisco's image. The elevated lines and trains are seen from a number of freeways, arterials, and residential areas, and the system is internationally known (see Fig. 27-5). It has, therefore, become something of a tourist attraction. Older subway systems, such as those in London, Tokyo, and Paris, have for many become the primary mode of structuring the city's image, since they are simpler and easier to use than the aboveground street networks.

In defining impacts, as already noted, it is essential to have a baseline or "no-build" situation with which to compare. A major environmental benefit, for example, would be the avoidance of construction of additional urban freeways because of the transit system. However, the difficulty of identifying such a one-for-one substitution should not be underestimated, since the two tend not to serve all the same purposes and also because many other factors are involved in the decision to build a major road. In BART's case, there was considerable discussion as to whether BART had been instrumental in preventing construction of a very large and environmentally disruptive bridge parallel to the Bay Bridge. An analysis of the events of that period indicated

Figure 27-5 *BART train on typical elevated trackway in residential area, with experimental "linear park." (courtesy of Bay Area Rapid Transit District)*

that the proposed bridge would probably have been stopped for other reasons, so it was not included as a component of the "no-BART" alternative. Clearly, this critically affected the outcome of the BART impact analysis. The "no-BART" scenario against which BART was compared emphasized the use of more express buses on existing roads, which had no discernible environmental effects. As a result, the net environmental impacts attributed to BART, although small, were largely adverse, even though this might not be so elsewhere. Obviously, such a base case must be carefully defined and defended (as it was with BART) in order to allow a fair and credible impact analysis.

BART's effects at stations are mixed. Impacts attributable to the downtown subway stations have been almost entirely positive as a result of the new plazas created around the stations and the street beautification projects that were undertaken by cities in cooperation with BART (see Fig. 27-6). Many of these environmental improvements

Figure 27-6 *BART station entrance plaza below street level in downton San Francisco. (courtesy of Gruen Associates, Inc.)*

have created lively social meeting places. As is true for the entire system, crime has not been a problem at these downtown stations. On the other hand, the coordinated planning of development around the BART stations has been much more limited than the multilevel pedestrian complexes that have been created around such stations as Place Bonaventure in Montreal, Shinjuku in Tokyo, or Insurgentes in Mexico City.

Neither have the suburban stations been closely integrated with new suburban centers, as at Vallingby near Stockholm or Senri near Osaka, Japan. At suburban BART stations, the large parking lots (up to 1500 cars) are often beyond convenient walking distance from adjacent centers (see Fig. 27-7). The opportunity to create suburban pedestrian centers or to reinforce existing ones has, therefore, been lost. Many suburban stations could have been located much closer to or even within already built suburban shopping centers. However, cost, the private nature of these centers, and the fragmentary nature of urban planning around BART, which resulted in BART's inability to plan beyond the right-of-way, precluded such packaging.[2] There is still the future option, however, of building on air rights over the BART parking lots.

As noted earlier, several parking lots were overfilled shortly after opening; others have become so as patronage has risen. Terminal stations are most affected. The severity of problems caused by this overflow and the associated station-area traffic varies widely, depending on the station location and parking-lot access to major streets. In

---

[2] R. BETTS, "Design of Bay Area Rapid Transit Stations" (unpublished Master's thesis in city planning, University of California—Berkeley, 1972).

Figure 27-7 *BART station and parking lot separated from shopping center by fenced drainage channel. (courtesy of Bay Area Rapid Transit District)*

general, it is a significant problem in residential areas—probably the system's largest effect on its surroundings—but not elsewhere. At the same time, solutions, such as either lot expansion or construction of multilevel facilities, are most difficult in existing residential areas.

There are few other station-area impacts. The visual effect of the stations is generally perceived by nearby residents as neutral or positive, and noise is slight. In general, nearby residents were found to be unhappy where there was an overflow parking problem and relatively happy otherwise. They seemed to discount most other effects. Finally, land value or land-use changes (after 5 years of limited operations) appear to be virtually nonexistent. For similarly short periods of operation, other recently developed systems have had similar experiences with station-area development, although Toronto is notable for its apparent land-use impacts over a longer period.

Impacts along BART's subway lines are nil where tunneled except around the stations, where large open excavations were necessary. Most cut-and-cover line sections were located in wide arterial streets—causing construction impacts, but limiting the numbers of dwellings taken. In the long run these are the lines that have had most beneficial impacts, reinforcing and enhancing existing centers, such as Market Street in San Francisco and Shattuck Avenue in Berkeley. BART's 113-km/h (70-mi/h) trains on its aerial lines, however, despite their quietness relative to other systems, cause some noise problems for many residents living within one or two blocks. A reduction of from 5 to 10 dB(A) is required to eliminate this problem in most places. Sound-barrier baffles on the guideway could do this, although they would increase the presently acceptable visual bulk of the structure as well as its shadow effects and cost. Future transit systems must deal with this through even-quieter trains, bulkier structures, wider rights-of-way, or line locations outside quiet residential areas.

Even these problems affect relatively few residents, since most of the BART aboveground trackway shares rights-of-way with other transportation facilities, such as freeways, arterial streets, and railroads (Fig. 27-8). It was found, however, that this is no guarantee of impact-free operation; where the system shares a little-used railway right-of-way, adjacent neighborhoods are not adapted to noise and suffer more than others. A 2-mi (3-km) landscaped strip (the "linear park" in Fig. 27-5) beneath the BART aerial structure in one such location was appreciated and actively used by local residents but apparently did not lessen their unhappiness with the BART train noise. Along the at-grade lines, which are potentially dangerous because of the high-voltage third rail as well as the high-speed trains themselves, protective cyclone fences now interrupt pedestrian flows, which freely crossed relatively unused railroads in some neighborhoods. However, this has been offset by pedestrian bridges and is apparently only a minor concern. All in all, the use of prior transportation rights-of-way appears to be a key factor in minimizing environmental impact.

Figure 27-8 *Low-impact BART right-of-way in freeway median.* (*courtesy of Bay Area Transit District*)

Apart from unexpected increases in use of the system, which could add to congestion problems at some stations, the major possible long-term environmental effects of a rapid transit system are those on local and regional land-use patterns. Experience with post-World War II transit improvements in the United States and Canada indicates that such effects are likely to be small unless encouraged by land-use policy and other factors in addition to the transit system itself.[3] Under such encouragement the most likely effects are an increase in high-rise office development and possibly some strengthening of retail activities in the central business district, plus some focusing of office and apartment construction at some outlying stations. Such effects are probably limited to intraregional transfers of activity rather than net new growth in a region.

How much the high-rise building boom in San Francisco was caused by BART may never be empirically established. Webber judges that it "would have happened anyway, but . . . BART . . . made it happen bigger and quicker."[4] The environmental effects of high-rise development in San Francisco have not been very positive. They have been the subject of a separate study, in which increases in noise levels, traffic generation, the blockage of views, shadowing and wind on downtown streets and open space, and their overpowering scale were cited among the negative impacts.[5]

Around local stations several Bay Area cities produced ambitious development plans prior to BART's opening, incorporating high-rise buildings and multilevel commercial and apartment complexes. Many of these were subsequently opposed by the neighboring residents, whose principal response to BART prior to its opening was one of fear about the effects of such development on neighborhood composition and character.[6] In a study of new townhouse developments in one of the Bay Area's suburban counties, Dingemans reports that only "some degree of sub-centering (of townhouse developments around BART) has occurred . . . ," and those more spread out within a mile radius than within the immediate area of the stations.[7] He offers four reasons why more clustering has not happened. First, there were few available building sites, and most were too small for the usual 10 acres (40,500 m²) or more required for such developments. Of the stations studied by Dingemans, most clustering has occurred around the one that had large sites available. Second, the construction of

[3]R. L. KNIGHT AND L. L. TRYGG, *Land Use Impacts of Rapid Transit*, Report no. DOT-TPI-10-77-29 (Washington, D.C.: U.S. Department of Transportation, 1977).

[4]MELVIN M. WEBBER, *The BART Experience—What Have We Learned?* reprinted from *The Public Interest*, no. 45 (Fall 1976), pp. 79–108. Copyright © by National Affairs, Inc.

[5]SAN FRANCISCO PLANNING AND URBAN RENEWAL ASSOCIATION, *Detailed Findings: Impact of Intensive High-Rise Development on San Francisco, Sec. 3: Environment*, prepared for HUD, San Francisco Foundation, and Mary A. Crocker Trust (San Francisco: San Francisco Planning and Urban Renewal Association, June 1975), chap. 6. Now available as PB 245 577.

[6]DONALD APPLEYARD AND OTHERS, *BART Impact Studies, BART-II: Pre-BART Studies of Environment, Land Use, Retail Sales, Part II: Residential Environment Impact Study, Volume III: Residential Quality Prior to the Opening of BART* and *Volume VI: Rationale and Procedures for Collection of Behavioral and Environmental Data*, Final Report, prepared for Metropolitan Transportation Commission, U.S. DOT and HUD (Berkeley, Calif.: University of California, Institute of Urban and Regional Development, 1973). Now available as PB 236 730 and 236 733.

[7]D. DINGEMANS, *Residential Subcentering and Urban Sprawl: The Location of Higher-Density, Owner-Occupied Housing Around the Concord Line BART Stations*, Working Paper no. 275 (Berkeley, Calif.: University of California, Institute of Urban and Regional Development, 1977).

large parking lots [up to 1500 cars, or 8 acres (32,400 m²)] has preempted close-in sites. Third, public opposition to townhouses emerged in the early 1970s partly because they had been allowed to locate in scattered sites. "Residents for Density Control," a local ad hoc group, effectively blocked proposals for townhouses in the vicinity of some stations. The fourth and final reason for little clustering was the willingness of the suburban cities to allow commercial centers to locate away from the station sites. Part of this was also due to BART's location policies, which emphasized the use of cheaper sites away from existing centers.

Inner-city neighborhoods have also opposed increasing densities around the stations and have sponsored "downzoning."[8] Environmental change around many stations is, therefore, almost at a standstill, even though it makes "regional" sense to increase densities in those locations. This may, however, only be a slowing down of the process rather than a permanent halt. Here is a case of conflicts among environmental qualities. Increased densities around stations are seen as decreasing comfort conditions for nearby residents, but they improve pedestrian access, encourage transit use, and can create fine urban environments. The need is for more sensitive and participatory planning for densification, identifying particular development sites, utilizing air rights, improving pedestrian access, and so on, while maintaining some continuity of character.

It is difficult to predict the scale and significance of future development around BART stations, since it is contingent on so many factors other than transit. In the BART Impact Program a preliminary analysis estimated that if clustering effects on the Bay Area similar in scale to those observed in Toronto could be induced, the currently projected consumption of new land for urban use by the year 2000 might be reduced by up to 10%.[9] Although this is not a dramatic effect, it is significant. This suggests that such long-term land-use effects (generally considered benefits) should be given serious consideration in impact evaluations, but are unlikely to completely offset or overshadow more direct system impacts, such as train noise and neighborhood parking. In any event, it seems clear that a public commitment to clustered development, including appropriate land-use controls, is necessary for such effects to occur.

Some observers have noted that low-density residential development has been strong in the BART suburban corridors around and beyond the terminal stations, and have offered this as evidence that BART has actually helped to further sprawl in these corridors.[10] Certainly the rapid transit service's long lines have made the distant suburban areas more attractive for residences of downtown commuters, and the combination of available land, low-density zoning, and large BART parking lots for auto access from such residential areas has encouraged a conventional spread-out form of development. The extent of BART's actual effect is not known, however, and this

---

[8]ANDREJS SKABURSKIS, "An Economic and Political Analysis of BART Land-Use Impacts: A Planning Study of the Rockridge Conflict" (unpublished Ph.D. dissertation, University of California—Berkeley, College of Environmental Design, 1976).

[9]GRUEN ASSOCIATES, INC., AND DE LEUW, CATHER & COMPANY, *Environmental Impacts of BART: Final Report*, prepared for Metropolitan Transportation Commission, U.S. DOT and HUD (Berkeley, Calif.: Metropolitan Transportation Commission, 1978).

[10]WEBBER, *The BART Experience.*

contention can be considered only a hypothesis. It suggests only that any such sprawl-inducing effects, if they do exist, would be reduced if rail transit lines were shorter or suburban auto access restricted.

OTHER TRANSIT MODES

The environmental impacts of other transit modes have not been well-documented, in comparison to the detailed studies of conventional rapid rail systems such as BART. However, the limited evidence available can be used in combination with the rapid rail findings to provide some indicators of how effects of these other modes compare with those of BART-like rail systems.

Systems of interest in addition to conventional rail rapid transit include commuter rail, light rail, innovative fixed-guideway systems, and regional all-bus operations. Not all of these modes are direct competitors, in that the differences in their service characteristics sometimes lead them to serve quite different markets and purposes. Light rail, for example, is usually not a reasonable substitute for a commuter rail system. Consequently, their environmental impacts should not be interpreted immediately as indications that one system is "better" than another.

COMMUTER RAIL

The environmental impacts of commuter rail systems are likely to be much smaller than even those of rapid rail systems such as BART. Typically, an existing freight rail right-of-way is used, service is infrequent relative to that of rapid rail systems, and suburban station facilities are less obtrusive and their patronage lower in most cases. Construction impacts are likely to be small even if new trackage is laid.

The typical baseline for commuter rail evaluation is an all-highway system. Regional effects on traffic and associated impacts can be estimated quite easily for given patronage levels, as with BART. At a corridor level, effects on parallel freeway traffic and downtown parking can be substantial, although on a regional basis these effects are not substantial except for the largest commuter rail networks. It would appear that other environmental concerns are unlikely to be significant in decisions concerning inauguration or expansion of commuter rail facilities. Their higher speeds, given the option of express trains, can, however, bring places as far as 97 km (60 mi) from urban centers into commuting range, as has happened in the southern region of London. This has resulted in the growth of many small towns, but sprawl has been prevented by green belt controls.

LIGHT RAIL

Light rail systems usually run at moderate speed and on separate at-grade rights-of-way. Attributes of modern light rail systems most relevant to environmental impact include their use of some grade crossings and small, relatively numerous stations or stops. To the degree that these characteristics are rejected in favor of high-speed, mainly grade-separated operation and large, widely spaced stations with parking (as in Edmonton, Canada), impacts will approach those of rapid rail systems. However, with the more standard configuration, impacts should be substantially less because of the lack of concentration of activity. Major concerns are likely to be limited to grade-crossing safety; other impacts, such as noise and visual effects, are less likely to be significant than for rapid rail systems.

INNOVATIVE FIXED-GUIDEWAY SYSTEMS

Impacts of unconventional guideway transit systems will vary substantially, depending on specific system characteristics. However, the types of impact and their causes identified as important in the BART study can provide useful indications of the key impact concerns for such systems. Most important, many impacts have little to do with guideway technology. For example, suburban station-area concerns focus on overflow parking and other access problems. Innovative guideway systems usually cannot avoid such problems, irrespective of the technology used for the system. Similarly, effects on regional air quality will not be substantial unless the system carries a very high proportion of the region's trips—again, irrespective of guideway technology.

Innovative guideway systems are most likely to have environmental impacts different from those of BART along the guideway itself. In particular, if the system is significantly noisier than BART, any residents within two or perhaps more blocks will probably have reason to complain. Conversely, a system slightly quieter than BART will cause almost no discernible effect on most acoustic environments. At the same time, some proposed guideway systems may involve either lighter or bulkier guideways than that of BART. Since the bulk or shadowing of BART's guideway is not a cause of significant complaint, lighter guideways are unlikely to produce a significant improvement. Bulkier guideways, such as those with side walls for guidance of untracked systems, may cause significant shadow and view-blocking problems, however. These problems are important when narrow rights-of-way are used in residential areas and of increasing concern for downtown people mover systems.

REGIONAL ALL-BUS SYSTEMS

As already noted, the BART study defined the system's environmental impacts as the differences between the existing situation (with BART) and a hypothetical "no-BART alternative" scenario which relied on a regional all-bus system large enough to carry about the same number of trips. The only significant environmental impact differences between BART and an all-bus system might be those occurring around the BART stations and guideways, where the "alternative" bus system would have few or no offsetting effects. However, if the regional bus system were to have terminals or if it were to disperse along arterial streets, its impacts could be more widespread than BART's. Comparative research on the environmental impacts of buses versus automobiles carrying equal numbers of passengers has not been carried out, but buses are known to have substantial negative impacts on residential streets.[11] However, bus systems are necessary even with a rail system, to serve shorter trips and the collector–distributor role. The important issue is whether the increase in total bus operations required by the all-bus alternative to serve the longer trip and express functions (otherwise covered by rail transit) would be enough to have significant environmental effects. In the BART study, it was concluded that it would not.

CONCLUSION

Overall, the experience cited in this discussion indicates that the negative environmental impacts of modern public transit systems are likely to be small compared with those of freeway systems. For all systems, the most important determinant of systemwide environmental effects is the proportion of a region's trips which are captured, both because of their diversion from other more disruptive modes, especially the auto (a benefit), and their resulting orientation to locations with transit stations (with both benefits and detriments).

For significant regional-scale environmental benefits such as air quality improvement to accrue, transit patronage must be very much larger than that accommodated either on most existing systems such as BART or on typical proposed systems. The only possible exception to this general conclusion is in long-term benefits of land-use intensification around rapid transit stations; on this no conclusion is yet possible, although such effects seem likely to be only moderate, even if significant.

At the same time, even the moderate patronage levels experienced on systems such as BART can cause significant adverse impacts at outlying transit stations in residential areas. With the higher levels of patronage needed to generate significant regional benefits, these localized adverse effects could become serious problems. Under such conditions, stations should be located away from sensitive environments such as quiet residential neighborhoods or be planned in ways to combine with regional centers and arterial street systems.

Different transit modes do have significant differences in environmental impact. But distinctions in impact among modes are complicated by the fact that the modes tend to occur not singly but in combinations. For example, rapid transit systems must be combined with bus feeder systems, and commuter rail (and to some extent light rail) systems serve other market segments. All are possible elements of a comprehensive transportation strategy. This chapter's contention is that immediate environmental impacts such as regional air quality and energy savings are not likely to be the dominant factor—either in selecting among transit options in instances where their roles might be substitutable or in implementing or expanding one of them in lieu of better regional traffic management to control automobile usage.

---

[11]DONALD APPLEYARD, M. SUE GERSON, AND MARK LINTELL, *Liveable Urban Streets: Managing Auto Traffic in Neighborhoods*, prepared for FHWA (Washington, D.C.: U.S. Government Printing Office, January 1976).

Some perspective on this conclusion may be provided through comparison with other transportation strategies. In particular, major regional benefits such as reduction of energy use and air pollution are much more likely through private ridesharing (car-and vanpooling) arrangements; an increase in average peak-period auto occupancy from 1.2 persons per vehicle to 1.4, which is only about one additional person in every sixth car, would do far more toward attainment of most regional environmental objectives than could a rapid transit system such as BART. Improvements in auto engine combustion efficiency, use of smaller cars with smaller engines, and a shift to electric power could also have larger effects in achieving benefits of this type.

The distribution of impacts can vary for different transit systems. The more transport flows can be concentrated on major channels (such as with rail transit), the fewer persons are impacted. This is all the more so if the rail system's typical level of impact is low, as it is with BART. The more dispersed the transit system, as with a regional bus system, the more it approaches the pervasive impact of the automobile. No one has yet calculated, to our knowledge, the relative distributions of impacts of different transit systems. However, there are some clues. A Bay Area study of noise, for instance, found that 40% of a randomly selected population complained of local street traffic, whereas those disturbed by freeway noise amounted to only 24%. Bus transit systems that use local streets may, therefore, cause more widespread environmental problems than regional rail systems. At the same time, concentration of transit and other traffic on arterial streets rather than neighborhood streets and the introduction of quieter and less polluting street transit vehicles may pay even greater environmental dividends.

A major issue outstanding in evaluation of the environmental impacts of transit options is that of long-term effects on urban form and function. Some transit modes, notably high-capacity fixed-guideway systems, may be instrumental in achievement of a more compact, multicentered urban configuration with major benefits in internal accessibility and opportunity as well as infrastructure efficiency, resource savings, and protection of the surrounding natural environment. Recent studies indicate that such transit systems have encouraged progress in this direction. At the same time, provision of rapid transit is but one ingredient, albeit a key one, in a necessary blend of closely related physical and policy inducements if cities are to be restructured to any significant degree. Given such interdependence of causal forces, rapid transit alone cannot be credited with long-range benefits of this nature.

Once a local commitment is made to mobilize such complementary forces to change the course of a city's future development, a new (or extended or improved) fixed-guideway form of mass transit must be given serious consideration as an element in the overall strategy. At this point the relative environmental merits of alternative systems must be considered, as outlined in earlier sections. Nonguideway systems appear to be much less likely to contribute to urban growth-focusing objectives than do either conventional or innovative fixed-guideway systems.

Where a guideway form of transit is adopted, the evidence indicates that effective steps can be taken to mitigate adverse guideway impacts. The major approaches include thoughtful location of stations, careful planning of their surrounding development, and selection of trackway configuration in keeping with the sensitivity of the urban environments to be traversed. This sensitivity is largely determined by factors such as ambient sound levels, local traffic intensity and capacity, right-of-way width, and presence of residential or similarly sensitive land uses. Other efforts to optimize impact may include rapid construction, high-quality architectural design, transit vehicle sound control, provision of adequate parking, extensive feeder bus service, landscaping, and other compensatory measures. With such efforts, rapid transit's environmental impact need not be a major problem, and indeed can offer some significant improvements in the quality and structure of urban environments.

APPENDIX A: POSSIBLE SOCIAL AND ENVIRONMENTAL IMPACTS OF TRANSIT SYSTEMS

Passive hazards	Characteristics that increase the chance of earthquake, flood, fire, unfenced heights, deep water, etc.
Vehicle hazards	Danger due to vehicles, live rails, etc.
Crime	Danger due to criminal activity, street assault, burglary, theft, etc.
Health	Threats to health through air pollution, loss of sunlight, water pollution, garbage, and trash.
Exercise	Constraints on physical exercise through loss of athletic facilities, walking difficulties, etc.
Overcrowding	Loss of space to carry out desired activities, loss of parking facilities, etc.
Facility loss	Loss of homes, work places, community, or other facilities.
Noise, vibration	Noise and vibration levels which interfere with desired activities or are unpleasant.
Air pollution	Fumes, smells, smoke, dust, and smog which are unpleasant to breathe, a nuisance to clean, and which obscure desirable views.
Darkness, glare	Blockage of light into buildings, shadowing of public and private spaces, glare of headlights into windows, bright reflective surfaces.
Microclimate	Exposure to wind, rain, snow, and unacceptable heat or cold.
Disruption of access	Local vehicular access to various parts of the community, cycle and pedestrian access, public access to valued environments and facilities such as shorelines, beaches, lakes, rivers, viewpoints, and other amenities.
Disorientation	Invisibility and poor signing of significant and desirable destinations.
Destruction of valued places	Destruction of, intrusion upon, erosion, and deterioration of valued natural, historic, and community environments.

Territorial invasion	Invasion of territory that individuals, streets, neighborhoods, and communities feel "belong" to them, for which they care and feel responsible even if they are not owned.
Privacy	Intrusion from prying eyes, the presence of strangers, distracting events.
Disruption of neighborhood	Reduction of contacts on the street, through noise, presence of strangers, unpleasant conditions.
Oppressiveness	Environments which, through their vast scale and authoritarian nature, diminish human identity.
Reduction of choice	Loss of activities, uses, and places that lend diversity and life to a community.
Ugliness	Environments that are unpleasant to the senses of sight, sound, smell, or touch or are cluttered, poorly maintained, littered with trash, or dilapidated.
Visual disruption, intrusion	Environments that disrupt the character of an existing landscape, neighborhood, or city, that block desired views.
Regional image	Reduction in quality and diversity of the regional image.
Natural loss	Loss of wildlife habitats, ecological niches, and other valued natural features.
Artificiality	Environments that lack natural materials, outdoor views, open windows, vegetation.

SELECTED BIBLIOGRAPHY

Many citations are no longer available from their original source. These citations are often available from the National Technical Information Service, U.S. Department of Commerce, 5285 Port Royal Road, Springfield, Va. 22161. We have verified the order numbers for many of these citations, and they are found at the end of the citation. Prices are available through NTIS at the address above.

APPLEYARD, DONALD, "Evaluating the Social and Environmental Impacts of Transport Investments," in *Conference Proceedings, Third International Conference on Behavioral Travel Modelling*, Tanunda, Australia, 1977, eds. D. A. Hensher and P. R. Stopher (to be published by Pergamon Press, London, 1978).

———, M. SUE GERSON, AND MARK LINTELL, *Liveable Urban Streets: Managing Auto Traffic in Neighborhoods*, prepared for FHWA. Washington, D.C.: U.S. Government Printing Office, January 1976.

———, AND OTHERS, *BART Impact Studies, BART-II: Pre-BART Studies of Environment, Land Use, Retail Sales, Part II: Residential Environment Impact Study, Volume III: Residential Quality Prior to the Opening of BART* and *Volume VI: Rationale and Procedures for Collection of Behavioral and Environmental Data*, Final Report, prepared for Metropolitan Transportation Commission, U.S. DOT and HUD. Berkeley, Calif.: University of California, Institute of Urban and Regional Development, 1973. Now available as PB 236 730 and 236 733.

BETTS, R., "Design of Bay Area Rapid Transit Stations" (unpublished Master's thesis in city planning, University of California—Berkeley, 1972).

CARP, F., R. ZAWADSKY, AND D. APPLEYARD, "Noise in the Urban Residential Environment" (unpublished paper, University of California—Berkeley, Institute of Urban and Regional Development, 1975.)

DINGEMANS, D., *Residential Subcentering and Urban Sprawl: The Location of Higher-Density, Owner-Occupied Housing Around the Concord Line BART Stations*, Working Paper no. 275. Berkeley, Calif.: University of California, Institute of Urban and Regional Development, 1977.

GRUEN ASSOCIATES, INC., AND DE LEUW, CATHER & COMPANY, *Environmental Impacts of BART: Final Report*, prepared for Metropolitan Transportation Commission, U.S. DOT and HUD. Berkeley, Calif.: Metropolitan Transportation Commission, 1978.

KNIGHT, R. L., AND L. L. TRYGG, *Land Use Impacts of Rapid Transit*, Report no. DOT-TPI-10-77-29. Washington, D.C.: U.S. Department of Transportation, 1977.

LANE, JONATHAN S., AND OTHERS, *The No-Build Alternative: Social, Economic, and Environmental Consequences of Not Constructing Transportation Facilities*, in 2 vols., prepared for NCHRP by David A. Crane & Partners/DACP, Inc., Economics Research Associates, Inc., and Alan M. Voorhees & Associates, Inc. Washington, D.C.: Transportation Research Board, December 1975.

SAN FRANCISCO PLANNING AND URBAN RENEWAL ASSOCIATION, *Detailed Findings: Impact of Intensive High-Rise Development on San Francisco, Sec. 3: Environment*, chap. 6, prepared for HUD, San Francisco Foundation, and Mary A. Crocker Trust. San Francisco: San Francisco Planning and Urban Renewal Association, June 1975. Now available as PB 245 577.

SKABURSKIS, ANDREJS, "An Economic and Political Analysis of BART Land Use Impacts: A Planning Study of the Rockridge Conflict" (unpublished Ph.D. dissertation, University of California—Berkeley, College of Environmental Design, 1976).

SKIDMORE, OWINGS & MERRILL, AND OTHERS, *Environmental Assessment Notebook Series*, Summary and vols. I–VI, prepared for U.S. DOT. Washington, D.C.: U.S. Government Printing Office, 1975.

VOORHEES, ALAN M., & ASSOCIATES, INC., AND OTHERS, *HUD's Areas of Environmental Concern*, prepared for HUD, Office of Policy Development and Research. Washington, D.C.: Department of Housing and Urban Development, 1974.

WEBBER, MELVIN M., *The BART Experience—What Have We Learned?* reprinted from *The Public Interest*, no. 45 (Fall 1976), pp. 79–108. Copyright © by National Affairs, Inc.

Chapter 28

ENERGY: CASE STUDIES

S. SOKOLSKY, *Director, Planning and Analysis Office, Transportation Group Directorate, Energy and Transportation Division, Aerospace Corporation*

The embargo on shipment of crude petroleum to the United States in late 1973 and early 1974 and the subsequent fourfold increase in wellhead prices arranged by the members of the Organization of Petroleum Exporting Countries (OPEC) has resulted in major efforts to assess the uses of and needs for petroleum to power this country's transportation systems. The proliferation of data and studies published since the embargo was lifted has revealed some interesting statistics[1-3]:

- Energy consumption by the transportation sector has remained between 24% and 26% of total energy used in the United States since 1950.
- If the use of energy to create transportation vehicles and systems is considered, the transportation sector's share of consumed energy rises to over 40% of the total for the United States.
- Transportation vehicles are almost totally dependent on petroleum and natural gas liquids, and utilized some 53% of the total of these fuels consumed in the United States in 1975.
- 69.5% of fuel devoted to transportation was used by highway vehicles, with the automobile accounting for roughly three-fourths of this amount.

[1] UNITED STATES DEPARTMENT OF TRANSPORTATION, *National Transportation Trends & Choices (to the Year 2000)*, issued by the Secretary of Transportation (Washington, D.C.: U.S. Government Printing Office, January 12, 1977).

[2] A. S. LOEBL AND OTHERS, *Transportation Energy Conservation Data Book*, ORN-5198 Special, prepared for the Energy Research and Development Administration (Oak Ridge, Tenn.: Oak Ridge National Laboratory, October 1976). Now available as ORNL-5198.

[3] MARGARET FELTON FELS AND ALAIN L. KORNHAUSER, "A Comparison of the Energy and Resources Required in the Manufacturing of Four Modes of Urban Transportation," in *Ground Transportation Symposium*, Santa Clara–Bay Area, May 31–June 1, 1973 (n.p.: University of Santa Clara, n.d.).

- 63.8% of fuel used by automobiles (and personal light trucks) was for home-to-work and other urban personal trips, and amounted to 36.1% of all energy used for transportation.
- Only two-thirds of 1% of energy consumed by the transportation sector was accounted for by urban common carriers (bus and rail).
- 36.8% of energy consumed by transportation vehicles in 1972 was for intercity transport of passengers and freight, excluding water and pipeline transport.

Notwithstanding the increased emphasis on common-carrier usage in the urban environment, indicated by the opening of new rail transit systems in several cities in recent years and the augmentation and improvement of bus systems in many cities, the trends indicated by these statistics have changed relatively little since 1972. For example, California has experienced record use of gasoline since 1976, indicative of the continuing surge in the use of private automobiles. Indeed, recent data indicate that the cost of gasoline has risen very little in relation to the total cost of operating an automobile, despite the rise in gasoline prices since 1974.[4] This trend is probably the result of a general shift to more efficient cars, both by users and producers.

The energy watershed represented by the oil embargo, in addition to focusing attention on the severe economic impact of high petroleum prices on world economics, also brought home to many people the realization of this country's growing dependence on oil from foreign sources. Actually, the beginnings of energy problems in this country were evident as early as 1955, when the United States became a net importer of energy.[5] The past availability of cheap foreign petroleum spurred the widening gap between energy demand and domestic production; imports rose from 1.8 million barrels (0.3 million m^3)/day in 1960 (19% of consumption) to 3.4 million barrels (0.5 million m^3)/day in 1970 (24% of consumption). In the same year, domestic production peaked at 9.6 million barrels (1.5 million m^3)/day, and has been declining ever since. Thus, in 1975, after the lifting of the oil embargo and in the face of much higher prices, the United States imported 6 million barrels (1 million m^3)/day (37% of consumption). During several days in 1977, the rate of imports actually exceeded 50% of consumption, surely a bellwether of a still dimmer energy future for the United States during the next decade or more.

The issue of petroleum resources has recently been studied by several groups, each of which reached a different conclusion about the extent of future availability and pricing. On the one hand, the Central Intelligence Agency (CIA) predicts worldwide petroleum shortages as early as the mid-1980s, leading to significantly higher fuel prices.[6] According to the CIA, 1990 world oil prices will increase to $36 per barrel (current dollars, or $15.96 per barrel in 1973 dollars) unless conservation measures are instituted to stem increasing demand. An independent study "corroborated" these

---

[4]LOEBL, *Transportation Energy Conservation.*

[5]ATOMIC ENERGY COMMISSION, *The Nation's Energy Future: A Report to Richard M. Nixon, President of the United States,* WASH-1281, submitted by Dixy Lee Ray (Washington, D.C.: U.S. Government Printing Office, December 1, 1973).

[6]T. O'TOOL, "Demand for Oil Will Exceed Output by 1985, CIA Says," *Los Angeles Times,* April 16, 1977, p. 1, col. 5, and p. 5, col. 1.

forecasts, and indicated that the high prices are a direct result of a world level of demand that outstrips supplies. On the other hand, the report of a conference organized by the United Nations Institute for Training and Research (UNITAR) and the International Institute for Applied Systems Analysis concludes that oil and gas from conventional sources would last at least until the year 2030, from which it may be inferred that prices would also be lower than those anticipated by the CIA.[7] Indeed, the Federal Energy Administration has taken a more optimistic view than its sister agency, indicating a price range of $6.74 per barrel to $13.47 per barrel (1973 dollars) in a series of scenarios of the 1990 time period.[8] This last analysis has been updated in an as-yet-unpublished study, increasing the 1990 price range from $8.25 per barrel to $14.44 per barrel (1973 dollars). Finally, at the most optimistic end of the spectrum is an estimate that fossil-fuel availability in terms of proved reserves is enough to supply the forecasted growth of world economies for more than 100 years and, taking account of potential but as yet unproved fossil resources and neglecting new energy sources, provides enough energy for forecasted world growth well into the distant future.[9]

The consensus at the federal level, however, is increasingly toward the establishment of programs to reduce the use of energy. A goal of these programs is to institute measures that would have the effect of conserving energy without lessening the national standard of living, limiting the mobility of the population, or lowering even the perceived quality of the transportation system. This issue has been the subject of considerable study in the past several years, both in terms of the urban transportation arena, where the largest potential gains are to be made because the largest fraction of transportation energy is used there, and the intercity transportation arena, where there is heavy reliance on the air mode. Before examining the approach and results of two such studies, it is of interest to consider the energy efficiency of the vehicles comprising the transportation system in order to better understand the methodology adopted by energy policy analysts. The following operational factors are pertinent:

1. *Automobile mode.* In the urban arena, five-eighths of all auto trips are less than 8 km (5 mi) in length, although nearly half the vehicle-miles traveled are for trips exceeding 34 km (21 mi). A large fraction of urban trips experience continual stop-and-go driving, thus reducing the average fuel economy. Highway trips are substantially more energy-efficient, but an intercity trip usually consists of urban access and egress portions, as well as the nearly nonstop highway portion, thus lessening the overall fuel economy. The limitation of highway speeds to 88 km/h (55 mi/h) has helped in improving overall intercity trip fuel economy.

2. *Bus mode.* Most urban and intercity buses are powered by relatively efficient

[7]UNITED NATIONS INSTITUTE FOR TRAINING AND RESEARCH, *Future Supply of Nature-Made Oil and Gas*, Summary Report, conference sponsored by UNITAR and the International Institute for Applied Systems Analysis, Laxemburg, Austria, July 5–16, 1976 (New York: Pergamon Press, 1977).

[8]FEDERAL ENERGY ADMINISTRATION, *National Energy Outlook*, FEA-N-75/713 (Washington, D.C.: U.S. Government Printing Office, February 1976).

[9]HERMAN KAHN, WILLIAM BROWN, AND LEON MARTEL, *The Next 200 Years: A Scenario for America and the World* (New York: William Morrow and Company, Inc., 1976).

diesel engines. Such vehicles are capable of highway fuel-economy levels nearly equal to that of a large, heavy automobile. A bus optimized for intercity use thus achieves quite good overall fuel economy, considering its weight and payload capability. An urban bus experiences continual stop-and-start conditions and, with the automatic transmissions usually found in such vehicles, suffers a substantial loss in economy relative to its intercity brethren (on the order of triple the fuel used per mile). Buses must also comply with the 88 km/h (55 mi/h) speed limit.

3. *Rail mode.* Heavy rail rapid transit systems, usually electrically powered, are limited to low average speeds and are characterized by continual accelerations from a full stop. Such systems exhibit fuel-economy figures similar to that of an urban bus (accounting for conversion of the raw energy source to electric power). Intercity rail fuel-economy figures are lower, as a result of the much higher cruise speeds characteristic of such systems. There are also fewer accelerations from full-stop conditions, thus tending to mitigate the reduction in economy of such systems relative to their rapid transit counterparts. Intercity trains powered by diesel-electric locomotives achieve lower fuel-economy levels than do electrically powered trains, partially because of the much higher mass of the diesel locomotive.

4. *Air mode.* The fuel economy of gas-turbine-powered aircraft is highly dependent on stage length and circuity. Turbine engines burn fuel at high rates at sea level but are quite economical at cruise altitude, where lower air density combines with favorable cruise specific fuel consumption (particularly for fan-jets) to yield good levels of fuel economy. In short-haul arenas, where circuity sometimes reaches 50% and cruise represents a relatively small portion of the trip as well as often being conducted at lower altitudes, use of fuel at high average rates is common. For long-haul trips, where cruise at high altitude predominates and circuity is usually less than 10%, much lower average rates of fuel use are observed.

It should be clear from this discussion that energy efficiency cannot be assessed for a vehicle without knowing the environment in which it operates, and that the relative ranking of the modes in terms of energy efficiency could change as the environment changed. The energy efficiency of transportation vehicles is often defined in terms of the number of passenger-miles per gallon (passenger-kilometers per liter) of fuel used, or it may, for consistency, be converted to Btu per passenger-mile (joule per passenger-kilometer). In this form, differences among the various fuels used in transportation are eliminated by means of appropriate conversion factors, and direct modal comparisons are facilitated. The usual definition of energy efficiency carries with it a built-in implication of load factor, so that a mode is penalized if it carries low passenger loads. A definition permitting modal comparisons on the basis of technology alone would utilize "seat-miles" rather than "passenger-miles," in effect putting all the modes at 100% load factor.

Considerable data on modal energy efficiency have been published, but modal comparisons are difficult to make because the conditions of the computations are usually omitted.[10] In general, indications are that peak-hour rail transit is the most energy-efficient mode, with intercity rail, peak-hour transit bus, and intercity bus tied for second place. Peak-hour transit mode conditions often include large numbers of standees, but even off-peak conditions, for which reductions in energy efficiency of one-half to one-fourth are indicated, carry sizable loads relative to the average number of seats installed. On the other end of the energy-efficiency spectrum is the automobile used for commuting, which many analysts have found exhibits an energy efficiency well below that of commercial jet aircraft. The fully loaded automobile is, however, shown to be more efficient than aircraft in both urban and intercity arenas. A recent forecast of travel between New York and Washington, D.C., in the 1980 time period provides a consistent set of data for a single intercity arena, as seen in Table 28-1.

TABLE 28-1
Short-Haul Intercity Modal Energy Efficiencies

Mode	Energy Efficiency[a] (Btu/pass.-mi)[b]
Bus	700
Rail	1695
Auto	2415
Air	7130

[a]Port-to-port except auto, which is door-to-door.
[b]Metric conversion: 1 mi = 1.6 km; 1 Btu = 1055 J.

Source: S. Sokolsky, *Short-Haul Airline System Impact on Intercity Energy Use*, ATR-74(7307)-1 (El Segundo, Calif.: Aerospace Corporation, May 31, 1974).

For this analysis, load factors of the common-carrier modes were set at historical levels, while auto-occupancy levels were determined in a modal-split analysis to average 2.6 travelers. The air mode fares poorly because this arena is characterized by high circuity, relatively low-altitude cruise, and delays due to heavy traffic in both the New York and Washington, D.C., terminal areas. The relatively high level of energy used by the rail system is due to the assumption of a high-speed line roughly equivalent to the Japanese Tokaido Line. Buses and automobiles were assumed in this scenario to be restricted to 88 km/h (55 mi/h) on intercity highways.

Using the data cited above, one may gain some insight into the potentialities for energy savings in urban home-to-work trips, accounting for probably the largest single portion of transportation energy consumption. Consider an arena in which there are only bus and auto trips, and let

$$P_A = \text{total auto passengers per rush-hour trip}$$

$$P_B = \text{total bus passengers per rush-hour trip}$$

---

[10]LOEBL, *Transportation Energy Conservation*.

M_A = average distance of auto trip

M_B = average distance of bus trip

G_A = total auto fuel consumed

G_B = total bus fuel consumed

F = fraction of total travelers using bus

Therefore,

$$P_B = F(P_A + P_B)$$

or

$$F = \frac{1}{1 + \frac{(PM/G)_A}{(PM/G)_B} \times \left(\frac{M_B}{M_A}\right) \times \left(\frac{G_A}{G_B}\right)}$$

Assume that

$$\left(\frac{PM}{G}\right)_A = 0.1\left(\frac{PM}{G}\right)_B \qquad \text{(footnote 2)}$$

$$M_A = M_B$$

$$G_B = 0.0065G_A \qquad \text{(footnote 1, but assuming that half the energy is in home-to-work trips)}$$

Therefore,

$$F = 0.06$$

i.e., 6% of total home-to-work trips are taken by bus. If it is further assumed that a fleet of 2000 buses are used during rush hours, each carrying an average of 50 passengers, and that the average automobile carries 1.5 passengers, it is found that 1.1 million commuter automobiles are required. Thus, it becomes quite clear that, barring a major shift to transit, great savings in energy are possible only through increases in the number of occupants per automobile through carpooling and vanpooling.

Now, given the information cited on relative energy efficiencies of the urban and intercity modes, the analyst may examine various policies designed to reduce energy consumption (in effect, make the arena more energy efficient). In these studies, the air and automobile modes are often taken to be the energy-inefficient modes, and strategies are formulated with the intention of diverting urban travelers from the automobile mode to transit modes, or intercity travelers from air and automobile modes to rail and bus modes. It is necessary to perform modal-split analysis to aid in measuring the shifts in traveler mode choice, and to compute the individual modal energies to determine the savings achieved, if any. Energy savings are only one aspect of policy analysis, however, since such secondary effects as regulatory and institutional constraints, societal implications, economic impacts, and land-use considerations may play an important role in ranking the policy alternatives studied. Nevertheless, the following discussion will be restricted to energy implications alone.

The Federal Energy Administration, in carrying out its role as energy policy advisor to the White House, has undertaken several modal alternatives studies in an attempt at assessing the overall implications of mode-shift strategies. Separate studies were performed of urban and intercity arenas. One study of the urban arena was concerned with a detailed analysis of four cities serving as proxies for four categories of cities considered to be representative of all urbanized areas in the United States.[11] The four groupings were based on the reported percentage utilization of transit for home-to-work trips and on the presence, or lack of, an extensive rail transit system. Two hundred forty urbanized areas were examined, and the final selection consisted of three cities (Albuquerque, New Mexico; San Diego, California; and Baltimore, Maryland) with no rail transit and less than 4%, between 4% and 7%, and greater than 7%, respectively, transit modal split; and one city (Chicago, Illinois) with rail transit and over 14% transit modal split. From the results of the mode-shift analyses and an estimate of the percentage of the total urbanized population represented by each city, it was possible to infer the extent of national energy savings. An interesting and important finding of this study was that, while the automobile proved to be less energy efficient than transit, it was not nearly as inefficient as has been claimed in some circles. The study found that the ratio of transit to automobile energy efficiency varied between 1.5 and 5, depending upon the type of service offered and the city involved. Another source indicated peak-hour ratios between 16 and 28.[12]

Two types of mode shifting strategies were considered:

- Those which resulted in rail and bus transit time-line improvements and also postulated various transit fare-reduction schemes.
- Those which resulted in cost increases for driving private automobiles.

Some 25 separate strategies were examined, and the individual results used to structure four scenarios covering a broad range of possible actions, from minimal federal and local government intervention to the imposition of substantial cost penalties for automobile use. In essence, the first three scenarios each included transit improvements as well as increasing driving penalties, while the fourth included minimal transit improvements but severe driving penalties. The results tended to be somewhat city-dependent, with Baltimore and Chicago exhibiting different sensitivities than Albuquerque and San Diego. In the former pair, where there were large, distinctive central business districts and well-developed transit systems, both transit improvements and automobile disincentives proved relatively effective, although overall energy savings amounted to only 5 to 6%. In the latter pair, where the central business district and the transit system were both less well developed, and the road system less congested, maximum induced energy savings were under 1%. When these data were aggregated to the national level, it was found that the greatest energy savings occurred when maximum transit improvements were combined with maximum automobile disincen-

---

[11]R. H. PRATT ASSOCIATES, INC., *The Potential for Transit as an Energy Saving Option*, prepared for FEA (Kensington, Md.: R. H. Pratt Associates, Inc., March 1976). Now available as PB 263 087.
[12]LOEBL, *Transportation Energy Conservation*.

tives, and were estimated to be in the range 2 to 4 %. This was translated into maximum savings of 28 million barrels (4.5 million m³) of gasoline per year, or less than 2 days' worth of U.S. gasoline usage, but this level of savings required up to threefold increases in transit ridership.

The study concluded that it was difficult to conserve significant amounts of energy through actions designed simply to shift travelers from the automobile to transit. A major drawback of this analysis, however, was that automobile party sizes were not permitted to rise with increasing automobile disincentives, a scenario that might have shown significantly higher fuel savings than was observed by mode shifts alone.

The Federal Energy Administration's study to assess the effectiveness of mode-shift strategies in conserving energy in intercity transportation was concentrated in high-density, short-haul arenas.[13] Incentives were considered for inducing travelers to choose rail and bus modes, since these were deemed to be energy-efficient, and disincentives were applied to air and automobile modes, which were deemed to be relatively energy-inefficient. The selected strategies were analyzed singly and in various combinations, and several scenarios were developed with both rail and bus incentives and air and automobile disincentives. The latter were designed to simulate balanced transportation policy options, with the dual goals of reducing energy consumption while minimizing negative impacts on transportation system quality. In fact, a major concern of this study was the reaction of the traveling public to qualitative transportation system changes. For example, it is known that an attractive new transportation mode, offering competitive fares, will cause some travelers to shift from other modes. It may also induce a substantial increase in travel, so that the total number of travelers in the arena rises above that which would otherwise be anticipated on the basis of historical (or "normal") growth. Conversely, certain disincentives could induce a large reduction in travel demand, causing economic and other disruptions.

This situation leads to two considerations:

1. While a shift of travelers from energy-inefficient to energy-efficient modes is desirable, an increase in total travel may not be desirable, because it could result in an overall increase in energy consumption.
2. A significant reduction in travel resulting from imposition of an energy-conservation strategy may be an indication of too great a reduction in transportation system quality, even though it might be accompanied by a large reduction in energy use.

In order that these conditions could be properly examined and accounted for in the analysis, it was necessary to adopt a methodology for predicting increased (induced) or reduced demand occasioned by the imposition of a given strategy. The essence of the model developed to forecast total demand was its recognition of two major forces driving demand:

---

[13]AEROSPACE CORPORATION, *Mode Shift Strategies to Effect Energy Savings in Intercity Transportation*, prepared for FEA (El Segundo, Calif.: Aerospace Corporation, April 1977).

- Evolutionary, or slowly varying, forces caused by changes in demographic and socioeconomic conditions, differences in trip distance, and the appeal of potential alternative travel destinations.
- Policy, or rapidly varying, forces, mainly concerning transportation system quality as perceived by the traveler.

A formulation was designed that included a term for each one of the slowly and rapidly varying forces. The major new factor was that related to transportation system quality. In the methodology used, simulated travelers optimized their mode selection on the basis of a perceived trip-cost algorithm. Each traveler was assigned to that combination of local and intercity modes producing the minimum trip cost. Transportation system quality was then measured by an aggregation of the perceived trip cost of the large number of simulated travelers and therefore included the overall effects of fare, block time, service frequency, and access time and cost.

The analysis had to be performed in arenas where major transportation system changes had occurred so that a data base from which induced demand information could be extracted was available. The Northeast and California corridors, selected for this analysis, are similar only in that they both exhibit extremely high levels of travel demand; their respective travel characteristics are otherwise very different. In the Northeast, which has a high population density along the entire spinal route from Boston through New York City to Washington, D.C., the four major transportation modes (air, automobile, rail, bus) are well represented, although by no means equally. In California, where the high-density regions are concentrated around Los Angeles and San Francisco and the average travel distance is longer than in the Northeast, almost all intercity travel is by air and automobile. Of additional significance is the fact that, in the Northeast, a 320-km (200-mi) air trip from New York to Washington takes longer than a 560-km (350-mi) air trip from Los Angeles to San Francisco, owing to the high density of operations at the major Northeast corridor airports. Furthermore, the highly developed Northeast corridor rail system offers travelers in that arena an important alternative to air. This is not true in California, where rail and bus travel requires an entire working day for trips between Los Angeles and San Francisco.

The baseline scenarios (1982 and 1990 time frames) developed for this study assumed that mainly evolutionary changes would occur in the transportation system, including, however, improvements in fuel economy of the air and automobile modes. Significant results of the analysis of the 1982 baseline scenario are the following:

1. In each of the seven city pairs examined, air and automobile together carry the largest number of travelers and consume the largest percentage of energy. The total for the two arenas combined indicates that 89% of all travel is by these modes, accounting for 97% of energy consumed.
2. Air mode split is lower than air energy split, while the opposite is true for the other three modes. In the Northeast, for example, air carries 26% of travelers while consuming 60% of energy.

3. On the average, half of all travel is by automobile, although longer city pairs exhibit relatively lower automobile travel while shorter city pairs exhibit relatively higher automobile travel. Some short city pairs exhibit almost no air travel.

4. Bus and rail are the clear minority modes and are almost nonexistent (in terms of modal split) in the California corridor.

5. Annual demand is approximately 20% higher in the Northeast than in California. A third more energy is consumed in California than in the Northeast, however, due to the longer average distance and much higher demand for air.

6. Total energy consumed per passenger-mile (an arena energy index) is similar for the two corridors, despite the higher energy consumption and lower demand in California relative to the Northeast, because average travel distance is much higher in California, thereby raising the number of passenger-miles.

The following fuel conservation strategies were studied in the 1982 time frame:

- Air fare adjustments (lower as well as higher).
- Rail fare reductions.
- Rail and bus fare reductions.
- Rail block time reductions.
- Rail and bus block time reductions.
- Automobile cost increases.
- Automobile availability (proxy for fuel allocation).
- Air frequency reductions (proxy for fuel allocation).
- Combinations of the above.

The method of approach was to select a range of values for each parameter and analyze each strategy for each parameter value while holding all other parameters unchanged. In most cases, this meant only a single change from case to case. In one instance, however, changes were made in both rail and bus parameters, in an attempt to improve both modes relative to air and automobile. The combinations of strategies studied were synthesized from these results. Significant findings of the single parameter cases are as follows:

1. Three scenarios resulted in an increase in energy consumption relative to baseline. The air-fare-reduction scenario indicated a large shift to air, as well as a significant increase in total travel. The two automobile-fuel-rationing strategies (simulated in terms of reduced automobile availability) also caused shifts to air, particularly in California, where modal choices were more limited by high travel times. Increases in energy consumption resulted, even though there was less total travel. In all three scenarios, the overall result was a reduction in efficiency of the transportation system, as measured by the arena energy index.

2. Two other scenarios also indicated a lessening in transportation system energy efficiency, although total energy consumption decreased. In these, increases in

the cost of automobile fuel were assumed. This caused a major decrease in total travel, as drivers elected to cancel trips rather than shift to other modes. Thus, the result was a reduction in energy use, despite the fact that some previous automobile travelers now found air more attractive. The increased use of air was the major cause of the observed deterioration in arena energy efficiency.

3. Eight scenarios modeled improvements in rail and bus, both in terms of lower fares and lower block times, but proved disappointing in terms of energy savings. For the best case (rail and bus fare at only 20% of baseline) energy consumption dropped by just over 4%. In both the Northeast and California corridors, there were large increases in rail and bus travel, with California showing improvements by factors of four or more (which still left rail at a mode split of just over 2%). Few air travelers elected to make the shift, so that rail and bus travelers either came from the automobile mode or were new travelers (demand rises above baseline in each of these scenarios). Arena energy efficiency rises in these scenarios.

4. The air-fuel-allocation strategy produced significant energy savings. A 75% allocation is modeled by changing air load factors. In California, these approach 80%, while in the Northeast they are 73%. There is a minimal drop in demand in this scenario, because the increase in air mode waiting times (reflecting lower frequency of service) is small in the high-density arenas modeled for this study. No attempt was made, however, to model the case where some potential air passengers are unable to board an aircraft when they want to because some aircraft depart with 100% load factors. Some shifting to other modes occurs, but it is minimal, and the result is a significant improvement in arena energy index. A zero-air-fuel-allocation scenario was also studied in order to set a minimum on energy consumption by removing the most-energy-consumptive mode. Large energy savings are produced, but there is also a drastic drop in demand, reflecting the poor quality of the remaining transportation system as perceived by air travelers. A 40% improvement in the arena energy index was noted.

5. An increase in air fare was very effective in producing energy savings. The two scenarios studied indicated large improvements, but at the price of substantial deterioration in transportation system quality. In fact, while this strategy does result in some shifting to other modes, the major reason for the drop in energy consumption is related to loss of travelers from the total system, since the remaining modes do not satisfy their transportation needs.

A 1982 scenario combining a number of the parameters tested was defined in an attempt at meeting the goal of finding a strategy that would result in significant energy savings without causing a serious deterioration in transportation system quality. Rail and bus improvements did not appear effective, in light of the disbenefits (subsidy and high capital investment) associated with them. Reducing the attractiveness of the automobile resulted in only a slight improvement, but since it could be readily implemented by federal action and also impacted an energy-intensive mode, it was adopted as one element of the combined strategy. Finally, because both an air fare increase (leading to lower patronage) and an air fuel allocation (leading to higher load factors) were effective strategies for reducing fuel use, each was applied in this scenario.

It was found that more than one-third of the energy consumed in the 1982 baseline scenario could be saved by means of a strategy combining an air fare increase of 50% above the baseline level, a doubling of auto fuel costs, and a reduction in the availability of aviation fuel to 75% of the baseline level. Air and automobile demand dropped off markedly as a result of the increase in costs to the traveler, while air load factors increased because of the reduction in the amount of fuel allocated to the air system. The overall result was a lessening of 15% in total annual transportation demand, and a major improvement in overall arena energy efficiency.

The 1990 baseline scenario indicated a further increase in energy consumption relative to the 1982 baseline scenario, despite the fact that air and automobile modes became more energy-efficient in 1990 than they were in 1982. The observed increase in energy consumption was due to the projected rise in demand (nearly 23%), occurring mainly through population and income growth in the modeled cities. Income growth, in particular, is effective in shifting travelers to the higher-cost air mode, and accounts for the reduction in arena energy efficiency reflected by the energy index.

The approach taken in designing the 1990 scenario combining several energy saving measures was to pattern it after that selected for 1982, but with a goal of maintaining energy use at the 1982 combined scenario level. This was done by imposing an additional increase in air fare while making no further changes in either automobile fuel cost or air fuel allocation. It was found that the 1990 total travel demand level dropped to that of the 1982 baseline scenario. This, in turn, resulted in no further increase in energy consumption compared with the 1982 combined scenario. While a significant increase in total demand occurred between the 1982 and 1990 combined scenarios, demand for air is significantly reduced in 1990, as evidenced by a further improvement in arena energy index. In fact, the energy index is nearly as good as that for the no-air case examined in 1982. The apparent benefits in energy savings represented by this scenario were, however, achieved at the price of a substantial alteration in mode choice and total demand, and the resulting transportation system might not adequately serve the mobility requirements of the population or the economy at that time.

In summary, this study demonstrated the potential effectiveness of certain strategies designed to promote energy conservation in short-haul intercity transportation. In many instances, these strategies were accompanied by reductions in total travel demand, a direct result of the fact that the quality of the transportation system perceived by travelers was reduced. This correlation between energy conservation and total demand reduction is indicative of the hazards of attempting to reduce transportation energy consumption through the arbitrary adoption of federal policies. Since most policies that tend to reduce energy consumption will impinge on demand, it is crucial that the full impact of such policies on travelers, on the economic well-being of common carriers, and on the national economy are considered before implementation is undertaken.

It was noted in this study that a significant fraction of total energy consumption is associated with the air mode. Furthermore, it was seen that diversion of air demand to modes exhibiting higher time lines is difficult to achieve. Thus, policies which encourage higher airline load factors offer the greatest potential for achieving significant energy savings while minimizing adverse effects on total demand. This point is particularly significant at a time when deregulation of the air carrier industry is under active consideration, since a reduction in air fares (often cited as a principal reason for promoting deregulation) can have an adverse effect on transportation energy consumption, unless the resulting increased demand for air travel is offset by measures that ensure higher productivity of the airline system.

SELECTED BIBLIOGRAPHY

Many citations are no longer available from their original source. These citations are often available from the National Technical Information Service, U.S. Department of Commerce, 5285 Port Royal Road, Springfield, Va. 22161. We have verified the order numbers for many of these citations, and they are found at the end of the citation. Prices are available through NTIS at the address above.

AEROSPACE CORPORATION, *Mode Shift Strategies to Effect Energy Savings in Intercity Transportation*, prepared for FEA. El Segundo, Calif.: Aerospace Corporation, April 1977.

FEDERAL ENERGY ADMINISTRATION, *National Energy Outlook*, FEA-N-75/713. Washington, D.C.: U.S. Government Printing Office, February 1976.

LOEBL, A. S., AND OTHERS, *Transportation Energy Conservation Data Book*, ORN-5198 Special, prepared for the Energy Research and Development Administration. Oak Ridge, Tenn.: Oak Ridge National Laboratory, October 1976. Now available as ORNL-5198.

PRATT, R.H., ASSOCIATES, INC., *The Potential for Transit as an Energy Saving Option,* prepared for FEA. Kensington, Md.: R.H. Pratt Associates, Inc., March 1976. Now available as PB 263 087.

UNITED STATES DEPARTMENT OF TRANSPORTATION, *National Transportation Trends & Choices (to the Year 2000)*, issued by the Secretary of Transportation. Washington, D.C.: U.S. Government Printing Office, January 12, 1977.

Chapter 29

PROVIDING FOR THE
TRANSPORTATION DISADVANTAGED

ARTHUR SALTZMAN, *Director, Transportation Institute, North Carolina A & T State University* (*on leave at University of California, Irvine, 1976–1978*)

At some time in his or her life, virtually everyone has been transportation disadvantaged. The most common occurrence that restricts mobility is when a person temporarily does not have an automobile available to make a trip. Good examples are when the one family auto needs repairs and it is out of commission or when it is temporarily being used by another member of the family. This is usually a temporary situation and the simple solution to this mobility problem is to wait for the auto to return home or to get it repaired.

A more serious problem occurs when a person is unable to drive an automobile or is not sufficiently wealthy to purchase and maintain one. Persons in this group are generally defined as *transportation disadvantaged*.

Practically all of the research, legislation, and demonstration projects concerning persons who could be considered transportation disadvantaged have focused on three subsets of this group: elderly persons, persons who are physically or mentally handicapped, and poor persons. These groups are by no means small. Various estimates indicate that in the United States between 47 million[1] and 70 million[2] are either elderly, handicapped, or poor. This wide numerical range is indicative of the definitional problem inherent in trying to count the number of persons who are transportation disadvantaged. For example, the definition of who is elderly is somewhat arbitrary. Usually persons above 65 years are considered elderly by federal and state agencies, but some local social service programs are extended to all those over 55. A more

---

[1]TRANSPORTATION RESEARCH BOARD, *Transportation Requirements for the Handicapped, Elderly, and Economically Disadvantaged*, NCHRP Report 39 (Washington, D.C.: Transportation Research Board, 1976).

[2]LYNN SAHAJ, "Mobility for the Disadvantaged," *Transportation Topics for Consumers*, 1, no. 4 (November 1973), 1, 4, 5, and 7.

serious issue is that not all persons over 65 have severe mobility problems. Equating age with immobility is a gross oversimplification.

Defining all persons who are physically or mentally handicapped as transportation disadvantaged also poses some problems. First, there is no professional consensus as to who is handicapped. Second, not all handicapped persons have severe transportation problems.

The problem of classifying poor persons is one that has vexed every agency that has tried to deal with low-income individuals. What should be the measure of poverty? It is generally accepted that household income is a reasonable measure of wealth and the ability to purchase adequate transportation is directly dependent on income level. Since some low-income persons do not own a car, but use other auto-oriented solutions to journey to work, the term "transportation disadvantaged" may apply for some trip purposes but not others.

TRAVEL NEEDS

The introductory statement defined the transportation disadvantaged as those who have no access to an automobile. While this is a useful statement for general descriptive purposes, a more precise and analytical definition is necessary in considering this group's travel needs, as well as proposed solutions.[3]

More precision can be achieved by using a measure that can be compared among each of the disadvantaged groups. Thus, for describing the degree of disadvantageness, data on trip frequency per person will be the prime determinant. A *transportation-disadvantaged* person is defined as one who takes fewer trips per person per day than one who is not disadvantaged. This procedure is modified from one used by researchers on a detailed study on the urban transportation disadvantaged.[4] Some caution is necessary in using this measure. Although the relative degree of transportation disadvantage can be indicated by comparing trip rates among groups, it should not be assumed that the transportation disadvantaged "need" or have a "latent demand" for as many daily trips as the general population. This fallacy has been pointed out here to prevent planners from using this gap-analysis technique as a way of predicting, for example, the additional trips a group of elderly persons will take if an innovative transit system is provided. Even when provided with vastly improved transit, few among the disadvantaged will take the number of trips per day of the nondisadvantaged population.

Trip rates do, however, provide one measure of transportation disadvantagedness. In the following sections the trip rates, major travel problems, and characteristics of

---

[3]ARTHUR SALTZMAN AND GEORGE AMEDEE, "Serving the Transportation Disadvantaged with Demand-Responsive Transportation," in *Transit Planning*, Transportation Research Record 559 (Washington, D.C.: Transportation Research Board, 1976), pp. 1–10.

[4]ABT ASSOCIATES, INC., *Transportation Needs of the Urban Disadvantaged*, prepared for FHWA (Cambridge, Mass.: Abt Associates, Inc., March 1974).

each of the prime groups identified as being transportation disadvantaged will be discussed.

THE POOR

The poor are one of the most readily identifiable groups of the transportation-disadvantaged. They are, because of a lack of sufficient income, unable to meet their travel needs and desires conveniently. Low incomes result in low trip-making rates, as indicated in Table 29-1. The household trip rates for those with annual incomes over $4000 is much higher than for those with lower incomes. Many trips desired by the poor are not being made. Of course, the intervening variable between incomes and trip rates is auto ownership. Data from 1971 show that while only 20% of all U.S. households were without an auto, 46% of households with under $3000 annual earnings did not own an auto.[5] Furthermore, since many of the autos owned by the poor were old and not in good operating condition, the mere availability of an auto did not necessarily guarantee mobility. If income was held constant, members of carless households seemed to take about one trip less per person per day than did people from one-car households. The difference in the total number of trips was much greater, however, between zero- and one-car households than between one- and two-car households.[6]

TABLE 29-1
Household Travel in the United States

Annual Household Income (dollars)	Annual Trip Rate per Household	Annual Vehicle-miles[a] per Household	Average Trip Length (miles)
Under 4000	580	4708	8.1
4000-9999	1433	12,262	8.6
10,000-14,999	1949	17,497	9.0
15,000 and over	2526	24,410	9.7

[a]Metric conversion: 1 mi = 1.6 km.

Source: Beatrice T. Goley, Geraldine Brown, and Elizabeth Samson, *National Personal Transportation Survey, Report No. 7, Household Travel in the United States* (Washington, D.C.: Federal Highway Administration, December 1972), p. 6.

The location of carless individuals also had a considerable effect on available transportation alternatives and therefore on trip making. In the larger cities where public transportation is more available, the trip frequency gap between individuals with and without an auto is reduced. In these cities, transit is used for a much larger percentage of trips taken by carless individuals. This is quite different from what occurs in sparsely populated areas. In smaller cities, ridesharing and car borrowing by carless

---

[5]ROBERT E. PAASWELL, *Problems of the Carless in the United Kingdom and the United States*, prepared for the Organisation of Economic Co-Operation and Development (Buffalo, N.Y.: State University of New York at Buffalo, Department of Civil Engineering, August 1972).

[6]ABT ASSOCIATES, INC., *Transportation Needs.*

households exist to a much greater degree.[7] These informal methods, however, do not allow poor residents of smaller cities the mobility afforded by the better transit systems of the larger cities.

INNER-CITY POOR AND MINORITIES

There are special transportation problems associated with the poor and minorities, including Blacks, Puerto Ricans, Chicanos, Orientals, and American Indians, who tend to live in inner cities of major metropolitan areas.

The lack of adequate areawide coverage by many inner-city public transit systems has been, in part, responsible for the lack of accessibility to jobs and to very critical services. More specifically, the decentralization of jobs and services as a result of suburban growth has not been followed by the development of a convenient transit system that inner-city residents can use to reach desired work and nonwork destinations outside the city core.[8] The section of this chapter on the federal role will describe some attempts that have been made to provide the link between jobs and areas of high unemployment.

Even when income is held constant, minority-group members across the nation take from 0.4 to 0.9 fewer nonwork trips per person per day than do whites.[9] This relationship between race and transportation may be partially caused by the historical pattern of racial housing segregation and may also depend on different cultural attitudes toward transit. Minorities are most disadvantaged, when compared with whites, in their trip rates to social/recreational activities and in the frequency with which they shop.

Mode choice data are also revealing. When comparing the percentage of public transportation used by both inner-city whites and minorities, it was found that minorities were more dependent on public transportation than whites. This relationship was true within each income group of inner-city residents. Finally, many of the trips made by the minorities and the poor are walking trips, partly because of the dense neighborhoods in which many of them live. This larger number of walking trips, however, does not change the fact that the poor and minorities make considerably fewer trips than higher-income and white persons.[10]

THE ELDERLY

One group of the transportation disadvantaged which has received considerable attention from researchers in recent years has been the elderly of our society. They are a significant portion of our population and will continue to increase as a proportion of

[7]ALICE E. KIDDER AND ARTHUR SALTZMAN, "Mode Choice Among Autoless Workers in Auto-Oriented Cities," in *Proceedings: International Conference on Transportation*, Bruges, Belgium, Transportation Research Forum (Oxford, Ind.: The Richard B. Cross Company, June 1973), pp. 647–54.

[8]CHARLES B. NOTESS, "Shopping and Work Trips in the Black Ghetto, "in *Proceedings of the American Society of Civil Engineers, Journal of the Urban Planning and Development Division*, 98, no. UP1 (July, 1972), 71–83.

[9]ABT ASSOCIATES, INC., *Transportation Needs*.

[10]Ibid.

our total population. In 1970, there were 20 million Americans over age 65, of which about 65% lived in urban or suburban areas. It is estimated that there will be 28 million by the year 2000.[11]

There are two major factors associated with the elderly's transportation problems. The first is that many have limited income and are not able to pay for automobile or taxi expenses. The second factor relates to the physical health of the elderly when it is an obstacle in operating an automobile, as well as in riding conventional transit systems. Auditory and visual problems of many senior citizens not only considerably reduce their ability to safely operate an automobile, but also impair their utilization of most transit systems. Those elderly who are less agile are also inhibited in using conventional public transportation by the design-related problems such as high entrance steps, overhead grips, and fast-acting doors. In addition, other problems occur when too many transfers are required and long waits are necessary at stops. An elderly person who is subjected to these discomforts and inconveniences is discouraged from using public transportation.

Some of the effects of not being able to afford an auto and the barriers to using public transit are evident in Table 29-2. The average number of trips per person per day, by income, age, and trip purposes, are given for SMSA (standard metropolitan statistical area) residents. Because of the aforementioned factors, the trip-making rate for the elderly is considerably lower than that of the nonelderly within each income group. The effect of income on trip-making rates for the elderly is also shown in Table 29-2. As income increases, the elderly take more trips for both work and nonwork purposes.

Mode choice data indicate that although the elderly are described as "captive riders," they do not use transit for a large number of their trips. In fact, they tend to use transit for a smaller proportion of their total trips than the nonelderly, according to nationwide data on the elderly within SMSAs.[12]

No description of the transportation characteristics of the elderly would be complete without some mention of the importance of transportation used solely as an activity for many of the elderly. "Transportation for the elderly needs to be provided not purely for getting from 'here to there' but also as an 'antidote' for the entire process of aging."[13]

HANDICAPPED PERSONS

The major transportation problem of the handicapped, like that of the elderly, lies in their inability to find a convenient mode of transportation which does not cause them serious discomforts. The U.S. Department of Transportation has estimated the

[11]U.S. DEPARTMENT OF TRANSPORTATION, OFFICE OF THE ASSISTANT SECRETARY FOR POLICY AND INTERNATIONAL AFFAIRS, *1972 National Transportation Report: Present Status–Future Alternatives* (Washington, D.C.: U.S. Government Printing Office, July 1972).

[12]ABT ASSOCIATES, INC., *Transportation Needs.*

[13]ADMINISTRATION ON AGING, OFFICE OF HUMAN DEVELOPMENT, U.S. DEPARTMENT OF HEALTH, EDUCATION, AND WELFARE, *Transportation for the Elderly: The State of the Art*, prepared by Institute of Public Administration (Washington, D.C.: U.S. Government Printing Office, January 1975), p. 13. Now available as HRP-0015165.

TABLE 29-2
Average Number of Trips per Person per Day by Income, Age,
and Trip Purpose for SMSA Residents[a]

Trip Purpose	Poverty $0-$4000		Low $4000-$6000		Middle $6000-$10,000		High $10,000+	
	Elderly	Nonelderly	Elderly	Nonelderly	Elderly	Nonelderly	Elderly	Nonelderly
Work	0.11	0.38	0.19	0.48	0.39	0.56	0.37	0.59
Nonwork	1.39	1.69	1.44	1.77	2.04	2.18	1.45	2.26
Total	1.50	2.07	1.63	2.25	2.43	2.74	1.82	2.85

[a]Sample size: 5187 persons.

Source: Adapted from *Nationwide Personal Transportation Survey, 1969-1970*, as reported by Abt Associates, Inc., *Transportation Needs of the Urban Disadvantaged*, prepared for FHWA (Cambridge, Mass.: Abt Associates, Inc., March 1974).

total of handicapped persons in the United States in 1970 who could not use transit or who used transit with difficulty.[14] A list of the dysfunctions of this transportation-handicapped group is shown in Table 29-3. The first interesting fact that is apparent from this table is that 53% of the handicapped were elderly persons. As discussed in the previous section, the problems of the elderly in driving and riding conventional modes of transportation are, to a large extent, associated with physical impairment.

TABLE 29-3
National Numbers of Handicapped with Transportation Dysfunctions[a]

Handicap Class	Elderly Handicapped	Nonelderly Handicapped	Total Handicapped
Noninstitutionalized chronic conditions			
Visually impaired	1,460,000	510,000	1,970,000
Deaf	140,000	190,000	330,000
Uses wheelchair	230,000	200,000	430,000
Uses walker	350,000	60,000	410,000
Uses other special aids	2,290,000	3,180,000	5,470,000
Other mobility limitations	1,540,000	1,770,000	3,310,000
Acute conditions	90,000	400,000	490,000
Institutionalized	930,000	30,000	960,000
Total	7,030,000	6,340,000	13,370,000

70 estimate of those who cannot use transit, or use transit only with difficulty.
Sources: HEW National Center for Health Statistics 1960 and 1970 Census of Population in *The Handicapped and erly Market for Urban Mass Transit* prepared by the Transportation Systems Center for UMTA (Cambridge, Mass.: nsportation Systems Center, October 1973). Now available as PB 224 821.

Crain and Associates, in a review of other recent reports, classify the transportation handicapped as persons with physical or mental conditions that reduce their ability to use transit or prevent them from using it. They review the inaccuracies of previous estimates (including the one in Table 29-3) and conclude that in 1975 there were approximately 4.8 million transportation handicapped persons in the U.S.[15] Whatever their total number, the difficulty experienced by the transportation handicapped in getting to and from the transit system, boarding the vehicles, and safely riding mean that they only ride public transit when absolutely necessary.[16] Their attempts to use inadequate public transit often result in both physical endangerment and psychological frustrations. The travel patterns of the handicapped, because of some of these impediments, result in a large gap between the trip frequency of the

---

[14]TRANSPORTATION SYSTEMS CENTER, *The Handicapped and Elderly Market for Urban Mass Transit*, prepared for UMTA (Cambridge, Mass.: Transportation Systems Center, October 1973). Now available as PB 224 821.

[15]CRAIN AND ASSOCIATES, eds., *Transportation Problems of the Transportation Handicapped, Volume I: The Transportation Handicapped Population, Definitions and Counts*, prepared for UMTA (Washington, D.C.: Urban Mass Transportation Administration, August 1976). Now available as PB 258 579.

[16]U.S. DEPARTMENT OF TRANSPORTATION, *1972 National Transportation Report.*

handicapped and that of the nonhandicapped. Data from a study in Boston showed that the handicapped took 1.13 trips/day compared to an average of 2.23 trips/day by the general population.[17]

Finally, modal split data reveal that a significant number of trips by the handicapped were taken by taxi. The handicapped, for example, took 15% of their trips by taxi compared with 2% by the nonhandicapped. Although the handicapped are generally less able to afford the taxi fare, they have need for door-to-door taxi service.[18]

CONVENTIONAL TRANSIT AS A SOLUTION

Adequate public transportation would seem to be one solution for the transportation disadvantaged. In fact, the literature often refers to these groups as "captive riders or transit dependents." But there are many indications that current transit systems are quite far from being adequate for that purpose. Both rail rapid transit lines and fixed-route bus operations do offer a solution to some transportation demands, but the services they offer are not sufficient to serve all the needs of those with mobility problems. Barriers to the use of conventional mass transit include some which are physical and others which are operational. For example, the difficulty a handicapped person would have in negotiating a high step on a bus is a physical barrier; whereas insufficient route coverage resulting in long walks to bus stops would be an operational barrier for many of the elderly. In addition to these physical and operational factors are psychological barriers, such as fear of assault, which can affect any potential rider. Finally, there is the fare, which can be an economic barrier to the poor.

Perhaps the overriding barrier in conventional public transportation is that it does not take people to where they want to go. Far from being ubiquitous, transit is still usually radially oriented and does not provide good service unless the destination or origin of travel is the central business district (CBD). With respect to convenience, conventional transit cannot provide door-to-door service.

Moreover, in the past, the transit industry has paid very little attention to the mobility needs of the transportation disadvantaged. It is extremely costly to provide the specialized transportation needed by this group. In an era of declining patronage, most operators have been more concerned with cutting costs than with expanding services for any special subgroups. Thus, until recently, providing special services for elderly, handicapped, and poor persons has been a low-priority item for transit operators.[19]

---

[17]ABT ASSOCIATES, INC., *Travel Barriers: Transportation Needs of the Handicapped*, prepared for U.S. DOT, Office of Economic and Systems Analysis (Cambridge, Mass.: Abt Associates, Inc., 1969). Now available as PB 187 327.

[18]Ibid.

[19]ALICE E. KIDDER AND GEORGE AMEDEE, *Assuming Responsibility for Mobility of Elderly and Handicapped: The Roles of Transit Properties, Transit Planners, and Social Service Agencies in Small Cities* (Greensboro, N.C.: North Carolina A & T State University, 1976). Now available as PB 267 231.

There have been a few isolated cases of innovation by the transit operator, but this has usually occurred when general services were being substantially improved as a result of a newly implemented dial-a-ride system, as for example in Rochester, New York. At other times, innovation has occurred when a public planning agency has made and implemented a specific policy of serving elderly and handicapped persons. For example, the Regional Transportation District in Denver decided to provide a special service for elderly and handicapped persons and implemented an effective, but rather costly, system. Several others have followed Denver's commitment to a substantial effort to serve the transportation disadvantaged.

Transit operators have been slow to respond to a clear congressional mandate to provide improved transit to elderly and handicapped groups. Although legislation designed to enhance the mobility of elderly and handicapped persons was enacted in the early 1970s, many representatives of disadvantaged groups felt that there had been few or no changes because of these laws. Thus, during 1974–1975, a number of court cases were initiated to force the federal Department of Transportation's Urban Mass Transportation Administration (UMTA) to implement the legislation that was passed by Congress. In Baltimore, for example, the city was enjoined from purchasing a large number of vehicles for its public transit system because they were not designed to accept a person in a wheelchair. UMTA finally agreed to provide a set of rules governing the provision of transit for elderly and handicapped persons.

The planning requirements promulgated by UMTA in the *Federal Register* of April 30, 1976, indicate that special attention must be given to the transportation needs of elderly and handicapped persons.[20] Projects designed to benefit elderly and handicapped persons are required from each urban area as a condition for receiving UMTA capital or operating assistance. The transportation improvement programs (TIPs) submitted to UMTA after September 30, 1976, must include these projects as part of the program's annual elements.

These rules give each area flexibility in the way they will comply. An area can opt for any one of three suggested minimum levels of effort or they may propose their own technique for serving the elderly, nonambulatory (those in wheelchairs), and semiambulatory persons. The three alternative minimum levels of effort are[21]:

1. 5% of Section 5 formula funds allocated to an urban area must be used to serve these groups. "Special efforts" in planning and implementing projects specifically designed for these groups are required.
2. All buses bought must be wheelchair-accessible until at least one-half of the fleet is accessible, or a substitute service that would result in comparable coverage and service must be provided.
3. A system must be available that would ensure that at least 10 round trips per week would be provided if requested for every nonambulatory or semiambulatory person in the urban area.

---

[20]URBAN MASS TRANSPORTATION ADMINISTRATION AND FEDERAL HIGHWAY ADMINISTRATION, "Transportation for Elderly and Handicapped Persons," *Federal Register*, 41, no. 85 (April 30, 1976), 18234.
[21]Ibid.

Prior to the rules, there was much public debate on the issue of "accessibility vs. mobility." That is, should every vehicle in transit service be accessible to all handicapped persons, including those in wheelchairs, or is it sufficient that some mobility is provided to elderly and handicapped persons by a specialized service? These UMTA rules have allowed each urban area to decide for themselves whether they want to provide an accessible transit system (at least half-accessible anyhow) or decide on solutions that focus on mobility.

Other legislation and rulings, however, seem to mandate that all vehicles purchased with federal funds will be accessible. This is required under Section 504 of the Rehabilitation Act of 1973 which provides that transportation facilities funded by federal programs shall be totally accessible to those in wheelchairs. A separate ruling by the Secretary of Transportation stipulates that all buses purchased with UMTA support after September 30, 1979, will include design features of "Transbus" which effectively make them fully accessible.

One other provision of the UMTA regulations requires a reduced-fare program. It specifies that, during off-peak hours, transit fares for elderly and handicapped persons shall be no more than one-half of the regular fare. Such reduced-fare programs had already been instituted in over 100 communities.[22] These existing reduced-fare programs have removed some economic barriers and resulted in increased ridership among the elderly.[23] However, they provide little relief for persons whose barriers are not economic.

FEDERAL ROLE

The UMTA regulations previously discussed were in response to the problems that the transportation disadvantaged face in using conventional transit. The proposed solutions do not focus on any specific types of trips, such as for shopping, working, or recreation. They were designed to raise the level of mobility for all types of trips for the target groups.

Prior to the promulgation of these regulations, many other federal agencies, including UMTA, had provided funds for various programmatic efforts to solve specific transportation problems of poor, elderly, and handicapped persons. These earlier efforts of the late 1960s were demonstration programs designed to provide prototype solutions that other areas could adopt. However, more recently, direct transportation subsidies from diverse social welfare, health, employment, and education programs have provided the impetus for a new type of paratransit service which has been implemented in virtually every area of the country. These human-services-agency[24]

---

[22]STEPHEN M. GOLANT, "Housing and Transportation Problems of the Urban Elderly, "in *Urban Policy-making and Metropolitan Dynamics: A Comparative Geographical Analysis*, ed. John S. Adams (Cambridge, Mass.: Ballinger Publishing Company, 1976).

[23]EDWARD K. MORLOK, WALTER M. KULASH, AND HUGO L. VANDERSYPEN, *The Effect of Reduced Fare Plans for the Elderly on Transit System Routes* (Evanston, Ill.: Northwestern University Transportation Center, 1971). Now available as PB 204 058.

[24]Human services include employment, health care, social services, and educational assistance programs.

transit operations are designed to serve specific travel needs of agency clients, as opposed to their general transportation problems.

In the following sections these programmatic efforts will be traced. The major federal responses to the special trip needs of the transportation disadvantaged will be discussed followed by a review of how special human-services-agency transit systems and conventional transit operators are sorting out their respective roles in providing better mobility for the transportation disadvantaged.

THE POOR

The first use of federal funds for the transportation disadvantaged occurred in the mid-1960s when the Department of Housing and Urban Development (HUD) initiated a series of demonstration projects that were aimed at solving some of the transportation problems of the poor.[25] These projects were in response to the national prominence that had come to the issue of the immobility of the poor with the 1965 racial riots in the Watts area of Los Angeles. Inadequate transportation to employment centers had been identified by the federally established McCone Commission as a factor leading to high unemployment rates in Watts.[26]

In response to these conditions, federally supported demonstration projects were launched in riot-prone major metropolitan areas. Buses were used to provide daily door-to-door service from workers' homes to outlying suburban jobs. These services had a number of demand-responsive characteristics. Routes were usually changed daily or weekly to accommodate new clients. Pickups were made at the clients' doors or very close by, and clients were provided direct access to their place of employment. Some of these projects improved employment access enormously, more than justifying the large initial investment in the operation by the consequent increase in lifetime earnings of new job holders. Others suffered from waning ridership and were not continued beyond the demonstration phase.

In contrast to these employment facilitation efforts, the poor have been the focus of a number of other federally funded demand-responsive transportation services primarily planned for non-work-related trips. Model Cities' agencies in Columbus, Ohio; Detroit and Grand Rapids, Michigan; and Buffalo, New York, have experimented with dial-a-ride services that allow residents better access to health and social service agencies.[27] In Grand Rapids, for example, a special supplement to the fixed-route system provided increased mobility to the poor and elderly. A demonstration grant to the Grand Rapids Transit Authority from UMTA funded a demand-responsive transportation system within the Model Cities' neighborhood. Five small buses were used to provide service to or from anywhere in the city, as long as one end of the trip was in the Model Cities' neighborhood.[28]

---

[25]KIDDER AND SALTZMAN, "Mode Choice," pp. 647–54.

[26]California Governor's Commission on the Los Angeles Riots, chr. John M. McCone, *Violence in the City—An End or a Beginning*, a report for submission to Governor Edmund T. Brown (Los Angeles: Jeffries Banknote Co., December 2, 1965).

[27]NOTESS, "Shopping and Work Trips," pp. 71–83.

[28]SAHAJ, "Mobility for the Disadvantaged," pp. 1, 4, 5, and 7.

The Office of Economic Opportunity (OEO) was a prime mover behind efforts to provide demand-responsive transportation to those in rural areas. Public transportation prototype systems have been started in rural areas with demonstration grants from OEO. In their effort to help people out of the poverty cycle, local OEO-funded community action agencies (CAAs) had consistently identified transportation as a major problem area. In response to these needs, by 1972 there had been over 50 rural transportation projects funded by OEO.[29] The dispersed nature of the trips and lack of high population densities have dictated that few of these systems have had conventional fixed routes or schedules. They have been primarily human services delivery systems that provide door-to-door service for agency clients.

ELDERLY AND HANDICAPPED

UMTA and the Department of Health, Education, and Welfare's Administration on Aging (AOA) are two federal agencies that have been very active in developing transportation that serves the elderly and handicapped.

UMTA has funded a number of demonstrations that have included demand-responsive transportation for the elderly and handicapped. Under their service and methods demonstration program, UMTA is experimenting with innovative transportation services for those with mobility constraints.

A project in the lower Naugatuck Valley, Connecticut, used a demand-responsive component to provide transportation services to clients of health and social service agencies.[30] Telephone requests for the door-to-door demand service were made in advance and served by van-type vehicles, most of which were modified to meet the special needs of the elderly and handicapped. The Valley Transit District also offered other specialized transportation services, including charters available to the local agencies. The project also featured a new concept in automated fare collection which used credit cards instead of cash and allowed agencies to pay all or part of a client's trip through a billing feature called FAIRSHARE.

Financial support of the project was also received from AOA. These additional funds have been used to help the agencies pay for client transportation. UMTA and AOA officials are hopeful that the consolidation of social- and health-service-agency transportation needs and the flexible service developed in this demonstration will be a model for serving the transportation needs of many small to medium-size communities.[31]

A major program to provide vehicles for human-services-agency transportation is administered by UMTA. Section 16(b)(2) of the Urban Mass Transportation Act

---

[29]IRA KAY, "Transportation Problems of the Older American in Rural Areas," in *Rural Development: 1971—A Year of Listening and Watching the Development of the Growing Consensus That Something Must Be Done for the People of the American Countryside*, 92nd Congress, 2nd Session, Committee Print, U.S. Senate Committee on Agriculture and Forestry, May 31, 1972 (Washington, D.C.: U.S. Government Printing Office, 1972), pp. 429–46.

[30]RRC INTERNATIONAL, INC., *Valley Transit District: Elderly/Handicapped Transportation*, prepared for Lower Naugatuck Valley Community Council, Ansonia, Conn. (Latham, N.Y.: RRC International, Inc., July 1974). Now available as HRP-0012180 and 0012181.

[31]TRANSPORTATION RESEARCH BOARD, *Transportation Requirements*.

provides for capital assistance grants to private nonprofit agencies who will purchase vehicles to serve the special needs of elderly and handicapped persons. This program provided $21 million in grants in fiscal year 1975 which were used to purchase over 2000 vehicles.

AOA. The Administration on Aging (AOA) of the Department of Health, Education, and Welfare (HEW) was authorized to conduct transportation research and demonstration programs under Title III and Title VII of the Older Americans Act.

One of the first pilot projects funded by AOA was the YMCA Senior Citizens Mobile Service in Chicago, which was funded from September 1966 through November 1969. Two seven-passenger vans provided door-to-door service to participating elderly persons on request. Access to health centers, welfare agencies, supermarkets, senior centers, and libraries were provided to senior citizens who called in their requests for transportation one day in advance. The project has shown that isolated persons living in a large city would use a free demand-responsive service to get where they needed and wanted to go.[32]

This is just one of some 920 projects involving the provision of transportation for the elderly that was enumerated by a research project conducted for the AOA.[33] All of this activity is taking place at the local and state government levels and a majority of the projects received funds under Titles III and VII of the Older Americans Act and Title VI of the Social Security Act.

PROVISION OF SPECIAL SERVICES

HUMAN SERVICES AGENCY RESPONSE

As indicated previously, a plethora of social service and health agencies have responded to the lack of adequate transit for their clients by initiating their own transit systems. These systems range in size from single vehicles that provide monthly trips, to large 300-vehicle statewide-coordinated systems such as the Delaware Authority for Special Transportation. Substantial amounts of public funds are being spent on these systems. In 1976, it was conservatively estimated that in the United States over $500 million annually was expended in providing special transit services for all human services agencies and that an annual growth rate of 13 to 18% was expected until 1978 and an 8% annual growth thereafter.[34] Inventories taken by many planning agencies have confirmed the large number of agencies that provide transportation for their clients. For example, among the 1900 human services agencies in the San Francisco

---

[32]JOHN H. BELL, "Senior Citizens Mobile Service," in *Transportation and Aging: Selected Issues*, based on proceedings of the Interdisciplinary Workshop on Transportation and Aging, May 24–26, 1970, eds. Edmund J. Cantilli and June L. Shmelzer (Washington, D.C.: Government Printing Office, 1971), pp. 138–50. Now available as HRP-001424.

[33]ADMINISTRATION ON AGING, *Transportation for the Elderly*.

[34]ARTHUR SALTZMAN, "Special Service Transportation Systems Which Serve the Transportation Disadvantaged: Current Operations and Future Projections" (unpublished report prepared for Alan M. Voorhees and Associates, Inc., 1976).

Bay area enumerated by Crain,[35] approximately half of them owned their own vehicles or purchased transportation services for their clients.

It is not surprising that these health and social service agencies have opted for nonconventional, paratransit operations. These paratransit options are usually more demand-responsive than the conventional fixed-route, fixed-schedule transit. Vehicles are dispatched only when some demand has been established. Operations are personalized, and frequently provide door-to-door service in small vehicles.

These systems were not initiated by transportation planners. Agency directors who perceived mobility needs among many of their clients decided to start systems to handle these needs. This is a significant fact and should not be overlooked in the future planning of transit for the transportation disadvantaged. The persons who developed these systems usually had no technical expertise in transit per se. They simply recognized the problem and went at it the best way they knew how. Fortunately, few of them were aware of the "urban transportation planning process" and did not use sophisticated models to develop their systems. Using a "seat of the pants" approach, they identified the location of their clients and tried to provide door-to-door service to meet their most critical transportation needs.

Often government-surplus vehicles were acquired and elderly or unemployed drivers were hired to drive them. Sometimes repairs were done by local garages or county maintenance departments, and when social service agency vehicles did not have priority, a reliable pattern of vehicle availability was not assured. In most cases a preventive maintenance schedule did not exist. It is very easy to be critical of the poor planning and management exhibited by most of these systems. They are fragmented and relatively costly on a per passenger-trip basis. But these operations have provided door-to-door services that have had significant positive impact on their passengers.

COORDINATING FOR BETTER EFFECTIVENESS AND EFFICIENCY

The way to have the most profound impact on transportation for clients of human services agencies is to find ways to more efficiently utilize the existing equipment and manpower that is used to provide paratransit services. Everyone seems to agree that having small uncoordinated systems is inefficient, but there is little unanimity on the best solution.

Consolidation of all special services within a given area has been a suggested solution and, in fact, is being attempted in some areas. But why doesn't public policy move toward capturing the advantages of large-scale operation and what should be done to facilitate this type of coordination? Unfortunately, the institutional impediments to changing restrictive regulations which constrain coordination are found at every level of government, starting with laws enacted by Congress which must ultimately be implemented by local agencies.

Laws that affect public transportation are developed by many different congressional committees. These various pieces of legislation have not, in the past, been

---

[35]John L. Crain, Sydwell D. Flynn, and Fred C. Stoffel, *Para-Transit Survey, Component of MTC Special Transit Service Needs Study*, prepared for the Metropolitan Transportation Commission, Berkeley, Calif., and UMTA (n.p.: Crain & Associates, April 1974).

coordinated to see that they do not create overlapping programs, or to ensure that they allow for sufficient flexibility so that some consolidation is possible. Of course, this is not unique to the area of transportation. The interfacing of many federal social service programs is made difficult by the uncoordinated nature of the congressional committee structure.

An interagency task force of the Southern Federal Regional Council has studied human services agency transportation. Suanne Brooks of this task force has documented the administrative jungle created by the many separate sources of federal funds for providing transportation service. She indicated that:

> The Departments of Health, Education, and Welfare, Labor, Transportation, and the U.S. Office of Economic Opportunity fund no less than fifty (50) human services categorical project and formula grant programs that authorize the provision of a payment for transportation services. . . . One fact remains; the person . . . must be "categorically" eligible for the program(s) to obtain the transportation service and eligibility restrictions (Federal and State imposed) are tedious at best. Many needful people who are categorically ineligible go unserved as a result.[36]

The same problem is found among various state-sponsored special transportation services, that is, too many uncoordinated, restricted sources of funds for transportation programs. Suggested improvements for state governments, however, need not stop with better coordination. In addition to enacting better legislation and implementing coordinated programs, states can establish umbrella agencies that are empowered to consolidate disparate sources of funds. Probably the best example of a state-created agency which was established to coordinate specialized transportation service was established in Delaware. The Delaware Authority for Specialized Transportation (DAST) embodied a successful approach for funding and operating specialized transportation services on a statewide basis. In essence, the legislature created an authority that could provide transportation services to a wide range of client agencies under purchase-of-service contracts.

Local county governments, the United Fund of Delaware, and numerous private agencies contracted with DAST to provide transportation services for their clients. In almost every case, the cost to the agency was less than was previously the case. This may not be a feasible solution in every area, but it is certainly indicative of the strong role a state agency can play in coordinating specialized transportation services.

Local efforts at coordination are also helpful in reducing costs and providing better services. For example, the 40 service providers in Chattanooga, Tennessee, have managed to substantially lower their cost per client-mile by pooling their resources into a single radio-dispatched pickup system which was operated by a coordinating agency.[37] Whereas before consolidation it cost an average of $2.93 per passenger-mile,

---

[36]Suanne Brooks, "Funding Specialized Transportation Systems: Policies and Problems," in *Toward a Unification of National and State Policy (and Action) on the Transportation Disadvantaged, Part II: Rural Perspectives*, Proceedings of the Fourth Annual Conference on the Transportation Disadvantaged, December 3, 4, 5, 1974, eds. William G. Bell and William T. Olsen (Tallahassee, Fla.: Florida State University, n.d.), p. 44. Later research produced 62 sources.

[37]Dolli Cutler, "Interagency Cooperation—A Federal Perspective," in *Proceedings of the First National Conference on Rural Public Transportation*, ed. Douglas J. McKelvey, prepared for U.S. DOT (Greensboro, N.C.: North Carolina A & T State University, Transportation Institute, October 27, 1976), pp. 103–12. Now available as PB 262 808.

the single provider technique offered an improved service at a cost of \$0.61 per passenger-mile.

But there are still many agencies who would rather continue to operate their own vehicles. They fear the loss of control and potential loss of accountability to their various funding agencies. Local agencies are loath to give up the vehicles, which provide a visible indication that they are using their public funds to provide services to the community. For these reasons, efforts at consolidation of vehicles are going to be less than 100% effective. However, there is a clear trend toward larger systems which are operated by an entity created especially to provide special transportation services for human services agencies.

CONVENTIONAL TRANSIT OPERATORS AS SPECIAL SERVICE PROVIDERS

Whether it is advisable or possible for the transit operator to provide special services to human-services-agency clients is a subject being discussed by many transportation planning agencies. Because of the previously referenced federal legislation, every transit operator will be making some special efforts to accommodate general travel needs of the elderly and handicapped population. But many planners want the local mass transit operator to assume total responsibility for providing special transit services for human-services-agency clients. They most often suggest that a subsidiary or special division would be operated by the transit system which would be devoted to the provision of special services. It is argued that the transit operators have the operating experience and capability to provide efficient services. A major concern among social service agencies who would be contracting for the services is the responsiveness of the transit operator to their needs. Studies by Kidder and Amedee[38] and Crain et al.,[39] note that most agencies doubt that the transit operator could ever be adequately responsive or sensitive to their clients.

The transit operators in general have not been aggressively pursuing the special-service market. As with the general services for the elderly and handicapped, they point out that these special services are extremely expensive to provide when compared with conventional transit on a per passenger-trip basis. Even with the recent influx of large amounts of federal funds, the transit industry still has financial woes. Escalating operating expenses make operators unwilling to assume additional responsibilities unless they receive additional funds to completely pay for the new services.

An additional deterrent to the provision of special services by the transit operator is their high labor cost. Transit bus drivers earn substantially more per hour than drivers of special-service vehicles. If the transit operator provided these services, then it is likely that drivers of the special-service vehicles would be elevated to higher transit wages. Even if these services were provided by a separate division of the transit operator, these higher wages might be incurred. Thus, it could be argued that the cost to the agencies will be higher even though the transit operator has the technical ability to provide services more efficiently than agency operated systems.

---

[38]Kidder and Amedee, *Assuming Responsibility*.
[39]Crain, Flynn, and Stoffel, *Para-Transit Survey*.

One technique conventional transit operators have used to reduce the cost of providing better mobility for elderly and handicapped persons is by contracting with taxi companies. By subsidizing taxi trips for these groups, the transit operator is usually able to offer a higher level of mobility for less cost than would be incurred if they were to operate a similar demand-responsive system.

CONCLUSION

Two trends are likely to dominate the future of transit for elderly and handicapped persons. The first is the federally induced programs that every urban area will have as part of their conventional transit operation. What is not clear is which of the available options will be chosen by each area and whether they will merely try to pass the minimum requirements or respond in an innovative and resourceful way. Will transit operators make a real commitment to either full accessibility or substantially improved mobility?

The second trend is in the area of human-services-agency transit. More coordinated and consolidated systems are emerging. As public officials begin to question the high costs and inefficiencies of current small-scale operations, they are forcing agencies into larger coordinated systems. In some cases, a separate entity not attached to any one agency is the service provider, while some large agency systems are becoming dominant in some areas.

Unfortunately, the transit operator is not willing or is unable to be the lead special-transit agency. Thus, as in the past, the human services providers are finding their own solutions.

SELECTED BIBLIOGRAPHY

Many citations are no longer available from their original source. These citations are often available from the National Technical Information Service, U.S. Department of Commerce, 5285 Port Royal Road, Springfield, Va. 22161. We have verified the order numbers for many of these citations, and they are found at the end of the citation. Prices are available through NTIS at the address above.

ABT ASSOCIATES, INC., *Transportation Needs of the Urban Disadvantaged*, prepared for FHWA. Cambridge, Mass.: Abt Associates, Inc., March 1974.

————, *Travel Barriers: Transportation Needs of the Handicapped*, prepared for U.S. DOT, Office of Economic and Systems Analysis. Cambridge, Mass.: Abt Associates, Inc., 1969. Now available as PB 187 327.

ADMINISTRATION ON AGING, OFFICE OF HUMAN DEVELOPMENT, U.S. DEPARTMENT OF HEALTH, EDUCATION, AND WELFARE, *Transportation for the Elderly: The State of the Art*, prepared by Institute of Public Administration. Washington, D.C.: U.S. Government Printing Office, January 1975. Now available as HRP-0015165.

BELL, WILLIAM G., AND WILLIAM T. OLSEN, eds., *Toward a Unification of National and State Policy (and Action) on the Transportation Disadvantaged*, in 3 vols., Proceedings of the Fourth Annual Conference on the Transportation Disadvantaged, December 3, 4, 5, 1974. Tallahassee, Fla.: Florida State University, n.d.

CANTILLI, EDMUND J., AND JUNE L. SHMELZER, eds., *Transportation and Aging*, selected issues based on the proceedings of the Interdisciplinary Workshop on Transportation and Aging, May 24-26, 1970. Washington, D.C.: U.S. Government Printing Office, 1971. Now available as HRP-0014247.

CRAIN AND ASSOCIATES, eds., *Transportation Problems of the Transportation Handicapped*, Volume I: The Transportation Handicapped Population, Definitions and Counts, Volume II: The Roles of Government and the Private Sector in the Provision of Mobility Systems for the Transportation Handicapped, Volume III: Alternative Planning Methodologies, and Volume IV: Transportation Solutions for the Handicapped, prepared for UMTA. Washington, D.C.: Urban Mass Transportation Administration, August 1976. Now available as PB 258 579, 258 580, 258 581, and 258 582.

CRAIN, JOHN L., SYDWELL D. FLYNN, AND FRED C. STOFFEL, *Para-Transit Survey, Component of MTC Special Transit Service Needs Study*, prepared for the Metropolitan Transportation Commission, Berkeley, Calif., and UMTA. n.p.: Crain & Associates, April 1974.

GOLANT, STEPHEN M., "Housing and Transportation Problems of the Urban Elderly," in *Urban Policymaking and Metropolitan Dynamics: A Comparative Geographical Analysis*, ed. John S. Adams. Cambridge, Mass.: Ballinger Publishing Company, 1976.

INSTITUTE OF PUBLIC ADMINISTRATION, *Coordinating Transportation for the Elderly and Handicapped: A State of the Art Report*, prepared for the Office of Service and Methods Demonstrations, UMTA, Washington, D.C.: U.S. Department of Transportation, November 1976. Now available as PB 265 079.

KIDDER, ALICE E., AND GEORGE AMEDEE, *Assuming Responsiblity for Mobility of Elderly and Handicapped: The Roles of Transit Properties, Transit Planners, and Social Service Agencies in Small Cities*. Greensboro, N.C.: North Carolina A & T State University, 1976. Now available as PB 267 231.

———, AND ARTHUR SALTZMAN, "Mode Choice Among Autoless Workers in Auto-Oriented Cities," in *Proceedings: International Conference on Transportation*, Bruges, Belgium, Transportation Research Forum, pp. 647–54. Oxford, Ind.: The Richard B. Cross Company, June 1973.

MCKELVEY, DOUGLAS J., ed., *Proceedings of the First National Conference on Rural Public Transportation*, prepared for U.S. DOT. Greensboro, N.C.: North Carolina A & T State University, Transportation Institute, October 27, 1976. Now available as PB 262 808.

MORLOK, EDWARD K., WALTER M. KULASH, AND HUGO L. VANDERSYPEN, *The Effect of Reduced Fare Plans for the Elderly on Transit System Routes*. Evanston, Ill.: Northwestern University Transportation Center, 1971. Now available as PB 204 058.

NOTESS, CHARLES B., "Shopping and Work Trips in the Black Ghetto," in *Proceedings of the American Society of Civil Engineers, Journal of the Urban Planning and Development Division*, 98, no. UP1 (July 1972), 71–83.

PAASWELL, ROBERT E., AND WILFRED W. RECKER, *Problems of the Carless*, prepared for U.S. DOT, Office of University Research. Buffalo, N.Y.: State University of New York at Buffalo, Department of Civil Engineering, June 1976, also available from Praeger Press, New York, 1978.

SALTZMAN, ARTHUR, AND GEORGE AMEDEE, "Serving the Transportation Disadvantaged with Demand-Responsive Transportation," in *Transit Planning*, Transportation Research Record 559, pp. 1–10. Washington, D.C.: Transportation Research Board, 1976.

TRANSPORTATION RESEARCH BOARD, *Transportation Requirements for the Handicapped, Elderly, and Economically Disadvantaged*, NCHRP Report 39. Washington, D.C.: Transportation Research Board, 1976.

TRANSPORTATION SYSTEMS CENTER, *The Handicapped and Elderly Market for Urban Mass Transit*, prepared for UMTA. Cambridge, Mass.: Transportation Systems Center, October 1973. Now available as PB 224 821.

URBAN MASS TRANSPORTATION ADMINISTRATION AND FEDERAL HIGHWAY ADMINISTRATION, "Transportation for Elderly and Handicapped Persons," *Federal Register*, 41, no. 85 (April 30, 1976), 18234–41.

U.S. GENERAL ACCOUNTING OFFICE, *Hindrances to Coordinating Transportation of People Participating in Federally Funded Grant Programs*, vol. 1. Washington, D.C.: U.S. General Accounting Office, 1977.

WACHS, MARTIN, AND ROBERT D. BLANCHARD, "Life Styles and Transportation Needs of the Elderly in the Future," in *Transportation Issues: The Disadvantaged, the Elderly, and Citizen Involvement*, Transportation Research Record 618, pp. 19–24. Washington, D.C.: Transportation Research Board, 1976.

Chapter 30

PUBLIC TRANSIT AND INSTITUTIONAL CHANGE

FRANK C. COLCORD, *Chairman, Department of Political Science, Tufts University*

Urban public transit has been in the eye of an institutional storm in the large cities of the United States and Canada since about 1945. In this chapter, we will describe the institutional changes that have occurred and are currently under way, and seek to identify the political and other reasons for them.

American and Canadian urban transit have experienced three institutional phases since the mid-1940s. The era began with most big-city transit operations still in the hands of private companies, and most typically, operated under state or provincial charter and regulation and restricted to the territorial jurisdiction of the city. The core-area transit company generally was augmented by subregional transit firms serving sections of suburbia. These institutional arrangements were marked by a high degree of autonomy of the separate parts. The previously ubiquitous trolley lines were being phased out, and buses were already the primary transit mode in both the large city and suburban operations. Only five North American cities (Boston, Chicago, Cleveland, New York, Philadelphia), all in the United States, had rail rapid transit systems.

The second model, installed in U.S. cities as early as 1948 and as late as 1974, was marked by three key characteristics: public ownership, metropolitan area service, and continued autonomy of transit vis-à-vis other related policy concerns.

The third model, still in process of adoption and refinement although first surfacing to any significant extent in the mid-1960s, is marked by an integration and subordination process. To varying degrees, and as a product of several separate but reinforcing pressures, transit is being drawn into a broader and more comprehensive decision-making pattern. Its metropolitan geographic scope remains as, of course,

TABLE 30-1
Urban Transportation Institutional Models

Model	Ownership	Territory	Political Character
I	Private	Submetropolitan	Autonomous
II	Public	Metropolitan	Autonomous
III	Public	Metropolitan	Subordinate (comprehensive)

does its public ownership. Table 30-1 illustrates the characteristics of these three models.

The same basic process of institutional change has occurred in both the United States and Canada. There are some interesting differences in detail which arise out of contrasting philosophies of government. Canada's political systems, at all levels, are often described as lying somewhere between those of the United States and Europe, and this indeed seems to be valid in this policy area. It is particularly evident in contrasting experience with and attitudes toward public ownership of transit.

The movements of cities from the first institutional model to the second and from the second to the third were generally preceded and accompanied by political controversy. Rarely were institutions the real subject of these controversies; however, institutional change has become an important symbol of major changes in policy, emphasis, or attitude on the part of the public and policy makers. Institutions have been viewed as significant instruments for achieving these other objectives.

The controversies involved in the shift from the first to the second model were generally very basic in character. In most instances, they reflected a concern over two issues:

- The declining quality and quantity of transit services.
- The ever-increasing costs of this deteriorating service.

The conflicts preceding the second institutional change were more complex, just as were the institutional changes themselves. They have concerned a collection of related policies including, but not restricted to, transit. While they still often relate to quality, quantity, and cost of service, they also usually have had to do with questions of access to the policy-making process and control over policy outcomes. A concern with "grass-roots participation" has been evident.

Institutions can be structured to (1) restrict policy determination essentially to technicians, (2) restrict it to "relevant" interests, or (3) provide for input to all concerned and affected parties. The first approach defines the policy as a nonpolicy, merely a technical matter of no interest to the public or even to the politician. This is the approach most typical of traditional European and Canadian practice. The second philosophy accepts certain "expert" politicians and interest groups into the decision-making fold, but still largely excludes other politicians, the public, and "irrelevant" interest groups. This has been the typical U.S. approach. The third recognizes that transportation affects the consumer and has important social and environmental impacts on many other elements of the policy.

Arguments over institutions can be generated when the public or groups within the public become concerned over the policy in question (i.e., they don't like it) and then become aware that the institution is structured to keep them out of the process. In addition to private sector groups, these may be existing or new government agencies or legislative committees who have not been dealt into the process. Institutions can be, and often are, designed to make coordination with other agencies and programs difficult, if not impossible.

To understand fully the changes in institutions for transit, we must be aware of the parallel changes that have been occurring in urban highway and metropolitan planning institutions. Sometimes, the institutional changes relating to transit have, in fact, been partly or largely the product of dissatisfactions with highway programs and their emphases. The following discussion draws on a number of studies the author has done in large U.S. and Canadian urban areas.

The three models described must be viewed as ideal types. In some instances, the transition from one model to the next occurs over a considerable period of time, with a number of changes occurring sequentially or simultaneously, eventually leading to the new model. Examples of the "pure" model or aberrations from the standard model will be noted subsequently.

MODEL I: TRANSIT UNDER PRIVATE OWNERSHIP

When the United States and Canada emerged from World War II, most of their urban transit systems were in private hands, as they had been since their inception. In the early decades of the industry, transit was not only private, but often absentee-owned. For many years the Seattle transit system, for example, was owned in Boston, while the Boston system was owned in New York, in both cases by large early versions of the "conglomerate." In addition to absentee ownership, corruption and mismanagement were not uncommon.

These firms began to become unprofitable, or only marginally profitable, as early as the post-World War I era. It was then that the Boston Elevated Railway first began to receive guarantees of a "fair profit" from the public treasuries of the cities and towns served by the system. A few companies had already become publicly owned in the early decades of this century, notably the Seattle and San Francisco municipal systems.

As the politics of American cities began to become less corrupt and raucous, so too did the transit industry. By the 1940s it seems to have become locally respectable, and often locally owned. While the earlier financial mismanagement of transit may have contributed marginally to the demise of the industry, the most important reasons lay elsewhere, principally in the great growth of affluence after World War II and the accompanying acquisition of automobiles and suburban homes.

By its very nature, the private corporate ownership of transit had certain key characteristics. First, the opportunities for public or political influence in the key decisions were relatively limited. Most city politicians did not see their mission as influencing development anyway. Urban transit development was not a product of urban planning objectives but rather a product of seeking profitable runs. In the early years of trolley-line extensions, these were often made to areas which the owners were interested in developing, and thus there was some coordination of transportation and housing development under private auspices. Again, this was certainly not done in accord with some popularly approved plan; there was no such thing. Partial exceptions to this approach occurred where underground rail transit was developed, inevitably requiring active governmental participation and financial assistance.

Private ownership of transit was, of course, an extreme case of a structure that excluded certain actors from access to decision making. Private ownership excluded the citizen almost completely, and for the most part—at least in substantive decisions—largely excluded the politician. Similarly, this institutional arrangement made it nearly impossible to coordinate transit policy with related policy concerns. The inputs into the decision-making system made only a limited array of policy outputs possible.

It should be noted here that more contemporary transit companies, especially those owned locally, seem often to have sought to be responsive to the ever-increasing popular and political demands of their times. But, again, the inherent necessity of operating for profit within the private enterprise system constrained them from considering certain policy options. A good case in point is the history of transit operation, planning, and ownership in Atlanta, a city that retained its private transit firm much later than most—until 1972. It was an innovative and profitable organization, strongly involved in local and metropolitan planning, and respected by users and political leadership alike. But its end became inevitable when the area decided to build a rail rapid transit system.

Most commonly, the demise of the private bus system has been fully agreeable to the bus company itself (except for the often vigorous debates over the price to be paid) because of many years of declining service and escalating prices. Milwaukee is one big-city example of this phenomenon. As has been the case elsewhere, local government (in this case the county) assumed ownership of the system only with the greatest reluctance, largely because of the threat of growing subsidies. Only the likelihood of both state and federal assistance made this acquisition palatable to the county.

The dates that cities have shifted from model I to model II vary considerably, and the shift itself, as we have defined it, can take a very long time. For example, Seattle took over its transit system from its private owners in 1918, Toronto in 1921, but it was not until 1953 in Toronto and 1973 in Seattle that "metropolitan" transit service was provided. In Boston, public operation began in the late 1940s in 14 cities and towns, but it was not until 1964 that the district encompassed the whole metropolitan area. The San Francisco Bay area has moved incrementally toward public ownership beginning in the second decade of the century in the city proper, adding cross-bay and East-bay service in the 1950s, establishing the three-county Bay Area Rapid Transit system (BART) in the early 1960s, and moving into Marin County in the early 1970s—all of these operated by different public agencies. Miami's system became public and metropolitan in 1960, following by a few years the establishment of metropolitan government. St. Louis and Kansas City, Missouri, took the plunge in the mid-1960s, the Twin Cities and Baltimore at the beginning of the 1970s, all of them becoming metropolitan and public simultaneously. In Canada, Montreal purchased the Tramways Company in 1951, but it did not become geographically enlarged until after 1970. In Vancouver, the B.C. Electric Company, which also operated transit, was bought out by the Province of British Columbia in 1961, and renamed B.C. Hydro. With the transfer of the Milwaukee system to public metropolitan ownership, this move from model I to model II is very nearly complete in the major U.S. and Canadian municipalities.

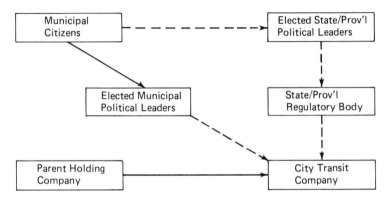

Figure 30-1 *Standard model I institutional structure*

This process has taken a long time, and in some instances has involved a number of incremental steps. In the United States, in particular, with its proclivity to free enterprise, it is a process that has been taken with great reluctance. As we will note, putting the next model into effect was often difficult, partly because of ideological predilections. While Canada is somewhat more pragmatic in these matters, similar problems have been evident there, especially in Toronto.

MODEL II: PUBLIC OWNERSHIP, METROPOLITANIZATION, AND AUTONOMY

The 1960s was the decade in which the new model II style of organizational structure became the predominant one in North America. A few preceded that decade, such as those of Boston, whose multicity Metropolitan Transit Authority (MTA) became something of a prototype, and Toronto and Miami. By the end of the 1960s such urban areas as Vancouver, San Francisco, Los Angeles, New York, Philadelphia, St. Louis, and Kansas City had created their new institutions, and Boston's had been enlarged to include the whole urban region. A number of important cities, however, did not move to this model until the 1970s, examples being Chicago, Minneapolis, Atlanta, Seattle, and Baltimore. By the mid-1970s this approach was nearly universal.

Much of the organizational and operating philosophy built into the new model II transit institutions in the 1960s was a direct outgrowth of their former private status. It has been the prevailing view that new public organizations should be operated like private corporations as much as possible, including showing a primary concern for balancing expenditures with revenues. Many of them were required by their organic statutes to operate within their revenues, thus forcing increased fares or reduced services whenever costs rose. The assumption seemed to be in most of the earlier cases that once these organizations were relieved of the necessity to pay local property taxes and state and federal income and excise taxes and could rationalize the formerly fragmented and duplicatory operations, they would be able to operate in the black. Business-type accounting procedures were generally required. Frequently, the organization was made immune from normal civil service requirements in order to allow freedom to hire and fire like a business. Unions were allowed to represent the workers, as before, and to bargain collectively.

These new "authorities," as they were usually called, were provided with a board of directors, appointed in a variety of ways. One arrangement was to have the counties, and sometimes the central-city political leadership, appoint persons or serve themselves as representatives of their jurisdictions. This was the approach contained in the original Bay Area Rapid Transit District (BARTD) legislation. The legislation establishing the Twin Cities Area Metropolitan Transit Commission (TCAMTC) and the Metropolitan Atlanta Rapid Transit Authority (MARTA) also adopted this model. Both BARTD and the TCAMTC have since had their appointment system altered by state legislation, so that neither board is now directly representative of the local governments served. The former board is now elected; the latter is appointed by the Metropolitan Council with its chairman being named by the governor.

Another approach is to give the governor, or in the case of bistate bodies, the governors, the appointive powers. Examples of this are the Boston, Baltimore, St. Louis, Kansas City, and New York organizations. Still another model is found where the transit authority's area falls within the jurisdiction of an authoritative areawide government; in such places, that governing body typically has the appointing power, e.g., Dade County (Miami), the metropolitan government of Toronto, Milwaukee County, and the Minneapolis–St. Paul Metropolitan Council (since 1974). Earlier examples, later changed, were the transit systems of the cities of Seattle, New York, and Chicago and many others that were once restricted to the core city. In keeping with the "businesslike" philosophy attendant upon the creation of these institutions, businessmen were frequent appointees to those boards that allowed for such extra-governmental appointments.

Whatever the method of appointment, in every U.S. and Canadian case known to the author, there is a board responsible for transit decisions under which is a manager or executive director generally appointed by that board. Seattle, St. Louis, and Vancouver are somewhat special cases, in which the board is multifunctional. In theory, "politics" is to be kept out of the decision making of the transit system; in practice, this is rarely the case. To some degree, this is because the organization is typically unable to operate within its revenues and, consequently, must come before various political bodies seeking subsidies. In a few instances, particularly in the United States, these organizations have become fair game for patronage demands from state legislators or local politicians as a quid pro quo for financial support.

The philosophical objective of creating a businesslike institution for transit has proved to be somewhat in conflict with the other basic necessity in such an organization—to make the agency responsible to the people and their political institutions. While the aim was to "keep transit out of politics," nonetheless, it was recognized that some sort of link needed to be forged to keep the agency responsible. The solutions chosen, in practice, placed greater emphasis on the "businesslike" objective and less on the political objective. The aim of autonomy has, for the most part, been successfully achieved, especially where the agencies were able to live within their revenues. Given their conservative financial policies (often required by law), the managements of these authorities rarely looked for ways to meet such social needs as enlarging employment opportunities for inner-city minorities or improving the mobility of the handicapped, the elderly, and so on. Given their autonomy, politicians and civic groups oriented toward meeting such needs have rarely been able to persuade these managements to think in such terms. Consequently, the new managements have not been very different from the old.

It seems to have mattered little whether the authority's board was made up of local government representatives or appointees of the governor(s); they have not provided easy access for social, environmental, or aesthetic demands. Neither of the two institutional approaches makes it easy to demand responsiveness; indeed, the organizational theory underlying the arrangments is to *provide* resistance to such "unbusinesslike" demands.

Even in instances where transit authorities are appointed by politicians of a single jurisdiction, serious controversy has developed between the politicians and their appointees, not only because of legal restrictions but also because of seemingly almost inevitable differences in perspective. Dade County and Metropolitan Toronto have been examples of this kind of ambiguous autonomy. Like conflicts elsewhere, both have experienced conflicts which ultimately have led to the shift to model III.

The autonomy of these authorities has made coordination with other agencies difficult; they have tended to overlook, indeed they have had little choice but to ignore, program solutions that lay totally or partially outside their purview.

The model II phase has shown mixed results. Costs have continued to spiral upward, increasingly met in more recent years by subsidy rather than fare increases. Indeed, a few cities, such as Milwaukee and Atlanta, have reduced fares at the time of public takeover. These growing costs, however they are paid, have kept transit in the public eye. Compared to the last few years of private ownership, the quality of service improved in most cities under this structural arrangement resultant from growing

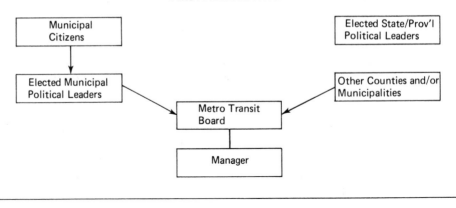

FIRST ALTERNATIVE

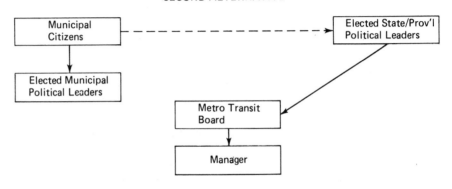

SECOND ALTERNATIVE

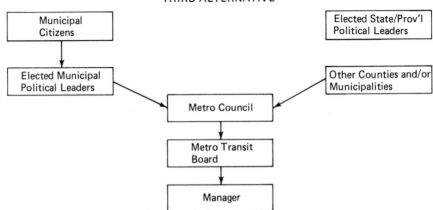

THIRD ALTERNATIVE

Figure 30-2 *Standard model II institutional structures*

federal and, in some instances, state capital subsidies. And, while hard to measure, there seems to be a real improvement in the quality of management in many cities.

While the controversies that have led to model III sometimes involved spiraling costs and continued dissatisfaction with service, they have focused more often on the failure of transportation policy to respond to social and environmental needs and concerns of the community. This perception, of course, encompasses policies related not only to transit but also to highways and other transport. Thus, the preceding events and the solutions sought in the shift from model II to III represent a more complex political phenomenon than was involved in the previous shift from I to II.

While Canada has adopted comparable institutions to those of the United States, Toronto has experienced some of the same problems with them; nonetheless, there are distinctive differences. Montreal's transit system is tied closely to the sources of power within the Montreal area and is formally a part of the "Urban Community." Toronto's system, although it has had a semiautonomous board since the establishment of the Metro Council, always has had some degree of authoritative policy direction from an established, duly constituted government. Vancouver's experience has been most like that of U.S. cities; there the question of authority over the location of planning powers is not yet resolved.

MODEL III: TOWARD RESPONSIVENESS AND COMPREHENSIVENESS

The shifts from private to public ownership and from municipal to metropolitan jurisdictions were important steps in recognition of the changing character of the city and the new role of urban public transit. They were taken in recognition that the "city" had long since outgrown its boundaries and that transit was a vital public need, but they did not provide an adequate mechanism to link transit decisions to the political process, or to tie it in with the broad metropolitan planning process.

In fact, it is little wonder that such goals were not realized. They hardly began to be recognized by the decision makers until the mid-1960s or so. In the 1950s and 1960s—and we would argue in most U.S. urban areas even in the 1970s—there was no effective metropolitan political process to which transit might be linked. Also, metropolitan planning hardly existed when many of these transit institutions were created, and it has continued to be a relatively weak process. The new metropolitan transit authorities had little choice but to make their own autonomous decisions.

We have noted previously that even where authoritative, metropolitan decision-making structures exist, transit authorities have shown what may be an inherent tendency to go their own way. In Dade County, Minneapolis–St. Paul, and Toronto, disagreements have occurred which have resulted in steps to strengthen the powers of the decision-making bodies vis-à-vis the transit units. In the Twin Cities, the Metropolitan Council sought and secured state legislation in 1974 which eliminated the former statutory ambiguities as to which agency had long-range planning powers, and also gave to the council appointive powers and approval authority over transit commission capital programs. In Toronto, the Metropolitan Council achieved review power over the Toronto Transit Commission through the devices of appointing its own members to the commission and agreeing, in 1964, to pick up the operating deficit. The Dade County Board has increased its involvement in transit decisions through initiating a successful campaign in 1972 for funding for a new rapid transit system, retaining control of the planning and (likely) eventual operation of that system, and increasing the effectiveness of its role in the areawide transportation planning body. Thus, although not without difficulty, these three areas, with their greater institutional capacity to govern at the metropolitan level, have made major strides in their shift to model III.

Elsewhere in the United States the changes are occurring only with great difficulty. The traditional view that local government is little more than a collection of services is dying hard. However, there has come to be an increasing recognition, thanks largely to transportation, renewal, and antipoverty programs, that political decisions are made by the complex of local (and state) governments which have differing, and sometimes disagreeable, impacts on various segments of the public. As a result, there does seem to be under way an effort to achieve the twin goals of responsiveness and comprehensiveness which is altering the institutional relationships in the urban areas.

These changes may not be directed primarily toward transit; nonetheless, they impact it. The establishment and evolution of metropolitan planning and policy-making bodies is the most important of the steps taken. The movement began by local initiative in the mid- to late-1950s in a few cities (examples are Detroit, Washington, San Francisco, Seattle, and Atlanta), but it was given several major boosts from federal legislation in the 1960s, which, in effect, required their establishment. The three major statutes were the Federal-Aid Highway Act of 1962, the Demonstration Cities and Metropolitan Development Act of 1966, and the Intergovernmental Cooperation Act of 1968, all of which required reviews by representative metropolitan bodies prior to approval of federal assistance for particular projects.

The institutions which resulted—typically called councils of governments (COGs)—rarely were given much more power over local governments and metropolitan single-function agencies than that deriving from these federal laws. But these federal statutes clearly represented a desire to assure that federal moneys were being spent for projects that were consistent with the policy objectives of the elected leadership of the urban area. Moreover, there were attempts to get the collective leadership to define such policies.

The "council of governments" movement was not aimed primarily at transit; it had a broader planning and political objective. But, it has significantly impacted transit. Despite the limited powers of the COGs, they often have had dedicated, high-quality staff with a comprehensive, regional perspective. Their responsibilities under the federal legislation inevitably have led them to identify inconsistencies between the plans of transit authorities and such approved metropolitan objectives as may exist, since these plans generally require federal aid.

In a number of cities, something resembling comprehensive thinking came about through noninstitutional means that can only be described as political. Perhaps the best two examples are San Francisco and Boston. In the former case, a "freeway revolt" became effective in the city at the end of the 1950s; this led informally into the ongoing debate over rapid transit which culminated in the 1962 decision to build BART. Thus, through political actions, a policy was fashioned giving priority to rapid transit over highways in the more urban sections of the area. That policy was subsequently confirmed in the 1970 regional plan of the Association of Bay Area Governments (the COG), and the obvious necessity for a comprehensive body to carry the policy into future planning and programming led to the creation of the Metropolitan Transportation Commission (MTC), with substantial powers over future capital investments.

In the Boston area, somewhat similar forces were at work, which resulted in very different institutional forms but in an equally comprehensive approach. There, strong opposition was registered in Boston, Cambridge, and a number of other municipalities, beginning in the early 1960s, to the interstate freeway plans then on the books. Also, the public was frustrated by the low level of competence and high level of expense of the Metropolitan Transit Authority. In 1964, an enlarged areawide transit authority (Massachusetts Bay Transportation Authority) was established with new state revenue resources and with a statutory obligation to plan cooperatively with the state's highway agency. In the same year, the Metropolitan Area Planning Council (the COG) was established, as well as a long-range planning unit in the state's Department of Public Works (the highway agency). A continuing determination on the part of then-Governor Volpe to proceed with the highway plans led to an intensification of political opposition. In 1969, the succeeding governor, Francis Sargent, established a task force to take a new look at Boston's transportation needs. This study, largely financed from federal assistance, led eventually to a moratorium and then later to a total, comprehensive, and innovative replan which eliminated most of the proposed highways and placed heavy emphasis on improved public transit. It also resulted in a greatly strengthened role for the state's new transportation secretary.

In neither the San Francisco nor the Boston cases was the shift toward greater comprehensiveness primarily the handiwork of the agency set up to provide such an overview (i.e., the COG). In both cases, it was strong political forces, using every resource at hand, that forced the issue. In both cases, the end result was a reduction in the autonomy of the functional transport agencies, both highway and transit. In both cases, a major factor, perhaps the dominant one, was an unwillingness on the part of citizens in densely populated urban areas to suffer the damages, both social and environmental, that would be wrought by superhighways. In Boston, the sense of dissatisfaction with transit was a stronger element than in San Francisco. In the latter city, dissatisfaction existed, but it was less "popular"; it was largely held by downtown businesspersons and their political allies, who saw transit as a stimulant to development. In both cases, however, transit emerged as the new emphasis.

Except for those cities with strong metropolitan governments or councils, the movement from model II to model III has been less dramatic and less positive than in Boston and the Bay Area, and it has been much more the product of external forces. Freeway revolts have occurred in many, indeed most, other big urban areas, such as

Baltimore, Washington, Philadelphia, Atlanta, Milwaukee, Kansas City, Miami, New Orleans, Louisville, San Antonio, Los Angeles, Seattle, Chicago, and New York. In all these areas, such popular uprisings have stimulated a greater interest and concern over transit and then a greater understanding of the interrelatedness of highways and transit.

Federal transportation statutes, notably the 1973 Federal-Aid Highway Act, have gone even further in recent years to strengthen the powers of metropolitan councils and, in effect, to force them to set priorities among competing transportation needs. The movement away from single-purpose federal grants and trust funds also has encouraged this approach.

The direction of institutional change in Canada has been quite different from that prevailing in the United States. The COG idea has not caught on there; instead, Canada has taken the step for which the COG is a weak substitute, namely, the establishment of metropolitan governments or multifunctional districts. Led by Toronto in 1953, most metropolitan areas have since followed. Montreal's "Urban Community" was established in its present form in 1969. The "Greater Vancouver Regional District," established in 1968, is a multipurpose metropolitan body with significant powers. North America's most dramatic structural reform occurred in Winnipeg, Manitoba, which in 1971 abolished all its 19 municipalities and established a single city council with a decentralized system of service delivery.

The second important development in model III is also one in which Canada has moved much more vigorously and universally than has been true of the United States—the growing involvement of the "parent" governments (states and provinces) in urban transit planning, programming, and financing. The states and provinces traditionally have been the major centers of authority in the planning and construction of intercity highways. In the United States, despite the strong presence and vast financing inputs of the national government since the 1956 Federal-Aid Highway Act, the most important contributor to policy decisions regarding highways in urban areas continues to be the states. In Canada, since the federal government is not involved except for the Trans-Canada Highway, the highway policy-making role of the provinces is and has long been stronger than that of our states.

In the United States, these state agencies for road planning and construction were, like their transit counterparts, unifunctional, and quite independent, in principle, of "political" influence. In Canada, their autonomy always has been considerably less by virtue of the parliamentary-cabinet form of government.

In the 1960s and 1970s, many U.S. states and Canadian provinces, like the U.S. national government, have moved in the direction of comprehensive departments of transportation. In some states, this has amounted to little more than a consolidation of already existing state transportation programs; but, increasingly, there has been a move toward assumption of new functions, the most important of which is urban public transit. By 1975 most of the more urbanized states and provinces had departments of transportation, and there is a continuing movement in the direction of greater comprehensiveness.

Meaningful state and provincial involvement in transit coincides closely with the provision of financial aid. State and provincial financial assistance came earliest in those cities which had rail transit and commuter railroads, but has since become quite common for bus-only cities as well. Most of the large urban states now budget substantial sums for urban transit, sometimes including both capital and operating subsidies. In Toronto and New York, the province/state is actually in the business of operating commuter railroads; and, in contrast to highways, the Canadian national government always has been heavily involved in the provision of commuter rail service through the nationally owned Canadian National Railway.

With the growing trend toward state/provincial involvement in, financing of, and even operation of transit (e.g., Boston, Baltimore, New York, Vancouver) and the inevitable accompaniment of a growing comprehensiveness of transportation interest at the state/provincial level, we find a very different intergovernmental institutional system evolving. Previously, one mode (transit) was the responsibility of an autonomous agency at the local level of government and the other (roads) was conducted by an equally autonomous agency at a different level (state/province), making any really comprehensive approach nearly impossible. The emerging model is one in which two comprehensive institutional systems and approaches are operating in parallel, both dealing with the same collection of modes.

As this model of dual comprehensiveness begins to emerge, the municipal and, in the United States, the federal levels of government continue to claim a portion of the power over transportation; in the instances where state and metropolitan powers remain weak, then other levels are particularly important. It is too early to tell how model III will work in many U.S. cities or, indeed, whether it will in fact prove workable. It seems to be the emerging *modus operandi* in Canada's largest cities and in the few U.S. cities with metropolitan governments.

It is a highly competitive operating system, inevitably involving conflict. With both levels capable of seeing the whole picture, but with each responding to rather different political pressures and cultures, an identity of interest seems most unlikely. And, given the constitutional powers and financial interest of the senior government and the inherent concern of the metropolitan unit, neither is likely to forego its interest.

In some U.S. cities which now have councils of government, despite, or perhaps because of, federal efforts to strengthen their authority, there are signs of revolt against powerful metropolitan bodies. Major local units have left the COGs of Los Angeles and Seattle, for example. It will remain to be seen whether metropolitan policy making can be imposed from Washington without a powerful assist from heretofore reluctant states.

In a number of urban areas, however, particularly in the crowded East, states have moved into the power vacuum—notably New York, Maryland, and Massachusetts. In a few other places, modest gains have been made by metropolitan forces. The Atlanta Regional Council (formed in 1972) has been given some limited powers beyond those normally held by such bodies. In the San Francisco Bay area, the Metropolitan Transportation Commission, which was given considerable powers when first created,

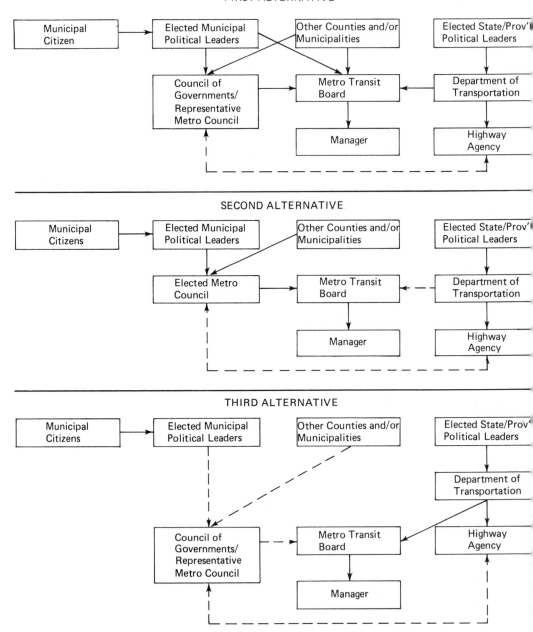

Figure 30-3 *Standard model III institutional structures*

has been strengthened further in the act creating the California Department of Transportation. Indeed, that act seems to do as much to strengthen metropolitanism in the urban areas of California as it does to strengthen the state role.

CONCLUSION

The changes being wrought at both the state and the metropolitan levels seem to be having one dominant effect on transit institutions. Their autonomy is clearly being reduced. In those places where strong metropolitan decision makers have emerged, they tend to battle over, and then destroy, the autonomy previously held by the transit agency. This need not affect the institution in any formal way, but the impact is nonetheless powerful. Similarly, where the state gains in powers, as in Massachusetts, it, too, has moved to reduce the planning and programming authority of transit through various devices. It appears, therefore, that transit's institutional autonomy phase is drawing to a close. Whether it is the metropolitan area or the state, or both, which will gain at transit's expense, will vary from place to place, but the result for transit will be the same. Comprehensiveness and responsiveness cannot exist side by side with an autonomous transit agency. The theories that led us to create such institutions seem now to be obsolete and unworkable.

An important group of related questions remains to be answered and cannot be definitively dealt with because the changes we noted are so recent. The point was made at the outset that reorganizations change the extent and distribution of access by citizens and their groups to the decision makers. We emphasized that in both models I and II, access by any but the transportation community was difficult indeed. The model II system led to frustration partly because politicians and citizens had no effective means of access. There was no democratic governing body giving the transit organization policy direction and political legitimacy.

With the strengthening of the metropolitan bodies and/or the state and provincial departments of transport, will there be better access? Will there be more effective citizen control?

Limited as our information is, there seems to be cause for optimism. The growth of comprehensive involvement by California in urban transportation has been accompanied by a greater sensitivity to local opinions and to the need for strengthened metropolitan democratic institutions than existed before. The assertion of initiative by the governor of Massachusetts was the means by which citizen inputs could at least be effectively heard and built into the planning process. The governor-appointed Metro Council of the Twin Cities seems to have been more responsive to popular inputs than was the Transit Commission, whose members represented the communities of the area. This seems also to be true in Toronto and Miami. The continuing evolution of institutions toward a dual comprehensive system—state and metropolitan—seems a promising direction in which to move, completely consistent with the checks-and-balances tradition in the United States, but relieved of the major road-blocks to comprehensiveness and responsiveness which have been present in our system in the past.

In Canada, where the provinces have already assumed stronger powers than is ever likely to occur in the U.S. states, there seems a greater likelihood of a more hierarchical system continuing, with the metropolitan institutions remaining subservient to the province, although continuing to be important initiators and implementors of policy.

SELECTED BIBLIOGRAPHY

Many citations are no longer available from their original source. These citations are often available from the National Technical Information Service, U.S. Department of Commerce, 5285 Port Royal Road, Springfield, Va. 22161. We have verified the order numbers for many of these citations, and they are found at the end of the citation. Prices are available through NTIS at the address above.

ALTSHULER, ALAN, *The City Planning Process*. Ithaca, N.Y.: Cornell University Press, 1965.

BOYCE, DAVID E., NORMAN D. DAY, AND CHRIS MCDONALD, *Metropolitan Plan Making*. Philadelphia: Regional Science Research Institute, 1970.

COLCORD, FRANK C., *Urban Transportation Decision Making 2: The Houston Case Study*, prepared for UMTA. Cambridge, Mass.: Massachusetts Institute of Technology, Urban Systems Laboratory, November 1970. Now available as PB 206 224.

————, *Urban Transportation Decision Making 3: The San Francisco Case Study*, prepared for UMTA. Cambridge, Mass.: Massachusetts Institute of Technology, Urban Systems Laboratory, May 1971. Now available as PB 204 954.

————, AND STEVEN M. POLAN, *Urban Transportation Decision Making 4: Miami-Dade, A Case Study*, prepared for U.S. DOT, Office of Secretary. Medford, Mass.: Tufts University, July 1973. Now available as PB 257 996.

————, AND STEVEN M. POLAN, *Urban Transportation Decision Making 5: Atlanta, A Case Study*, prepared for U.S. DOT, Office of Secretary. Medford, Mass.: Tufts University, July 1973. Now available as PB 257 997.

————, AND STEVEN M. POLAN, *Urban Transportation Decision Making 6: Minneapolis–St. Paul, A Case Study*, prepared for U.S. DOT, Office of Secretary. Medford, Mass.: Tufts University, July 1973. Now available as PB 257 998.

————, AND RONALD S. LEWIS, *Urban Transportation Decision Making 9: Toronto, A Case Study*, prepared for U.S. DOT, Office of Secretary. Medford, Mass.: Tufts University, March 1974. Now available as PB 257 999.

————, AND RONALD S. LEWIS, *Urban Transportation Decision Making 11: Stockholm and Gothenberg, A Case Study*, prepared for U.S. DOT, Office of Secretary. Medford, Mass.: Tufts University, January 1974.

————, AND RONALD S. LEWIS, *Urban Transportation Decision Making 12: Hamburg, A Case Study*, prepared for U.S. DOT, Office of Secretary. Medford, Mass.: Tufts University, January 1974.

————, AND RONALD S. LEWIS, *Urban Transportation Decision Making 13: Amsterdam, A Case Study*, prepared for U.S. DOT, Office of Secretary. Medford, Mass.: Tufts University, February 1974.

————, *Urban Transportation Decision Making: Summary*, prepared for U.S. DOT, Office of Secretary. Medford, Mass.: Tufts University, September 1974. Now available as PB 257 995.

JACOB, HERBERT, AND KENNETH N. VINES, eds., *Politics in the American States*. Boston: Little, Brown and Company, 1971.

LUPO, ALAN, FRANK COLCORD, AND EDMUND P. FOWLER, *Rites of Way: The Politics of Transportation in Boston and the U.S. City*. Boston: Little, Brown and Company, 1971.

MEYER, J. R., J. F. KAIN, AND M. WOHL, *The Urban Transportation Problem*. Cambridge, Mass.: Harvard University Press, 1965.

MOGULOF, MELVIN B., *Five Metropolitan Governments*. Washington, D.C.: The Urban Institute, 1972. Now available as PB 234 358.

————, *Governing Metropolitan Areas: A Critical Review of Councils of Government and the Federal Role.* Washington, D.C.: The Urban Institute, 1971. Now available as PB 220 905.

PIERCE, NEAL R., *The Megastates of America: People, Politics and Power in the Ten Great States.* New York: W. W. Norton and Company, Inc., 1972.

PLUNKETT, THOMAS J., *Urban Canada and Its Government.* Toronto: Macmillan of Canada, Ltd., 1968.

RICHARDSON, BOYD, *The Future of Canadian Cities.* Toronto: New Press, 1972.

RICKER, JOHN, AND JOHN SAYWELL, *How Are We Governed?* Toronto: Clark, Irwin and Company, Ltd., 1971.

WHITE, W. L., R. H. WAGENBERG, AND R. C. NELSON, *Introduction to Canadian Politics and Government.* Toronto: Holt, Rinehart and Winston of Canada, Ltd., 1972.

Chapter 31

LABOR AND THE MANAGERIAL PROCESS *

KENNETH M. JENNINGS, JAY A. SMITH, JR., and EARLE C. TRAYNHAM, JR., *College of Business Administration, University of North Florida*

Labor represents a vital part of the problems and opportunities mass transit management faces in serving the public. While suffering a decline in passengers, the mass transit industry has been experiencing a steady increase in costs of operation. All systems have had to meet sizable wage increases in the inflationary period since 1967, e.g., from 1967 to 1977, the cost of transit labor increased over 100% in many cities, with the bill for labor ranging from 60 to 85% of total annual operating costs. Increased fringe costs have been added to overall expenses, as well as expenditures for new equipment and sharply increased fuel costs. If mass transit is to be revitalized, one critical factor will be viable labor–management relations which can ensure stability and maintain financial integrity for the transit systems.

Noting the particular importance of transit labor, the 1974 National Transportation Report stated:

> Labor costs constitute a substantial portion of the cost to operate public transportation systems, particularly bus systems. As the financial condition of the transit industry has worsened, there has been a growing concern about the relationship of labor compensation and productivity to the transit industry's financial and operating performance. Transit management has argued that the financial condition of transit systems has deteriorated partly because labor costs have increased more rapidly than other costs and, more important,

---

*The authors are indebted to the U.S. Department of Transportation for funding of research related to this topic. It should be mentioned that two portions of this research (interviews with management and union officials, and computerized analysis of the labor agreements) were confined to nine southeastern states. However, our additional literature review and discussions with union and management officials in other regions suggest nationwide applicability.

For a complete discussion of labor-management relations for mass transit, see KENNETH M. JENNINGS, JAY A. SMITH, JR., AND EARLE C. TRAYNHAM, JR., *Labor Relations in a Public Service Industry* (New York: Praeger Publishers, 1978).

faster than revenues. Moreover, management claims labor productivity has decreased. Transit labor, on the other hand, argues that its compensation has not increased at a rate greater than the cost of living, annual earnings per employee are not out of line with respect to other transportation workers, and transit labor productivity has not decreased.

When one examines the data . . . it becomes clear why so much confusion exists regarding this issue. First, management's argument that labor cost is rising faster than other costs appears correct, although not in dramatic terms. For the period 1962–72, labor costs increased 65.8 percent, whereas total costs increased 63.0 percent. Payroll as a percent of total expenses increased from 67.2 percent in 1962 to 68.4 percent in 1972. Labor cost also increased faster than revenues, but this is mainly because patronage declined 22.8 percent during the period.[1]

The report also commented that management arguments concerning productivity decreases seemed valid, as did labor's contention that employees' annual earnings were not out of line with respect to other transportation workers. While the report suggested several alternatives to the dilemma facing the transit industry, the important fact is that significant attention must be given to the issues and process of labor–management relations.

Underlying the character and quality of labor–management relations is the collective bargaining process, which represents a continuing joint decision-making process between union and management representatives over terms of employment and working conditions. The remainder of this chapter will be devoted to collective bargaining in mass transit, with emphasis on influences affecting the process and representative collective bargaining issues.

INFLUENCES ON COLLECTIVE BARGAINING

STRUCTURAL CONSIDERATIONS IN BARGAINING

Collective bargaining *structure* refers to the organizational scope of collective bargaining; more specifically, the nature and number of bargaining units, either formally or informally recognized, which are either directly involved or influential in the negotiation of the labor agreement. The inclusion or exclusion of various bargaining units from formal negotiations can have a serious impact on the resultant labor agreement. To illustrate, if a municipality negotiated a common labor agreement covering most of its employees (e.g., motor pool, recreation department, sanitation department, streets and highways, mass transit), there would probably be few provisions pertinent to the issues and complexities confronting mass transit. However, relatively few of the publicly owned agencies include mass transit operations in a centralized bargaining process—the negotiated labor agreement applies solely to mass transit employees. This finding is in part due to the unique legal considerations affecting mass transit as well as the usual separate governmental administration of the transit properties. Consequently, most mass transit sites experience decentralized bargaining—management

---

[1]U.S. DEPARTMENT OF TRANSPORTATION, *1974 National Transportation-Report: Current Performance and Future Prospects* (Washington, D.C.: U.S. Government Printing Office, July 1975), pp. 233–34.

and union officials negotiating a labor agreement pertaining to the exclusive interests of each mass transit property. A somewhat more common occurrence, particularly in privately owned companies, is more than one bargaining unit at the facility. Few of these locations have experienced *coordinated bargaining*—joint efforts of the units to bring coordinated pressure upon management, or *parity*—each union using the other union's settlement as a starting point for their own negotiation settlement. However, some of the management officials attribute significant impact to multiunit bargaining as "it makes it more difficult in trying to please two groups who are quite competitive in their bargaining demands." Another influence in multiunit bargaining is the extent that mass transit operations affect the total operations of the facility. Management officials at some of the privately owned utility firms indicate that mass transit employees represent a minority of the operation's total employees and are, therefore, subject to the pattern established by the more dominant union.

While the preponderance of mass transit agencies has one bargaining unit representing the exclusive interests of its employees, there are nonetheless informal, internal differences which influence the negotiation process and outcome, as two authorities note:

> In an important sense, collective bargaining consists of no less than three separate bargains — the agreement by different groups within the union to abandon certain claims and assign priorities to others; an analogous process of assessing priorities and trade-offs within a single company or association; and the eventual agreement that is made across the bargaining table.[2]

Perhaps the most vivid internal distinction occurs between the bus operators and craft employees.

Craft employees typically represent one-fifth of total bargaining unit employees. These employees have traditionally represented a "significant minority" in some labor organizations—their interests, influence, and obtained settlements often extend beyond their proportional representation of bargaining unit employees, creating a structural controversy as old as the labor movement.[3] However, many management officials indicate that the transit union is "driver-oriented." For example, various economic issues (bonus time, spread time, pay for time not worked, fringe benefits, etc.) are negotiated for the operators who "dominate the negotiation committees and ratification vote," and are subsequently applied to craft employees.[4] Additionally, there are typically low negotiated wage differentials between craft employees and operators to substantiate their contentions; and a subsequent review of labor agreements containing both craft and operator classifications indicates an average wage differential of only 10%. However, one reason for the relatively low wage differential is that many of the detailed craft assignments often calling for a higher wage differential are either contracted out or are the responsibility of the vendor.

---

[2]Derek C. Bok and John T. Dunlop, *Labor and the American Community* (New York: Simon and Schuster, 1970), p. 225.

[3]Harold W. Davey, *Contemporary Collective Bargaining*, 3rd ed. (Englewood Cliffs, N.J.: Prentice-Hall, Inc., 1972), p. 32.

[4]This situation is not limited to mass transit operations. For example, see Arvid Anderson, "The Structure of Public Sector Bargaining," in *Public Workers and Public Unions*, ed. Sam Zagoria (Englewood Cliffs, N.J.: Prentice-Hall, Inc., 1972), p. 39.

Union officials usually indicate there are no problems arising from this proportional difference. While contract ratification is usually on the basis of "one-man one-vote," there are many instances where at least one position of the negotiation team is always reserved for a craft employee. Some unions specify that only craft employees vote on those issues which pertain solely to craft classifications. In summary, some difference of opinion appears to exist between management and union officials regarding the effects of bargaining unit composition upon the negotiated settlement.

A final, potential structural influence on collective bargaining is the amount of services furnished by competitors in the local area. This influence can be twofold: (1) management officials may feel pressured to stabilize or reduce labor costs in order to remain competitive; and (2) union officials may use competitors' wages as a starting point in their negotiation demands. However, one author suggests that:

> Most transit firms, therefore, can be classified as monopolies, with each monopolist limited to one locality. The systems are only monopolies in the most literal sense, as they do compete with other modes of transportation—the most important being the private automobile. Nevertheless, transit bargaining structure and processes are directly affected by this industrial and market structure.[5]

Our findings suggest competitive service exerts a minimal influence on the collective bargaining process. Few locations indicate that privately run competitive bus services affect agency revenues or negotiated work rules. Additionally, there appears to be little union concern (at the local level) over the competitive aspects of taxis or jitney services.

ORGANIZATIONAL CHARACTERISTICS

Public/private ownership. Perhaps one of the most commonly cited organizational characteristics affecting labor relations in mass transit is the shift from private to public ownership of the agency.[6] Some authors have suggested that the differences between private- and public-sector bargaining are negligible.[7] Typically cited contentions for this reasoning are (1) many public employee classifications are not different from their private-sector counterparts, in terms of their job responsibilities; (2) the collective bargaining issues are somewhat identical; and (3) the determination of the negotiation outcome in both public and private sectors is a function of the respective bargaining power of union and management. Other academicians and practitioners have suggested that the shift from private to public ownership has resulted in profound differences in the labor–management relationship.[8]

[5]DAROLD T. BARNUM, "From Private to Public: Labor Relations in Urban Transit," *Industrial and Labor Relations Review*, 25, no. 1 (October 1971), 96. © 1971 by Cornell University. All rights reserved.

[6]FREDERICK MEYERS, "Organization and Collective Bargaining in the Local Mass Transportation Industry in the Southeast," *Southern Economic Journal*, 15 (April 1949), 425.

[7]For example, see A. BILIK, "Close the Gap: NLRB and Public Employees," *Ohio State Law Journal*, 31 (Summer 1970), 456–89.

[8]For a concise statement of these potential differences, see JAY F. ATWOOD, "Collective Bargaining's Challenge: Five Imperatives for Public Managers," *Public Personnel Management*, 5, no. 1 (January–February 1976), 24–32.

Most union and management practitioners indicate that the shift from private to public ownership has had little impact on the collective bargaining process. Perhaps this attitude is best reflected by the comments of one union official, "The key to bargaining is the individual negotiator, not the particular organization." One possible reason for this response is that most or all of the labor agreement provisions (e.g., arbitration, the right to strike) were negotiated when the agency was privately owned and included in the transition to public ownership to facilitate application for federal funding.

However, there are two cited influences associated with the transition of public ownership: heightened union expectations for wage increases and diminution of the management negotiator's authority. A related study by Daniel Hamermesh examined 48 publicly operated bus systems for the years 1963–1971 and found that government takeover of privately owned facilities was statistically significant in explaining wage increases even when several variables (e.g., regional differences, cost of living, the "quality of labor") were held constant.[9]

The potential wage impact associated with public ownership has not gone unnoticed by some transit managers; for example, Louis J. Gambaccini, then vice-president and general manager, Port Authority Trans-Hudson Corporation, commented:

> We in the industry certainly do not begrudge labor the gains that were made in the period following public takeovers. Many of these gains were overdue and more than justified by the years of neglect in working conditions even as transportation service was declining. However, labor in the transit industry has more than made up for the erosion of its position in the late days of private ownership. Studies of transit wages reveal that labor costs in the industry have increased dramatically in recent years—the years in which many of these systems came under public ownership. At present, transit wages are significantly higher than wages in the private sector—and these wages have been increasing at a faster pace than the general wage rates in private industry.[10]

The wage "catch up" afforded by some public takeovers of private mass transit properties has been acknowledged by at least one national union official; however, this individual does not think that management requires an ownership profit incentive to bargain effectively:

> These ancient "market forces" theories may be popular with those seeking an excuse for political interference in collective bargaining, but the history of transit bargaining under tax supported public operation provides no evidence that management cannot do its job.[11]

---

[9]DANIEL S. HAMERMESH, "The Effect of Government Ownership on Union Wages," in *Labor in the Public and Nonprofit Sectors*, ed. Daniel S. Hamermesh (Princeton, N.J.: Princeton University Press, 1975), pp. 227–38. For a similar study having opposite conclusions, see DAROLD T. BARNUM, "Collective Bargaining and Manpower in Urban Transit Systems" (unpublished Ph.D. dissertation, University of Pennsylvania, 1972), pp. 227, 301.

[10]LOUIS J. GAMBACCINI, "A Common Purpose: Labor and Management in the Future of Public Transportation" (unpublished speech made at the Conference on Unions, Management Rights, and the Public Interest in Mass Transit, sponsored by the U.S. DOT Program of University Research and the University of North Florida, Jacksonville, Fla., March 22, 1976).

[11]DANIEL V. MARONEY, JR., "Collective Bargaining in Mass Transit" (unpublished speech made at the Conference on Unions, Management Rights, and the Public Interest in Mass Transit, sponsored by the U.S. DOT Program of University Research and the University of North Florida, Jacksonville, Fla., March 22, 1976).

Our investigation only partially supports the relationship found in Hamermesh's study; more specifically, almost one-third of the respondents believe the shift from private to public management has resulted in greater economic benefits. This transition has resulted in greater access to governmental financial assistance, which, in the opinion of one management official, increases union bargaining power, as management needs union agreement on certain grant provisions. Many of the management respondents indicate their "inability to pay higher wages" argument under the privately owned system is not currently accepted by the union in the publicly owned agency because of the agency's access to government subsidies. Almost all of the public takeovers were due to the dire financial situation of the private organization; under public ownership, unions maintain that, as employees and contributing taxpayers, they receive the same treatment and consideration available to other public employees. This sentiment was reflected by one union official:

> We think public transit should be treated the same way as fire and police and garbage collection or whatever other type city service. I've never had to use a policeman. I know they are essential. I've never had to use a fireman, but I know they are essential and I pay my taxes to support it. And I know there are complicated work rules regarding the fire department as well as there is in the transit industry, and I know that you can't have a man fighting a fire 24 hours a day at 8-hour shifts because we hope there's not that many fires, but the man that's a fireman has got to make a living, so therefore, he's got to have a day's work and a day's pay. The same is true with transit. . . . I don't read too much about the deficit operation of the police department . . . or the other departments. All we hear is how much deficit is in transit. But if we could get the people back on the buses and out of the cars, I think you would find that all of the cities, especially the large cities, would be better off.[12]

An often cited element of public-sector bargaining is *sovereignty*—the government is the sole possessor of final power as it represents the interests of all its constituents. This concept makes it impossible for labor and management to bargain as equals because the government must remain the sole authority in resolving labor's interests in terms accommodative to the larger constituency.[13] Sovereignty presents a paradox because the public employee working for a government which guarantees and maintains his democratic rights finds his employment rights are severely limited. A sometimes cited rationale for this paradox is that "the government employee's share in the control of his working life should be exercised through his capacity as a voting citizen of the state rather than as an employee of the state."[14] Interestingly, none of the union and management officials indicate any concern over this issue—apparently, sovereignty is neither discussed nor invoked during collective bargaining or other aspects of the

---

[12]Remarks made by a union panelist at the Conference on Unions, Management Rights, and the Public Interest in Mass Transit, sponsored by the U.S. DOT Program of University Research and the University of North Florida, Jacksonville, Fla., March 23, 1976.

[13]NEIL W. CHAMBERLAIN, "Public vs. Private Sector Bargaining," in *Collective Bargaining in Government: Readings and Cases*, eds. J. Joseph Loewenberg and Michael H. Moskow (Englewood Cliffs, N.J.: Prentice-Hall, Inc., 1972), pp. 11–16. See also WILLIAM H. HOLLEY, JR., "Unique Complexities of Public Sector Labor Relations," *Personnel Journal*, 55, no. 2 (February 1976), 73.

[14]LOUIS V. IMUNDO, JR., "Some Comparisons Between Public Sector and Private Sector Collective Bargaining," *Labor Law Journal*, 24, no. 12 (December 1973), 812.

labor–management relationship. Perhaps this is attributable to two interrelated factors:

- The long-established labor–management relationship at most of the mass transit properties, which tends to remove barriers inherent with the sovereignty principle.
- The "private-ownership heritage" found at most of these properties.

Yet another aspect of sovereignty pertains to its exercise in an independent system:

> The operation of government is organized around a system of checks and balances that delimit the exercise of power by an individual or group. The check and balance system exists because of separation of powers, elections, and constitutions. Employment and personnel policies are shared by legislatures, governors, departments, independent agencies, commissions, and even political parties.[15]

The diffusion of decision-making authority extended to the labor relations functions differs among the investigated properties. For example, most of the chief management negotiators have to consult with various governmental officials before tentatively agreeing on any economic issue, with some indicating that the morass of approval associated with public ownership has reduced the initiative and interest in labor negotiations they enjoyed under private ownership.

Management service organizations. With the decline and closure of many transit properties, the mass transit industry has been hard pressed to attract, develop, and train qualified managerial talent. Added to this managerial demise has been the conversion of private transit operations into public ownership by cities desiring to maintain some semblance of transit service for their communities. Publicly owned systems are, for the most part, service-oriented rather than profit-dependent and have the advantage of financial assistance from several levels of government. One major difficulty with public ownership and the attempt to revive existing transit systems has been the lack of qualified local government personnel with existing knowledge and experience in transit operations—a deficiency that can be best observed in the areas of collective bargaining and marketing. The use of services offered by management service organizations has been utilized by many cities as a means of maintaining and improving these areas.

Since about 1967, there has been a nationwide demand for competent, progress-oriented senior and middle managers in the transit industry. The major thrust of the management service organizations has been to provide managerial talent to publicly owned transit systems. Management service organizations offer similar, competitively bid services for contract to their clients, typically through a resident manager, a resident management team, or by the corporate staff, depending upon the needs of the

---

[15]Ibid., p. 813. See also MICHAEL H. MOSKOW, J. JOSEPH LOEWENBERG, AND EDWARD CLIFFORD KOZIARA, *Collective Bargaining in Public Employment* (New York: Random House, 1970), pp. 16, 211.

operation. There appear to be two basic management levels common to transit systems operated by management service firms. The upper level generally assumes overall responsibility for the system and usually includes top management of the contract firm along with an existing public entity such as the city council, county governing body, or an authority, board, or commission specifically created to make final decisions relative to policy, planning, and financing.

The other managerial level consists of the general manager (frequently called the resident manager) and his staff. This operational level of management is basically responsible for the day-to-day administration of the property. The general manager is usually, as are key members of his staff, contracted from the management service organization. The general manager is responsible to the upper managerial level for implementing its plans, policies, and directives. The nonresident corporate staff of the management service firm provides direct assistance to the resident management team. Frequently, a nonresident corporate staff member is assigned the task of conducting labor agreement negotiations. Contract interpretations may involve nonresident corporate staff depending upon the complexity and monetary significance of the issue involved.

There appear to be two major advantages to publicly owned transit properties which utilize contract management services: a method for facilitating financial assistance to the public agencies, and increased operational and labor relations expertise. The first advantage dealing with facilitating the acquisition of governmental financial assistance is illustrated by the "Memphis formula." Under this arrangement, the transit system's governmental owners contract with a management service firm, which, in turn, bargains with the unions. Since the management service organization is a private firm, state law prohibiting bargaining by public employees is assumed to be inapplicable. It appears that the two most difficult issues to resolve in dealing with the communities are the questions of labor costs due to the labor agreement and the provisions of 13(c) agreements.[16] As one management respondent (a resident manager) noted, "13(c) agreements scare the authority members to *death!*" It appears that the unknown qualities and "feared" costs believed to be associated with the employee protection provisions of Section 13(c) present authority members with a dilemma; however, the continuation of collective bargaining, which may be in opposition to state laws affecting publicly owned transit systems, does not seem to be of major concern to the authority members.

One study, in reporting on the advantages of contract management which were considered by public officials as most important, lists that, "A management company brings to the operation the expertise and know-how accumulated from years of experience, including extensive experience in the negotiation of labor contracts and public take-overs."[17] In discussions with the "professional" labor staff members of

---

[16]URBAN MASS TRANSPORTATION ADMINISTRATION, *Urban Mass Transportation Act of 1964 and Related Laws*, as amended through February 5, 1976 (Washington, D.C.: U.S. Government Printing Office, 1976), p. 21.

[17]M. M. BAKR, DANIEL ROBEY, AND THOMAS S. MILLER, *Role and Effectiveness of Contract Management in the Transit Industry*, prepared for UMTA (Milwaukee, Wis.: Marquette University, 1974), p. 37.

four management service firms, it was found that each has had extensive labor relations experience, including a wide variety of negotiation settings. In response to on-site interviews, several union respondents commented that, "Negotiations for labor agreements have substantially improved since a professional bargainer has taken over." It is interesting to note that this expression of confidence in the professionalism of contract management firms' "labor experts" extends to international union officers. In fact, where a certain degree of animosity could have been expected in such relationships, just the opposite seems to be the case. Several explanations have been offered, ranging from "the infrequent contact with the labor–management specialists" to "they bring a comprehensiveness to the bargaining table which allows for the 'petty' tactics of aggravation to be eliminated." Regardless of the reason, it seems apparent that the local labor respondents have a healthy respect for the labor specialists and also believe that the management service companies provide for good labor relations. Not one union respondent feels that the management service company impeded bargaining, but rather that bargaining has improved since the management service company had become involved.

Our research and discussions with management service firms seem to confirm the prominence of the role of their labor experts; in fact, these firms seem to place great emphasis on their labor experts serving as chief negotiators at the bargaining table. In one instance, it appears that the labor expert has direction of overall labor–management strategy for the firm, and in another instance, the individual has responsibility for overall direction of labor relations for his geographical territory. In commenting on these responsibilities, a panelist representing one of these firms, at a 1976 conference on labor relations in the transit industry, stated:

> I think our reponsibility is an educational process in that many of the public authorities or municipalities have individuals in decision-making positions who seem to have a natural reaction to criticize anything which they know little about. The fear, particularly in the South, is that when you mention labor, the municipality officials think strike. In some instances, the municipality believes that in dealing with labor that labor is going to pound the table and then go on strike. So I think that a very big part of our program has to be the education of some of these authorities and municipalities to the fact that labor does have some basic rights and those rights are given to them in a great part in Section 13(c) of the UMTA Act.[18]

BUDGETARY INFLUENCES IN COLLECTIVE BARGAINING

Budget making is traditionally a unilateral management activity necessary for organizational funding, planning, and control of operational activities. Yet, collective bargaining between labor and management officials can introduce new considerations that might alter the traditional view of budget making. More specifically, managerial speculations regarding the amount of the negotiated settlement might delay the

---

[18]Remarks of a management panelist serving as a member on the Management Service Panel, at the Conference on Unions, Management Rights, and the Public Interest in Mass Transit, sponsored by the U.S. DOT Program of University Research and the University of North Florida, Jacksonville, Fla., March 23, 1976.

budget-making process, whereas subsequent negotiation settlements might render initial budgets obsolete.

Our research[19] revealed two related findings. First, there appears to be little relationship between the fiscal year, final budget submission dates, and the collective bargaining process. Second, there appears to be a great deal of flexibility in the budget making–collective bargaining relationship in the form of supplemental or amended budgets, "padding," and lump-sum budgeting. Consequently, negotiated settlements can alter budget figures at a majority of the locations.

COLLECTIVE BARGAINING ISSUES AND OUTCOMES

MANAGEMENT RIGHTS: SCOPE AND LIMITATIONS

The issue of management rights in a unionized setting can be placed into proper perspective with the following questions: (1) "How is the management of labor in American industry affected by trade unions and collective bargaining?"[20] and (2) To what extent can management unilaterally decide where people work and what they are going to do?[21] This is perhaps the most controversial issue in the labor–management relationship: managerial defense of their prerogatives has historically been steeped in intense emotion. Currently, many management officials maintain that their "property rights" enable them to determine unilaterally the disposition of issues not specifically covered by the labor agreement. However, in the case of private-sector establishments, one authority noted:

> As for inherent property rights, the contention is that management has been authorized by the stockholders to manage the enterprise, including the right to direct employee activity. This is not the case. Management's legal rights are restricted to deciding how the property or assets of the firm will be utilized. These rights do not include the employee. There is no question that management can organize, arrange, and direct the machinery, materials, and money of the enterprise; however, it has no comparable right to direct the employee.[22]

Indeed, legislation has given the unions legal sanction and encouragement in challenging management's vested authority. Thus, the organization (either privately or publicly owned) becomes a "debating society" where employees, through their union representatives, challenge managerial directives and policies. A few issues are sealed off from bilateral consideration or joint decision making between management and the union. However, the vast remainder (either specified in or excluded from the

---

[19]The relationship between budget making and collective bargaining is more fully explored by KENNETH M. JENNINGS, JAY A. SMITH, JR., AND EARLE C. TRAYNHAM, JR., "Budgetary Influences on Bargaining in Mass Transit," *Journal of Collective Negotiations*, 6 (1977), 333–39.

[20]SUMNER H. SLICHTER, JAMES J. HEALY, AND E. ROBERT LIVERNASH, *The Impact of Collective Bargaining on Management* (Washington, D.C.: The Brookings Institution, 1960), p. 4.

[21]NEIL W. CHAMBERLAIN, "The Union Challenge to Management Control," *Industrial and Labor Relations Review*, 16, no. 2 (January 1963), 185.

[22]STANLEY YOUNG, "The Question of Managerial Prerogatives," *Industrial and Labor Relations Review*, 16, no. 2 (January 1963), 242. © 1963 by Cornell University. All rights reserved.

written labor agreement) are subject to management's procedural authority or administrative initiative. Management reserves the right in all instances to act on the basis of its interpretation of the labor agreement, as illustrated by the following quotation:

> The union cannot direct its members to their work stations or work assignments. The union does not tell people to go home because there is no work. The union does not notify people who are discharged to stay put. . . . The union does not start or stop operations unless perhaps some urgent safety matter is involved and there is some contractural or other basis for such action.[23]

Unions do not usually want to be "partners with management," as this practice could foster concerns from their constituents. However, unions do desire the option to challenge or appeal management's procedural rights through at least four possible avenues: contract negotiations, joint union–management committees, the negotiated grievance procedure, or informal discussions.

Our labor-contract analysis and interviews attempted to determine the extent of union involvement in managerial decisions, more specifically, the extent and substance of those issues under management's unilateral domain. Management officials tend to have complete discretion in the following areas: selection of employees, determination of when employee layoffs are needed, length of runs and time standards of runs, scheduling changes (routes and times), technological changes, and apprenticeship programs. It appears that the only administrative issues qualified by labor agreement provisions are employee layoff procedures and the bidding of runs. Thus, the findings generated from interview questions, as well as the more comprehensive contract analysis,[24] suggest that management has a relatively unencumbered hand in dealing with operations at the mass transit facilities. While no questions specifically asked the effects of union involvement on managerial discretion, it is important to note that no management official volunteered any concern over the issue during the rather lengthy interviews.

ECONOMIC ISSUES

The economic issues are the heart of the labor agreement, especially in mass transit operations where employee compensation accounts for approximately 60 to 85% of total operating expenses. Indeed, our research shows economic issues dominate current collective bargaining negotiations. Economic issues indicate to the employee how much pay he will get for work on a given job, and to the employer how much it will cost—in money—to get desired performance. There is often a tendency to view employee compensation narrowly in terms of wages. However, the wage is merely the most obvious, and often the most variable, part of employment compensa-

---

[23]ARTHUR G. GOLDBERG, "Management's Reserved Rights: A Labor View," in *Proceedings of the Ninth National Academy of Arbitrators*, ed. Jean T. McKelvey (Washington, D.C.: Bureau of National Affairs, Inc., 1956), p. 124.

[24]For additional discussion of management rights, see KENNETH M. JENNINGS, JAY A. SMITH, JR., AND EARLE C. TRAYNHAM, JR., "Managerial Discretionary Capability in Affecting the Public Interest in a Unionized Setting," in *Proceedings of Southern Management Association*, eds. Dennis F. Ray and Thad B. Green (Atlanta, Ga.: n.p., 1976), pp. 22–24.

tion. A substantial portion of the economic issues consists of contingent benefits such as sick leave, insurance programs, pension programs, provisions for premium or extra pay, and payment for time not worked (e.g., vacation pay and jury duty).

Union and management respondents were asked the open-ended question, "What were the major issues during your last contract negotiations?" It was anticipated that an industry, such as mass transit, with a declining output would have different labor problems/issues than an expanding industry (e.g., that job security issues would be relatively more important than wage demands). One would expect, even in inflationary times, that wages and wage demands would be moderated in a situation where price (fare) increases are often necessitated by wage increases, thereby resulting in fewer riders and fewer jobs. However, wages were mentioned as a major, if not "the" major, issue by all union and management respondents. An explanation for this emphasis on economic issues, aside from inflation, would appear to be the long history of collective bargaining in the transit industry; that is, most labor agreements reflect established and somewhat detailed criteria for promotion, layoff, and selection of runs, with systemwide or departmental seniority as the prime criteria. A merit system considering the critical issues of promotion, security, and run selection is somewhat difficult to attain because of the inherent inability to measure superior performance. With seniority issues so critical and because of the high proportion of minority workers, it was anticipated that work conditions or seniority issues would have been listed by respondents as one of the prominent issues in the most recent negotiations concluded before our study; however, this was not found to be the case. Perhaps this economic emphasis reflects the opinion expressed by several union respondents that federal and local financial assistance given to the transit industry belongs, in part, to the transit employees both as a factor of production in the creation of transit services and as taxpayers.

In assessing economic issues it appears most appropriate to relate briefly the mass transit industry to economic and institutional theories of wage determination. Generally, economic wage theories tend to view employees and employers as economic agents, trying to maximize wages and profits, respectively. When employees organize, the union becomes the economic agent, attempting to maximize the wage bill for its members. The union's efforts are typically constrained by a desire to maintain membership, a constraint which discourages pushing wages so high that employment is significantly reduced. Economic theories focus on productivity as the principal determinant of wages. Institutional wage theories, on the other hand, emphasize the importance of market structures (e.g., existence of monopoly powers and administrative and political forces in the determination of wages) and pay less attention to productivity as a wage-determining factor. According to Richard Lester, "The more 'mixed' the economy becomes, the less controlling is the market mechanism and the greater tends to be the influence of group psychology, public opinion, and political, social, and institutional factors."[25] Professor Lester adds that any theoretical formula-

---

[25]RICHARD A. LESTER, "A Range Theory of Wage Differentials," *Industrial and Labor Relations Review*, 5, no. 4 (July 1952), 485. © 1952 by Cornell University. All rights reserved.

tion that allows for multiple motivation and includes the influences just mentioned must necessarily be "eclectic and unprecise, devoid of simple solutions and subject to zones of indeterminacy."[26] Relatively little attention has been devoted to the public sector in the formulation of wage theories. However, there are some marked differences between private and public sectors, particularly with respect to employer goals and, frequently, output characteristics. The public employer generally responds to political motivations, and is less likely to be concerned about agency survival or relative labor costs and product price vis-à-vis his competition than his private counterpart.

The output or product of public employees and the price of this product often make application of economic wage theory difficult, if not impossible. In order to assign a value to the productivity of a public employee, it is first necessary to determine (1) the price of the product or service, and (2) the output of the public employee. In many cases, this information is not obtainable. Current conditions in the mass transit industry illustrate these problems well. It is not an easy matter to identify the output of a mass transit system or to measure the productivity of transit employees. Without elaborating, the services provided by a mass transit system affect many people in addition to the riders, and it is precisely these external effects which make the output uncertain. Furthermore, to the extent that the system receives governmental financial assistance and does not rely solely on voluntary purchases for revenue, the price of mass transit services is also unclear.

Because of these inherent problems, many public agencies must rely heavily on wage comparisons as a means of setting wages. This practice, commonly referred to as the *prevailing wage* principle, is given a legal basis by the Federal Salary Reform Act of 1962, which requires that federal pay rates be comparable with private enterprise pay rates for the same levels of work. Application of the prevailing wage technique is not a simple statistical undertaking devoid of discretion, but involves elements of negotiation. According to Bok and Dunlop, the final decision is influenced by the geographical area from which comparable wages are selected, the particular firms and occupations included, the data of the survey, and the methods of combining the survey data.[27]

An examination of the application of the prevailing wage principle leads Fogel and Lewin to conclude that public-sector wage rates tend to be higher than private-sector rates for low-skill and craft jobs for the following reasons: (1) government employees tend to exclude small firms from their wage surveys, giving an upward bias to the results of such surveys; (2) where private-sector wage rates are considered relatively low, the public sector tends to pay wage rates higher than existing private rates; (3) where private-sector wage rates are considered relatively high, the public sector tends

---

[26]Ibid.

[27]BOK AND DUNLOP, *Labor and the American Community*, pp. 318–20. For a cogent discussion of some of the merits and problems of using comparability as a wage-determining process, see NEIL W. CHAMBERLAIN, "Comparability Pay and Compulsory Arbitration in Municipal Bargaining," in *Collective Bargaining in Government: Readings and Cases*, eds. J. Joseph Loewenberg and Michael H. Moskow (Englewood Cliffs, N.J.: Prentice-Hall, Inc., 1972), pp. 342–46; and STEPHAN A. KOCZAK, "Collective Bargaining and Comparability in the Federal Sector," in *Industrial Relations Research Proceedings of the Twenty-Eighth Annual Winter Meeting*, eds. James Stern and Barbara Dennis (Madison, Wis.: Industrial Relations Research Association, 1976), pp. 197–204.

to pay rates at least equal to private rates; and (4) in setting wage rates, public-sector agencies do not take into account (i.e., adjust public wage rates downward to offset) favorable nonwage aspects of public-sector employment, such as greater job security.[28]

The conclusion that an upward bias exists in wages for low-skill and craft jobs in the public sector is contradicted, however, in a study by James Annable.[29] Annable concluded that the range of acceptable wages for any given public employee is generally more narrow, and eventually lower, than his private-sector counterpart. For the public employer, the upper limit of the acceptable range of wages is determined by the desire to maintain stable or decreasing tax levels. The lower limit is determined by the minimum wage at which the public employer can attract sufficient labor to provide stable or increasing levels of service. Pressures forcing these two boundaries to be very close to each other come essentially from the interaction of two facts: (1) the outputs of most public agencies are largely labor-intensive services, and (2) the productivity growth trend in the service-producing sector is less than half that of the goods-producing sector (approximately 1.1% per annum and 2.4% per annum, respectively). If the minimum wage required to attract qualified labor is set by the private sector, it is likely that this wage will increase at a rate roughly equal to the growth rate in the goods-producing sector. Since wage gains not offset by productivity increases must result in increases in per unit labor cost, the public employer must choose between paying higher labor costs for a stable level of public service or stabilizing labor costs by permitting public services to deteriorate. Since public output is labor-intensive, any rise in labor costs results in higher taxes. The public employer, according to Annable, faces a dilemma that gives the employer very little flexibility in setting wages and exerts constant downward pressure on public employee wages. He suggests that the unionization of labor is probably the only effective means available to public employees to combat this severe wage constraint.

On a priori grounds, we would expect that both of the hypotheses discussed previously about public-sector wage levels have some applicability to the mass transit industry. First, the decade of the 1960s was characterized by a substantial growth in per capita earnings. Significant increases in private-sector earnings would have exerted upward pressure on public-sector wages. Comparability was unavoidable. Second, continued declining ridership and farebox revenues coupled with the labor intensity of mass transit services would have made wage increases impossible without large increases in tax subsidies. If subsidy levels are to be stabilized or if transit services are to be expanded, it seems likely that the transit employer's range of acceptable wages must become subject to the same constraints discussed by Annable. However, this pressure upon the employee wage levels may be mitigated by the source of external financial assistance—that is, because of the inability to adequately associate increasing taxes at, say, the federal level with the wage level, municipal employers may feel less constrained in permitting wage increases. Also, it seems likely that unions will vigor-

---

[28]WALTER FOGEL AND DAVID LEWIN, "Wage Determination in the Public Sector," *Industrial and Labor Relations Review*, 27, no. 3 (April 1974), 410–31.

[29]JAMES E. ANNABLE, JR., "A Theory of Wage Determination in Public Employment," *The Quarterly Review of Economics and Business*, 14, no. 4 (Winter 1974), 43–58.

ously pursue wage increases comparable to those received by workers in other industries.

In bridging the theoretical-reality gap we find data furnished by the Bureau of Labor Statistics (BLS) tend to support the effectiveness of transit unions in obtaining substantial wage increases. Nationally, union wage rates for local transit operating employees averaged $6.25 per hour on July 1, 1975, an average increase of 11.3% over the previous year.[30] Between 1960 and 1975, union hourly wage rates of transit operating employees increased approximately 160%, and between 1965 and 1975, the average annual rate of increase was 7.9%.[31]

While these wage-rate increases indicate substantial gains enjoyed by unionized transit operating employees, it must be noted that a significant part of these wage-rate increases resulted from the cost-of-living escalator clauses found in most contracts. In fact, of the 11.3% average increase between July 1, 1974, and July 1, 1975, only 1.5 percentage points represented an increase in real wages.[32]

It is unlikely that traditional market forces such as productivity increases or increased demand for transit services explain these wage gains. As Darold Barnum points out, "The fact that transit wages have rapidly increased at the same time that productivity and profits have decreased is just one more indication that these (productivity and profits) have not been controlling criteria."[33] He suggests that comparisons with other transit systems are likely to be an important criterion.

In order to determine the extent that comparability is used as a basis for wage determination, we examined contracts for provisions pertaining to wage comparisons, and asked union and management officials specific, related questions. The only wage-setting practice specified in the contracts is a cost-of-living adjustment. None of the contracts examined contain a provision requiring the use or consideration of a wage survey, a wage formula, or the payment of a "prevailing" wage rate.

In on-site interviews, union and management officials were asked, "To what extent was comparability used in the negotiation of the present labor agreement, e.g., wages and specific noneconomic issues?" One-half of the respondents indicate that comparability is extensively used in economic issues, whereas only one respondent indicates that comparability is extensively used in noneconomic issues. Perhaps more significant is the perceived effect that comparability has in persuading each side to accept the other's position. A sizable number of the respondents indicate that comparability is only used as "a talking point" to "illustrate rationales behind union and management demands." One management official appears to sum up this statement with the following remark: "You can get a list and I can get a list. You won't convince me and I won't convince you, so let's work with what we have here."

---

[30]U.S. DEPARTMENT OF LABOR, BUREAU OF LABOR STATISTICS, Bulletin 1903, *Union Wages and Hours: Local-Transit Operating Employees, July 1, 1975* (Washington, D.C.: U.S. Government Printing Office, 1976).

[31]Ibid., p. 5.

[32]Ibid., pp. 2–3.

[33]DAROLD T. BARNUM, *From Private to Public: Labor Relations in Urban Mass Transit* (Lubbock, Tex.: Texas Tech University Press, 1977), p. 116.

This issue can be examined in terms of the extent technological change has affected the mass transit industry as well as the degree of union involvement in technological change. Technological change can have several potential effects on the jobs of mass transit employees. First, innovations can alter the work patterns of employees— requiring them to alter their work schedules, job duties, or skill levels. None of the union and management respondents maintain that recent technological changes (1971–1976) have materially altered their job characteristics, although a few of the respondents indicate that operators and maintenance employees had to undergo some training when new braking and transmission systems were introduced. Also, no job classifications have been seriously altered or eliminated due to recent technological changes. A second, more profound effect of technological change occurs when the number of bargaining-unit jobs are either increased or decreased as a result of the innovation.[34] One Amalgamated Transit Union (ATU) national official has succinctly placed this possibility in historical perspective:

> The transit industry, over the years, has participated in many innovations and technological changes. We have learned to live with them, sometimes at a great cost to ourselves. Originally, our first fight against innovation and technological change—first and last one, I believe—was our resistance to the changeover from the two-man car to the one-man car. We got soundly defeated at great price to our own inner wealth within our union and in our stature before our own membership. Our own members stated in public testimony that they drove the one-man car and felt so good after their 8 hours on the one-man car that they were able to play a round of golf. Now this sort of testimony defeated us. Since that time we have accommodated ourselves to the transition from the street car to the bus, from the small bus to the large bus, from the gasoline engine to the diesels; which almost overnight reduced our maintenance department and therefore our membership by 50 percent.[35]

Our interviews revealed no current impact of technological change on job loss or gain for the visited transit properties.

Unions can impact upon technological change through three general procedures: suggesting the change to management, assisting management in planning the change, and implementing the technological change on the job.[36] Our discussions with scores of union and management officials indicate a unanimous contention that unions have little or no influence through any of these procedures. Three reasons are given by the union representatives for their lack of influence: (1) "The unions and employees have

---

[34]GARDNER ACKLEY, "Automation: Threat and Promise," *The New York Times Magazine*, March 22, 1964, pp. 16, 52, 54, 57.

[35]W. BIERWAGON, "Labor's Response to Innovation in the Transit Industry," in *Proceedings of a Series of Conferences on Organized Labor, Transportation Technology and Urban Mass Transit in the Chicago Metropolitan Area*, eds. Stanley Rosen and Scott Schiave (unpublished, conferences sponsored by Chicago Labor Education Program, University of Illinois Institute of Labor and Industrial Relations, Office of Continuing Education and Public Service, in cooperation with College of Engineering, University of Illinois at College Circle), pp. 236–37.

[36]This classification roughly parallels that of MARTIN WACHS, "Fostering Technological Innovation in Urban Transportation Systems," *Traffic Quarterly*, 25, no. 1 (January 1971), 41.

worked to develop new techniques and tools for which no rewards have been given; in fact, management employees have claimed credit"; (2) "Employer maintains unions have no right to suggest or influence planned technological change"; and (3) "Union doesn't desire that much input but would seek protection if employees were laid off as a result."

This latter reason was echoed by many management officials who contend that most of the changes so far have been for the employee's betterment. However, if employees were adversely affected by the introduction of new equipment, the unions would seek greater involvement in related decisions. Some management officials speculate that the protection provisions in 13(c) reduce the possibility of the afore-mentioned situations.[37] Another indication of little union involvement in technological change emerges from the labor-agreement analysis—very few labor agreements contain provisions for joint union–management committees, and none of these agreements specify technological change as a topic for joint discussion.

A final dimension of union involvement in technological change relates to their overall policy position on this issue. One observer of the union movement has noted that, "From the viewpoint of history it is notable that outright union obstruction to technological change is conspicuously absent in the contemporary situation."[38] An ATU national official places this observation in the context of the mass transit industry:

> It is not my impression, but it may be yours, that transit labor, more than any other group, has powerful individual and institutional self-interests impelling it to resist the introduction of advanced systems of urban transportation. Of course, labor does not look with favor upon every proposal for change. But it can generally be counted as friendly to innovation if public policies and programs for implementation are sound and collective bargaining is preserved.
>
> Much depends, however, upon the facts and circumstances of a particular situation. So long as the workings of these future systems in a real-life setting can only be imagined, we have only the most rudimentary knowledge of their likely attributes and impact. We do not know yet what our attitudes may ultimately be.[39]

However, this official also suggested that dial-a-ride (a flexible scheduling system initiated by customers' telephoned request) could make the service more demand-responsive and fill in the gaps left unserved by present transit services, and may create better service to more people.

---

[37]At least one observer of mass transit operations suggests that management's lack of influence in tech-nological innovation matches that of the union—management officials are often given the technology "as is" with little involvement in the development or planning process. STANLEY ROSEN, "Organized Labor, Tech-nology and Innovation in Mass Transit" (unpublished speech made at the Conference on Unions, Manage-ment Rights, and the Public Interest in Mass Transit, sponsored by the U.S. DOT Program of University Research and the University of North Florida, Jacksonville, Fla., March 22, 1976). Our investigation did not attempt to verify empirically this contention, although it appears to be a most appropriate dimension for future, related research.

[38]JACK BARBASH, "The Impact of Technology on Labor–Management Relations," in *Contemporary Labor Issues*, eds. Walter Fogel and Archie Kleingartner, Wadsworth Continuing Education Series (Belmont, Calif.: Wadsworth Publishing Company, Inc., 1966), p. 340.

[39]JOHN M. ELLIOTT, "Labor's Response to Innovation in the Transit Industry" (unpublished address by the President, Amalgamated Transit Union, to the AFL–CIO, May 27, 1970), p. 1.

Subsequent to this official's comments, the San Francisco Bay Area Rapid Transit (BART) system, which was designed to be completely automated, was implemented. This same official expressed the national union's concern about a BART accident which occurred October 2, 1972:

> All those reponsible for allowing the BART trains to operate under the control of mechanical gadgets instead of under the direct control of a motorman are guilty of gross negligence. We believe the general public who ride these automated systems should insist that safe operation requires a human hand at the controls of BART trains.[40]

An increased number of rapid transit systems, projected by some union officials to equal 20 in approximately 15 years, would have profound effects on the jobs of mass transit employees. The potential impact of rapid transit systems on jobs was expressed by the following statement:

> Many of the rapid transit systems that will be developed over the next decade are expected to be run automatically through the use of computers. Accounting functions, maintenance operations and scheduling may also be performed largely through the use of computers. In addition, ticket sales and collection and analysis of power equipment functioning could be handled by automatic methods. The use of such equipment will probably limit employment opportunities in many operating, clerical, and maintenance occupations.[41]

It appears that the national unions have anticipated and have attempted to mitigate the possibility of technological displacement of employees:

> Work and work hard, against any and all attempts to establish a transit authority in your community until and unless you receive written assurances or legislative assurances that your membership will be employed by the proposed transit authority with all your rights and privileges.[42]
>
> We are accommodating ourselves to that in two ways; we are asking that the legislation that inaugurated these systems must bear reference and guarantees of collective bargaining and protection of the employees who are affected, not just adversely, who are affected because we do not want to be in the position of proving the adverse affect. That is sometimes difficult. They may argue that the adverse affect came from some other factor than the rapid transit or the use of federal funds or whatever they were making. If they are affected we want to be protected by legislation and we are insistent insofar as we are able that our local unions in supporting such legislation attempt and insist that it be placed in the legislation at the time the systems are being inaugurated in the state legislature at the first level, not at the level where they first say, "Well, let's put this thing on the tracks first—let's get the thing off the ground, then we will take care of you." . . . We are also taking care of ourselves, to a large extent, by our contracts which to a greater degree are now insisting that these changes be accommodated by attrition, that the immediate employee not be affected and that the present employees not be shouldered with the total cost of innovation and technological change.[43]

---

[40]JOHN M. ELLIOTT, "From the President's Desk," *In Transit*, November 1972, p. 11.

[41]NATIONAL COMMISSION ON TECHNOLOGY, AUTOMATION, AND ECONOMIC PROGRESS, *Technology and American Economy, Appendix Volume I: Outlook for Technological Change and Employment* (Washington, D.C.: U.S. Government Printing Office, 1966), p. 83.

[42]JOHN M. ELLIOTT, "From the President's Desk," *In Transit*, May 1971, p. 2.

[43]BIERWAGON, "Labor's Response," p. 237.

In summary, local mass transit unions currently have little influence in technological innovations, and appear to be relatively unconcerned about their role unless technological innovations make serious inroads into job content or employment positions. National union concern over this issue appears more pronounced, at present, than that found at the local level.

EMPLOYEE PROTECTION: SECTION 13(C)

The shift in ownership of transit properties from private to public could have had substantial effects on the collective bargaining rights of transit employees. As Barnum noted, when a transit system is in private hands, its collective bargaining is governed by the National Labor Relations Act (NLRA) and the ruling court cases.[44] However, the shift to public ownership causes a change in the collective bargaining relationships, for the NLRA is no longer the governing statute. The various local and state laws governing labor relations with public employees become effective, and the result is generally an inferior set of collective bargaining rights for the worker relative to those of the private sector.[45] But Section 13(c) of the Urban Mass Transportation Act of 1964 provides for a continuation of the collective bargaining rights as well as employee protection provisions for transit employees when their system becomes publicly owned.

Labor argued for a section in the transit assistance legislation that would require employee protection provisions be made, including the prevention of any curtailment of collective bargaining rights to the extent that such provisions would not be inconsistent with state or local law, prior to any federal aid. In the debates that took place in both the Senate and House, several amendments were offered modifying the language of the employee protection provision. Organized labor argued that past collective bargaining rights must be guaranteed, regardless of state or local laws, for even with a revised section that removed the specific language permitting preemption by state and local policy, the unions felt that the opportunity was present for destruction of bargaining rights.

The language that was contained in the final draft of the bill that became the Urban Mass Transportation Act of 1964 mandates that employees and their unions will not lose any rights as a result of the conversion from private to public ownership. As the act stated:

> It shall be a condition of any assistance . . . that fair and equitable arrangements are made, as determined by the Secretary of Labor, to protect the interests of employees affected by such assistance. Such protective arrangements shall include, without being limited to, such

---

[44]DAROLD T. BARNUM, "National Public Labor Relations Legislation: The Case of Urban Mass Transit," *Labor Law Journal*, 27, no. 3 (March 1976), 168.

[45]See JAMES J. MCGINLEY, *Labor Relations in the New York Rapid Transit Systems 1904–1944* (New York: King's Crown Press, Columbia University, 1949); ARTHUR W. MACMAHON, "The New York City Transit System: Public Ownership, Civil Service, and Collective Bargaining, "*Political Science Quarterly*, 56, no. 2 (June 1941), 161–98; P. FREUND, "Labor Relations in the New York Rapid Transit Industry, 1945–1960" (unpublished Ph.D. dissertation, New York University, 1964); and U.S. DEPARTMENT OF LABOR, *First Summary of State Policy Regulations for Public Sector Labor Relations* (Washington, D.C.: U.S. Government Printing Office, 1975).

provisions as may be necessary for . . . (2) the continuation of collective bargaining rights. . . .[46]

Although the act does not specify the exact procedure for protecting collective bargaining and employee rights, the legislative history indicates that Congress intended employee protections to be negotiated by the parties involved, not imposed by the government on the parties. Two emerging problems are implementation of Section 13(c) procedures and practitioner attitudes.

Several national agreements arising from transportation statutes form the precedent for the labor protection provisions in the transit industry. While these agreements concerning employee protection deal with rail operations, the Urban Mass Transportation Act sought to protect transit employees through similar language; for example, one of the key provisions of Section 13(c) is the guarantee of a continuation of collective bargaining rights. However, it is necessary to understand that if a strike or binding arbitration is prohibited by state law, then the means for resolving bargaining impasses need not be included in that guarantee. Larry Yud notes that many people confuse a specific provision negotiated for a given Section 13(c) agreement and the wording of Section 13(c) in the Urban Mass Transportation Act. The act does not require continuation of the right to strike in order to satisfy the requirement of the continuation of collective bargaining rights or employee protection. If the state law, by right of operation, does not allow the employee the right to strike or management the right to lock out their employees, but at some future time that state law might allow such actions, Section 13(c) will not prohibit this right in advance.[47]

Normally, when the U.S. Department of Transportation (DOT) receives a request for financial assistance, it sends a copy to the U.S. Department of Labor (DOL), which, in turn, notifies the union holding bargaining rights for that property, as well as other unions and transit members that might be affected by the project. If there is difficulty in settling upon mutually agreeable terms by the union and management, the Department of Labor provides advice and mediation services. In practice, DOL has the philosophy of approving any agreement between the parties, as long as there is no outright violation of the law.

Actual agreements vary because of the local conditions which recognize the individual properties and the sets of relationships that have developed between the local unit and management; however, in an examination of the Section 13(c) agreements collected from the visited properties, there were few differences, and then only minor variations, among the various Section 13(c) agreements.

----

[46]URBAN MASS TRANSPORTATION ADMINISTRATION, *Urban Mass Transportation Act*, p. 21. BARNUM, "National Public Labor Relations," p. 171. For a detailed analysis of the history of Section 13(c), see JEFFERSON ASSOCIATES, "Administration of Section 13(c)—Urban Mass Transportation Act," prepared for U.S. DOL (January 1972), pp. 5–19; and an unpublished U.S. Department of Labor study conducted in 1971 by W. L. Horvitz.

[47]L. F. Yud is Special Assistant for Mass Transit in the Office of the Under Secretary, U.S. Department of Labor, and is in charge of employee protection for DOL. The comments were answers to audience questions concerning employee protection at the Conference on Unions, Management Rights, and the Public Interest in Mass Transit, sponsored by the U.S. DOT Program of University Research and the University of North Florida, Jacksonville, Fla., March 23, 1976.

The similarities of 13(c) agreements probably should be increased as a result of the National Employee Protective Agreement for application to operating assistance grants under the Urban Mass Transportation Act, which is designed for use by individual transit employers and organizations representing employees in the area of proposed operating assistance projects.

It has been charged that labor unions use Section 13(c) to prevent transit innovation, and some management officials appear to be distrustful of the procedures adopted by DOL. Based upon the results of in-depth interviews at transit properties with both union and management respondents, there was no experience to ascertain costs under the application of Section 13(c) agreements. The field interviews were conducted in a nonstructured, informal, confidential manner in order to obtain both positive and negative comments concerning the advantages and disadvantages to both union and management from Section 13(c) agreements. While there is not wholehearted approval of Section 13(c) by management respondents, the decision makers seem to recognize that under the existing law, without Section 13(c) agreements, there could be no federal funding assistance. Management objections seem to be basically that Section 13(c) agreements tend to limit management rights and that there is no clear indication of the cost of the employee protection.

Our field interviews provided for a variety of responses about the difficulties concerning Section 13(c) negotiations; the main problem appears to be with city and local area governments, and their representatives, who, first, do not necessarily have the comprehensive skills to understand the complexity of employee protection provisions, and second, do not have the consummate negotiation skills to effectively complete a Section 13(c) agreement. Many of the comments about the problems of Section 13(c) negotiations, which have been publicized, do not necessarily agree with the comments from the professional negotiators (management respondents who have decision-making positions with respect to collective bargaining).

However, our field interviews found that a related concern in implementing Section 13(c) agreements is a lack of understanding on the part of all management respondents of the complete background of Section 13(c). This confusion might lead to fears by public officials that Section 13(c) would cause the extension of collective bargaining to all public employees. Of course, Section 13(c) requires that only past collective bargaining rights must be continued. Legislation applying to other public employees would have to go further and establish a uniform set of rights for all covered workers. This is so because almost all the nation's transit employees had already bargained under the NLRA when Section 13(c) was passed, so 13(c) needed only to extend to public-sector transit the uniform and comprehensive rights granted by the NLRA. Since other public employees do not have a common legal history of collective bargaining, legislation applying to them would have to include a uniform set of guidelines that would apply to all, regardless of past activity.[48] Perhaps some dispute between the two federal agencies handling federal assistance to transit has added some fuel to the fire of misunderstanding. The professional management negotiator seems much less

[48]BARNUM, "National Public Labor Relations," p. 176.

concerned about Section 13(c) agreements than do the resident managers, public officials, and trade association representatives and even some union officers at the local level. In the main, our survey results reflected the attitude of Mr. Gambaccini:

> On the subject of 13(c), I certainly accept the premise that employees who are adversely affected as a result of federal aid are entitled to some protection against the impact of that assistance. In fact, 13(c) negotiations, to the extent that they involve labor at the outset in the planning, policy and decision-making process, may even be helpful in obtaining union acceptance of needed improvements. I am also satisfied that the Department of Labor would not acquiesce in any attempt to use 13(c) as a vehicle to improperly "blackmail" management in an effort to force it to accept substantive contractual terms having no relation to 13(c). Nor, so far, have 13(c) agreements resulted in anything like the catastrophic charges to the industry which were feared.[49]

SELECTED BIBLIOGRAPHY

Many citations are no longer available from their original source. These citations are often available from the National Technical Information Service, U.S. Department of Commerce, 5285 Port Royal Road, Springfield, Va. 22161. We have verified the order numbers for many of these citations, and they are found at the end of the citation. Prices are available through NTIS at the address above.

ANDERSON, ARVID, "The Structure of Public Sector Bargaining," in *Public Workers and Public Unions*, ed. Sam Zagoria, pp. 37–52. Englewood Cliffs, N.J.: Prentice-Hall, Inc., 1972.

BARNUM, DAROLD T., *From Private to Public: Labor Relations in Urban Mass Transit.* Lubbock, Tex.: Texas Tech University Press, 1977.

————, "From Private to Public: Labor Relations in Urban Transit," *Industrial and Labor Relations Review*, 25, no. 1 (October 1971), 95–115.

BOK, DEREK C., AND JOHN T. DUNLOP, *Labor and the American Community.* New York: Simon and Schuster, 1970.

CHAMBERLAIN, NEIL W., "Public vs. Private Sector Bargaining," in *Collective Bargaining in Government: Readings and Cases*, eds. J. Joseph Loewenberg and Michael H. Moskow, pp. 11–16. Englewood Cliffs, N.J.: Prentice-Hall, Inc. 1972.

HAMERMESH, DANIEL S., "The Effect of Government Ownership on Union Wages," in *Labor in the Public and Nonprofit Sectors*, ed. Daniel S. Hamermesh, pp. 227–55. Princeton, N.J.: Princeton University Press, 1975.

LEWIN, DAVID, PETER FEUILLE, AND THOMAS A. KOCHAN, *Public Sector Labor Relations: Analysis and Readings.* Glen Ridge, N.J.: Thomas Horton & Daughters, 1977.

MEYERS, FREDERICK, "Organization and Collective Bargaining in the Local Mass Transportation Industry in the Southeast," *Southern Economic Journal*, vol. 15 (April 1949).

MOSKOW, MICHAEL H., J. JOSEPH LOEWENBERG, AND EDWARD CLIFFORD KOZIARA, *Collective Bargaining in Public Employment.* New York: Random House, 1970.

YOUNG, STANLEY, "The Question of Managerial Prerogatives," *Industrial and Labor Relations Review*, 16, no. 2 (January 1963), 240–53.

---

[49]GAMBACCINI, "A Common Purpose."

Chapter 32

PERCEPTIONS OF PUBLIC TRANSPORTATION

GEORGE E. GRAY, *Chief, Division of Mass Transportation,*
California Department of Transportation

Today the public seems to be reassessing its perceptions of the role expected of public transit. Not long ago, there was relatively little public thought given to the subject, but a number of factors have changed that. It is important that the industry, planners, decision makers, and others involved in public transportation understand that changes in public attitude are occurring which, collectively, may be the single most important determinant of the future roles of such service. Richard Reed has summarized the opportunities as follows:

> Today is clearly a turning point in the story of the automobile. And public transportation could gain from the new public perceptions of the auto and its consequences. If concern with a continued gasoline shortage or pollution control or the environment remains high, transit could regain patrons and once again become a prominent mover. The energy crisis is real, and transit use could be one of the patterns that result as the country adjusts to costly energy. The alternative, equally likely, is that the auto industry will provide smaller, less obtrusive vehicles and the country will decide to continue the pattern of individualized vehicles as the basic means of transport, the transit industry returning to its role as a welfare organization requiring subsidy to help the disadvantaged.[1]

The constantly changing values of modern societies often create conflict as well as opportunity for change. The fundamental facts of physics and reduced natural resources are impacting existing values to a greater extent than the general public yet completely realizes—but that realization will come and with it will come the call for change.

---

[1]RICHARD R. REED, *Market Segmentation Development for Public Transportation*, Research Report no. 8, prepared for UMTA (Stanford, Calif.: Stanford University Department of Industrial Engineering, August 1973), pp. 38–39. Now available as PB 227 178.

The ability of the transit industry to provide a quality service as an alternative to the automobile will be one of the key elements in influencing the reaction to the problems of air pollution, energy restrictions, and congestion. Most transportation authorities agree that these external factors, presently pressuring for changes in our mobility and our methods of achieving that mobility, will be major determinants of the growth and acceptance of public transit. However, it is obvious that the industry must improve its service—and image—in order to overcome the general public's formidable resistance, which presently inhibits significant increased use of most systems. In 1977, about 95% of the *choice riders*—those who have the option of using an auto or taking transit—always use the auto. Several attitude surveys taken in the mid-1970s have indicated that even if considerable disincentives are established on auto use, many people would continue using that mode.

In this chapter, various groups and their attitudes toward transit will be identified. Based on numerous studies, factors that appear to be significant to the groupings will be assessed. Finally, the major factors that impact on perceptions will be discussed and some strategies that may help in strengthening public acceptance of transit use suggested.

Government at all levels has a tremendous responsibility in addressing the problems of mobility. Those engaged in the current energy, environmental, and political tugs of war are directing much of their rhetoric to this problem without any prior determination as to the basic need for transportation. At this writing, there is still no articulated national policy on the subject, and state and local governmental units have little more to offer in this regard. The "shotgun" approach with categorical emphasis appears to be the accepted practice, with uncoordinated "band-aid" programs proliferating. Establishment of requirements for transportation improvement plans (TIPs) and their transportation systems management elements (TSMEs) in 1976 has helped to focus on this area and should increase coordination efforts. However, although these new requirements have the potential to change the basic planning process considerably and to orient it more toward being an effective programming tool, the changed process has not yet been fully developed. Given the history of past changes in the planning process, several years will be necessary to develop an effective process (see Chapters 16 and 17). The Carter administration's 1978 transportation program, as submitted to Congress, goes a long way in recommending consolidation of programs, but still misses the mark as far as being a national policy is concerned. The recently established National Transportation Policy Study Commission may be able to draw the conflicting transportation interests together enough to develop a policy that will receive the needed legislative and administrative endorsement to become the basis of national commitment. Obviously, the changing times are forcing reappraisal of many aspects of our present society. Transportation is but one of these. Unfortunately, it is so ubiquitous and so influential that even minor changes in the methods of providing transportation will have ripple effects in almost all aspects of our lives. These consequences have been largely ignored by our government. Except during times of tremendous highway development, governmental bodies in the United States have not used transportation, to any great extent, as a major tool to help achieve other goals, such as to control land use, or reinforce a national energy program.

The present federal emphasis on energy conservation will have impacts on all aspects of transportation, since the potential savings in that sector are so large. However, as important and necessary as energy use is, it is unfortunate that mobility needs are not considered more. They are the cause, and energy consumption is the effect. Assuming that this situation, lack of attention to mobility needs, will soon change as we learn to live at a less extravagant pace and consume less of our irreplaceable resources, it is apparent that it is necessary to learn more about the various groups most impacted by public transit so that service can be better adapted to address their concerns. At the same time, we may learn how to attract more choice riders to public transit.

THE CONCERNED GROUPS

One of the problems is to identify the various viewpoints that should be considered in looking at transit service. One early study broke the viewpoints into four groups but had a stratification resulting in a total of 79 categories.[2] Four major groups are self-evident: the transit users, the nonusers, the providers (operators), and the community as a whole (a classification that will be used to represent the spectrum from a small town to the nation as a whole).

THE USERS

The users group can be considered to be composed of the *captive users*, who have no alternative method for making a particular trip, and the *choice users*, who do have an alternative available. The captive market in this country is much larger than many realize. It is about half of the population at any one time. Included in this group are not only the elderly, the young, and certain of the handicapped, but also those without an automobile available, including the stranded housewife. The choice riders—the rest of the population except for a relatively small number who because of age or health are restricted from using public transit—are those who have an alternative transportation mode readily available.

Although the choice user group presents a large potential market for transit, it is also one that is difficult to attract. Tehan and Wachs propose using psychological considerations in the development and evaluation of new transit services in an attempt to meet the fundamental satisfactions of these possible users.[3] Their paper discusses methods of improving both the image and quality of mass transit, with these users' fundamental needs in mind, and draws parallels with the development and marketing

---

[2] J. L. SORENSON, "Identification of Social Costs and Benefits in Urban Transportation," in *Systems Analysis of Urban Transportation: Study in New Systems of Urban Transportation, Volume III: Network Flow Analyses*, prepared for HUD (Santa Barbara, Calif.: General Research Corporation, January 1968), pp. 22–25.

[3] CLAIRE TEHAN AND MARTIN WACHS, "The Role of Psychological Needs in Mass Transit," *High Speed Ground Transportation Journal*, 9, no. 2 (Summer 1975), 35–50.

of the automobile. At present, such psychological considerations, while not ignored, are largely not adequately considered.

Besides conventional transit, a number of specialized services have been developed to meet the needs of the captive users. These special services range from those provided by various human services agencies to meet the needs of their clients to those established for a portion of the market, such as the wheelchair-confined and the elderly. Such services may be provided by transit districts normally dedicated to operating conventional services, a variety of paratransit agencies, or other social and human services organizations.

THE NONUSERS

Nonusers include those who are unable to use transit as well as the choice riders who do not choose to use it for a variety of reasons. No doubt a large number of these reasons are psychological, but many are based on either physical limitations or mobility needs which cannot be served by transit. Of course, these deterrents will vary in accord with the particular type of service provided, but there will still always be a large number of "nonusers" who cannot be adequately accommodated. An example would be the television technicians, who must carry their tools and repair parts with them.

THE PROVIDERS (OPERATORS)

The providers group is rapidly changing its perspective. Until fairly recently, for most of them, the major concern was to provide service at a profit, or at least a minimal loss. As all major and many smaller systems have come under public ownership, transit managers have been increasingly interested in how to provide better service at a reasonable cost, even though operating costs are not recovered in the farebox. The emphasis has changed, but the main constraint—limited resources—still dominates their perceptions and resulting actions since the deficits must always somehow be covered. Increasing socially oriented services, such as reduced fares for selected groups during certain periods, cause conflicting objectives for the providers. Providing such human-services programs distorts the financial picture for the transit organization, and the resulting costs are often not adequately understood by the public. In only a few isolated cases are such human-services costs subsidized by their respective social programs.

THE COMMUNITY

Perspectives of the community group are becoming more and more the major determinants of establishing programs for newly developing public transit. Meanwhile, perceptions among this group are probably the least stable and, currently, are undergoing considerable change.

In most areas of this country, mobility has been dominated—even overwhelmed—by the automobile. However, recent indications are that this is causing severe impact problems. Among these impacts are (1) air and sound pollution; (2) increasing auto congestion, which lowers the efficiency of the auto and all those services which share its delegated space; (3) the high social and economic costs of extending or expanding the highway network; (4) land-use concerns focused on providing for the auto; (5) concern for those not served by the auto except at a very high cost—many of these people, the elderly, disabled, and young, feel that they have a civil right to economical, accessible transportation; and (6) diminished resources, specifically the energy problem, which, by itself, will eventually cause severe changes in existing transportation patterns.

CHANGING PERCEPTIONS

Obviously, the attitudes of individuals will differ with their particular circumstances. The transportation service needs of a home-to-work trip are quite different from those felt necessary to go to a society ball. Although both can be made in comfort by many of the same modes, the range of "acceptableness" of alternatives is different. Peer-group attitudes, financial resources, and a host of other factors can influence "acceptableness." To make it even more complex, attitudes change over time and space. Our involvement in the war in Viet Nam is an obvious example of the former, and one has only to compare travel habits of a San Franciscan or New Yorker with the average Los Angeleno to exemplify the latter.

It is this propensity toward changed attitudes which offers transit the opportunity for performing an increased role in providing mobility, especially urban mobility. If the industry can determine the major service attributes to meet user needs and provide them at a reasonable level of public investment, external pressures such as gasoline prices, congestion, and environmental concerns which will modify attitudes can be expected to cause significant modal shifting in the next 10 years.

TRANSIT USERS' ATTITUDE STUDIES

A number of studies have been made to identify and rank the factors which the public considers important in using conventional fixed-route transit. A few of these will be cited to illustrate the broad coverage of study types and the results obtained. The INTERPLAN study, one of the more recent, identifies six general attribute categories relative to mobility choice decisions[4]: accessibility, efficiency, reliability, comfort, safety, and cost. However, this study made no attempt to rank these factors.

A system to measure the effectiveness of the transportation services of local government was developed for the U.S. Department of Housing and Urban Development (HUD) by the Urban Institute.[5] The system uses the quality of transportation as seen by the citizen-consumer, and cites the major objectives of a local transportation system: "ease of access to the places people want to go, convenience, travel time (reasonable speed), comfort, safety, economy, maintenance of a habitable environment, and satisfaction among citizens with the overall adequacy of the system."[6]

---

[4]ROMAN KRZYCZKOWSKI AND OTHERS, *Integration of Transit Systems, Summary*, prepared for UMTA (Santa Barbara, Calif.: INTERPLAN Corporation, October 1973). Now available as PB 241 273.
[5]RICHARD E. WINNIE AND HARRY P. HATRY, *Measuring the Effectiveness of Local Government Services: Transportation*, prepared for HUD (Washington, D.C.: The Urban Institute, n.d.).
[6]Ibid., p. *v*.

One of the most comprehensive early studies was attitudinal research, conducted by a University of Maryland team over a 3-year period.[7] It included pilot studies in Baltimore and Philadelphia. These studies ranked variables in order of importance for both work and nonwork trips and found that the differences in relative importance were slight except for the travel-time factor. They concluded that the following list of factors[8] (in order of importance) suggests the basic attributes of a generalized, ideal transit system:

- Reliability of destination achievement (including elements of safety and confidence in the vehicle).
- Convenience and comfort.
- Travel time (but with large trip-purpose differences).
- Cost.
- State of vehicle (with cleanliness overshadowing newness).
- Self-esteem and autonomy (with emphasis on independence rather than pride).
- Traffic and congestion (both in and out of the vehicle).
- Diversions (including nature of travel companions, availability of radio, and scenery).

A mail questionnaire in the Twin Cities area by F. J. Beier attempted to identify why auto use dominated over bus transit. His study resulted in the following top-ranked factors[9]:

- Quickest travel time.
- Eliminate waiting periods.
- Freedom from schedules.
- Reliability of the car.
- Protection from the weather.

F. J. Stephenson, in a study of commuter attitudes of graduate students at the University of Minnesota, came up with the following listing of the 10 top factors favoring the auto[10]:

- Reliability.
- Able to leave when you desire.
- Shortest door-to-door time.
- Able to stop when you wish.
- Weather protection.
- Adequate space to carry items.

[7]ALLAN N. NASH AND STANLEY J. HILLE, "Public Attitudes Toward Transport Modes: A Summary of Two Pilot Studies," in *Public Attitudes Toward Highway Improvements*, Highway Research Record 233 (Washington, D.C.: Highway Research Board, 1968), pp. 33–46.

[8]Ibid., p. 43.

[9]FREDERICK J. BEIER, *The Attitudes of Drivers Toward Mass-Transit*, prepared for UMTA (Minneapolis Minn.: University of Minnesota, 1971). Now available as PB 207 131.

[10]F. J. STEPHENSON, JR., *Commuter Attitudes and Modal Choice in a Twin Cities Submarket* (Minneapolis, Minn.: University of Minnesota Graduate School of Business Administration, 1973).

- Transfer not needed.
- Independence.
- Clean vehicle.
- Able to travel at own speed.

A national survey of transportation attitudes conducted under the sponsorship of the American Association of State Highway Officials and the now-nonexistent Bureau of Public Roads identified many of the same items.[11] This survey, however, besides being somewhat dated, was evidently structured toward the use of the auto. Although it was comprehensive, it is of questionable value for the purposes of determining the relative factors which inhibit transit use. It does include valuable information on the segmented transportation market of the 1950s.

A more recent study by C. H. Lovelock agrees substantially with the earlier investigations and recommends three basic strategies operators could use to stimulate patronage: change physical attributes of vehicles and stations for comfort and safety, change operational characteristics for better service, and use persuasive communication to change nonuser attitudes and preferences.[12]

A comprehensive study by the Orange County Transit District in California focused on identification and assessment of the relative importance of the attributes of transit as conceived by the consumer and determination of the extent to which consumers consider that existing modes satisfy their needs.[13] The results are in general agreement with the earlier studies but indicate that the public places much more importance on bus-driver attitude than previously identified. Strong general support for transit was found, with 84% responding that benefits of transit are well worth the cost and 90% feeling that bus transport would make their city more livable. The strongest support for transit was found in the demographic groups least likely to use transit—those with incomes over $25,000 per year or with two or more autos.

This study provides a good example of how results can be used for policy guidance and management decisions. For example, interpretation of study results points out that in this country more effort is needed to market transit—an interested but largely uninformed public was identified.

This study also disclosed that attitudes concerning other transportation services are evidently not basically different than those focused on fixed-route transit. As part of a program to increase auto occupancy through formation of carpools, insight into the reasons for basic modal choice decisions was researched so that proposed actions could address the identified reasons behind transportation mode choice. Each person in the survey was asked to rate attributes of work travel as to importance in the mode selection for work trips. A total of 11 factors were included. The four receiving

[11]Robert K. McMillan and Henry Assael, *National Survey of Transportation Attitudes and Behavior, Phase I: Summary Report*, NCHRP Report 49 (Washington, D.C.: Highway Research Board, 1968).

[12]Christopher H. Lovelock, *Consumer Oriented Approaches to Marketing Urban Transit*, prepared for UMTA (Stanford, Calif.: Stanford University, March 1973). Now available as PB 220 781.

[13]Gordon J. Fielding, Douglas P. Blankenship, and Timothy Tardiff, "Consumer Attitudes Toward Public Transit," in *Public Transportation Planning*, Transportation Research Record 563 (Washington, D.C.: Transportation Research Board, 1976), pp. 22–28.

highest importance were reliability, safety from accidents, convenience, and safety from crime. Costs were not specifically identified as an attribute.

Battelle, Columbus Laboratories, in a 1972 report for the Urban Mass Transportation Administration (UMTA), noted that, although there is no consensus on the relative importance of user-conceived attributes, the apparent lack of consensus on *what* is important arises mostly from differing definitions of the attributes themselves.[14] Battelle further notes that all researchers tend to include travel time, travel cost, comfort, convenience, and safety.

A more recent review (1976) by Martin Wachs of various studies indicates that the relevant factors influencing modal choice are travel time, reliability, convenience, comfort, safety, cost, and amenities.[15]

A 1976 survey by Hoey and Levinson, covering a medium-size community, found radical differences between transit users and nonusers regarding acceptable transit service levels.[16] Even with an acceptable level of service, nonusers indicated that external factors would be needed to change their travel habits. The study concludes:

> The survey indicates that existing transit riders have a much lower expectation regarding bus service attributes than car drivers. Thus, radically improved service concepts and levels will be necessary to divert motorists to transit use; and they may be feasible only in selected corridors. *If energy, environmental, or public policy considerations require large scale diversions of commuters to transit, then selected auto disincentives may be necessary. Increased motor fuel taxation appears to be more productive than parking taxes and controls—at least in medium-sized cities.*[17]

The results of these various studies are far from identical, or even similar in some cases. That, however, does not detract from their value. Attitudinal surveys similar to these are finding increasing popularity and proving to be valuable in helping to determine the type of service that should be considered in a particular area. They are also frequently used in planning studies in ranking proposed alternatives for new systems.

THE *SCARCE* AMENITIES

Analysis of the various surveys and readings in the field suggests grouping the factors influencing use of transit into the acronym "SCARCE"—unfortunately, a most appropriate description of their present availability in some transit operations. "SCARCE" stands for:

---

[14]R. D. Leis, E. S. Cheaney, and N. Simons, Jr., *Functional Specifications for New Systems of Urban Mass Transportation*, prepared for UMTA (Columbus, Ohio: Battelle, Columbus Laboratories, November 1972). Now available as PB 217 613.

[15]Martin Wachs, "Consumer Attitudes Toward Transit Service: An Interpretive Review," *Journal of the American Institute of Planners*, 42, no. 1 (January 1976), 96–104.

[16]William F. Hoey and Herbert S. Levinson, "Attitude Surveys, Transit Planning, and Auto-Use Constraints" (unpublished paper presented at the 56th Annual Meeting, Transportation Research Board, January 1977).

[17]Ibid., p. 14.

Safety.
Comfort.
Accessibility.
Reliability.
Cost comparative.
Efficiency.

These attributes cover all the major items listed in the cited studies as well as many others not referenced.

It is important to note that there is no rating of importance implied in this acronym. It is obvious from a review of the numerous studies that this is not practical. People just are not consistent enough. They have different needs for different trips at different times in their life cycles. Besides, there is lack of uniformity in the terminology used in the various studies or surveys.

A short description of the elements constituting these various attributes follows.

Safety (on vehicles and at stops) includes not only safety from accidents but also passenger safety from theft and physical violence, as well as vehicle safety from vandalism. Chapter 23 covers this item in more detail.

Comfort embraces the physical comfort of the passenger within the vehicles and at stops (ride quality, adequate environmental controls, effectual seating, handholds, sufficient entrances and exits with easy fare collection, package accommodations); the aesthetic qualities of the system (clean and pleasingly designed vehicles, attractive stops, terminals, guideways, and other facilities); environmental protection of the community (noise and exhaust emissions); facilities for the handicapped; and pleasant, helpful operators.

Accessibility implies adequacy of route distribution over the area served, vehicle capacity, service frequency and operating time span, identification of stops and vehicles, and distribution of information on fares, schedules, etc., as well as ease of fare paying and well-placed stops and terminals.

Reliability depends on low breakdown rate with special services provided when breakdowns do occur, adherence to schedules with adequate information about any service changes, and guaranteed availability of transfer.

Cost comparative means reasonable, guaranteed fares with minimum zone fares (if any), and easy transfer mechanisms and possibly cost reductions for passes (weekly, daily, etc.) and special groups (students, children, senior citizens, etc.).

Efficiency includes high average speeds with minimum dwell times and the absence of traffic delays, sufficient stops for minimum walking (but not too many so as to increase travel time), coordinated schedules and transfer points with minimum user discomfort, direct routing, and express and special-event service when warranted. Efficiency also requires an easily maintained system with adequate maintenance facilities, an efficient management system, and minimal staff necessary to sustain efficient service.

Again, it should be recognized that the outlook toward transit of the three most interested groups (the user, the provider, and the community) toward these factors will vary. For instance, the users' requirements vary, depending upon being a commuter, new traveler to a system (such as a tourist), or a regular user frequenting certain routes (such as the captive rider going shopping).

In some of the identified attributes, there is obvious conflict between the goals of the various groups. For instance, the user and the provider have difficulty agreeing on the amount of service to satisfy certain elements of accessibility, such as adequacy of route distribution, vehicle capacity, and service frequency and time span. This disparity of interests is an example of why conventional transit often cannot compete favorably in an open market with the auto—and also indicates why private conventional transit systems are rapidly disappearing from the scene. In order to attract the choice rider, which is the main market for increased ridership, cost-effective service levels cannot be the sole determining criteria for establishing routings, headways, etc.

FACTORS AFFECTING THE SCARCE AMENITIES

INTERPLAN identifies seven factors as being the major causes of the present deficiencies in public transit in this country.[18] A short discussion of these items follows.

Finances. Over the years, lack of funding has severely restricted development of transit systems. This, coupled with inadequate allocation of the available funds, contributes to failures to make investments in maintaining the physical plant and equipment as well as to provide for modernization of systems. In many cases, it has resulted in transit systems that will be inadequate to provide for the increased services that will be needed as the energy crisis becomes more pronounced. It must be remembered that lead times to provide added services are substantial with, for instance, 2 years for changes which require more buses not uncommon.

The addition of Section 5 UMTA funding and similar funding which provides flexibility for capital additions or operating costs gave temporary relief in the mid-1970s, but the basic problem of inadequate funds, especially to cover ever-increasing operating costs, remains (see Chapter 25).

Transportation policies. Lack of transportation policies has caused imbalances in providing for competitive modes. With few exceptions, parking policies, highway funding, integrated services, rate setting—all seem to be developed separately. There is no coordinated effort to develop transportation as a whole; only elements of service are addressed. This fractured approach cannot be allowed to continue. A comprehensive national transportation policy is long overdue. The American Public Transit Association, American Association of State Highway and Transportation Officials, and others have developed policies reflecting their organizational positions, but the need for an accepted national policy is only more apparent as these more biased policies proliferate. Some state plans which provide policy guidance have been developed, but without a well-established national policy, such efforts can, at best, be temporary expedients subject to change as federal programs change.

---

[18]KRZYCZKOWSKI, *Integration of Transit Systems.*

Local political factors. Local political factors often create a havoc of multiple jurisdictions, legal barriers to coordination, rate constraints, and resistance to cooperation. All too often, local jealousies and the narrow interests of political bodies are allowed to overshadow the public good.

Technology. At present, the development of such necessary programs as vehicle improvement, automated ticket devices, and computerized management systems are hindered by a number of factors. Among these are lack of funds, unclear development rights, governmental "red tape," and, until recently, apathy on the part of both manufacturers and the general public. The problem of short-range programs based on existing technology vs. innovation and development of new concepts is especially difficult to address in an area faced with decisions involving major financial commitment for providing transit services.

Labor. In many instances, labor restrictions cause uneconomical operations to continue. There is considerable evidence that, in many cases, increased labor costs, if not counterbalanced by increased productivity, will eliminate much of the existing conventional bus service as a viable alternative. To provide for reliable transit service, it may become necessary to eliminate, or at least severely restrict, not only the right to strike but some of the more restrictive work rules.

Management. For many years, the industry has been in a declining market; now that the demands for increased service are growing, there are complicated managerial problems to overcome. George M. Smerk (see Chapter 20), among others, makes a strong case that "management has almost always been the weakest link in the mass transit chain."[19]

Lack of integration and coordination. Lack of integration and coordination includes such problems as fragmentation of transit service among different agencies, lack of cooperation among agencies, and uncoordinated services within a single agency.

LEVELS OF SERVICE AND THE SCARCE FACTORS

The SCARCE factors are all related to levels of service to some extent. Therefore, one of the best ways to reduce the adverse effects of the SCARCE factors is to increase the quality and quantity of service in general.

Several UMTA programs are already under way which potentially will have considerable impact on levels of service. The major constraint to the realization of this potential may be lack of adequate funding. However, there is considerable recent evidence that public attitudes soon are going to force increased levels of financial support; therefore, this may not be a continuing problem. UMTA programs to improve

---

[19]GEORGE M. SMERK, "Mass Transit Management," *Business Horizons*, 14, no. 6 (December 1971), 5.

transit equipment are covered in Chapter 34 and therefore this second element to improved service will not be addressed here.

Besides adequate funding and equipment, assured effective management and marketing are the remaining necessary elements in providing a high level of service. To improve capability in the management of transit systems, several tools are being made available. UMTA is developing a package of computer programs to provide for management information needs—including cost accounting (FARE), scheduling (RUCUS), maintenance (SIMS), and planning (UTPS). The greatest additional needs in this area appear to be training for middle management and an established forum for resolution of operational problems caused by institutional barriers. Needed is an accelerated and improved effort aimed at increasing the supervision capability of the industry by using modern techniques. Both improved and expanded training of existing practitioners and university programs to produce graduates oriented toward entering the transit field are also positive steps which would help produce improved and efficient management.

WHAT ELSE TO DO TO CHANGE PERCEPTIONS

There are a variety of actions which can be undertaken to improve the public attitude toward public transit and mitigate the adverse aspects of the SCARCE factors. It is important to keep in mind that attitudes are the product of perceptions. You must change the way people perceive a service before you can expect to change their attitudes toward it.

Improved services resulting from increased capital investment, improved management, diversification of types of service, and so on, all have a prominent place. However, as early as 1970, L. M. Schneider pointed out:

> The prospect of new capital is not the transit industry's salvation, for capital can too easily be misallocated through investments in inappropriate facilities or dissipated by poor maintenance. The industry is still caught up in the vicious circle of declining productivity, high operating costs, poor service, increasing fares, and level or declining patronage. A radical approach is needed. It is hoped that new marketing-oriented transit strategies will provide the answer.[20]

Although ridership is increasing in most areas, the basic concept behind this statement is still appropriate. Smerk,[21] Lovelock,[22] Davis,[23] and Reed[24] have all given emphasis to this position and agree that focus on market segmentation holds considerable promise.

Lovelock concludes his study with the opinion that by highlighting the consumer's need for information and the relationship between modal choice behavior and attitudes,

---

[20]Lewis M. Schneider, "Marketing Urban Transit," in *Mass Transportation*, Highway Research Record 318 (Washington, D.C.: Highway Research Board, 1970), p. 19.

[21]Smerk, "Mass Transit Management."

[22]Lovelock, *Consumer Oriented Approaches.*

[23]Davis; see Chapter 22.

[24]Reed, *Market Segmentation Development.*

relatively inexpensive marketing and communication programs might be extremely effective in encouraging use of public transit.[25] His study also contains several proposed strategies involving elements of the market. Reed takes this last approach considerably further and gives a comprehensive analysis of the value of using a segmented marketing approach for promotion of transit.[26] Many of these concepts are further developed in Chapter 22.

Although this chapter has concentrated on perceptions directed at conventional bus systems, there is no evidence that the attitudes underlying the perceptions cannot be applied to other types of transit service. Some of the paratransit services better address certain attributes for certain trips, but since there is such a variety of service combinations, no attempt to address the perceptual differences relating to this important growing transit sector has been attempted.

CONCLUSION

Attitude surveys in the public transit sector are relatively new, although their use is growing. They have the potential of providing needed information leading to improved service at a reasonable cost and over a short time frame.

A study of the literature on transit attitudes indicates considerable agreement on the major factors that influence the level of transit use of the choice rider, although the priority of importance of the factors is varied. The factors can be represented by the acronym SCARCE, standing for: *S*afety, *C*omfort, *A*ccessibility, *R*eliability, *C*ost, and *E*fficiency. These are six major factors reflecting present deficiencies in public transit service. Strategies to mitigate these six elements and improve the SCARCE amenities include improvement of service levels, equipment, management techniques, and marketing.

SELECTED BIBLIOGRAPHY

Many citations are no longer available from their original source. These citations are often available from the National Technical Information Service, U.S. Department of Commerce, 5285 Port Royal Road, Springfield, Va. 22161. We have verified the order numbers for many of these citations, and they are found at the end of the citation. Prices are available through NTIS at the address above.

BEIER, FREDERICK J., *The Attitudes of Drivers Toward Mass-Transit*, prepared for UMTA. Minneapolis Minn.: University of Minnesota, 1971. Now available as PB 207 131.

BURKHARDT, JON E., AND MARGARET T. SHAFFER, "Social and Psychological Impacts of Transportation Improvements," *Transportation*, 1, no. 2 (August 1972), 207–26.

BYRD, JOSEPH P., "Characteristics, Attitudes, and Perceptions of Transit Nonusers in the Atlanta Region," in *Public Transportation Planning*, Transportation Research Record 563, pp. 29–37. Washington, D.C.: Transportation Research Board, 1976.

---

[25]LOVELOCK, *Consumer Oriented Approaches.*
[26]REED, *Market Segmentation Development.*

CRAIN, JOHN L., "Notes on Factors Affecting Acceptance of Travel Modes" (unpublished paper presented at the 26th Annual California Transportation and Public Works Conference, March 27–29, 1974).

FIELDING, GORDON J., DOUGLAS P. BLANKENSHIP, AND TIMOTHY TARDIFF, "Consumer Attitudes Toward Public Transit," in *Public Transportation Planning*, Transportation Research Record, 563, pp. 22–28. Washington, D.C.: Transportation Research Board, 1976.

GOLOB, THOMAS F., "The Survey of User Choice of Alternate Transportation Modes," in *Urban and Regional Ground Transportation: Surveys and Readings*, ed. James J. Murray, pp. 175–85. Durham, N.C.: Planning-Transport Associates, Inc., 1973.

———, RICARDO DOBSON, AND JAGDISH N. SHETH, "Perceived Attribute Importance in Public and Private Transportation" (unpublished paper presented at the National American Institute for Decision Sciences Meeting, Boston, Mass., November 14–16, 1973).

———, AND OTHERS, "An Analysis of Consumer Preferences for a Public Transportation System," *Transportation Research*, 6, no. 1 (March 1972), 81–102.

HARTGEN, DAVID T., *Variations in Reference Scale and Perception of Modal Attributes for Different Traveler Groups*, Report no. PRR 55. Albany, N.Y.: New York State Department of Transportation, Planning Division, Planning and Research Bureau, December 1973.

KRZYCZKOWSKI, ROMAN, AND OTHERS, *Integration of Transit Systems*, Summary, prepared for UMTA. Santa Barbara, Calif.: INTERPLAN Corporation, October 1973. Now available as PB 241 273.

LOVELOCK, CHRISTOPHER H., *Consumer Oriented Approaches to Marketing Urban Transit*, prepared for UMTA. Stanford, Calif.: Stanford University, March 1973. Now available as PB 220 781.

NOTESS, CHARLES, "Life-Style Factors Behind Modal Choice," *Transp. Eng. Journal of ASCE*, 99, no. TE3 (August 1973), 513–20.

PAINE, FRANK T., AND OTHERS, "Consumer Attitudes Toward Auto Versus Public Transport Alternatives," *Journal of Applied Psychology*, 53, no. 6 (1969), 472–80.

REED, RICHARD R., *Market Segmentation Development for Public Transportation*, Research Report no. 8, prepared for UMTA. Stanford, Calif.: Stanford University Department of Industrial Engineering, August 1973. Now available as PB 227 178.

STEPHENSON, F. J., JR., *Commuter Attitudes and Modal Choice in a Twin Cities Submarket*. Minneapolis, Minn.: University of Minnesota Graduate School of Business Administration, 1973.

TARDIFF, TIMOTHY J., "Comparison of Effectiveness of Various Measures of Socioeconomic Status in Models of Transportation Behavior," in *Travel Behavior and Values*, Transportation Research Record 534, pp. 1–9. Washington, D.C.: Transportation Research Board, 1975.

TEHAN, CLAIRE, AND MARTIN WACHS, "The Role of Psychological Needs in Mass Transit," *High Speed Ground Transportation Journal*, 9, no. 2 (Summer 1975), 35–50.

TRANSPORTATION RESEARCH BOARD *Behavioral Demand Modeling and Valuation of Travel Time*, Special Report 149. Washington, D.C.: Transportation Research Board, 1974.

WACHS, MARTIN, "Consumer Attitudes Toward Transit Service: An Interpretive Review," *Journal of the American Institute of Planners*, 42, no. 1 (January 1976), 96–104.

WICKSTROM, GEORGE V., "Transportation System Performance Measurement and Application," *Institute of Traffic Engineers: Compendium of Technical Papers*, 43rd Annual Meeting, ed. Walter P. Youngblood, Minneapolis, Minn. (1973), pp. 159–63.

PART VII

The Future

INTRODUCTION TO PART VII

The purpose of this section is to present several possible directions for public transportation that are likely to occur in the coming decades. Forecasting the future is a hazardous activity at best, and while the seeds of change are now germinating, the results will not be known for many years. For example, jet engines, computers, television, and interstate highways existed in the 1950s, yet the impacts on society by the 1970s of these developments were not fully appreciated then. So it is with attempts to now describe transportation in the twenty-first century.

In the short run it can be expected that continued emphasis will be placed on using existing facilities more efficiently through a variety of techniques referred to collectively as transportation systems management (TSM). The objectives of TSM are to increase capacity and reduce energy consumption and pollution by more effective use of the present highway system and by reductions in travel during peak periods.

A variety of TSM techniques have been proposed or tested, and during the next decade many of these will become an integral part of regular transportation services in cities. Streets and highways dedicated to exclusive use by buses and carpools represent a TSM technique that has been adopted in a relatively short time. Other ideas, such as flexible work times, vanpools, transit coordination, parking management, and dial-a-ride, are within present technological capabilities and may see widespread use as incentives change and new organizational arrangements are created.

The role of new technology and systems in meeting future urban transportation needs is yet to be determined. Although the basic ideas for automated guideway transit (AGT) were developed in the late 1960s, the application of these advanced concepts has been limited. Computer-controlled personal rapid transit (PRT) that operates single vehicles on an integrated areawide network on lightweight aerial guideways may become a reality in the future if the cost and benefits prove favorable and the systems can be designed to operate reliably. Two classes of AGT systems, shuttle-loop transit (SLT) and group rapid transit (GRT), are operating in several airports and other major activity centers. Experience with these forms of high-technology transportation, as well as the Downtown People-Mover Program, will help to determine the potential of this mode in the future.

The long-range trends in transportation are dependent upon changes in population and the economy, energy availability, and institutional arrangements. The evolutionary process should see replacement of older facilities with new, and possibly different, forms of fixed-guideway transit. Coordination between modes will be essential if each is to serve its best suited function and as dependency on the personal auto is further diminished. These changes will affect the future of freight and passenger transportation for both urban and intercity systems.

LESTER A. HOEL, Professor and Chairman,
Department of Civil Engineering,
University of Virginia

Chapter 33

IMPROVED UTILIZATION OF EXISTING FACILITIES

DONALD A. MORIN, *Transit and Traffic Engineering Branch,*
Federal Highway Administration

No urban public transportation operation is a self-contained system. It functions as an integral part of the total urban transportation system. In most cases, the transit operation must share a common right-of-way, typically the highway network, with other modes. Even fixed-rail systems, on exclusive rights-of-way, rely on a variety of complementary facilities for the collection and distribution portions of the trip. Terminal areas, modal transfer points, pedestrian facilities, bicycle access and parking facilities, fringe parking, and passenger shelters must be developed concurrently with public transportation services to provide complete and convenient transportation service for diverse urban trips. Planning for new major public transportation capital facility investments or service improvements should include consideration of these peripheral facilities that can enhance utilization by improving the service characteristics of the operation. Furthermore, the development of these facilities as a part of a transportation system management (TSM)[1] program can increase the utilization of the existing public transportation system without the delay, disruption, and heavy capital expense associated with major new construction.

The highway network with its extensive coverage of the urban area provides the backbone of any public transportation system, since the majority of all public transportation operations in the United States utilize the highway network. In most cases, highway improvements, be they new or expanded facilities, traffic engineering improve-

---

[1] The terms "system" and "systems" are currently used interchangeably in discussing TSM. In the Code of Federal Regulations, Title 23 (Chapter I), Subpart A, Part 450 uses "systems" and Title 49 (Chapter VI), Subpart B, Part 613 uses "system."

ments, or only safety improvements, will also enhance transit service by improving transit schedules. Signal timing improvements, prohibitions of turns, and modifications to increase capacity at bottlenecks can reduce bus travel times as well as auto travel times. On the other hand, highway improvements can be detrimental to transit service if the projects are not properly coordinated with transit operations. Turn prohibitions, one-way street designations, and blocked cross streets that interfere with established bus routes can impede bus movements and cause inconvenience for bus passengers.

Since most transit operations rely on the existing highway network, either directly as the right-of-way for bus operations or indirectly as the collection and distribution network for fixed-guideway systems, highway system improvements play an integral role in short-range transit planning. Buses as highway vehicles, and bus passengers as highway users, share in the benefits of these types of improvements.

The effectiveness of traffic-engineering-type TSM techniques can often be limited by the sheer volume of traffic. In that case, the efficiency of the existing road network can be improved by increasing the number of persons per vehicle. Buses, for example, can carry 40 to 50 persons in the space of two automobiles. Since the objective of the transportation system is to provide for movement of persons and goods, buses and other high-occupancy vehicles such as carpools, which use limited highway space more efficiently, should be granted priority use of highways. A wide range of highway strategies have been used to give these vehicles an advantage in the competition for highway space. Typically, these projects involve only minor physical modifications to the highway system, although in some cases major new facilities have been built. Projects range from adding bus bays to provide for the safe and convenient discharge of passengers without sacrificing highway capacity, to constructing exclusive bus roadways in congested urban corridors to provide a substantial travel-time saving. Projects that afford high-occupancy vehicles a travel-time advantage have been particularly effective in attracting patrons.

While the condition and management of the highway network has a substantial impact on bus transit operations, other nonhighway TSM strategies can influence transit service and utilization as well. These strategies can help improve the efficiency and utilization of the existing transit operation by making the system more accessible, convenient, and comfortable for the traveling public. Programs and projects as diverse as carpool promotional activity, fringe parking, bicycle and pedestrian facilities, encouraging staggered work hours, and traffic-regulations enforcement are all interrelated with the quality and utilization of the transit system. With appropriate coordination the transit system can benefit from these strategies, which attempt more to manage the use of the transportation system than to expand facilities.

This chapter presents examples showing the wide range of TSM treatments available to increase utilization of existing systems. A comprehensive short-range program would include many types of strategies—both highway and nonhighway projects—to increase the utilization of existing facilities.

HIGHWAY-TYPE TRANSIT STRATEGIES

A high degree of bus use requires service levels that compare favorably with automobile travel in terms of trip times, costs, and service dependability. This can be aided by such actions as (1) providing adequate route coverage and service frequency to more of the metropolitan area; (2) operating express bus service on longer routes; (3) effectively coordinating bus and highway operations, planning, and construction; (4) adjusting street routing patterns and traffic controls to more effectively meet bus needs; and (5) providing bus priority facilities, such as busways, bus streets, bus lanes, and bus ramps. These opportunities exist in most cities.

Applied in isolation, individual bus priority treatments have slight impact relative to random variations in traffic flow or speeds, yet the cumulative effect of a large number of small-scale treatments may radically alter system performance and utilization.

Bus priority treatments have been increasingly implemented throughout the world. The types of treatment, the number of people served, and the design details vary widely. Treatments can be grouped into three broad categories: those relating to freeways, major arterials, and downtown streets.

PRIORITY LANES ON FREEWAYS

Freeway bus service is increasingly common in large cities. The rise in express bus service parallels the growth in urban freeway mileage and underlies the increasing emphasis on freeway-related bus priority treatments. Buses can substantially increase the peak-hour person-capacities on urban freeways. The proportion of peak-hour bus passengers on existing urban freeways, which on many facilities exceeds 25% and on the I-495 Lincoln Tunnel approach to New York is 85% of the total person movement, underscores the importance and potential of freeway bus operations in larger cities. A freeway lane can carry 2000 to 3000 persons/hour in cars without any priority treatment, or 35,000 to 40,000 people/hour in buses using off-line stations and adequate downtown distribution. When buses must stop in travel lanes, however, capacity is reduced to about 120 buses or 6000 persons/hour.

Buses operate efficiently on uncongested urban freeways; however, many freeways, particularly radial routes leading to downtown areas, become routinely congested in peak hours, delaying buses as well as other users. As a result, many cities are considering bus priority treatments on freeways or special busways to achieve faster and more reliable bus travel. Exclusive bus roadways on their own rights-of-way with complete control of access provide the highest type of service.

A preferential bus facility may be located as a separate or shared roadway within a freeway right-of-way, either in the freeway median or along one side of the freeway. On the Shirley Highway serving northern Virginia commuters to Washington, D.C., the two-lane reversible median roadway was initially reserved for buses along an 18-km (11-mi) section during peak periods. Since December 1973, carpools with four or more persons have been permitted to use the busway. The specially constructed San Bernardino Busway serving Los Angeles commuters now provides one lane for buses and carpools in each direction along 18 km (11 mi) of I-10 approaching the central business district (CBD). The lanes were constructed in the freeway median for one section and alongside the freeway for another section.

These two examples are in a special category of preferential treatment since they required extensive construction, and consequently a substantial investment of time and money. Existing road space can be reserved for buses and other high-occupancy vehicles, usually at much lower cost and with much shorter lead times.

The concept of reserved freeway lanes applies freeway traffic operations and control techniques to reserve a lane for buses and/or other designated vehicles (such as emergency vehicles, trucks, or high-occupancy cars). It involves minimum physical construction. However, it is difficult to provide stations or interim access.

Experience with reserving normal-flow bus lanes is limited because of concern over the impact of reducing the number of lanes available for other vehicles. Bus lanes can be provided in the normal direction of traffic when ample reserve capacity exists or where additional lanes are created (by widening or upgrading shoulders, for example). In particular, a queue bypass lane upstream from a bottleneck, with buses merged back into the general traffic stream at the head of the queue, can provide significant benefits.

Projects reserving normal-flow freeway lanes have been implemented on Route 101 in Marin County, California, on the Moanalua Freeway (Fig. 33-1) in Hawaii, on I-93 in Boston, on I-95 in Miami, on the Banfield Freeway in Portland, Oregon, and on I-280 in San Francisco. These projects were all implemented after construction of an additional lane. The Marin County operation initially provided priority treatment for buses only, but was later opened to carpools, while buses and carpools of three or more were provided for in the initial operations of the others. There is no physical separation between the priority lanes and the regular traffic lanes on any of these projects.

On the Santa Monica Freeway in Los Angeles, an extensive and extremely controversial priority-lane project was in operation for 5 months before being stopped by a court order for failure to follow correct environmental assessment procedures. The project involved reserving one of the existing lanes next to the median in both directions for buses and carpools with three or more for 20.3 km (12.6 mi). Extensive ramp metering with bus and carpool bypass was also used to control the volume of traffic entering the freeway.

A "wrong-way," or contra-flow, bus lane using a portion of the roadway that serves relatively light opposing traffic flow is a prime candidate, in that it will not reduce peak directional highway capacity or efficiency. It is an adaption of the reversible-lane concept used for more than three decades, now being applied to urban freeways. Potential problems include the need to remove median barriers at crossovers or transition points, blocking of the exclusive lane by accidents or stalled buses, and possible congestion in the remaining off-peak direction. It is usually not possible to

Figure 33-1 *Reserved bus and carpool lane on Moanalua freeway. (courtesy of Federal Highway Administration)*

provide stations or interim access for buses, and successful application is contingent on a high directional imbalance in traffic volumes.

Existing contra-flow bus lanes operate only in peak hours on freeways that are at least six lanes wide and provide at least two lanes for general traffic in the off-peak direction. Such bus lanes have been implemented in the New York, San Francisco, and Boston areas. In the New York area two contra-flow projects are operational: a 4-km (2.5-mi) lane on I-495 in northern New Jersey approaching the Lincoln Tunnel and a 3.2-km (2-mi) lane on the Long Island Expressway approaching the Queens Midtown Tunnel. Both of these projects operate in the morning peak period. The longest contra-flow operation in the United States was implemented along 13.5 km (8.4 mi) of the Southeast Expressway in the Boston area. The lane, which has since been discontinued, operated in the morning peak period, but only from April to October, owing to the safety problems of manually placing the cones during hours of darkness on the unlighted freeway. The 6.4-km (4-mi) contra-flow lane on Route 101 in Marin County (Fig. 33-2) north of the Golden Gate Bridge connects with the normal-flow reserved bus and carpool lane previously mentioned to provide priority treatment for a total of 12.9 km (8 mi) along the freeway. The contra-flow lane operates northbound in the evening peak period, with a buffer lane separating the contra-flow buses from the two southbound lanes.

Figure 33-2 *Contra-flow bus lane on Route 101 in Marin County. (courtesy of Federal Highway Administration)*

Most freeway bus operations take place in mixed freeway traffic. Thus, measures that assure steady freeway flow will simultaneously benefit bus passengers. As long as freeways operate above level of service D, as defined in the *Highway Capacity Manual*,[2] mixed-traffic operations are more efficient than providing exclusive bus lanes or roads. This allows buses to reach speeds of 80 km/h (50 mi/h). Person delay—even where freeway congestion develops—often can be minimized by expediting general traffic flow, rather than by reducing freeway capacity for cars and giving it to buses. Thus, mixed operation of cars and buses with bus priorities around bottlenecks will usually have wider applicability. Treatments such as special ramps to or from freeways, metering of ramps with special bus and/or carpool bypass lanes, and bus stops alongside or adjacent to freeways can be applied singly or in combination to expedite priority-vehicle flows at minimum cost and with minimum delay to other road users.

Ramp metering, in conjunction with priority freeway entry for high-occupancy vehicles, can extend the preferential treatment concept without restricting freeway capacity for general traffic. In this case, special traffic signals on entrance ramps allow only those vehicles to enter the freeway that can be accommodated without seriously reducing mainline speeds. Bypass lanes or special ramps at these metered entry points allow buses and/or carpools to bypass automobile queues and avoid delay.

[2]HIGHWAY RESEARCH BOARD, *Highway Capacity Manual: 1965* (Washington, D.C.: Highway Research Board, 1965).

In the Minneapolis area special bus bypass ramps were constructed at nine metered entrance ramps along I-35W south of the CBD. In California bypass lanes for high-occupancy vehicles (Fig. 33-3) have been provided at numerous metered ramps, mostly in the Los Angeles area.

Providing exclusive bus ramps to major terminals is another technique to allow preferential access to freeways. For example, exclusive bus ramps provide access to the San Francisco–Oakland Bay Bridge from the Transbay Bus Terminal in San Francisco and to the Lincoln Tunnel from the Port Authority Midtown Bus Terminal in New York. Seattle's Blue Streak bus service uses an exclusive bus ramp (Fig. 33-4) from the reversible lanes of I-5 for access to and from the CBD. In Reston, Virginia, exclusive bus access ramps were constructed allowing commuter buses to use the Dulles Airport Access Road for express service to Washington, D.C.

Where freeway congestion results from a bottleneck caused by lane reduction or convergence, special bus bypass facilities may be appropriate. An example of a short bus lane to bypass congestion is in operation on Route 163 in San Diego. The bus lane uses the parking lane and the right shoulder for about 1.6 km (1 mi) where the road transitions from a downtown street to a freeway. In the toll plaza approaching the San Francisco–Oakland Bay Bridge, lanes have been reserved for high-occupancy vehicles. The project was initiated as a single bus lane through the 17-lane toll plaza area, but was later extended to carpools with three or more when two additional lanes were reserved. Furthermore, tolls have been eliminated for the high-occupancy vehicles.

The time and expense involved in specially constructed busways generally preclude consideration as a TSM technique. While the quality of transit service on such facil-

Figure 33-3 *Typical bypass lane at metered ramp in Los Angeles area. (courtesy of Federal Highway Administration)*

Figure 33-4 *Exclusive bus ramp to I-5 in Seattle.* (*courtesy of Federal Highway Administration*)

ities is very good, substantial diversion to the transit service is possible, and the capacity of the system approaches that of fixed-rail facilities; this type of project should be more appropriately viewed as a long-range transit development strategy. Reserving existing freeway lanes and providing preferential freeway access will have more widespread application.

Different types of operational concerns are involved in each of different types of freeway bus-priority operations. The most common concerns associated with these projects fall into three general areas: public acceptance, enforcement, and safety.

The public reaction to preferential treatment projects is largely dependent on the impact on regular traffic and the level of utilization of the reserved lane. Contra-flow lanes should have a favorable impact on traffic in the peak direction of flow since buses are removed from the traffic stream. Traffic in the light direction may be somewhat restricted. Reserved bus lanes in the peak direction of flow have a greater potential for increasing delays to regular traffic. As a result, normal-flow reserved lanes are generally designated when new lanes have been added to the freeway or supplemental roadspace is added by minor construction. This avoids adverse public reaction that may be caused by aggravated traffic conditions if an existing lane is closed to general traffic.

Even though passenger volumes on bus lanes typically far exceed those of normal mixed-traffic lanes, bus lanes may appear underutilized because of long bus headways. To fill the gaps, carpools often are permitted to use normal-flow reserved lanes or ramp bypasses. The capacity of the lane can be fully utilized by extending the priority treatment to more high-occupancy vehicles.

Enforcement of lane restrictions can be a problem on normal-flow reserved lanes or ramp bypass lanes if proper enforcement planning and public information has been overlooked. On these types of projects, signs and pavement markings with the "diamond" symbol are used to designate the preferential treatment without physical barriers separating the priority lane from regular traffic. The priority vehicles are usually free to enter or leave the lane anywhere along the reserved portion. Violators, as well, can weave into and out of the preferential lane with relative ease; therefore, enforcement is essential to maintain the integrity of the preferential treatment. Usually a median shoulder or stopping bay can be used for enforcement activities. Enforcement on contra-flow bus lanes is less of a problem because of the limited number of access points and the high visibility of violators.

Safety is a prime consideration in the implementation of contra-flow lanes. Adequate traffic control devices, such as changeable message signs, delineators, and traffic cones, are an integral part of any project. Where possible, a buffer lane similar to the U.S. 101 Marin County contra-flow project is desirable. Many safety problems anticipated with contra-flow operations have failed to materialize. However, safety considerations should be a major factor in project design. On normal-flow preferential lane projects, the speed differential between priority vehicles and regular traffic in the adjacent lane creates a potential safety problem that should be carefully monitored. Adequate enforcement should mitigate the problem of violators weaving in and out of the priority lane posing a hazard for the faster-moving priority vehicles. In some instances special provisions may be required to allow priority vehicles to safely reenter the traffic stream without delay.

The principal advantage of reserving freeway lanes for the exclusive use of buses and/or carpools is that such preferential treatments have the potential of increasing the passenger-carrying capacity of the highway by several orders of magnitude. An exclusive freeway bus lane can comfortably accommodate peak-hour volumes of over 25,000 passengers, or over eight times more people than the peak-hour mixed-traffic lane. Thus, the preferential treatment concept is an effective tool to make more efficient use of existing vehicle and highway capacities. The I-495 contra-flow lane carried nearly 26,000 passengers on 600 buses during the highest hour recorded. In a normal daily peak hour, 480 buses carry about 21,000 passengers. On the Long Island Expressway, the contra-flow lanes carry about 6000 persons on 120 buses during the peak hour. On Route 101 in Marin County, nearly 4000 persons on about 105 buses use the exclusive lane, part contra-flow and part concurrent-flow, during the peak hour. The two Shirley Highway (Fig. 33-5) reversible lanes carry 18,500 persons in 250 buses and 2100 carpools in the peak hour. Even low bus volumes can be given preferential treatment by sharing the lane with carpools. The Moanalua Freeway priority lane in Honolulu carries 11 buses and 1300 carpools during the peak period.

The travel-time savings possible by providing bus priority treatment around congested bottlenecks provide a strong incentive to divert auto users to the more efficient bus mode. Generally, where preferential treatment schemes have been imple-

Figure 33-5 *Shirley Highway reversible bus and carpool lanes. (courtesy of Federal Highway Administration)*

mented, the bus service is well patronized. Peak-hour travel-time savings range from 5 to 30 minutes. To preserve the travel-time advantage in case of an incident in the bus lane, there should be space available to clear disabled vehicles from the traveled way. The I-495 contra-flow is only 3.4 m (11 ft) wide with no shoulders, so a tow truck remains on standby during the operation to clear stopped vehicles.

A considerable variety of freeway priority treatments for buses and carpools have been implemented to date and many more projects are in the planning stages. The particular type of preferential treatment appropriate to any highway situation must be determined by an analysis of the specific traffic conditions. The applicability of specific treatments depends on (1) the intensity and location of existing and future demands, (2) the suitability of existing and proposed freeways to meet these demands, (3) the location and extent of peak-hour congestion, and (4) the extent to which user demand should be modified.

To fully utilize the capacity of a reserved bus lane, carpools should be permitted in the lane if this can be done safely. Even where bus volumes are low, a lane reserved for carpools and buses will invariably be able to serve more people. In any case, the occupancy requirements (i.e., size of pool to qualify) should be set so as not to overload the preferential lane.

Allowing carpools to use contra-flow lanes requires special precautions. Buses can use single contra-flow lanes where mixed traffic could not do so as safely because (1) the bus lane traffic stream is homogeneous, variation in vehicle performance is minimal, and there is no need for overtaking slower vehicles; (2) buses are highly visible to other drivers, especially when emergency flashers are used; (3) professional bus drivers are generally well-trained, experienced, and highly disciplined; (4) bus lane volumes are relatively low (generally under 200 vehicles per hour), making risk of a collision no greater than on an undivided urban arterial or rural highway; and (5) the probability of a disabled vehicle is very low. These considerations would preclude carpools using contra-flow lanes on most freeways. However, this may not be the case on freeways that have an adequate median shoulder and/or mountable median refuge strip.

Use of normal-flow preferential lanes by carpools will increase weaving traffic into and out of the lane, which may increase the accident potential. Furthermore, the greater number of vehicles in the lane may create difficulties in merging back into the regular traffic. Enforcement would be necessary to keep violators out of the lane, especially since violators are not quite as noticeable once carpools are admitted. Enforcement experience to date indicates that it is possible to keep violations to an acceptable level without excessive enforcement expense.

PRIORITY LANES ON ARTERIALS

Most urban bus service will continue to operate on arterial streets. Radial bus routes generally converge on a few downtown streets where bus priority treatments can expedite flow. Buses frequently travel at headways ranging from 30 seconds to 3 minutes and often carry more than one-half of all peak-hour travelers to the downtown area.

Bus priorities along arterial streets represent a minimum-cost approach to increasing road-use efficiency, improving bus service, and enhancing the bus transit image. Corridor priority measures along major arterials expedite line-haul local and express movements through intermediate and outlying areas. Such treatments offer excellent potential for increasing urban mobility and altering modal choice patterns.

Bus priority treatments should be provided along arterial streets when they will minimize total person delay. This basic goal should be based on expected ridership considering the improvements and subject to (1) land access considerations, (2) environmental constraints, and/or (3) policy objectives to maximize transit use in specific corridors. Bus priority treatments along extended sections of major arterials have been implemented in several locations around the country:

1. A contra-flow bus lane (later changed to a concurrent-flow lane) along 8.9 km (5.5 mi) of the South Dixie Highway in Miami. Left turns were prohibited during peak hours, morning and evening, so that buses could use the median lane in the opposite-flow direction on this six-lane median-divided arterial with at-grade intersections.
2. Contra-flow bus lanes along nearly 18 km (11 mi) of a one-way couplet in San Juan, Puerto Rico. The left curb lane of these four-lane one-way streets has been reversed for the use of buses only.
3. Experimental bus priority treatments along nearly 16 km (10 mi) of N.W. 7th Avenue in Miami. Depending on the cross section along the route, the

priority bus lane takes the form of a reversible center lane or a reserved lane along the median divider. The project includes bus priority at traffic signals, including bus preemption of signals and signal progression.

4. A 3.2-km (2-mi) bus/carpool lane along the Kalanianaole Highway approaching Honolulu. A three–one directional split is in operation during the morning peak period on this four-lane arterial (Fig. 33-6), with the third inbound lane reserved for buses and carpools.
5. A 2.4-km (1.5-mi) median busway on Canal Street in New Orleans. Heavy bus traffic utilizes the paved median right-of-way that replaced the streetcar line.
6. A 3.5-km (2.2-mi) contra-flow lane in Madison, Wisconsin, implemented in conjunction with the designation of a one-way street couplet.

Nearly any existing street can be converted to provide bus lanes. The particular type of treatment appropriate to an arterial highway will depend on several factors, including roadway cross section and geometrics, traffic conditions, and bus service in the corridor. Types of preferential lane treatments include curb bus lanes, median bus lanes, and contra-flow bus lanes (either on one-way streets or across the median of a divided arterial). A major two-way arterial can usually support a bus lane either moving with or against traffic. The major difference between limited access and arterial streets is the interaction of traffic on intersecting streets. The resulting traffic operating patterns associated with reserved lanes may be complex. Another problem is that reserved lanes may complicate access to abutting land.

Bus lanes generally involve removing a travel lane from automobile use and giving it to buses. They are sometimes implemented in conjunction with one-way street

Figure 33-6 *Bus and carpool lane on major arterial approaching Honolulu. (courtesy of Federal Highway Administration)*

systems and curb parking prohibitions. In these cases, there is usually no net loss in street capacity. In other cases, buses normally dominate the lanes used and the designation of bus priority lanes causes no appreciable change in automobile capacity.

Curb bus lanes in the normal direction of flow are easy to implement and involve minimum street routing changes at little cost. However, they are often difficult to enforce and may produce only marginal benefits to bus flow. Right-turning vehicles either conflict with buses or must be prohibited.

Median bus lanes are an outgrowth of streetcar operations. These lanes may be in effect during peak periods or throughout the day. They remove buses from traffic conflicts along the curb and allow other traffic to make right turns without interfering with buses. Median lanes can serve express bus service exclusively; otherwise, they require wide streets with provisions for service stops and pedestrian refuge in the median. Passengers are required to cross active traffic lanes to reach bus stops along the route. Left turns must be prohibited or controlled to minimize interference with buses.

Contra-flow bus lanes, in which buses operate opposite to normal traffic flow, are increasing in number. Contra-flow lanes on one-way streets usually operate throughout the day. Contra-flow lanes in the median lane of the opposing roadway can be provided in conjunction with peak-hour bus service. Buses using the lanes are separated from other traffic flow and are not, therefore, affected by peak-hour congestion at signalized intersections. They are largely "self-enforcing." They frequently are located to permit more direct bus routing. Furthermore, they can create a sense of transit identity, and separate bus-loading delays from the peak-direction traffic flow. The lanes may, however, complicate loading and access to adjoining properties. They increase left-turn conflicts with opposing traffic, and on one-way streets with frequent signals, buses may have to operate against timed signals.

Owing to the high visibility of buses in a contra-flow lane and the lower operating speeds on arterial streets, safety problems arising from vehicle conflicts have failed to materialize, particularly on contra-flow operations on one-way streets. In fact, in the San Juan contra-flow project, as people became familiar with the bus lane, accidents declined below rates experienced before the bus lane was put into operation. With contra-flow bus lanes in the opposing median lane of a divided arterial, a particular safety problem arises with left turns across the bus lane, especially from traffic flowing in the same direction as the buses as drivers are not accustomed to looking for such traffic.

Another safety problem associated with contra-flow operations concerns pedestrians. Particularly where contra-flow operations are initiated on long-standing one-way streets, pedestrians may be unaccustomed to watch for buses traveling opposite the normal one-way flow. Since accidents involving pedestrians usually result in a serious injury or fatality, one or two accidents can discredit the entire operation.

Serious pedestrian accidents have occurred on the Madison, Wisconsin, and South Dixie Highway contra-flow operations, resulting in unfavorable publicity and community reaction. Special precautions should be taken to avoid these unfortunate incidents. Signs at pedestrian crossings warning of the bus operation and barriers in midblock to prevent pedestrian crossing can be used to mitigate potential hazards.

The principal objective of priority lanes on major arterial streets is to reduce transit travel times for the line-haul portion of the trip and thereby enhance the quality of service. Furthermore, the person-carrying capacity of the roadway can be increased because of the greater space efficiency of buses. To maintain the travel-time advantage in cases where stops are necessary on part of the route, it may be advisable to provide pull-offs so that buses behind are not delayed. If such pull-offs are not possible, a two-lane exclusive bus facility with one lane for nonstop vehicles should be considered.

Bus priorities along arterial streets form a logical component of a transportation improvement program that manages street use by spatially and/or temporally segregating bus from car traffic. Treatments should be developed as part of a system of improvements that expedite general traffic flow and bus service. This system should (1) reduce bus and car travel times, (2) improve bus service reliability and schedule adherence, (3) improve passenger safety, (4) increase bus service "visibility" (or route identity), and (5) reduce bus operating costs. Improved on-schedule operation may make it possible to provide additional bus runs without more equipment or cost.

Effective enforcement of bus lanes is essential. Bus lane proposals should be accompanied by active enforcement programs. The volume of buses in a reserved lane can help enforce the bus lane, since more buses will provide reassurance to the public that the lane is being effectively utilized.

Sharing of preferential facilities by carpools and even different types of bus service can cause additional complexities which require special consideration. Along routes with substantial local bus service, carpools using the bus lane, as well as express buses, may suffer a travel-time penalty. In such a case, carpools and express buses should use the mixed-traffic lanes or, if justified, a separate reserved lane.

PRIORITY LANES ON CBD STREETS

Major downtown streets generally carry a high concentration of bus traffic. Typical peak-hour bus and passenger characteristics underscore the importance of bus use of downtown streets and the need for bus priority treatments. Buses on Hillside Avenue (New York City), State Street (Chicago), Market Street (Philadelphia), and Pennsylvania Avenue (Washington, D.C.) carry more than 85% of the peak-hour travelers on those streets. Buses on downtown streets in Los Angeles, Atlanta, Pittsburgh, and Milwaukee carry more than 70% of all peak-hour travelers.

Downtown bus priority treatments far outnumber those along corridors, mainly because bus flows are heaviest within the CBD, and many of the same types of priority treatments described under arterial priority lanes apply. In planning downtown priority projects, the additional objective of providing for the safe loading and unloading of passengers must be kept in mind.

Curb bus lanes in the normal direction of flow are the most common. Cities as diverse as Atlanta, Baltimore, Denver, Buffalo, Dallas, New York, San Francisco, and

Washington, D.C., among others, have implemented curb bus lanes. These lanes are usually in effect during peak periods, although some operate continuously. In some cities the curb bus lanes are designated only on one or two of the main downtown streets. In other cities, curb lanes are designated on several arterial streets in and around the CBD. In Baltimore, for example, curb bus lanes operate on 11 streets, aggregating about 60 blocks. Similarly, in New York City about 24 km (15 mi) of curb bus lanes operate on several midtown Manhattan streets. In Washington, D.C., express buses from the Shirley Busway, as well as from other corridors, use curb bus lanes for downtown circulation.

Median bus lanes are not as common for downtown circulation because of the difficulty of accommodating loading and unloading passengers. Special provisions for passengers are required, such as pedestrian islands. However, median lanes can overcome some of the operational problems associated with curb lanes such as interference from turning traffic, problems with access to roadside land uses, and violations of no-parking restrictions. Examples include the 1-km (0.6-mi) Washington Street median bus lane in Chicago and the Canal Street Busway in New Orleans. The right-of-way along the Canal Street Busway is wide enough to accommodate pedestrians without interfering with mixed traffic.

Although not as common as curb lanes, contra-flow lanes on CBD streets have been in use for more than 10 years in many cities. The typical CBD operation involves reserving the left-side curb lane along a one-way street for buses traveling in the opposite direction, usually throughout the day. Contra-flow lanes are in operation in Chicago; Indianapolis; Harrisburg, Pennsylvania; and San Antonio. In Seattle and Los Angeles (Fig. 33-7), downtown contra-flow bus lanes form part of the downtown circulation pattern for express bus service using freeway priority bus facilities.

Another type of preferential treatment becoming more popular in CBD areas is the bus street. Bus streets represent a major commitment to downtown transit and development. They fully separate bus and car traffic, increase bus service reliability, enhance bus identity, and provide downtown distribution for regional express routes. They enhance pedestrian access and, when accompanied by amenities, can improve the downtown environment. Bus streets where implemented should penetrate the heart of the city center, thereby providing priority access to major activity concentrations. Nicollet Mall in Minneapolis and the Halsted and 63rd bus streets at Englewood in Chicago are examples of bus streets combined with pedestrian malls. In Portland, Oregon, the two main CBD streets for a length of 12 blocks have been developed into a transit-pedestrian mall.

The workability of CBD bus priority treatments depends on how effectively they are enforced. The problems are similar to those covered in the discussion of arterial streets. Many CBD land uses require frequent access by cars and trucks. As a result, many curb lanes have low efficiency and are avoided by bus operators. Many transit operators believe that effective enforcement of curb parking regulations is more important than the specific allocation of curb lanes to bus use. Where curb parking takes up a needed traffic lane, restriction of parking may be a more acceptable alternative, particularly where bus use is small relative to general traffic. The problem of

Figure 33-7 *Contra-flow bus lane on CBD street in Los Angeles. (courtesy of Federal Highway Administration)*

access to adjoining property makes bus streets particularly difficult to implement, and in most cases, some access by automobiles to specific uses such as parking garages and hotels is permitted.

The complexity of traffic interaction and movement patterns in the CBD area creates operational problems in the implementation of almost any type of priority treatment for buses, but it is precisely this complexity and the congestion resulting from conflicts of mixed traffic and pedestrians that make bus priority treatments advantageous. Separating buses from mixed traffic on congested downtown streets has three basic advantages in the CBD area: (1) improved transit service, that is, improved travel time, service dependability, and operating efficiency; (2) reduced pedestrian conflicts between bus passengers and vehicle traffic; and (3) improved general traffic flow because the buses making frequent stops in the CBD are removed from the traffic stream.

In some cases, bicycles and taxis have been permitted in CBD bus lanes. The prime consideration in sharing bus lanes is to utilize the full capacity of the lane without delay and inconvenience to bus passengers. Carpool use of CBD bus lanes could be detrimental to bus operations and would not necessarily be advantageous to the carpools. Joint bus and carpool use should be limited to streets with very low bus volumes and/or off-street loading facilities. In Denver, bus priorities and carpool priorities have been implemented on different streets in and around the CBD to provide incentives to all high-occupancy vehicles without unnecessarily mixing the vehicle types.

NON-HIGHWAY-TYPE TRANSIT STRATEGIES

The highway is the medium for bus travel, so naturally the highway system is a critical element in the quality of transit service. The public transportation operation includes many other elements that contribute to the total system and opportunities exist for TSM improvements in these other areas to enhance the overall quality of service.

PASSENGER LOADING AND TRANSFER IMPROVEMENTS

Since public transportation passengers frequently rely on other travel modes to complete their travel requirements, facilities for passenger waiting, loading, and modal transfer should be provided and designed for the comfort and convenience of patrons.

The residential collection portion of the transit trip can be accomplished in two ways: (1) by bus circulation through residential neighborhoods or (2) by feeder mode. For those who live within 0.4 km (0.25 mi) of a bus line, walking is usually the principal means of access. To avoid excessive travel times and operator costs, bus circulation in residential areas is usually limited to areas of at least moderate density development. For those beyond walking distance and those in the lower-density suburban fringe, access to transit requires a supplementary mode—private auto, paratransit, or bicycle.

Fringe parking has long been a vital service provided for park-and-ride transit passengers. In the case of fixed-rail transit, including commuter rail, parking facilities are often constructed around stations where sufficient space is available. Bus transit, being more flexible, can often take advantage of existing underutilized parking space, eliminating the expense of specially constructed fringe parking facilities. Perhaps the most common source of available fringe parking is the regional shopping center. Such facilities have been implemented in many metropolitan areas across the country, usually in conjunction with express bus service. These include Minneapolis–St. Paul; Milwaukee; Atlanta; Miami; Kansas City, Missouri; and Washington, D.C.

Another source of fringe parking space is often available at major recreational facilities (e.g., stadiums, sport arenas, civic centers). These nearby spaces provide an opportunity for peripheral parking with shuttle service to the CBD. This type of service has been implemented in Atlanta; Washington, D.C.; and San Diego, for example.

Another opportunity exists for the development of fringe parking at outlying freeway interchanges. Right-of-way is usually available for a limited number of spaces, or major facilities can be developed by expanding into adjacent undeveloped land. The primary advantages of locating a park-and-ride facility at a freeway interchange are: (1) the easy access of both motorists to the site and buses onto the freeway for the express trip, and (2) the high visibility of a location near the freeway. Fringe parking at highway interchanges has become common in outlying areas of many cities, particularly in the northeastern states of Connecticut, Massachusetts, New York, and New Jersey. The State of Connecticut is now providing facilities in the vicinity of the interchanges to accommodate the demand. These fringe lots serve carpool passengers as well as transit riders.

One example of a comprehensive approach to providing park-and-ride facilities is the experience of Portland, Oregon. The program was sparked by an association of ministries in the area who felt that church parking lots could be put to a useful purpose on weekdays. As a result, more than 70 lots have been identified, predominantly at churches, but also at abandoned service stations, late-evening restaurants, supermarkets, and other parking lots which are not fully utilized on normal commuting days and are located within about 70 m (75 yd) of the boarding area for inbound buses.

Interest in bicycling has been growing for several years, not just for recreational trips, but for shorter functional urban travel needs as well. Access to transit service appears to be highly amenable to bicycle transportation. Bicycles provide an opportunity to substantially increase the catchment area for transit stations and bus stops without expensive and space-consuming parking facilities. For this potential to be realized, however, it is necessary to provide special bicycle facilities—provisions for the safe storage of bicycles. Racks suitable for locking bikes provide a minimum of security, and fully enclosed lockers are preferable. Bike lockers have been installed at the El Monte terminal of the San Bernardino Busway, for example. Equally important to realizing the full potential of bicycles as a useful feeder mode is the provision of a network of safe travel facilities for bikes. Cities and communities are just beginning to evaluate areawide needs and plans to serve bicycle transportation. Coordination with transit operators can assure that networks of bicycle routes serve the transit access function and, in some cases, provision has been made to take the bike along with the rider.

The versatile demand-responsive transit services, such as dial-a-ride, can also provide feeder service to and from regularly scheduled bus or rail transit.

At the other end of the transit trip, the downtown distribution portion, the problem is to accommodate concentrated volumes of passengers loading and unloading without excessive delay and inconvenience to passengers and other traffic. The three key ingredients of efficient downtown distribution are (1) to provide service in proximity to major activity centers, (2) to load large volumes of passengers quickly, and (3) to utilize limited roadway and pedestrian-movement space efficiently.

Off-street bus terminals, bus bays, and reserved CBD lanes are useful techniques to avoid conflicts with other vehicles and reducing already limited highway capacity. Although some terminal development requires long-range construction, smaller-scale terminal areas can be developed relatively inexpensively in the short run by utilizing oddly shaped vacant parcels of land, by coordination with other downtown development, or by reserving short sections of downtown streets for buses.

To speed passenger loading and bus travel times in the downtown portion of the trip, several operational improvements are possible. Bus stops should be located to minimize delay to buses. A review of traffic conditions and signal timings is needed to determine the most efficient location for stops. Downtown travel times can be further improved by *skip-stop operations* (buses pick up or discharge passengers at selected stops instead of every one). Different routes would be assigned to different stops to equalize the passenger load and avoid crowding and bus platooning. The travel time saved by such an operation should be balanced against the possible disadvantages of more difficult transfers between routes and greater walking distances to final destinations. Also, in this type of operation buses must be able to bypass the stopped buses in leapfrog fashion or the travel-time advantage is lost.

Streamlining the actual fare-collection procedure, including transferring, can also affect transit service positively. The exact-fare requirement—in addition to its security —also shortens the passenger boarding time, as does requiring exiting passengers to use specific doors.

REVISED SCHEDULING AND ROUTE INFORMATION

For many commuters, time is the single most important factor in choosing a method of travel. Increasing the frequency of buses and offering express bus service can attract new ridership by making travel time more competitive with that of the automobile. Many transit agencies are using results of market research to modify routing patterns. Cincinnati, Dallas, and Minneapolis have had considerable success in attracting new riders by these methods.

In Cincinnati, additional buses increased the frequency of service on designated routes and realized an 80% increase in ridership. Forty-eight percent of these new riders had previously been automobile commuters. Dallas and Minneapolis both improved already established express bus service which resulted in ridership gains of 90% and 136%, respectively. Again, in Dallas, 36% of the new riders had been in the automobile "driver-only" category before the bus service was expanded.

Another way to improve total transit travel times is to selectively design transit services for the commuting needs of specific groups. Many commuter bus clubs have been formed using buses and drivers from local transit operators. The users of the service determine the neighborhood circulation pattern, park-and-ride pickup points if needed, and the scheduling to arrive promptly at work each day. The key to organizing the service is identifying groups of commuters with similar commuting needs. This requires close cooperation with community groups, employee associations, the employer, or any other interested group. In Reston, Virginia, a nonprofit corporation organized by community residents developed a commuter bus operation predominantly serving commuters to Washington, D.C. The service is provided under contract with the transit operator. In Knoxville, Tennessee, express bus routes designed to serve the commuting needs of employees at the Tennessee Valley Authority have been provided by the transit operator. In Portland, Oregon, the transit operator offers tailor-made express bus service to any employer who can guarantee 30 riders and work hours that precede the normal rush period.

Automatic vehicle monitoring systems of various types are being used to monitor bus scheduling in Chicago and give buses priority at intersections in Washington, D.C.; Louisville, Kentucky; and Miami. A monitoring system can also be integrated into passenger information systems to provide passengers waiting at major bus stops with up-to-the-minute information on exact arrival time, route number, seating availability, and boarding location for the next vehicle. Rochester, New York, has experimented with this approach.

Another approach to improved urban mobility would be to reduce or modify the time of travel. Changes can be instituted which adjust the demand for transportation facilities so that urban mobility is improved.

Some relief for the rush-hour crunch may lie in the technique of staggered working hours. Programs that stagger employee arrival and departure times spread out the peak hours to smooth out the difference between peak and nonpeak and thus ease the flow of people into and out of the central city. Extending the peak-hour demand over a long period of the working day spreads out the demand and permits more efficient use of street space and transit vehicles.

There are several alternative methods of staggering work hours. The "traditional" 9-to-5 workday can be adjusted to stagger employee arrival and departure times over a short time period. In 1971, New York City launched a campaign to shift people working in lower Manhattan out of the 9-to-5 pattern. Today, the expanded program is credited with switching more than 200,000 employees in 400 Manhattan firms to staggered hours that permit them to travel to and from lower and midtown Manhattan with less difficulty. Most of the participating companies chose an 8:30-to-4:30 schedule, some an 8-to-4, and others a 9:30-to-5:30. The transit systems, the road systems, and the people are all benefiting. Among employees, the plan has an 85% approval rating; employers credit it with increased employee punctuality (resulting from increased transit punctuality) and reduced elevator congestion; and transit managers credit the plan with a 26% cut in the size of the rush-hour crush at neighboring subway stations and a corresponding increase in passenger trips during the previously underutilized periods.

Other major cities are implementing such programs. In Philadelphia, a program began in 1970 as a test project at a pharmaceutical laboratory. The Chamber of Commerce and the Regional Planning Commission, coordinating the extension of the program, are aiming at a goal of 50,000 participants in the downtown area. Since 1970, 50,000 employees in six federal departments in Washington, D.C., have been arriving at their offices in 15-minute intervals from 7 a.m. to 9 a.m. with corresponding staggered departing times. State and local governments have taken the lead in setting up a staggered work schedule for their employees in Albany, New York; Raleigh, North Carolina; and Inglewood, California. Several companies have also launched staggered-hour programs on their own to help employees avoid traffic snarls and improve punctuality.

Staggered working hours can also take the form of flexible hours—also called Flextime, Gleitzeit, or gliding hours. This generally consists of a prescribed block of time during which all employees in an organization must be present, but allows employees to select their own starting and quitting schedules to fit their individual needs and preferences. This enables employees to take advantage of carpooling and other ridesharing opportunities and scheduled public transit services. In a regulation published by the General Services Administration of the federal government, all federal agency supervisors were reminded of their prerogative to adjust the schedule of an employee to facilitate carpooling and the use of public transit.

There are two general types of shortened workweek programs. One type, the reduced workweek, actually reduces the total number of hours worked each week. The "compressed" workweek retains the same number of hours per week but condenses them into fewer days. For example, a 40-hour workweek can take the form of a 4-day, 10 h/day schedule instead of the familiar 5-day, 8 h/day routine.

In theory, if the 4-day workweek were adopted by the entire working population in a given metropolitan area and the extra "day off" were evenly distributed from Monday to Friday, the demand for transportation services and facilities to serve commuters could be reduced by 20%. If the extra day off were to be distributed over 6 days, there would be a theoretical reduction in demand of $33\frac{1}{3}\%$. Even further easing of demand could be gained by staggering the starting and quitting times within the 10-hour day.

Some 600 firms in the United States have put into practice some version of the 4-day workweek for at least some of their employees where such a system was compatible with the interests of both the company and its employees.

However, a well-intentioned staggered workweek program could have unintended negative consequences. For example, a staggered workweek program could seriously jeopardize ridesharing programs and public transit service if it encouraged—by reducing street congestion—more people to drive private automobiles to work. Another negative effect could occur if the program, designed in part to conserve fuel resources by reducing the number of home-to-work trips an employee must make per week, resulted in the extra time off being spent driving the private automobile for recreational or pleasure purposes.

What this suggests is that any program aimed at shifting the work pattern of a number of people must pay careful attention to all possible consequences and try to find a proper balance.

RELATED ACTIVITIES

Other transportation-related activities can also have an impact on transit use. For one, parking supply, management, and cost are crucial factors in the modal decision to use transit or private autos for commuting. The plentiful free parking at suburban employment locations only encourages continued commuting by single-occupant automobile. Parking facilities downtown—more costly, more scarce, and less frequently provided by the employer—provide a deterrent to driving downtown. Parking management strategies can further accentuate the disadvantages to driving downtown to discourage downtown parking. Discount monthly rates, for example, tend to favor commuters who drive every day over those who drive occasionally because they happen to need a car on a particular day. Taxing strategies can readjust the cost so those who drive every day do not receive discounts. Employer-provided free or subsidized parking distorts the relative costs of modal choices. Automobile users fail to pay the full economic costs of reserving scarce urban space for vehicle storage. Air quality control programs have recently attempted to regulate employer-provided parking in an effort to reduce automobile travel. Reduced parking availability forces a shift to the ridesharing modes—transit or carpooling. Recently, a few major employers have begun to subsidize transit fares of employees. In downtown areas, this is a more appreciated and civic-minded fringe benefit for employees than free parking.

These subsidy programs can be coordinated with prepaid fare systems. Employees in some cases can buy passes at a discount rate direct from the employer through payroll deductions.

Enforcement of rush-hour parking restrictions can further enhance transit service, since buses rely heavily on the curb lane for passenger loading and unloading, particularly downtown. Parked or standing vehicles can interfere with curb bus lane operations, create inconvenience for passengers at bus stops, and reduce highway capacity during critical peak hours. To maximize available highway space during peak hours, parking restrictions should be actively enforced.

In response to the energy crisis, state and local public agencies and other public service agencies, throughout the country, began to encourage carpooling and provide carpool matching as a community service. While several programs predate the energy crisis, it was not until gas lines grew and gas prices rose that carpool-matching services became widespread. The benefits to be realized from increased carpool use, not only in reduced energy consumption, but in reduced traffic congestion, air pollution, commuting costs, and parking facilities as well, suggest that ongoing promotional programs are warranted. The potential benefits of carpool promotion to transit operations far outweigh initial fears that widespread carpool matching would decimate transit ridership. In several metropolitan areas the carpool matching and promotional campaign is conducted by the transit operating authority. This arrangement allows a comprehensive and complementary ridesharing effort with each high-occupancy mode aimed at serving the appropriate portion of the diverse urban travel market and provides a valuable source of commuter travel information that allows more effective routing and scheduling of transit services.

On preferential treatment projects, carpools and buses frequently share priority lanes to fully utilize available capacity. Joint use frequently enhances public acceptance of the project, especially when carpool-matching services are available to assist the traveling public in using the preferential lane.

Although carpool matching may cause some diversion from transit, the overall benefits to transit operations—in terms of the useful commuter information, a more favorable attitude, and growing reliance on ridesharing of all types—warrant the close cooperation between transit and carpool programs.

INSTITUTIONAL CONSIDERATIONS

The strategies that can be implemented to increase the utilization of existing systems are so many and varied that a wide range of institutional units need to be involved in any systematic, comprehensive TSM planning effort. While the basic control of transit service lies with the transit authority or other operating entity, implementation of most of the strategies described here falls beyond the jurisdiction of the transit operator. A cooperative effort is required among all the agencies involved in planning and management of the urban transportation system, including the hierarchy of agencies from the state to the local level and the many jurisdictional units in the metropolitan area.

The general policy direction for all transportation development in an urban area is provided by the metropolitan planning organization in cooperation with the state and operators of public transportation services. It is usually a council of governments or similar regional association of elected representatives of general-purpose governments. This organization provides a forum for discussion and resolution of issues with regional interest and impacts. The long-range transportation plan, developed by the planning organization, establishes a framework for all transportation developments. The policies adopted by the regional forum should be reflected in the transportation improvement program, which is a multiyear program of transportation improvement projects that is updated annually. It is through this process that agreement is reached on the TSM as well as the long-range elements of the transportation plan which should be implemented.

Once areawide policy has been established, the development of TSM strategies proceeds to the corridor level of the planning process. Depending on the institutional arrangements, corridor studies may be undertaken by a state department of transportation, regional planning agency, or other responsible department. The objective of this level of analysis is to identify a range of appropriate actions based on a review of existing transportation facilities in a specific corridor. Input to this type of analysis would include data on the level of transit service, existing highway facilities, traffic conditions, demand characteristics, and already programmed improvements.

Individual project proposals identified through this corridor or subarea level analysis should assure an optimum operational improvement among all the alternatives. Depending on the extent of the improvement, proposals may be initiated by the transit authority in response to a particular operational deficiency, by a local traffic department that has identified a particular opportunity for an improvement, or by the metropolitan planning organization in response to regional interest. In any event, at the project level, the principal agencies involved are the transit authority and the traffic department with jurisdiction over the segment of highway involved. In cooperation these agencies determine the operational improvements that can best accommodate the transit service within the constraints of the existing highway characteristics and traffic conditions.

The principal responsibility for the implementation of different types of TSM strategies will fall to different agencies depending on the work involved. Highway strategies would be the principal responsibility of the transportation department with jurisdiction over the facility. Usually, the traffic department would be most directly involved, since many of the projects require only operational changes to control traffic movements. Minor construction may also be needed in some cases. The transit operator would be responsible for modifying the transit services to take advantage of priority highway treatments. During the planning and implementation of highway strategies, the appropriate police departments should be involved to assure adequate consideration of enforcement requirements.

Federal financial aid is available to assist state and local governments in the planning and implementation of these types of strategies. The programs of the Urban Mass Transportation Administration and the Federal Highway Administration provide funding for TSM operational improvements as well as long-range capital programs. Urban planning funds channeled through the metropolitan planning organization can be used to identify opportunities and coordinate the TSM development program.

SELECTED BIBLIOGRAPHY

Many citations are no longer available from their original source. These citations are often available from the National Technical Information Service, U.S. Department of Commerce, 5285 Port Royal Road, Springfield, Va. 22161. We have verified the order numbers for many of these citations, and they are found at the end of the citation. Prices are available through NTIS at the address above.

FEDERAL HIGHWAY ADMINISTRATION, *Bicycles and Pedestrian Facilities in the Federal-Aid Highway Program.* Washington, D.C.: U.S. Government Printing Office, 1974.

———, *Preferential Facilities for Carpools and Buses: Seven Reports.* Washington, D.C.: U.S. Government Printing Office, May 1976.

———, *Preferential Treatment for High Occupancy Vehicles.* Washington, D.C.: U.S. Government Printing Office, January 1974.

———, AND URBAN MASS TRANSPORTATION ADMINISTRATION, "Transportation Improvement Program," *Federal Register*, vol. 40, no. 181 (September 17, 1975).

KIRBY, RONALD F., AND KIRAN U. BHATT, *Guidelines on the Operation of Subscription Bus Services*, prepared for UMTA. Washington, D.C.: The Urban Institute, August 1974. Now available as PB 237 076.

———, AND OTHERS, *Para-Transit: Neglected Options for Urban Mobility.* Washington, D.C.: The Urban Institute, 1975. Now available as PB 234 320.

LEVINSON, HERBERT S., AND OTHERS, *Bus Use of Highways: Planning and Design Guidelines*, NCHRP Report 155. Washington, D.C.: Transportation Research Board, 1975.

———, AND OTHERS, *Bus Use of Highways: State of the Art*, NCHRP Report 143. Washington, D.C.: Highway Research Board, 1973.

MCQUEEN, JAMES T., AND OTHERS, *Evaluation of the Shirley Highway Express-Bus-on-Freeway Demonstration Project: Final Report*, prepared for UMTA. Washington, D.C.: U.S. Department of Consumers, National Bureau of Standards, August 1975. Now available as PB 247 637.

REICHART, BARBARA K., *Improving Urban Mobility: Through Better Transportation Management.* Washington, D.C.: Federal Highway Administration, May 1975.

SMITH, DAN, JR., *Bikeways: State of the Art*, prepared for FHWA. San Francisco: De Leuw, Cather & Company, July 1974.

U.S. DEPARTMENT OF TRANSPORTATION, *Carpool Incentives and Opportunities*, Report of the Secretary of Transportation to the United States Congress pursuant to Section 3(e), Public Law 93–239, Emergency Highway Energy Conservation Act. Washington, D.C.: U.S. Government Printing Office, February 1975. Now available as PB 241 823.

Chapter 34

NEW TECHNOLOGY

CLARK HENDERSON, *Staff Scientist, SRI International*
(*formerly Stanford Research Institute*)

The subjects discussed here are urban public transportation systems that represent major technical advances beyond the equipment, facilities, and operations of conventional rail and bus, taxi, and other street modes. The focus is on system-level advances rather than subsystem-level or component-level changes, such as new vehicles or new propulsion systems for existing modes. The system classes of main interest are discussed under the following headings:

- Automated guideway transit (AGT).
- Fast transit links (FTL).
- Dual-controlled AGT (D-AGT).
- Automated mixed-traffic vehicles (AMTV).
- Accelerating moving ways (AMW).
- Rent-by-the-trip public automobile service (PAS).

The term "advanced systems" is used to refer to all such systems.

RATIONALE FOR SYSTEM-LEVEL INNOVATIONS

There is considerable interest in the development and use of advanced systems, and it is reasonable to ask, "How has the interest evolved?" and "Why are innovations needed?"

Interest in exploiting some of the advanced systems listed can be traced back to the nineteenth century, but most of the development and use have occurred during the past decade. In 1966 Congress passed the Reuss–Tydings Amendments to the Urban

Mass Transportation Act of 1964 and required the Secretary of Housing and Urban Development to

> undertake a project to study and prepare a program of research, development, and demonstration of new systems of urban transportation that will carry people and goods within metropolitan areas speedily, safely, without polluting the air, and in a manner that will contribute to sound city planning. The program shall (1) concern itself with all aspects of new systems of urban transportation for metropolitan areas of various sizes, including technological, financial, economic, governmental, and social aspects; (2) take into account the most advanced available technologies and materials; and (3) provide national leadership to efforts of States, localities, private industry, universities, and foundations.[1]

The resulting report, *Tomorrow's Transportation: New Systems for the Urban Future*, was submitted by President Johnson to the Congress in May 1968.[2] That report and backup studies prepared by contractors stimulated widespread interest in the exploitation of technically advanced systems in the United States and abroad.

During the past decade interest has been evidenced by inventors, private sector research and development institutions and firms, transportation planning consultants, transportation agencies at all government levels, industrial firms seeking roles as suppliers, and prospective owners and operators. In the United States, Western Europe, and Japan several hundred million dollars have been spent on research, development, prototype fabrication and testing of advanced systems of all types, and on the installation and operation of automated guideway transit systems in airports, recreation parks, and other special settings. These activities have produced useful and encouraging experience. Nevertheless, deployment of advanced systems in ordinary urban settings has not made significant progress.

The interests of the various parties concerned with the exploitation of advanced systems in urban settings are not yet focused on specific programs or goals. There is no consensus regarding the usefulness of various system types, the rates at which installations would be made, or the ultimate scale of exploitation. The delay in assessing the potential of advanced systems and initiating deployments is understandable. The needed programs are proving to be more complex than first envisioned. Parties who must work together to achieve substantial results have not yet found cooperative and mutually supportive ways of doing business. There is considerable uncertainty regarding the physical, operating, and economic characteristics obtainable through utilization of advanced systems. Evidence regarding benefits, costs, and adverse impacts has not been gathered and evaluated, and it appears that new evaluation techniques will have to be developed for the purpose. Many specialists in transportation planning and related fields hope and expect that advanced systems will begin to find large-scale applications in urban settings by the mid-1980s. However, the supply of an adequate

---

[1]URBAN MASS TRANSPORTATION ADMINISTRATION, *Urban Mass Transportation Act of 1964 and Related Laws*, as amended through February 5, 1976 (Washington, D.C.: U.S. Government Printing Office, 1976), Section 6(b), p. 16.

[2]LEON MONROE COLE, ed., *Tomorrow's Transportation: New Systems for the Urban Future*, prepared by U.S. Department of Housing and Urban Development (Washington, D.C.: U.S. Government Printing Office, 1968).

range of advanced system types remains to be established, and the demand for advanced systems remains to be defined.

Specific arguments for the development and exploitation of advanced systems can usually be related to these themes:

- Certain needs of society can only be satisfied by increasing travel via urban public transportation modes.
- The supply of service from the predominant modes, for example, conventional taxi, bus, and heavy rail systems, will always be limited by certain inherent economic and service characteristics.
- Advanced systems promise a variety of attractive economic and service characteristics that can be exploited in efforts to provide good service to all travelers for all trips in metropolitan areas.

NEEDS OF SOCIETY

The case for improving and expanding urban public transportation service to benefit society is based on two premises. There is a need to shift a greater fraction of existing urban travel from the private auto to public modes to achieve a variety of objectives, such as protecting the environment; conserving land, energy, and the time of travelers; reducing accidents; and controlling urban development. There is a need for transportation service by certain members of society who now suffer limited mobility via automobile—the young, the old, the poor, the handicapped, the unlicensed driver, and other persons who are underserved by the auto. The carless members of society make up about 40% of the population old enough and otherwise able to travel alone: 20% live in households without autos, 10% are under driving age, and 10% have no license. They need improved mobility to gain access to opportunities of all kinds—employment, residences, schools, recreation, cultural resources, professional services, retail stores, and intercity passenger terminals.

If good urban public transportation service is available in the future—for all travelers, for all trips, and at all times of day—transit patronage by the limited mobility groups, plus some "choice users," would probably be in the range of 25 to 50% of all urban travel rather than the 3% observed in 1976.

LIMITATIONS OF CONVENTIONAL MODES

Heavy rail rapid transit systems, buses on city streets, and taxis supply most of the urban public transportation service in the United States, but have limited potential for growth or improvement.

Heavy rail rapid transit systems, which carry about 24% of the transit riders in the United States, are limited in the extent of exploitation by their high capital costs. For example, BART—the San Francisco Bay Area Rapid Transit—had a capital cost of about $1.6 billion. The network, which contains 114 rte-km (71 rte-mi) and 34 stations, was designed to carry maximum loads of about 22,500 seated passengers per hour per direction (p/h/d) on two route segments, 15,000 p/h/d on two route segments, and 7500 p/h/d on one route segment. In 1976 the system served about 130,000 one-way trips, or the equivalent of about 65,000 round-trip riders on a typical workday.

The BART system was constructed in the 1960s and early 1970s at prices less than half those likely to prevail in future years. Even so, the capital costs of BART, prorated to the system characteristics cited above, appear high. If all capital costs are prorated to route-miles, the average cost is about $14 million per rte.-km ($22.5 million per rte.-mi). If all capital costs are prorated to stations, the average cost is about $47.1 million per station. If prorated to round-trip, weekday patronage, the average cost is about $25,000 per patron. If prorated to system capacity measured on the most heavily traveled routes, the cost is about $1000 per pass.-mi/unit of capacity/h, for example, about $14 million per rte.-km ($22.5 million per mi) for a system with a capacity of about 22,500 seated p/h/d.

Operation of heavy rail rapid transit systems is also costly. BART's budget for 1976–1977 was $77.1 million or $1186 annually per daily patron. All operators find it necessary to reduce or stop service in periods of low patronage. When service is reduced, travelers are inconvenienced by longer waits to board trains and sometimes by additional en route stops and transfers. When service is discontinued, some travelers suffer inconvenience or hardship.

The economic case for heavy rail rapid transit is most favorable on routes oriented to serve central business districts (CBDs) where high peak-hour patronage makes reasonably full use of high capacities. Such routes are found only in a few major cities, and even there the maximum extent of the rail network must be limited because of costs. It is unrealistic to expect that heavy rail systems will ever be constructed in fine-mesh networks with closely spaced routes and many stations that will be needed to serve all travelers and all trips throughout a metropolitan area.

Buses carry about 73 % of the transit riders in the United States. Most buses operate on city streets in mixed traffic at average speeds ranging from about 32 km/h (20 mi/h) in residential areas to 8 km/h (5 mi/h) on congested streets in the downtown areas. In some cities a small fraction of the buses operate on highways, diamond lanes, and busways, and achieve higher average speeds.

Bus operating costs outweigh capital costs by a great margin—usually of the order of 9:1. The major operating cost categories are related to the number of hours of bus operation. Examples are wages of drivers, mechanics, and supervisors; and expenditures for fuel, oil, and replacement parts. Many of the benefits of bus service vary with the number of patrons or the number of passenger-miles of service provided. Consequently, there is reason to consider variations in the productivity of buses over the full range of conditions. Productivity of buses can be expressed in terms of passenger-miles per hour of bus operation (pass.-mi/b-h). Productivity varies greatly depending on the day of the week, the time of day, the direction of travel, the position of the bus on its route, and the average speed of the bus.

In slack periods buses are often lightly loaded and have very low productivity. For example, a bus in light traffic traveling at an average speed of 32 km/h (20 mi/h) and carrying an average load of five passengers over its round trip would generate 160 pass.-km/b-h (100 pass.-mi/b-h). Productivity of a bus on the same route under peak load conditions may be higher than 1000 pass.-mi/b-h for short periods of time. For example, one may observe a heavily loaded bus approaching a downtown area during the peak carrying 70 passengers at an average speed of 24 km/h (15 mi/h). However, productivity declines sharply in the CBD as the bus is slowed to 8 km/h (5 mi/h) by congestion and as passengers unload. Productivity for round trips during hours of peak traffic is likely to be about 300 pass.-mi/b-h.

It is easy to understand why bus operators often find it necessary to reduce the frequency of service or to stop service entirely during midday and night hours and on weekends and holidays. In addition, there are deficiencies of bus service when it is supplied. Among these are crowding of vehicles during peak hours, indirect routing, long waits, slow travel, and the need for transfers.

Taxis are the third important element of urban public transportation. Although historically not regarded as a part of the transit industry, taxis serve many travelers and earn revenue comparable in magnitude to conventional transit. Taxis usually provide door-to-door service in response to the demands of individual travelers, although in a few cities they are allowed to serve two or more travel parties on a shared basis.

Taxi costs are dominated by wages, and the service is regarded as expensive by most users. Taxi service is usually good for trips originating at major traffic generators such as airports and downtown hotels. Street hailing is seldom practical except downtown. In other areas travelers must walk to a taxi stand or telephone for service. Delay awaiting service is often excessive in places where the density of demand for taxi service is too low to warrant keeping empty vehicles in the vicinity. Also, the supply of taxi service often drops when demand is highest because taxi drivers elect to leave the street in bad weather and at other times to avoid difficult driving conditions.

ADVANTAGES OF ADVANCED SYSTEMS

Each of the advanced systems discussed here promises one or more important advantages over conventional modes, yet no single system combines all the desired features. The main avenues for improvement are:

1. Low labor costs can be sought through automation, continuous or process-type operations, and self-service operations. These characteristics permit frequent service or service on demand 24 hours per day and every day of the year.
2. Low capital costs and conservation of land can be sought through the use of small vehicles, structures, and stations, and, in some cases, by the operation of automated or self-service systems on existing pavement in mixed traffic streams with autos and pedestrians. These characteristics will provide improved access to urban public transportation service by allowing the construction of many routes and stations and the installation of other access facilities such as rental automobile stands.
3. Environmental improvements can be sought by electric propulsion and design of small, aesthetically pleasing facilities.

4. Short travel times can be sought mainly by providing reasonably direct routes for all trips and by eliminating delays awaiting vehicles and for stops at en route stations. However, some systems also promise speeds much higher than buses or trains, for instance, up to 240 km/h (150 mi/h).
5. Reductions in the effort and inconvenience of travel can be sought by coupling network links at the nodes to eliminate the need for some transfers and by mechanizing stations to make it easier to board and leave vehicles.

AUTOMATED GUIDEWAY TRANSIT (AGT)

Automated guideway transit (AGT) systems employ self-powered vehicles and have two distinguishing features:

- Exclusive roadways or guideways are employed. Guideways may be elevated, at or near ground level, or underground.
- Vehicles are automated—they are able to carry passengers without having a driver on board. Personnel may monitor operations from a remote position and are free to perform other functions.

AGT systems of many kinds can be conceived. Discussion is aided by adopting a scheme of classification, although any such scheme is necessarily somewhat arbitrary. Three classes have received fairly general acceptance[3] and are used here:

- Shuttle-loop transit (SLT).
- Group rapid transit (GRT).
- Personal rapid transit (PRT).

The main attributes of each class are summarized in Table 34-1.

Designers of AGT systems have considerable freedom to tailor capacity to match expected demand. On routes where the capacities needed are lower than the normal capacities of heavy rail transit, it is expected that the capital costs per route-mile and per station of AGT systems will be lower than rail. It is also expected that AGT systems will have lower operating costs, but higher capital costs, than buses at most capacity levels. Thus, AGT systems will often have to be evaluated as alternatives to heavy rail and bus systems, and cost comparisons will be required. Such comparisons need to recognize both capital and operating costs and to make expenditures over future time periods commensurate by means of equivalence calculations at appropriate discount rates. Data on AGT costs needed to illustrate such comparisons are not available.

---

[3]For other systems of classification based on different criteria, see Chapter 4. The terminology and acronyms used in Chapter 34 were established by the U.S. CONGRESS, OFFICE OF TECHNOLOGY ASSESSMENT, in a report entitled *Automated Guideway Transit: An Assessment of PRT and Other New Systems*, including supporting panel reports, prepared for Senate Committee on Appropriations, Transportation Subcommittee (Washington, D.C.: U.S. Government Printing Office, 1975). Now available as PB 224 854.

TABLE 34-1
Characteristics of AGT Classes

	SLT	GRT	PRT
Availability	Presently available	Conditionally available	Not available
Operations	• Simple—single route • Switching in a constant manner	• Complex—multiple routes, prescheduled • Switching reacts to vehicle identity	• Very complex—multiple routes, vehicles actively responsive to demand • Switching is tailored for each passenger's destination
Passenger convenience	• Passengers use any vehicle • Stop at each station • All passengers on a route travel together	• Passengers must select vehicle • May bypass some stations • Passengers travel in groups	• Passengers are assigned vehicle • No en route stops • Passengers travel alone, or in small, private groups
System configuration	• Shuttles and loops • On-line stations • Switches seldom required	• Lines branch and merge • On-line and off-line stations • Switches required	• Coupled guideways • Off-line stations • Many switches required
Areawide network formation	• Employ many interfacing shuttles or loops	• Employ multiple interfacing GRT systems	• Employ a single integrated PRT system

SLT systems are the simplest of the three classes of AGT systems and are by far the best understood and most widely used. SLT systems are distinguished by one characteristic: their vehicles follow unvarying paths and therefore make little or no use of switches.

The performance of SLT systems can be tailored to a wide range of needs. Vehicles may travel at any reasonable speed, may be of any size, and may be operated singly or in trains of any length. In existing systems the capacities of single operating units vary from about 10 passengers in a single vehicle to about 200 passengers in a two-car train. Both higher and lower unit capacities are possible.

In 1977 there were 16 shuttle and loop installations in the United States (see Table 34-2). Four installations contain one or two shuttles on a single route, and 10 installations employ a single loop. Two installations contain multiple routes arranged in networks and are discussed separately.

Shuttles. The simplest system is now operating in a shopping complex at Pearl-ridge, Honolulu, Hawaii (Fig. 34-1a). The system was produced by Rohr Industries, Inc. It includes a single four-car train, two stations, an elevated guideway about 305 m (1000 ft) long, and a guideway extension for vehicle storage and maintenance. There are no switches. The train is double-ended or bidirectional. It "shuttles" between the two stations and is the horizontal equivalent of an express elevator. The train carries

TABLE 34-2
U.S. AGT Systems

Subclass	Type of Application	Location	Supplier	Status in 1977
SLT	Airports	Hartford, Conn.	Ford	Idle
		Miami, Fla.	Westinghouse Electric	Construction
		Tampa, Fla.	Westinghouse Electric	Service
		Seattle, Wash.	Westinghouse Electric	Service
		Houston, Tex.	Rohr	Service
		Dallas, Tex.	Braniff/Stanray	Retired
	Commercial centers	Dearborn, Mich.	Ford	Service
		Honolulu, Hi.	Rohr	Service
	Parks	Ashland, Va.	Universal Mobility	Service
		Charlotte, N.C.	Universal Mobility	Service
		Disney World, Fla.	Mapo/Walt Disney Productions	Service
		Hershey, Pa.	Universal Mobility	Service
		Kings Mill, Ohio	Universal Mobility	Service
		Sacramento, Calif.	Universal Mobility	Service
		Valencia, Calif.	Universal Mobility	Service
		Williamsburg, Va.	Westinghouse Electric	Service
GRT	Airport	Dallas-Ft. Worth Airport, Tex.	Vought	Service
	University	Morgantown, W. Va.	Boeing	Service

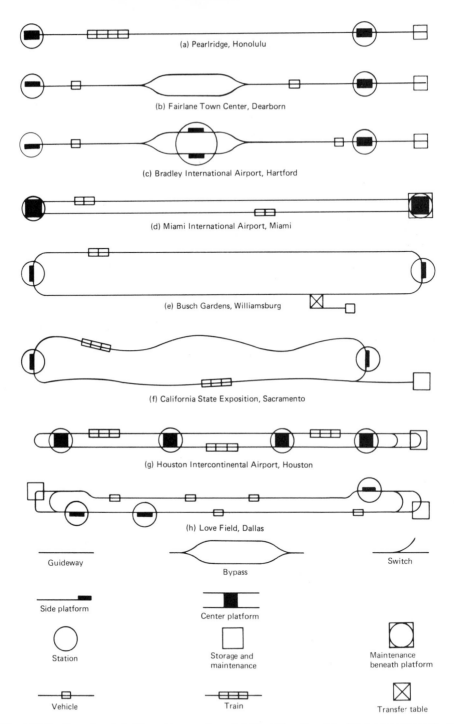

Figure 34-1 *Examples of shuttle and loop systems. (a) Pearlridge, Honolulu. (b) Fairlane Town Center, Dearborn. (c) Bradley International Airport, Hartford. (d) Miami International Airport, Miami. (e) Busch Gardens, Williamsburg. (f) California State Exposition, Sacramento. (g) Houston Intercontinental Airport, Houston. (h) Love Field, Dallas.*

up to 48 passengers—24 seated and 24 standing. Speed is modest—about 16 km/h (10 mi/h). The train makes about 15 round trips per hour and has a maximum capacity of about 720 p/h/d. (See Fig. 34-2.)

Figure 34-2 *Pearlridge, Honolulu, Hawaii. Rohr Monorail "P" Series Monotrain on test track. (courtesy of LEA TRANSIT COMPENDIUM)*

A shuttle system at the Fairlane Town Center, Dearborn, Michigan, links a shopping center with a hotel (Figs. 34-1b and 34-3). A similar system installed at Bradley International Airport near Hartford, Connecticut, links the air terminal with a remote parking lot and a hotel at an intermediate station (Figs. 34-1c and 34-4), but it has not been activated, because of failure to agree as to operating cost responsibility. Ford Motor Company installed both systems.

The Fairlane installation is elevated and includes a special guideway feature called a bypass near the center of the route. The entire route is about 793 m (2600 ft) long and includes a single guideway section about 274 m (900 ft) long at each end of the route, and a bypass section about 244 m (800 ft) long. The bypass has three parts—a length of double guideway and two transition sections connecting the double guideways to the single guideways. The purpose of the bypass is to allow two shuttle vehicles to start from opposite ends and pass each other near the midpoint of the route. This technique allows two shuttle routes to share single guideways on about 70% of the route. The Fairlane vehicles carry up to 10 seated passengers and 14 standees (or 20 standees with severe crowding). Each vehicle makes about 20 round trips per hour. The entire system has a maximum capacity of about 960 p/h/d. Waiting and riding times average about 2.5 minutes per trip or an effective speed of 19 km/h (12 mi/h) as viewed by users. The Bradley installation would have similar performance.

Figure 34-3 *Fairlane Town Center, Dearborn, Michigan. Ford ACT (Automatically Controlled Transportation) system. (courtesy of Ford Motor Company)*

Figure 34-4 *Fairlane vehicle. (courtesy of LEA TRANSIT COMPENDIUM, N. D. LEA Transportation Research Corp., Huntsville, AL.)*

Miami International Airport's shuttle is a large-capacity system manufactured by Westinghouse Electric to connect the main air terminal with a new international terminal (Fig. 34-1d). The system includes two parallel guideways on an elevated structure with stations at the ends. Each guideway carries a single two-car train with each train accommodating 200 standing passengers. The route is about 427 m (1400 ft) long, and vehicles are capable of making about 22 round trips per hour. The system has a maximum capacity of about 8800 p/h/d. Train speeds can approach 48 km/h (30 mi/h), with an effective speed of about 17 km/h (10.5 mi/h), including both waiting and riding times.

Loops. Loop systems have closed-circuit guideways and may include multiple vehicles or trains of any capacity and any number of stations. Most loop systems employ switches or transfer tables to insert or remove vehicles, but not for passenger operations.

Opened in 1976, the loop system located at Busch Gardens, Williamsburg, Virginia, was produced by Westinghouse Electric (Figs. 34-1e and 34-5). The guideway is 2134 m (7000 ft) long and contains two stations. The system has a single two-car train similar to the equipment at Miami International Airport. The train carries up to 180 passengers—24 seated and 156 standing. Maximum speed is about 48 km/h (30 mi/h). With the single train, system capacity is 2000 p/h/d. Up to seven vehicles could be added. With three 3-car trains capacity would be 9000 p/h/d.

Figure 34-5 *Westinghouse Transit Expressway vehicles. Vehicle type used for Busch Gardens and Miami International Airport on test track at West Miflin. (courtesy of Westinghouse Electric Corporation)*

Six loop systems have been installed in recreation facilities in the United States by Universal Mobility, Inc. (See Fig. 34-6.) A number of other systems of the same kind have been installed in Canada and abroad. The installation at the California Exposition and State Fairgrounds near Sacramento, California, best represents the potential of the system for urban public transportation service (Fig. 34-1f). The main purpose of the system is to transport passengers from the gate to a major attraction on the

Figure 34-6   *Unimobil/Habegger system. (courtesy of Universal Mobility, Inc.)*

opposite side of the grounds. A 50-cent fare is charged. The installation includes 2.7 km (1.7 mi) of route, two stations, and four trains. Each train includes eight vehicles and carries 50 to 60 passengers. Maximum speed is about 16 km/h (10 mi/h), and each train makes four to five round trips per hour. Maximum capacity is about 1500 to 2000 p/h/d.

The Houston Intercontinental Airport employs a loop system installed in 1972 by Westinghouse Air Brake Company (Fig. 34-1g). The product line was later sold to Rohr Industries, Inc. Trains used at Houston are similar to the one at Pearlridge. (See Fig. 34-7.) The system provides two-way service in a tunnel which passes beneath two air terminals, a hotel, and two parking lots. The route includes eight station stops—four stations each serving two-way traffic. The route is about 914 km (3000 ft) long and includes 1890 km (6200 ft) of guideway. A maintenance facility at one end of the loop is connected to the passenger route by switches. The system uses three-car trains, each with a capacity for 36 passengers—18 seated and 18 standing. Maximum speed is 13 km/h (8 mi/h). With six trains, headways can be as low as 3 minutes, and capacities as high as 720 p/h/d. With improved controls and a larger fleet—18 trains in service—headways could be as low as 1 minute, and capacities as high as 2160 p/h/d.

A loop system was installed at Love Field near Dallas, Texas, in 1970 by Braniff Airlines (Fig. 34-1h). The system, idle since Braniff moved to the new Dallas–Ft. Worth airport, contains a number of unique features. The guideway is an elevated monobeam with vehicles suspended beneath it. Stations at the end of the route are equipped with switches and sidings for the storage of empty cars held in reserve for surges of travelers. There is one intermediate station. The route is about 1280 m (4200 ft) long and contains about 2560 m (8400 ft) of guideway. Maximum vehicle speeds are about 27 km/h (about 17 mi/h). Single vehicles carry six seated passengers and up to eight standees. With 10 vehicles in service, the system capacity is about

Figure 34-7 *Houston Intercontinental Airport, Houston, Texas. Rohr Monorail "P" Series Monotrain. (courtesy of Rohr Industries, Inc.)*

600 p/h/d. With an additional 10 vehicles in service, the capacity would be doubled. After the end of revenue service the guideway and certain elements of the system were used as a test and demonstration facility for vehicles employing magnetic suspension and propulsion.

Existing SLT networks. An SLT network contains two or more shuttle or loop systems on routes that come together or *interface* at common stations. Passengers can transfer from one route to another at the route interfaces, but vehicles in normal passenger service cannot move from one route to another. Such networks are said to be *uncoupled.* Two SLT networks have been installed at airports in Tampa, Florida, and Seattle–Tacoma, Washington.

The *Tampa SLT network* entered service in 1971 and is one of the most significant accomplishments in the brief history of AGT exploitation (Fig. 34-8a). The airport terminal complex served by the network is unique in design—it includes a single "landside" central terminal building and four "airside" satellite terminals. The distances between landside and airside terminals are in the range 238 to 305 m (780 to 1000 ft). Each satellite terminal is connected to the central terminal by an elevated structure containing two shuttle guideways and a broad pedestrian walkway reserved for emergency use. The central terminal is the common station for four shuttle routes. Originating and terminating passengers ride only one shuttle. Some passengers changing planes at Tampa use two shuttles to transfer between satellites via the central terminal.

The eight shuttle guideways have a total length of about 2195 m (7200 ft). There are eight vehicles, one on each guideway. The vehicles have no seats—each carries up

EXISTING SLT NETWORKS

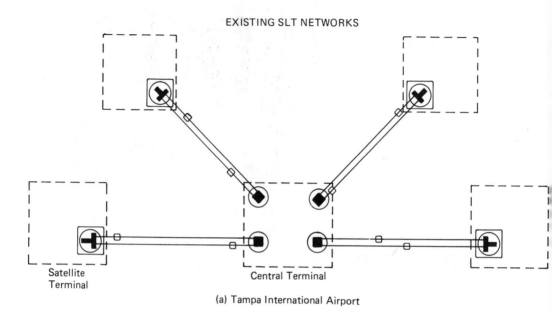

Satellite
Terminal

Central Terminal

(a) Tampa International Airport

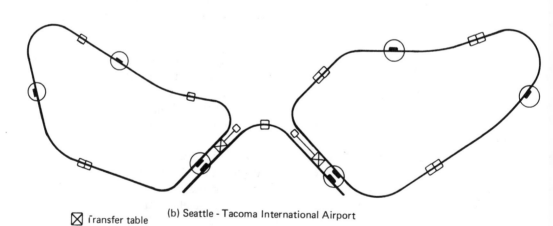

⊠ Transfer table

(b) Seattle - Tacoma International Airport

Figure 34-8 *Existing SLT networks*

to 100 standing passengers normally and up to 125 standing passengers with crowding. (See Fig. 34-9.) Vehicle maximum speeds are 48 to 56 km/h (30 to 35 mi/h). Time to travel 305 m (1000 ft) is about 40 seconds, and dwell time is about 30 seconds. Each vehicle can make about 25 round trips per hour and has a capacity of up to 2500 p/h/d with normal loading. The two shuttles on each route have combined capacities of up to 5000 p/h/d. The average time needed for a 305-m (1000-ft) trip is 75 seconds,

Figure 34-9 *Seattle-Tacoma International Airport. Westinghouse Transit Expressway. (courtesy of Westinghouse Electric Corporation)*

including 40 seconds riding and an average wait of 35 seconds for boarding. The effective speed is about 15 km/h (9 mi/h). Service is provided on demand during slack periods.

The Tampa network is outstanding in many ways and is a success by any test. The system carried about 65 million passengers during the first five years of operation and transports an average of about 38,000 passengers per day. It can provide service on each route almost constantly—99.99% of the time. When stoppages occur the system fails gracefully. Individual vehicles are stopped involuntarily about once every 20 hours on the average—usually for very minor incidents—and they are restored to service with a mean delay of less than 7 minutes. The stoppage of one vehicle does not impede the vehicle on the parallel path, and passengers are usually delayed only briefly. In the rare case when both vehicles on a route are out of service—about once a week on each line—travelers simply leave the stopped car—which is always possible—and finish the trip on the walkway. The walk requires less than 4 minutes. There have been no accidents in which vehicles were damaged. In one case power was reversed on a moving car and two passengers received significant injuries. There have been reports of minor injuries and a few claims. Each vehicle runs about 76,000 km (47,000 mi) per year—comparable to the average New York City subway car. A total work force of six employees is required to maintain and operate the entire system 24 hours per day every day of the year.

It has been estimated that, for 1976, the total equivalent annual cost of capital, operations, and maintenance was $2.18 million and that the unit cost per rider was 15 cents.[4] Capital cost estimates involved the assumption that a duplicate system was installed at 1976 price levels with $6.46 million expended for construction and $7.81 million expended for hardware. Service lives were 35 years and 15 years, respectively. The discount rate was 10% and salvage values were neglected. Operating and maintenance costs for 1976 were $487,000.

Direct energy consumption averaged 2100 Btu's (2216×10^3 joules) per rider or 69 passenger-trips per gallon (3.8 liters) of petroleum fuel. Indirect and capital energy demands averaged 1300 and 2140 Btu's (1372×10^3 and 2258×10^3 joules) per rider, respectively. Thus the estimated total, long-term, average energy demand was 5500 Btu's (5803×10^3 joules) per rider or the equivalent of 26.6 passenger-trips per gallon (3.8 liters) of petroleum fuel burned.[5]

The *Seattle–Tacoma (Sea-Tac) SLT network* began service in mid-1973. It employs hardware similar to that of the Tampa network, and has also achieved a high degree of success. The network has three interfacing routes—one shuttle about 305 m (1000 ft) long and two loops about 1128 and 1280 m (3700 and 4200 ft) long (Fig. 34-8b). The shuttle is located beneath the main terminal building and contains two stations. Each loop connects the main terminal with a satellite terminal. The loops are in tunnels beneath the terminal and the aircraft parking apron. Each loop contains three stations,

[4]A. M. YEN AND OTHERS, *Assessment of the Passenger Shuttle System (PSS) at the Tampa International Airport*, prepared for UMTA, Report no. UMTA-IT-06-0135-77-4 (Menlo Park, Calif.: SRI International, December 1977).

[5]CLARK HENDERSON, ROBERT H. CRONIN, AND HAZEL T. ELLIS, *Energy Study of Automated Guideway Transit (AGT) Systems*, prepared for Energy Research and Development Administration (Menlo Park, Calif.: SRI International, February 1978).

one of which shares a platform with the shuttle. Passengers can use any two or all three elements of the network and transfer on foot at the interfacing stations.

Single guideways are used on all three routes. There are two maintenance and storage facilities located between the ends of the shuttle and the two loops. Each contains a transfer table connecting maintenance and storage guideways with both the shuttle and loop guideways. Transfer tables are used only for movements of empty vehicles. Vehicles can be shifted from line to line as desired.

The Sea-Tac vehicles are generally similar to those used at Tampa, Miami, and Busch Gardens. Vehicle maximum speed is about 42 km/h (26 mi/h). Vehicles normally carry up to 102 passengers—12 seated and 90 standing. There are 12 vehicles in service. When fully equipped the system will employ 25 vehicles—1 on the shuttle and 12 on each loop. Capacities will then be 14,400 p/h on each loop and 1800 p/h/d on the shuttle.

Possible future SLT networks. Shuttles and loops can be utilized as modular routes or "building blocks" to form networks of any size and complexity. For example, 305-m (1000-ft) shuttles similar to those installed at the Tampa airport could be arranged in a grid network to provide excellent circulation service for an activity center. A grid using 40 such elements would serve an area as large as the Chicago Loop district—about 2.6 km² (1 mi²). With a shuttle or loop system on each network link, passengers would have to transfer at every node. Other network configurations are possible. For example, the same grid could be served by a combination of 305-m (1000-ft) shuttles and longer runs.

Grids offer no special advantage, except where dictated by existing streets. Any pattern can be served, and any mix of technical equipment can be used in an SLT network. The variety of hardware available is quite limited, but SLT systems could be designed to provide a great variety of speeds and capacities and service frequencies. Economic considerations are likely to rule out the extremes, but, from the technical viewpoint, capacities over an enormous range can be obtained. For example, a system using four-passenger cars and 5-minute headways would have a capacity of 48 p/h/d—about the same as a standard urban bus on a 1-hour schedule. At the other extreme, a loop system with 400-passenger trains operating with 1-minute headways would have a capacity of 24,000 p/h/d—generally comparable to rail rapid transit.

SLT networks have been considered for urban service but none has been constructed. In 1976 the Urban Mass Transportation Administration (UMTA) initiated a Downtown People Mover Program in four cities—Cleveland, Houston, Los Angeles, and St. Paul. The program was later broadened to include eleven candidate cities. This program could bring one or more urban systems into revenue service by the early 1980s.

GROUP RAPID TRANSIT

GRT systems represent a level of technical sophistication and promise a quality of service intermediate between SLT and PRT systems. GRT systems are characterized by the use of switches to allow vehicles to follow multiple paths. Specifically, the guideways of GRT networks branch and merge. Thus, where traffic volumes are moderately high, GRT stations may be located off the main guideway. Vehicles will then stand on station sidings, clear of the passenger service line, while other vehicles pass the station without stopping. Passengers must board the correct GRT vehicle to reach a specific destination and may have to wait while several vehicles with other destinations stop at a station. GRT systems are only advantageous when used to connect several stations. Analytical comparisons of SLT and GRT systems on identical networks show that GRT systems can allow users to make fewer en route station stops and few transfers but can also require longer boarding delays. As with SLT technology, multiple GRT systems can be used together to form large networks.

Existing GRT systems. Two GRT systems are now in existence—one at West Virginia University, Morgantown, West Virginia, and one at the Dallas–Ft. Worth Regional Airport.

The Morgantown GRT system was designed, fabricated, and installed by a team headed by Boeing Aerospace Company. The system contains 3.5 km (2.2 mi) of double guideway, three stations, 45 cars, and a maintenance and operations center (see Fig. 34-10). The intermediate station has a number of guideway paths and platform positions. Vehicles can be commanded to bypass the intermediate station without stopping, to stop at a platform and continue in the same direction, or to stop at a platform and turn back in the opposite direction. Morgantown vehicles carry up to 21 passengers—8 seated and 13 standing. The maximum vehicle speed is 48 km/h (30 mi/h). Riding time from one end of the system to the other is about 7 minutes or at a speed of 31 km/h (19 mi/h). Waiting time varies from 5 minutes in slack periods to 2 minutes at peak periods. The Morgantown system can operate in both *scheduled* and *demand* modes. During peak hours the scheduled mode is used. Each vehicle follows a predetermined path, and passengers must board the correct vehicle. At other times the demand mode is used. The passenger indicates a desired destination, and the system routes a vehicle to provide that service. The minimum headway is 15 seconds. The maximum theoretical capacity is about 5000 p/h/d. In practice the capacity is about 3500 p/h/d because average headways exceed 15 seconds and average loads fall below 21 passengers.

The Morgantown system began transporting passengers in October 1975 while in the "shakedown" stage. By April 1976 it had transported 500,000 passengers and had achieved 94% service availability.

The Morgantown system was planned as a research, development, and demonstration project with the intention that it would continue in revenue service. From the service viewpoint the existing Morgantown system, with three stations, is not large enough to provide significant advantages over a simpler SLT system or network on the same route. Funding is being provided for construction of an additional 2.3 km (1.4 mi) of dual guideway and two stations. The more extensive GRT network may provide better service than SLT systems on the same route and will surely provide a more significant demonstration of GRT technology.

The Dallas–Ft. Worth GRT system, called Airtrans, has been in service since January 1974. It was designed, fabricated, and installed by The Vought Corporation.

MORGANTOWN CONFIGURATION

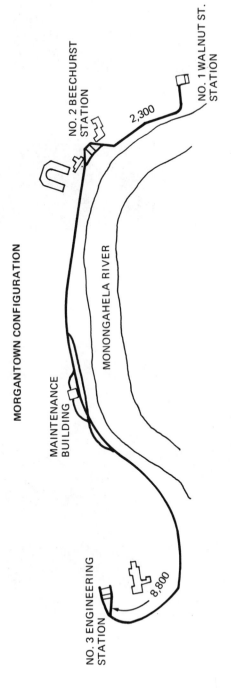

NO. 2 BEECHURST STATION

NO. 1 WALNUT ST. STATION

2,300

MAINTENANCE BUILDING

MONONGAHELA RIVER

NO. 3 ENGINEERING STATION

8,800

Figure 34-10 *Morgantown, West Virginia, system.*

(a)

(b)

Figure 34-11   *Morgantown vehicle. (courtesy of The Boeing Company)*

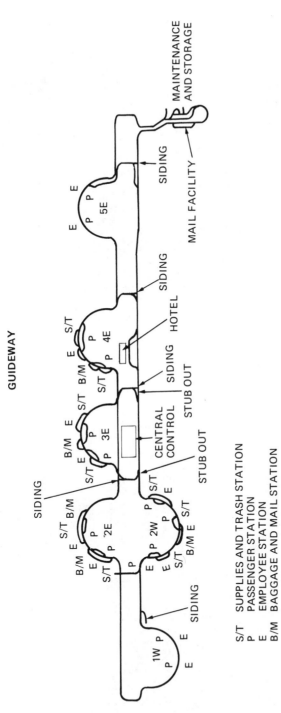

Figure 34-12 *Dallas-Fort Worth Airport system.*

S/T   SUPPLIES AND TRASH STATION
P   PASSENGER STATION
E   EMPLOYEE STATION
B/M   BAGGAGE AND MAIL STATION

Figure 34-13 *Airtrans vehicles.* (*courtesy of LEA TRANSIT COMPENDIUM and Vought Corporation*)

Figure 34-14 *Interior of Airtrans vehicle.* (*courtesy of Vought Corporation*)

Figure 34-15   *Airtrans passenger station. (courtesy of Vought Corporation)*

As of 1977 the system was the largest, most complex, and most versatile AGT system constructed (Fig. 34-12).[6] It contains the following major elements:

- 21 km (13 mi) of one-way guideway.
- 55 station stops: 14 for passengers and visitors, 14 for airline employees, and 27 for mail, baggage, supplies, and solid waste.
- 68 vehicles: 51 for passengers and 17 for material.
- 74 switches.

Routes were designed to allow vehicles to operate in a scheduled mode over 17 distinctly different service loops as follows:

- Five loops for passengers and visitors: two between remote parking and terminals and three among terminals.
- Two loops for airline employees between remote parking lots and terminals.
- Two loops for mail between terminals and the air mail facility.

---

[6]RONALD KANGAS AND OTHERS, *Assessment of Operational Automated Guideway Systems—Airtrans (Phase I)*, prepared for UMTA (Cambridge, Mass.: Transportation Systems Center, September 1976). Now available as **PB 261 339.**

- Four loops for interline baggage and mail transfer.
- Four loops for solid waste and supplies.

As of late 1977 the mail and baggage services have not yet been utilized.

The design of the Dallas–Ft. Worth airport allows most air passengers and visitors to do all necessary travel on foot. Airtrans is provided for persons using remote parking lots or transferring between airlines. When Airtrans is out of service for more than about 15 minutes, it is necessary to use buses to serve these people. Although seldom used, the buses and drivers are kept on standby. Drivers also serve as station attendants.

The capacity of the entire Airtrans system was specified at 9000 p/h, although no single route would need to carry that large a load. Each vehicle carries up to 40 passengers—16 seated and 24 standing—and can be operated singly or in two-vehicle trains. With a minimum headway of about 18 seconds, the theoretical capacity of a line is about 16,000 p/h/d. This high capacity is never fully realized, because average headways are longer than 18 seconds, and average train loads are less than 80 passengers. The specifications call for a maximum speed of 8 meters per second or 27 km/h (25 ft/s or 17 mi/h). Average trip times should not exceed 10 or 20 minutes, depending upon the origin and destination of the trip. Maximum trip times should not exceed 20 or 30 minutes.

The Airtrans system had an estimated total cost of about $81 million, including losses borne by the supplier. Operating and maintenance costs in 1976-1977 were about $2.94 million, including about $228,000 for electrical power.[7] Fares are 25 cents per ride.

Possible future GRT networks. Many GRT system variations can be envisioned, and it should also be possible to use two or more GRT systems as modules or building blocks to form networks of any desired size and complexity. The modules would interface at some stations, and passengers would transfer on foot. The separate systems or modules would not necessarily use the same hardware. Also, any number of SLT and GRT modules could be combined in a single network. As with SLT systems, there is the opportunity to develop a variety of GRT systems having capacities, performance characteristics, and costs quite different from the two existing systems. UMTA is sponsoring engineering studies of three advanced GRT systems.

PERSONAL RAPID TRANSIT

PRT systems have yet to be fully developed and installed; therefore, discussions must focus on conceptual designs. The term PRT was first used in 1968, in *Tomorrow's Transportation*,[8] to identify a system that would employ small automated vehicles capable of following paths tailored to the personal needs of an individual or small group traveling together by choice (i.e., a single travel party). Vehicles would have

---

[7]N. D. LEA & ASSOCIATES, *Summary of Capital and Operating Cost Experience for Automated Guideway Transit Systems* (Washington, D.C.: N. D. Lea & Associates, October 1977).

[8]COLE, *Tomorrow's Transportation.*

capacities similar to automobiles—two to four seats. Average loads would likely fall in a range of 1.2 to 1.5 persons depending on the purpose of the trip. However, vehicles would also travel without loads some part of the time.

The PRT system concept embodies all of the guideway and station characteristics and vehicle operating capabilities that are needed to provide prompt, nonstop, transfer-free service among all the stations of an extensive PRT network. The name "personal rapid transit" is well suited to represent this package of service characteristics.

The guideways of a PRT system would form a single network that could be arranged in a gridlike pattern, similar to the major streets and highways of a metropolitan area, or in other patterns to suit the particular site. An ideal network, from the viewpoint of users, would form a fine mesh—it would have closely spaced routes throughout the area served—and stations would be closely spaced to make them accessible via walking from all addresses in the area served.

A unique quality of PRT networks is that the guideways are coupled at the junctions. Vehicles can pass straight through junctions, change directions (i.e., turn right or left), or turn back. This means that a PRT vehicle can travel from any origin station to any destination station in a network—passengers do not have to make transfers between vehicles within the PRT network. Also, vehicle-trips can be distributed among alternate routes to avoid congestion or to detour around temporary blockages.

PRT system concepts call for vehicles to follow one another with very short time intervals or headways. Experience with autos on typical freeway lanes can be used to place this characteristic of PRT systems in perspective. Assume that a freeway lane carries 1800 autos/h under peak load conditions—headways average 2 seconds. With average auto loads of 1.33 persons, which is an observed value, the freeway lane will carry 2400 travelers/h.

To achieve that capacity a PRT system would also need to carry 1800 loaded vehicles each hour with an average of 1.33 passengers per loaded vehicle. In addition, the link would have to carry some empty vehicles since it would be necessary to redistribute vehicles for reuse, and some of that traffic would necessarily fall on heavily loaded routes. Assume that the combined load on the link is 1800 loaded vehicles and 200 empties, or 2000 PRT vehicles/h. This means that the *average* headway would need to be 1.8 seconds. The *minimum* headway must be significantly shorter to provide unoccupied spaces needed for the separation and remerging of many traffic streams. It is reasonable to assume that a PRT link designed to match the capacity of a typical freeway lane devoted to auto traffic and to carry 2400 p/h in the peak direction under peak load conditions would need headways of 1.5 seconds or less.

Reducing headways is a major technical challenge for PRT system engineers. Existing rail rapid transit systems seldom operate with headways below 100 seconds. Safety, reliability, comfort, and cost become matters of concern as headways are reduced. The two GRT systems now in revenue operation each aim to achieve a minimum headway in the range of only 15 to 18 seconds. There is every reason to believe that reducing PRT headways to 1.5 seconds will be achieved only with a major research and development effort.

Case studies treating PRT systems in a major U.S. city indicate that all links of a network do not require 1.5 seconds or any other standard headway.[9] Many routes could be served by PRT links with capacities of 240 p/h. That capacity is equivalent to bus service every 12 minutes and to one-tenth of the capacity of a freeway lane carrying autos. PRT headways on such a link would need to average only 18 seconds—a figure already surpassed. On the other hand, there are links on which capacities of 12,000 p/h and average headways of 0.36 second could be utilized, if attainable. Headways as short as 0.36 second will be achieved only by very great effort and are likely to require multiple technical breakthrough. Designers of early PRT systems can sidestep that challenge by using one of several alternative approaches. Networks can include multiple links on heavily traveled routes or can have many closely spaced routes—a very fine mesh—to distribute loads. Planners may find it even more desirable to substitute rail transit or other forms of AGT for PRT on heavily loaded routes.

PRT stations must be off-line to gain enough time to unload and load the vehicle without risk of end-to-end collisions, and to allow through passengers to bypass intermediate stations with little or no delay. The design of PRT stations presents especially difficult problems where a large number of vehicles must be processed. For example, a major PRT station may need the capacity to unload or load at rates of up to 1000 vehicles per hour or at average rates of 1 vehicle/3.6 seconds. The standing time required to unload or load a PRT vehicle is likely to be 10 seconds or longer. Therefore, such stations require something more than a simple siding. Several approaches are available to designers. One is to use dynamic platforms—a technique that has been used successfully in many places, especially at Disneyland and Disney World. Vehicles do not stop—they approach, pass, and exit the platform at a steady speed of about one-third to one-half walking speed [e.g., 0.6 m/s (2 ft/s)]. Platforms are equipped with pedestrian conveyors traveling at the same speed as the passing vehicles. Passengers moving between the conveyor and the vehicle experience little or no difficulty since both walking surfaces are moving at the same speed. Users boarding and leaving the conveyor need only the same degree of agility required to use moving walkways and escalators. A second approach uses two or more station platforms in parallel and makes each platform long enough to accommodate several vehicles in series. Unloading operations are accomplished in serial order on one platform while loading is accomplished in serial order on another, and operations alternate from one platform to the other as needed. A third approach uses a dock to slide a vehicle from the siding to an unloading–loading position.

The three approaches are not mutually exclusive. Parallel dynamic platforms could be used to achieve high capacity. Static platforms or docks can be used to accommodate handicapped passengers while the main unloading–loading operations proceed at a dynamic platform. Docks can also be used to remove malfunctioning cars to storage to await repair.

The most sophisticated PRT prototype system was developed in Japan in a program started in 1968. The program was sponsored by the Ministry of International

---

[9]CLARK HENDERSON AND OTHERS, *Future Urban Transportation Systems: Descriptions, Evaluations, and Programs*, Final Report I, prepared for UMTA and HUD (Menlo Park, Calif.: Stanford Research Institute, March 1968).

Trade and Industry and had numerous participants, including Tokyo University and eight industrial firms. The prototype system is called the Computer Controlled Vehicle System (CVS). A 4.7-km (2.9-mi) network of guideways was constructed near Tokyo, and 84 passenger and cargo vehicles were fabricated. Passenger vehicles carried four seated passengers and no standees. Cargo vehicles carried payloads of 300 to 400 kilograms (660 to 880 pounds). Speeds ranged from 39 to 77 km/h (24 to 48 mi/h). The goal was to achieve theoretical capacities of 3600 vehicles/h and 14,000 seats/h with 1-second headways. Headways of 1 second were achieved in tests with three vehicles at speeds up to 29 km/h (18 mi/h). The extensive test facility has been dismantled, and the future of the system is uncertain.

The ARAMIS system in France and the Cabinentaxi system in West Germany also achieved some PRT characteristics. Full development of PRT systems will require much work, and it is likely to be many years before PRT systems are available for urban service.

FAST TRANSIT LINKS (FTL)

The fast transit link (FTL) concept was represented by the U.S. Department of Transportation's Urban Tracked Air Cushion Vehicle (UTACV) system developed to the prototype stage by Rohr Industries. The system was designed for a top speed of about 240 km/h (150 mi/h). The vehicle operated on a special guideway and used air cushions for suspension and guidance and linear induction motors for propulsion and normal braking. The prototype vehicle carried an operator but could be fully automated. A revenue system would employ on-line stations. Similar systems have been developed in France and England. Technology developed in Germany and Japan utilizes magnetic suspension.

Opportunities to utilize FTL systems in urban settings are limited—long routes and long intervals between stations would be needed to realize significant time savings, and large passenger loads would be needed to justify capital costs. These conditions may exist on some intercity routes but not on urban or suburban routes. All development programs for urban FTL systems appear to have been abandoned. Presumably the cost of development has been found to be excessive in the light of the limited scope for applications.

DUAL-CONTROLLED AGT (D-AGT)

D-AGT systems would operate on city streets under driver control and on guideways under automatic controls. Dual-controlled SLT, GRT, and PRT systems have been conceived and described.[10] In the United States the most thoroughly studied

---

[10]HENDERSON AND OTHERS, *Future Urban Transportation Systems*, and TRANSPORTATION RESEARCH BOARD, *Dual-Mode Transportation*, Special Report 170 (Washington, D.C.: Transportation Research Board, 1976).

example of the class is the dual-controlled bus, often called "dual-mode transit." Networks envisioned for such systems would include a "belt route" around a central business district and several radial routes extending to the suburbs. The guideway part of the network would have the basic characteristics of a GRT system, including branching and merging junctions and off-line stations. Prototypes have not yet been developed in the United States. An UMTA program aimed at the development of a dual-mode bus system was stopped in 1974.

A small AGT system, designed by a Japanese consortium for the 1975 International Ocean Exposition in Okinawa demonstrated some dual-mode features. Vehicles seated four passengers and traveled at 19 km/h (12 mi/h). Eighteen vehicles were employed—15 were captive to the guideway and 3 were dual-controlled. The guideway was about 1.9 km (1.2 mi) long and included five off-line stations.

AUTOMATED MIXED TRAFFIC VEHICLES (AMTV)

Automated vehicles capable of transporting passengers over roadways shared with pedestrians or manually controlled vehicles would avoid the high labor and capital costs that limit the exploitation of many other systems. Two passenger-carrying AMTV systems with this basic capability have been developed in the United States to the prototype stage. However, these systems have not reached regular passenger service because of concern for safety and the problems of achieving speed high enough to make the service attractive.

There are several hundred AMTV systems in use for materials handling in factories and warehouses. Vehicles are powered by batteries and are designed to follow an electrical signal carried in a wire attached to the running surface or in a slot cut in the surface. The industrial systems travel at about one-third normal walking speed[11] and depend upon sensitive bumpers to apply brakes when the vehicle contacts anything in its path. Better sensors are needed to increase speed and for operation in public places. Acoustical and optical sensors have had limited use in industrial systems.

General Motors Corporation has demonstrated a passenger-carrying system capable of operating among pedestrians at about one-third walking speed. Jet Propulsion Laboratories has installed within its laboratory complex a prototype system on a street where both motor vehicles and pedestrians are present. Its maximum speed is about 11 km/h (7 mi/h)—more than double normal walking speed. An operator is always carried aboard the vehicle, although controls are fully automatic.

The key to the design of an AMTV system suitable for urban public transportation service is the development of a sensing subsystem that will allow vehicles to operate at a relatively high average speed—say, double or triple normal walking speed—while avoiding unreasonable risk of injuries and property damage. This is likely to require use of advanced optical sensors as well as other devices such as wayside sensors, lane markers, and signals.

---

[11]Normal walking speed is about 3 mi/h or about 5 km/h.

ACCELERATING MOVING WAYS (AMW)

AMW systems use wayside propulsion devices to accelerate, transport, and decelerate passengers either in vehicles or as pedestrians standing on the surface of a conveyor. Escalators and pedestrian conveyors are moving-way systems, but they transport passengers at one-third to one-half walking speed. Both vehicular and nonvehicular AMW systems have been developed. (See Figs. 34-16 and 34-17.) Only the vehicular system has entered regular transportation services.

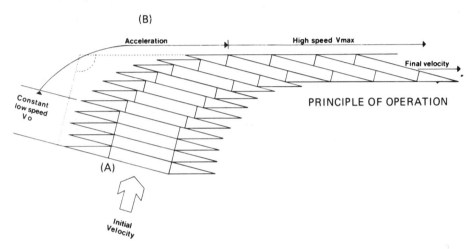

Figure 34-16 *Dunlop Speedaway. High-speed passenger conveyor.* (*courtesy of LEA TRANSIT COMPENDIUM*)

The WEDway People Mover at Disneyland is a vehicular AMW system. It has been in service since 1967 and has transported more than 30 million passengers. Trains pass through the station at a low speed—about one-third walking speed—but do not stop. The station uses a circular conveyor—a dynamic platform—to unload and reload passengers as trains pass through the station. Loaded trains then accelerate, travel about 1.2 km (0.75 mi) at about 9.7 km/h (6 mi/h), decelerate, and unload as they again pass through the station. The trains have reaction plates mounted on their undersides and are propelled by rubber wheels mounted in the guideway and driven by electric motors. A similar system propelled by linear induction motors (LIMs) has been in operation at Disney World since 1975. The LIM windings are in the guideway and the reaction plates are on the vehicle. The Disney World system has been classed as an AGT system by UMTA and is eligible for consideration in the Downtown People Mover Program.

In nonvehicular AMW systems, passengers step from a station platform to a conveyor surface moving at one-third to one-half walking speed. The surface is then accelerated to a speed several times the boarding speed, travels at, say, double walking

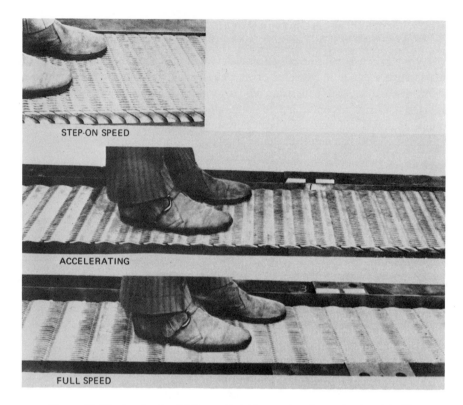

STEP-ON SPEED

ACCELERATING

FULL SPEED

Figure 34-17 *Accelerating Walkway. Variable-speed walkway developed by The Johns Hopkins University Applied Physics Laboratory. (courtesy of LEA TRANSIT COMPENDIUM)*

speed, and finally is decelerated back to the original low speed to permit a passenger to step back to a stationary platform in the station.

Prototype acceleration pedestrian conveyors have been developed in Switzerland, France, and the United States; production versions of the Swiss system have been fabricated in England and in Japan. No systems are in regular passenger service.

RENT-BY-THE-TRIP PUBLIC AUTOMOBILE SERVICE (PAS)

PAS systems would supply small automobiles to accredited drivers at self-service stands or lots located at close intervals throughout designated service areas. One conceptual design assumes that each accredited driver would carry a key or magnetically coded card containing an account number. This device would allow the driver to unlock and activate a rental car. It would also start a tape recorder which would note the account number together with start time, end time, and the distance driven. Tapes would be read periodically, and the data would be used to compute charges for services and to prepare a monthly bill.

tekening Bas Janmaat

Figure 34-18 *PAS station. Artist rendition of a Witkar station. (courtesy of Cooperative Association Witkar)*

PAS storage places would be located at all transit stations and other major trip-generating points. Small-capacity PAS stands would be located in the parking strip of streets at points within easy walking distance of every address in the service area. The number of vehicles on hand at each place would be monitored from a central control facility, and empty vehicles would be redistributed from time to time in anticipation of shifting demands.

PAS systems could be started with presently available small automobiles, but special governors, locks, and recorders would have to be added. Over a longer period, purpose-built vehicles and other equipment could be developed to achieve efficient redistribution of empty cars and other desirable features.

Conceptual designs for rent-by-the-trip autos were prepared by Stanford Research Institute and the University of Pennsylvania in 1968.[12] A small experimental system was initiated in the downtown area of Amsterdam. Another small-scale experiment was conducted in France. However, no system is commercially available.

The PAS system has attractive service and economic features. It would provide most of the conveniences of taxi service for many trips, but could be much less expensive since the cost of the service would not include wages of a driver. Parking burdens

---

[12]HENDERSON AND OTHERS, *Future Urban Transportation Systems*, and VUKAN R. VUCHIC AND OTHERS, eds., *Minicar Transit System*, Final Report, prepared for UMTA (Philadelphia: University of Pennsylvania, 1970). Now available as PB 196 370.

Figure 34-19 *Witkar vehicle. Amsterdam, Netherlands. (courtesy of Cooperative Association Witkar)*

imposed by the system would be light in comparison with private autos—the vehicles would be small; they would be parked in more compact patterns than private autos; and the number of vehicles to be parked would be small since each vehicle would serve many travelers each day. However, rent-by-the-trip autos might increase vehicular traffic on city streets by encouraging more circulation travel and by shifting pedestrian traffic into the new street vehicles.

CONCLUSION

The need for innovation and the main avenues for development of advanced urban public transporta ion systems have been generally recognized. Progress has been slow, however, and many programs have been aborted. The problems of planning, developing, producing, installing, and operating advanced systems have proved to be complex far beyond early expectations.

The benefits claimed to be available through exploitation of advanced systems have not been fully assessed and are not recognized at all by most of the potential beneficiaries of such systems or by institutions that might install them. Consequently, there is no powerful constituency or political force pressing for innovation and exploitation, and it is not politically feasible for federal, state, regional, and local agencies to develop aggressive programs.

Potential suppliers of advanced systems demonstrated an enormous capability to develop and produce systems in the early 1970s, but then became discouraged by the lack of market opportunities. The number of major firms with active programs in advanced systems declined substantially after 1974. Industry interest will not be revived until markets are assured.

What is most needed is competent and innovative planning of advanced systems at the regional and local levels. For this planning to be effective, there must be active cooperation of national professional organizations and all federal agencies directly and indirectly concerned with urban transportation and all related environmental, resource, and land-use problems.

SELECTED BIBLIOGRAPHY

Many citations are no longer available from their original source. These citations are often available from the National Technical Information Service, U.S. Department of Commerce, 5285 Port Royal Road, Springfield, Va. 22161. We have verified the order numbers for many of these citations, and they are found at the end of the citation. Prices are available through NTIS at the address above.

COLE, LEON MONROE, ed., *Tomorrow's Transportation: New Systems for the Urban Future*, prepared by U.S. Department of Housing and Urban Development. Washington, D.C.: U.S. Government Printing Office, 1968.

HENDERSON, CLARK, ROBERT H. CRONIN, AND HAZEL T. ELLIS, *Energy Study of Automated Guideway Transit (AGT) Systems*, prepared for Energy Research and Development Administration. Menlo Park, Calif.: SRI International, February 1978.

————, AND OTHERS, *Future Urban Transporation Systems: Descriptions, Evaluations, and Programs*, Final Report I, prepared for UMTA and HUD. Menlo Park, Calif.: Stanford Research Institute, March 1968.

KANGAS, RONALD, AND OTHERS, *Assessment of Operational Automated Guideway Systems—Airtrans (Phase I)*, prepared for UMTA. Cambridge, Mass.: Transportation Systems Center, September 1976. Now available as PB 261 339.

LEA TRANSIT COMPENDIUM, *Group Rapid Transit*, vol. III, no. 3, 1976–77, a supplement to vol. II, no. 3, 1975. Huntsville, Ala.: N. D. Lea Transportation Research Corporation, 1976.

————, *Light Guideway Transit*, vol. I, no. 3, 1974. Huntsville, Ala.: N. D. Lea Transportation Research Corporation, 1974.

————, *Light Guideway Transit*, vol. II, no. 3, 1975. Huntsville, Ala.: N. D. Lea Transportation Research Corporation, 1975.

————, *Moving Way Transit*, vol. I, no. 2, 1974. Huntsville, Ala.: N. D. Lea Transportation Research Corporation, 1974.

————, *Moving Way Transit*, vol. II, no. 2, 1975. Huntsville, Ala.: N. D. Lea Transportation Research Corporation, 1975.

————, *Moving Way Transit*, vol. III, no. 2, 1976–77, a supplement to vol. II, no. 2, 1975. Huntsville, Ala.: N. D. Lea Transportation Research Corporation, 1976.

————, *Personal Rapid Transit*, vol. I, no. 4, 1974. Huntsville, Ala.: N. D. Lea Transportation Research Corporation, 1974.

————, *Personal Rapid Transit*, vol. II, no. 4, 1975. Huntsville, Ala.: N. D. Lea Transportation Research Corporation, 1975.

————, *Personal Rapid Transit*, vol. III, no. 4, 1976–77, a supplement to vol. II, no. 4, 1975. Huntsville, Ala.: N. D. Lea Transportation Research Corporation, 1976.

N. D. LEA & ASSOCIATES, *Summary of Capital and Operating Cost Experience for Automated Guideway Transit Systems*. Washington, D.C.: N. D. Lea & Associates, October 1977.

SIDDIQEE, W., AND OTHERS, *Summary Discussion Report: The Assessment of Six Domestic Automated Guideway Transit (AGT) Systems*, prepared for UMTA, Report no. UMTA-IT-06-0135-7. Menlo Park, Calif.: SRI International, January 1978.

TRANSPORTATION RESEARCH BOARD, *Dual-Mode Transportation*, Special Report 170. Washington, D.C.: Transportation Research Board, 1976.

U.S. Congress, Office of Technology Assessment, *Automated Guideway Transit: An Assessment of PRT and Other New Systems*, including supporting panel reports, prepared for Senate Committee on Appropriations, Transportation Subcommittee. Washington, D.C.: U.S. Government Printing Office, 1975. Now available as PB 224 854.

Vuchic, Vukan R., and others, eds., *Minicar Transit System*, Final Report, prepared for UMTA. Philadelphia: University of Pennsylvania, 1970. Now available as PB 196 370.

Yen, A. M., and others, *Assessment of the Automatically Controlled Transportation (ACT) System at Fairlane Town Center*, prepared for UMTA, Report no. UMTA-IT-06-0135-77-2. Menlo Park, Calif.: SRI International, December 1977.

————, and others, *Assessment of the Passenger Shuttle System (PSS) at Tampa International Airport*, prepared for UMTA, Report no. UMTA-IT-06-0135-77-4. Menlo Park, Calif.: SRI International, December 1977.

————, and others, *Assessment of the Satellite Transit System (STS) at the Seattle-Tacoma International Airport*, prepared for UMTA, Report no. UMTA-IT-06-0135-77-1. Menlo Park, Calif.: SRI International, December 1977.

————, and others, *Assessment of the UMI Type II Tourister AGT System at King's Domain*, prepared for UMTA, Report no. UMTA-IT-06-0135-77-6. Menlo Park, Calif.: SRI International, November 1977.

————, and others, *Assessment of the WEDway People Mover System at Walt Disney World*, prepared for UMTA, Report no. UMTA-IT-06-0135-77-5. Menlo Park, Calif.: SRI International, November 1977.

————, and others, *Assessment of Tunnel Train System at the Houston Intercontinental Airport*, prepared for UMTA, Report no. UMTA-IT-06-0135-77-3. Menlo Park, Calif.: SRI International, December 1977.

Chapter 35

A LOOK AHEAD

JERRY D. WARD, *U.S. Department of Transportation, Office of the Secretary*

In this chapter we will try to peer as far into the murky crystal ball of the future as seems useful. We will deal in possibilities, not predictions; remember that talking about the year 2000 is roughly analogous to describing today from the vantage point of the early 1950s. One might do it correctly; the seeds of many current conditions were visible then. But it would have taken extraordinary vision, and perhaps more important, even if correct, such predictions would have been unbelievable to most people. Thus such vision would have had, at best, entertainment value only; it would have been unlikely to have brought forth support for actions that might have alleviated today's problems or enhanced our opportunities.

But it is not important to be right. It is only important that we alert ourselves to possibilities, to sharpen our sensitivity to the portends of coming problems and opportunities, and to give ourselves lead time to provide options for an always uncertain future.

In 1950, the jet engine that has revolutionized air travel was about a dozen years old. The first commercial digital computer was to be delivered the following year. It was made using vacuum tubes; the solid-state electronic components that have permitted the cheap, compact, and reliable computers of today were still a laboratory dream. But in the perspective of the day we could not afford many big computers or much air travel anyway. Nor could we afford television in 95% of our houses or 10 million new cars a year because each person's share of the national output (GNP) was only $2900 per year in 1973 dollars.

With rising affluence many of yesterday's luxuries have become today's necessities. In 1973 GNP per capita was $6110, more than twice that of 1950 in equivalent purchasing power. From the perspective of 1950 we can afford not only more leisure but also to concern ourselves more deeply about things other than personal subsistence. And we do; our activities and expenditures to protect the environment and to increase the opportunity for greater social equity would have seemed incredible 25 years ago.

Can we reasonably expect the next 25 or so years to bring the same percentage rise in affluence that the last brought? Will GNP per capita really be $14,000 in 1973 dollars? As is discussed later, probably not. But it is likely to be substantially up from today. How will we spend it? How will it affect our values, life-styles, and national priorities? And more specifically, how will it affect transportation?

The point of all this is to remind ourselves that in 25 years a lot can change; and while many of the changes are conceivable today, they will still be viewed as surprises when they mature. And there will be changes that seem inconceivable today. Above all, when we discuss transportation systems for the future, we should continuously remind ourselves not to view them as predictions but as options and possibilities. The criteria and the conditions under which future choices will be made are highly unlikely to be those that exist today, and we should be wary of too quickly foreclosing alternatives because they represent a departure from current thinking.

In subsequent sections, we will begin to examine some of the possibilities. Because there is such a large variety of specific alternatives, we will also try to identify some of the principles that now seem likely to guide the way the transportation system evolves. We will start with urban transportation.

URBAN TRANSPORTATION EVOLUTION

The automobile is a marvelous device. It dominates both urban and intercity travel today, and, we will conclude, it will continue to be the single most important transportation mode as far into the future as we can see. From the point of view of energy efficiency, emissions, and safety, it will get better. But it has one key deficiency that appears essentially incurable: it requires 7 to 10 times as much street space per passenger as a bus, plus space for parking. The car, while tremendously attractive in many ways, is not efficient in its use of space.

This is the root of the urban transportation dilemma. If we continue to use the car as we now do, we have two choices. First, we can continue to live with the congestion that is so onerous to large city dwellers. Our second choice is to limit the density of development by allocating a higher ratio of space to streets and parking per traffic generator—shops, apartments, offices, hotels, etc.—than has been our past practice. This latter implies a major overhaul of cities now in place. It implies more low-density development, or, to use a more value-laden term, sprawl. Many people contend that a city designed around the automobile cannot be made a good city for the pedestrian; it becomes a kind of dehumanized city. (We might observe that there is a fundamental incompatibility between our two most popular means of transportation: the automobile and the elevator.)

The third option is to modify the pattern of car usage, to induce a shift out of the car into more space-efficient modes downtown and in other areas of high-density development. Most people, on the face of it, opt for the third choice, not only because it would make our high-density urban areas more pleasant places to live and work, but because it would imply the existence of a better public system that can help provide mobility for the transportation disadvantaged: the young, the old, the poor, and the handicapped. But it will clearly not be easy to get people out of their cars, and it probably cannot be done unless the alternative offered in the car-inhibited zones provides very good service.

Then there is the issue of what to do about the suburbs. Roughly half our urban population now lives in low- to medium-density areas outside the central cities. Most of them do not have easy access to bus service, because conventional fixed-route buses are too expensive when ridership density is low. Good bus service means many buses serving many destinations; where there are few riders per square mile this results in mostly empty buses. Rail systems obviously have the same deficiency. At some point as ridership density decreases, it becomes cheaper to switch to flexible-route service with the vehicle (car, van, or minibus) going directly to each customer. While this kind of service is expensive, it is not as expensive as conventional fixed route in low-density areas.

Why should we bother about offering suburban service? We clearly have the option of confining conventional transit to areas where we have congestion problems, and provide park-and-ride access to it, and offering taxi and special-purpose services in the suburbs for those who do not have access to autos. And this may be the way it turns out. On the other hand, the commuter still leaves one car in a parking lot all day; the suburban aged, youth, and poor may or may not get adequate transportation; and while it has not been proved, the total cost of transportation is probably higher than if a good, coordinated system is available throughout the suburbs as well as downtown.

How might we provide such service? We have the situation that the fixed-route bus or rail that is effective for high-density circulation and line-haul movement of lots of people is ineffective in low-density areas. On the other hand, the flexible-route private car and taxi that are good where there is no premium on road space are too land hungry downtown and in other high-density areas and along the arterials leading to them.

The conclusion is obvious. There is no single system that can serve all the diverse needs of a medium- to large-size urban region. The only way to provide good public transportation that is available everywhere and can serve all the diverse destinations of the modern multinucleated city is through a mix of systems, each serving the neighborhood or functions for which it is best suited, functionally integrated so that the individual parts behave cooperatively instead of competitively.

Such systems will take time to evolve. There are many obstacles, some institutional and some operational, with which we will have to learn to cope. A few such mixed, integrated systems have already been started, some successfully so far, while others have had financial or operational difficulty. But we think that this is the most desirable direction for the evolution of urban transportation in the future, reflecting the fairly simple and obvious principle that the complete urban system should be a multimodal system in which the various modes and elements behave cooperatively.

If this comes to pass, we will see many different kinds of organizational arrangements and operating schemes, and different mixes of system elements. Some may be just conventional fixed-route bus plus shared-ride taxi or some other demand-responsive system in the suburbs. Some may have fixed rail or light rail elements. Some cities may place heavy emphasis on private car- and vanpooling to take the pressure off the commuter peak. Some will have taxi or limousine operators offering a wider variety of services, perhaps receiving some subsidy from the conventional transit whose per passenger costs have been reduced by the larger ridership enjoyed by an integrated system. There may need to be use of auto disincentives: limited or high-priced downtown parking, or congestion pricing schemes. But all these variant possibilities reflect the principle cited: multimodal systems, behaving cooperatively, governed by coherent policies.

As we move further along in time, improved versions of today's systems will likely become available and replace incrementally the older mode serving that same function. For example, in the mid-1980s, new automated transit may replace light rail as we know it today, offering improved comfort and a much higher proportion of express service. The trend will be toward an expanding grid or network of automated guideway systems that allows good accessibility to most of the built-up nuclei of metropolitan areas, including good access to the airports and other intercity travel modes.

SOME GENERAL PRINCIPLES

In the discussion of urban systems the point was made that the car that serves the low-density areas of the city so well is not the best system at high densities. As more cars flow in from the various sections of the suburbs, arterial congestion increases, suggesting that in the high-density part of the network, larger capacity vehicles that are more space efficient would be preferred. These, in turn, are not efficient at low density. The drawback is that if people are to get out of the vehicle that served the low density and into a larger vehicle, a transfer is involved—a source of inconvenience and time lost (even though the conditions of transfer should be very much better in the future than they generally are today).

This illustrates a general dilemma, or trade-off, that applies to all transportation networks, whether they be urban or intercity, passenger or goods. Every transportation mode has a set of conditions, a "window," in which it operates best. When it operates outside its optimum window, it pays a penalty. The trade-off is between this penalty and the cost or penalty of transferring to the optimum mode. How this trade-off turns out should be the fundamental determinant as to whether unimodal or multimodal operation is the preferred approach to a given situation or market.

Now the reason such simple principles are important in the context of this chapter is that they may be one guide to the direction of transportation system evolution in the future. However, implicit in that postulate is the assumption that economic efficiency will be an important criterion for transportation in the future. One could seriously question this, asking if the system we have today is a consequence of a search for the most economically efficient transportation system. This assumption may seem even more questionable in the future in what is likely to be a more highly politicized and affluent world. It has been noted that most political bodies sometimes seem to show only a peripheral interest in efficiency of resource allocation.

On the other hand, the regulations and practices that have helped mold today's system into its often nonoptimal behavior patterns are likely to change in the future, and the impetus for change seems, in general, to be based largely on reaction to economic difficulties. The changes will not be optimal, but it is hard to argue that the changes will deliberately discourage efficiency. It thus seems reasonable that while many other factors will help shape the transportation of tomorrow, the general desire for efficiency of resource use—at whatever service level is desired—will remain a valid goal for system design and operation. While changing cultural norms and values may impact resource allocation between transportation and competing uses, and how trade-offs are made between, say, environmental protection and cost, changing values will not overcome resource scarcity. If the nation is rich, we may all want luxury cars, but we will still, in general, want the least expensive car that embodies the luxury desired, because we may also want yachts. At any level of reasonably conceivable affluence, resources are not unlimited, and it is hard to believe the interest in efficiency of their use will not continue to be an important shaping influence for transportation.

FREIGHT: AN EXAMPLE

Let us see where this thinking leads us as we consider the direction of evolution of the future freight system. Figure 35-1 shows a simplified network that depicts a portion of a transportation system, which we will now view in the context of freight. Each link in the system can be a different mode, either truck, rail, water, or air. The nodes represent the transfer points between them. Alternatively, the same mode may carry its cargo through the whole network, from origin to destination—unimodal operation.

The heavy segment might be ships, connecting at either end to truck or rail. Or airplanes connecting to urban truck collection and distribution. In these cases the total trip almost always involves multimodal handling; unless the origin or destination is located at the port or airfield, there is no option.

With truck and rail there is an option, because for many years rail dominated freight traffic and many large shippers and receivers are located on rail lines. But for a number of reasons rail has been losing to truck. Today trucks carry slightly more than half the ton-miles of the rail but, according to Transportation Association of America statistics, receive nearly 7 times as much revenue. This compares to 4 times in 1962. The market differentiation is based primarily on the nature of the goods shipped, and only secondarily on the distance or the volume of flow. These figures show clearly that truck has been capturing the higher-value cargo and the more expensive shipments.

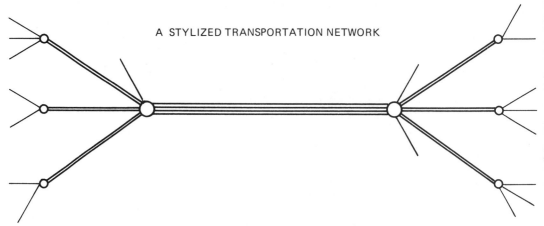

Figure 35-1 *A stylized transportation network*

If we could set aside the reasons the truck and rail systems have evolved as they have, a potentially different picture emerges. We can observe, first, that rail service would be improved and costs reduced if the train *consist* (the combination of cars) could remain the same from origin to destination; that is, if it were not necessary to take the train apart and recombine it as it picked up or discharged cars coming from or going to different destinations. Trains operated without this reshuffling, and on good track, have the potential for offering cheaper and faster service than the best intercity trucks. The problem today is that much of the track needs substantial investment to be put in first-class condition, and in very few cases is the volume of flow large enough to make up trains where every car is going to the same destination; since they cannot, the trains must frequently stop to drop off some cars and pick up others. The result is that the average rail car is moving loaded less than 10% of the time.

Now the number of "yardings" could be reduced by either smaller trains or larger shipments. Smaller trains are more expensive to operate, and larger shipments are the shipper's decision, not the railroads! What we can observe then is that the inherent capability of the rail to offer good, long-distance high-density service is being compromised by their need to handle shipments that involve small numbers of cars. Such long-distance high-density service is rail's "window" of optimal performance; operating outside it costs it some of its potential comparative advantage within it.

Truck, on the other hand, is to some degree doing the same kind of thing. In an effort to better compete for long-distance medium-density haulage, trucks and truck trailers are getting larger, and in some states, getting permission to operate as highway "trains" of two and even three trailers in one unit, called double and triple bottoms. These large units are clearly less well suited to urban streets, and must be broken down or transfer their goods to smaller trucks for urban collection and distribution.

The inference one might draw from these observations is that, in the future, it would be desirable to move toward a much higher degree of truck–rail multimodal operation, with truck serving more of the small-load movement over shorter distances and as a feeder/distributor to rail, which would specialize primarily in long-haul high-density movement. Each mode would begin to curtail its operation outside its own window of optimal performance. We would be moving toward optimizing the performance of the system rather than that of the individual links. This is schematically illustrated in Fig. 35-2.

AN OPTIMIZED TRUCK-RAIL FREIGHT SYSTEM

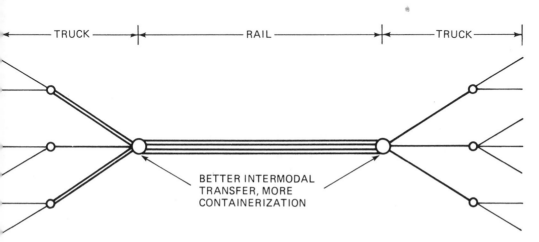

Figure 35-2 *An optimized truck–rail freight system*

While this seems logical on the face of it, there are many impediments to the total truck–rail system evolving in this direction. Probably the most important are built into regulatory practices and industry structure. But there is also a need for better physical facilities, for much better intermodal transfer terminals and methods of loading and unloading. If one were to ask what change might be expected in the next 5 years, the best guess might be "almost none." But in 25 years, things will change; and it seems reasonable that the multimodal system described above might be the best guide as to the direction of that change.

GENERALIZED COST BEHAVIOR

Threaded through the conjectures about the freight system and the urban transportation system discussed earlier has been another general principle: as flow volume increases, *ceteris paribus*, unit costs decrease. These unit costs can be either cents per passenger-mile, or ton-mile, or volume-mile. Obviously other things impact costs, but the preceding statement is generally true for two reasons: first, the fixed investment costs are spread over more units as volume increases, and second, operating costs are reduced because higher volume permits better trade-offs between frequency of service, vehicle (or train) load factor, and vehicle size (or train size). A full DC-10 is cheaper per person than a full DC-9. A full bus is cheaper per person than a full taxi.

This principle is depicted in Fig. 35-3. Applying it to our generalized transportation network of Fig. 35-1, we would expect the costs to be higher in the lower-density collection/distribution ends of the network than in the high-density line-haul portions. This fits with what we observe in the real world. It also explains why the demands for subsidy are almost always to reduce the prices charged at the low-density ends of a system.

Higher levels of aggregation also offer the potential for better efficiency in the use of energy and the use of space. These economies of aggregation are the incentive for the kind of truck–rail freight movements already discussed; the trade-off is the cost of transfer from one mode to another and the extra distance introduced by potentially more circuitous routing. We see the principle in the greater use of buses and rapid transit where passenger flows are very high; the aggregation of people provides higher capacity per unit of space used, which is absolutely essential in most of our larger cities.

The problem is that aggregation of passengers and goods is becoming increasingly hard to bring about as more people and activities are diffusing into low-density suburbs. It is likely that in the future we will see even more intense efforts to encourage higher-density growth patterns as well as more attention to transportation system and network design that takes greater advantage of the economies of aggregation.

THE UNIT COSTS OF TRANSPORTATION

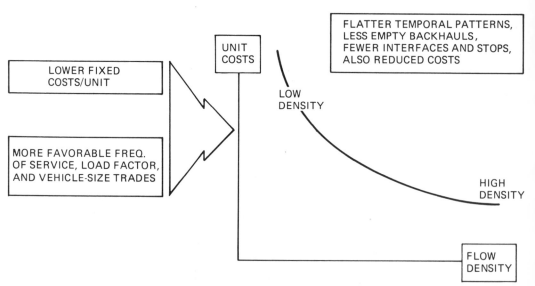

Figure 35-3 *The unit costs of transportation*

The Census Bureau has produced a number of population projections based on different birth and net immigration rates. One is shown in Fig. 35-4. It is based on Census Series P, which assumes a fertility rate of 1.8 children per woman per lifetime. It shows the population continuing to grow for the next 50 years (because we have disproportionately more young in the mix today), leveling at about 275 million people. This adds about 60 million more people to the current population.

This assumed fertility rate is just slightly lower than the roughly 1.83 rate that was obtained in 1975. Whether this lower rate will continue is obviously conjectural; it was substantially higher for the 20 or so years before the 1970s. On the other hand, it is on the long-term trendline going back to 1800, when the fertility rate was seven live children per woman per lifetime.

The first conclusion is that even if we continue the low fertility rate path toward zero population growth, the nation's economy will have to accommodate, in the form of jobs, houses, goods, and services, some 60 or so million more people between 1975 and 2025. In fact, job formation and the capital required therefor may be one of the tougher challenges to our economic well-being over the next 10 to 20 years. This is illustrated by Fig. 35-5, which shows the historical labor force growth since 1950, with the extrapolation based on the population of Fig. 35-4 and the assumption of the same rate of participation in the work force as a function of age and sex as we had in 1973. If female participation continues to increase, this could underestimate the potential work force; if we take growing productivity in the form of increased leisure, it could overestimate it, in the sense that each member works less.

These work-force figures take on significance if we look at them as ratios as in Fig. 35-6. The first curve indicates that workers per capita will increase by about 10 to 15% by 2010 if work-force participation rates hold. Given full employment and no dramatic change in the average workweek, real GNP per capita should increase correspondingly, but magnified by whatever improvements in labor productivity we are able to achieve. If productivity increases at only 2% per year, compared to a 3.0% rate between 1950 and 1973, GNP per capita should reach $11,000 in 2000 in 1973 dollars (compared to $6110 then). At 3.0%, it would reach nearly $14,000 in 2000.

The second curve in Fig. 35-6 shows that the potential retiree roles begin to swell rapidly about 2010 as the young adults of today begin to reach their 60s and the number of workers/retirees drop. Throughout this whole period the average age of the work force and the population has been increasing, with whatever sociological impacts that may imply. The post-World War II baby boom that swelled the schools in the 1950s and 1960s and the work force in the last quarter of this century starts to retire in the beginning of the next. If this retirement is paid for on the current pay-as-you-go basis, it could mean a very dramatic loss in earnings-after-taxes for those still doing the working. And unless for some reason the population starts to grow again, this new ratio of workers/retirees will be the new norm.

What does this mean for transportation? First, labor-intensive systems, such as the urban system described earlier, may not be all bad: they offer socially desirable

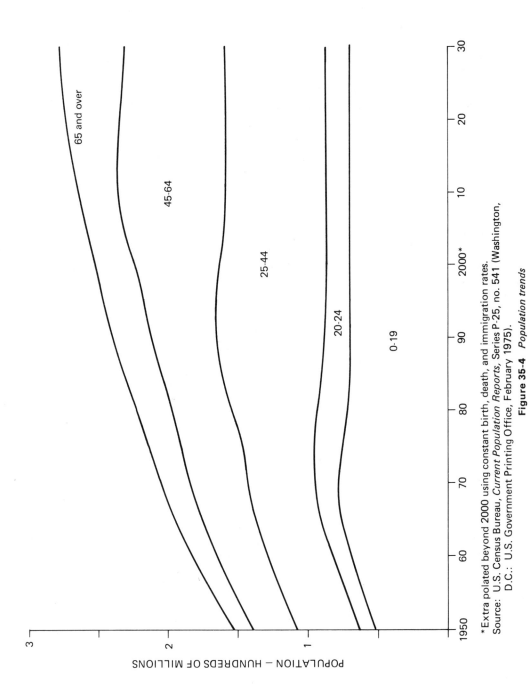

POPULATION — HUNDREDS OF MILLIONS

65 and over

45-64

25-44

20-24

0-19

1950   60   70   80   90   2000*   10   20   30

*Extrapolated beyond 2000 using constant birth, death, and immigration rates.
Source: U.S. Census Bureau, *Current Population Reports*, Series P-25, no. 541 (Washington, D.C.: U.S. Government Printing Office, February 1975).

Figure 35-4 *Population trends*

LABOR FORCE TRENDS

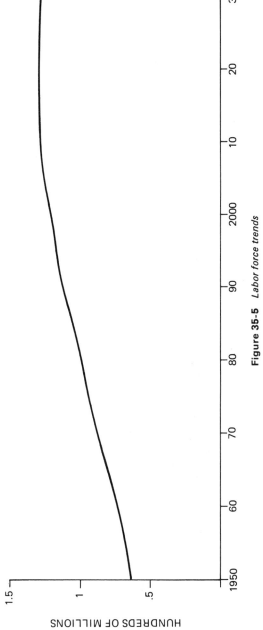

Figure 35-5   *Labor force trends*

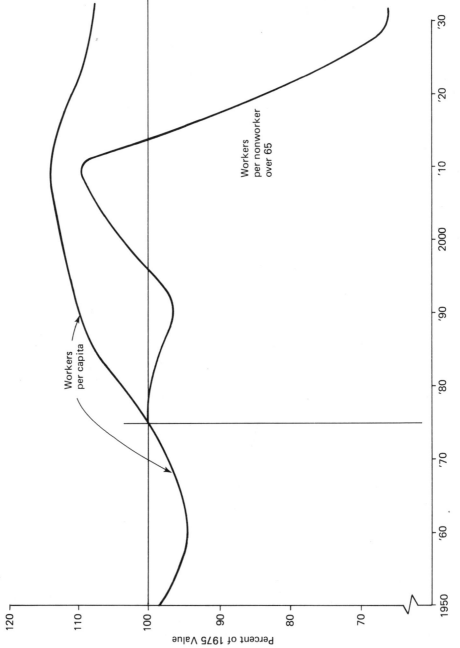

Figure 35-6 *Trends in workers per capita and workers per dependent*

jobs requiring relatively low capital input. Second, total affluence is not likely to be an impediment to continuing transportation improvement, barring major catastrophies or really inept handling of the shifting of our energy and resource base. But the observations about the changing age mix and the transition to a new worker/retiree ratio is harder to interpret. It clearly is a phenomenon that deserves more thought. Here we will make some superficial observations, but basically leave the question of its implications for transportation unanswered.

One might say an older population would have less tendency to drive. Maybe, but cars may get easier to drive; this will be discussed later. More time to travel? Probably. A more fundamental impact might be through its effect on the whole economy. This impact could be alleviated through later retirements, higher work-force participation rates, or through swelling paychecks so the larger transfer payments hurt less. The latter could be brought about by longer workweeks or by rapidly rising labor productivity. The perspective with which this will be viewed 15 years from now is hard to fathom, but it is just possible that by about 1990-2000 improving labor productivity will acquire a new significance, and by circa 2010 we would prefer not to be dependent on highly labor-intensive transportation.

It can be argued that we should be concerned with labor productivity improvement now, not just 20 years from now. Many believe that the large capital needs of the nation will require a higher ratio of investment to consumption as we build more jobs, convert our energy plants, and put more investment into safety and environmental protection; if this is to be politically possible it probably implies the need for a GNP/per capita growth that is rapid enough to supply the higher investment levels without sacrifice of per capita consumption.

The most important route to improved labor productivity of transportation is the familiar substitution of capital for labor through increased automation. This brings us back to the need for capital; refurbishing the neglected rail system, building an improved intermodal freight network, and improving urban and intercity transportation require substantial capital infusion. From our current perspective we probably cannot do them all at once; something will have to be deferred. Because of its obvious importance to the economy, first priority is likely to go to the freight system.

We should remind ourselves once again that conjectures such as these are fraught with uncertainties. Their only purpose is to sensitize us to possibilities.

ENERGY SCENARIOS

Waiting so long to mention energy does not imply that it is not an important uncertainty. There are so many possibilities, and selecting one over another is more an act of faith than a reasoned judgment. At one end of the spectrum of possibilities is the "great plenty breakthrough": we solve our problems and all forms of energy are abundant at reasonable costs. Should this happy state arrive, then evolution of the transportation system will be molded by other considerations.

At the other end is a restricted supply at very high prices for an indefinite future. This is a dull world of no or slow economic growth and constrained mobility, with emphasis on low-speed systems that sacrifice service to high load factors. New systems are introduced only if they improve energy efficiency.

In between are the multiple scenarios that derive from different technical outcomes in the shift from petroleum-based energy to coal- and nuclear-based energy. If it turns out that there is an important comparative advantage for systems that can use electricity directly over those which are dependent on petroleum or petroleum substitutes, then a bias against highway systems is introduced; unless batteries are very much improved highway systems may become range-limited. The implications of this particular scenario for energy are explored further in the next section.

With any reasonable scenario, however, it is highly likely that there will be an increasing premium on energy efficiency, at least for several decades. The car is already reflecting this, and it seems reasonable to expect continuing improvement into the 1980s, producing cars that have a different and, hopefully, better trade-off between energy efficiency, harmful emission output, safety, and economy. Producing more energy-efficient cars is the most important single thing we could do to make mobility require less energy.

What appears to be another general principle can be noted here. The energy required for vehicle propulsion increases roughly as the square of the speed, so that slow vehicles require less energy per seat-mile (or freight capacity-mile) than high-speed vehicles. On the other hand, unless energy prices rise very, very dramatically, it costs less to go fast. This point, probably surprising to some, follows from the fact that higher speeds mean higher vehicle productivity (seat- or ton-miles per hour). Fewer vehicles are needed to provide the same total capacity. Thus, costs decrease as speed increases until the point is reached that the continuing gain in labor and capital productivity is canceled by the higher individual costs of faster vehicles. For ground systems, it now appears that somewhere around 325 km/h (200 mi/h) is about optimum for distances over about 120 km (75 mi); lower speeds would be optimum for shorter distances. Higher energy prices lower the speed for the best economic performance.

These points are just one more of the many cross currents that muddy our vision of future transportation: the rising cost of labor drives us toward higher speeds to save on labor and capital resources; the rising cost of energy drives us toward lower speeds to save on energy resources. We cannot have it both ways.

MORE FIXED-GUIDEWAY SYSTEMS?

The term "fixed-guideway systems" is often used to designate the broad class of systems now primarily typified by trains. The first problem with the term is that it is ambiguous: all transportation systems are "fixed guideway" to some degree. Cars operate very poorly off roads and highways, aircraft often follow electronic guideways, and ships follow channels (and water!). Worse, it connotes an image that impacts the way we think. We often impute a permanence to a new rail line without considering that the highway or road that might be an alternative has no less permanence. The fact is that building roads and highways is relatively habitual and familiar, a product not of permanence or impact but of a more widespread acceptance that has made it easier to justify and build roads than other alternatives.

A more accurate term when we wish to consider nonhighway ground systems is "guideway-steered systems." But its unfamiliarity makes it awkward; we will stick with "fixed-guideway systems."

Today the most familiar fixed-guideway system is the train. But there is little reason to think that the systems of two or three decades from now will either look or behave like trains; there are too many alternative possibilities for physical design, network structure, and operational employment. Schemes such as high-speed moving pallets for small urban cars or moving rendezvous trains are possibilities. In the latter, the individual vehicles from different origins join up while in motion so that the passengers can redistribute themselves for the "car" going to their destination, giving express service to each customer. Networks could be richer; speeds could be higher. The applications might be in intercity travel, or as a backbone for a metropolitan regional system.

Such systems enjoy three advantages over conventional highway systems. First, operation is easier to automate. In a direct sense this advantage in terms of improved labor productivity may be small, but it opens up design possibilities that would not now be considered because of the labor implication. With automation, both urban and intercity freight and passenger systems might be designed to substitute several smaller vehicles for one larger one, thus offering service improvement through better frequency and direct nonstop routing. To do this manually is not now seriously considered, because of both labor costs and control difficulties.

Second, fixed-guideway systems can use electrical energy directly. Whether or not this is an advantage depends on how the energy picture evolves. If petroleum or petroleum substitutes are as cheap as electricity, then it does not matter in a primary way. If, however, electrical energy is relatively cheaper, then there is a comparative advantage to systems that can use electricity directly. As noted, unless batteries or other electrical energy storage devices become very much better than they are now, electric highway vehicles will become range-limited.

Third, fixed-guideway systems do not have the same constraints on top speed that are likely to continue to be imposed on highway systems. As also noted, whether or not this is an advantage also hinges at least partly on the energy picture; while higher speeds provide higher labor and capital productivity, they also consume more energy.

Given energy availability, higher speeds could be important for three possible reasons. The first follows from the potential impact of speed on the spatial organization of our society; this is a very knotty issue that is discussed later. The second is its impact on system costs discussed earlier in the energy section; if deployment is on a large-enough scale, they can offer more productive systems with lower operating costs. The third is its influence on patronage, or modal split; the evidence is fairly clear that if other things are equal, fast systems attract more patronage than slower ones.

Reiterating, we have made the following points. First, the technical and operational possibilities for nonhighway fixed-guideway systems are far broader than we are now exploiting. Second, moving toward these types of systems has at least three potential advantages: they can use electrical energy directly without having to generate it or store it on board, a characteristic that appears more technically difficult for highway vehicles and impossible by available techniques for air; they are easier to automate; and they are not constrained to highway speeds. Their disadvantage is that their costs are high unless the volume of traffic is high, so that their network richness is unlikely ever to reach that of roads and highways. This means that good ubiquitous service requires good connectivity to the road/highway system as an integral part of the design.

The purpose of this section has not been to make a prediction but to illuminate the possibility that our current thinking habits tend to reject. It is not to suggest that the highway/road system might go away; it will not. The car dominates passenger travel today, and it will continue to do so into the foreseeable future; its convenience and its economies are hard to beat. It does suggest, however, that there are reasons to think that a supplementary network of a new variety and family of fixed-guideway systems may assume a much larger role than fixed-guideway systems now have.

INTERCITY SYSTEMS

The purpose of this section is to compare the fundamental properties of the various kinds of intercity passenger systems, including the fixed-guideway systems just discussed, and infer the relative roles for each, now and in the future.

Today intercity travel is dominated by the automobile. Air is second, and does better than the aggregate statistics imply, becoming an important component in those corridors where travel is heavy enough that reasonably frequent service is available. For example, air captures nearly half the trips between Los Angeles and San Francisco, but only about one-fifth of all the trips of that distance in the aggregate. Bus serves only 1 to 2% of total trips, but it is important in that it is the only alternative to car for many low-density routes which service small cities. Train also captures a relatively small portion of trips, and only in the denser corridors. The Northeast corridor (Washington–Philadelphia–New York–Boston) is the first target for trying to improve rail modal share through service improvement.

What of tomorrow? Can we expect dominance by the car to continue? The answer is probably yes, but the degree may decrease somewhat. It is useful to consider the characteristics of the other modal options to see where each might fit.

In Fig. 35-3 we noted that the costs of all systems decrease as patronage increases. But there is a very marked difference in the relative importance of this trend between air and ground systems, because of the differences in the relative costs of the supporting infrastructure. For air, this infrastructure is the airports and the air traffic control system. As distance between airports grow, the contribution of these costs to total costs on a per mile basis drops very rapidly. For ground systems, however, an extra mile of travel adds the cost of an extra mile of track or highway, so that infrastructure costs remain a major contribution to total costs, and do not vary appreciably with distance traveled.

On the other hand, air system operating costs increase rapidly at short distances, because the time lost in landing, taxi, loading and unloading, taxi, and takeoff and climb-out become a major portion of trip time. The net result is that air systems have total costs that are quite high at short distances, say 240 km (150 mi), but which decrease very rapidly with increasing stage length. Their costs vary some with density, but it is a less important variable. Ground system costs, including highway system, are, conversely, very sensitive to density (patronage level) and much less so to stage length. Thus, air systems tend to be better for low-density route segments and, at any density, improve relative to ground as distance increases. High-speed trains, say 240 km/h (150 mi/h), can beat air in travel time up to about 160 km (100 mi), but in cost only if patronage is very heavy. Very high-speed ground transportation, say 400 km/h (250 mi/h), extends this superiority to 300 to 500 km (200 to 300 mi), but again only if patronage is reasonably heavy. A quiet helicopter-equivalent might serve low-density markets.

There is a very important qualification about the cost of highway systems, not because the former observations are not generally valid, but because of the way the system is financed. Individual links in the highway network do not have to cover costs on a link-by-link basis (with the partial exception of some toll roads). Users pay a flat rate through gas taxes and fees whether operating on a heavily used link or a lightly used link. Thus, the heavily used links generate more taxes than they cost, and low-density links generate less. There is, in effect, an internal cross subsidy with the infrastructure, even in rural or lightly traveled areas. Whether or not this same policy is applied to any fixed-guideway network in the future could have a profound impact on how (or even if) that network might evolve, because it relieves a constraint on building medium- to low-density links that might otherwise not be able to be financed.

There are obviously a lot of ifs. If energy remains constrained, it is likely to be associated as well with a slower growth in personal income, a key determinant of intercity travel demand. Under this if, new intercity systems are unlikely. If the opposite occurs, then a new network of high-speed fixed-guideway ground systems could very well start to evolve. Coupled to better urban collection and distribution, a new kind of travel opportunity and habit pattern could begin to take shape near the end of the century.

CARS AND ROADS

If we doubled the percentage of travel by all other modes, cars would still furnish 80% of all travel. What happens to the car will continue to be the most important aspect of transportation to most of our population. The car is already evolving into a more energy efficient, less polluting, and safer machine. With the continuing trend toward cheaper, smaller electronics, it seems highly likely that these readily available computational and "thinking" capabilities will increasingly substitute for electro-mechanical virtuosity, leading possibly to a mechanically simpler, easier to operate, automobile.

At the same time the vehicle is changing, so might the roadway change. Signs are supplemented by traffic lights. Traffic lights are getting smarter, also being operated by computers. Sensors in the road register the traffic and adapt the signal control to better regulate the flow.

The really interesting breakthrough might come when we shift from having the roadway tell the driver what to do (who then hopefully controls the car) and start having the roadway control system "talk" to the car directly. This could greatly simplify driver functions and should be a marked improvement in safety. Ten-year-olds and eighty-year-olds could have drivers' licenses.

The idea of a car that one does not need to "drive," that you could send home for someone else to use after it delivered you to your destination, that was almost 100% safe, sounds like dreaming. But remember 1950: wouldn't an electronic computer for every kid or satellites for live TV halfway around the world sound like a dream? This kind of step would clearly have to evolve slowly, and is very unlikely in the near term. But it is a fascinating possibility that appears technically feasible.

While such a development would clearly change our urban transportation systems, it is hard to see now how these new automated cars would be appreciably less space hungry than today; our city centers will still need more space-efficient systems. The new urban systems might become automated fixed-guideway within high-density areas and a high-speed grid to tie them together, with the automated cars furnishing a safe and convenient collection and distribution service in the low-density areas.

One can also conjecture about numerous alternative institutional arrangements for car ownership and operation. Rental of special-purpose vehicles could become considerably more commonplace than it is today.

Another possibility often mentioned is to have the roadway transfer electric propulsion energy to the vehicles. The principal problem here is technical feasibility.

SUMMARY OF POSSIBLE TRENDS

We have talked about a number of currents and crosscurrents that may mold the transportation system of the future. We have hypothesized four primary trends:

1. The car will continue to be the most important form of personal mobility, but our degree of dependence on it will decrease. In urban areas its access to high-density areas will be constrained. In the quest for better urban alternatives, we will move toward multimodal systems that supplement the conventional fixed-route bus or rail with multiple forms of smaller, more operationally flexible

taxi variants that can offer service anywhere, even in low-density suburbs. Perhaps in the 1980s we will see nonroadway, automated fixed-guideway transit beginning to replace bus networks.

2. Freight systems will follow the same multimodal principle as urban passenger transport, with better transfer terminals and handling factilities permitting greater specialization for both truck and rail: truck tending toward the lower-density collection/distribution function and rail the long-distance, high-density line-haul function. Increased containerization is an integral part of this hypothe-sized trend. Pipelines may become more versatile. This shift will occur slowly; there are many impediments to be overcome.

3. How the intercity system evolves depends very much on the energy picture. Given the availability of abundant electrical energy, coupled with a reasonably healthy economy, we could see the highway and the air system supplemented with a high-speed fixed-guideway system. Such a system would tie into a similar fixed-guideway urban and regional network, further blurring the demarcation between "city" and "intercity." The timing is likely to be post-1990, based on the need to develop the energy supply, the required technology, and the support to attract the required investment.

4. The fourth trend is the evolution of the car and its operating environment toward a more energy efficient, safer, and easier to operate form of mobility.

In the course of the discussion of these possibilities, several general principles were noted. One was that the choice between unimodal or multimodal approaches to any given transportation requirement should logically depend on the cost of transfer from one mode to another, with each operating in its "window" of optimal performance, compared to the cost penalty on a single mode performing the same job but being forced to operate outside its natural window. A second was that the cost of any mode decreases as the volume or density of use increases, other things equal. The third was the observation that there is an operating cost (and labor productivity) penalty in operating at low speeds to conserve energy, and that the speed for minimum operating costs is well above highway speeds. Obviously, the optimum speed decreases as stage length decreases.

TRANSPORTATION AND SPATIAL EVOLUTION

Let us now offer a few more principles concerning transportation characteristics and the spatial organization of our economy and society—often referred to as transportation and land use. It is hoped that they will give added significance to some of the points just summarized and illuminate the nature of some policy options for the future.

First, access is a necessary but not sufficient condition for development. Transportation does not cause development, it enables it; the causal forces are economic and sociological. The trick, and the basic problem of transportation policy, is to recognize the link between spatial form and quality of life, to know what kind of transportation system is most likely to enhance our social and economic well-being in the long run.

One tool for preventing undesired development is withholding transportation; this is a common ploy in preserving our natural areas. Transportation is also a tool for permitting development in a form deemed desirable; the location of potential development can be controlled by controlling points of access to the transportation network.

Let us consider two extremes for an intercity transportation network. Consider a rich network, many linkages with many points of access to the system. It seems reasonable to expect that associated with such a network is a city structure uninhibited by a dearth of transportation and therefore primarily shaped by socioeconomic forces. This would make possible, over time, more medium-size and small cities. Travel over the various links would, in general, be low to medium density.

In contrast, consider a sparse intercity network, consisting of a relatively few high-density corridors, and access only at the nodes. This we would associate with fewer but larger cities at these nodes, and much heavier travel over the fewer links in the network.

Here is a policy alternative. If, in the future, more effort goes into fostering modes suitable to low and medium densities, and supports a richer intercity network, then the small/medium city form is enabled. If the focus is on improving high-density forms of transportation, then the large city form is encouraged.

If we look back to Fig. 35-3 and the discussion accompanying it, it is clear that the latter approach is cheapest from a transportation point of view. The policy problem, though, involves a multiplicity of considerations, most of which transcend the transportation issue per se. Given the differences in costs (of all kinds) what would people choose?

This discussion is couched in terms of the intercity spatial network and city size. It is obvious that on a different scale the same principle applies to urban structure as well.

A second major variable besides network richness is speed. There is considerable evidence that people's travel habits are dictated less by distance traveled than by time traveled. Thus, the limits of habitual mobility are a function of speed. Clearly, costs increase as distance increases, so that the upper limits may be determined by cost as well as time. But if our conjectures about rising affluence are correct, these cost constraints may continue to decrease in importance.

If we typify the "casual intercity trip" as one requiring less than 1 hour, at highway speeds this implies that only cities less than roughly 80 km (50 mi) away are in our "weekly intercity set" (travel to which does not involve a major decision).

At 400 km/h (250 mi/h) this system reaches out beyond 350 km (200 mi), unless price makes it a "biweekly intercity set." At these speeds the cities 80 km (50 mi) away have become 14 minutes away and could very well have become part of our "daily urban system" rather than our "weekly intercity system (set)." Speed permits enlarging the spatial dimensions of the network without increasing travel time over it or, if the network dimensions remain constant, permits casual access to a larger proportion.

What might this mean to our society and economy? What does it imply for institutions to have larger "catchment" areas from which to draw their employees or members or clients? Or from the individual's point of view, to have access to such a rich choice of destinations? Would it cause greater specialization, leading to more intercity travel? A higher degree of multinucleation with less sprawl? A new lifestyle? These are very fundamental questions to which we have very poor answers. They deserve more attention than they have received.

A third variable is communication, as a substitute for some forms of travel and a stimulant for others. Which role is more important is debatable, and there is no clear answer. But it clearly should be part of our thinking.

In all of this it is clear that there are more questions than answers, and the questions about transportation are inextricably intertwined with much more fundamental questions about the nature of our individual lives and our civilization. It has become almost trite to say that transportation should be considered in the context of land use; it is equally important to say land use should be considered in the context of impact on society in the broadest sense of the word. There is much that needs to be thought about; it is hoped that some of the conjectures here help stimulate that thought.

SELECTED BIBLIOGRAPHY

Many citations are no longer available from their original source. These citations are often available from the National Technical Information Service, U.S. Department of Commerce, 5285 Port Royal Road, Springfield, Va. 22161. We have verified the order numbers for many of these citations, and they are found at the end of the citation. Prices are available through NTIS at the address above.

U.S. TASK FORCE ON RAILROAD PRODUCTIVITY, *Improving Railroad Productivity*, Final Report to the National Commission on Productivity and the Council of Economic Advisors. Washington, D.C.: U.S. Government Printing Office, November 1973.

WARD, JERRY D., *An Approach to Region-Wide Urban Transportation*, DOT-TST-75-108. Washington, D.C.: U.S. Department of Transportation, July 1975. Now available as PB 244 638.

———, "The Future Roles for Tracked Levitated Vehicle Systems," *Journal of Dynamic Systems, Measurement, and Control*, June 1974, pp. 117–27, in *Transactions of the American Society of Mechanical Engineers*, vol. 96.

ZAHAVI, YACOV, *Traveltime Budgets and Mobility in Urban Areas*, prepared for FHWA. Washington, D.C.: U.S. Department of Transportation, May 1974. Now available as PB 234 145.

INDEX